Global Challenges and Strategic Disruptors in Asian Businesses and Economies

Patricia Ordóñez de Pablos
The University of Oviedo, Spain

Miltiadis D. Lytras
American College of Greece, Greece & Effat University, Saudi Arabia

IGI Global
PUBLISHER of TIMELY KNOWLEDGE

A volume in the Advances in Business Strategy and Competitive Advantage (ABSCA) Book Series

Published in the United States of America by
IGI Global
Business Science Reference (an imprint of IGI Global)
701 E. Chocolate Avenue
Hershey PA, USA 17033
Tel: 717-533-8845
Fax: 717-533-8661
E-mail: cust@igi-global.com
Web site: http://www.igi-global.com

Library of Congress Cataloging-in-Publication Data

Names: Ordóñez de Pablos, Patricia, 1975- editor. | Lytras, Miltiadis D., 1973- editor.
Title: Global challenges and strategic disruptors in Asian businesses and economies / Patricia Ordonez de Pablos and Miltiadis D. Lytras, editors.

Description: Hershey, PA : Business Science Reference (an imprint of IGI Global), [2021] | Includes bibliographical references and index. | Summary: "The book presents a collection of chapters exploring and discussing the state-of-the-art, emerging topics, challenges and success factors in business, big data, innovation and technology in Asia, exploring how IoT, big data and AI can provide solutions for global challenges and companies"-- Provided by publisher.
Identifiers: LCCN 2020018662 (print) | LCCN 2020018663 (ebook) | ISBN 9781799847878 (hardcover) | ISBN 9781799858317 (paperback) | ISBN 9781799847885 (ebook)
Subjects: LCSH: Economic development--Technological innovations--Asia. | Technological innovations--Economic aspects--Asia. | Business enterprises--Technological innovations--Asia. | Information technology--Economic aspects--Asia. | Disruptive technologies--Asia.
Classification: LCC HC415.I55 G56 2021 (print) | LCC HC415.I55 (ebook) | DDC 338/.064095--dc23
LC record available at https://lccn.loc.gov/2020018662
LC ebook record available at https://lccn.loc.gov/2020018663

This book is published in the IGI Global book series Advances in Business Strategy and Competitive Advantage (ABSCA) (ISSN: 2327-3429; eISSN: 2327-3437)

British Cataloguing in Publication Data
A Cataloguing in Publication record for this book is available from the British Library.

Advances in Business Strategy and Competitive Advantage (ABSCA) Book Series

Patricia Ordóñez de Pablos
Universidad de Oviedo, Spain

ISSN:2327-3429
EISSN:2327-3437

Mission

Business entities are constantly seeking new ways through which to gain advantage over their competitors and strengthen their position within the business environment. With competition at an all-time high due to technological advancements allowing for competition on a global scale, firms continue to seek new ways through which to improve and strengthen their business processes, procedures, and profitability.

The **Advances in Business Strategy and Competitive Advantage (ABSCA) Book Series** is a timely series responding to the high demand for state-of-the-art research on how business strategies are created, implemented and re-designed to meet the demands of globalized competitive markets. With a focus on local and global challenges, business opportunities and the needs of society, the **ABSCA** encourages scientific discourse on doing business and managing information technologies for the creation of sustainable competitive advantage.

Coverage

- Joint Ventures
- Economies of Scale
- Small and Medium Enterprises
- Balanced Scorecard
- Competitive Strategy
- Value Creation
- Strategic Alliances
- Customer-Orientation Strategy
- International Business Strategy
- Co-operative Strategies

IGI Global is currently accepting manuscripts for publication within this series. To submit a proposal for a volume in this series, please contact our Acquisition Editors at Acquisitions@igi-global.com or visit: http://www.igi-global.com/publish/.

The Advances in Business Strategy and Competitive Advantage (ABSCA) Book Series (ISSN 2327-3429) is published by IGI Global, 701 E. Chocolate Avenue, Hershey, PA 17033-1240, USA, www.igi-global.com. This series is composed of titles available for purchase individually; each title is edited to be contextually exclusive from any other title within the series. For pricing and ordering information please visit http://www.igi-global.com/book-series/advances-business-strategy-competitive-advantage/73672. Postmaster: Send all address changes to above address.

Titles in this Series

For a list of additional titles in this series, please visit:
http://www.igi-global.com/book-series/advances-business-strategy-competitive-advantage/73672

Handbook of Research on Multidisciplinary Approaches to Entrepreneurship, Innovation, and ICTs
Luísa Cagica Carvalho (Instituto Politécnico de Setúbal, Portugal & CEFAGE, Universidade de Évora, Portugal) Leonilde Reis (Instituto Politécnico de Setúbal, Portugal) Alcina Prata (Instituto Polytechnic of Setúbal, Portugal) and Raquel Pereira (Instituto Polytechnic of Setúbal, Portugal)
Business Science Reference • © 2021 • 455pp • H/C (ISBN: 9781799840992) • US $295.00

Ethical Standards and Practice in Managerial and Financial Accounting
Ionica Oncioiu (Titu Maiorescu University, Romania)
Business Science Reference • © 2021 • 300pp • H/C (ISBN: 9781799840121) • US $195.00

Sustainability Reporting, Ethics, and Strategic Management Strategies for Modern Organizations
Ionica Oncioiu (Titu Maiorescu University, Romania) Sorinel Căpuşneanu (Titu Maiorescu University, Romania) Dan Ioan Topor (1 Decembrie 1918 University, Romania) and Dana Maria (Oprea) Constantin (University of Bucharest, Romania)
Business Science Reference • © 2021 • 320pp • H/C (ISBN: 9781799846376) • US $195.00

International Perspectives on the Youth Labor Market Emerging Research and Opportunities
Samir Amine (Université du Québec en Outaouais, Canada)
Business Science Reference • © 2020 • 217pp • H/C (ISBN: 9781799827795) • US $170.00

Open and Innovative Trade Opportunities for Latin America and the Caribbean
Pablo Alberto Baisotti (University of Costa Rica, Costa Rica)
Business Science Reference • © 2020 • 255pp • H/C (ISBN: 9781799835035) • US $215.00

Cases on Performance Improvement Innovation
Darlene M. Van Tiem (Capella University, USA & University of Michigan – Dearborn, USA) and Nancy Crain Burns (Crain Burns Associates LLC, USA)
Business Science Reference • © 2020 • 377pp • H/C (ISBN: 9781799836735) • US $195.00

Handbook of Research on Entrepreneurship Development and Opportunities in Circular Economy
Neeta Baporikar (Namibia University of Science and Technology, Namibia & University of Pune, India)
Business Science Reference • © 2020 • 696pp • H/C (ISBN: 9781799851165) • US $265.00

IGI Global
PUBLISHER of TIMELY KNOWLEDGE

701 East Chocolate Avenue, Hershey, PA 17033, USA
Tel: 717-533-8845 x100 • Fax: 717-533-8661
E-Mail: cust@igi-global.com • www.igi-global.com

Editorial Advisory Board

Muhamad Rusliyadi, *Polytechnic of Agricultural Development Yogyakarta Magelang, Indonesia*
Susheela Shetty, *Brindavan College, Bangalore, India*
Archana Shrivastava, *Jaypee Business School, JIIT University, India*
Ayuphita Tiara Silalahi, *Binus Business School, Bina Nusantara University, Indonesia*
Tanmay Singh, *Birla Institute of Technology and Science, Pilani, India*
Sachin Soonthodu, *Garden City University, India*
Heru Susanto, *The Indonesian Institute of Sciences, Indonesia*
Josephine Alexandra Susilo, *Petra Christian University, Indonesia*
Josua Tarigan, *Petra Christian University, Indonesia*
Kanchan Chandar Tolani, *Shri Ramdeobaba College of Engineering and Management, Nagpur, India*
Shamila Rasanjani Wijesundara, *Uva Wellassa University, Sri Lanka*
Xi Zhang, *Tianjing University, China*

Table of Contents

Preface xix

Chapter 1
Analysing the State of Sector-Specific CSR Reporting: Evidence From Pakistan 1
Muzammal Khan, University of the West of Scotland, UK

Chapter 2
The Institutional Impact and Community Perception Implementation of Food Security Policy on Poverty Reduction: Case of Food Self-Sufficiency Village Programme, Indonesia 29
Muhamad Rusliyadi, Polytechnic of Agricultural Development Yogyakarta Magelang, Indonesia
Azaharaini Bin Hj. Mohd. Jamil, College IGS Brunei Darussalam, Brunei
Ratna Tri Kumalasari, Agricultural and Food Security Office, Kebumen Regency, Indonesia
Ari Abdul Rouf, Gorontalo Assessment Institute for Agricultural Technology, Ministry of Agriculture Indonesia, Indonesia

Chapter 3
Institutional Role and Asisstance Service Analysis on Food Security Policy Case in Indonesia 43
Muhamad Rusliyadi, Polytechnic of Agricultural Development Yogyakarta Magelang, Indonesia
Azaharaini Bin Hj. Mohd. Jamil, College IGS Brunei Darussalam, Brunei
Ratna Tri Kumalasari, Agricultural and Food Security Office, Kebumen Regency, Indonesia
Ari Abdul Rouf, Gorontalo Assessment Institute for Agricultural Technology, Ministry of Agriculture Indonesia, Indonesia

Chapter 4
Food Security Policy Analysis of Household Level: Case of Food Security Village Programme in Indonesia 60
Muhamad Rusliyadi, Polytechnic of Agricultural Development Yogyakarta Magelang, Indonesia
Azaharaini Bin Hj. Mohd. Jamil, College IGS Brunei Darussalam, Brunei

Chapter 5
Human-Centered Design to Enhance the Usability, Human Factors, and User Experience Within Digital Destructive Ecosystems 76
Heru Susanto, Brunei University of Technology, Brunei & The Indonesian Institute of Sciences, Indonesia
Fahmi Ibrahim, Brunei University of Technology, Brunei
Saleem Haja Nazmudeen, Brunei University of Technology, Brunei
Fadzliwati Mohiddin, Brunei University of Technology, Brunei
Desi Setiana, Ministry of Law and Human Right, Indonesia & University of Brunei Darussalam, Brunei

Chapter 6
Active Social Listening and Its Impact on Firm Strategies: Study of Indian Context 95
Som Sekhar Bhattacharyya, National Institute of Industrial Engineering, Mumbai, India
Neenu Neenu, National Institute of Industrial Engineering, Mumbai, India

Chapter 7
Demonetization and Movement Towards Digital Cashless Indian Economy: Its Macroeconomic Effects 115
Rajib Bhattacharyya, Goenka College of Commerce and Business Administration, Kolkata, India

Chapter 8
Augment Human Resource Proximity Plumbing Cybernation 131
Anant Deogaonkar, Shri Ramdeobaba College of Engineering and Management, India
Sampada Nanoty, M. S. University Vadodara, India
Archana Shrivastava, Jaypee Business School, Jaypee Institute of Information Technology, India
Geetika Jain, Amity University, Noida, India

Chapter 9
Huawei, China, and Ideological Tensions in the 5G Telecommunications Platforms 141
Bruno Mascitelli, Swinburne University of Technology, Australia
Mona Chung, North China University of Technology, China

Chapter 10
What Are the Leading Bank-Specific and Macroeconomic Factors Influencing Islamic Bank Performance? New Evidence From MENA Countries 153
Mosharrof Hosen, Universiti Tunku Abdul Rahman, Kampar, Malaysia

Chapter 11
Disruption and Innovation Trends in the QSR Industry: Perspectives Drawn From India 172
Gaurav Nagpal, Birla Institute of Technology and Science, Pilani, India
Kanika Dawar, Birla Institute of Technology and Science, Pilani, India
Srutadipta Roy Choudhury, Birla Institute of Technology and Science, Pilani, India
Tanmay Singh, Birla Institute of Technology and Science, Pilani, India

Chapter 12
The CSR Performance and Earning Management Practice on the Market Value of Conventional Banks in Indonesia 196
Saarce Elsye Hatane, Petra Christian University, Indonesia
Amadea Nathania Pranoto, Petra Christian University, Indonesia
Josua Tarigan, Petra Christian University, Indonesia
Josephine Alexandra Susilo, Petra Christian University, Indonesia
Ang Jonathan Christianto, Petra Christian University, Indonesia

Chapter 13
Retailing in Indonesia: A Deeper Look Into the World's Growing Market 214
Adilla Anggraeni, Binus Business School, Bina Nusantara University, Indonesia
Ayuphita Tiara Silalahi, Binus Business School, Bina Nusantara University, Indonesia

Chapter 14
Automation of VAT System: A Pathway of Domestic Resource Mobilization 224
Biplob Kumar Nandi, East West University, Bangladesh
Md. Humayun Kabir, East West University, Bangladesh
Nandini Roy, University of Dhaka, Bangladesh

Chapter 15
An Overview of Emerging Technologies in the Indian Retail Industry 247
Nilesh Kumar, Amity University, Jharkhand, India

Chapter 16
Innovative Technology and Human Resource Management 257
Sachin Soonthodu, Garden City University, India
Susheela Shetty, Brindavan College, Bangalore, India

Chapter 17
Consumer Perception and Purchase Intention Towards Refurbished Smart Phones: A Circular Consumption Perspective 270
Nishant Kumar, Amity University, Noida, India
Divya Mohan, Delhi Institute of Advanced Studies, India

Chapter 18
Women Managers and Generations: A Study of Obstacles 285
Kanchan Chandar Tolani, Shri Ramdeobaba College of Engineering and Management, Nagpur, India
Pritam Bhadade, Shri Ramdeobaba College of Engineering and Management, Nagpur, India
Kavita Patil, Dhanwate National College, Nagpur, India
Archana Shrivastava, Jaypee Business School, Jaypee Institute of Information Technology, India

Chapter 19
Perceived Tourist Harassment in Tourist Destinations: A Study of Southern Coastal Belt of Sri Lanka....... 299
Shamila Rasanjani Wijesundara, Uva Wellassa University, Sri Lanka
Athula Gnanapala, Sabaragamuwa University of Sri Lanka, Sri Lanka

Compilation of References 314

About the Contributors 350

Index 356

Detailed Table of Contents

Preface xix

Chapter 1
Analysing the State of Sector-Specific CSR Reporting: Evidence From Pakistan 1
Muzammal Khan, University of the West of Scotland, UK

This chapter aims to deepen understanding of trends in corporate social responsibility reporting (CSRR) practices in Pakistan since the introduction of voluntary reporting guidelines in 2009 by the Securities and Exchange Commission Pakistan (SECP) and their updating in 2013. Quantitative content analysis was applied to CSRR for the chemicals, oil and gas, banking, cement, and manufacturing industries in Pakistan. The results were benchmarked to the guidelines issued on social and environmental aspects by the SECP. It was found that the reports issued by the highly polluting industries such as oil and gas, cement, and chemical industries reported significantly higher levels of information than the other sectors. The results indicate the appropriateness of industry-specific reporting and suggest, in line with local guidelines, that further standardisation is required to level the playing field of CSRR in Pakistan.

Chapter 2
The Institutional Impact and Community Perception Implementation of Food Security Policy on Poverty Reduction: Case of Food Self-Sufficiency Village Programme, Indonesia 29
Muhamad Rusliyadi, Polytechnic of Agricultural Development Yogyakarta Magelang, Indonesia
Azaharaini Bin Hj. Mohd. Jamil, College IGS Brunei Darussalam, Brunei
Ratna Tri Kumalasari, Agricultural and Food Security Office, Kebumen Regency, Indonesia
Ari Abdul Rouf, Gorontalo Assessment Institute for Agricultural Technology, Ministry of Agriculture Indonesia, Indonesia

Indonesia has established various types of agrarian policies in line with poverty reduction initiatives. Various policies on poverty reduction schemes that have been implemented before were not successful because many of them lacked sustainability. Most strategies on the activity of the programme called for direct assistance to the unfortunate. The Food Self-Sufficiency Village Programme (Desa Mandiri Pangan) gives support financially and offers intensive assistance to the community. The principal targets of the programme are to empower the community, alleviate rural poverty and sustain food security at the village level. Active institutions play a very important role in supporting the DMP Programme. There were institutions in the village sites before the introduction of the DMP Programme, such as the village leader, village councils, farmer groups, rice milling units, a village health station unit, a school, a mosque, a church, private lenders, village shops, and traders.

Chapter 3
Institutional Role and Asisstance Service Analysis on Food Security Policy Case in Indonesia......... 43
Muhamad Rusliyadi, Polytechnic of Agricultural Development Yogyakarta Magelang, Indonesia
Azaharaini Bin Hj. Mohd. Jamil, College IGS Brunei Darussalam, Brunei
Ratna Tri Kumalasari, Agricultural and Food Security Office, Kebumen Regency, Indonesia
Ari Abdul Rouf, Gorontalo Assessment Institute for Agricultural Technology, Ministry of Agriculture Indonesia, Indonesia

The chapter aims to analyze on the role of institutions, sources of funding/assistance, source information in terms of food security and extension policy. The result of the research shows the information on problematic areas in policy implementation with respect to food security and extension policy in terms of poverty reduction. The role of the institutions, assistance, and source information is useful in the implementation of other policy sectors in the future because similar issues or problems may be avoided by taking precautions not to repeat the same mistakes or by applying measures that address the implementation issues. In this way, policy implementation can be carried out effectively, and the outcomes will meet the policy objectives.

Chapter 4
Food Security Policy Analysis of Household Level: Case of Food Security Village Programme in Indonesia.. 60
Muhamad Rusliyadi, Polytechnic of Agricultural Development Yogyakarta Magelang, Indonesia
Azaharaini Bin Hj. Mohd. Jamil, College IGS Brunei Darussalam, Brunei

The study focuses on analyzing the food self-sufficiency village program at household level in Indonesia. The before and after analysis and food and security composite analysis at household level are used as tools. It involved comparing the implication and impact between indicators before and after the implementation of policy. Quantitative data were used to compare major indicators and qualitative data for minor indicators. In general, the impact of the DMP Programme on the villages was positive. The level of poverty in each village has been significantly reduced by 8-40% after the introduction of the programme. Composite food security analysis at household level shows the positive impacts of DMP Programme implementation. This is shown by several indicators, including the rise of 4-7% availability, reduction in poverty by 8-40%, and decrease in people working fewer than 15 hours per week by 10-20%.

Chapter 5
Human-Centered Design to Enhance the Usability, Human Factors, and User Experience Within Digital Destructive Ecosystems.. 76
Heru Susanto, Brunei University of Technology, Brunei & The Indonesian Institute of Sciences, Indonesia
Fahmi Ibrahim, Brunei University of Technology, Brunei
Saleem Haja Nazmudeen, Brunei University of Technology, Brunei
Fadzliwati Mohiddin, Brunei University of Technology, Brunei
Desi Setiana, Ministry of Law and Human Right, Indonesia & University of Brunei Darussalam, Brunei

Human-centered design is an approach that focuses on involving the end user throughout the product development and testing process which can be crucial in ensuring that the product meets the needs and capabilities of the user, particularly in terms of user experience and safety. The structured and iterative nature of human-centered design can often be a challenge for the design team when faced with the necessary, rapid, product development life cycles associated with the competitiveness in the industry. This ensures that the needs of the user are taken into account throughout the design process whilst also maintaining a rapid pace of development, and its rationale before outlining how it was applied to assess and enhance the usability, human factors, and user experience within destructive digital ecosystem era. The authors encouraged a system approach such as human-centered design for prevention on further damages being done on data breaches through the application of each steps of the process.

Chapter 6
Active Social Listening and Its Impact on Firm Strategies: Study of Indian Context 95
Som Sekhar Bhattacharyya, National Institute of Industrial Engineering, Mumbai, India
Neenu Neenu, National Institute of Industrial Engineering, Mumbai, India

Due to the present customer voice in a digital world, keeping a watchful eye on what customers were expressing on social media became a necessary firm imperative. For this study, the authors found that rather than using FGDs and survey research, digital tools like the applications of social media listening could serve as a valuable platform for gathering insights about a firm's latest strategy. This could be complemented by the existing channels of feedback. This research study focused on customer perspective. Data was collected from Indian consumers and social media handling experts regarding social listening based upon a semi structured open-ended questionnaire. The data collected was content analyzed based upon thematic content analysis. Customer voices were reading majorly complaints and compliments followed by advocacy. This helped to comprehend how well firm managers aligned and helped in getting insights regarding marketplace reflections for assessing a firm, its products, and its brands.

Chapter 7
Demonetization and Movement Towards Digital Cashless Indian Economy: Its Macroeconomic Effects 115
Rajib Bhattacharyya, Goenka College of Commerce and Business Administration, Kolkata, India

One of the greatest painful, un-stabilizing self-imposed macroeconomic blows on the Indian economy occurred in the absence of a short-term crisis when the government decided to announce a major change in the macroeconomic environment by demonetizing the high value currency notes – of Rs 500 and Rs 1000. These two denominations ceased to be legal tender from midnight of 8th of November 2016. The reasons offered for demonetization are two-fold: one, to control counterfeit notes that could be contributing to terrorism, in other words a national security concern; and second, to undermine or eliminate the "black economy." It has also been a step forward towards a digital cashless economy. In this study an attempt is being made to present a discussion on both the short- and long-run effects of demonetization. It attempts to throw light on the impact of some macroeconomic variables—GDP, sectoral composition, industrial production, inflation, employment—using secondary time-series analysis. The empirical analysis clearly reveals that contraction of currency in circulation was one of the most important factors responsible for decrease in GDP in India after the period of demonetization. Apart from the issue of transition, confronted by the banking system, the government initiative was needed to neutralize the short-term, medium-term, and long-term effects particularly on regularization of cash flows, withdrawals, income, employment, inflation, consumption, and production. Moreover, cyber and other digital security measures were also essential to curb any kinds of frauds and encourage people towards a more digital cashless economy.

Chapter 8
Augment Human Resource Proximity Plumbing Cybernation 131
Anant Deogaonkar, Shri Ramdeobaba College of Engineering and Management, India
Sampada Nanoty, M. S. University Vadodara, India
Archana Shrivastava, Jaypee Business School, Jaypee Institute of Information Technology, India
Geetika Jain, Amity University, Noida, India

The expeditious proliferation of artificial intelligence in the mainstream has rejigged the simplest processes of the various sectors in the most efficient way. With the advent of the era of cybernation, the work culture has been curbed with the timely developments and upgradation of the technology. Cybernation has propelled the growth of every respective sector of the vast corporate diaspora with time. The main aim of the cybernation being that of smoothening the complex, bulk tasks which exploit mass human energy, has seen much success in its purpose so far. But certain domains of the corporate diaspora still await the technological transformation of their respective processes. One such prominent domain and the real fuel of the corporate diaspora, the human resource has yet to expand its purview to imbibe and imbue cybernation in its certain processes. Human resource domain being the custodian of the corporate, wherein it is for the people and by the people though with the niche of Industry 4.0 beholds more space to expand the angle of understanding the term resource for the human, than human as an element of resource in itself. Multifarious human resource processes can be enhanced further with apt utility of digitization in order to optimize the user interface and user experience, boosting the overall employee experience amidst the corporate. Several certain customary functions of the human resources entail the adaptation of automation in more nuanced way to evolve parallel with the digitalization. Moreover, the millennial era further looks up to a transformed human resource with higher echelons of functions to be performed, digitally evolved jobs, an automated work environment, work culture well acquainted with the artificial intelligence. The effect of cybernation on the business acumen of futuristic human resource leaders, working in the rapid concurrent era of disruptions, without losing the human touch, will carve the future human resource structure. Therefore, the intent of this chapter is to study the detailed implications of automation, digitalization, and cybernation in the domain of human resources and to study and examine the dynamically changing HR functions with technological interventions and disruptions by proposing a literature review.

Chapter 9
Huawei, China, and Ideological Tensions in the 5G Telecommunications Platforms 141
Bruno Mascitelli, Swinburne University of Technology, Australia
Mona Chung, North China University of Technology, China

While the COVID 19 pandemic has captured the attention of the geo-political agenda throughout 2020, pushing the Huawei controversy off the front pages of the news, the hysteria and suspicions around Huawei providing their lower cost telecommunications equipment to Western nations reached new crescendos in the move towards 5G communication platforms. The purpose of this chapter is to examine the recent series of escalating tensions between Huawei and Western nations. While there was a first run of tension with the 4G networks, it was to be repeated with the preparations for the 5G telecommunications platforms. Alongside this expansion was the parallel development of geo-political tensions between China and Western powers. This included ongoing tensions over the South China Sea, Taiwan's relationship with

China, the Hong Kong issue, the trade war with the United States, and general diplomacy between China and the West. The chapter seeks to provide the likely result on how these tensions would be resolved.

Chapter 10
What Are the Leading Bank-Specific and Macroeconomic Factors Influencing Islamic Bank Performance? New Evidence From MENA Countries 153
Mosharrof Hosen, Universiti Tunku Abdul Rahman, Kampar, Malaysia

Despite the proven sustainability and growth of Islamic banks during the financial crisis period, many scholars criticise the current performance of Islamic banks. Therefore, policymakers are continuously getting worried due to inconclusive finding of different research related to Islamic bank profitability. To shed the light of raising concern, this study investigates the issue from considering both macroeconomic and bank-specific factors. The annual cross-sectional data has been collected from 46 Islamic banks in 10 selected MENA countries over the period 2015-2019. The standardized pooled ordinary least square (OLS) approach's findings revealed that bank size, capital adequacy, GDP, and inflation have a significant positive impact on Islamic banks' return on asset, but asset quality has no significant effect on ROA. In contrast, most of the variables have an insignificant effect of ROE. Investors, financial analysts, and policymakers will get benefits from this study's results to secure their investment by successfully controlling the above-mentioned leading factors.

Chapter 11
Disruption and Innovation Trends in the QSR Industry: Perspectives Drawn From India 172
Gaurav Nagpal, Birla Institute of Technology and Science, Pilani, India
Kanika Dawar, Birla Institute of Technology and Science, Pilani, India
Srutadipta Roy Choudhury, Birla Institute of Technology and Science, Pilani, India
Tanmay Singh, Birla Institute of Technology and Science, Pilani, India

The QSR (quick service restaurants) industry in the emerging economies such as India is undergoing a wave of disruption and re-engineering. Many global brands in QSR food servicing have resorted to technology and innovation in one or more aspects of their value chain in order to maintain leadership positions in a market that is facing some fast-growing competition from various channels, especially with the penetration that service aggregators like Zomato, Swiggy, and Uber Eats have managed to gain. This study aims to establish a general direction towards which the QSR industry is progressing in India by examining not only the current trends in India but also the trends that are prevalent worldwide and which have the potential of diffusion to emerging economies like India.

Chapter 12
The CSR Performance and Earning Management Practice on the Market Value of Conventional Banks in Indonesia 196
Saarce Elsye Hatane, Petra Christian University, Indonesia
Amadea Nathania Pranoto, Petra Christian University, Indonesia
Josua Tarigan, Petra Christian University, Indonesia
Josephine Alexandra Susilo, Petra Christian University, Indonesia
Ang Jonathan Christianto, Petra Christian University, Indonesia

This study examined the effect of the components of corporate social responsibility (CSR) and earnings management on market value, measured using Tobin's Q. CSR is measured by using KLD Index, while earnings management used discretionary loan loss provision. The GMM-SYS (generalized method of moment system) dynamic panel data method is employed to examine the research framework on conventional banks listed in Indonesia Stock Exchange. Among six components in CSR disclosures, only corporate governance, environmental and product disclosures are favorable for bank's market value. Furthermore, earnings management had a positive impact on market value. Empirical result indicated that CSR functions as a part of bank strategic moves in order to survive the highly dynamical business environment. Since CSR inflicts additional costs for the company, they must perform CSR efficiently while maintaining a strong relationship with shareholders. This study contributes to CSR and financial management literature by finding the nature of CSR effects as future strategic investment.

Chapter 13
Retailing in Indonesia: A Deeper Look Into the World's Growing Market.. 214
Adilla Anggraeni, Binus Business School, Bina Nusantara University, Indonesia
Ayuphita Tiara Silalahi, Binus Business School, Bina Nusantara University, Indonesia

The chapter discusses Indonesia's retailing landscape. The retail sector itself can be considered to be one of the most promising in Asia due to the high populations, growing middle class, higher purchasing power, and shifting spending habits. The discussion revolves along the state of online and offline retailing in Indonesia, including the current trends and discussion of luxury retailing. The technological advancement was proven to have shifted how people do retailing activities. The chapter discusses the trends in luxury retail as well as the challenges facing luxury retailers doing business in Indonesia, which may include counterfeiting. Counterfeiting is one of the prevailing issues in Indonesian retailing behaviours, targeting consumers who are aware that they have indeed purchased counterfeited items.

Chapter 14
Automation of VAT System: A Pathway of Domestic Resource Mobilization 224
Biplob Kumar Nandi, East West University, Bangladesh
Md. Humayun Kabir, East West University, Bangladesh
Nandini Roy, University of Dhaka, Bangladesh

The automated tax system has been taken as an effective tool for modernizing the tax system. The automated tax system can easily store all types of reported income, and it makes the tax submission procedure easy and convenient, resulting in reducing the compliance cost. The main objective of this chapter is to explain the necessity of an automated value added tax (VAT) system for raising domestic resource mobilization and how automation can be a better alternative to finance sustainable development goals projects. The secondary data was collected from the National Board of Revenue, Bangladesh. This study explains that the entire VAT system's automation can reduce the taxpayers' incentive to evade tax by reducing the tax compliance and taking bribes of tax officials. In sum, automation of the tax system would ultimately be pragmatic tax reform for the financing in the SDG projects.

Chapter 15
An Overview of Emerging Technologies in the Indian Retail Industry 247
Nilesh Kumar, Amity University, Jharkhand, India

With the arrival of several new players, Indian retail has become one of the most dynamic and fast industries. With the advancement in technology, internet, engineering, many retailers are adopting and using the internet of things, big data technology, RFID, and other technical software and programs to enhance customer experience, customer engagement through which retailers are improving efficiency. In particular, many customer-oriented internet of things technologies, such as augmented reality, smart shopping carts, smart displays, and RFID tags, are expected to change the way customers experience retail shopping. For this study, the secondary data has been explored and studied. The purpose of this chapter is to study how emerging technologies like big data and IoT implementation are transforming organizational practices and thereby generating potential benefits in the retail industry.

Chapter 16
Innovative Technology and Human Resource Management.. 257
Sachin Soonthodu, Garden City University, India
Susheela Shetty, Brindavan College, Bangalore, India

Technology plays a crucial role in inclusive growth of modern human management systems. Recruitment, hiring, training, retaining, workplace administration, and optimizing workforce environment are the major functions of human resources management. Adopting innovative technology within the organisation enables the managers to accumulate and deliver the information as well as communicate with employees more effectively. India, as one of the developed countries, is successfully integrating technology in human resource management systems to ensure market-driven product and service development. Technology makes jobs easy; at the same time, it threatens the job market by reducing the human resource requirement to perform particular tasks. An effective human resource management should have the ability to integrate technology and the human resource for the better development of an organisation. This theoretical study focuses on various technologies adopted by the human resource management to make the workplace effective and highly productive.

Chapter 17
Consumer Perception and Purchase Intention Towards Refurbished Smart Phones: A Circular Consumption Perspective.. 270
Nishant Kumar, Amity University, Noida, India
Divya Mohan, Delhi Institute of Advanced Studies, India

Circular economy is a global economic model that focuses to transform linear consumption in a circular system by minimizing waste and preserving the cost of materials. Refurbishment can be useful to recover value from old products and to minimize waste. Based on the insights from literature, a deductive research approach has been used to examine consumer understanding about refurbished smart phone and their purchase intention. A survey based on barriers, perceived risk, and benefits associated with refurbished phones was conducted. Multiple analyses of variance were employed to identify the effect of demographic parameters on refurbishing dimensions. Multiple regression was used to identify prominent predictors in determining purchase intention towards refurbished products. The study demonstrates a fine level of awareness among people about refurbished phone, and they link it to environmental benefits. A major concern among consumers was performance issue and financial risk involved in purchasing refurbished smart phones. Financial benefits are key aspects behind promoting refurbished.

Chapter 18
Women Managers and Generations: A Study of Obstacles 285
Kanchan Chandar Tolani, Shri Ramdeobaba College of Engineering and Management, Nagpur, India
Pritam Bhadade, Shri Ramdeobaba College of Engineering and Management, Nagpur, India
Kavita Patil, Dhanwate National College, Nagpur, India
Archana Shrivastava, Jaypee Business School, Jaypee Institute of Information Technology, India

The number of women in organizations is increasing in most countries, but the representation of women in managerial positions is still disproportional. The percentage of women in leadership positions globally is only 29%. Grant Thornton annual survey 2019 reveals that India still ranks the fifth lowest in having women in managerial roles. Thus, though diversity at work is increasing, there are still fewer women in the boardroom. The main reason for this is the hurdles and obstacles that women managers face. The chapter studies the various obstacles faced by women managers. Also, it takes into account the role of generation and aims at comparing the hurdles faced by women managers belonging to Generations X and Y. The study is undertaken with special reference to the banking sector. Major findings reveal that there is a difference in obstacles faced by women managers belonging to Generations X and Y.

Chapter 19
Perceived Tourist Harassment in Tourist Destinations: A Study of Southern Coastal Belt of Sri Lanka.. 299
Shamila Rasanjani Wijesundara, Uva Wellassa University, Sri Lanka
Athula Gnanapala, Sabaragamuwa University of Sri Lanka, Sri Lanka

Tourism is a fast-growing industry in the world. Many developing countries have recognized the economic contribution of the tourism industry towards to country; therefore, it has been included as an integral part of their development strategies. Sri Lanka continues to use tourism as one of the incomes earning strategy of its nation. At present, a huge tourism development is continued while accepting severe issues occurs itself like tourist harassment. The nature of the harassment is different from destination to destination, and this study mainly aims to identify the harassment in Sri Lanka. The study carried out in Southern Coastal Belt, considering foreign tourists as the sample to the study. A pretested questionnaire was distributed among 600 foreigners to collect primary data for the study, and 530 questionnaires were valid for the analysis. The collected data was analyzed through exploratory factor analysis, which revealed six major types of harassment in Sri Lanka as a result of tourist consumption process throughout the vacation.

Compilation of References 314

About the Contributors 350

Index 356

Preface

INTRODUCTION

The book presents a rich collection of chapters exploring state of the art, new and emerging topics, challenges and success factors in business, big data, innovation, and technology in Asia. It will explore how innovative technologies and business practices can provide solutions for global challenges and companies. The book emphasizes empirical studies and case studies in Asia. It aims to be an international platform to bring together academics, researchers, lecturers, decision makers, policy makers, and practitioners to share new theories, research findings, and case studies, to enhance understanding and collaboration in business, disruptive innovation and technology in Asia.

The book will explore the role of strategic disruptors and major trends and challenges in companies, organizations and economies in Asia and how they can contribute to the creation of new business opportunities, jobs and growth towards a greener and more inclusive and resilient societies and economies. The interesting studies and examples focused Bangladesh, China, India, Indonesia, and Pakistan, to name a few, will help readers to develop a better understanding of the complex dynamics in this region of the world.

The target audience of the book is mainly professors in academia, deans, heads of departments, directors of masters, students (undergraduate and postgraduate level), politicians, policy makers, corporate heads of firms, senior general managers, managing directors, information technology directors and managers, libraries, etc.

CONTENTS OF THE BOOK

The book consists of a collection of 19 chapters that discusses relevant topics for the Asian businesses, economies and societies.

Chapter 1 titled "*Analysing the State of Sector-Specific CSR Reporting: Evidence from Pakistan*" (by Muzammal Khan, University of the West of Scotland, Great Britain) provides "an understanding of trends in corporate social responsibility reporting (CSRR) practices in Pakistan since the introduction of voluntary reporting guidelines in 2009 by the Securities and Exchange Commission Pakistan (SECP) and their updating in 2013. Quantitative content analysis was applied to CSRR for the Chemicals, Oil and Gas, Banking, Cement and Manufacturing industries in Pakistan. The results were benchmarked to the guidelines issued on social and environmental aspects by the SECP. It was found that the reports issued by the highly polluting industries such as oil and gas, cement, and chemical industries reported significantly higher levels of information than the other sectors. The results indicate the appropriateness of industry-specific reporting and suggest, in line with local guidelines, that further standardisation is required to level the playing field of CSRR in Pakistan".

Chapter 2 titled "*The Institutional Impact and Community Perception Implementation of Food Security Policy on Poverty Reduction: Case of Food Self Sufficiency Village Programme, Indonesia*" (by Muhamad Rusliyadi, Polytechnic of Agricultural Development Yogyakarta Magelang, Indonesia) states that "Indonesia has established various types of agrarian policies in line with poverty reduction initiatives. Various policies on poverty reduction schemes that have been implemented before were not successful because many of them lacked sustainability. Most strategies on the activity of the programme called for direct assistance to the unfortunate. The Food Self-Sufficiency Village Programme (Desa Mandiri Pangan) gives support financially and offers intensive assistance to the community. The principal targets of the programme are to empower the community, alleviate rural poverty and sustain food security at the village level. Active institutions play a very important role in supporting the DMP Programme. There were institutions in the village sites before the introduction of the DMP Programme, such as the village leader, village councils, farmer groups, rice milling units, a village health station unit, a school, a mosque, a church, private lenders, village shops and traders".

Chapter 3 titled "*Institutional Role and Assistance Service Analysis on Food Security Policy Case in Indonesia*" (by Muhamad Rusliyadi, Polytechnic of Agricultural Development Yogyakarta Magelang, Indonesia) explores "the role of institutional, sources of funding/assistance, source information in term of food security and extension policy. The result of the research shows the information on problematic areas in policy implementation with respect to food security and extension policy in term of poverty reduction. The role of the institutional, assistance and source information is useful in the implementation of other policy sectors in the future, because similar issues or problems may be avoided by taking precautions not to repeat the same mistakes or by applying measures which address the implementation issues. In this way policy implementation can be carried out effectively and the outcomes will meet the policy objectives".

Chapter 4 titled "*Food Security Policy Analysis of Household Level: Case of Food Security Village Programme in Indonesia*" (by Muhamad Rusliyadi, Polytechnic of Agricultural Development Yogyakarta Magelang, Indonesia) studies "food self-sufficiency village program at household level in Indonesia. The Before and After Analysis food and security composite analysis at household level used as tools. It involved comparing the implication and impact between indicators before and after the implementation of policy. Quantitative data were used to compare major indicators and qualitative data for minor indicators. In general, the impact of the DMP Programme on the villages was positive. The level of poverty in each village has been significantly reduced by 8-40% after the introduction of the Programme. Composite food security analysis at household level shows the positive impacts of DMP Programme implementation. This is shown by several indicators, including the rise of 4-7% availability, reduction in poverty by 8-40%, and decrease in people working fewer than 15 hours per week by 10-20%".

Chapter 5 titled "*Human-Centered Design to Enhance the Usability, Human Factors, and User Experience within Digital Destructive Ecosystem*" (by Heru Susanto, The Indonesian Institute of Sciences, Indonesia) affirms that "human-centered design is an approach that focuses on involving the end user throughout the product development and testing process which can be crucial in ensuring that the product meets the needs and capabilities of the user, particularly in terms of user experience and safety. The structured and iterative nature of human-centered design can often be a challenge for the design team when faced with the necessary, rapid, product development life cycles associated with the competitiveness in the industry. In ensuring that the needs of the user are taken into account throughout the design process whilst also maintaining a rapid pace of development, and its rationale before outlining how it was applied to assess and enhance the usability, human factors, and user experience within Destructive Digital Ecosystem Era. We encouraged a system approach such as human centered design for prevention on further damages being done on data breaches through the application of each steps of the process".

Chapter 6 titled "*Active Social Listening and its Impact on Firm Strategies: Study of Indian Context*" (by Som Sekhar Bhattacharyya, National Institute of Industrial Engineering, India; and Neenu Neenu, National Institute of Industrial Engineering, India) states that "due to the present customer voice in a digital world, keeping a watchful eye on what customers were expressing on social media, became a necessary firm imperative. For this study, the authors found that rather than, using FGDs and survey research, digital tools like the applications of social media listening could serve as a valuable platform for gathering insights about a firm's latest strategy. This could be complemented by the existing channels of feedback. This research study focused on customer perspective. Data was collected from Indian consumers and social media handling experts regarding social listening based upon a semi structured open-ended questionnaire. The data collected was content analyzed based upon thematic content analysis. Customer voices were reading majorly complaints and compliments followed by advocacy. This helped to comprehend how well firm managers aligned and helped in getting insights regarding marketplace reflections for assessing a firm, its products and its brands".

Chapter 7 titled "*Demonetization and Movement towards Digital Cashless Indian Economy- its Macroeconomic effect*" (by Rajib Bhattacharyya, Goenka College, Kolkata, University of Calcutta, India) considers that "one of the greatest painful, un-stabilizing self-imposed macroeconomic blows on the Indian economy occurred in the absence of a short term crisis when the government decided to announce a major change in the macroeconomic environment by demonetizing the high value currency notes – of Rs 500 and Rs 1000. These two denominations ceased to be legal tender from the midnight of 8th of November 2016.The reasons offered for demonetization are two-fold: one, to control counterfeit notes that could be contributing to terrorism, in other words a national security concern and second, to undermine or eliminate the "black economy". It has also been a step forward towards a digital cashless economy. In this study an attempt is being made to present a discussion on both the short and long run effects of demonetization. It attempts to throw light on the impact of some macroeconomic variables- GDP, sectoral composition, industrial production, inflation, employment using secondary time-series data".

Chapter 8 titled "*Augmenting Human Resource Proximity Plumbing Cybernation*" (by Anant Deogaonkar, Shri Ramdeobaba College of Engineering and Management, India; Sampada Nanoty, M S University Vadodara Gujarat, India; Archana Shrivastava, Jaypee Business School, JIIT University, India; and Geetika Jain, Amity University, Noida, India) states that "the expeditious proliferation of Artificial Intelligence in the mainstream has rejigged the simplest processes of the various sectors in the most efficient way. With the advent of the era of cybernation, the work culture has been curbed with the timely developments and upgradation of the technology. Cybernation has propelled the growth of every respective sector of the vast corporate diaspora with time. The main aim of the cybernation being that of smoothening the complex, bulk tasks which exploit mass human energy, has seen much success in its purpose so far. But certain domains of the corporate diaspora still await the technological transformation of their respective processes. The effect of cybernation on the business acumen of futuristic Human Resource leaders, working in the rapid concurrent era of disruptions, without losing the human touch, will carve the future Human Resource structure. Therefore, the intent of this chapter is to study the detailed implications of automation, digitalization and cybernation in the domain of Human Resource".

Chapter 9 titled "*Huawei, China and Ideological Tensions in the 5G Telecommunications Platforms*" (by Bruno Mascitelli, Swinburne University of Technology, Australia and Mona Chung, North China university of Technology, China) proposes that "while the covid 19 pandemic has captured the attention of the geo-political agenda throughout 2020, pushing the Huawei controversy off the front pages of the news, the hysteria and suspicions around Huawei providing their lower cost telecommunications equipment to western nations reached new crescendos in the move towards 5G communication platforms. The purpose of this chapter is to examine the recent series of escalating tensions between Huawei and western nations. While there was a first run of tension with the 4G networks, it was to be repeated with the preparations for the 5G telecommunications platforms. Alongside this expansion was the parallel development of geo-political tensions between China and western powers. This included ongoing tensions over the South China Sea, Taiwan's relationship with China, the Hong Kong issue, the trade war with the United States and general diplomacy between China and the West. The chapter seeks to provide the likely result on how these tensions would be resolved".

Chapter 10 titled "*What are the Leading Bank-Specific and Macroeconomic Factors Influence Islamic Banks Performance? New Evidence from MENA Countries*" (by Mosharrof Hosen, Universiti Tunku Abdul Rahman, Kampar Campus, Perak, Malaysia) proposes that "despite the proven sustainability and growth of Islamic bank during the financial crisis period, many scholars criticise the current performance of Islamic banks. Therefore, policymakers are continuously getting worried due to inconclusive finding of different research related to Islamic bank profitability. To shed the light of raising concern, this study investigates the issue from considering both macroeconomic and bank-specific factors. The annual cross-sectional data has been collected from forty-six Islamic banks in ten selected MENA countries over the period 2015-2019. The standardized pooled ordinary least square (OLS) approach's finding revealed that bank size, capital adequacy, GDP and inflation has a significant positive impact on Islamic banks' return on asset, but asset quality has no significant effect on ROA. In contrast, most of the variables have an insignificant effect of ROE. Investors, financial analysts and policymakers will get benefits from this study's results to secure their investment by successfully controlling the above-mentioned leading factors".

Chapter 11 titled "*Disruption and Innovation Trends in The QSR Industry: Perspectives Drawn from India*" (by Gaurav Nagpal, Kanika Dawar, Srutadipta Roy Choudhury and Tanmay Singh, Birla Institute of Technology and Science, Pilani, India) affirm that "The QSR (Quick Service restaurants) industry in the emerging economies such as India, is undergoing a wave of disruption and re-engineering. Many global brands in QSR food servicing have resorted to technology and innovation in one or more aspects of their value chain in order to maintain leadership positions in a market that is facing some fast-growing competition from various channels, especially with the penetration that service aggregators like Zomato, Swiggy and Uber Eats have managed to gain. This study aims to establish a general direction towards which the QSR industry is progressing in India by examining not only the current trends in India but also the trends that are prevalent worldwide and which have the potential of diffusion to emerging economies like India".

Chapter 12 titled "*The CSR Performance and Earning Management Practice on the Market Value of Conventional Banks in Indonesia*" (by Saarce Elsye Hatane, Amadea Nathania Pranoto, Josua Tarigan, Josephine Alexandra Susilo and Ang Jonathan Christianto, Petra Christian University, Indonesia) presents a study that examines "the effect of the components of Corporate Social Responsibility (CSR) and earnings management on market value, measured using Tobin's Q. CSR is measured by using KLD Index, while earnings management used discretionary loan loss provision. The GMM-SYS (generalized method of moment system) dynamic panel data method is employed to examine the research framework on conventional banks listed in Indonesia Stock Exchange. Among six components in CSR disclosures, only corporate governance, environmental and product disclosures which favorable for bank's market value. Furthermore, earnings management had a positive impact on market value. Empirical result indicated that CSR functions as a part of banks' strategic move in order to survive the highly dynamical business environment. Since CSR inflicts additional costs for the company, they must perform CSR efficiently while maintaining a strong relationship with shareholders. This study contributes to CSR and financial management literatures by finding the nature of CSR effects as future strategic investment".

Chapter 13 titled "*Retailing in Indonesia: A Deeper Look into The World's Growing Market*" (by Adilla Anggraeni and Ayuphita Tiara Silalahi, Bina Nusantara University, Indonesia) explores retailing landscape in Indonesia. According to the authors, "the retail sector itself can be considered to be one of the most promising in Asia due to the high number of populations, growing middle class, higher purchasing power and shifting spending habits. The discussion revolves along the state of online and offline retailing in Indonesia, including the current trends and discussion of luxury retailing. The technological advancement was proven to have shifted how people do retailing activities. The chapter discusses he trends in luxury retails as well as the challenges facing luxury retailers doing business in Indonesia, which may include counterfeiting. Counterfeiting is one of the prevailing issues in Indonesian retailing behaviours, targeting consumers who are aware that they have indeed purchased counterfeited items".

Chapter 14 titled "*Automation of VAT System: A Pathway of Domestic Resource Mobilization*" (by Biplob Kumar Nandi, East West University, Bangladesh; Md. Humayun Kabir, East West University, Bangladesh and Nandini Roy, University of Dhaka, Bangladesh) state that "the automated tax system has been taken as an effective tool for modernizing the tax system. The automated tax system can easily store all types of reported income, and it makes the tax submission procedure easy and convenient, resulting in reducing the compliance cost. The main objective of this chapter is to explain the necessity of an automated value added tax (VAT) system for raising domestic resource mobilization and how automation can be a better alternative to finance sustainable development goals projects. The secondary data was collected from the National Board of Revenue, Bangladesh. This study explains that the entire VAT system's automation can reduce the taxpayers' incentive to evade tax by reducing the tax compliance and taking bribes of tax officials. In sum, automation of the tax system would ultimately be pragmatic tax reform for the financing in the SDG projects".

Chapter 15 titled "*An Overview of Emerging Technologies in Indian Retail Industry*" (by Nilesh Kumar, Amity University Jharkhand, India) states that "with the arrival of several new players, Indian retail has become one of the most dynamic and fast industries. The advancement in technology, internet, engineering, many retailers are adopting and using the internet of things, Big Data technology, RFID, and other technical software and programs to enhance customer experience, customer engagement through which retailers are improving efficiency. In particular, many customer-oriented Internet of Things technologies, such as augmented reality, smart shopping carts, smart displays, and RFID tags, are expected to change the way customers experience retail shopping. For this study the secondary data has been explored and studied like The purpose of this article is to study how emerging technologies like big data; IoT implementation is transforming organizational practices and thereby generating potential benefits in the retail industry.

Chapter 16 titled "*Innovative Technology and Human Resource Management*" (by Sachin Soonthodu, Garden City University, India; and Susheela Shetty, Brindavan College, Bangalore, India) affirm that "technology plays crucial role in inclusive growth of modern human management system. Recruitment, hire, training, retain, workplace administration and optimizing workforce environment are the major functions of Human Resource Management. Adopting innovative technology within the organisation enables the managers to accumulate and deliver the information as well as communicate with employees more effectively. India, as one of the developed countries is successfully integrating technology in human resource management system, to ensure market driven product and service development. Technology makes job easy, at the same time it threatens the job market by reducing the human resource requirement to perform particular tasks. An effective human resource management should have the ability to integrate technology and the human resource for the better development of an organisation. This theoretical study focuses on various technologies adopted by the Human Resource Management to make the workplace effective and highly productive".

Chapter 17 titled "*Consumer Perception and Purchase Intention towards Refurbished Smart Phones A Circular Consumption Perspective*" (by Nishant Kumar, Amity University, India and Divya Mohan, Delhi Institute of Advanced Studies, India) states that "circular economy is a global economic model focuses to transform linear consumption in a circular system by minimizing waste and preserving the cost of materials. Refurbishment can be useful to recover value from old products, and to minimize waste. Based on the insights from literature a deductive research approach has been used to examine consumer understanding about refurbished smart phone and their purchase intention. A survey based on barriers, perceived risk and benefits associated with refurbished phones was conducted. Multiple analyses of variance was employed to identify the effect of demographic parameters on refurbishing dimensions. Multiple Regression was used to identify prominent predictors in determining purchase intention towards refurbished products. Study demonstrates fine level of awareness among people about refurbished phone and also they link it to environmental benefits. Major concern among consumer was performance issue and financial risk involved in purchasing refurbished smart phones. Financial benefits are key aspect behind promoting refurbished".

Chapter 18 titled "*Women Managers and Generations: A study of obstacles*" (by Kanchan Chandar Tolani, Shri Ramdeobaba College of Engineering and Management, Nagpur, India; Pritam Bhadade, Shri Ramdeobaba College of Engineering and Management, Nagpur, India; Kavita Patil, Dhanwate National College, Nagpur, India and Archana Shrivastava, Jaypee Business School, Noida, India) proposes that "the number of women in organizations is increasing in most countries but the representation of women in managerial positions is still disproportional. The percentage of women in leadership position globally records to only 29%. Grant Thornton annual survey 2019 reveals that India still ranks the fifth lowest in having women in managerial roles. Thus, though diversity at work is increasing, the number of women in the boardroom level is still less. The main reason for this is the hurdles and obstacles that women managers face. The current paper studies the various obstacles faced by women managers. Also, it takes into account the role of generation and aims at comparing the hurdles faced by women managers belonging to Generation X & Y. The study is undertaken with special reference to the banking sector. Major Findings reveal that there is a difference in obstacles faced by women managers belonging to Generation X and Y".

Chapter 19, titled "*Perceived Tourist Harassment in Tourist Destinations: A Study of Southern Coastal Belt of Sri Lanka*" (by Shamila Rasanjani Wijesundara, Uva wellassa university, Sri Lanka and Athula Gnanapala, Sabaragamuwa University of Sri Lanka, Sri Lanka) state that "tourism is a fast growing industry in the world. Many developing countries have recognized the economic contribution of the tourism industry towards to country, therefore, it has been included as an integral part of their development strategies. Sri Lanka continues to use tourism as one of the income earning strategy of its nation. At present, a huge tourism development is continued while accepting severe issues occurs itself like tourist harassment. The nature of the harassment is differed from destination to destination and this study mainly aims to identify the harassment occurred in tourist destination in Sri Lanka. The study carried out in Southern coastal belt, considering foreign tourists as the sample to the study. A pre tested questionnaire was distributed among 600 foreigners to collect primary data for the study and 530 questionnaires were valid for the analysis. The collected data was analyzed through exploratory factor analysis which the result revealed major six types of harassment happen in Sri Lanka as a result of tourist consumption process throughout the vacation".

Patricia Ordóñez de Pablos
University of Oviedo, Spain

Miltiadis D. Lytras
American College of Greece, Greece & Effat University, Saudi Arabia

Chapter 1
Analysing the State of Sector-Specific CSR Reporting:
Evidence From Pakistan

Muzammal Khan
https://orcid.org/0000-0001-9729-5412
University of the West of Scotland, UK

ABSTRACT

This chapter aims to deepen understanding of trends in corporate social responsibility reporting (CSRR) practices in Pakistan since the introduction of voluntary reporting guidelines in 2009 by the Securities and Exchange Commission Pakistan (SECP) and their updating in 2013. Quantitative content analysis was applied to CSRR for the chemicals, oil and gas, banking, cement, and manufacturing industries in Pakistan. The results were benchmarked to the guidelines issued on social and environmental aspects by the SECP. It was found that the reports issued by the highly polluting industries such as oil and gas, cement, and chemical industries reported significantly higher levels of information than the other sectors. The results indicate the appropriateness of industry-specific reporting and suggest, in line with local guidelines, that further standardisation is required to level the playing field of CSRR in Pakistan.

INTRODUCTION

Organisational reporting practice has received significant interest over the last two decades, with growth in the recognition of CSRR globally (de Villiers et al., 2014; Gao, 2011; Tilt, 2016; Vurro & Perrini, 2011). Research has found an increase in regulations and an increase in voluntary guidelines for CSRR. For example, the UK regulatory body (The Environment Agency) introduced the regulation in 2013 requiring all listed companies to disclose information on businesses' impact on the environment. Many other countries, e.g. Australia, Malaysia and South Africa have introduced reforms and voluntary guidelines in CSRR practices (de Villiers et al., 2014).

This recent trend in introducing voluntary CSRR guidelines has since emerged in developing countries (Kansal et al., 2016; Tilt, 2016). SECP issued voluntary guidelines in 2009, followed by detailed

DOI: 10.4018/978-1-7998-4787-8.ch001

Corporate Social Responsibility (CSR) voluntary guidelines in 2013, encouraging listed companies to disclose on CSRR matters (Malik & Kanwal, 2016). The guidelines emphasised the reporting of CSR aspects, for example, a quote from the guidelines highlights this urgency stating that "companies are expected to report concise and material information regarding their CSR policy and activities that may be consolidated and reported in the form of a separate CSR" (Securities and Exchange Commission of Pakistan, 2013). the implementation of voluntary guidelines in Pakistan is intended to improve the reputation and attractiveness of Pakistan in the global business market.

In Pakistan, both CSR and the debate on CSRR is on the rise. Companies adopting voluntary CSRR practices are becoming more focused on internationalising business, and Pakistan is already a home for more than 50 multinational companies (Javaid Lone et al., 2016). Pakistan has cultural, social, political, and economic aspects that make it both different and interesting to study. There has been fluctuating levels of economic development in Pakistan, yet the economy survives due to the abundance of natural resources and human capital (Bowering et al., 2012).

Significance of the Study

The theme of this study is to consider how Pakistani companies, within the sectors that are identified, have responded to the guidelines set out in 2009 by SECP, and how these directed attention to CSRR up to the revised guidelines issued in 2013. This is important as, prior to SECP releasing their original framework in 2009, there were no specific requirements or guidelines helping Pakistani companies to focus on issues relating to environment, social, and stakeholder issues, and no evidence of any study following the introduction of these guidelines during the period under consideration. This study examines reporting behaviours of Pakistani companies in five important sectors since the launch of the first set of guidelines and provides an overview of patterns of reporting practices. This study will benefit organisations within the sectors which were investigated, identifying how guidelines have helped to improve CSRR, whilst outlining best practice in relation to social and environmental reporting. This should help management of these companies, and other Pakistani companies that are less familiar with these guidelines, to develop best practice, or to introduce CSRR.

The issuance of guidelines and other initiatives, such as best reporting awards, may encourage companies to increase reporting, especially in those polluting sectors with a greater need to maintain legitimacy to satisfy the needs of stakeholders. Guthrie et al., (2008, p.2) noted that "the levels of social and environmental impacts can vary greatly from industry to industry due to its affiliation and nature", further justifying the need to conduct an analysis in these sectors in Pakistan. Only limited analysis has been previously undertaken, such as in the pharmaceutical (Malik & Kanwal, 2016) and aviation sectors (Kemp & Vinke, 2012), with Khan et al., (2018) comparing the impact of the institution on CSRR and also comparing Pakistan with a developed country. Studies relating to other countries (Abukari & Abdul-Hamid, 2018; Dong & Burritt, 2010; Kirat, 2015; Kolk et al., 2010; Pahuja, 2009; Patten & Zhao, 2014; Tran et al., 2016) investigated different sectors, such as oil and gas, manufacturing, and retail in order to understand the state of CSRR. There is a need to gain understanding of overall impacts and developments of CSRR in Pakistan since the introduction of guidelines.

Aim and Research Objectives

The aim of this study is to explore the impact that voluntary regulations have had on CSRR practices in various Pakistani sectors by comparing two years, namely 2009 and 2013. In attempting to achieve this aim the study considers the following research objectives:

(1) To examine how the volume and focus of CSRR has changed in Pakistan since the 2009 release of the first voluntary reporting guidelines up until the revised 2013 guidelines.
(2) To assess the degree to which legitimacy has played a part in how reporting has been conducted since the first guidelines were introduced and up until the revised 2013 guidelines.

This study focusses on changes in the volume and focus of CSRR in Pakistan between the first and second SECP guidelines on CSRR. It identifies the impact that initial guidelines had on the companies within sectors where there is greater pressure to provide justification for ethical and corporate decisions, such as industries in the polluting sectors. These are compared with companies not in the more controversial industries. Legitimacy Theory (LT) is considered to draw inferences and make sense of the state of CSRR in Pakistan during this period. The use of LT is referred to later in this paper.

Study Contribution

This study offers multiple contributions to corporate non-financial reporting practice and research. The study has theoretical implications because it assesses motivation of companies by evaluating the impact of legitimacy perspectives. This study provides evidence that, in corporate CSRR, there is potential to apply improvements regarding levels and content found in the presentation of voluntary reporting. In view of future guidelines, this study serves as the basis for taking actions in this direction (Tamvada, 2020). The analysis conducted, and results obtained, open the possibility for developing future lines of research. Finally, this study provides results from a sample of companies on the extent and focus of reporting.

The remaining sections of the paper are structured as follows. The next section explains the literature and discusses the theoretical stance used. This is followed by discussion on the research methods used, the next section presents the research findings and discussions, and the final section concludes the paper and sets out the implications, limitations, and recommendations, for future research.

LITERATURE REVIEW

Previous studies have argued that the concept of CSR is still in its infancy (Nazir, 2010, Kemp & Vinke, 2012). Malik and Kanwal (2016, p.4) noted that “it (Pakistan) is gradually moving toward CSR actions”. One of the earliest studies by Ahmad (2006, p. 127) concluded that “the motivation to engage in CSR (…in Pakistan), the types of CSR emphasised, as well as the relative importance of certain types of CSR activity appear to be moderated by the cultural values and Islamic beliefs prevalent in the country”. In terms of CSRR, the study by Nazir (2010, p.9) concluded that “despite of the fact that, there is no strict law and regulation regarding these CSR initiatives of the company, they are making it possible on the volunteer basis”. Another study found that there are no laws available which force companies towards CSR and its reporting; it is still a voluntary practice (Kemp & Vinke, 2012). There are now a few studies from the Pakistani context that have examined CSRR and which reveal the emergence of the phenomenon in the country, as is the case in many other developing countries. For example, Majeed et al. (2015) and Syed and Butt (2017) found that there was a positive impact of board, ownership and firm size on the quality and quantity of CSRR. Muttakin and Khan (2014), who completed a content analysis on listed companies in Bangladesh, concluded that these were export-oriented, and that firm size and industry type could have a positive impact on the extent of CSRR in a developing country. Finally, several authors made reference to the banking and finance sector, all of whom used content analyses, including Nobanee and Ellili (2015), who identified the overall level of sustainability disclosure in the UAE and found this to be low, with conventional banks disclosing more than Islamic banks, and suggested that this had a positive impact on the financial performance of the conventional banks; Ullah and Afjalur (2015) who suggested that the level of CSRR varied within annual reports, and contained mostly linguistic explanations rather than graphs or images to portray important information to stakeholders, but identified that regulatory change significantly impacted on the nature and extend of CSRR; Andrikopoulos et al. (2014) listed company size, financial leverage and corporate visibility as factors that impacted on CSRR; and Bonsón and Bednárová (2015) concluded that a company's sector and listing in the Dow Jones Sustainability Index influenced the extent of sustainability reporting. For some developed countries, (Gao et al. 2005) found industry differences and corporate size have positive effects on the level of CSR disclosure in Hong Kong-based companies. Branco and Rodrigues (2008) highlight that banks with higher market visibility tend to give more importance to corporate non-financial disclosures than those with lower visibility as part of their reputational management strategy. Corporate size appeared to be a significant factor and was highlighted by several of the above articles in relation to both developed and developing countries. This indicates that CSRR is common in large firms as they have access to resources and are more visible, which convinces them of the need to report to gain advantages such as improving corporate reputation and instilling confidence in stakeholders. smaller firms find it difficult to engage in CSRR due to underlying structural reasons such as lack of awareness and resources.

The Global Integrity Report, cited by Kemp and Vinke (2012), noted that legal framework and voluntary mechanisms remain ineffective. The government in Pakistan has allowed NGOs and other institutes to adopt international standards and promote the issue of social accountability certificates to encourage CSR. Organisations, such as the CSR centre of Pakistan, the Sustainable Development Policy Institute, the Pakistan Centre for Philanthropy, the Pakistan Poverty Alleviation Fund, the Institute of Cost and Management Accountants and the Institute of Chartered Accountants of Pakistan, are active in promoting the CSR agenda. The most prominent development has been the introduction of CSRR voluntary guidelines, issued in 2009, which encouraged listed companies to adopt CSR activities whilst emphasising reporting of social and environmental aspects of business. Since the introduction of CSR guidelines in 2009 by SECP[1], the level of awareness of the need to report has increased. SECP deals with regulations for the corporate sector and has established a Code of Corporate Governance to promote good corporate governance practices. In 2013[2], they again introduced voluntary guidelines (which were more detailed than the previous guidelines published in 2009) on CSR and disclosure, which encouraged listed companies to engage in CSR, and to report on CSR performance for transparency purposes. To test the impact of these guidelines, Javaid Lone et al. (2016) and Khan et al. (2018) investigated Pakistani companies and found the extent of CSRR had increased since the introduction of CSR voluntary guidelines by SECP. The study by Javaid Lone et al. (2016) only focused on stand-alone reports while overlooking CSRR in annual financial reports, the medium most frequently used to communicate CSR related information by companies in developing countries (Kemp & Vinke, 2012). Khan et al. (2018)

adopted instead a very small sample and is unrepresentative of many sectors that operate in Pakistan. This current study focuses on both annual financial and stand-alone reports and refers to a much larger sample of Pakistani companies, focussing on five major sectors to assess the extent of reporting and the impact of voluntary guidelines.

LEGITIMACY THEORY UNDERPINNING

Researchers have often applied LT to draw inferences while researching voluntary non-financial reporting practice (Archel et al., 2009; Branco & Rodrigues, 2008; Hahn & Kühnen, 2013; Rahaman et al., 2004). It is argued that legitimacy is a powerful tool to create a picture of companies' possible intentions behind non-financial reporting (Bebbington et al., 2014). Reporting practices are used to create a dialogue between an organisation and relevant stakeholders to address emerging incidents by disclosing relevant information (Killian & O'Regan, 2016). Companies implement various reporting approaches in response to emerging problems, depending on how the company aims to construct, preserve, or re-establish credibility (Ching & Gerab, 2017). Organisations, for example, may raise, sustain, or decrease the degree of reporting to achieve organisational legitimacy (de Villiers & van Staden, 2006; Deegan et al., 2000; Dumay et al., 2010).

Several authors have referred to the impact that legitimacy has on reporting practices of firms across the globe. These include Mahadeo et al. (2011) who identified that, between the years 2004 and 2007, there had been a selective increase in the quantity and quality of social and environmental reporting in Mauritius, and argue that the firms selected changed reporting practices due to legitimacy reasons; de Villiers and van Staden (2006) who identified a similar pattern in South African firms, but suggest that legitimising objectives may be served by altering the type and volume of disclosure in order to avoid a legitimacy crisis; Choi et al. (2013) who suggested that legislation may have enhanced the levels of voluntary carbon emission disclosures in Australian firm, in line with the claim made by legitimacy theory; and Cho et al. (2013) who noted that authoritative guidance for separate reports may improve corporate environmental disclosure practice in South Korea.

Similar research has looked at how controversial industries in developing countries have used CSRR. These include Odera et al. (2016) who used content analysis to examine the CSRR of oil companies; Chaudhry et al. (2014) who carried out interviews in petroleum companies to access the level of focus on being seen to be green and suggested that these companies were doing so in order to portray themselves in a positive way; and Finally, Khan and Hassan (2019) investigated oil and gas companies in Pakistan and claimed that legitimacy theory linked with company disclosure of environmental issues such as health and safety, emissions, carbon footprint, energy conservation and environmental protection.

Islam's (2010) review revealed that existing research only provided a partial understanding of CSRR practices of organisations operating in developing countries and research lacked theoretical support. In comparison to developed nations, the phenomenon of CSRR practices in developing nations remains under-theorised, as also suggested in a recently revised study by Khan et al., (2020). Few attempts have applied LT to CSRR practices within the context of developing countries. For example, Islam and Deegan's study (2008) studied the CSRR practices of Bangladeshi companies' and found that companies adopted reporting due to pressures from industry. The clothing sector of Bangladesh is the country's leading exporter, with international buyers and contractors exerting influence on local clothing firms to report on CSR activities. Islam and Deegan (2008, p.871) concluded in their study that "Legitimacy theory would suggest that for an organisation to maintain its "license to operate" then it must comply with the expectations of the community in which it operates". LT offers a basis for the future researcher who wants to theorise and explain similar phenomena. In the case of Pakistan, there is a lack of evidence on the application of LT, especially in comparing how LT matters in different sectors, including environmentally sensitive sectors, such as oil and gas and non-environmentally sensitive sectors, such as financial. The insights offered by LT indicate that organisations need to be sensitive to the evolving expectations of people (Azizul Islam, 2017).

METHODOLOGY

Content Analysis Process

Content analysis is a well-used research method in CSRR studies and is considered a valid research strategy (Beck et al., 2010; Khan et al., 2020; Lock & Seele, 2016; Michelon et al., 2015), and is useful for analysing trends and patterns in documents (Krippendorff, 2012), and includes drawing deductive, inductive, and abductive inferences from data to uncover tacit and explicit significances of messages. Given the degree of subjectivity involved in content analysis, researchers are advised to address the reliability of the coding process and the validity of the research instrument to ensure consistency and replication of research findings (Dumay & Cai, 2014, 2015). Researchers must ensure that research data is trustworthy and unbiased and that the research technique used represents what should be assessed (Dumay & Cai 2015). Several steps have been taken to address the potential validity and reliability of the research data in this study.

Secondary data is often researched while searching for trends in patterns of corporate reporting. The quantitative content analysis measures the volume of reporting to draw inferences about meaning and significance of the disclosed text (Krippendorff, 1980; Unerman, 2000). The research objectives are best served by the use of quantitative methods because companies engage with various stakeholders using corporate annual reports which are published in documentary form, and such records are deemed appropriate for a quantitative technique, namely content analysis (based on archival research). It is argued that such techniques can allow the researcher to assess the importance given to CSR related data in companies (Cho et al., 2015; de Villiers & Staden, 2012; Michelon et al., 2015). Corporate reporting can signal importance that organisations give to the subject (Michelon et al., 2015). This paper focuses on secondary data to examine CSRR in different sectors of Pakistan. The researcher focuses on CSR reports made available by companies as digital publications because this type of publication provides information on a longitudinal scale and is suited for comparative analysis.

Although there are many sectors in Pakistan, only five major sectors have been explored: Financial, Cement, Oil & Gas, Chemical and Energy. Previous studies have investigated these sectors in different countries (Bakhtina & Goudriaan, 2011; Eljayash et al., 2012; Kamla & Rammal, 2013; Laine, 2009; Vani & Murali, 2015), yet there is a lack of evidence to explain the CSRR of these sectors from a Pakistani context. These sectors are classified as having high carbon footprints because their operations impact on the environment and people. The financial sector has been included to test whether industry classification impacts on the patterns, extent, and level of CSRR. The data has been collected from the annual reports of companies listed on the Pakistan Stock Exchange (PSE). Sixty-three (n=63) companies were selected from five (5) major sectors – Financial Institutions (n=17), Cement (n=5), Oil and Gas (n=11),

Manufacturing (n=21) and Chemical (n=9). These companies were selected based on two criteria. Firstly, the firm must have been registered with PSE since 2009 as most companies started reporting on CSR after the introduction of voluntary guidelines by SECP. Secondly, the company must have committed to publishing CSR related information (in English and, in some cases, in Urdu).

The aim was to compare two different years to identify differences in trends and patterns of CSRR periods since the introduction of voluntary guidelines in 2009. To achieve this the focus of the study compares the change in the levels of CSRR as well as the focus of CSRR between the years 2009 and 2013. Despite SECP's motivation for issuing voluntary guidelines in 2009 was to create an environment in which companies were encouraged to disclose CSR related information to enhance transparency levels in Pakistan, the responsiveness of the businesses to this important development by SCEP needs to be investigated further. This paper does not consider the impact following the 2013 guidelines but examines the impact between 2009 and the 2013 guidelines. Statistical analysis was performed on reports published in those two years and examined how many pages companies devoted to CSRR as a way of assessing reporting practices (Odera et al., 2016). Descriptive statistical analysis was adopted to understand trends and patterns of reporting. This study also observes trends in using reporting guidelines in each sector, and which sectors use the annual financial report, and which use stand-alone reports for CSR related information. The extent of environmental and social information is also examined in different sectors in Pakistan.

Research Instrument and Scoring Method

This research implements the technique of content analysis to examine the scope of company CSRR. This method has been well-established among social, environmental and accountability fields and has been used considerably in CSR literature (Khan et al., 2020). The 2009 voluntary guidelines, and other items (such as philanthropic related aspects, as well as environmental) identified in previous literature, specifically in studies from developing countries (environmental and philanthropy related), were included in the research. These issues can be classified using two main dimensions: the environmental dimension is represented by the concepts 'emissions', 'energy conservation', 'environmental protection', 'water management'; and the concepts 'health/safety', 'community investment (education and health)', 'consumer protection', 'employees' protection' and 'welfare investment (donations)' can be allocated to the social dimension. Previous studies have suggested that companies are more likely to place emphasis on environmental and social indicators to maintain a positive brand image (Hsieh, 2012). This is because companies seek to obtain or maintain legitimacy of their business to legitimise the company operations with stakeholders (Faisal et al., 2012; Kuruppu & Milne, 2010; Tilling & Tilt, 2010). The purpose of comparing environmental and social aspects is to examine the extent and importance given to items from the reporting index in these sectors. Many other research studies have relied on a checklist-based approach while conducting content analysis (de Aguiar & Fearfull, 2010; Marzouk et al., 2017; Muttakin & Khan, 2014). In this study, 'Yes' and 'No' was used to code the presence or absence of coding criteria (Casadei & Amadei, 2010; Ding et al., 2016; Kent & Zunker, 2013; Stanny, 2013). For example, one of the coding criteria relates to the presence of environmental policy. The researcher investigated the company's report and searched for related words such as "environmental policy," "environmental values," "environmental mission," "environmental objective," or texts pertaining to any environmental statement. The size of the text was counted in the form of pages to cover related pictorial information. Many companies used images and graphs to portray information relating to environmental and social performance and activity (Beattie, 2014; Gray, 2006). The more that reporting is provided on an activity in CSRR, the more it is perceived by the company as achieving legitimacy. For example, if a polluting industry provides more environmental related discourse in their reports, this might show that the company values environmental aspects more than other aspects (Bebbington et al., 2014). To record this, if a company had reported a specific item from the index that is created for this study, one (1) was assigned, otherwise it was recorded as zero (0) (Al-Tuwaijri et al., 2004; Guthrie et al., 2004; Lu & Abeysekera, 2015; Muttakin & Khan, 2014). To determine the extent of a company's CSRR, total numbers of items reported were counted and recorded. Using descriptive statistics, simple average was used to ascertain the number of pages dedicated by companies in each sector to CSRR. In this document, in the analysis section, narrative discussion will identify the key items within the environmental and social indices that these sectors concentrate most on.

In the study, the researcher used only publicly available data. No sensitive personal information was used. The company website was targeted to check the availability of the reports and once the report was found it was downloaded and saved in a folder. Due to the lack of standardisation of reporting in Pakistan (Khan & Hassan, 2019), the researcher considered the length of reported materials in terms of number of pages. The number of pages also covered the pictorial reporting (Duff, 2014; Nyahunzvi, 2013; Odera et al., 2016), and all pages from each report were considered. Attention was focussed on environmental and social activities, ignoring irrelevant information for example financial information.

DESCRIPTIVE ANALYSIS

The study now examines the changes in CSRR across different sectors in Pakistan.

The Volume of CSR Reporting – A Comparison

Table 1 shows the amount of CSRR in different sectors of Pakistan. The result shows a different scope of CSRR across different sectors. Compared to other sectors some tend to report more on CSR. For example, the levels of CSRR are significantly higher for environmentally sensitive industries such as Chemical, Oil and Gas and Cement and are lowest for Financial. These environmentally sensitive companies follow international reporting standards such as GRI or Integrated Reporting and are required to be more transparent due to industry relevance and higher visibility in the market.

By comparing reporting practices between 2009 and 2013, a significant change for reporting has been observed, particularly in the cement sector. This suggests that CSRR has gained momentum among different sectors in Pakistan. Reporting appears to be still in its infancy in some sectors, for example, manufacturing.

Table 1 shows that the amount of paper committed to CSRR has increased between 2009 and 2013, particularly in the cement and chemicals industry sectors. Across all five sectors the average number of papers allocated has more than trebled, although Financial and Manufacturing sectors, despite having the largest percentages changes have had the smallest impact in terms of page numbers. The impact results in a wider disparity between those sectors which have committed to publishing on CSRR than was evident in 2009.

Table 1. Volume CSRR

Sector	Average page(s) 2009	Average page(s) 2013	% change
Financial (n=17)	0.5	1.6	220
Cement	1	22.5	2150
Manufacturing	1	2	100
Oil and gas	14	20	43
Chemical	15	49	227
Descriptive Statistics			
Mean	6.3	19.02	
Standard Deviation	7.5	19.4	
Minimum	0.5	1.6	
Maximum	15	49	

Reporting Guidelines

In terms of using reporting guidelines, it can be seen from Table 2 that the trend of using guidelines among some sectors has increased to some extent. The guidelines that were adopted by companies vary between sectors. Smaller local companies have adopted SECP guidelines whereas companies, for example from the polluting industries, as well as larger companies, have used GRI reporting guidelines as these provide comprehensive coverage of environmental and social aspects.

Table 2. Comparison of the trend of using reporting guidelines

Sector	No. of companies 2009	No. of companies 2013
Financial (n=17)	0	2
Cement (n=5)	0	1
Manufacturing (n=19)	0	2
Oil and Gas (n=11)	2	4
Chemical (n=9)	2	3

As argued above. companies from highly polluting sectors e.g. oil and gas are expected to be more transparent due to the significant negative impact of their operations.

Compared to other sectors in the sample, the manufacturing sector appears to have a very low interest in adopting CSRR guidelines. Hossain and Andrew (2006) found that polluting manufacturing industries tend to provide more CSR information than those manufacturing industries or service industries with a lower environmental impact. In the manufacturing sector, only two companies appeared to be using reporting guidelines, and these two companies mainly adopted local voluntary guidelines issued by SECP. Despite using some guidelines, these two companies have a minimal amount of reporting rather than comprehensive. The majority of companies report on CSR issues within their annual financial report, allowing them to describe what is important to them (e.g. most reported on community related reporting) rather than considering any voluntary guidelines to expand the focus on their reporting practices. It is noted that companies that did not follow any guidelines were found to have a descriptive and low level of reporting. To improve this, it is suggested that the adoption of reporting guidelines has a significant impact on companies' comprehensiveness and expansion of their reporting scope.

Type of Reports

The environmentally sensitive sectors, namely oil and gas, cement, and chemical appear to be using stand-alone reports, unlike the manufacturing and financial sectors as can be seen in Table 3. In a comparison of the annual financial reports and the stand-alone reports, it is noted that where the company used a stand-alone report and guidelines to provide detailed information on CSR performance, this significantly increased their level of reporting. As evidenced in previous research, sectors such as Oil and Gas, Cement and Chemical, have a significant impact on the environment and such companies prefer to present detailed CSR related information. By issuing a stand-alone report, as per GRI guidelines, this could suggest an attempt to maintain legitimacy of a company's business practices.

Even though CSRR is a voluntary practice in Pakistan, and a market which is not heavily regulated by environmental laws; companies still appear to be issuing stand-alone reports, resulting in greater levels of reporting.

Table 3. The type of reports used for CSRR

Sector	2009		2013	
	Annual report	**Stand-alone report**	**Annual report**	**Stand-alone report**
Financial	17	0	17	0
Cement	5	0	4	1
Manufacturing	21	0	21	0
Oil and gas	9	2	9	2
Chemical	7	2	6	3

This is arguably motivated by legitimacy perspectives, as these companies reflect upon CSR performance in reports in a detailed manner to avoid legitimacy risks. This is supported by the findings of Jo and Na (2012), which suggested that the impact of risk reduction through CSRR is more economically and statistically significant in 'controversial' industries than in the non-controversial sector (Kilian & Hennigs, 2013, p.79). They also found that CSRR helps companies to manage risks. This may be the result of industry affiliation and size as the polluting firms in Oil and Gas, Chemical and Cement in Pakistan are mainly larger, for example, Engro Corporation and Fauji Fertilizer Limited are two of the largest firms in Pakistan. It is well documented in previous research that, when businesses release a stand-alone report, reporting volumes increase substantially (Khan & Hassan, 2019; Michelon et al., 2015). In the case of oil and gas companies, four companies were found to be using a stand-alone report which relied on GRI guidelines. These companies' reporting levels were found to be significantly higher, as seen in Table 3 above. Studies have indicated that oil and gas companies have had a greater environmental footprint; maintaining legitimacy is essential for oil and gas companies (Berthelot et al., 2013). It may be suggested that businesses in this field pay close attention to their transparency as a way of achieving stakeholder trust by issuing a stand-alone report to increase the volume, as well as coverage of CSRR. Other strategies involve the application of international guidelines, such as GRI, to provide extensive coverage of CSR performance indicators. This is consistent with results from the analysis by Alazzani and Wan-Hussin (2013), which showed that businesses made fair attempts to comply with GRI reporting guidelines because these offered a rigorous and detailed tool for reporting. The voluntary adoption by oil and gas companies of GRI reporting guidelines increases transparency, credibility, and comparability as this helps organisations to create a good impression on their stakeholders.

THE EXTENT OF SOCIAL AND ENVIRONMENTAL REPORTING

In each sector, the state of social and environmental reporting was reviewed to gain insights into what was reported more frequently and, therefore, what was most important to the sector. Some of the key sectors were studied and discussed separately to observe the differences in the reports.

Financial

In Figure 1, it can be observed that, even though the banking sector is not an environmentally sensitive industry, some companies chose to provide environmental information. For example, the annual reports of Askri Bank (2013, p.52) claimed that: "In order to contribute positively to a better and healthy environment, we aim to promote paperless culture, renewable energy sources, reduction of carbon emissions and increasing plantation".

Figure 1. Social and Environmental Reporting - Oil and Gas Sector

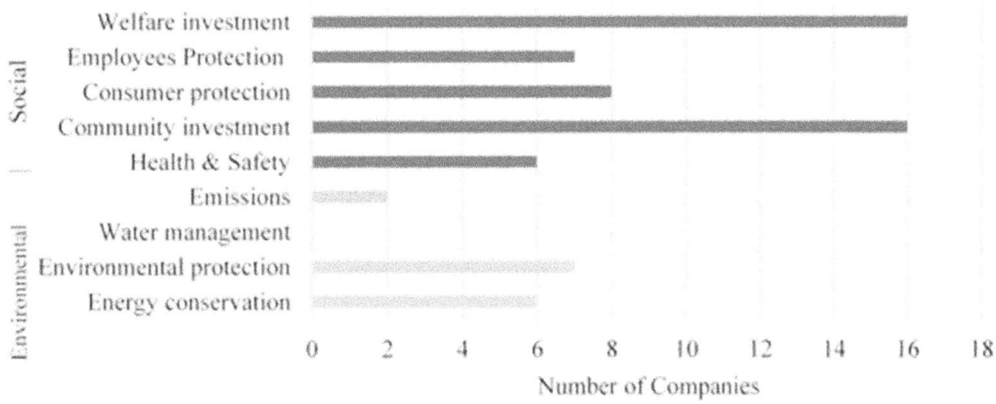

Out of seventeen companies, 7 provided some sort of environmental information. In contrast, the level of social aspect reporting was considerably greater than environmental information; in particular, sixteen companies issued information regarding community investment and welfare investment. This indicates that the financial sector considers social information or social aspects of CSR to be more important to them. This is in line with the findings of Aribi & Gao (2012); Kamla & Rammal (2013; Khan et al. (2011); Kiliç et al. (2015); and Krasodomska (2015), who found that a sample of financial companies disclosed more on Islamic aspects, such as Zakat, charity donations, philanthropy, and community. This current study also finds greater levels of reporting on community investment and welfare investment in the financial sector in Pakistan. The main statements derived from the annual reports were:

During the year, Bank spent Rs.21.4 million on the general welfare of the community. This included contributions towards Sadqa for feeding the poor, Jashan-e-Baharan (spring) celebrations, Literary Festival, Awareness Activities on the eve of International Anticorruption Day and sponsorship of sports activities. Further, the Bank sponsored various organisation including Human Rights Society of Pakistan, Karachi Stock Exchange Guarantee Limited, Quetta Development Authority, in social events, conferences and awareness programs, during the year 2015 by spending Rs.10.9 million (Askari Bank, 2013).

Sharif and Rashid (2014) supported this notion and argued that the level of CSRR was not low in the commercial banks of Pakistan and that the reporting had been impressive. This could be due to banks or other financial companies believing that their practices have no significant impact on society or the environment, in contrast to manufacturing industries where cases such as child labour and poor working conditions were found. In this regard, Saeed, cited in Relano and Paulet (2012, p.382), argued that "they (Banks) all claim to be the most virtuous institutions as far as the environment and society are concerned". It may also be that banks want to obtain confidence of stakeholders by revealing CSR information in line with the claim made by LT. This is one strategy that companies use to maintain a positive relationship with their customers. As Branco and Rodrigues (2008) argued, banks which want to be more visible to customers showed more concern with enhancing their corporate image through CSRR and their study suggested that LT may be an explanation of CSRR by the sampled banks.

Cement

The cement industry is a major sector in Pakistan, and it is playing a vital role in the economic development of the country (Ali, 2015), however, it also has a greater impact on the environment.

As shown in Figure 2, information on both environmental protection and health and safety is disclosed by all companies in the cement industry. This supports LT perspectives that polluting industries significantly impact upon the environment and companies issue environmental performance information in annual reports to alter/maintain/change stakeholders' perceptions (Bebbington et al., 2014). The reporting on energy conservation and water management appears to be low, whilst the trend of social reporting in the cement industry is significantly higher. Almost all companies give information on social aspects of their CSR performance and companies in developing countries tend to give information on their social performance, as argued by many studies Elijido-Ten (2011); Islam & Deegan (2008); Lund-Thomsen et al. (2016); Momin & Parker (2013); Sumiani et al. (2007). The overarching trend of disclosing social information shows that companies want to justify themselves as responsible citizens so that the company may operate in society more effectively (Jayanti & Rajeev Gowda, 2014). It is noted

Figure 2. Social and Environmental Reporting - Cement Sector

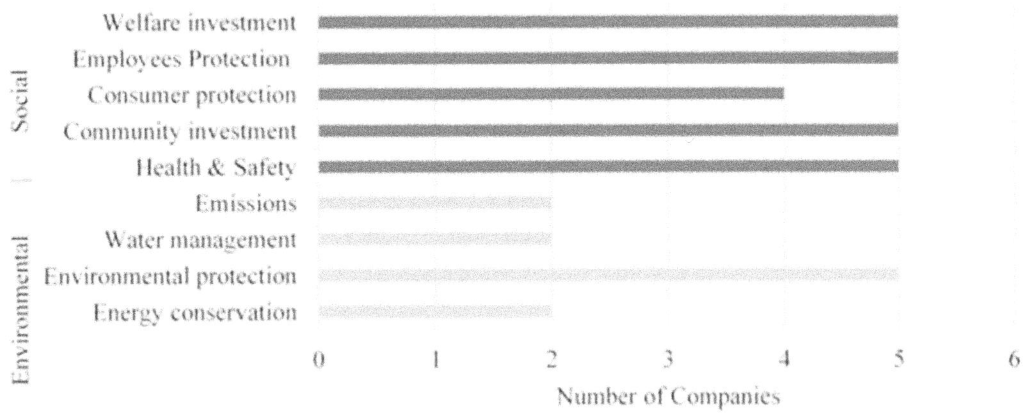

that the large cement companies of Pakistan, such as Lucky Cement, disclosed a great amount of CSR information; this company is large (Total assets 50,196.175 million Pak rupees) and is a significant exporter of the cement of other companies. It issues annual CSR reports, whereas other local Pakistani cement companies do not. The influence of customers from other countries may have brought pressure upon this company to be more transparent. It could be a result of trying to project a better corporate image for local and international buyers (Belal & Cooper, 2011). This is in line with the findings of Vani and Krishna (2015), who found that the larger players of the cement industry in India were contributing towards CSR. Furthermore, the findings are also in line with the study conducted on the Pakistani cement industry by Awan and Akhtar (2014), which found that CSR practice has proved to be a positive tool for cement companies to enhance their brand image and reputation to local and global customers. Furthermore, according to Aruwa and Hemen (2011), the cement industry of Nigeria paid compensation to the stakeholders affected by their operations, which enhanced their corporate image.

Oil and Gas

Oil and gas are valuable resources and many developing nations flourish in these natural resources (Alazzani & Wan-Hussin, 2013). Oil and gas companies tend to publish substantial detail on both environmental and social issues in their annual reports. Several companies in Pakistan's oil and gas sector reported information on the environment, and on health and safety (see Figure 3). Similar results have been found by Kilian and Hennigs (2013, p.79) who argued that "companies in controversial industries are more active in CSR communication".

It could be argued that the reporting of environmental information gives them environmental credibility as transparency is also used as a tool for creating a better corporate image (Friedman & Miles, 2001, Branco & Rodrigues, 2007, Dragomir, 2010, Kilian & Hennigs, 2013). This generates questions around whether CSRR is an actual reflection of socially responsible activities of companies, as companies might be using claims to be being socially responsible. Du and Vieira (2012, p.425) suggested a solution to this question:

Figure 3. Social and Environmental Reporting - Oil and Gas Sector

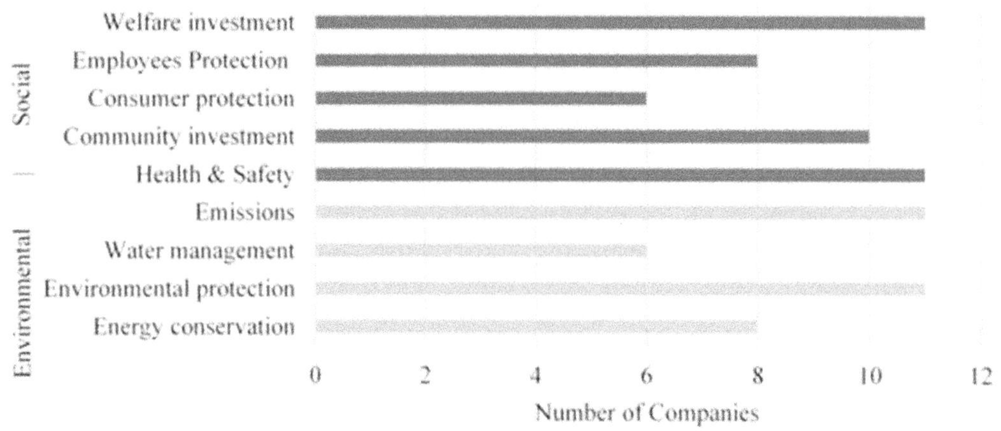

Despite a wide variety of CSR initiatives and prevalence of cross-sector partnerships, oil companies need to abandon the ''CSR as public relations'' mentality, and instead work proactively in minimizing the negative externalities of their business operations, and take a long-term approach to CSR by investing substantially in renewable energies and going beyond simple financial donations in their cross-sector partnerships.

The results of their research are consistent with this paper in that they confirm that the major oil and gas firms revealed more CSR information than their smaller counterparts. According to Banerjee (2020), oil and gas companies significantly embraced regulated CSR and explicitly reported their CSR practices and spending in India. They also have increasingly developed sophisticated reporting approaches to connect with stakeholders about CSR issues and in line with regulations, such as Schedule VII of the Act. Dealing with such important issues and complying with voluntary/mandatory guidelines may improve the company's reputation, in line with the perspectives of the legitimacy theories.

Chemical

Figure 4 provides information on environmental information disclosed in the chemical industry of Pakistan. Many companies disseminated information on environmental protection, energy conservation and health and safety.

The study reveals that companies are proactive and provide relevant information so that they can maintain or gain legitimacy. It can be argued that chemical companies work with MNCs and have partnerships with other businesses, which provides a positive influence on reporting. Companies respond to such pressure to attain a competitive advantage and to satisfy their crucial business partners.

All companies disseminated information on society in their annual reports. This supports the argument that companies operating in developing countries tend to provide more social information due to prevalent issues such as poverty, lack of education, and poor health which exist within Pakistan (Idemudia,

Figure 4. Social and Environmental Reporting - Chemical Sector

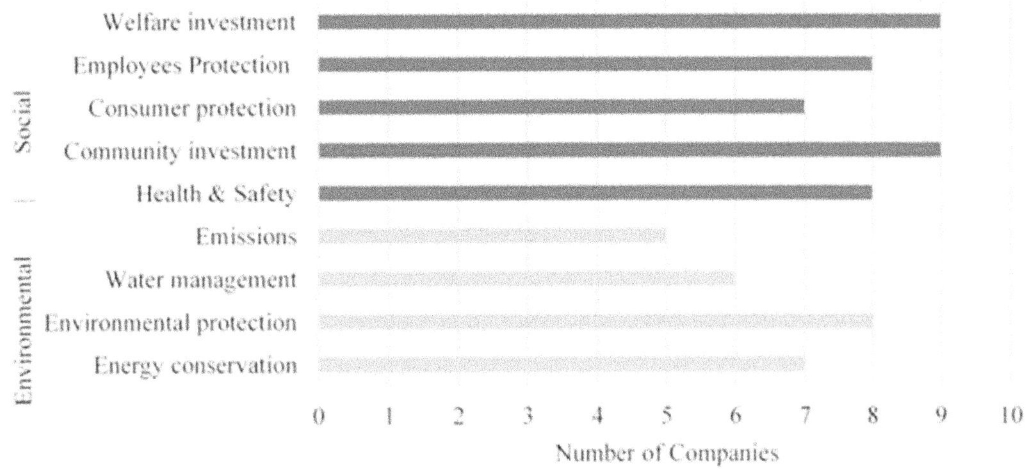

2011; Momin & Parker 2013; Naser et al., 2006). The chemical industry's practices have the potential to make a negative impact on the environment, hence the need to give justifications of CSR practices. Companies in this industry use reporting as a tool to affect stakeholders' perceptions – mostly by giving positive information. Aerts & Cormier (2009) found that environmentally sensitive industries. such as the chemical industry. provide more environmental, information as it is considered important to that industry. In addition, according to Salomone and Galluccio (2001), the chemical industry has different types of environmental concerns to other industries, which is in line with Lock and Seele's (2015) study that found that the chemical industry's CSRR is extensive as compared to industries with a lower environmental impact, such as banking. This could be mainly due to the increased risks observed in the Pakistani chemical industry in the use of stand-alone reports and reporting guidelines. This may be the result of industry affiliation and size as generally chemical firms in Pakistan are larger, for example, Engro Corporation and Fauji Fertilizer Limited. The same trend was found in Jiufang et al. (2009) and Zhang et al.'s, (2008) study that investigated the chemical industry and the findings indicate that firms' size has a stronger impact on determining the disclosure of environmental information. Furthermore, Adams (2002) found that the country of original and its sector significantly impacts on the reporting trends of social and environmental issues, as well as on the content and extensive reports protects legitimacy as non-reporting might generate possible threats. However, in light of the results of Jahdi and Acikdilli's (2009) study, it can be argued that CSRR is a marketing tool. In addition, for chemical companies, the communication of CSR is a necessary effort to maintain their 'license to operate'.

Manufacturing

The type of businesses included in the manufacturing sector are textiles, packaging, food, sugars, cables, tyres, and tobacco. The results showed that all companies sampled discussed health and safety issues in their annual reports, likely in response to the call for maintaining safety standards after incidents in factories (Waheed, 2014), for example, the collapse of a garment factory, Rana Plaza, in 2013 in Bangladesh. Information on the environment protection activities reported in annual reports has tended to provide basic and descriptive content. Hossain and Andrew (2006) found that polluting manufacturing industries tend to provide more CSR information than those manufacturing industries or service industries with lower environmental impact.

As can be observed in Figure 5, most companies report on social aspects of CSR, particularly in relation to community and welfare investment, whereas there is less reporting observed in employee-related aspects of CSR.

Figure 5. Social and Environmental Reporting - Manufacturing Sector

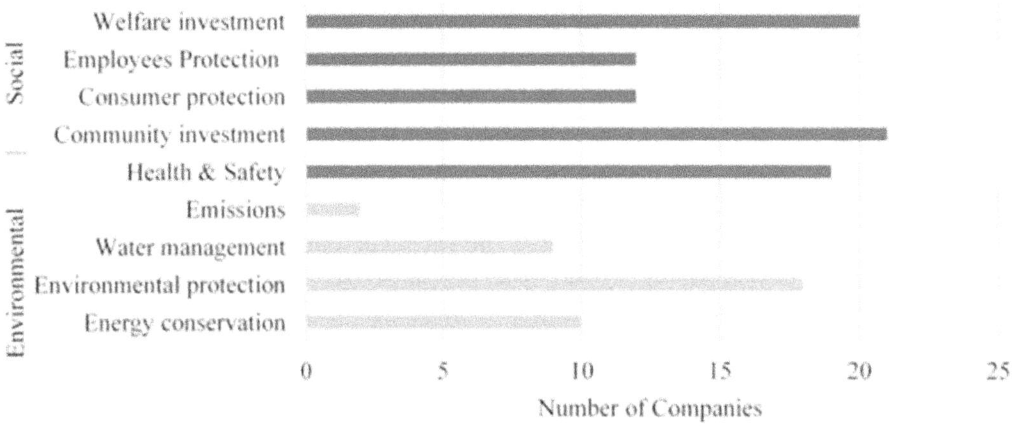

It can be argued that the reason behind high levels of social information in the reports is due to cultural reasons because in South Asia, especially in Muslim countries, giving donations, and helping the community is important. In a general sense, the emphasis on environmental issues receives less focus in Pakistan as the public has limited awareness of this area. The current government is making efforts to increase people's awareness of environmental issues (Kamal et al., 2019). In addition, some NGO's run initiatives to create awareness about environmental and social issues, but only in particular areas. At a mainstream level, there are no such initiatives to encourage the public to become aware of environmental issues. The government also places less emphasis on the environmental side of CSR.

Following the introduction of voluntary guidelines in Pakistan, some studies have examined the extent of CSRR before, and after, the introduction of SEPC guidelines (Chaudhry et al., 2014; Kemp & Vinke, 2012; Khan & Hassan, 2019; Nazir, 2010). Khan and Hassan (2019) also found that the level of CSRR increased considerably in Pakistan's Oil and Gas sector of Pakistan. The findings are limited to only a few sectors in Pakistan's context and this study explores the application of CSRR over time in five major sectors in Pakistan (Chemical, Oil and Gas, Financial, Cement and Manufacturing).

Further findings relate to controversial industries in developed countries, such as Yapa et al. (2005) who found that environmentally sensitive companies in Australia were disclosing more environmental information than other companies; Guthrie et al. (2008) discussed the reporting by companies, again in Australia, where more specific issues were involved; they suggested that companies tended to use corporate websites more than annual reports when discussing CSRR; and Kilian and Hennigs (2013) in a study which focussed on German companies, identified that companies in controversial industries were found to be more active in CSRR than those in non-controversial industries.

CONCLUSIONS

This study examines the level of the adoption of CSRR in specific Pakistani sectors between the years 2009-2013, a time when SECP's influence was shaping the nature of reporting in a way that had not previously been witnessed. The justification for carrying out such research is to identify how key sectors of Pakistani industry and commerce are faring in adopting CSRR approaches. A comparison is made between the reporting of CSRR issues of Pakistani companies and those of equivalent sectors in the developed nations.

Changes in CSRR Volume Since Introduction of Voluntary Guidelines

The current study concludes that companies in the different sectors in Pakistan engage in CSRR with varying levels of disclosures. One important conclusion which this study presents is the fact that, since the introduction of voluntary guidelines by SECP, the levels of CSRR has increased in Pakistan with significant changes in the amount of disclosures on CSRR since the first emergence of voluntary guidelines from SECP. It is observed that there is a clear difference between reporting in annual financial reports and stand-alone reports. Companies provide broader and more comprehensive coverage of CSRR issues in stand-alone reports, whereas reporting appears to be low and narrative in annual financial reports. In addition, the adoption of reporting frameworks enhances a company's reporting practices. The results suggest that only large companies appear to be using these frameworks whilst for small-medium companies, using reporting guidelines might be a complicated and costly option.

This study also concludes that highly polluted sectors or larger sized organisations have more levels of CSRR compared to those in the financial and manufacturing sectors. In terms of CSRR within different industries, the results suggest that CSRR varies across industries and significantly differs according to the nature of the sector, which is consistent with Sweeney and Coughlan (2008) who investigated reports of 28 FTSE4Good firms and found that significant variations appeared in how different sectors disclosed CSR information. Similar trends were also shared by Giannarakis (2014). Companies do not report in the same manner and the sector affiliation impacts the level, quality, and nature of information being disclosed. Deegan (2002) argued that the industry type was also associated with the level of the reporting; he argued that sectors producing high carbon footprints, such as automobile and oil and gas, were more likely to have a higher volume of reporting than those producing lesser carbon footprints, such as the financial sector. As was the case within this study, it can be observed that companies prefer to report on what they think is more important to their business. In other words, and to their stakeholders. For example, in the banking sector, stakeholders expect to be provided with information on social performance and stakeholders in oil and gas companies are more interested in the company's environmental performance, and these drivers encourage companies to provide relevant information to their stakeholders.

Link Between CSRR and Legitimacy

This study identifies that there are differing practices in CSRR between companies in Pakistan who tend to use CSRR as a means of providing a rationale to stakeholders for their existence, particularly focusing on the good they provide to society. These sorts of practices are identified as legitimising the existence of the company and this notion is widely debated in CSRR literature, yet prior to this study there appears to be limited evidence of studies on Pakistani businesses that support any connection being made to the legitimacy concept. The lack of previous studies in this area adds to the significance of this paper. The financial sector is found to make more social and community-related reporting, whereas the industrial sectors heavily focus on environmental aspects, which indicates that companies often report according to the expectations of industry stakeholders to gain their confidence, consistent with LT claims. From LT perspectives, Cho and Roberts, (2010) have argued that poorer environmental performing companies provide more extensive environmental reporting, and also present their reporting on better-presented websites. Many companies in both developed and developing countries face ongoing threats to their legitimacy, including environmental degradation, workplace treatment, child labour, and corruption, which means that pressure from legitimacy threats can be a motivational factor in seeking organisational legitimacy.

Study Implications

CSRR is an important practice that helps companies to enhance the trust that is constituted as a basic moral expectation, hence companies should not just take reporting practice as an image building or maintaining activity (Merkelsen, 2011). Public scrutiny is on the rise, hence CSRR and reports are subject to investigation by various bodies e.g. academics, NGOs, shareholders, and the government, and just "greenwashing" could be a potential risk for a company's reputation. Such a practice could distort reputation, lead to mistrust or a weakening of trust. Reporting standardisation can help businesses resolve the drawbacks of having varied reporting material and can help corporations fulfil the needs of their most significant stakeholders. The shift to integrated reporting standardisation can help to accomplish the goal of enhanced trust between the various groups and close the gap in knowledge among stakeholders and companies (Bloxham, 2011).

There is a need for industry specific guidelines to make CSRR explicitly relevant in different sectors. It appears that reputation-related motives are common in various sectors, and to encourage companies to provide comprehensive account and coverage of their CSRR, more guidelines could be issued which take industry-specific issues into consideration, as current codes (GRI) and SECP guidelines have been found to be excessively rigid and difficult to follow. A framework that fits the contextual needs should be encouraged and needs to take account of industry-specific requirements of companies and stakeholders. The analysis performed in this study can provide initial guidance in this area.

The government of Pakistan and policy-makers need to play a vital role in putting pressure on companies to improve social and environmental aspects of businesses and address ethical concerns in a comprehensive manner, rather than taking CSRR practice as a means of impressing stakeholders. The current study also provides insights for management who could use it to enhance efficiency of CSRR practice. For investors, it provides guidance on the long-term financial worthiness of their investments and gives them an understanding of expectations for CSRR.

Limitations of the Study

Top listed companies on the PSE were considered according to their market capitalisation, hence the findings of this paper cannot be applied to small and medium firms. The results are not to be considered as generalised and should only be taken for the sectors investigated, as well as for the years investigated.

FUTURE RESEARCH RECOMMENDATIONS

To enhance future research in this important area, other media of communication should be included in any sampling, for example, websites, brochures, and company social media accounts, to have a broader understanding of company CSRR practice. It is recommended that content analysis be applied to other sectors and nations to identify potential cultural variations. Finally, since this paper compares the impact of the SCEP guidelines between 2009 and 2013, there is a clear opportunity for future researchers to focus on a comparison that looks at the evolution of CSRR in the years since the issue of the 2013 guidelines, examining reporting trends that have since taken place in the Pakistani sectors. and suggesting what further areas should be covered by future voluntary guidelines.

REFERENCES

Abukari, A. J., & Abdul-Hamid, I. K. (2018). Corporate social responsibility reporting in the telecommunications sector in Ghana. *International Journal of Corporate Social Responsibility*, *3*(1), 2. doi:10.118640991-017-0025-9

Adams, C. A. (2002). Internal organisational factors influencing corporate social and ethical reporting. *Accounting, Auditing & Accountability Journal*, *15*(2), 223–250. doi:10.1108/09513570210418905

Aerts, W., & Cormier, D. (2009). Media legitimacy and corporate environmental communication. *Accounting, Organizations and Society*, *34*(1), 1–27. doi:10.1016/j.aos.2008.02.005

Al-Tuwaijri, S. A., Christensen, T. E., & Hughes, K. (2004). The relations among environmental disclosure, environmental performance, and economic performance: A simultaneous equations approach. *Accounting, Organizations and Society*, *29*(5–6), 447–471. doi:10.1016/S0361-3682(03)00032-1

Alazzani, A., & Wan-Hussin, W. N. (2013). Global Reporting Initiative's environmental reporting: A study of oil and gas companies. *Ecological Indicators*, *32*, 19–24. doi:10.1016/j.ecolind.2013.02.019

Ali, N. (2015). *The Role of Cement Industry in the Economic Development of Pakistan*. EduPedia Publications (P) Ltd.

Andrikopoulos, A., Samitas, A., & Bekiaris, M. (2014). Corporate social responsibility reporting in financial institutions: Evidence from Euronext. *Research in International Business and Finance*, *32*, 27–35. doi:10.1016/j.ribaf.2014.02.001

Archel, P., Husillos, J., Larrinaga, C., & Spence, C. (2009). Social disclosure, legitimacy theory and the role of the state. *Accounting, Auditing & Accountability Journal, 22*(8), 1284–1307. doi:10.1108/09513570910999319

Aribi, Z. A., & Gao, S. S. (2012). Narrative disclosure of corporate social responsibility in Islamic financial institutions. *Managerial Auditing Journal, 27*(2), 199–222.

Aruwa, S., & Hemen, A. (2011). Corporate social responsibility and organizational performance in Nigeria: A survey of the cement industry. *Journal of Entrepreneurship Research, 1*(1), 57–74. doi:10.1093/icesjms/16.3.384

Askari Bank. (2013). *Annual Report of Askari Bank Limited for 2013.* http://akbl.com.pk/wp-content/uploads/2014/12/Askari-AR-2013.pdf

Awan, A. G., & Akhtar, N. (2014). The impact of Corporate Social Responsibility (CSR) on profitability of firms: A case study of fertilizer and cement industry in Southern Punjab, Pakistan. *International Journal of Development and Economic Sustainability*, 2(4), 1682–1690.

Azizul Islam, M. (2017). CSR Reporting and Legitimacy Theory: Some Thoughts on Future Research Agenda. In M. Aluchna & S. Idowu (Eds.), *The Dynamics of Corporate Social Responsibility* (pp. 323–339). doi:10.1007/978-3-319-39089-5_17

Bakhtina, K., & Goudriaan, J. W. (2011). CSR reporting in multinational energy companies. *Transfer: European Review of Labour and Research, 17*(1), 95–99. doi:10.1177/1024258910396308

Banerjee, S. (2020). Institutionalization of Corporate Social Responsibility (CSR) in India and Its Effects on CSR Reporting: A Case Study of the Petroleum and Gas Industry. In N. Mitra & R. Schmidpeter (Eds.), *Mandated Corporate Social Responsibility* (pp. 141–157). CSR, Sustainability, Ethics & Governance. doi:10.1007/978-3-030-24444-6_8

Beattie, V. (2014). Accounting narratives and the narrative turn in accounting research: Issues, theory, methodology, methods and a research framework. *The British Accounting Review, 46*(2), 111–134. doi:10.1016/j.bar.2014.05.001

Bebbington, J., Unerman, J., & O'Dwyer, B. (2014). *Sustainability accounting and accountability* (2nd ed.). Routledge.

Beck, A. C., Campbell, D., & Shrives, P. J. (2010). Content analysis in environmental reporting research: Enrichment and rehearsal of the method in a British–German context. *The British Accounting Review, 42*(3), 207–222.

Belal, A. R., & Cooper, S. (2011). The absence of corporate social responsibility reporting in Bangladesh. *Critical Perspectives on Accounting, 22*(7), 654–667.

Berthelot, S., Coulmont, M., & Thibault, K. (2013). Sustainability Content on Oil and Gas Company Websites. *Business and Management Research, 2*(1), 94–103. doi:10.5430/bmr.v2n1p94

Bloxham, E. (2011). Corporate governance and sustainability: New and old models of thinking. *Journal of Sustainable Finance and Investment, 1*(1), 77–80. doi:10.3763/jsfi.2010.0003

Bonsón, E., & Bednárová, M. (2015). CSR reporting practices of Eurozone companies Prácticas en la presentación de informes sobre RSC de las empresas de la Eurozona. *Cómo Citar Este Artículo*, *18*(2), 182–193. doi:10.1016/j.rcsar.2014.06.002

Bowering, G., Crone, P. P., & Kadi, W. (2012). *The Princeton Encyclopedia of Islamic Political Thought*. Princeton University Press., doi:10.2307/j.ctt1r2g6m

Branco, M. C., & Rodrigues, L. L. (2007). Issues in corporate social and environmental reporting research : An overview. *Issues in Social and Environmental Accounting*, *1*(1), 72–90.

Branco, M. C., & Rodrigues, L. L. (2008). Social responsibility disclosure: A study of proxies for the public visibility of Portuguese banks. *The British Accounting Review*, *40*(2), 161–181.

Casadei, A., & Amadei, F. (2010). The competitive influence of corporate social responsibility and corporate social disclosure in Italian small and medium sized companies: Focus on disclosure and competitive drivers 1. *Social and Environmental Accountability Journal*, *30*(1), 13–25.

Chaudhry, M., Mughal, S. L., & Zafar, F. (2014). Corporate Social Disclosure : A Case Study On Petroleum Industry Of Pakistan. *International Journal of Business and Marketing*, *2*(1), 1–18.

Ching, H. Y., & Gerab, F. (2017). Sustainability reports in Brazil through the lens of signaling, legitimacy and stakeholder theories. *Social Responsibility Journal*, *13*(1), 95–110. doi:10.1108/SRJ-10-2015-0147

Cho, C. H., Choi, J.-S., Kwak, Y.-M., & Patten, D. M. (2013). An Empirical Investigation of the Extensiveness of Stand-Alone Environmental Reporting in South Korea. *Social and Environmental Accountability Journal*, *33*(2), 91–103.

Cho, C. H., Michelon, G., Patten, D. M., & Roberts, R. W. (2015). CSR disclosure: The more things change…? *Accounting, Auditing & Accountability Journal*, *28*(1), 14–35. doi:10.1108/AAAJ-12-2013-1549

Cho, C. H., & Roberts, R. W. (2010). Environmental reporting on the internet by America's Toxic 100: Legitimacy and self-presentation. *International Journal of Accounting Information Systems*, *11*(1), 1–16. doi:10.1016/j.accinf.2009.12.003

Choi, B. B., Lee, D., & Psaros, J. (2013). An analysis of Australian company carbon emission disclosures. *Pacific Accounting Review*, *25*(1), 58–79.

de Aguiar, T. R. S., & Fearfull, A. (2010). Global climate change and corporate disclosure: Pedagogical tools for critical accounting? *Social and Environmental Accountability Journal*, *30*(2), 64–79. doi:10.1080/0969160X.2010.9651824

de Villiers, C., Low, M., & Samkin, G. (2014). The institutionalisation of mining company sustainability disclosures. *Journal of Cleaner Production*, *84*(1), 51–58. doi:10.1016/j.jclepro.2014.01.089

de Villiers, C., & van Staden, C. J. (2006). Can less environmental disclosure have a legitimising effect? Evidence from Africa. *Accounting, Organizations and Society*, *31*(8), 763–781. doi:10.1016/j.aos.2006.03.001

de Villiers, C., & van Staden, C. J. (2012). New Zealand shareholder attitudes towards corporate environmental disclosure. *Pacific Accounting Review, 24*(2), 186–210. doi:10.1108/01140581211258470

Deegan, C. (2002). Introduction: The legitimising effect of social and environmental disclosures - a theoretical foundation. Accounting. *Auditing and Accountability, 15*(3), 282–311. doi:10.1108/09513570210435852

Deegan, C., Rankin, M., & Voght, P. (2000). Firms' Disclosure Reactions to Major Social Incidents: Australian Evidence. *Accounting Forum, 24*(1), 101–130. doi:10.1111/1467-6303.00031

Ding, D. K., Ferreira, C., & Wongchoti, U. (2016). *Does it pay to be different? Relative CSR and its impact on firm value.* doi:10.1016/j.irfa.2016.06.013

Dong, S., & Burritt, R. (2010). Cross-sectional benchmarking of social and environmental reporting practice in the Australian oil and gas industry. *Sustainable Development, 18*(2), 108–118.

Dragomir, V. D. (2010). Environmentally sensitive disclosures and financial performance in a European setting. *Journal of Accounting & Organizational Change, 6*(3), 359–388.

Du, S., & Vieira, E. T. (2012). Striving for Legitimacy Through Corporate Social Responsibility: Insights from Oil Companies. *Journal of Business Ethics, 110*(4), 413–427. doi:10.100710551-012-1490-4

Duff, A. (2014). Corporate social responsibility reporting in professional accounting firm. *The British Accounting Review, 48*, 74–86. doi:10.1177/0021943608317111

Dumay, J., & Cai, L. (2014). A review and critique of content analysis as a methodology for inquiring into IC disclosure. Journal of Intellectual Capital, 15(2), 264–290. doi:10.1108/JIC-01-2014-0010

Dumay, J., & Cai, L. (2015). Using content analysis as a research methodology for investigating intellectual capital disclosure: A critique. *Journal of Intellectual Capital, 16*(1), 121–155. doi:10.1108/JIC-04-2014-0043

Dumay, J., Guthrie, J., & Farneti, F. (2010). Gri Sustainability Reporting Guidelines For Public And Third Sector Organizations. *Public Management Review, 12*(4), 531–548. doi:10.1080/14719037.2010.496266

Elijido-Ten, E. (2011). Media coverage and voluntary environmental disclosures: A developing country exploratory experiment. *Accounting Forum, 35*(3), 139–157.

Eljayash, K. M., James, K., & Kong, E. (2012). The Quantity and Quality of Environmental Disclosure in Annual Report of National Oil and Gas Companies in Middle East and North Africa. *International Journal of Economics and Finance, 4*(10), 201–217. doi:10.5539/ijef.v4n10p201

Faisal, F., Tower, G., & Rusmin, R. (2012). Legitimising Corporate Sustainability Reporting Throughout the World. *Australasian Accounting Business & Finance Journal, 6*(2), 19–34. https://ro.uow.edu.au/aabfj/vol6/iss2/3/?utm_source=ro.uow.edu.au%2Faabfj%2Fvol6%2Fiss2%2F3&utm_medium=PDF&utm_campaign=PDFCoverPages

Friedman, A. L., & Miles, S. (2001). Socially Responsible Investment and Corporate Social and Environmental Reporting in the UK: An Exploratory Study. *The British Accounting Review, 33*(4), 523–548. doi:10.1006/bare.2001.0172

Gao, S., Heravi, S., & Xiao, J. Z. (2005). Determinants of corporate social and environmental reporting in Hong Kong: A research note. *Accounting Forum*, *29*(2), 233–242.

Gao, Y. (2011). CSR in an emerging country: A content analysis of CSR reports of listed companies. *Baltic Journal of Management*, *6*(2), 263–291.

Giannarakis, G. (2014). The determinants influencing the extent of CSR disclosure. *International Journal of Law and Management*, *56*(5), 393–416. doi:10.1108/IJLMA-05-2013-0021

Gray, R. (2006). Social, environmental and sustainability reporting and organisational value creation?: Whose value? Whose creation? *Accounting, Auditing & Accountability Journal*, *19*(6), 793–819. doi:10.1108/09513570610709872

Guthrie, J., Cuganesan, S., & Ward, L. (2008). Industry specific social and environmental reporting: The Australian Food and Beverage Industry. *Accounting Forum*, *32*(1), 1–15. doi:10.1016/j.accfor.2007.10.001

Guthrie, J., Petty, R., Yongvanich, K., & Ricceri, F. (2004). Using content analysis as a research method to inquire into intellectual capital reporting. *Journal of Intellectual Capital*, *5*(2), 282–293. http://www.emeraldinsight.com/doi/abs/10.1108/14691930410533704

Hahn, R., & Kühnen, M. (2013). Determinants of sustainability reporting: A review of results, trends, theory, and opportunities in an expanding field of research. *Journal of Cleaner Production*, *59*, 5–21. doi:10.1016/j.jclepro.2013.07.005

Hossain, M., & Andrew, J. (2006). *Corporate Social and Environmental Disclosure in Developing Countries : Evidence from Bangladesh*. Asia Pacific Conference on International Accounting Issues. https://ro.uow.edu.au/commpapers/179/

Hsieh, Y.-C. (2012). Hotel companies' environmental policies and practices: A content analysis of their web pages. *International Journal of Contemporary Hospitality Management*, *24*(1), 97–121.

Idemudia, U. (2011). Corporate social responsibility and developing countries: Moving the critical CSR research agenda in Africa forward. *Progress in Development Studies*, *11*(1), 1–18. doi:10.1177/146499341001100101

Islam, M. Azizul, & Deegan, C. (2008). Motivations for an organisation within a developing country to report social responsibility information: Evidence from Bangladesh. *Accounting, Auditing & Accountability Journal*, *21*(6), 850–874.

Islam, M. A. (2010). Social and Environmental Accounting Research: Major Contributions and Future Directions for Developing Countries. *Social and Environmental Accounting Research: Major Contributions and Future Directions for Developing Countries*, *16*(2), 27–43.

Jahdi, K. S., & Acikdilli, G. (2009). Marketing Communications and Corporate Social Responsibility (CSR): Marriage of Convenience or Shotgun Wedding? *Journal of Business Ethics*, *88*(1), 103–113. doi:10.100710551-009-0113-1

Javaid Lone, E., Ali, A., & Khan, I. (2016). Corporate governance and corporate social responsibility disclosure: Evidence from Pakistan. Corporate Governance. *The International Journal of Business in Society*, *16*(5), 785–797.

Jayanti, R. K., & Rajeev Gowda, M. V. (2014). Sustainability dilemmas in emerging economies. *IIMB Management Review*, *26*(2), 130–142. doi:10.1016/j.iimb.2014.03.004

Jiufang, T., Xiaohua, L., & Jiuhong, T. (2009). Environmental Disclosure of Chemical Industry: Evidence from Chinese A-Share Market. *Zhongguo Renkou Ziyuan Yu Huanjing*, *7*(1), 23–29. doi:10.1080/10042857.2009.10684906

Jo, H., & Na, H. (2012). Does CSR Reduce Firm Risk? Evidence from Controversial Industry Sectors. *Journal of Business Ethics*, *110*(4), 441–456. doi:10.100710551-012-1492-2

Kamal, A., Yingjie, M., & Ali, A. (2019). Significance of Billion Tree Tsunami Afforestation Project and Legal Developments in Forest Sector of Pakistan. *International Journal of Law and Society*, *1*, 157.

Kamla, R., & Rammal, H. G. (2013). Social reporting by Islamic banks: Does social justice matter? *Accounting, Auditing & Accountability Journal*, *26*(6), 911–945. doi:10.1108/AAAJ-03-2013-1268

Kansal, M., Joshi, M., Babu, S., & Sharma, S. (2016). Reporting of Corporate Social Responsibility in Central Public Sector Enterprises: A Study of Post Mandatory Regime in India. *Journal of Business Ethics*, 1–19.

Kemp, L. J., & Vinke, J. (2012). CSR reporting: A review of the Pakistani aviation industry. *South Asian Journal of Global Business Research*, *1*(2), 276–292.

Kent, P., & Zunker, T. (2013). Attaining legitimacy by employee information in annual reports. *Accounting, Auditing & Accountability Journal*, *26*(7), 1072–1106. doi:10.1108/AAAJ-03-2013-1261

Khan, L. J. C., & Bathurst, R. J. (2018). Institutional impacts on corporate social responsibility: A comparative analysis of New Zealand and Pakistan. *International Journal of Corporate Social Responsibility*, *3*(1). Advance online publication. doi:10.118640991-018-0026-3

Khan, M., & Hassan, A. (2019). Environmental Reporting in Pakistan's Oil and Gas Industry. *International Research Journal of Business Studies*, *12*(1), 15–29. doi:10.21632/irjbs.12.1.15-29

Khan, M., Hassan, A., Tarbert, H., & Harrison, C. (2020). CSR reporting: A review of research and agenda for future research. *Management Research Review*.

Khan, M., Lockhart, J. C., & Bathurst, R. J. (2018). Institutional impacts on corporate social responsibility: A comparative analysis of New Zealand and Pakistan. *International Journal of Corporate Social Responsibility*, *3*(1). Advance online publication. doi:10.118640991-018-0026-3

Khan, M. H.-U.-Z., Halabi, A. K., & Samy, M. (2011). Corporate social responsibility (CSR) reporting: A study of selected banking companies in Bangladesh. *Journal of Business and Management*, *6*(2), 42–47. doi:10.1108/17471110910977276

Kilian, T., & Hennigs, N. (2013). Corporate social responsibility and environmental reporting in controversial industries. *European Business Review*, *26*(1), 79–101. doi:10.1108/EBR-04-2013-0080

Kiliç, M., Kuzey, C., & Uyar, A. (2015). The impact of ownership and board structure on Corporate Social Responsibility (CSR) reporting in the Turkish banking industry. Corporate Governance. *The International Journal of Business in Society*, *15*(3), 357–374. doi:10.1108/CG-02-2014-0022

Killian, S., & O'Regan, P. (2016). Social accounting and the co-creation of corporate legitimacy. *Accounting, Organizations and Society*, *50*, 1–12. doi:10.1016/j.aos.2016.02.004

Kirat, M. (2015). Corporate social responsibility in the oil and gas industry in Qatar perceptions and practices. *Public Relations Review*, *41*(4), 438–446. doi:10.1016/j.pubrev.2015.07.001

Kolk, A., Hong, P., & van Dolen, W. (2010). Corporate social responsibility in China: An analysis of domestic and foreign retailers' sustainability dimensions. *Business Strategy and the Environment*, *19*(5), 289–303. doi:10.1002/bse.630

Krasodomska, J. (2015). CSR disclosures in the banking industry. Empirical evidence from Poland. *Social Responsibility Journal*, *11*(3), 406–423. doi:10.1108/SRJ-02-2013-0019

Krippendorf, K. (1980). *Content analysis: An introduction to its methodology*. Sage Publications.

Kuruppu, S., & Milne, M. J. (2010). Dolphin deaths, organizational legitimacy and potential employees' reactions to assured environmental disclosures. *Accounting Forum*, *34*(1), 1–19. doi:10.1016/j.accfor.2009.12.001

Laine, M. (2009). Ensuring legitimacy through rhetorical changes?: A longitudinal interpretation of the environmental disclosures of a leading Finnish chemical company. *Accounting, Auditing & Accountability Journal*, *22*(7), 1029–1054.

Lock, I., & Seele, P. (2015). Analyzing sector-specific CSR reporting: Social and environmental disclosure to investors in the chemicals and banking and insurance industry. *Corporate Social Responsibility and Environmental Management*, *22*(2), 113–128. doi:10.1002/csr.1338

Lock, I., & Seele, P. (2016). *The credibility of CSR (corporate social responsibility) reports in Europe. Evidence from a quantitative content analysis in 11 countries*. doi:10.1016/j.jclepro.2016.02.060

Lu, Y., & Abeysekera, I. (2015). What Do Stakeholders Care About? Investigating Corporate Social and Environmental Disclosure in China. *Journal of Business Ethics*. https://link.springer.com/content/pdf/10.1007%2Fs10551-015-2844-5.pdf

Lund-Thomsen, P., Lindgreen, A., & Vanhamme, J. (2016). Industrial Clusters and Corporate Social Responsibility in Developing Countries: What We Know, What We do not Know, and What We Need to Know. *Journal of Business Ethics*, *133*(1), 9–24. doi:10.100710551-014-2372-8

Mahadeo, J. D., Oogarah-Hanuman, V., & Soobaroyen, T. (2011). Changes in social and environmental reporting practices in an emerging economy (2004–2007): Exploring the relevance of stakeholder and legitimacy theories. *Accounting Forum*, *35*(3), 158–175.

Majeed, S., Aziz, T., & Saleem, S. (2015). The Effect of Corporate Governance Elements on Corporate Social Responsibility (CSR) Disclosure: An Empirical Evidence from Listed Companies at KSE Pakistan. *International Journal of Financial Studies*, *3*(4), 530–556.

Malik, M. S., & Kanwal, L. (2016). Impact of Corporate Social Responsibility Disclosure on Financial Performance: Case Study of Listed Pharmaceutical Firms of Pakistan. *Journal of Business Ethics*, ●●●, 1–10.

Marzouk, M., Linsley, P., & Verma, S. (2017). Risk reporting. *The Routledge Companion to Accounting and Risk*, *24*(1), 64–81. doi:10.4324/9781315716756

Merkelsen, H. (2011). Institutionalized Ignorance as a Precondition for Rational Risk Expertise. *Risk Analysis*, *31*(7), 1083–1094. doi:10.1111/j.1539-6924.2010.01576.x PMID:21284683

Michelon, G., Pilonato, S., & Ricceri, F. (2015). CSR reporting practices and the quality of disclosure: An empirical analysis. *Critical Perspectives on Accounting*, *33*, 59–78. doi:10.1016/j.cpa.2014.10.003

Momin, M. A., & Parker, L. D. (2013). Motivations for corporate social responsibility reporting by MNC subsidiaries in an emerging country: The case of Bangladesh. *The British Accounting Review*, *45*(3), 215–228. doi:10.1016/j.bar.2013.06.007

Muttakin, M. B., & Khan, A. (2014). Determinants of corporate social disclosure: Empirical evidence from Bangladesh. *Advances in Accounting*, *30*(1), 168–175.

Naser, K., Al-Hussaini, A., Al-Kwari, D., & Nuseibeh, R. (2006). Determinants of Corporate Social Disclosure in Developing Countries: The Case of Qatar. *Advances in International Accounting*, *19*, 1–23.

Nazir, M. (2010). Corporate Social Disclosure in Pakistan: A Case Study of Fertilizers Industry. *Journal of Commerce*, *2*(1), 1–11. http://www.ciitlahore.edu.pk/Papers/Abstracts/146-8588969319825962058.pdf

Nobanee, H., & Ellili, N. (2015). Corporate sustainability disclosure in annual reports: Evidence from UAE banks: Islamic versus conventional. *Renewable & Sustainable Energy Reviews*, *55*, 1336–1341.

Nyahunzvi, D. K. (2013). CSR reporting among Zimbabwe's hotel groups: A content analysis. *International Journal of Contemporary Hospitality Management*, *25*(4), 595–613.

Odera, O., Scott, A., & Gow, J. (2016). An Examination of the Quality of Social and Environmental Disclosures by Nigerian Oil Companies. Corporate Governance. *The International Journal of Business in Society*, *16*(2), 400–419.

Pahuja, S. (2009). Relationship between environmental disclosures and corporate characteristics: A study of large manufacturing companies in India. *Social Responsibility Journal*, *5*(2), 227–244.

Patten, D. M. (1992). Intra-industry environmental disclosures in response to the Alaskan oil spill: A note on legitimacy theory. *Accounting, Organizations and Society*, *17*(5), 471–475. doi:10.1016/0361-3682(92)90042-Q

Patten, D. M., & Zhao, N. (2014). Standalone CSR reporting by U.S. retail companies. *Accounting Forum*, *38*(2), 132–144. doi:10.1016/j.accfor.2014.01.002

Rahaman, A. S., Lawrence, S., & Roper, J. (2004). Social and environmental reporting at the VRA: Institutionalised legitimacy or legitimation crisis? *Critical Perspectives on Accounting*, *15*(1), 35–56. doi:10.1016/S1045-2354(03)00005-4

Relano, F., & Paulet, E. (2012). Corporate responsibility in the banking sector: A proposed typology for the German case. *International Journal of Law and Management*, *54*(5), 379–393. doi:10.1108/17542431211264269

Salomone, R., & Galluccio, G. (2001). Environmental Issues and Financial Reporting Trends: A Survey in the Chemical and Oil & Gas Industries. *SSRN Electronic Journal* (FEEM Working Paper No. 32.2001). doi:10.2139srn.278240

Securities and Exchange Commission of Pakistan. (2013). *CSR Guidelines*. https://www.sustainablebankingnetwork.org/upload/file/2019/0819/1566184721324559.pdf

Sharif, M., & Rashid, K. (2014). Corporate governance and corporate social responsibility (CSR) reporting: An empirical evidence from commercial banks (CB) of Pakistan. *Quality & Quantity*, *48*(5), 2501–2521. doi:10.100711135-013-9903-8

Stanny, E. (2013). Voluntary Disclosures of Emissions by US Firms. *Business Strategy and the Environment*, *22*(3), 145–158.

Sumiani, Y., Haslinda, Y., & Lehman, G. (2007). Environmental reporting in a developing country: A case study on status and implementation in Malaysia. *Journal of Cleaner Production*, *15*(10), 895–901. doi:10.1016/j.jclepro.2006.01.012

Sweeney, L., & Coughlan, J. (2008). Do different industries report Corporate Social Responsibility differently? An investigation through the lens of stakeholder theory. *Journal of Marketing Communications*, *14*(2), 113–124. doi:10.1080/13527260701856657

Syed, M. A., & Butt, S. A. (2017). Financial and non-financial determinants of corporate social responsibility: Empirical evidence from Pakistan. *Social Responsibility Journal*, *13*(4), 780–797. doi:10.1108/SRJ-08-2016-0146

Tamvada, M. (2020). Corporate social responsibility and accountability: A new theoretical foundation for regulating CSR. *International Journal of Corporate Social Responsibility*, *5*(1). Advance online publication. doi:10.118640991-019-0045-8

Tilling, M. V., & Tilt, C. a. (2010). The edge of legitimacy: Voluntary social and environmental reporting in Rothmans' 1956-1999 annual reports. *Accounting, Auditing & Accountability Journal*, *23*(1), 55–81.

Tilt, C. A. (2016). Corporate social responsibility research: The importance of context. *International Journal of Corporate Social Responsibility*, *1*(1), 1–9. doi:10.118640991-016-0003-7

Tran, T. T. M., Aluko, O., & Beddewela, E. (2016). The Impact of Institutional Environment on Corporate Social Responsibility Disclosure. *Academy of Management Proceedings*, *2016*(1), 17827. doi:10.5465/ambpp.2016.17827

Ullah, H., & Afjalur, M. (2015). Corporate social responsibility reporting practices in banking companies in Bangladesh. *Journal of Financial Reporting and Accounting*, *13*(2), 200–225.

Vani, M., & Murali, K. P. (2015). Corporate Social Responsibility: A Glance At the Practices of Cement Industry. *International Journal Of Marketing*, *4*(8), 79–100.

Vurro, C., & Perrini, F. (2011). Making the most of corporate social responsibility reporting: Disclosure structure and its impact on performance. *Corporate Governance*, *11*(4), 459–474. doi:10.1108/14720701111159280

Waheed, M. A. A. (2014). Approach to fire-related disaster management in high density urban-area. *Procedia Engineering*, *77*, 61–69. doi:10.1016/j.proeng.2014.07.007

Yapa, P. W. S., Harvey, D., & Ellis, G. (2005). Disclosure of Corporate Environmental Policies in Annual Reports: Further Evidence Incorporating a National Ideology–An Australian Study. *Journal of Asia-Pacific Business*, *6*(1), 75–90.

Zhang, J., Guo, H. T., Li, B., & Wang, W. (2008). *The Influence of Financial Factors on Environmental Information Disclosure in China Chemical Industry*. doi:10.2139srn.1305005

KEY TERMS AND DEFINITIONS

Content Analysis: A research technique that examines and review themes, patterns, words, images within documents, for example, newspapers and published company annual reports.

Corporate Social Responsibility: The moral duty of the firm to recognise the needs of the society in which it operates by acting in an ethical and responsible manner.

Developing Country: A country that has not yet economically and socially advanced but is in a process of doing so, for example, Pakistan, India, and Bangladesh.

Legitimacy Theory: A theoretical stance that predicts companies' behaviour towards managing and maintain the perspectives of key stakeholders though company disclosure.

Polluting Sectors: Sectors that have a significant negative impact on the natural environment, for example, CO2 emissions, greenhouse gases, air and water pollutants and plastic waste.

Securities Exchange Commission of Pakistan: A government body that regulates financial and capital markets within Pakistan.

Voluntary Guidelines: A set of guiding notes that is often issued by a Government to promote and encourage certain behaviours or trends in a market. For example, promoting ethical and environmental transparency.

ENDNOTES

1 See details of guidelines (2009) - https://jamapunji.pk/sites/default/files/CSR.pdf

2 See details of guidelines (2013) - https://www.secp.gov.pk/document/voluntary-guidelines-for-csr-2013/

Chapter 2
The Institutional Impact and Community Perception Implementation of Food Security Policy on Poverty Reduction:
Case of Food Self-Sufficiency Village Programme, Indonesia

Muhamad Rusliyadi
https://orcid.org/0000-0003-4632-5671
Polytechnic of Agricultural Development Yogyakarta Magelang, Indonesia

Azaharaini Bin Hj. Mohd. Jamil
College IGS Brunei Darussalam, Brunei

Ratna Tri Kumalasari
Agricultural and Food Security Office, Kebumen Regency, Indonesia

Ari Abdul Rouf
Gorontalo Assessment Institute for Agricultural Technology, Ministry of Agriculture Indonesia, Indonesia

ABSTRACT

Indonesia has established various types of agrarian policies in line with poverty reduction initiatives. Various policies on poverty reduction schemes that have been implemented before were not successful because many of them lacked sustainability. Most strategies on the activity of the programme called for direct assistance to the unfortunate. The Food Self-Sufficiency Village Programme (Desa Mandiri

DOI: 10.4018/978-1-7998-4787-8.ch002

Pangan) gives support financially and offers intensive assistance to the community. The principal targets of the programme are to empower the community, alleviate rural poverty and sustain food security at the village level. Active institutions play a very important role in supporting the DMP Programme. There were institutions in the village sites before the introduction of the DMP Programme, such as the village leader, village councils, farmer groups, rice milling units, a village health station unit, a school, a mosque, a church, private lenders, village shops, and traders.

INTRODUCTION

The growth in agriculture has been a guiding source of poverty reduction in most developing nations, particularly in the case of rural poverty. The agriculture sector contributes to poverty reduction in terms of employment generation to the poor and supports the development of non-agricultural employment generation in rural fields. Development in agriculture also contributes to a larger supply of food and lower food prices benefiting both rural and urban poor (Grewal *et al.*, 2012).

Agricultural development is important in a developing country for achieving industrialization. Farming is the backbone of economic growth in many growing countries, because it provides food security, food self-sufficiency, diversification, and value-added enhancement of competitiveness of exports. Moreover, it increases the wellbeing of farmers and leads directly to poverty reduction.

Indonesia has shifted from an agricultural economy to an industrial one. Nevertheless, the agriculture sector remains a key sector for millions of those who depend directly on agriculture for their livelihood. The agriculture sector has been playing a key role in improving living standards and alleviating poverty. Poverty in rural areas, where most people depend on agriculture for their livelihoods, is one of the immense problems in Indonesia. The poverty level indicates that 16.56% of people in rural areas are poor (CBS, 2010). The increasing numbers of poor people are due to the fact that the bulk of the people cannot satisfy their basic needs and survive at the subsistence level, and therefore ensuring household food security via affordable agricultural workplaces and sustainability scheme policies on the basic demands of the farming sector is vital, especially in terms of food security policy.

According to Darwis and Rusastra (2011), the Food Self-Sufficiency Village Programme (*Desa Mandiri Pangan*) implemented by community groups was supported by agricultural and non-agricultural capital programmes, as well as by rural financial institutions. It was facilitated by agricultural extension workers and expert consultants. This programme is directed at several other objectives: raising the availability of foodstuffs, growing the family unit entitlement, recovering the efficiency of food supply and access programmes, enhancing the local marketplace availability for selling and buying food products, raising capital and industrial options through the introduction of high-yielding varieties of seeds that agriculture community in rural area can develop to increase income, as well as improving the quality of food consumption handling at the household level, and so forth.

The reasons for choosing the Food Self-sufficiency Village Programme (*Desa Mandiri Pangan*) as the subject of the study are that: 1) The programme has a comprehensives scheme and assistance; 2) The programme has a direct or an indirect beneficial impact on poverty alleviation and food security efforts; 3) This programme is aimed at resolving the existing problems at the grassroots level; 4) It is expected to contribute importantly to rural growth; and, 5) The programme has been implemented in most of Indonesia's provinces.

MATERI AND METHOD

This research is focused on the existing food security policy in Indonesia with regard to the DMP Programme that has been implemented since 2006. The methodology used in the study was mainly quantitative, but a qualitative approach was also used to enrich the findings of the quantitative study. Primary data were analysed using Microsoft Excel and Statistical Program for Social Science (SPSS). Research site in Java island has the largest number of population in Indonesia. It was chosen to represent the research site. Central Java was chosen for this case study because it constitutes 17.0% of the population experiencing poverty (CBS, 2011). Secondly, it has many poor villages when compared to other provinces. Four villages were selected purposively[1].

Two villages from Kebumen Regency, Kedung Dowo Village at Poncowarno District and Selogiri Villlage at Karanggayam District, and the others in Magelang Regency at Madukoro Village Kajoran District and Candirejo Village Borobudur District were selected. These villages have been implementing the programme in varying stages with different characteristics and success rate. (Rusliyadi, et al 2019)

Data related to the DMP Programme and extension service were collected using unstructured and semi-structured questionnaire. The survey was conducted in four villages, each of which involved 100 samples. Samples were selected using a purposive and clustered sampling technique based on some particular sample criteria. Criteria of the sample chosen were based on farmer characteristics such as rich farmer, poor farmer, farmer leader, the village leader, man and women. The Scoring o the data preseterd is by author perception and the investigate scoring exercises using replication, cross-check scoring exercises, and interviews. These activities were undertaken with scoring exercises were developed to assess how local people perceived the importance of various environments and resource (Sheil, D & Liswanti, N 2006).

The purposive sampling technique is a type of non-probability sampling that is most effective when one needs to study a certain cultural domain with knowledgeable experts within. Purposive sampling may also be used with both qualitative and quantitative research techniques. The sample that is selected based on characteristics of a population and the objective of the study. This type of sampling can be very useful in situations when you need to reach a targeted sample quickly, and where sampling for proportionality is not the main concern (Rusliyadi, M and Libin, W, 2018)

RESULT AND DISCUSSION

Villagers' Rating Scale and Community Perceptions

In general, villagers' rating scale and community perceptions describe the implementation of poverty policy. Policies analysed include the DMP policy and the implementation of agricultural extension at village level. Several questions were asked of individuals and groups in FGDs, the results of which can be seen in Table 1.

Table 1. Villagers's and Community's Perceptions Towards the DMP and Extension Programmes

Performance Indicator/ Instrument	Kebumen Regency		Magelang Regency	
	Kedungdowo Village	Selogiri Village	Candirejo Village	Madukoro Village
Is the implementation of the programme in line with its objectives?	7	6	8	8
Is it received by the targeted recipients (well-targeted)?	7	7	9	8
Is it pro-poor?	8	9	9	9
Community perception towards implementation of the programme	6	6	7	8
The improvement of the programme according to the community	7	7	7	8
Benefits enjoyed from the DMP Programme and agriculture extension	7	8	7	9
Implementation of agricultural technology information delivered by extension officer	6	8	9	8
Perception towards the agriculture extension in the village	8	7	8	9
Impacts of agricultural programmes for you/your village	8	8	7	8
Total Score	64	66	71	75

NB: Scoring is out of 10; the higher the score, the better the perceptions of the villagers
Source: Field work primary data, (2013)

In this section, the analysis is divided into two parts. The first is the villagers' and community's perceptions on the performance indicators of the DMP Programme and extension. The second is on the impacts of institutions on poverty reduction as a result of the DMP Programme. The results show that the perceptions of the community and villagers on the DMP and extension programmes are generally a 'high' score. There are scores greater than 6 for all performance indicators. Based on the perceptions and opinions of the villagers the DMP Programme is one programme that deserves to be continued in villages with some improvements in terms of collaboration with extension services. The community also said that the DMP Programme should score a high rating on its implementation. This is because the Programme has significant impact on poverty reduction in their village in terms of raising income and food security.

Table 1 also shows that the highest total score (75 points) for the community perception is achieved by Madukoro. This shows that poor families in Madukoro are relatively enthusiastic about the DMP Programme. The villager as user policy has the role to evaluate the programme in order to know the rating score showed successful implementation. The output of the section here is to know the performance of the programme in terms of poverty.

Institutions can have a big impact on economic development and are considered a determining factor for growth. The indicator of the institution in terms of capability, for example, capital, skilled labour and technology, is usually a substantial factor in rural development. Institutional dynamism explains why growth and development output varies between regions, countries, and even villages from time to time.

A study by Gandhi and Marsh (2003) found a substantial number of both formal and informal local institutions in the villages and a substantial degree of interaction between households and institutions. These include formal and informal local institutions such as service cooperatives, dairy cooperatives, savings groups, community associations and labour groups. The study found that, apart from standard determinants of land, capital, labour and education, local institutions appear to play a significant role in explaining the variation in poor household incomes and the gain in capital assets over time. Membership in these institutions is not related to high asset levels or high caste – indeed, it is often inversely so. This indicates a stronger developmental role of institutions. The direct and indirect responses of households also support these findings on the nature, impact and the beneficial role of local institutions. The findings confirm that institutions matter, and local institutions can and do play a significant role in helping economic development in rural areas, especially for lower-income households.

Kedungdowo Village

Selogiri Village

The scores of impact of institutions on Selogiri development can be seen in the Table below. The institution receiving the highest score is the village health station units. This is in line with the result that

Table 2. Scores of Institutional Impact on Poverty Reduction of The DMP Programme at Kedungdowo Village

No.	Institution	Criteria					Overall Importance *(ranking 1 = most important)*
		Trust	Effective	Provide help when needed	Influence	Total score	
1.	District agricultural and forestry extension	8	9	7	10	34	4
2.	District education	7	3	5	4	19	13
3.	District Health	7	7	4	5	23	8
4.	Village health stations unit	8	10	9	8	35	3
5.	Village Food Team	4	7	8	9	28	5
6.	Farmer Groups/Affinity Groups	10	9	9	9	37	1
7.	Village shopkeeper/trader	5	7	6	4	22	11
8.	Private lender	3	6	8	5	22	10
9.	Village head	9	9	8	10	36	2
10.	Village councils	7	6	6	8	27	6
11.	Party	6	5	8	7	26	7
12.	District bank	9	4	5	5	23	9
13.	Military force	5	5	6	4	20	12
14.	Police	5	2	3	4	14	14

NB: Scoring is out of 10; the higher the score, the better the performance of institution
Source: Field work primary data (2013)

Table 3. Scores of institutional Impact on Poverty Reduction of the DMP Programme at Selogiri Village

No.	Institution	Criteria					Overall Importance (ranking 1 = most important)
		Trust	Effectiveness	Provide help when needed	Influence	Total score	
1.	District agriculture and forestry	7	8	7	8	30	4
2.	District education	6	4	5	7	22	11
3.	District health	6	7	5	6	24	8
4.	Village health stations unit	9	9	9	9	36	1
5.	Village Food Team	4	5	6	8	23	12
6.	Farmer Groups/Affinity Groups	9	8	10	9	36	2
7.	Village shopkeeper/trader	4	6	7	5	22	13
8.	Private lender	6	5	8	7	26	6
9.	Village head	8	8	8	9	33	3
10.	Village councils	7	7	4	7	25	7
11.	Party	7	6	7	8	28	5
12.	District bank	8	5	6	5	24	9
13.	Military force	6	6	7	5	24	10
14.	Police	4	4	7	4	19	14

NB: Scoring is out of 10; the higher the score, the better the performance.
Source: Field work primary data (2013)

the village is actually lacking in health infrastructure and a midwife or personal health officer. The villagers were proposing that the number of health workers or doctors in the village be increased so that sick villagers can be treated imediately without the need to call on doctors living some distance away. The second in rank of the impact of institutions on poor households is the farmer groups. The activities of farmer groups are based on the poor farmers helping other poor farmers. The routine meeting every week for *yasinan* (reciting Al-Qur'an) provides a medium for meeting and helping each other if there are members in difficulties. The monthly meeting routinely held for villagers has strengthened kinship between them by *arisan* (social gathering) and has enabled them to discuss problems in farming and issues in the village.

Candirejo Village

Candirejo has witnessed improvements in rural development since its inception as a tourism village. Institutional efforts in conducting the DMP activities through affinity groups have resulted in good impact, as they are supported by the village head. Candirejo's village head is a respected person in the village. He has a high education level and is always thinking of the people's needs. In the interviews conducted by the researcher, it was said that the village head continuously strived to provide solutions for their village in order to distribute the benefits of development to a greater number of people. This explains

Table 4. Scores of Institutional Impact on Poverty Reduction of the DMP Programme at Candirejo Village

No.	Institutions	Criteria					Overall Importance Rank (ranking 1 = most important)
		Trust	**Effectiveness**	**Provides help when needed**	**Influence**	**Total score**	
1.	District agriculture and forestry	9	9	8	9	35	3
2.	District education	8	5	5	7	25	8
3.	District health	8	8	8	5	29	5
4.	Village health stations unit	9	8	8	9	34	4
5.	Village Food Team	6	7	8	6	27	6
6.	Farmer Groups/ Affinity Groups	9	9	9	8	35	2
7.	Village shopkeeper/ trader	6	5	7	5	23	11
8.	Private lender	4	7	7	6	24	10
9.	Village head	8	10	9	9	36	1
10.	Village councils	7	6	6	8	27	7
11.	Political Party	4	7	6	6	23	12
12.	District bank	8	5	6	6	25	9
13.	Military force	4	6	5	7	22	13
14.	Police	4	6	5	3	18	14

NB: Scoring is out of 10; the higher the score, the better the performance
Source: Field work primary data (2013)

the reason why the village head received the highest score given by the villagers. The perceptions of villagers on poverty reducation of institutional impacts are shown in Table 87. The village leader's effort is ranked first and villagers perceived that this institution has made a big contribution to the welfare of poor society in Candirejo. The learning point of this finding is that it is important for village leaders to give more attention to the poor by giving assistance and motivating poor families to be involved in various development programmes in the village. The community leader in Candirejo has been awarded high trust by the villagers. Leadership is the main contributing factor in making programme implementation a success in Candirejo.

Madukoro Village

The impact of the DMP Programme in terms of institutional contribution to rural development at Madukoro is shown in Table 88. In general, the contributions and performances of the institutions in Madukoro are better than in the other villages. Programme activities ranging from agricultural programmes, health, fisheries, forestry, and poverty reduction have all showed good performance in practice. Public awareness of the farmer groups and women group in Madukoro has resulted in village members being actively engaged in the activities of the village. Farmer Groups/Affinity Groups are given the highest score by the villagers. This finding shows that the farmer groups (including groups of farmers in agriculture and

Table 5. Scores of Institutional Impact on Poverty Reduction of the DMP Programme at Madukoro Village

No.	Institution	Criteria					Overall Importance (ranking1 = most important)
		Trust	Effectiveness	Provides help when needed	Influence	Total score	
1.	District agriculture and forestry	9	9	8	10	36	2
2.	District education	6	7	7	5	25	8
3.	District health	6	7	6	6	25	7
4.	Village health stations unit	9	9	9	9	36	3
5.	Village Food Team	5	6	7	8	26	6
6.	Farmer Groups/Affinity Groups	9	10	9	9	37	1
7.	Village shopkeeper/ trader	5	7	4	5	21	12
8.	Private lender	4	5	7	6	22	11
9.	Village head	8	7	8	9	32	4
10.	Village councils	5	7	7	6	25	9
11.	Political Party	7	7	6	8	28	5
12.	District bank	7	5	6	6	24	10
13.	Military force	6	4	5	6	21	13
14.	Police	4	6	4	3	17	14

NB: Scoring is out of 10; the higher the score, the better the performance
Source: Field work primary data (2013)

livestock) in Madukoro are perceived by the villagers as helping the poor. The DMP Programme provides direct benefits to the poor by increasing their income.

Analysis of the Roles and Responsibilities of Men and Women (Gender) in the Household and in the Community

The perception of villagers on the responsibility of men and women in the household is relatively different. However, in fact there was no clear difference, if one side (people or wives) had a condition such as sickness or something to do in another place it will be handled by the other side. Research data indicate that work outside the house is the responsibility of men, while work inside the house is the duty of women.

The tasks of women in general can be seen in Table 5: most of their activities involve outside as well as inside the house. Women tend to hold fewer responsibilities than men at community level because it is the villages' culture that women are mostly responsible for looking after their homes, whereas men are in charge of businesses. Similarly, in decision making there are significant differences between them at household and community levels.

In line with Quisumbing (2003), decisions were reported as being made by men alone, the women, jointly (and possibly with others), and by someone other than the husband or wife. The most striking finding was heterogeneity in decision making among villagers. While managing household expenses on food and routine items was largely the wife's domain, the husband either took charge or played a role in the decision in about 20% of households. On the other hand, the decision to use contraceptives was largely a joint decision. Between these extremes, there was a spectrum of distribution of decision makers. The data show that many households appear to behave as if spheres of influence differ for men and women. For all decisions except use of contraceptives the excluded group (modern or non-traditional groups) was the most likely to be individualistic in its decision-making. Controlling for the husband's education, the wife's education can be interpreted as relative education (or a measure of relative power). According to the wives, an increase in a wife's education reduces the probability of her husband making decisions about food expenditure and increases the probability that she makes the decisions. This pattern holds for all decisions except for one: as the wife's education increased, she was more likely to make decisions about child health jointly. Men from higher-status families were more likely to make decisions about the health of their children, expenditure on the education of their children, durable expenditure, and the couples' use of contraceptives.

Gender analysis seeks to look at certain issues from the perspective of male and female. This analysis is a very important component in poverty assessment because men and women usually have different roles and responsibilities, both within the household and in their social place in the community. Therefore, they possess different life experiences and ways of viewing poverty. The impact and benefits of certain policies or programmes on women and men also vary. Thus, to fully understand the problem of poverty requires an understanding of the patterns of relationship, as well as different experiences, problems and opinions from both women and men. To comprehend these distinctions requires separate discussions with men and women to divulge various issues. The team implementing community-level consultations needs to have an understanding of gender analysis and local customs related to gender, to ensure that they utilise an approach and method that does not trigger conflict, which is usually harmful to women (for example, they may be reprimanded by their husbands or forbidden to attend the meetings).

Kedungdowo Village

The position of women in the household and community differs in rural society. This is reflected in the results of group discussions: the roles of women in the household are much more significant than their roles in the community. A patriarchal tradition is observed, where men have a higher position in society than do women. Gender comparisons in Table 90 show that there are fundamental differences of responsibility and authority that the policy should take into account. Gender is a concept used to describe the roles and social relations of men and women. Gender formulates what role should attach to men and women in society. The gender identities of men and women are introduced, maintained, and disseminated through written and unwritten social and legal norms in society. If there is a related mistake in the implementation of development policies, it will have implications that are not small. This mistake will cause the policies to lose effectiveness and not achieve their expected goals.

Selogiri Village

In Selogiri, the scores on responsibilities and authorities (scores) of men and women can be seen in Table 8. There is a general increase among women in household responsibilities in the past compared with the present, as well as authority in the family. The score for women in Responsibility in Social

Table 6. The Roles and Responsibilities in the Household and in the Community

No	Topic/issue	Gender	
		Female	Male
1.	Responsibilities of women and men in the household	Gather firewood, cook, washing clothes, fetch water, clean house, pond rice, sew, care for children, feeding animals Plant seedlings, transplant rice, winnow the rice, transport rice to barn, sell chicken, sell eggs	Chop firewood, cut trees for construction, build house, saw lumber, repair house, take children to school and clinic, drive the tractor, adjust water level of paddy land, harvest, construct rice barn, clear vegetation, build fence, sell cows, sell goats
2.	Responsibilities of women and men in the community	Health volunteer, teacher, woman activator, environment	Village elder, village chief, Spirit Healer, religious leaders, study
3.	Role of women and men in decision making in the household	Food dishes, child education, child health, consumer durables, contraception, food expenditures	Food dishes, child education, child health, consumer durables, contraception, investment
4.	Role of women and men in decision making in the community	Head Village election, woman farmer group,	Head Village election, farmer group
5.	Violence against women in the household and in the community	Violence to women less than three cases in one year	
6.	Women's perceptions of control in the household and community compared to the past	Women have almost the same rights on household assets and decision making	
7.	Are the conditions of women in the community getting better?	Conditions of women are getting better: women have their own role in the village community	

Source: Field work primary data (2013)

Table 7. Scores on Responsibilities and Authority of Women and Men in Kedungdowo Village

No.	Indicator	Past		Present	
		Men	Women	Men	Women
1.	Responsibility for family or housework	4.3	10	5.3	10
2.	Responsibility in social community	10	4.3	10	5.6
3.	Right to decide within family	9.8	5.4	9.6	6.7
4.	Right to decide in social community	10	5	10	6.1

NB: Scoring is out of 10; the higher the score, the higher is his/her responsibility and authority
Source: Field work primary data (2013).

Community showed increase from 4.6 points to 5.6 points. This shows that there is a gender imbalance in the community, since the social role of women should be less dominant than that of men. Policy implementation should pay more attention to the role of women in development by making women the main subject of the policy, for example, as in the Grameen Bank project. Basically the appearance of women in the community has a significant function, since many programmes are run by women. The

Table 8. Scores on Responsibilities and Authority of Women and Men in Selogiri Village

No.	Indicator	Past		Present	
		Men	Women	Men	Women
1.	Responsibility for family or housework	4.6	9.8	5.7	10
2.	Responsibility in social community	10	4.6	10	5.6
3.	Right to decide within family	10	5.4	9.8	6.9
4.	Right to decide in social community	10	5.1	10	6.6

NB: Scoring is out of 10; the higher the score, the higher the responsibility and authority
Source: Field work primary data (2013)

responsibility and awareness of women is higher than men in terms of social activity. In some cases, policy empowerment by women has high sustainability. This study finds that in Kedungdowo the DMP Programme has women group activity (*Arisan*) which is still running and in good standing to date by raising capital in the women financial community.

Candirejo Village

In general, the conditions in Candirejo are the same as in other villages. Women play a more dominant role in the family than they do at community level. Men's significant role in society means that they have better opportunities in discharging their responsibilities. The government should consider giving more attention to making gender-based policies, as opposed to generalised policies.

Madukoro Village

In Madukoro women generally have a considerable role in the household and community. The study data show that women have relatively higher social roles in this village than in the other villages. The

Table 9. Scores on Responsibilities and Authority of Women and Men at Candirejo Village

No.	Indicator	Past		Present	
		Men	Women	Men	Women
1.	Responsibility in family or housework	4.4	10	5.7	10
2.	Responsibility in social affairs	10	5.8	10	6.6
3.	Right to decide within family	9.4	6.1	10	6.2
4.	Right to decide in social affairs	10	6.5	10	6.9

NB: Scoring is out of 10; the higher the score, the higher the responsibility and authority
Source: Field work primary data (2013)

result of discussions involving three groups of men and three groups of women shows that the average scoring of women participants was found to be higher than the men's average score. Women's farmer groups in Madukoro are relatively more active than in the other villages. The learning point from this case is that programme implementation is likely to be more successful with the participation of women. The women-based programme in Madukoro was found to be successful in the monitoring sessions of the programme by local government. An example is the pilot project of the village operated by the Regency Health Center. Another example is the DMP Programme, such as a Family Planning Services - Integrated Healthcare (IHC).

Table 10. Scores on Responsibilities and Authorities of Women and Men in Madukoro Village

No.	Indicator	Past		Present	
		Men	Women	Men	Women
1.	Responsibility in family or housework	6.5	10	7.3	10
2.	Responsibility in social community	10	7.3	10	8.1
3.	Right to decide within family	10	7.3	9.6	7.7
4.	Right to decide in social community	10	6.5	10	7.1

NB: Scoring is out of 10, the higher the score the higher is the responsibility and authority
Sources: Field work primary data (2013)

CONCLUSION AND RECOMMENDATION

Conclusion

Active institutions play a very important role in supporting the DMP Programme. There were institutions in the village sites before the introduction of the DMP Programme, such as the village leader, village councils, farmer groups, rice milling units, a village health station unit, a school, a mosque, a church, private lenders, village shops and traders. New institutions introduced by the Programme are affinity groups, food village teams, rice barns and microfinance institutions. In Kedungdowo, the village leader is serving his second elected term. This shows the trust that villagers have for the village head. The relationship of village leader and village council should be harmonious in order to ensure good consultation with the village council, which typically advises and monitors every village activity.

The institutions, organisations, groups and individuals represented Analysis provide information on the relationships between these entities in the delivery of programme activities and these help planners in identifying and characterising the different factors (impacts, cooperation's, linkages, leadership) involved in different circumstances to bring about successful implementation in rural development. Firstly, in Kedungdowo, the important institution is the RMU. Although it is relatively small, it is useful because it is close by. Its function is like a rice barn or financial institution. It provides villagers with farming inputs and stores of rice stock. Since the launching of the Programme in Kedungdowo, village rice barns and micro financial institution (LKD) have been established, making the function of the RMU less important and its role has been taken over by farmer groups now managing the rice barn and LKD. Low interest loans are an important factor for poor farmers to be motivated to apply and the loan applications are processed in the regular meeting of farmer groups. The poor families find the rice barn beneficial, especially during periods of food shortages. Secondly, in Selogiri, the Affinity Group (AG) formed as a result of the DMP activities consists of four groups of farmers with different business areas of agriculture, livestock, fisheries and cassava cracker manufacturers. Fifty percent of funds are channelled to agricultural groups, so that many more farmers can become involved. The village food team (FVT), which consists of representatives of each affinity group, holds regular meetings every month attended by the head of the village and the village council. The constraints faced in the implementation of activities and future implementation plans are being worked out together so as to encourage the participation of all levels of the society. Thirdly, in Candirejo, farmer groups are relatively more dynamic than those in other villages. The fundamental difference is absence rice milling units because farmers grind their rice in a neighbouring village. Grants are not allocated to the building of rice barns, but are used to purchase livestock (local and *etawa* goats). The allocation of funding is for poor families who are involved as farmer groups. Their tourism resources contribute to revenue. Some villagers earn money through sales to local and foreign tourists. Fourth, in Madukoro, an individual or group has self-motivation initiated by the village leader. High responses of the public to the programme makes it easy to introduce and implement. The important success factor is the efforts of the leader driving activities initiated by the DMP Programme. The the role of the leader is critical to the village's development. The leader should have the ability to mobilise the community to be active in most programmes. A key person with great influence can have a significant impact on programme success through community participation. Policies targeted at the family level such key people to have a significant impact on rural development.

Recommendations

Several programmes have been implemented successfully in one of the villages associated with the Programme, various agencies' cooperation gave rise to high impact contribution to the development of the village. In some villages the Programme was not implemented with other programmes but different times, making them less successful. Programmes should be integrated for more significant impact.

REFERENCES

Central Bureau of Statistics (CBS). (2010). Indonesia in Number Book. In Statistical Yearbook of Indonesia 2010. Badan Pusat Statistik, BPS.

Central Bureau of Statistics (CBS). (2011). Indonesia in Number Book. In Statistical Yearbook of Indonesia 2011. Badan Pusat Statistik, BPS.

Darwis, V., & Rusastra, I. W. (2011, June). Optimizing Rural Community Empowerment through Integrating PUAP and Desa Mandiri Pangan Programs. *Agricultural Policy Analysis Journal.*, *9*(2), 125–142.

Gandhi, V. P., & Marsh, R. (2003). *Development and Poverty Reduction: Do Institutions Matter? A Study on the Impact of Local Institutions in Rural India*. Contributed Paper, The 25th International Conference of Agricultural Economists, Durban, South Africa.

Grewal, B., Grunfeld, H., & Sheehan, P. (2012). *The contribution of agricultural growth to poverty reduction.* ACIAR Impact Assessment Series Report No. 76. Australian Centre for International Agricultural Research.

Quisumbing, A. R. (2003). Household Decisions, Gender, and Development A Synthesis of Recent Research. An earlier. Food Policy, 20, 407–423.

Rusliyadi, M., Bin Hj. Mohd. Jamil, A., Maseleno, A., Tri Kumalasari, R., & Othman, M. (2019). Agricultural extension policy, agricultural growth and poverty reduction in Indonesia. *IACSIT International Journal of Engineering and Technology*, *7*(4), 5539–5550. doi:10.14419/ijet.v7i4.13337

Rusliyadi, M., Jamil, A., Mohd, B., & Kumalasari, R. T. (2019). Analysis of household food security policy: Case of food security village programme, Indonesia. *Asian Journal of Agriculture and Rural Development*, *9*(1), 19–32.

Rusliyadi, M., & Jamil, A. B. (2020). Participatory Poverty Assessment Effort in Food Security and Extension Policy: Evidence From Indonesia. In V. Erokhin & T. Gao (Eds.), *Handbook of Research on Globalized Agricultural Trade and New Challenges for Food Security* (pp. 481–499). IGI Global. doi:10.4018/978-1-7998-1042-1.ch024

Rusliyadi, M., & Libin, W. (2018). Agriculture development programs for poverty reduction evidences from Indonesia and china - comparative study case. *Asian Journal of Agriculture and Rural Development*, *8*(2), 104–118.

Rusliyadi, M., Mohd, H., Jamil, A., & Anshari, M. (2020). Analysis of Food Security Policy by Participatory Poverty Assessment (PPA) Effort: Case in Indonesia. In P. Ordoñez de Pablos, M. Almunawar, & M. Abduh (Eds.), Economics, Business, and Islamic Finance in ASEAN Economics Community (pp. 105-127). Hershey, PA: IGI Global. doi:10.4018/978-1-7998-2257-8.ch006

Sheil, D., & Liswanti, N. (2006). Scoring the importance of tropical forest landscapes with local people: Patterns and insights. *Environmental Management*, *38*(1), 126–136. doi:10.100700267-005-0092-7 PMID:16508796

ENDNOTE

1 Purposive sampling is also known as judgmental, selective, or subjective sampling. Based on the recommendation by the Agricultural and Food Security Agency in Regency Level.

Chapter 3
Institutional Role and Asisstance Service Analysis on Food Security Policy Case in Indonesia

Muhamad Rusliyadi
https://orcid.org/0000-0003-4632-5671
Polytechnic of Agricultural Development Yogyakarta Magelang, Indonesia

Azaharaini Bin Hj. Mohd. Jamil
College IGS Brunei Darussalam, Brunei

Ratna Tri Kumalasari
Agricultural and Food Security Office, Kebumen Regency, Indonesia

Ari Abdul Rouf
Gorontalo Assessment Institute for Agricultural Technology, Ministry of Agriculture Indonesia, Indonesia

ABSTRACT

The chapter aims to analyze on the role of institutions, sources of funding/assistance, source information in terms of food security and extension policy. The result of the research shows the information on problematic areas in policy implementation with respect to food security and extension policy in terms of poverty reduction. The role of the institutions, assistance, and source information is useful in the implementation of other policy sectors in the future because similar issues or problems may be avoided by taking precautions not to repeat the same mistakes or by applying measures that address the implementation issues. In this way, policy implementation can be carried out effectively, and the outcomes will meet the policy objectives.

DOI: 10.4018/978-1-7998-4787-8.ch003

INTRODUCTION

The growth in agriculture has been a guiding source of poverty reduction in most developing nations, particularly in the case of rural poverty. The agriculture sector contributes to poverty reduction in terms of employment generation to the poor and supports the development of non-agricultural employment generation in rural fields. Development in agriculture also contributes to a larger supply of food and lower food prices benefiting both rural and urban poor (Grewal et al., 2012).

Agricultural development is important in a developing country for achieving industrialization. Farming is the backbone of economic growth in many growing countries, because it provides food security, food self-sufficiency, diversification, and value-added enhancement of competitiveness of exports. Moreover, it increases the wellbeing of farmers and leads directly to poverty reduction.

Indonesia has shifted from an agricultural economy to an industrial one. Nevertheless, the agriculture sector remains a key sector for millions of those who depend directly on agriculture for their livelihood. The agriculture sector has been playing a key role in improving living standards and alleviating poverty. Poverty in rural areas, where most people depend on agriculture for their livelihoods, is one of the immense problems in Indonesia. The poverty level indicates that 16.56% of people in rural areas are poor (CBS, 2010). The increasing numbers of poor people are due to the fact that the bulk of the people cannot satisfy their basic needs and survive at the subsistence level, and therefore ensuring household food security via affordable agricultural workplaces and sustainability scheme policies on the basic demands of the farming sector is vital, especially in terms of food security policy.

According to Darwis and Rusastra (2011), the Food Self-Sufficiency Village Programme (Desa Mandiri Pangan) implemented by community groups was supported by agricultural and non-agricultural capital programmes, as well as by rural financial institutions. It was facilitated by agricultural extension workers and expert consultants. This programme is directed at several other objectives: raising the availability of foodstuffs, growing the family unit entitlement, recovering the efficiency of food supply and access programmes, enhancing the local marketplace availability for selling and buying food products, raising capital and industrial options through the introduction of high-yielding varieties of seeds that agriculture community in rural area can develop to increase income, as well as improving the quality of food consumption handling at the household level, and so forth.

The reasons for choosing the Food Self-sufficiency Village Programme (Desa Mandiri Pangan) as the subject of the study are that: 1) The programme has a comprehensives scheme and assistance; 2) The programme has a direct or an indirect beneficial impact on poverty alleviation and food security efforts; 3) This programme is aimed at resolving the existing problems at the grassroots level; 4) It is expected to contribute importantly to rural growth; and, 5) The programme has been implemented in most of Indonesia's provinces.

Active institutions play a very important role in supporting the DMP Programme. There were institutions in the village sites before the introduction of the DMP Programme, such as the village leader, village councils, farmer groups, rice milling units, a village health station unit, a school, a mosque, a church, private lenders, village shops and traders. New institutions introduced by the Programme are affinity groups, food village teams, rice barns and microfinance institutions. In Kedungdowo, the village leader is serving his second elected term. This shows the trust that villagers have for the village head. The relationship of village leader and village council should be harmonious in order to ensure good consultation with the village council, which typically advises and monitors every village activity.

MATERI AND METHOD

This research is focused on the existing food security policy in Indonesia with regard to the DMP Programme that has been implemented since 2006. The methodology used in the study was mainly quantitative, but a qualitative approach was also used to enrich the findings of the quantitative study. Primary data were analysed using Microsoft Excel and Statistical Program for Social Science (SPSS). Research site in Java island has the largest number of population in Indonesia. It was chosen to represent the research site. Central Java was chosen for this case study because it constitutes 17.0% of the population experiencing poverty (CBS, 2011). Secondly, it has many poor villages when compared to other provinces. Four villages were selected purposively[1].

Two villages from Kebumen Regency, Kedung Dowo Village at Poncowarno District and Selogiri Villlage at Karanggayam District, and the others in Magelang Regency at Madukoro Village Kajoran District and Candirejo Village Borobudur District were selected. These villages have been implementing the programme in varying stages with different characteristics and success rate. (Rusliyadi, et al 2019)

Data related to the DMP Programme and extension service were collected using unstructured and semi-structured questionnaire. The survey was conducted in four villages, each of which involved 100 samples. Samples were selected using a purposive and clustered sampling technique based on some particular sample criteria. Criteria of the sample chosen were based on farmer characteristics such as rich farmer, poor farmer, farmer leader, the village leader, man and women. The Scoring o the data preseterd is by author perception and the investigate scoring exercises using replication, cross-check scoring exercises, and interviews. Theseactivities were undertaken with scoring exercises were developed to assess how local people perceived the importance ofvarious environments and resource (Sheil, D & Liswanti, N 2006).

The purposive sampling technique is a type of non-probability sampling that is most effective when one needs to study a certain cultural domain with knowledgeable experts within. Purposive sampling may also be used with both qualitative and quantitative research techniques. The sample that is selected based on characteristics of a population and the objective of the study. This type of sampling can be very useful in situations when you need to reach a targeted sample quickly, and where sampling for proportionality is not the main concern (Rusliyadi, M and Libin, W, 2018)

RESULT AND DISCUSSION

Institutions, Organisations, Groups and Individuals (Venn Diagram)

The following Venn diagrams show the institutions, organisations, groups and important individuals in each village site. The institution on the Venn diagram is involved directly with villagers in terms of importance activity in the community. The closeness of the relationship between institutions and communities in the group is shown by placing them in the same area. The Venn diagrams also provide information on external and internal factor such us institutions, organisations, groups or individuals linking in the community. The expectation from this diagram is the provision of information on the direct impact of and influential institutions in the community. This tool helps identify and characterise different institutions in terms of impact, cooperation, and link integration in different circumtances in a rural village. The output is the information and provision of relationships between the institutions in terms of delivery of programme activities.

Each Venn diagram shows the importance of institutions in a village community. The assessment of the DMP Programme in this analysis is focused on food security and nutrition issues at household level. The institutional collaboration needs adjustments in measurement, especially closeness relative to other institutions. However, each programme has different target groups or institutions in the community, for example, not all member groups receive allocation of aid from the programme. The cooperation is the key to identifying institutional problems in the community and programme implementation.

The Venn diagrams can be used to discover what formal and informal institutions exist in each village and their relationships and benefits for the local community. The distance between the circles in the diagrams indicates the closeness of their relationship, while their sizes indicate their relative sizes or influence in the community.

Kedungdowo Village

As shown in *Figure 1*, institutions within the village all lie within a larger circle, while outside institutions are shown outside the large circle, with their respective estimated distances from Kedungdowo. The distance here is very important, because the process of assisting a programme will be more effective and efficient when the distance between the donor and recipient policies is not too great so that monitoring and implementation can be maximised. The influence and availability of institutions when needed is determined by the symbiotic relationship between villagers and importance institutions in the village.

Each institution shown is an active institution that plays a role in supporting the DMP Programme. There were institutions in the village before the introduction of the Programme. These were village leaders, village councils, farmer groups, rice milling units, the village health station unit, a school, a mosque, a church, private lenders, village shops or traders. New institutions introduced by the Programme are affinity groups, a food village team, rice barn and microfinance institutions. In Kedungdowo, the village leader is serving his second elected term. This shows that the trust that villagers have in the village head is high. The relationship of village leaders and village councils should be harmonious, since activity in the village needs to be consultative with village councils. Normally the village council gives advice and monitors every activity in the village.

The rice milling unit (RMU) in Kedungdowo is relatively small but useful, because it is not far away for villagers to grind their rice. The RMU is an important institution in the village since its function is like a rice barn or financial institution. The RMU assists villagers by providing farming inputs and store for rice stock. The mechanism involves the villagers being given cash or input in the pre-planting stage and they repay this after harvest in the form of rice or money that is equivalent to the value of inputs provided at the pre-planting stage. It is like a soft loan with low interest, but in some cases the RMU charges double the price of the inputs given to farmers, with the result that the villagers have low earnings. Since the implementation of the DMP Programme in Kedungdowo the introduced rice barns are also providing farmers with microfinancing (LKD), which reduces the function of theRMU. The role of the RMU has been taken over by the farmer groups who run the operation of the ricebarn and the LKD. Low interest is an important factor for poor farmers in making a decision to seek a loan, which is handled at the regular meeting of farmer groups. The poor members of society find the rice barn beneficial, especially during periods of food shortages.

The nearest institutions outside the village, such as the district office, the agriculture and forestry office, the military/police outpost and the market are about 7km distant. This is relatively far from the village, which makes coordination less optimal. According to villagers, "a far distance from the district office means lack of information for their development". The centres of district municipalities in general are the centres of economic activity for some villages. The point is that economic development in villages depends on the distance from the village to the district centre. The nearest market is about 7km from the village. It is important to understand that the closer the village is to the market, the more it is developed. The market is, therefore, central to village activity and employment opportunity. The local daily market that provides the basic needs of the rural community is an economic buffer (food security) for surrounding villages to do business. It is related to the previous observation that the availability of a market makes it easier to start or do business.

Selogiri Village

Institution/group activity in Selogiri is generally not very dynamic. Village institutions would be involved only if there was a government programme for the village. The village leader has uneasy relations with some community leaders, according to the interviews. This has reduced the effectiveness of existing programmes in the village. Affinity groups as drivers in the DMP Programme are quite active, but the effectiveness level is still below the level of effectiveness in other villages.

Figure 1. Venn Diagram for Kedungdowo Village
NB: RMU = Rice Milling Unit, FVT = Food Village Team, FG = Farmer Gorups, AG = Affinity Groups. Sources: Field work primary data (2013)

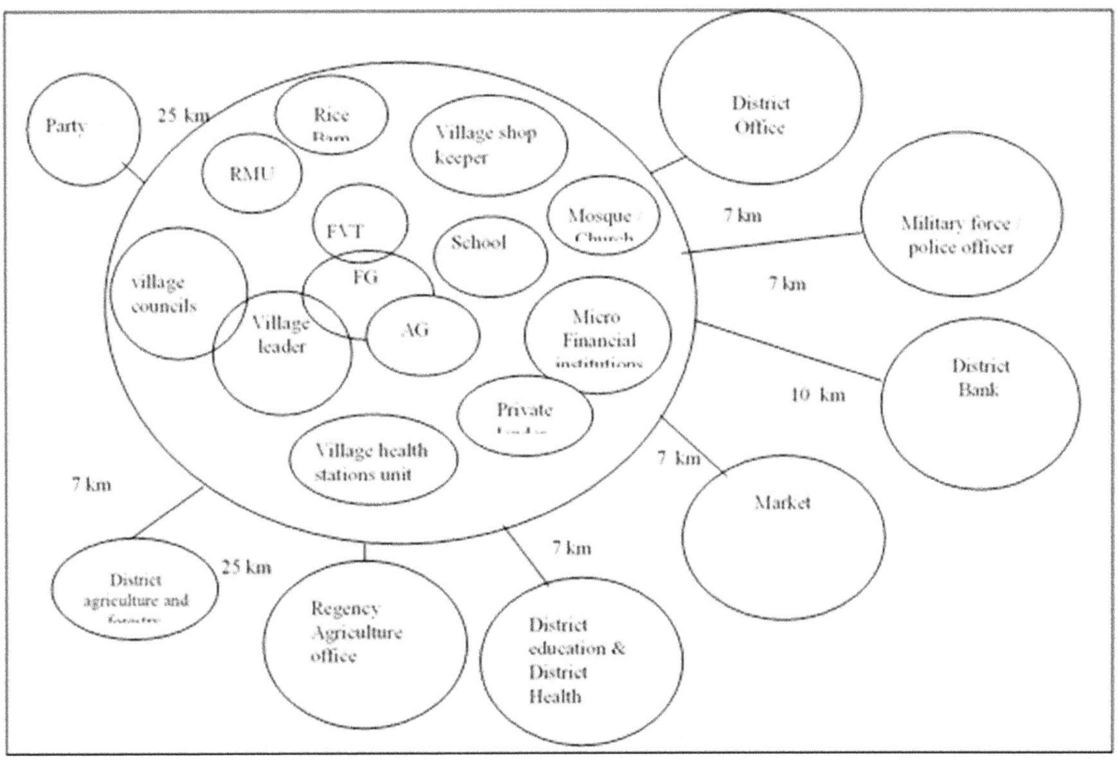

Figure 2 describes the general institutional Venn diagram for Selogiri. The distance of the village from the district office is less compared to the situation in Kedungdowo, but the distance to the regency office is considerable – about 35 kilometres. The Affinity Group (AG) formed as a result of the DMP activities consists of four groups of farmers with different business areas of agriculture, livestock, fisheries and cassava cracker manufacturers. Fifty percent of funds are channeled to agricultural groups so that many more farmers are involved in the programme. The village food team (FVT) which consists of representatives of each affinity group holds regular meetings every month attended by the head of the village and the village council. The constraints faced in the implementation of activities and future implementation plans are being worked out together so as to encourage the participation of all levels of society.

Figure 2. Venn Diagram at Selogiri Village
NB: RMU = Rice Milling Unit, FVT = Food Village Team, FG = Farmer Gorups, AG = Affinity Groups. Sources: Field work primary data (2013)

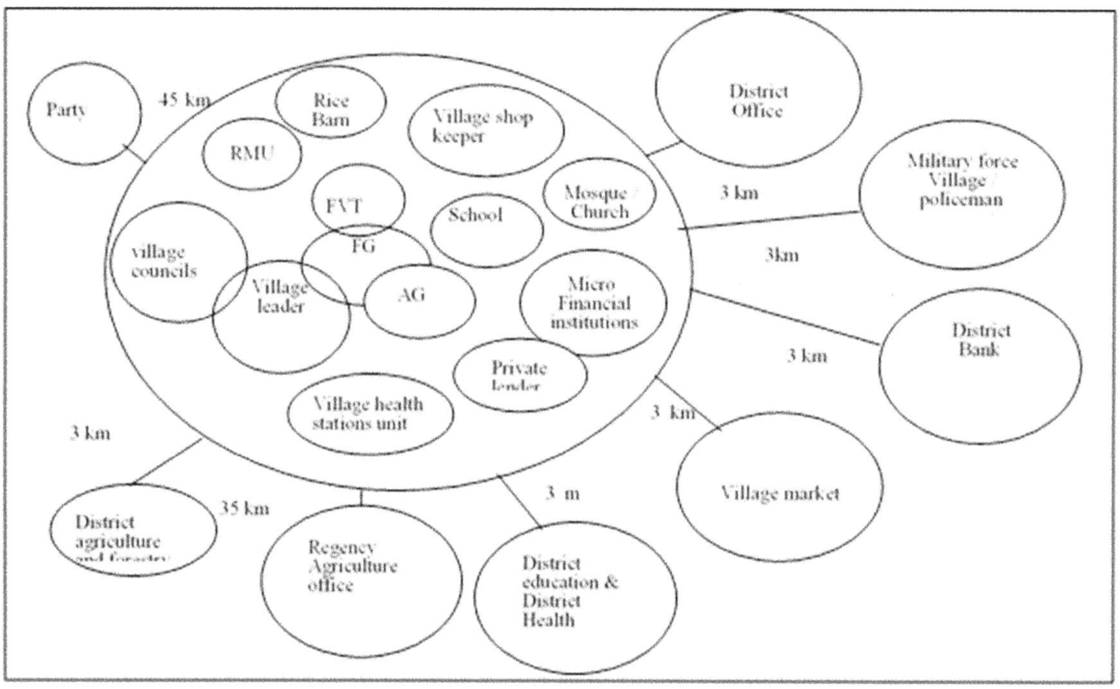

Candirejo Village

The farmer groups in Candirejo are relatively more dynamic than in the other villages. The fundamental difference in the diagram below compared to other villages is, firstly, an absence of rice milling units (RMU) in the village, as farmers grind their rice in a neighbouring village. Secondly, grants are not allocated to the building of rice barns, but are used to purchase livestock in the form of local and *etawa* goats. The allocation of funding is for poor families, which is involved as a farmer group (affinity group). Thirdly, the distance from the village to the district office is 4km. Finally, tourism resources are contributing to the revenue of the village, such as a handicraft store and homestay facilities. Some villagers earn money by selling when local and foreign tourists visit Candirejo.

Madukoro Village

Madukoro Village is located on the border between Purworejo Regency and Magelang Regency, relatively far from the centre of the district (about 7km). DMP activities run well as the farming group in this village is much better in terms of their participation. In Madukoro an individual or group has self-motivation initiated by the village leader. High response of the public to a programme makes it easy to introduce and implement it. The important success factor is the efforts of the village/hamlet leader in driving the activity initiated by the DMP Programme. The influence of the hamlet leader in Madukoro is greater than village's head because the village head is relatively young and pays less attention to villagers. The important point of this case is the role of the village head or chief of the hamlet, which is a critical factor in the village's development. Village leaders should have the ability to mobilise the community to be active in most village programmes. Key persons who have great influence in the village have a significant impact on the success of a programme, measured by the highest participation of

Figure 3. Venn Diagram for Candirejo Village
NB: RMU = Rice Milling Unit, FVT = Food Village Team, FG = Farmer Groups, AG = Affinity Groups. Sources: Field work primary data, (2013).

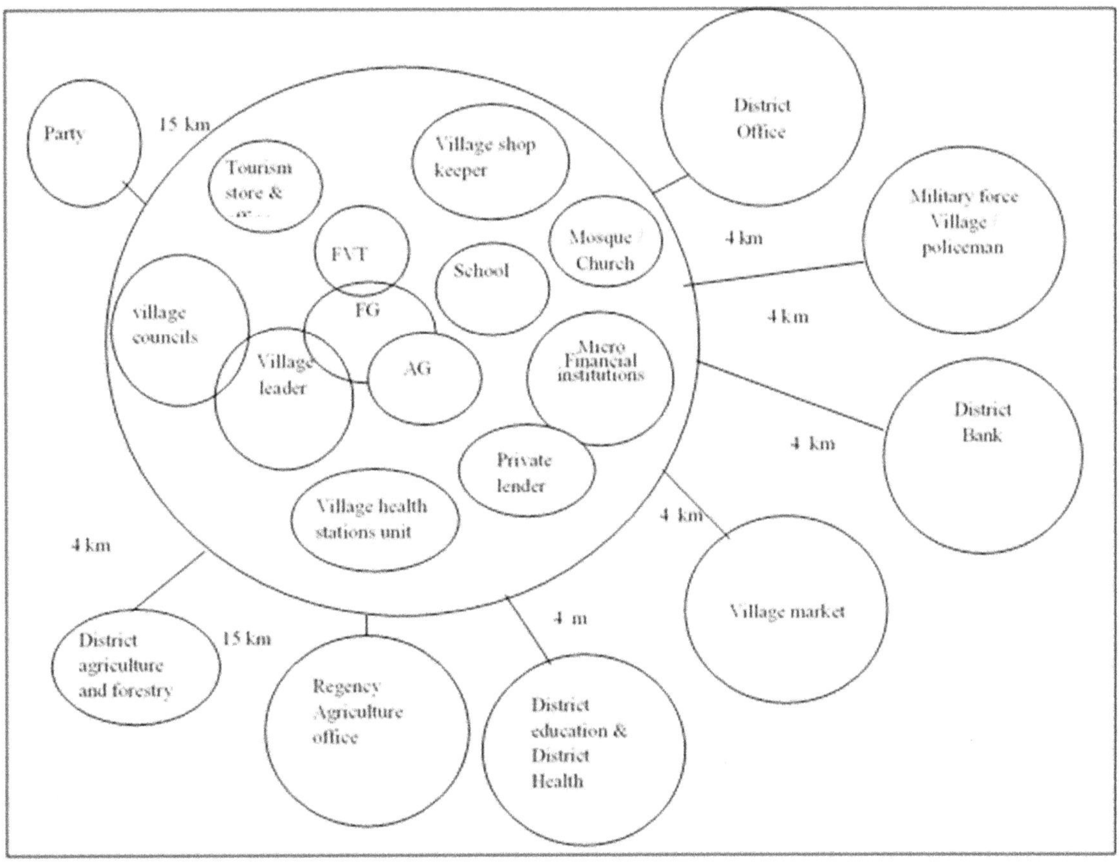

the community. The policies at village level require effort and involvement from several key persons to achieve implementation impact.

Analysis of the Sources of Information and Assistance

This analysis is the result of focus group discussions (FGD) and randomly surveyed poor households as respondents. Information is a source of knowledge that can be used by farmers to contribute to their income by practical business. To villagers, knowledge is difficult to obtain due to village remoteness. Education alone is not enough for development to take place at village level. Villagers need experience and accurate information. Starting businesses (the opportunity to open/start a business) in the village is difficult because of lack of information and capital. Therefore, information is very helpful for villagers to start a business and information on the latest technologies should also be useful for them to promote business development.

Figure 4. Venn Diagram at Madukoro Village
NB: RMU = Rice Milling Unit, FVT = Food Village Team, FG = Farmer Gorups, AG = Affinity Groups. Sources: Field work primary data (2013)

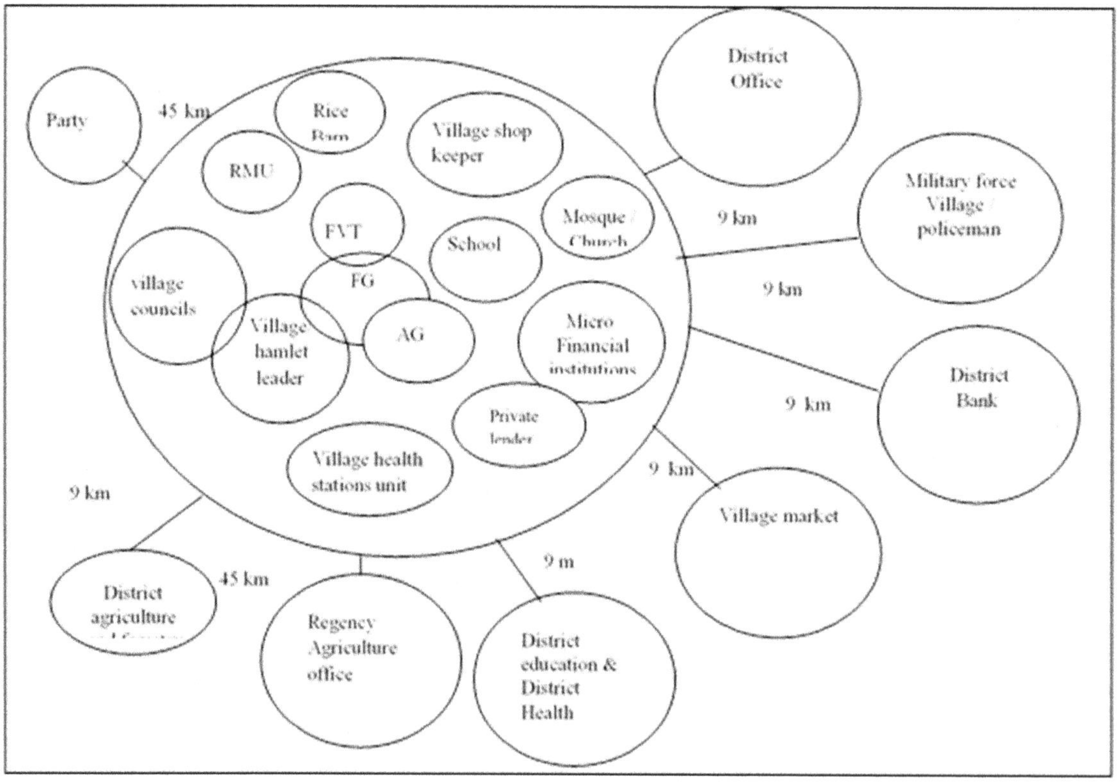

The sources of funding received by the villages are identified and analysed based on perception of the randomly selected villagers. The funding resources are categorised on the basis of where the funding comes from: the State budget (National budget), local budget (Province or Regency budget), International funds, and NGOs. There are four types of assistance made available to the research sites for rural village development: cash funding, physical assistance, aid-type of goods, and types of integrated programmes such as the DMP Programme.

Kedungdowo Village

Based on discussions and analysis of several groups in Kedungdowo (Table 1), villagers receive information from friends, relatives and parents. This shows that verbal information obtained through discussion and conversations is influential. Information obtained through formal schooling is less influential, because it tends to contain theoretical knowledge with little information on practices. Villagers expressed their desire to be continuously trained and exposed to the latest technologies for agriculture, fisheries and husbandry. Extension officers need to be more active at village level in providing information and knowledge-based resources in village workshops.

Table 1. Information Source Scoring of Kedungdowo Village

No.	Information type required	Information Source				
		Media (TV, Newspapers, magazines)	Schools	Extension Officers	Friends, relative, parents	Score
1	Agriculture	3	4	8	9	24
2	Livestock	4	3	7	8	22
3	Fisheries	5	4	7	7	23
4	Forestry	7	3	9	8	27
5	Business opportunity	7	6	6	9	28
6	Markets	8	3	6	8	25
7	Employment	8	4	5	8	25
	Score	42	27	48	57	

NB: Scoring is out of 10; the higher the score, the greater is the information obtained
Sources: Field work primary data (2013)

Funds in Kedungdowo mostly come from the National budget. The majority of the financial resources coming from the central government are distributed through local government. This means that, in the distribution of financial resources, the central government should still consider the local situation by administering a proper allocation of funds. The local government is currently striving to boost revenue by looking to local and foreign investors and persuading them to invest in their areas so that more funding is available for rural development. The local government should be proactive in generating sources of funds through local revenue – *Pendapatan Asli Daerah* (PAD). This point is very important for rural development and the gap between the national and regional budgets can be minimised.

Table 2. Sources of Assistance Scoring of Kedungdowo Village

No.	Type of poverty Assistance	Sources of Assistance				Score
		APBN National Budget	APBD Provinces or Regency Budget	International Funds	NGO	
1	*Bantuan IDT* - National Aid for underdeveloped villages	6	-	-	-	6
2	*Kartu Sehat/Gakin* Health Card	9	-	-	-	9
3	*Raskin* (rice for the poor)	9	-	-	-	9
4	*Bantuan langsung Tunai BLT* - Direct cash assistance	8	-	-	-	8
5	*Desa mandiri pangan (DMP) Programme*	9	-	-	-	9
6	*PAMSIMAS* - Community-Based Water Supply and Sanitation	0	-	8	-	8
7	*Bedah Rumah* - House Renovation Programme	5	7			12
8	Agricultural Extension assistance	8	-	-	-	8
9	*Programme Nasional Pemberdayaan Masyarakat - PNPM Mandiri perdesaan* -National Programme for Community Empowerment - Rural PNPM Mandiri	10	-	-	-	10
	Score	64	7	8		

NB: Scoring is out of 10; the higher the score, the higher its impact
Sources: Field work primary data, (2013).

Selogiri Village

In Selogiri, information obtained from friends, relatives and parents also received high score from respondents. Why are these information sources significant for farmers' farming knowledge? This is because other resources, such as the mass media, are rarely accessed by villagers or they must actively obtain this information, while information from friends, relatives and parents is readily available through daily interactions in the village. Also, this information is free of charge. Villagers might have no time to seek information through the media because of working in the fields.

The sources of financial assistance in Selogiri (Table 4) are almost the same as in Kedungdowo, that is, the majority of financial assistance comes from state funds. The biggest aid funds are derived from the National Programme for Community Empowerment (Rural PNPM Mandiri) at 252 million IDR. These funds were directed to the construction of concrete rural roads with partial support employment comes from the community. Villagers in the group discussions said that the national budget has the greatest impact on physical development in PNPM and the highest score (value of 10: see Table 4) in terms of impact on social development through the Health Card/household health scheme. The agricultural

Table 3. Information Source Scoring of Selogiri Village

No.	Information type required	Information Source				
		Media (TV, Newspapers, magazines)	Schools	Extension Officers	Friends, relative, parents	Score
1	Agriculture	2	4	7	8	21
2	Livestock	3	4	8	10	25
3	Fisheries	5	5	6	6	22
4	Forestry	6	4	8	9	27
5	Business opportunity	5	7	5	8	25
6	Markets	7	3	5	7	22
7	Employment	7	3	4	9	23
	Score	35	30	43	57	

NB: Scoring is out of 10; the higher the score, the greater the amount of information obtained
Source: Field work primary data (2013)

Table 4. Sources of Assistance Scoring of Selogiri Village

No.	Type of poverty Assistance	Sources of Assistance				Score
		APBN National Budget	APBD Provinces or Regency Budget	International Funds	NGO	
1	*Bantuan IDT* - National Aid for underdeveloped villages	5	-	-	-	5
2	*Kartu Sehat/Gakin* Health Card	10	-	-	-	10
3	*Raskin* (rice for the poor)	8	-	-	-	8
4	*Bantuan langsung Tunai BLT* - Direct cash assistance	7	-	-	-	7
5	*Desa mandiri pangan (DMP)* - Food Self-Sufficient village Programme	8	-	-	-	8
6	*PAMSIMAS* - Community-Based Water Supply and Sanitation	0	-	9	-	9
7	*Bedah Rumah* - House Renovation Programme	0	6	-	-	6
8	Agricultural Extension assistance	8	7	-	-	15
9	*Programme Nasional Pemberdayaan Masyarakat - PNPM Mandiri perdesaan* National Programme for Community Empowerment	9	-	-	-	9
	Score	55				

NB: Scoring is out of 10; the higher the score, the higher its impact
Source: Field work primary data (2013).

extension programme receives assistance from two fund sources with the same pattern and type but different commodities (wetland rice and upland rice). This programme was initiated by School Field of Integrated Rice Crop Management (*Sekolah Lapang Pengelolaan Tanaman Terpadu* - SLPTT) funded by APBN. The upland rice SLPTT is funded by the Local Budget APBD. The collaboration programme implementation by national and local budgets in the same time but different commodities is possible, but it needs different targets (villagers) and areas (location).

Candirejo Village

Candirejo is a village which enjoys good access to information. It is a tourist village that often interacts socially and culturally with people from outside the village. The information obtained by villagers is varied and spreads quickly in the village. One example is about business opportunities in other places and success stories become special information for villagers. However, not all villagers have access to the information. It depends on the distance between the village centre where they live and the other villages where their relatives live. The neighbourhood activity in the village is very important, since information resources are mostly transmitted and received from the interactions of people and relatives. Thus the information obtained by villagers is very limited. The important implication from this case is that rural development policy should be focused on providing information through actual practical training in agriculture and business development opportunities, rather than through information provided through various media sources. An additional solution is training on how to get information from reliable resources such as the Internet and news media.

Table 5. Information Source Scoring of CandirejoVillage

No.	Information type required	Information Source				
		Media (TV, Newspapers, magazines)	Schools	Extension Officers	Friends, relative, parents	Score
1	Agriculture	4	3	9	10	26
2	Livestock	6	4	8	9	27
3	Fisheries	6	7	9	9	31
4	Forestry	7	3	9	8	27
5	Business opportunity	7	6	6	9	28
6	Markets	7	4	5	9	25
7	Employment	7	6	4	8	25
	Score	40	30	41	52	

NB: Scoring is out of 10; the higher score, the higher the information
Sources: Field work primary data (2013)

The sources of funding assistance in Candirejo can be seen in Table 6. Unlike the previous villages, funds from NGOs are provided. This aid comes in the form of mentoring activities provided near the famous Borobodur Temple in the field of hospitality and tourism. From 2009 until 2011 Candirejo was

Table 6. Sources of Assistance Scoring of Candirejo Village

No.	Type of poverty Assistance	Sources of Assistance				Score
		APBN National Budget	APBD Provinces or Regency Budget	International Funds	NGO	
1	*Bantuan IDT* - National Aid for underdeveloped villages	7	-	-	-	7
2	*Kartu Sehat/Gakin* Health Card/Gakin scheme	8	-	-	-	8
3	Raskin - Rice for the poor	9	-	-	-	9
4	*Bantuan langsung Tunai BLT* - Direct cash assistance	6	-	-	-	6
5	*Desa mandiri pangan (DMP) Programme* – Food Self-Sufficient village	8	-	-	-	8
6	*PAMSIMAS* - Community-Based Water Supply and Sanitation	0	-	8	-	0
7	*Bedah Rumah* - House Renovation Programme	7	6	-	-	13
8	Agricultural Extension assistance	6	7	-	-	13
9	*PNPM Mandiri perdesaan* - National Programme for Community Empowerment	9	-	-	-	9
10	*Desa Wisata* Tourism Village	9	-	-	8	14
	Score	69	13	8	8	

NB: Scoring is out of 10; the higher score, the higher its impact
Source: Field work primary data (2013)

provided with full assistance by NGOs from Yogyakarta. In 2012 the local government assisted Candirejo through the *Program Nasional Pemberdayaan Masyarakat* - PNPM programme to build infrastructure and support facilities to become a tourist village. The community believes that the tourism programme can contribute significantly to their economy if some villagers take the opportunity to make their homes into guesthouses. In terms of the DMP Programme, its activities are more focused on agriculture development, including introduction of livestock farming packaged with management training, and skills training based on local resource availability. The goal of the Programme is to increase the income of poor families living on the village's border where the impact of tourism is less obvious.

Madukoro Village

Based on the results of group discussions (Table 7), extension officers have an important role in every activity in the village. The expected function of the extension officers is to successfully disseminate knowledge and information on programme implementation activities. However, the scoring results show that the sources of information are mostly friends, relatives and parents, with total of 63 points, whereas information disseminated by extension officers only scored 57. This means that extension officers need to improve their performance to the expected level, for example, by frequently visit the villages and visiting their friends or relatives so that they know the problems of villagers. In other words, the extension officers need more creativity and innovation in disseminating information. The villagers at Madukoro suggested that the extension activities should not only come from the district level but also from the regency level and even from the provincial level. The extension officers in this case are from various sectors such as agriculture, husbandry, fisheries and even health. In addition, the variety of information from experienced extension officers is very important. The important issue to be borne in mind is the need for information about the villagers to be known deeply by extension officers through observations. Information to be disseminated should include updated technology and knowledge associated with programme implementation.

Madukoro enjoys considerable aid from the government. Many programmes implemented successfully in a village benefit from cooperation by many agencies in implementation and this gives rise to high impact contribution in terms of village development. In the case of Madukoro, the DMP Programme was not implemented in conjunction with other programmes; they were implemented at different times. The point to be learned is that many programmes should be integrated and implemented at the same time so that the impact is more significant.

Table 7. Information Source Scoring of MadukoroVillage

No.	Information type required	Information Source				
		Media (TV, Newspapers, magazines)	Schools	Extension Officers	Friends, relative, parents	Score
1	Agriculture	4	4	7	10	25
2	Livestock	5	4	9	9	27
3	Fisheries	6	5	10	9	30
4	Forestry	6	4	8	9	27
5	Business opportunity	8	6	8	8	30
6	Markets	7	4	7	9	27
7	Employment	7	6	8	9	30
	Score	43	33	57	63	

NB: Scoring is out of 10; the higher score, the higher the information
Source: Field work primary data (2013)

CONCLUSION AND RECOMMENDATION

The DMP Programme has resulted in the establishment of a microfinancial institution (*Lembaga Keuangan Desa* - LKD) in the village, participated in by farmer groups. However, the funds allocated for the LKD are limited and they cannot cover the needs of all villagers. There remains a lack of capital necessary to start businesses for some farmers. The villagers proposed establishing a farmer cooperative in the village to support 'off-farm' and 'on-farm' activities and to be managed by farmer groups. The aim of the cooperative is to provide the place for savings and loans with low interest rates and to gain profits for the villagers.

Table 8. Sources of Assistance Scoring of Madukoro Village

No.	Type of poverty Assistance	Sources of Assistance				Score
		APBN National Budget	APBD Provinces or Regency Budget	International Funds	NGO	
1	*Bantuan IDT* - National Aid for underdeveloped villages	6	-	-	-	6
2	*Kartu Sehat/Gakin* Health Card/Gakin scheme	10	-	-	-	10
3	Raskin/ rice for the poor	9	-	-	-	9
4	*Bantuan langsung Tunai BLT* - Direct cash assistance	8	-	-	-	8
5	*Desa mandiri pangan (DMP) Programme* – Food Self-Sufficient village	9	10	-	-	19
6	*PAMSIMAS* - Community-Based Water Supply and Sanitation	0	-	7	-	7
7	*Bedah Rumah*/House Renovation Programme	5	6	-	-	13
8	Agricultural Extension assistance	7	7	-	-	14
9	*Programme Nasional Pemberdayaan Masyarakat - PNPM Mandiri perdesaan* National Programme for Community Empowerment	8	-	-	-	8
10	Fishery fishpond programme	8	-	-	-	8
11	*Kawasan Rumah Pangan Lestari (KRPL)* Sustainable Food House zones	8	-	-	-	8
	Score	62	23	7	0	

NB: Scoring is out of 10; the higher score, the higher its impact
Source: Field work primary data (2013).

On the issue of information sources, analysis shows that the villagers receive information related to the Programme mostly from friends, relatives and parents. Verbal information obtained through discussion and conversations is influential. Information obtained through formal schooling is less influential because it tends to contain theoretical knowledge with little information on practices. Villagers want to be trained and exposed to the latest technologies for agriculture, fisheries and husbandry. Extension officers need to be more active at the village level in provided information and knowledge-based resources.

Analysis on sources of funding shows that villages receive funding mostly from the national budget, implemented through local government. To ensure sustainability in efforts to alleviate poverty central government should continue to consideration the local situation in allocation of funds. The local government is currently striving to boost revenues by looking to local and foreign investors to invest in their villages so that the budget can be increased. The local government should be proactive in generating financial sources through local revenue. In this way the gap between the national and regional budgets can be reduced.

Extension officers play an important role in every activity in the village. Their function is to disseminate knowledge and information on programme implementation. However, that information is mostly obtained from friends, relatives and parents. If extension officers are to play their role they need to frequently visit villages and come to the problems faced. Extension activities should not be only from the district level but also from regency or province level. Information dissemination is more effective if officers are experienced and come from various sectors, such as agriculture, husbandry, fisheries and health. Extension officers need to know villagers' problems through close observation. Information should include up-to-date technology and information in terms of programme implementation.

REFERENCES

Central Bureau of Statistics (CBS). (2010). Indonesia in Number Book. In Statistical Yearbook of Indonesia 2010. Badan Pusat Statistik, BPS.

Central Bureau of Statistics (CBS). (2011). Indonesia in Number Book. In Statistical Yearbook of Indonesia 2011. Badan Pusat Statistik, BPS.

Darwis, V., & Rusastra, I. W. (2011, June). Optimizing Rural Community Empowerment through Integrating PUAP and Desa Mandiri Pangan Programs. *Agricultural Policy Analysis Journal.*, *9*(2), 125–142.

Gandhi, V. P., & Marsh, R. (2003). *Development and Poverty Reduction: Do Institutions Matter? A Study on the Impact of Local Institutions in Rural India.* Contributed Paper, The 25th International Conference of Agricultural Economists, Durban, South Africa.

Grewal, B., Grunfeld, H., & Sheehan, P. (2012). *The contribution of agricultural growth to poverty reduction.* ACIAR Impact Assessment Series Report No. 76. Australian Centre for International Agricultural Research.

Quisumbing, A. R. (2003). Household Decisions, Gender, and Development A Synthesis of Recent Research. An earlier. Food Policy, 20, 407–423.

Rusliyadi, M., Bin Hj. Mohd. Jamil, A., Maseleno, A., Tri Kumalasari, R., & Othman, M. (2019). Agricultural extension policy, agricultural growth and poverty reduction in Indonesia. *IACSIT International Journal of Engineering and Technology*, *7*(4), 5539–5550. doi:10.14419/ijet.v7i4.13337

Rusliyadi, M., Jamil, A., Mohd, B., & Kumalasar, R. T. (2019). Analysis of household food security policy: Case of food security village programme, Indonesia. *Asian Journal of Agriculture and Rural Development*, *9*(1), 19–32.

Rusliyadi, M., & Jamil, A. B. (2020). Participatory Poverty Assessment Effort in Food Security and Extension Policy: Evidence From Indonesia. In V. Erokhin & T. Gao (Eds.), *Handbook of Research on Globalized Agricultural Trade and New Challenges for Food Security* (pp. 481–499). IGI Global. doi:10.4018/978-1-7998-1042-1.ch024

Rusliyadi, M., & Libin, W. (2018). Agriculture development programs for poverty reduction evidences from Indonesia and china - comparative study case. *Asian Journal of Agriculture and Rural Development*, *8*(2), 104–118.

Rusliyadi, M., Mohd, H., Jamil, A., & Anshari, M. (2020). Analysis of Food Security Policy by Participatory Poverty Assessment (PPA) Effort: Case in Indonesia. In P. Ordoñez de Pablos, M. Almunawar, & M. Abduh (Eds.), Economics, Business, and Islamic Finance in ASEAN Economics Community (pp. 105-127). Hershey, PA: IGI Global. doi:10.4018/978-1-7998-2257-8.ch006

Sheil, D., & Liswanti, N. (2006). Scoring the importance of tropical forest landscapes with local people: Patterns and insights. *Environmental Management*, *38*(1), 126–136. doi:10.100700267-005-0092-7 PMID:16508796

ENDNOTE

1 Purposive sampling is also known as judgmental, selective, or subjective sampling. Based on the recommendation by the Agricultural and Food Security Agency in Regency Level.

Chapter 4
Food Security Policy Analysis of Household Level:
Case of Food Security Village Programme in Indonesia

Muhamad Rusliyadi
https://orcid.org/0000-0003-4632-5671
Polytechnic of Agricultural Development Yogyakarta Magelang, Indonesia

Azaharaini Bin Hj. Mohd. Jamil
College IGS Brunei Darussalam, Brunei

ABSTRACT

The study focuses on analyzing the food self-sufficiency village program at household level in Indonesia. The before and after analysis and food and security composite analysis at household level are used as tools. It involved comparing the implication and impact between indicators before and after the implementation of policy. Quantitative data were used to compare major indicators and qualitative data for minor indicators. In general, the impact of the DMP Programme on the villages was positive. The level of poverty in each village has been significantly reduced by 8-40% after the introduction of the programme. Composite food security analysis at household level shows the positive impacts of DMP Programme implementation. This is shown by several indicators, including the rise of 4-7% availability, reduction in poverty by 8-40%, and decrease in people working fewer than 15 hours per week by 10-20%.

INTRODUCTION

Food security policy will be a paramount concern for the economic development of many countries for at least the next two decades. (FAO, 2006).. The rate of increase in population is rising significantly in many countries, but especially in developing countries. Governments are trying to address their food problems, and they need good analysis and good implementation of development policies, especially in

DOI: 10.4018/978-1-7998-4787-8.ch004

rural areas where most people live. Food security analysis, carried out at nationally and household or village level, is indispensable.

The challenges in food security development in general are linked to high population growth, limited natural resources and shifting functions of agricultural soil, inadequate infrastructure for businesses in the food sector, increased competition with imported merchandise in the marketplace, and the sheer number of poor people (Paasch et al., 2010). Moreover, demand for food per capita increases over time, driven by increased revenue, awareness of health and diet changes, because of the influence of globalization and various community activities. In Indonesia, poverty and the attainment of food security have been the main problems. Food insecurity is widely experienced in many regions and is positively linked to impoverishment. (Weiler, Anelyse M et al. 2014).

Rural development aims to achieve food security in a region. It requires integration and collaboration of the aspects of availability, distribution, and consumption of food security at a household level. Therefore, a good system is a prerequisite for the realisation of food security by the Food Self-Sufficiency Village Programme (DMP Programme). The rural areas are very important, especially in terms of supplying nutrients for the population, providing labour, providing industrial raw material, and providing food for export.

The performance of DMP Programme has enabled to provide significant impact with some major indicators such as poverty, income and food security in the villages. However, rural areas have classical problem in some villages. The participation rate for farmers in the program is low and most farmers in villages face the problem of limited capital resources hindering their success. Policy programs such as DMP Programme need to be effectively developed in collaboration and cooperation with others sectors so that the rural development targets have to be more focused on poverty reduction and maintenance of food security at village level. (Darwis, V 2012).

According to Darwis and Rusastra (2011), the DMP Programme implemented by community groups was supported by agricultural and non-agricultural capital programmes, as well as by rural financial institutions. It was facilitated by agricultural extension workers and expert consultants. This programme is directed at several other objectives: raising the availability of foodstuffs, growing the family unit entitlement, recovering the efficiency of food supply and access programmes, enhancing the local marketplace availability for selling and buying food products, raising capital and industrial options through the introduction of high-yielding varieties of seeds that agriculture community in rural area can develop to increase income, as well as improving the quality of food consumption handling at the household level, and so forth.

MATERIAL AND METHOD

This research is focused on the existing food security policy in Indonesia with regard to the DMP Programme that has been implemented since 2006. The methodology used in the study was mainly quantitative, but a qualitative approach was also used to enrich the findings of the quantitative study. Primary data were analysed using Microsoft Excel and Statistical Program for Social Science (SPSS). Research site in Java island has the largest number of population in Indonesia. It was chosen to represent the research site. Central Java was chosen for this case study because it constitutes 17.0% of the population experiencing poverty (CBS, 2011). Secondly, it has many poor villages when compared to other provinces. Four villages were selected purposively[1].

Two villages from Kebumen Regency, Kedung Dowo Village at Poncowarno District and Selogiri Villlage at Karanggayam District, and the others in Magelang Regency at Madukoro Village Kajoran District and Candirejo Village Borobudur District were selected. These villages have been implementing the programme in varying stages with different characteristics and success rate.

Data related to the DMP Programme and extension service were collected using unstructured and semi-structured questionnaire. The survey was conducted in four villages, each of which involved 100 samples. Samples were selected using a purposive and clustered sampling technique based on some particular sample criteria. Criteria of the sample chosen were based on farmer characteristics such as rich farmer, poor farmer, farmer leader, the village leader, man and women. The purposive sampling technique is a type of non-probability sampling that is most effective when one needs to study a certain cultural domain with knowledgeable experts within. Purposive sampling may also be used with both qualitative and quantitative research techniques. The sample that is selected based on characteristics of a population and the objective of the study. This type of sampling can be very useful in situations when you need to reach a targeted sample quickly, and where sampling for proportionality is not the main concern (Muhamad Rusliyadi and Wang Libin, 2018).

MAIN FOCUS OF THE CHAPTER

Food security is achieved when every household can continuously have access physically and economically to food that is dependable and healthy for all household members (FAO, 1996). This is the main focus of food security conditions at the home level. Food security should include availability, accessibility, security and sustainability. Accessibility here means every household is able to meet food self-sufficiency. Food availability is the average amount of food in consumption needs in the region and at household level. In food safety the emphasis is on the quality of food that meets nutritional needs.

The indicators used in the analysis of food security at the household level are food availability, food access and food consumption or food absorption. An indicator of food availability is normative per capita consumption for food production and normative consumption ratio. The ratio indicates whether or not a region has a surplus production of cereals and tubers. The normative consumption ratio is the ratio between the production of food commodity cereals (rice, maize, cassava, and sweet potato) net of the normative population food consumption per day, which is as much as 300 grams of cereals (DKP, 2005).

Food access has indicators that are expressed in the percentage of household poverty, working people and the percentage working less than 15 hours per week. The research finding is the percentage of those who did not finish elementary schooling, the percentage of households without access to electricity, and the length of roads per square kilometer are indicators which reflect limitation factors in accessing food availability at the village level. (Katarzyna Boratynska and Raqif Tofiq Huseynov. 2017)

Indicators of food consumption or absorption used in the study include: one-year life expectancy of children (amount/1000), underweight children less than 5 years of age (%), percentage of illiterate women, percentage of children who are not immunised, percentage of people with access to clean and safe water, percentage of people who live more than five kilometers from the health center, and the ratio of the number of people per physician to population density.

Calculation of food production at village and district levels is by using data on average production of three years (2010-2012) for rice, maize, cassava and sweet potatoes, because the main energy source of food energy intake comes from cereals and tubers. Patterns of food consumption in Indonesia show that nearly 50% of total caloric needs come from cereal crops. Data on average net gains from rice, maize, cassava and sweet potatoes are calculated using standard conversion factors. For the average net production of cassava and sweet potatoes that are equivalent to rice, this should be multiplied by 1/3 (1 kg of rice or corn is equivalent to 3 kg of cassava and sweet potato in terms of calorific value). Per capita net availability of cereals is calculated by dividing the total cereal availability by a population. Under the Indonesian consumption profile, the normative consumption of cereals/day/capita is 300 grams (DKP. 2009).

FOOD SECURITY COMPOSITE ANALYSIS AT HOUSEHOLD LEVEL

Availability of Food

In general, in most villages few people store staple food in their houses. They mostly buy staple food (rice) and this is part of their daily lifestyle. This trend also occurs in rural areas, where the majority of household heads work in agriculture. This lifestyle suggests that a low income is the most common problem facing many households, contributing to vulnerability to food insecurity and to disease, because they cannot afford food prices. In most cases, it is only rice that is kept in stores as food commodities obtained from the previous harvest or labour fees in harvesting rice. These stores are kept in the house in a sack or barrel. Only a small amount of harvested rice is sold, so that they normally seek for other employment whenever they have free time, particularly after planting rice, and mainly in agricultural sector and as workers in other economic sectors. (Falcon, W P & Naylor, R L, 2005)

The availability of adequate food is an absolute prerequisite for food security; however, it is not a sufficient precondition to ensure food security at the household and individual level. Many efforts have to be made to ensure the availability of food security at village level. The causes of the deficit in the availability of cereals food in some districts, include: (1) expansion of oil palm plantations, black pepper, rubber, cashew, and cocoa; (2) expansion of open-pit mining areas; (3) swamp areas; (4) upland rice production systems that have low productivity; and (5) lack of availability of arable land compared to population density. In addition, many areas of surplus cereal crops are often affected by disasters due

Table 1. Net Cereal Production Per Capita Per Day (G) and Normative Consumption Ratio in Villages Before and After Programme Implementation

No	Indicators	Kebumen Regency				Magelang Regency			
		Kedungdowo Village		Selogiri Village		Candirejo Village		Madukoro Village	
		Before	After	Before	After	Before	After	Before	After
1	Net Cereal Production per Capita per Day (g)	521	542	483	502	481	497	465	486
2	Normative consumption ratio	0.58	0.55	0.62	0.60	0.62	0.60	0.65	0.62

Source: primary data from survey (calculated, 2013).
Note:
Before: Before programme implementation; After: After programme implementation (2013)2

to deforestation, drought or flood. This threatens the sustainability of current production levels and in the future.

Table 1 above is a representation of food availability indicators at the village level sampled in the study. Villages showed an average positive outcome after the implementation of the DMP Programme. This shows that, in the first indicator, the Net Cereal Production per capita per day (g) in all villages increased after the programme was implemented. The highest increase in the value of the indicator is in Madukoro by 21 grams, whereas Kedungdowo is lower. Thus it is possible to say that there is some food in the village. The performance of food security in the two villages was high. This result shows that the Programme can raise enough agricultural production, especially in the cereal crops sector, with the support of training activities and efforts to increase rice productivity through field extension services, that is, provision of assistants in every village.

The normative consumption ratio is a key indicator in the context of food security in a region. Food insecurity of the area is already self-sufficient or does not use this indicator as a reference. The four villages showed that they have a medium surplus in some. After implementation of the DMP Programme, almost all the villages in the Kebumen Regency and Magelang Regency have shown a positive response to a decrease in the value of the normative consumption ratio, which can be interpreted as moving towards surplus food or food self-sufficiency.

Food Access

Table 2 shows data before and after implementation of the DMP Programme. The first indicator, the Percentage of household poverty, shows that most villages were poor and they were in a very vulnerable category before implementation of the Programme. After implementation, however, the percentage of poor households decreased significantly, especially in Selogiri (29.8%). The impact of the has been positive up to the present time, with a significantly decrease in poverty after implementation. The Programme has resulted in the development of productive business activities, which increase the income of farmers.

This Programme is not the only factor contributing to poverty reduction, there are also other programmes, such as social safety assistance, social direct funds for community, rice for the poor and other activities that have encouraged the villages to become independent in food self-sufficiency. The other indirect impact of the DMP Programme is the initiation of other programmes in villages. The lowest percentage of poor people (34.53%) after implementing the Programme is found in Candirejo. The villagers, apart from being farmers, are also engaged in tourism activities. Three out of four villages have the potential to become tourism village because of their natural resources.

A second indicator is the percentage of people who work fewer than 15 hours per week. This is a category of the community who are less productive on a daily basis. Ideally, a normal person works at least 35 hours a week, assuming more than five hours a day. The data in Table 8 above shows the result, a data range of 10-20% (quite resistant). Kedungdowo shows a low percentage (3.74%), before the Food Self-Sufficiency Village Programme was implemented prior to 2013. This situation shows that the duration of Programme, which started from 2009, has been over an extended period and should have reached the stage of self-sufficiency.

When comparison is made with the data of Central Java province, based on the number of hours of work in August 2013, a total of 10.95 million people (68.60%) worked over 35 hours per week, while the working population in the study area by the number of hours worked fewer than 15 hours per week reached 1.33 million, equivalent to 8.30% (CBS/BPS, 2013). These findings show the average data

Table 2. Food Access Indicators in Villages Before and After Programme Implementation

No	Indicators	Kebumen Regency				Magelang Regency			
		Kedungdowo Village		Selogiri Village		Candirejo Village		Madukoro Village	
		Before	After	Before	After	Before	After	Before	After
1	Percentage of household poverty	61.54	56.46	69.42	39.60	42.36	34.53	61.14	35.56
2	Percentage of people working less than 15 hour per weeks	12.36	8.62	14,65	12.59	9.26	8.21	10.32	7.85
3	Percentage of those who did not finish elementary schooling	28.75	25.67	34.56	32.20	20.21	18.95	25.87	23.23
4	Households without access to electricity (%)	3.53	3.24	3.50	3.45	1.45	1.22	1.32	1.27
5	The length of road per square kilometer	2.3	4.5	2.7	3.8	4.6	6.3	1.3	1.9

Source: primary data from survey and Villages Monograph (calculated, 2013). [3]

jobless at village level (real survey) is more than data from the provincial statistical level. This means the policy should pay attention to the real condition of the people in the village by creating more job opportunities. (Boratynska, K & Huseynov, R, 2017).

The third indicator is the percentage of those who did not complete elementary schooling at the village level. This is the main and important indicator in this case study because it is concerned with most of the population. The finding shows an interesting result, that is, there were more people who completed elementary schooling after the implementation of the Programme. This means that the more they are educated, the more productive they are. In terms of the indicator on the percentage of households without access to electricity, the Table above revealed that they were only a few villagers without access to electricity (below 5%). This is because the island of Java has a more developed infrastructure and, therefore, it is relatively easy for people to access electricity. If the study was conducted outside Java island, the figure would be more than 20% of the people unable to afford electricity.

Food Utilization/Absorption/Consumption

The indicator in food absorption is one-year life expectancy of children (amount/1000); this is also the number of deaths of infants (0-12 months) per 1,000 live births in the period of one year. These indicators describe the level of public health issues related to the causes of infant mortality, the level of antenatal care, maternal nutritional status, success rates of maternal and child health programmes, and family planning, as well as environmental and socio-economic conditions. When the indicator in one area is high, it means that the health status in the region is low and the mean levels of food security are also low. Children with one-year life expectancy (amount/1000) in the villages is low, below 12%. This means that the villages' health level is quite good and food supply is secured. There is a decrease in the number of children dying after the implementation of the Programme. This shows the success of the Programme in terms of improving health care and food security for community.

The percentage of underweight children less than 5 years of age is an important indicator in determining the level of utilisation or absorption of food in food security analysis of households. In public

Table 3. Food Utilization/Absorption/Consumption Indicators in Villages Before and After Programme Implemention

No	Indicators	Kebumen Regency				Magelang Regency			
		Kedungdowo Village		Selogiri Village		Candirejo Village		Madukoro Village	
		Before	After	Before	After	Before	After	Before	After
1	One-year children life expectancy (amount/1000)	9.21	9.17	11.92	10.41	10.39	10.25	9.63	9.21
2	Percentage of Underweight Children < 5 years	16.70	14.1	17.34	16.65	14.87	13.4	15.93	15.46
3	Percentage of illiterate women	15.54	14.78	16.37	16.03	20.21	19.29	23.31	21.56
4	Percentage of children who are not immunized	19.23	19.11	24.28	23.87	21.34	21.02	10.23	10.12
5	Percentage of people with access to clean water	80.34	89.72	87.32	83.46	69.56	72.35	85.35	90.59
6	Percentage of people who live more than five kilometers from the health center	6.79	6.79	10.35	10.35	16.76	16.76	9.37	9.37
7	Ratio of the number of people per physician to population density	0.29	0.29	0.39	0.39	0.08	0.08	0.6	0.6

Sources: primary data from survey and Village Monograph (calculated in 2013) [4]

health, children under the age of 5 years is an important component of how health and food programmes achieve success in alleviating malnutrition in rural children. The result shows in fact that most villages are highly resistant (have high resistance to absorption of food) because the village has less than 30% underweight children. The DMP Programme collaboration with other programmes, such as maternal and child health activities, and neighbourhood health centers in every village, has resulted in low percentages of underweight children in the four villages. In spite of a small change of percentage underweight children less 5 years after the implementation of the DMP Programme, it did decrease the number of malnourished children.

The percentage of illiterate women in the villages in Table 3 is in the range 14 – 23%, which falls under the category of 'quite resistant' (food absorption 10 - <20%), near to 'rather vulnerable' (food absorption 20 - <30%). Before the implementation of the DMP Programme, Madukoro recorded the highest percentage for this indicator (23.31%). However, after implementation this fell to 21.56%. The DMP Programme is not aimed at purely educational purposes; it aims at providing more intensive assistance to farmers through extension field services which ultimately should contribute to the acquisition of modern farming skills by farmers.

Problem and Impact of Implementation Food Self-Sufficiency Policy

Social conditions in the study areas mostly consisted of poor villages with their main income and livelihood from agricultural activities and where food availability is relatively limited and the proportion of poor population is more than 30%, so that the villages are justifiably the target for implementing the DMP Programme.

In general, the four villages are densely populated and some have more than 5,000 residents, which is the characteristic of villages on Java island. a high population creates job competition, especially in the agricultural sector, because more people depend on one sector. The relatively low formal and informal education level of the people in most villages makes it necessary to undertake greater effort to increase the level of knowledge of the people in order for them to become more productive. Special efforts in the DMP Programme are expected to be incorporated to enable the rural economy to be developed through enhancing people's knowledge of productive activities so as to develop society.

Socio-cultural attitudes of the people in the villages have contributed to the problems of implementing the Programme. Low participation in awareness-raising activities has led to a lag in the Programme in the two villages in the Kebumen Regency. The involvement of the village people in the implementation of specific activity of food self-sufficiency is impacted by the level of awareness of these people about the Programme. This is partly because of the lack of village officials to socialise the Programme to the community. The result is that the sustainability of the Programme is difficult to achieve. In Candirejo, the social and cultural aspects involve people's inability to maximise creativity in the utilisation of the available resources. For example, people sell pandan leaf directly to the sellers who come to the village. If the available resources such as pandan leaf are sold in the the form of 'handcrafts', this will give added value to the resources and the people could earn more, rather than selling the resources in 'raw' form.

Limited capital availability has become a major problem for many Indonesian farmers. This is a hindrance to the application of farming technology. In the Programme, the funds disbursed by the government for it are very low and it is impossible to meet the capital needs of the entire society. However, if farmers in this Programme are successful and are able to influence other farmers in a positive direction, this will reach out to those farmers who have not received any funds.

Agricultural technology used by farmers in the most villages is very rudimentary due to capital constraints in their farming, which is why farmers are using simple technology that is within their capabilities, but yielding low productivity. Constraints of this technology are found almost all the rural areas, and therefore the role of agricultural extension is to enhance the role of farmer knowledge in agriculture technology. Another problem is a low level of education in the four villages, which contributes to most people's lack of ability to create or perform a productive business. This is obviously seen in cultivation, maintenance and post-harvest in agriculture, animal husbandry and fishery.

Other problems include the lack of access to market information and the length of the marketing chain of agricultural products, which are sold at low prices by farmers. The Programme connects and is able to bridge the farmer activities into affinity groups' engagement in agriculture-based small businesses, livestock, farms and home industry. All four villages under study have very few business networks and strategies for marketing local products with other business partners or investors who can push upwards the rural products to the district level and thus access reliable markets. Lack of transportation facilities also affects market accessibility, because access to the village is very difficult. This causes farmers or villagers to sell their products to merchants who come to the village (middlemen), rather than selling to district-level or regency traders, where they can sell their commodities at higher prices.

The main problem in Candirejo and Kedungdowo is water. The availability of water for farming depends on topography: both villages use water flowing from the hills, and it is too difficult to obtain ground water directly. Dry-land farming practice relies on harvested rain water. Rain-fed rice is harvested once a year, only during the rainy season, which is insufficient to sustain the income of the villagers.

Rural development issues in Indonesia are generally very complex, as can be seen in the matrix based on the research case study. Complexity refers to the linkage between agricultural development and the subject of the actual conditions in the community. The context of the problem in the matrix refers to how the relationship between development actors is represented by groups of farmers or farmer's groups, institutions and village agricultural service officers, with the indicators cited above.

Limited capital is a major problem for many Indonesian farmers, including the four villages under study. The rate of participation of farmers in the DMP Programme is low and most farmers in the have problems of limited capital resources that hinder their success. Two villages, Candirejo and Kedungdowo, also have problems with water. Availability of water for farming depends on topography: both villages use water flowing from the hills and it is too difficult to obtain ground water directly.

The problem indicators impacting poverty/low income farmer's groups are shown in the matrix below table 6. One can see that the number of problem indicators impacting poverty is 10. The number of problem indicators causing 'low investment capacities' of farmer's groups is eight. The 'dependence on aid' by farmer's groups is also impacted by six problem indicators. The main cause for existing problems from agricultural service institutions' perspective is the lack of understanding of the farmers' problem. This problem is most significant at the local government level. The difficulty in policy implementation is because the farmers' problems have not been well-explored and understood. The problem is that civil servants have very limited time to work in the field (real conditions). They normally produce very nice plans on papers, but, when it comes to implementation in the village, they are confused, because of not knowing the root cause of the problem and also because of lack of commitment and funding.

The matrix further shows that problem indicators originate or are located in the organisation and implementation of the DMP Programme, affecting the performance of farmer's groups in most villages. For example, 'limited access to inputs' makes farmers more dependent on other parties such as brokers/traders; this situation exacerbates the persistence of poverty. Most villages need financial support to implement the DMP Programme to be able to meet the farmers' needs. Lack of funds or capital contributes to the inability of farmer groups to invest and become innovative. Other prominent issues are imperfect information, low levels of knowledge and skills, and uncertainty. Access to information and knowledge are important to farmers, as these may help mostly poorly educated farmers to access good prices for their produces, which ultimately solves their problems in the countryside. Future policy makers should consider these crucial issues as a top priority to mitigate problems and to achieve the Programme's success.

Impact of the Self-Sufficiency Village Programme at Village Sites

Table 4 below shows the survey results before and after Programme implementation in 2013. The data reveal the extent to which the Programme has benefited people in the four villages in terms of social welfare and rural development, especially in terms of poverty reduction. The income of the people has shown a relatively low increase in all four villages after Programme implementation. Although it increased at least 5-15%, this still benefits the farmer. The low involvement of farmers and rural communities in the DMP Programme was one of the reasons why people's income has been low. This is an important point for policy intervention in the future. The Programme needs more farmer involvement or participation so that the impact is more visible and realised.

The main social problem in this research is poverty, because all other indicators (problems) tend to contribute the context of poverty. The data below are taken and processed from the data companion extension of food self-sufficient villages and tabulation was done with village officers in each village and was then adjusted with data from village monographs and the CBS at sub-district level. The result is surprisingly significant. The level of poverty in each village declined after the introduction of the DMP Programme by 8-40%. However, the poverty rate in the villages under study (34.5% to 56.5%) is relatively higher than the national average of poverty rate in rural areas (14.3% to 16.0%) of Central Java province (CBS, 2013). Thus the expectation is that the provincial governments should introduce programmes that focus on empowering rural communities to promote their economic activities. One example is the implementation of the Food Self-Sufficiency Village Programme which is complemented by other cross-sectoral programmes to all villages in the whole country.

The Programme allocates funding for social assistance targeted at the poor households who participate in farmer groups. With these funds, productive business activities have been implemented, especially in agriculture, livestock, fisheries and small businesses, contributing to households earning income in the community. Stimulation funding of 7143 US Dollars per village from the government is hoped to become a revolving fund scheme for all citizens. The development funds managed by the financial institutions have increased in amount after a few years of DMP Programme implementation. This increase is generally not very large, except for Madukoro, which has shown a significant level of increase at 78%. The affinity group of the village has managed to achieve a good performance. Most of the funds in the villages are allocated to livestock such as goats. At the start of the programme the Food Self-Sufficiency Village Programme started with 40 goats and this number has increased to 89 goats during the research period.

The increasing number of institutions for farmer's groups has created a new cluster of affinity groups that can make villages' economies act independently. This is reflected in the data below, where there is an increase in farmer's groups before and after Programme implementation. These groups are important because of their strengthening effect on the community groups. It is part and parcel of building social capital, where a programme is initiated by groups which eventually become self-reliant. The socio-economic benefits of the system can be extended to other surrounding villages to strengthen farmer groups.

Table 4. Impact of the Self-Sufficiency Village Programme at Village Sites

No	Indicators	Kebumen Regency				Magelang Regency			
		Kedungdowo Village		Selogiri Village		Candirejo Village		Madukoro Village	
		Before	After	Before	After	Before	After	Before	After
1	Average Income/month (IDR)	1,457,920	1,681,902	1,393,342	1,647,436	1,467,850	1,687,667	1,290,245	1,589,000
2	Poverty (%)	61.54	56.46	69.42	39.62	42.36	34.53	61.14	35.56
3	Village Aid fund/year (Million IDR)	100	109	100	111.6	100	113.78	25	44.5
4	Institutional/farmers groups	2	5	3	6	2	6	2	4
5	Rice Yields productivity (ton/ha)	2.65	2.87	4.58	4.84	3.76	3.88	3.87	4.23
6	Livestock population (Cows and goats)	139	171	245	261	598	805	195	268
7	Average aid funding from other sources/year (Millions IDR)	65.3	146.9	193.1	264.7	76.86	123.42	46.39	93.67
8	Infrastructure	-	Rice barns and roads	-	Rice barns and roads	-	3 km roads	-	2 km roads
9	Participation of villagers in the Programme	75	86	68	71	65	72	78	83
10	Extension officer visit (per month)	1	5	2	4	1	6	2	4

Sources: Primary data from survey (2013)

Note: Before: Before Desa Mandiri Pangan implementation, After: After Desa Mandiri Pangan implementation, (2013)

RESPONSES TO THE FOOD SELF-SUFFICIENCY PROGRAMME FOR POVERTY REDUCTION

Comparative Profile of the Programmes in Villages

The comparative profile of the DMP Programme level for the villages under study. The findings indicate the variability of implementation in each village. Although the villages are at different stages of implementation, they have virtually the same issues. Poor household involvement in the DMP Programme is a major issue common to all villages. The procedures outlined in the Programme's activities are implemented by farmer leaders at district level involving over 60% of poor households for each activity. This initiative can have a direct impact on poor families in gaining their livelihood.

The impacts of the DMP Programme on two regencies are different. Kebumen Regency is less responsive to the Programme compared to Magelang. The study confirms that the impacts and adoption of the Programme in Kebumen are producing lower results compared to Magelang. Local government showed less concern for the Programme in Kebumen compared to local government's concern in the Magelang Regency. For example, the local government did not allocate a budget for a replication village in DMP Programme in Kebumen Regency. The regency is dependent on the allocation of funds from the central government. In contrast to what happened in the Magelang Regency, local government allocated funds for replication villages for DMP Programme development. The important point is that local government should be proactive in programme development. In general, local government concern is important in the rural sector development, which depends on leadership quality in terms of paying attention and providing budget allocations.

Indicators of Outcomes of the Self-Sufficiency Village Programme

The changes in the community after the implementation of the DMP Programme are shown in Table 5 and they are very impressive. The data show that there is a significant increase in the amount of funds managed by farmer groups. The increase of 78% in Madukoro is unexpected, because it is a village replication which received social grants that are relatively small compared to other villages. This indicates that the DMP Programme enables augmentation of the local economy through productive activities like animal husbandry, e.g., goats, home industries and fisheries. The result shows that other programmes associated with the implementation of the DMP Programme are generating benefits every year. For example, some villages obtained funding of more than a 100% increase. The collective efforts in imple-

Table 5. Community Gains from the DMP Programme

Gains Indicator (%)	Kebumen Regency		Magelang Regency	
	Kedungdowo Village	Selogiri Village	Candirejo Village	Madukoro Village
Knowledge of farmers about the Programme	87	67	93	78
Community response to the Programme in terms of their actions	76	69	72	87
Participation of community in the Programme	86	71	72	83

Sources: Primary data from survey (2013)

mentation of the intensive DMP villages programmes allocated to the Madukoro and Kedungdowo are working well to the endpoint of this research study.

As can be seen in Table 5, the DMP Programme has benefited communities. Its implementation has directly impacted significantly on people at grassroots level.

CONCLUSION

Composite food security analysis at household level shows the positive impacts of DMP Programme implementation. This is shown by several indicators, including the rise of 4-7% availability, reduction in poverty by 8-40%, and decrease in people working fewer than 15 hours per week by 10-20%.

In general, the impact of the DMP Programme on the villages was positive. The level of poverty in each village has been significantly reduced by 8-40% after the introduction of the Programme. The poverty rate in these villages (34.53% to 56.46%) is relatively higher than the national average in rural Central Java (14.32% compared to 15.99%) (CBS, 2013). This is the justification for selecting the four villages to be the sites of the DMP Programme. Thus the expectation is that the national and provincial governments should introduce programmes of this nature in areas or villages where the gap between the poverty level at the grassroots and the national average is high. The programme introduced should be focused on empowering rural communities to enable them to carry out their economic activities. Such empowerment should be complemented by other cross-sectoral programmes that should be widely practised throughout the entire country.

REFERENCES

Boratynska, K., & Huseynov, R. T. (2017). An innovative approach to food security policy in developing countries. *Journal of Innovation & Knowledge*, *2*(1), 39–44. www.elsevier.es/jik. doi:10.1016/j.jik.2016.01.007

Boratynska & Huseynov. (2017). An innovative approach to food security policy in developing countries. *Journal of Innovation & Knowledge*, *2*, 39–44. www.elsevier.es/jik

Central Bureau of Statistics (CBS). (Badan Pusat Statistik, BPS) (2010). Indonesia in Number Book. Statistical Yearbook of Indonesia 2010. Badan Pusat Statistik, BPS. ISSN/ISBN: 0126-2912

Central Bureau of Statistics (CBS). (2011). Indonesia in Number Book. Statistical Yearbook of Indonesia 2011. Badan Pusat Statistik, BPS. ISSN/ISBN: ISSN/ISBN: 0126-2912

Central Bureau of Statistics (CBS). (2013). *CBS Strategies Data*, CV. Nasional Indah. ISSN: 2087-2011

Darwis, V. (2012). Food Self-Reliance Movement through the Village Food Resilience Program: Analyses and Constraints. *Agricultural Policy Analysis Journal*, *10*(2), 159–179.

Darwis, V., & Rusastra, I. W. (2011, June). Optimizing Rural Community Empowerment through Integrating PUAP and Desa Mandiri Pangan Programs. *Agricultural Policy Analysis Journal.*, *9*(2), 125–142.

DKP. (2005). A food insecurity atlas of Indonesia, 2005. Dewan Ketahanan Pangan.

DKP. (2009). Panduan Penyusunan Peta Ketahanan dan Kerentanan Pangan di Indonesia: A Food Security and Vulnerability Atlas of Indonesia (FSVA). Jakarta: Dewan Ketahanan Pangan dan World Food Programme.

Falcon, W. P., & Naylor, R. L. (2005). Rethinking food security for the twenty-first century. *American Journal of Agricultural Economics*, *85*(5), 1113–1127. doi:10.1111/j.1467-8276.2005.00797.x

FAO. (1996). Rome Declaration on World Food Security and World Food Summit Plan of Action. World Food Summit, Rome, Italy.

FAO. (2006). The State of Food Insecurity in the World 2006. Food and Agriculture Organization of the United Nations.

Paasch, A., Garbers, F., & Hirsch, T. (2010). Agricultural Trade and the Human Right to Food: The Case of Small Rice Producers in Ghana, Honduras, and Indonesia. In Food Ethics. DOI doi:10.1007/978-1-4419-5765-8_8

Rusliyadi, M., Bin Hj. Mohd. Jamil, A., Maseleno, A., Tri Kumalasari, R., & Othman, M. (2019). Agricultural extension policy, agricultural growth and poverty reduction in Indonesia. *IACSIT International Journal of Engineering and Technology*, *7*(4), 5539–5550. doi:10.14419/ijet.v7i4.13337

Rusliyadi, M., Jamil, A., Mohd, B., & Kumalasari, R. T. (2019). Analysis of household food security policy: Case of food security village programme, Indonesia. *Asian Journal of Agriculture and Rural Development*, *9*(1), 19–32.

Rusliyadi, M., & Jamil, A. B. (2020). Participatory Poverty Assessment Effort in Food Security and Extension Policy: Evidence From Indonesia. In V. Erokhin & T. Gao (Eds.), *Handbook of Research on Globalized Agricultural Trade and New Challenges for Food Security* (pp. 481–499). IGI Global. doi:10.4018/978-1-7998-1042-1.ch024

Rusliyadi, M., & Libin, W. (2018). Agriculture development programs for poverty reduction evidences from Indonesia and china - comparative study case. *Asian Journal of Agriculture and Rural Development*, *8*(2), 104–118.

Rusliyadi, M., Mohd, H., Jamil, A., & Anshari, M. (2020). Analysis of Food Security Policy by Participatory Poverty Assessment (PPA) Effort: Case in Indonesia. In P. Ordoñez de Pablos, M. Almunawar, & M. Abduh (Eds.), Economics, Business, and Islamic Finance in ASEAN Economics Community (pp. 105-127). Hershey, PA: IGI Global. doi:10.4018/978-1-7998-2257-8.ch006

Satriawan, Oktavianti. (2012). Upaya Pengentasan Kemiskinan Pada Petani Menggunakan Model Tindakan Kolektif Kelembagaan Pertanian. *Jurnal Ekonomi Pembangunan*, *13*(1), 96–112.

Weiler, A. M., Hergesheimer, C., Brisbois, B., Wittman, H., Yassi, A., & Spiegel, J. M. (2014). Food sovereignty, food security and health equity: A meta-narrative mapping exercise. *Health Policy and Planning*, *30*(8), 1078–1092. doi:10.1093/heapol/czu109 PMID:25288515

ENDNOTES

1 Purposive sampling is also known as judgmental, selective, or subjective sampling. Based on the recommendation by the Agricultural and Food Security Agency in Regency Level.

2 Classification for Normative consumption ratio: > 1.5 - high deficit, 1.25 - <1.50 - moderate deficit, 1.00 - <1.25 - low deficit, 0.75 - <1.00 - low surplus, 0.50 - <0.75 - moderate surplus, <0:50 - high surplus

3 Note:
Before: Before programme implementation; After: After programme implementation (2013)
Classification:
Indicator 1: Percent of Population Below Poverty Line (%): > = 35 - Highly vulnerable, 25 - <35 - Vulnerable, 20 - <25 - Rather vulnerable, 15 - <20 - Quiteresistant, 10 - <15 - Resistant, 0 - <10 - Highly resistant.
Indicator 2: Percentage of people working fewer than 15 hour per weeks (%): <50 - Highly vulnerable, 50 - <30 - Vulnerable, 30 - <20 - Rather vulnerable, 20 - <10 – Quite resistant, 10 - <12:01 - Resistant, 0:01 - 0.0 - Highly resistant.
Indicator 3: Percentage who did not finish elementary schooling ; > = 50 - Highly vulnerable, 40 - <50 - Vulnerable, 30 - <40 - Rather vulnerable, 20 - <30 – Quite resistant, 10 - <20 - Resistant, 0 - <10 - Highly resistant
Indicator 4: Percentage of Population without access to electricity; = 50 - Highly vulnerable, 40 - <50 - Vulnerable, 30 - <40 - Rather vulnerable, 20 - <30 – Quite resistant, 10 - <20 - Resistant, 0 - <10 - Highly resistant.

4 Note: in the village physician = health officer/midwife
Before: Before programme implementation, after: After programme implementation (2013).
Classification:
Indicator 2: Percent Less Toddler Nutrition ; > = 55 - Highly vulnerable, 50 - <55 - Vulnerable, 45 - <50 - Rather vulnerable, 40 - <45 – Quite resistant, 31 - <40 - Resistant, <31 - Highly resistant
Indicator 3: Percent of Women Literacy ; > = 40 - Highly vulnerable, 30 - <40 - Vulnerable, 20 - <30 - Rather vulnerable, 10 - <20 – Quite resistant, 05 - <10 – Resistant, <05 - Highly resistant
Indicator 4: Infant Mortality ; > = 55 - Highly vulnerable, 50 - <55 - Vulnerable, 45 - <50 - Rather vulnerable, 40 - <45 – Quite resistant, 31 - <40 - Resistant, <31 - - Highly resistant.
Indicator 5: Percent of population with access clean water ; > = 70 - Highly resistant, 60 - <70 - Resistant, 50 - <60 – Quite resistant, 40 - <50 - Rather vulnerable, 30 - <40 - Vulnerable, <30 - Highly vulnerable
Indicator 6: Percent of Population Living ; > 5 km from the health center ;> = 60 - Highly vulnerable, 50 - <60 - Vulnerable, 40 - <50 - Rather vulnerable, 30 - <40 – Quite resistant, 20 - <30 - Resistant <20 - Highly resistant.

APPENDIX

Table 6. Matrix Showing the Problems in General at Research Village Sites for Poverty and Programme Implementation

Problems due to:	Problems Indicators	Farmer groups			Agricultural service institutions		Village officers	Amount
		Problems			Problems		Problems	
Institutional issues	-	Poverty	Dependence on Aid	Low investment capabilities	Function not optimal	Lack of understanding of farmers' problems	Dependence on funds	
Farmer groups	Limited access to input		X	X				2
	Imperfect information	X	X	X		X		4
	Limited availability of technology			X		X		2
	Low level of knowledge and skills	X	X	X		X		4
	Limitations of capital	X		X			X	3
	Moral hazard behaviour	X						1
	Price instability	X	X					2
	Uncertainty	X	X	X		X		4
	Price taker	X	X					2
	High transaction cost	X		X		X		3
	Poor organisational management			X	X		X	3
Agricultural service institutions	Limited human resources				X	X		2
	Limited funding	X			X		X	3
Village officers	Not the decision makers	X			X		X	3
	Number	10	6	8	4	6	4	

Sources: Primary data and modified from Satriawan et al. (2012).

Table 7. Comparative Profile of the Programmes in Villages

Indicators	Kebumen Regency		Magelang Regency	
	Kedungdowo Village	Selogiri Village	Candirejo Village	Madukoro Village
Year start	2009	2010	2012	2011
Type of Program	Core Village	Core Village	Core Village	Replication
Alocation Aid fund programme (million IDR)	100	100	100	25
The number of farmer groups involved	4	4	6	1
The number of people involved	75	67	71	35
Number of poor household	79	513	422	214
Percentage poor household in the programme	65.8	68.4	71.3	75.2
Kinds of activity in the programme	Livestock Fishery Financial Agriculture Small Home industry Empowerment society	Livestock Agriculture Small Home industry Empowerment society	Goat Livestock Women Empowerment society	Goat Livestock Empowerment society

Sources: Primary data from survey (2013).

Table 8. Some Impact Indicators on the Community as a Result of the Self-Sufficiency Village Programme

Impact Indicators (%)	Kebumen Regency		Magelang Regency	
	Kedungdowo Village (%)	Selogiri Village (%)	Candirejo Village (%)	Madukoro Village (%)
The number of farmer groups involved	100	100	100	25
Increase in number of people (farmers) involved	15	17	5	32
Increase of programme funds	9	11.6	13.78	78
Reduction in poverty	8.25	29.8	7.83	25.58
Increase in income of farmers	15.36	19.75	14.96	22.33
Raising aid funds from other sources	124.96	37.079	60.57	101.92

Sources: Primary data from survey (2013)

Note: the percentage stated in the Table shows the value after DMP Programme implementation.

Chapter 5
Human-Centered Design to Enhance the Usability, Human Factors, and User Experience Within Digital Destructive Ecosystems

Heru Susanto
https://orcid.org/0000-0002-1823-357X
Brunei University of Technology, Brunei & The Indonesian Institute of Sciences, Indonesia

Fahmi Ibrahim
Brunei University of Technology, Brunei

Saleem Haja Nazmudeen
Brunei University of Technology, Brunei

Fadzliwati Mohiddin
Brunei University of Technology, Brunei

Desi Setiana
Ministry of Law and Human Right, Indonesia & University of Brunei Darussalam, Brunei

ABSTRACT

Human-centered design is an approach that focuses on involving the end user throughout the product development and testing process which can be crucial in ensuring that the product meets the needs and capabilities of the user, particularly in terms of user experience and safety. The structured and iterative nature of human-centered design can often be a challenge for the design team when faced with the necessary, rapid, product development life cycles associated with the competitiveness in the industry. This ensures that the needs of the user are taken into account throughout the design process whilst also

DOI: 10.4018/978-1-7998-4787-8.ch005

maintaining a rapid pace of development, and its rationale before outlining how it was applied to assess and enhance the usability, human factors, and user experience within destructive digital ecosystem era. The authors encouraged a system approach such as human-centered design for prevention on further damages being done on data breaches through the application of each steps of the process.

INTRODUCTION

Human-centered design has roots that go back hundreds of years and build on concepts of sociology, psychology. On the other hand, as a cohesive process, the idea can be traced back to 1950s thank to Buckmister Fuller, who described human-centered design engineering as "...the effective application of the principles of science to the conscious design of our total environment in order to help make the Earth's finite resources met the needs of all humanity without disrupting the ecological processes of the planet". Human-centered systems used in economics, computing and design, aim to preserve or develop human skills, in manual and office work, in environment in which technology tends to challenge the skills that people use in their work. As for the terminology, in 1989, Mike Cooley created the term "human-centered systems" in the context of the transition in his profession from traditional drafting at a drawing board to computer-aided design. Designers have focused on enhancing the look and functionally of products. Designers started to practice tools to challenge more complex problems. Now businesses are to embrace a new approach called Human-Centered Design, and they begin to adopt it.

This study to reveal the needs of the user are taken into account throughout the design process whilst also maintaining a rapid pace of development, and its rationale before outlining how it was applied to assess and enhance the usability, human factors, and user experience on steps taken to prevent breach of data within Destructive Ecosystem Era. It offers a broadly-applicable problem-solving framework and methods for developing an in-depth understanding of people who are directly impacted by development challenges, generating creative ideas, and rapidly learning from small-scale pilots. The process aims for better understanding an issue from the human perspective and focuses on how it looks and feels to consumers and users within their environment and context. This study also outlines the differences between human centered design and User Centered Design. The main principle of Human Centered Design is they describe how to use insights about human beings – users, customers or other stakeholders – to design products or services that meet their needs and aspirations. In this study also, discussed the traditional thinking approach, why it fails to meet the goals and why Human Centered Design is better than Traditional Thinking Approach.

THEORETICAL CONCEPTS AND DISCUSSIONS

Any design activity is the identifying of the meaning which the product or service should offer to people (Krippendorff, 2004). Such a view suggests that design activity should concentrate first and foremost on questions of learning previously proceeding to identify the means of implementation. The definition of human-centered designs, is a logical and practical approach that make sense. Human-centered design is suitable for incremental innovation but not likely to lead for radical innovation because of the repetition on observation, ideation and testing. Human-centered knowledge and practices is one of the main roles in the design innovation which can create an opportunity for the fields of human-centered design to be more strategic. Not only this but also the human-centered design was also criticized for not having the sufficient skills and knowledge that were required to operate a strategic innovation context. Central to this application and exploitation is the knowledge in design process. Creating and and sharing knowledge is essential to fostering innovation and is the key challenge of knowledge-based economy (Ibrahim and Barr, 2009). Hence, by applying the Human-Centered Design it can enhance the success of the business.

The direct measurement of how the subjective experience of the products, systems and services might influence on the human nervous system. Whereas according to Norman and Verganti (2011), it says that "Today's human-centered design is based on the use of techniques which communicate, interact, empathize and stimulate the people involved, to obtain an understanding of the people's needs, experiences and desires which often exceeds the people's expectation and their realization. Human Centered Design is usually in its basic form used for products, systems and services which are physically, spontaneous, perceptually and cognitively. Where it is consistent with the definition proposed. Human-centered design tool is a growing set which used for simulating intuitions, opportunities and also possible futures for the purpose of emersion, discussion and reflection from the currently popular approach of co-design. Also, Sklar and Madsen, 2010, believed that "Human-Centered Design is a problem-solving approach that is focused on learning from the customer of the intended solution, particularly through empathic methods – its defining feature".

Human-Centered Design (HCD) is the process of integrating human perspectives in all aspects of the problem-solving process. The process aims for better understanding an issue from the human perspective and focuses on how it looks and feels to consumers and users within their environment and context. This process aims to achieve an understanding of an issue and focuses on how this is on a customer or consumer point of view within their environment and context. As an approach, Human-Centered Design taps into capacities we all have but that are overlooked by more conventional problem-solving practices. Not only its emphasis on producing product and services that are human centered but the process is as well deeply human. Human-Centered Design depends on the capability to be intuitive, to identify the outlines, to constructs ideas that have the meaning as well as being useful, and to express in media other than words or symbols. Human-Centered Design, the integrated approach at the essential of the design process, provide the way.

The nature of designing product or services development within organizations has altered dramatically over the past few decades as products and services have become more complex. For example, within the automotive industry, integrated product development processes based around multi-functional Integrated Product Teams are becoming the norm. Integrated product team members are not only multi-functional, but likely to work for different companies and subsidiaries, have different nationalities and stem from different sites of one company or even be scattered across the globe. Decades ago an automobile design team would reside on a single site and would deal principally with local suppliers compared, whereas, human-based knowledge is harder to share, transfer and codify. Knowledge particularly tacit knowledge is hard to assimilate and internalize (i.e. knowledge entails the knower's understanding). This highlighting of the design aspect often associated with the use of the term *data* (symbolic representation of numbers, letters and facts), *information* (data arranged in meaningful way) and *knowledge* demonstrates the key difference between knowledge (application, analysis, and productive use of data and information). The terms 'tacit knowledge' and 'explicit knowledge' have become popular as a way of differentiating between personal knowledge and that which has been codified as a company information resource (Nonaka, 1991). This distinction was made to emphasize the need for organizations to, wherever possible, convert the personal knowledge of employees into tangible, sharable information resources, but it also emphasizes that all knowledge cannot be codified and quantified by those involved (Hislop, 2005). These considerations indicate that the important tasks in Human-Centred design both people-involvement (creating and fostering these skills and attitudes in the participants in the design process and technology-based (collecting and organizing information and other resources associated with the encoded knowledge)(Ibrahim and Barr, 2009). For example and an automotive company have been experimenting with technology-based approaches to capture and share knowledge (Ibrahim et. al., 2009). The initiative is centred on the development and utilisation of knowledge-based tools C3Ps (CAD/CAM/CAE) programme and Automated Design Process (ADP) that seek to capture information and knowledge in the design process. The utilisation of knowledge-based tools supports the function of Product Development Manufacturing (PDM) systems. On the other hand, central to effective human-centred design is the management of knowledge in the product development design process in which the involvement of people-participants are vital to the design outcome.

These characteristics have been the subject of a number of empirical studies such Marsh (1997) noted the importance of personal experience and informal networks of contacts in design, as did Court et al. (1996), who emphasized the importance of colleagues and of the designer's own memory as sources of design information. Badke-Schaub and Frankenberger (1999) distinguish between 'critical situations' work in design. The critical situations involve those actions taken by designers (e.g. when choosing conceptual design solutions or at design review meetings) that determine the overall direction of a design programme. In their study of designers in German industry, they found that although designers worked individually for some 85% of their working time, nearly 90% of 'critical situations' are carried out while interacting with colleagues. At these times the nature of the communication and social interaction between participants is also critical. This is in line with Hong and Choi (2011) as it is suggested *reflective thinking* where human-based is one of the critical factors in solving design problems.

In the era of destructive digital ecosystem, the world has become more complex and competitive, with distractions from all directions which have created newer problems and new solutions are needed. Whether the solutions are for the products, services, processes or the interaction between the customers and others. It is great when people are cooperative and energized, creating a solution that no one has thought before. Nonetheless, that does not happen at all times. From time to time, people get to think of figuring out what exactly the problems are, doing presentations and discussions but is still not able to decide on which one is the best solution. Many ideas have been brainstormed and created which initially was great but turns out to be something that people could not even use. However, there is a way that empowers the whole world to solve problems faster, with better results which is the Human-Centered Design approach. Human-Centered Design is one of the approaches that can create solutions for problems and any opportunities through focusing on the behaviors, needs and emotions of people. Therefore, this report outlines on how importance Human-Centered Design is and to understand the three phases of it which are Inspiration, Ideation and Implementation. In Human-Centered Design, it is essential is to understand about people – their needs, constraints, context, behaviors and wants, in order to build the empathy and to make sure that the design solution can provide the people that will give impact the most. When talking about 'design', it is not talking about stylish or aesthetic. Particularly, 'design' in human-centered design is the methodology used to capture human needs, and define solutions, processes and outcome that are designed to meet the needs. Whereas, 'human' in the context of human-centered design are not necessarily just the user of a product or service. Besides that, this can also include the other people involved in a project such as employees and stakeholders. Human-Centered Design is used to create beneficial products and services to buy and businesses want to sell.

Why Human Centered Design?

With human-centered design, people are involved in the design of products and services right from the start. The human-centered design process ensures the product is based on human-centric design solutions to problems, provides optimum user experiences, effortless interaction, and ultimately, business benefits. Human-Centered Design aims to put the consumer in the heart of the design process through balancing between three main factors which are human desirability, business viability and technology feasibility (Figure 1). The business part aims to put the project in a solid business viability model, meanwhile the human desirability part focuses on the design, add the tool to create a user-friendly and appealing visual design and lastly the technology feasibility target the design that implements technology trends to address the consumers problems with an efficient solution. Principles of HCD are belief that are used to form rules that guide to behave and decide what to do in given situations. In human-centered design, it develops solution to problems by involving the human perspective in all steps of the problem-solving process. Human-Centered Design principles are used in fields such as customer experience, user experience and service design. The key principles of human-centered design are as follows:

- Focus upon the people

Before designing a product, the product creator must think who will be using the product. In other words, the product/ services is a tool that helps them to reach their goal. Therefore, it is important to identify the real goal of real people who will be using the product. It needs to identify the target market by questioning: "who am I building this for?" "who will be using this product?". After defining the target users, then it needs to plan what are the ways that are needed in the process. Always question yourself with this simple question before designing the product/services:

- When _______ (Situation)
- I want to _______ (Motivation)
- So I can ________ (Expected outcome)
- Find the right problem

It is true that, not all problems can be solved. There are two types of problems, firstly, fundamental problems and secondly, problems caused by other problems. The later is usually the symptoms of the fundamental problems. It is important to solve the fundamental problem because it will be easier to solve the causes of other problems. In addition, conducting research and identifying the problem requires time and product which will then the team might argue that they don't have enough time. Therefore, when a better research is conducted, they will save more time and energy towards coming in the future.

- Think of everything as a system

This means that is it the ability or skill to perform problem solving in a complex system. This also focuses on the way of thinking interrelate and how systems work overtime within the larger system. It also needs to reach the goal from the user's experience and then, the result can be seen.

- Always test the design decision

It needs to test on the real people, this is because by testing /prototyping the product will then give feedback and helps you to understand what part of the product or service that require improvements The process can be tested out with real people such as family or friends or team members. The reason is if the designer or the developer tend to test the product or service, they might suffer from the false-consensus effect. This can be assuming that, the creator of the product will assume that the people who use their created product will like them.

Figure 1. Human-Centered Design Components

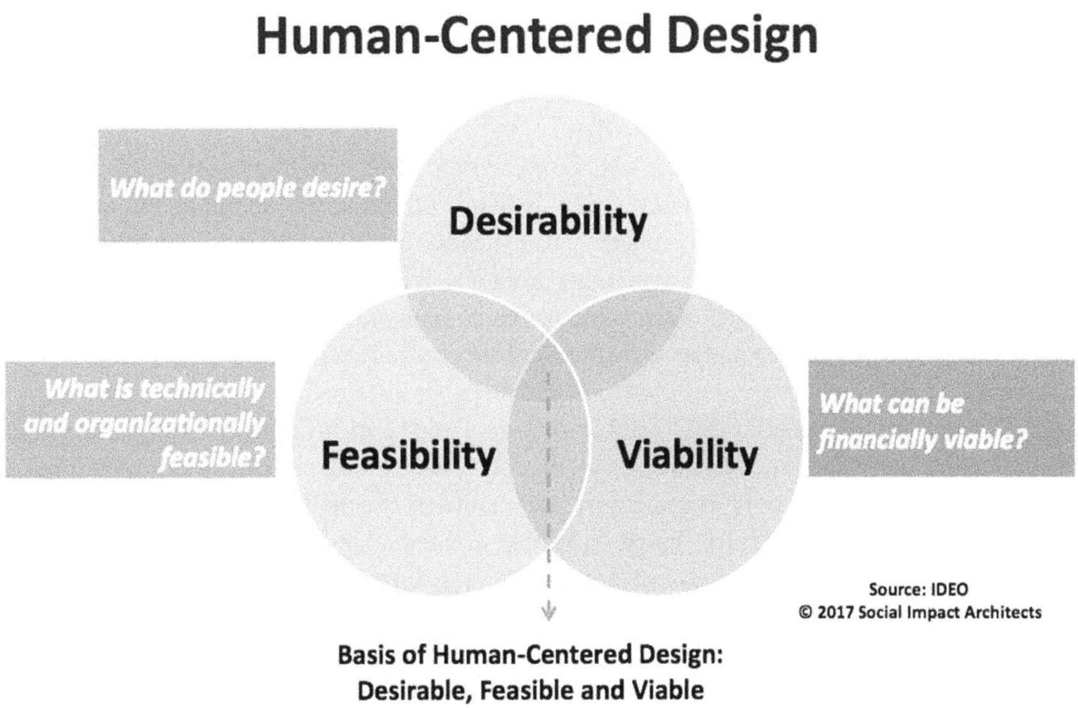

One of the reasons that we need human-centered design is that the method and mindset of human-centered design that strengthens the focus on making the product/ services that can create value for people in real-life situation. If their idea meets all of these three criteria, then it contains these essentials features: Feasibility, Desirability, Viability.

Feasibility focuses on building the strength of the current operational capabilities. In other words, whether the producer is able to implement the solution in an effective manner to ask on, "what do the producer need to make this happen?", "What kind of technology do we need?". By this, it may not only affect the company's operation but it seeks as to implement the product and services, but also give impacts to users' experience directly. Desirability focuses on the customers really needs, how can they create an experience that is human-centered and give answers to important needs to customers. In this case, this is to test whether the innovation solves the right customer problem. In addition, this can be explored through analyzing the customer segments, customer relationships and value proposition. The viability lens focuses on the business-focused discussion around marketing and finance. It is one of the important factors this is because it affects its sustainability and also long-term success. This can be questioned as, "how are we going to make money with this or cut costs?". Therefore, to conduct an evaluation of solution's viability, they should analyze the value proposition of the product and services, potential revenue sources and also to consider the various stakeholder that can be use.

When feasibility, desirability and viability overlapped, it will be being the desirability to what the user wants that can lead to innovation. However, when one of the elements is missing, the plan and implementation cab become riskier and costlier. In order, to test all of the three features, it needs to be built during implementation stage, therefore, the adjustment can be made to keep on the right track. As a result, it depends on the type of project that the producer is going to create, as long as the process of human-centered design is used, that is: inspiration, ideation and also implementation.

When to use Human-Centered Design?

HCD involves people right from the start and places them at the center of the problem-solving design process. HCD focuses on the people's problem, goals, needs, thinking, emotions and behavior in order to come up with an effective design solution to the problems. it is important for all product and services, it helps to have a clear understanding of consumer needs to maintain efficient and effective delivery this creative framework uses various approaches to problem-solving and keeps the consumer at the heart of the solution, also can help businesses to be more innovative, better differentiate their brands and bring their products and services to market faster. Other than that, applying Human-Centered Design is important as the businesses can have a better understanding on the consumer's problems. Business professionals need to develop plans to introduce or to increase customer centricity among the organizations. They'll have to prototypes the product and services based on Human-Centered Design in addition, they also need to Interview real consumers to learn their needs in an evolving digital world. However, Human-Centered design can use as an approach to any challenges, the description is as follows:

Product design

When talking about design the first application that comes to people mind is the stylish product however the implementation of the Human-Centered Design takes a holistic approach to include the following, the product is interfering to pull physical and digital product while physical products include fashion design, automated design, light design, digital design that includes the application, website design, interaction design and games design. For example, how we design a toothbrush that can be easily gripped by the toddler.

Service Design

The service design targets the services provided for the consumers rather than the product itself. It aims to provide a consumer-centered service that provides effective solution for consumers. The services need to be considered from the top to bottom, from how it is advertised and how it will be delivered? Example how should a new service be delivered in order to get attraction from the consumers.

Space Design

The space design aims to apply that provides a positive experience for the consumers when using the space around them including but not limited to classrooms, banks, hospitals and public transportation. Example how might the universities come up with an idea that could allocate their business students when all the classes in business faculty are full.

Systems Design

This includes the holistic eco-systems inside the organization building including the business strategy process and how is this reflective understand and the organization management process, as for example it may involve redesigning the company's structure to unleash the employee's potentials through friendly working environments.

How to Apply the Human-Centered Design

The ideas presented in an efficient model for the human-centered design process that includes three phases which are Inspiration, Ideation and Implementation (Figure 2).

Inspiration Phase

In the first stage is the inspiration. Inspiration is the opportunity that motivates the search for solutions. In order to build an efficient problem solution, a deep understanding of consumer needs and problems are required in the first phase. The design teams aim to achieve the following, define the design challenges that needs to be addressed. It is the target that needs to be achieved. Create a project plan this will include the timeline about the project, about the team and logistics. Form the team that will be involved in the process. Apply a secondary research about previous researchers that address the specific problems. And lastly apply a primary research that includes observation and proper research methods.

In the inspiration phase, this is where they learn about the problem in hand and as well as the users, as a result to build a cleaner knowledge about the problem. It is important for people to understand their problems and what they need as an individual. These are the type of questions that needed to be asked in the inspiration stage.

- "Who are the users we're designing for?"
- "What are their pain points?"
- "What do they need to succeed?"
- "How do they currently solve these things?"

Figure 2. Human-Centered Design Implementation

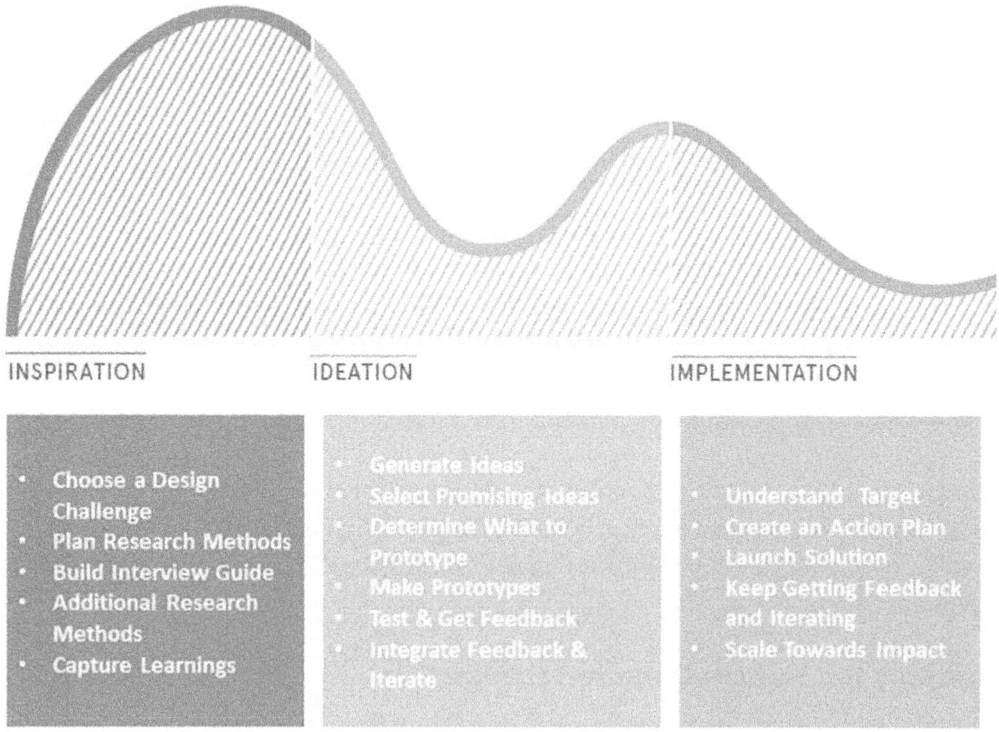

Ideation Phase

In this stage, where it makes sense of everything that has been heard, generates tons of ideas. The collected data is shared among the team through a brainstorm meeting to decide which solution will be taken to the next stage. A prototype will be created to visualize the ideas, after creating the prototype, it will be shared with the team and consumer sample in order to evaluate and give feedback to improve as a part of an iterative process (Iterative Process is the act of testing and refining an output with the aim of approaching a desired goal).

Once the problem is clearly defined and the information is analyzed, it can move to the suggested solutions into prototypes that can be tested and iterated. With human-centered design, people work as a team to generate tons of ideas. Everyone in the team, should participate in this process through workshop and brainstorming sessions, which they should come up with lots of ideas and narrow it to the most important points.

After testing and improving the prototype, the team can implement the solution through an action plan that the team can follow during the product development process. Through this inspiration, the ideas through a usable prototype. Usability testing and user interviews help to validate assumptions and answering critical questions. In which this can be asked,

- "Does our solution work?"
- "is there anything that we can improve?"

Implementation Phase

Lastly, this stage is the solution. The designers develop the best ideas into a concrete plan of action. The solution is brought to life and to the market starting with, throughout this stage the designers create a live prototype for a long-term testing. By using the prototype, it can get funding and help to build the relationship. Then getting feedback from the consumer and the users based on to improve the future versions of the products or the service. This Human-Centered Design process can provide an efficient strategy than can help builds and innovation user-driven products and services. The solution in this stage is to ensure that the design team can create products that are both scalable and sustained. In the implementation stage is finding the solution If the solution is bad, therefore had to leave the idea behind and move to the next idea. If the solution is moving in the right direction, then it needs the feedback to improve. Through implementation, it can undergo to multiple of prototypes before getting the best possible solution.

Consequently, all of these processes can be used as agile process. The meaning of agile process is the practice that helps continuous iteration of development and testing process. By developing and testing activities are concurrent; this process also allows more communication between customers, developers, managers and testers. The process is entirely based on the incremental progress. Therefore, the team needs to know exactly what is complete and what is not. As a result, to reduce risk in the development process.

CHALLENGES IN ADOPTING HUMAN-CENTRED DESIGN (HCD)

As it has been acknowledged, Human-centered design (HCD) is a group methods and principles that are aimed at designing useful, usable, pleasurable and meaningful products of services for people. The main principle of these methods is they describe how to use insights about human beings – users, customers or other stakeholders – to design products or services that meet their needs and aspirations. Taking human-centered design approach means leading with people wants, needs and behavior; developed a deep thoughtful of task, workflow, culture, environment and technology; and also ensuring users that are involved throughout the design process. However, there are challenges in adopting human-centered design, where it can be difficult for some organizations. This is because it will be varying from different views and ideas between users and also organizations. There are internal and external challenges with this approach to product development. One of the top reasons is time. Scheduling and conducting interview, they need do adequate research and proper synthesis of different inputs before jumping into giving solutions.

Externally, finding the 'target group' of Human-Centered Design, is the target group that is not something that can be deliberately choose. By having a strategy can help to have broaden knowledge on market research, and often, by filling in the gaps can be difficult and resource-intensive. Another point is that, when involving outside parties in the process, there will be a new view invented where the organization may be aware and lack of experts that could deter to come up with appropriate solutions. By hiring an expertise or outsourcing would incur cost to the organization that could lead to over budgeting.

Furthermore, by maintaining the quality of the idea is also an important process. If the process is failing, this may cause time wastage and the idea might not be used to challenge the problem. As humans we've come a long way when it comes down to resolving problems and creating varieties of solutions to solve different types of problems. Maybe hundreds or thousands of years ago we would throw rocks at a problem in hopes of solving it. Well even now we might throw or smash the TV remote control that's not working properly. But overall, we don't really use brute force all that often. Nowadays we tend to actually think things through properly in hopes of coming up with a valid solution. Yet there is more than one way of coming up with a solution in this way. One way, the traditional way, appears to be going back to the way of rock throwing, and the other way is what should be practiced by the majority in the future which is known as design thinking. We will distinguish and explain about the difference in the next part of this report

Human Centered Design Versus Design Thinking

We have explained what is Human Centered Design and Design thinking so what are their differences? They may seem similar on the surface but really there are quite a bit of a difference in terms on how they serve as a purpose or tools. Design thinking can simply be defined as a process that you go through to develop solutions or products that will actually be adopted by people. HCD or Human Centered Design on the other hand can be defined in simpler terms as a mindset that overlays design thinking to ensure that the solutions or products are actually relevant, useful and beneficial in the long run for the people they were created to serve.

To make this easier to understand, any businesses or organization can utilize Design Thinking to create a solution that is able to make money. For example, a broadcasting media company may use Design Thinking to develop a TV show in an attempt to target kids. Applying Human Centered Design on top of that Design Thinking will ensure that the show actually benefit the people watching it, in this case for example making it so that it meets the learning objectives of the children watching the show).

Ergo, Design Thinking is typically used to create a commercial product for the market. Human Centered Design take it a step further by enabling tools and mindset that can ensure these products to actually improve the lives of the end-users or consumers. As you can see, by utilizing both Human Centered Design and Design Thinking and then applying it to a scenario, they provide a process and mindset that creates self-sustaining solutions to some of the challenges that companies may face.

Design Thinking

If the implemented solution doesn't work out as expected, it is not surprising as traditional problem-solving approach were used and there are actually many flaws which can cause problems. To better understand why, we will go over the design thinking approach which is a design methodology that delivers a solution-based approach to solving problems. It is also a flexible approach of coming up with a customized solution based on continuous data input. Let's take a closer look at the four different stages of Design Thinking.

- Empathizes with the user Stage

The first stage of design thinking process is to gain an emphatic understanding of the users of the product and the problem you are trying to solve. In our case, it is more than just reading the reviews of the hiking bag that says the product is not very comfortable. What is different in Design Thinking is that you will also need to try to understand why users deem your product uncomfortable. You will have to observe, engage and empathizing with people to understand their experiences and also immerse and imagine yourself in their position. Traditional thinking assumes that we understand the user while the modern design thinking actually goes out there and interact or lives the life of the user.

- Divergent thinking Stage

In the traditional approach, we used our collected data (the reviews) to converge and come up with one solution which is to add more support padding for the hiking bag in our example. With design thinking, we use the data to create as many ways to solve the problem as we possibly can. Other than adding more support padding at the back, we can also add more padding on the shoulder strap as well as at the hip belt, lighter material to reduce weight, more sturdy material to improve stability, etc. After all, level of comfort can be affected by many different kinds of reasons and sometimes users don't distinctly state why something is an issue or they might just simply do not know why it is uncomfortable!

- Create prototype Stage

You will now produce a number of inexpensive, scaled down versions of the product or distinct features found within the product so you can have a better look and investigate the product if it actually is able to solve the previous issue. By the end of this stage, you should have a better idea on the constraints of the product and the problems that are present, and have a more accurate vision on how real users would behave, think and feel when using the end product. Design thinking is about coming up with the optimum solution for the end user, not the solely just benefiting the company.

- The testing Stage

This stage is all about learning more about the product you've created and the customer you've created it for. It is an iterative process meaning the results obtained during this phase are often used to redefine one or more problems. It gives you an opportunity to observe customers interacting with your product or service and to seek for feedbacks about what you've created. Even during this stage, alterations and improvements are made in order to produce the best final product as possible before delivering it to the consumers.

Traditional Thinking Approach

The main elements are solving the problems or feeding the problems in the future. If continued to feed the problems, it will never get the solutions. The traditional thinking approach grossly underestimate the economic trends and shifts that world are facing. How can be aware of something that were not aware of and how you can say yes or no to ideas that you don't even know exists. In traditional thinking the problems your facing has some solutions but the solutions they're offering you also contains the problems that your trying to avoid. Traditional thinking that deals with a very specific problems and a very specific answers then if draws a straight line it creates with a specific formula. Traditional thinking discusses the thinking that has traditionally permeated the approaches, models, choices, and studies of management. Its source is in analysis and analytical thinking.

The traditional thinking approach is a direct and structured approach to express and resolves an issue. It takes a set of data and works off of that same data to come up with a solution. If we added to traditional thinking the abstract of idea of change our world become enormously complex. The way we manage the difficulty is that we produce, we produce by introducing simplification plus another concept. The author of "The age of fallibility" George Soros says that "Once it comes to generalizations, the more general they are, the more simplify matters. Thinking up the world as the usual response which represented by unchanging situation. Changing the situation and the same identification will applying to all past and also with the future situations, which called the critical thinking. George Soros also identifies that the traditional thinking with an 'Organic Society'.

Furthermore, he also identifies that the critical thinking with the 'open society'. Each society must find a means to deal with factors that do not conform to the will of the members of society. In the traditional approach, even though it focuses primarily on phenomena that are generally static, nature can be obdurate. As for traditional thinking the principles is that things are as they have always been and the future will be the same, hence they cannot be in any different way. The status quo is fate and all we need do is to learn and to organize lives in accordance. In logic world and argumentation has no place since there is no alternatives. When we examine the nature of epistemology, what does it mean to say that we know something, what can we know and how can we know about it, in such thinking we quickly light up the advantages and the limitations.

In a certain society there will be no bifurcation between thought and actuality. There only unprejudiced relationship between knower and known. The validity of traditional truth is undoubted, there can be no dissimilarity between ideas and reality. Traditional thinking approach does not explicate but it performs entirely in accordance with the nature. There is no dissimilarity between the natural and supernatural between reality and thought that are arise in denial. The traditional thinking is flexible as long as there are no alternatives are voices out and become traditional faster and as long as the situation meets the needs of the consumers such a situation will carry on. In order to understand the traditional way of thinking, we must maintain the habits of thinking that are embedded within us, especially the conceptual of an individual. The traditional approach to change management or organizational development is to look for the issues, do a diagnosis and then look for ways to overcome them. This approach emphasizes and amplifies problems but also draws effort away from innovative work and creative thinking. In simpler terms, with this approach you basically identify the problem, theorize why it happened and then find a solve.

Example of Traditional Thinking Approach

It is best to use a simple and general example to explain the differences between these two-problem solving method. Let's pretend that you work for a sports equipment company. This company recently launched a line of hiking bags, but the sales and reviews have been dismal and mostly negative.

So, what's the problem? After going through the reviews, you realized that the hiking bag your company produced is not very comfortable. The data collected evidently indicates that people say it's uncomfortable over and over again. How are you going to solve this problem?

One way is by using the traditional problem-solving approach. The traditional thinking approach is a more linear and structured approach to describing and resolving an issue. It takes a set of data and works off of that same data to come up with ways to solve the issue. Anyhow, traditional problem solving in a business environment often begins with the identification of a problem, which you've already done in the example! Your hiking bag is not very comfortable. Next, you sit and think of various possible reasons for why it's uncomfortable and solutions to those reasons. In your case, you believe the problem lies in not having enough support padding on the back side of the bag. After all, people usually sweat a lot when hiking and not having enough bag padding can cause the bag to irritate their backs especially when they carry heavy loads' After that, you will try to come up with alternative solutions to the issue such as reducing bag weight and then rank them according to how feasible and viable those solutions appear to be based on your own thought and circumstances. You will then choose the solution that seems the most effective and efficient and hope that your plan successfully solves the problem and doesn't cause any further problems.

Therefore, traditional thinking approach in a business setting often begins with the identification of a problem, which it has already done! Running shoe is uncomfortable. Next, sit and think of possible reasons for why it's uncomfortable and results to those reasons. After all, people run over running track and so the shoes should be lighter enough for them to sprint in order to get the first place. After that, coming up with the alternate solutions to the problem and rank them according to how viable and feasible they appear to be based on the circumstances. Choosing the solution that is most viable and feasible and hope the plan comes off without a hitch.

Why Design Thinking (HCD) is Better Than Traditional Thinking Approach?

In traditional approach, for assessing any business plan, the two most vital aspects that are taken into account by businesses are Viability and Feasibility. This approach looks at the business utility of the aspects of viability and then evaluate whether it is achievable in real manner, with through own resources or partnering with some in a timely fashion or not feasibility.

The initiative which ranks the highest on these tow metrics. It seems like a very reasonable way of solving problems but more than of their initiative do not live up to the expectation. Several reasons were because both viability and feasibility projections are based on assumptions about the future, the approach follow waterfall methodology to plan for a long time and implement for even longer time and then shove the solution down stakeholders' throats, it is usually compartmentalized. It also takes months or even years before the stakeholders get the solutions and lastly it focused on how and what. Traditional thinking approach usually takes a methodical and scientific procedure. It identifies a problem, define the stages and tools in order to get generate a solution, then follows the plan and hope for the expected outcomes. This kind of problem-solving is easy as pie, however it is not always innovative, operative and effective, in fact, it brings some question with vague answers to our mind such as what if the concern recognized isn't the actual source of the problems and what if the stages can't lead to the correct solutions.

Meanwhile for the design thinking, it is a process that is best practiced with following mindsets. With this Human Centered Design categorized as a design thinking, it starts with understanding the needs of stakeholder the desirability and bringing the viability and feasibility together. The process of Human centered design has been elaborate in the process parts. Regarding the concept of Human Centered Design, it is something that really surprising, the way that we approach a problem. Human considered that as a design thinker, instead of starting with a problem. It starts with an observation which helps to identify the context and culture of a problems and what people needs, rather than just a narrow idea of the problem. Truly, need to understand every aspects of the problems that has an exclusive context and unique culture which define by the human. In HCD, trying to understand the values, needs and beliefs that make the audiences tick. Actually, the reason behind starting with an observation and listening in HCD is to understand the consumer and get engage or interact with them in order to identify their unmet needs and the roots of their problems. It is all about seeing new and creative innovative solutions to the problems in a human and their need at priority.

Why Traditional Thinking Miscarries to Reach Its Goals?

There are several reasons why traditional thinking approach miscarries to reach its goals, the first one was jumping to Solutions, in traditional problem solving, a lot of time is used up in protecting ideas, proposed solutions, and lack of time getting the facts that was needed to consider and choose from the solutions. Challenging short-term results even at the cost of long-term results are also the factors that leads to miscarries Traditional Thinking are puts focus on short-term results, or immediate relief from problems. This causes people to put band-aids on problems or even sweep them under the rug, rather than take the time to address their underlying causes. This solution within the problems will reappear with a greater cost. When new and old problems rear their heads at the same time, this creates a savage cycle of having time only for short-term relief. Continuous improvement recognizes the need for short-term problem containment and relief but keeps the focus on long-term countermeasures at the source.

Next will be, Solving the wrong problem, it is still surprisingly common to find people attempting to solve a problem which may or may not be the problem that matters to the customer. The continuous enhancement requires that what thoroughly clarify and express the gap and prioritize the perceived problem, from the customer's eyes, before setting out a target.

Accelerating rather than slowing down, traditional thinking approach tends to be addictive. Speeding up the process in order to get more output. In increasing the output and lead to spending more time. With a continuous improvement that acknowledges the works in a short term but is not sustainable. In the long run, by reducing the system to results wide losses, work harder, eliminate unnecessary measurements. This will often slow things down here and there, build quality into the process and improve the whole. Traditional thinking approach, does not always urge that to see for ourselves to understand the current situation, while continuous improvement does.

Failure to socialize, as traditional problem solving can outshine at providing the technical solutions, but the results often don't live up to promise when it falls short on change management. The new actions, policy and result needs to be "socialized" sufficiently, which just means listening and talking to people throughout the problem-solving stages. Or else known as respect for humanity, this is something that goes hand-in-hand with continuous improvement.

And finally, Experts vs. everybody, the confidence in few of experts of involving everybody in problem-solving may be the major failing of traditional thinking approach. This is just subjective but others will find otherwise. There are no doubt other significant differences between how problems-solving is practices before and after adopting a continuous improvement mindset.

Human Centred Design	Traditional Design
Consumer centric	Process Centric
Inspiration to implementation	Structured approach
Empathizing with users	Feed further problems
Prototyping	Provide solution based on assumptions
Rigorous Testing	

CONCLUSION

The human-centered design is an important approach that can be used today. This is because without our realization Human-Centered Design is used in our daily life in solving problems which that can be used in various fields, even subjects in which they have limited or no expertise. Also, this paper has outlined a process and examples which demonstrate some of the potentials of Human Centered Design. With the practice of Human Centered Design, has identified the problems and solutions by using the three phases. It is ensured that Human-Centered Design can lead to improvements in the destructive digital economy era

ACKNOWLEDGMENT AND AUTHOR CONTRIBUTIONS

Heru Susanto, and Fahmi Ibrahim are the main contributors; Heru Susanto is the lead author. We wish to thank Saleem Haja Nazmudeen, Fadliwati Mohiddin, and Desi Setiana who helped to improve the manuscript and helped with the literature review. All authors have read and approved the final manuscript.

REFERENCES

Agentestudio.com. (2019). *User-Centered Design: Principles, Processes and Examples | AGENTE.* Available at: https://agentestudio.com/blog/user-centered-design-examples

Babich, N. (2019). *Principles of Human-Centered Design.* Available at: http://babich.biz/principles-of-human-centered-design/

Badke-Schaub, P., & And Frankenberger, E. (1999). Analysis of design projects. *Design Studies, 20*(5), 465–480. doi:10.1016/S0142-694X(99)00017-4

Court, A. W., Culley, S. J., & And Mcmahon, C. A. (1996). Information access diagrams: A technique for analysing the usage of design information. *Journal of Engineering Design, 7*(1), 55–75. doi:10.1080/09544829608907927

Designorate. (2019). *Characteristics of Human-Centered Design.* Available at: https://www.designorate.com/characteristics-of-human-centered-design/

Designorate. (2019). *Characteristics of Human-Centered Design.* Available at: https://www.designorate.com/characteristics-of-human-centered-design/

Hong, Y. C., & Choi, I. (2011). Three dimensions of reflective thinking in solving design problems: A conceptual model. *Educational Technology Research and Development, 59*(5), 687–710. doi:10.100711423-011-9202-9

Hoover, C. (2019). Human-Centered Design vs. Design-Thinking: How They're Different.... *Moving-Worlds Blog*. Available at: https://blog.movingworlds.org/human-centered-design-vs-design-thinking-how-theyre-different-and-how-to-use-them-together-to-create-lasting-change/

Ibrahim, F., & Barr, S. (2010). Reconfiguring IT and the Cultural Dimension in Knowledge Management Practices, International Journal of Knowledge. *Culture and Change Management, 9*(11), 27–43.

Ibrahim, F., Edgar, D., & Reid, V. (2009). Assessing The Role Of Knowledge Management In Adding Value: Moving Towards A Comprehensive Framework. *Journal of Information & Knowledge Management, 8*(4), 1–12. doi:10.1142/S0219649209002397

Invisionapp.com. (2019). *User-centered design: Definition, examples, and tips | Inside Design Blog*. Available at: https://www.invisionapp.com/inside-design/user-centered-design-definition-examples-and-tips/

Keen To Design. (2019). *Human Centred Design and it's Process - Keen to Design*. Available at: https://www.keentodesign.com.au/human-centred-design/

Krippendorff, K. (2004). Intrinsic Motivation and Human-Centered Design. *Theoretical Issues in Ergonomics Science, 5*(1), 43–72. doi:10.1080/1463922031000086717

Lindstrom, M. (2008). *Buyology: How Everything we believe about, why we buy is wrong*. Random House Business.

Linstrom, M. (2005). *Brand Sense: How to Build Powerful Brands through Touch, Taste, Smell, Sight and Sound*. Kogan Page Publishers.

Marsh, J. R. (1997). *The capture and utilization of experience in engineering design*. Cambridge University.

Medium. (2019). *Top 4 Principles of Human-Centered Design*. Available at: https://uxplanet.org/top-4-principles-of-human-centered-design-5e02751e65b1

Nonaka, I. (1991, Nov.). The Knowledge Creating Company. *Harvard Business Review*, 96–104.

Norman, D. A., & Verganti, R. (2011). *Incremental and Radical Innovation: design research versus technology and meaning change*. 5th Conference on Designing Pleasurable Products and Interfaces, Politecnico di Milano, Milano, Italy.

NovoEd. (2019). Available at: https://plusacumen.novoed.com/#!/courses/design-kit-2019-3/flyer

Static1.squarespace.com. (2019). Available at: https://static1.squarespace.com/static/55ca3eafe4b05bb65abd54ff/t/574737f89f7266ddad87a3cf/1464285179544/294+van+der+Bijl-Brouwer.pdf

Studio Frankly. (2019). *Desirable, Feasible and Viable: three important lenses - Studio frankly*. Available at: https://frankly.studio/desirable-feasible-and-viable-three-important-lenses/

Susanto, H., Chen, C. K., & Almunawar, M. N. (2018). Revealing Big Data Emerging Technology as Enabler of LMS Technologies Transferability. In *Internet of Things and Big Data Analytics Toward Next-Generation Intelligence* (pp. 123–145). Springer. doi:10.1007/978-3-319-60435-0_5

The Interaction Design Foundation. (2019). *From Prototype to Product: Ensuring Your Solution is Feasible and Viable.* Available at: https://www.interaction-design.org/literature/article/from-prototype-to-product-ensuring-your-solution-is-feasible-and-viable

Von Hippel, E. (2005). *Democratizing Innovation.* MIT Press. doi:10.7551/mitpress/2333.001.0001

Wired. (2019). *Why Human-Centered Design Matters.* Available at: https://www.wired.com/insights/2013/12/human-centered-design-matters/

WiseStep. (2019). *How to Solve Unemployment in a Country: Best Tips - WiseStep.* Available at: https://content.wisestep.com/solve-unemployment-country-best-tips/

ADDITIONAL READING

Almunawar, M. N., Anshari, M., Susanto, H., & Chen, C. K. (2018). How People Choose and Use Their Smartphones. In *Management Strategies and Technology Fluidity in the Asian Business Sector* (pp. 235–252). IGI Global. doi:10.4018/978-1-5225-4056-4.ch014

Almunawar, M. N., Susanto, H., & Anshari, M. (2015). The Impact of Open Source Software on Smartphones Industry. In *Encyclopedia of Information Science and Technology* (3rd ed., pp. 5767–5776). IGI Global. doi:10.4018/978-1-4666-5888-2.ch569

Almunawar, M. N., Susanto, H., & Anshari, M. A. (2013). Cultural Transferability on IT Business Application: iReservation System. *Journal of Hospitality and Tourism Technology*, *4*(2), 155–176. doi:10.1108/JHTT-05-2012-0015

Nograšek, J., & Vintar, M. (2014). E-government and organisational transformation of government: Black box revisited? *Government Information Quarterly*, *31*(1), 108–118. doi:10.1016/j.giq.2013.07.006

Olphert, W., & Damodaran, L. (2007). Citizen participation and engagement in the design of e-government services: The missing link in effective ICT design and delivery. *Journal of the Association for Information Systems*, *8*(9), 27. doi:10.17705/1jais.00137

KEY TERMS AND DEFINITIONS

Automation: Automation is machine-controlled execution of actions, based on artificial intelligence and machine learning that do not require human intervention. It enables speed to action to help reduce time taken by human operators.

Digital Ecosystem: A distributed, adaptive, open socio-technical system with properties of scalability, sustainability, and self-organization, inspired from natural ecosystems. This is achieved through the use of digital technologies.

DSS (Decision Support System): A decision support system (DSS) is a computer-based application that collects, organizes, and analyzes organizational data to facilitate quality decision-making for management, operations and planning.

Innovation Management: This refers to the reinventing of management process in an organisation such as strategic planning project management, knowledge management, employee assessment. Innovation management can create an enduring success if the organisations are able to meet one of the three conditions: 1) it is systemic, 2) it consists of a range of processes and methods and 3) it is part of an ongoing program of inventions.

Innovation Management Capabilities: These refer to organisation's ability to manage resources including employees and meeting their customer/user demands. New skills and capabilities can ensure growth and development in the long term and for organisations to improve their digital transformation efforts, they need to source fresh talent and nurture current skills within the organisations. In innovation management, the capabilities aspect mainly revolves around people's abilities, unique insights, and practical skills in the organisation.

Innovation Management Culture: In every organisation, culture is very integral and unique and different organisations have different cultures that might work for some organisations but not for others. Organisational Culture is "The sum of values and rituals which perform as 'glue' to integrate the members within an organisation". It may include experiences, ways of thinking, future expectations, and beliefs. This aspect of innovation management is dominated by emotional energy and influence. When the culture within the organisation is positive and in sync with the organisation's strategic priorities, it can increase and improve the organisation operations and achieve its strategic goals.

Innovation Management Strategy: Strategy is about positioning for longevity, and making decisions around the organisation on which services and products to deliver, and allocating resources efficiently to achieve the long-term and superior performance. With organisational strategy, it can help to create alignment between the employees in achieving the organisational goals as they know which activities to prioritize more. Furthermore, it can also help to align the organisation's resources and efficiently use them to maximise the strategic success.

Innovation Management Structure: This key aspect of innovation management includes organisational structure, processes, and infrastructure of the organisation. Having the right organisational structure is very important as it can help the organisation to be innovative and achieve its goals as well as ensuring its survival. Traditionally, most organisations are using hierarchical models in which decisions are taken in a top-down manner. This approach had faced some challenges especially in developing their digital strategies as per an adage that state for every products and services created by a company are reflected by their organisational charts and communication structures i.e. by having a traditional and hierarchical organisation in which the product development teams have a very thick layers with their users, project managers, and so on will mostly having a hard time to ensure acceptance of the products or services from the users.

UEBA (User and Entity Behaviour Analytics): This is in the context of computer security. UEBA is a tool that uses AI to collect, track and analyse data from computer activities to indicate suspicious behaviours. It utilizes deep learning and machine learning to shape user behaviour and devices that are connected to the organization's network.

Chapter 6
Active Social Listening and Its Impact on Firm Strategies:
Study of Indian Context

Som Sekhar Bhattacharyya
https://orcid.org/0000-0003-3259-0319
National Institute of Industrial Engineering, Mumbai, India

Neenu Neenu
National Institute of Industrial Engineering, Mumbai, India

ABSTRACT

Due to the present customer voice in a digital world, keeping a watchful eye on what customers were expressing on social media became a necessary firm imperative. For this study, the authors found that rather than using FGDs and survey research, digital tools like the applications of social media listening could serve as a valuable platform for gathering insights about a firm's latest strategy. This could be complemented by the existing channels of feedback. This research study focused on customer perspective. Data was collected from Indian consumers and social media handling experts regarding social listening based upon a semi structured open-ended questionnaire. The data collected was content analyzed based upon thematic content analysis. Customer voices were reading majorly complaints and compliments followed by advocacy. This helped to comprehend how well firm managers aligned and helped in getting insights regarding marketplace reflections for assessing a firm, its products, and its brands.

INTRODUCTION

Social listening has been defined as the monitoring of digital conversations in determining what consumers voiced online about a brand, product or a company (Steimer, 2017). Social listening as a novel concept was derived from social monitoring (Meg, 2015). Social monitoring provided a reactive approach, whereas social listening could be used as a platform for proactive business decision making and crisis management (Lee, 2018; O'Leary, 2011; Singh, Shukla, & Mishra, 2017). Social monitoring was also

DOI: 10.4018/978-1-7998-4787-8.ch006

used to analyze the strategy of a firm (Booth & Matic, 2011). However, when firm managers failed to fully engage with its customers, firm managers also failed to fully exploit the capabilities of social media platforms, which gave rise to the importance of social listening (Bhimani et al., 2019). Social listening, thus, provided an alternative to the conventional way of data gathering. Data gathered via social listening enabled firm managers to tap into the right consumer insights which were being generated in real-time (Booth & Matic, 2011). In India, with a billion plus population and hundreds of millions of young internet users social media has become very important. Social media in India has been very popular and thus social listening could be very pertinent. One should note that a significant number of Indian FMCGs, had started unlocking the potential of customer perspectives via social media listening (Sangani, 2019). India had about 241 million Facebook users, 7.75 million Twitter users and 69 million instagram users (Pragati, 2019). India had one of the highest numbers of internet and mobile device users in the world by the close of the second decade of the millennium (Fuscaldo, 2019). However, most social media and internet-based engagements were still at the nascent stage, using share-of-voice, delivering sentiment, and influencer analysis. Additionally, in India some brands were leveraging social data to understand the purchase journey, customers' views, perception or expectations from the products and service offering (Shaikh, 2018). In the present-day context in India, social media was used to such an extent that 93% of users believed that a good company should have a good social media presence (Cone, 2008). One DEI worldwide report indicated that 49% of users undertook purchase decisions based on the information they found on social media (DEI,2008). Another report by Hootsuite noted that 42% of users were likely to use social media websites to exchange information via mobile devices (Hootsuite, 2019). Statista predicted that Ad spending in the Social Media Advertising segment would amount to US$3,770m by the year 2020 and grow at a CAGR of 7.4% (Statista, 2019). This would result in a market volume of US$4,677m by the year 2023. This substantive size would make social media even more crucial for firms' success and branding (statista,2019).

It would be important to note that COVID-19 and the physical social distancing changed the lives of people around the world and it also had a massive impact on their social media habits (Banerjee, 2020). Social media like Facebook reported an increase in messaging of around 50% in March (Schultz & Parikh, 2020). Similarly, COVID-19 Tweets were being shared every 50 milliseconds on twitter (Josephson & Lambe, 2020). Further, according to Sprinklr, a platform which highlighted where and in which context a brand was being mentioned on social media, the presence of a global pandemic has made it even more important to listen to what customers had to say. Most importantly, getting alerts of a potential crisis, which varied on the basis geographical location made it furthermore important to make strategies which worked best for a particular geography (Conn, 2020). Given this one could argue that social media had become the new word of mouth for companies and every single day, millions of customers, brand enthusiasts, investors, business students, budding entrepreneurs, customers and others have started to voice their thoughts on social media platforms (Cui, *et al.,* 2018). I would be important to note that such discussions were majorly about what they had bought, where their purchases were done, what did they think about the latest marketing campaign of a brand, and their good and bad experiences related to services or goods offered by firms (Cui, Gallino, Moreno, & Zhang, 2018; Paniagua & Sapena, 2014). The presence of such substantial information was nothing less than a gold mine for several consumer-facing industries, such as retail, insurance, consumer goods, retail banking, and healthcare (Reiter et al., 2017). Nevertheless, so far, most Indian companies were not actively turning this information into valuable insights. In this article, the authors focused on how customers who voiced their opinion for native company and the subsequent data generated could be used by firm managers to gain insights and device strategy for firm level advantage.

In this research study, the authors attempted to understand and validate the role of social listening towards planning of firms' strategies. This was achieved through comprehending the shift in the behavior of consumers with respect to voicing concerns on social media platform. The authors have also tried to understand both the supply as well as the demand side view of data generation and arrive at a decision-making framework regarding social media perspectives. This study would help managers and researchers to comprehend the factors influencing consumers the most. Further, it would help in increasing positive brand performance and better stakeholder relations of Indian firms. This study finding would also help generate clearer and better interpretation of activities on social media for proactive decision making by firms' managers. One needs to note that this could be achieved by adjusting and using the right set of data from social media. Managers could re-evaluate their firms' current social media strategy to enhance the reach their firms' brand, product or firm objective they had set out to achieve in the first place.

LITERATURE REVIEW

In this section, the authors have presented the literature review has been presented. First a bibliometric analysis was carried out. Keyword string search on social listening was carried out for Scopus listed journals. Based upon the search results, a total of 5443 articles got considered. The initial search indicated that the number of articles in business and management domains to be just 2.6% of the 5443 articles. The search analysis indicated that the number of articles written on social media listening have been on an increasing trend. Some other findings of bibliometric analysis have been depicted in figures 1,2 and 3.

As one could notice that the study of social listening took a steep upturn post the year 2000. The reasons for this was the introduction of internet and subsequently ubiquitous sprouting and presence of social media in daily life of customers and society in general. One must note that MySpace became the first platform to have more than one million active users by the year 2004 and the journey of exploring managerial insights from social media commenced (Esteban Ortiz-Ospina, 2019).

It is evident from figure1 and 2 that, social listening (offline) was a thoroughly researched field in social science and medicines. However, Social listening via social media platforms and its managerial implications was a budding area which had 2.6% contribution in the total search results.

The United States of America followed by United Kingdom were the top ten countries of research in this domain in the world. India with the second highest population in the world, did not hold any position in the top ten countries by research output in this space. This as a tautological logic, indicated the lack of research from India and its context. Thus, social listening has often been more actively researched in developed countries than in developing countries. One of the reasons for this could be the number of active users and necessary infrastructure in the countries. As one could notice from figure 3, that maximum research has been done in the developed world, leaving only a very small fraction of research coming from the developing countries. The authors then read through the abstracts and keywords of the listed articles and narrowed down the search to twenty-one articles based upon relevance as well as immediacy. In Scopus listed journals data base, the keywords string search of Social listening was done. Based upon the immediacy and relevance of articles twenty-one articles were short listed for detailed study. These twenty-one articles were studied in depth by the authors. The findings, methodology and

Figure 1. Documents by Year

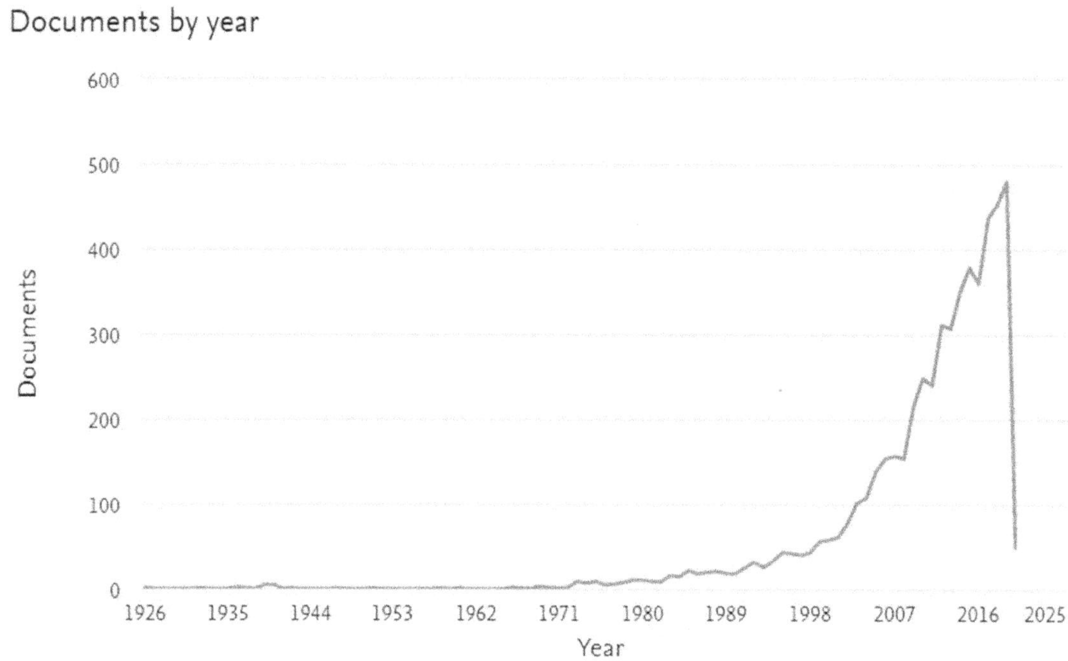

the remarks of these twenty-one articles has been presented in table 1 in columns whereas the articles have been presented in rows.

The study of twenty-one articles listed in table-1, helped the authors to arrive at the researchable gaps in Indian social media listening context with the help of remarks. The study conducted by Enginkaya and Yilmaz, (2014) have explored the use of social media in predicting consumer motivation. Similarly, Kohli, Suri and Kapoor, (2015) found out the potential of social media to upend traditional branding. However, like several other researches even the mentioned research studies in table 1, didn't dwell deeper into the prospect of using social media listening as a proactive tool. The vast amount of data generated by social media website wasn't organized to gather insights. Even when Indian companies have been using social media listening tools such as "Going up", "Simplify360", and "Locobuzz" for quite some time now, none of the papers explained how managers could use active social listening to overcome the information barrier. Social media listening also played a crucial role in firms decision making process, strategy formulation and innovation (Chae, McHaney and Sheu, 2019). However, the amount of research done on this topic was limited to a few sectors. Thus, expanding the scope was beneficial for example, a firm making personalized or bespoke items, could finetune its supply chains based on what social media users were voicing on various social media platforms. Thus, the research objectives of this study were set. The primary goal of the research was to investigate the proactiveness of companies in responding to social media vis a vis the viewpoint of consumers. In particular, this research attempted to answer the following objectives to study:

1. customers involvement in voicing their concerns, praise, advocacy, criticism, and other remarks on social media.

Figure 2. Documents by subject Area

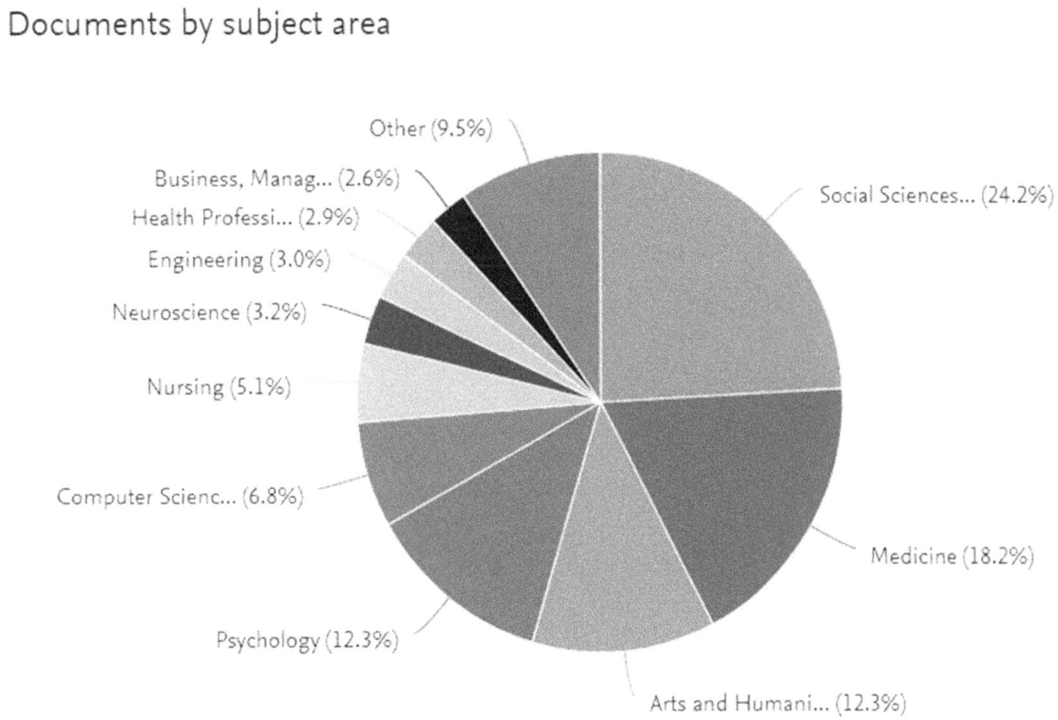

2. how social media managers were engaging in social listening.

Subsequently, this research answered, why should firms' managers use social media listening as a proactive tool. This was done with the help of questionnaires distributed to customers and the answers were secured and analyzed. Thus, two separate open-ended semi structured research questionnaires were developed. One was for customers and the other for organizational social media handlers. This has been tabulated in table 2.

RESEARCH METHODOLOGY, DATA ANALYSIS AND FINDINGS

In this section the research methodology has been presented. In order to gather insights about social listening and its impact on firm's strategy, 31 interviews were carried out. The subjects of interviews were taken from customers who were active social media users. Further, 11 in-depth interviews were conducted with social media experts. Exploratory qualitative interviews were conducted. Interviews were conducted till thematic saturation was reached (Marshall,1996). The respondents were managers of brands of different categories including service, technology, and Fast-moving consumer goods (FMCG) sectors. This study was an exploratory qualitative study as the topic of enquiry was exploratory (Silverman, 2016 ; Denzin & Lincoln, 2008). The data was content analyzed for thematic content analysis

Figure 3. Documents by country or territory

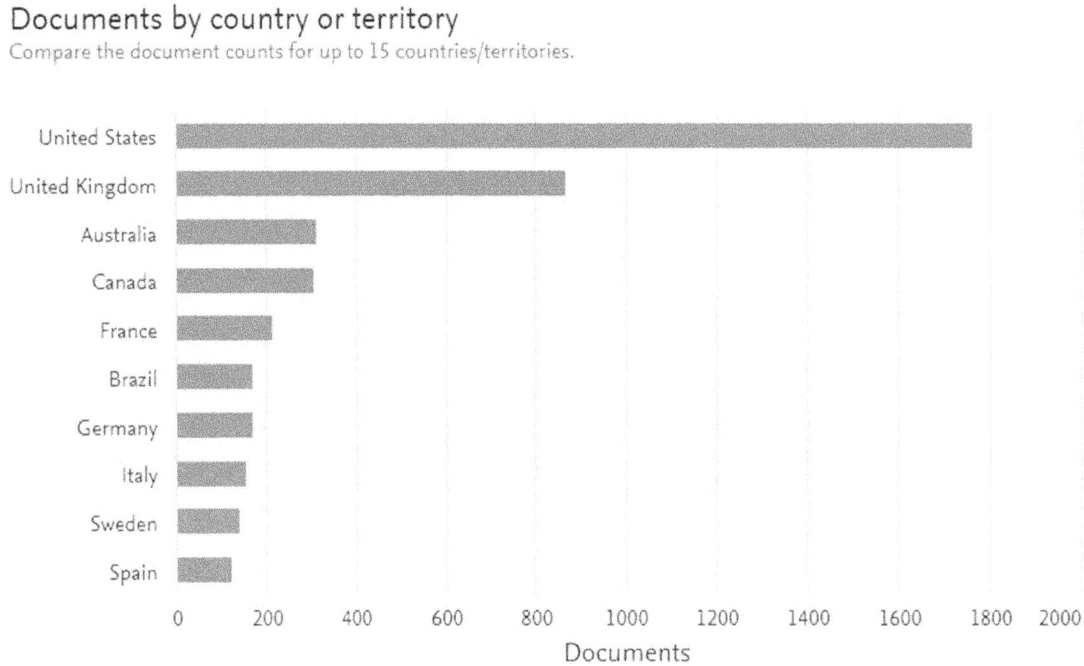

(Vaismoradi, Turunen & Bondas, 2013; Scherl & Smithson,1987). This qualitative phase and previous research findings regarding social listening and social media monitoring usage provided the basis for this study. The respondent's characteristics has been tabulated in table 3.

The data collection was carried out between January to February 2020. The data was transcribed within 72 hours of collection. The protocols of qualitative research as advocated by Seale, (1999) was followed. In this section, the findings of the study have been presented. The authors conducted interviews of 32 customers to gather insights about when and what they commented about a firm on social media. The response of the customers has been presented in table 4.

The eleven responses by social media managers has been tabulated in table 5.

The authors based upon the response of customer as well as the experts on social media extracted the key themes. The frequency count of the key themes has been presented in table 6. Thus table-6 was based upon the analysis carried out on table 4 & 5.

One must note that some respondents had different responses for different firms' actions or initiatives, thus the sum was more than 100%.

DISCUSSION

One must note that the results indicated that social media listening was a powerful tool for Indian firms as pointed out by Tuten and Perotti, (2017). Social media listening should be widely used both inside as well as outside an organization. In depth interviews with customers, it became evident that customers

Table 1. Literature Review on Social Listening

S. No.	Author (s)	Findings	Methodology	Remarks
1.	Patroni, Briel and Recker, (2020)	The authors identified three types of consumer conversations on social media that provided innovation impetus for retailers. They also described the process of how a retailer leveraged these conversations for innovation.	Due to the absence of empirical evidence, the authors adopted an inductive, qualitative research design to generate theory from case study in the retail sector.	One could state that since the case study involved in depth research, it demonstrated how one of the worlds' largest retailers developed a capability to leverage consumer conversations that were publicly available on social media. Further innovation could be facilitated from insights generated.
2.	Zubielqui and Jones, (2019)	The researchers identified that social media was significantly positively related to innovation. The authors also made a structural model and tested it with environmental moderators to identify when and how social media impacted innovations in start-ups.	The authors collected the initial data from Management Capabilities Module (MCM) 2015/16 using a questionnaire. The authors did final data analysis in two stages 1. The first stage involved descriptive analysis. 2. The second stage employed structural equation modelling (SEM) to analyse structural models using STATA version 15.	With this model, one could reason that social media represented an effective channel for new ventures to access information, knowledge and managerial learning to facilitate innovation.
3.	Chae, McHaney and Sheu, (2019)	The authors found out the managerial implications of social media in supply chain.They summarized these implications into 3 steps: (1) learn the capabilities of social media for B2B operations, (2) begin to use social media tools, and (3) be proactive to new challenges.	The authors conducted primary research and gathered insights on B2C context. This they then applied on B2B operations.A survey was also conducted to validate the findings.	One could argue that just like in B2C context, social media could play extremely vital role in the context of B2C supply chain. The involvement of supply chain managers in social media helped make it easier and more useful.
4.	Tam and NamKim, (2019)	The authors described how Social Media analytics (SMA) tools were useful for generating real-time data and its quick analysis. They also found that SMA can clarify the networks of issues concerning different respondents. Another finding was that SMA should be used as a supplementary, rather than a primary, tool to guide strategy.	The authors made use of Social Media Monitoring (SMM) tools for User Generated Content (UGC).The authors interviewed public relation managers and then organized the data to find insights.	One could state that the major challenges in using Social Media Analytics (SMA) had been that social networks, such as Facebook, Twitter and Instagram, were increasingly restricting third-party access to the data.It could also be said that to better develop a brand the presence of leader on social media could be harnessed.
1. 5.	Curran, Treiber and Rosenblatt, (2018)	The authors analyzed and discovered the impact of social media advertisement on purchase decisions and reported that 1. Advertisements were posted daily (majorly on Facebook) 2. Maximum respondents scrolled past advertisements 3. Customer comments and ratings were the primary factors behind purchase decision for most of the respondents.	The authors monitored social media data in the USA for 3 brands for a month. They conducted a student survey. They applied two monitoring tools namely *SimilarWeb* and *Brand24* for the study	One could argue that the brand post had good impression on customers. It could also be said that the sub brands needed different approach than brands. Facebook advertisement success also appeared to decline (as twitter trends became more influencing).
6.	Reida and Duffy, (2018)	The authors argued that adopting a netnographic sensibility was a way to approach the value of social listening research towards securing holistic consumer understanding.	The authors used Social Media Monitoring (SMM) tools for User-generated content (UGC).	One could comprehend that netnographic sensibility helped in differentiating value from the noise in data Further, a single dataset could be used in various ways to find suitable applications.
7.	Tuten and Perotti, (2017)	The authors proved how false information and media sentiment which were spread via social media could ultimately affect consumer sentiment and attitude towards a brand.	The authors started with google search and continued with analysis of media articles discussing a brand. They utilized brand related conversation on social media and developed a team to further analyze the scraped data.	It could be argued that the media coverage of a false claim revealed, brand sentiment was more negative than positive. It could also be argued that brand managers just have to be beyond vigilant regarding the news media. They had to use social media to amplify the scientiðc facts as organic sharing failed often.
8.	Eysenbach, (2017)	The authors analyzed Social Listening data to monitor misuse and nonmedical use of Bupropion and discovered that the nonmedical use was discouraged by 40.6% users. Bupropion and Venlafaxine were most commonly procured from health care providers, whereas amitriptyline was most commonly obtained from third parties	The authors used data from publicly available harm-reduction forums (like Bluelight and Opiophile). Once the data was collected, post monitoring was done by a team.	One could state that social listening, along with harm-reduction Web forums, could offer a valuable new data source that could be applied for better monitoring.
9.	Bashir, Papamichail and Malik, (2017)	The researchers found out that that MNC managers' viewed information as a key success factor in today's dynamic and complex market environment. Their research also revealed that social media played an essential role in acquiring customers' information from outside the firm. Their findings confirmed that social media had more relevance as an informal knowledge source for new product development (NPD) processes.	The authors selected five multinational companies and collected data for 6 months. A total of 25 interviews were collected from the employees of these companies. The authors devised a process of descriptive coding followed by interpretative coding to identify key concept in analysis.	One could argue that even when the use of social media was quite prominent in companies and towards New Product Development (NPD) but the usage wasn't formal. This was despite the scope towards better usage of insights gathered from social media.
10.	Lewis, Heather, Pugatch and Jillian, (2015)	The authors studied online sentiment towards cigarette and found that the sentiment percentage for cigarette was mainly positive.By doing a user description study, the authors were also able to gauge the user types, namely celebrity, government, foundations/organization, reputable news source, Retailer and Tobacco companies.	The authors applied strategic keyword search on twitter (via Gnip). They used refinement tools on the gathered data set. The team conducted final assessment with the help of a set of analysts.	One could argue that Gnip was no longer useful because of less data sharing for third parties. It could also be noted that social listening as a new methodology could be used to find a social media landscape around a new brand or product type.

continued on following page

Table 1. Continued

S. No.	Author (s)	Findings	Methodology	Remarks
11.	Pham and Gammoh, (2015)	The authors studied how companies utilized social media practices to strengthen its Customer Based Brand Equity (CBBE) and provided a framework for building social media marketing strategies.	The authors applied a conceptual model to propose and examine the influence of important dimensions of social media marketing strategy on CBBE.	One could argue that the content sharing sites could generate brand imagery and brand feeling. Further, Social networking sites provided the purpose of building brand resonance.
12.	Kohli, Suri and Kapoor, (2015)	The researchers found out that social media had the potential to upend traditional branding. They also discovered that social media could strengthen or kill a brand. The key to success was based on how quickly companies could change its mindset and adopt new strategies in response to consumer preferences.	The authors started with primary research and then gathered data from different studies (including the studies done by Golder, Irwin, and Mitra (2013), and Divol, Edelman, & Sarrazin, (2012). These researches were then studied to gather insights on how social media effected branding and the best way to use it for firms benefit.	One could argue that social media could be both a boon or a bane. It depended entirely on firm management to use the insights gathered towards its benefit.
13.	Habibi, Hamilton and Valos, (2015)	The authors explored the contribution of social media on the B2B marketing. They also developed an E-marketing orientation (EMO) model with four components (namely philosophical, initiation, implementation and adoption) to help managers on B2B marketing in decision making.	The authors did exploratory research and drew on the existing B2B marketing, social media and organizational orientation literature.	It could be noted that the research propositions could provide managers with details regarding a number of cultural, structural and job design changes required for better B2B marketing using social media.
14.	Graffigna and Riva, (2015)	In this article the authors proposed a mixed methods approach to social media analysis and proved that it provided a balance between the systematization of quantitative measurement with the ecological and situated nature of qualitative research strategies.	The authors started with primary research and referred to a real case research work to arrive at a set of conclusions.	One could argue that the current social monitoring method lacked in ecology and creativity part. Applying mixed method could be a better approach.
15.	Elena, (2015)	The author coined the term social customer relationship management (SCRM) and its numerous benefits for an organization were mentioned.	The author did primary research and conducted interviews with company managers.	One could notice that an SCRM strategy allowed feedback and follow up. It further generated reminders which helped the specific departments to schedule activity. This whole process in turn could help the company in its overall branding.
16.	Enginkaya and Yilmaz, (2014)	The authors developed a social media motivation scale which could help in predicting consumer motivation. Five distinct and reliable motivations explored were – brand affiliation, conversation, opportunity seeking, entertainment and investigation	The authors conducted two focus groups and four depth interviews, after which an online survey was conducted. The authors surveyed 854 respondents. After this, the authors analyzed the data with a random sample split approach.	The scale obtained from this research could be utilized by scholars, researchers, marketing professionals and strategists to target and understand social media users. However, there might be some omitted motivation factors which could be ignored if one totally relied on this scale.
17.	Zhang and Vos, (2014)	The authors explored the use and challenges of social media monitoring on international business. The authors also found out that monitoring methods were grouped into four categories, namely word search, thematic and sentiment analysis, analysis of spread patterns and combination of methods.	The authors did an exploratory research based on a systematic literature review of peer-reviewed journals. The authors then made a data extraction table with summery of relevant research papers and answered a few relevant questions to reach the conclusion.	One could note that monitoring was important for both international and local business, but they needed to acquire a precise information on the return on investment (ROI) of such activities and only if it was positive then they moved forward with the decision.
18.	Wu He, Zha and Li, (2013)	The authors found out how three pizza companies fared on twitter and Facebook. They discovered that a company could gain more traction and profit if the firm managers made ordering easy and linked social media accounts with the order process.	The authors did a primary research with the help of an IT study published in MIS quarterly by Chiasson and Davidson (2005) and social media handles of companies. They did secondary research in three steps namely, text pre-processing, analysis, and actionable intelligence.	One could argue that with the help of social media, data harvesting, decision making of a company could be improved significantly.
19.	Berthon, Pitt, Plangger and Shapiro, (2012)	The authors found out 5 axioms for effective application of social media. These were: 1. Social media was a function of the technology and government of a country. 2. In social media era, local events seldom remained local. 3. Similarly, general issues seldom remained general. 4. The actions of creative consumers tended to be a function of the technology, and government of a country. 5. Technology tended to be historically dependent.	The authors conducted a primary research on social media contents mainly through blogs, graphs and videos.	One could note that rather than marketing being reactive in a dynamic world, it could in fact be one of the primary drivers of change.

continued on following page

Table 1. Continued

S. No.	Author (s)	Findings	Methodology	Remarks
20.	Johansson and Brynielsson, (2012)	In this paper the authors presented a tool for social media monitoring and analysis, which they referred to as the screening of new media (SNM) tool.	The authors used two step process for gathering data followed by tool development. 1. Data acquisition was done by web harvesting. 2. Data analysis included sentiment and affect analysis on the acquired data as well as visualization of relevant results.	One could understand that this tool would come handy in crises for providing authorities with an understanding of how citizens were reacting to communicated alert messages. This use could further be applied by firm managers for crisis management for their firms.
21.	Kasper, Koleva and Kett, (2012)	The authors introduced an instrument for companies to choose social media activities based on corporate goals.	The authors started with primary research and then took six structured expert interviews with practitioners who were in charge of social media activities in various firms.	One could reason that this work developed the foundation of a more sophisticated tool for planning and controlling corporate social media activities.

did exchange their thoughts about a brand on social media as Enginkaya and Yilmaz, (2014) had mentioned. However, the type of information shared varied with individual experience and service level. It was found that the way brands posted, published and advertised about its products or company made a big impression amongst the digital native followers. Further, this was also pointed out by Curran, Treiber and Rosenblatt, (2018). The impression that was left when firm managers responded to customers wasn't researched so much. The interviews with customers helped the authors gauge an idea of how well a brand image was formed if they secured timely responses which could thereby help firms to tap into the pulse of Indian population. Also, in case of crisis, individuals often tended to move to social media platforms for complaints. This was in line with the work of Kohli, Suri and Kapoor (2015) who also reported that the timely response that customers received defined the image of a brand in their minds. Firm managers much appreciated the response trends in the market to introduce products with new advantages as stated by Hamel and Prahalad, (1996). However, the authors also found that consumer sentiments varied according to the response rates of companies as much as they were influenced by brilliant offerings. In practice, this implied that a firm could have positive impression amongst the customers if it could positively utilize opinions voiced on social media. Competitive advantage could be achieved by such

Table 2. Questionnaire for Customers and Firms' social media handlers

Questionnaire for customers	Questionnaire for firm social media managers /handlers
1. When do you comment on a firm strategy on Social Networking sites? What are the reasons behind making comments? 2. When do you compliment a firm and why? 3. When do you criticize a firm and why? 4. When do you advise a firm and why? 5. Do you think your point of view is heard by firms? 6. Any other point that you would like to mention?	1. What were the cases in which you had engaged in social media listening but couldn't act? 2. What were the underlying reasons behind this? 3. How long does the decision-making process take, once you've identified something on social media? What was the process followed? 4. Any other point that you would like to mention?

Table 3. Descriptive Statistics for the sample characteristics

Gender	Age	Daily Online time
Male 56% Female 44%	18-30 67% 30-45 21% 45 and above 12%	0-2 hours 36% 2-5 hours 46% 5-10 hours 13% More than 10 hours 5%

Table 4. Response by customers on social remarks

Respondent	Question 1 Do you voice your concerns on social media?	Question 2 What was the type of conversation (criticism, appreciation, advice, feedback)?	Question 3 Do you think you're heard?
1.	*"Sometimes, when it matters."*	· *"Appreciate the firm when I like their product or service."* · *"Criticize the firm when the service is not as expected."*	*"Rarely heard if I don't call the customer care. Only one or two companies respond to twitter tagging."*
2.	*"Yes, When the decision making affects the general public."*	· *"Compliment for their CSR initiatives."* · *"Criticize in case of an unruly behavior towards the society."* · *"Advise when the stakeholders are at a loss and it becomes difficult to invest with unhappy stakeholders."*	*"Sometimes heard but the number of brands doing that is severely limited."*
3.	*"Sometimes."*	· *"Appreciate when the product is exceptionally good."* · *"Criticize when I am unhappy with the product."*	*"Sometimes I get a mail or callback but often its limited to a few brands."*
4.	*"Yes, if I can relate or connect to it."*	· *"Compliment Based on how genuine and honest they are with what they say and what they actually do, without compromising on the performance."* · *"Not an advice per se, but usually we among our closed groups, discuss and debate on a particular firm, when it effectively fails by making naive decisions and thereby failing."*	*"No, since I've never got a response to my comments on any social platform till now."*
5.	*"Yes, when I have an attachment towards that product or brand (especially if I use it a lot)."*	· *"Compliment when the product or service is good."* · *"Criticize by calling customer care first and if they fail then commenting on social media."* · *"Advice when I think they might listen and there is a scope of improvement, which is very rare."*	*"Yes, often I've got responses and replies on social media platforms via comments and emails."*
6.	*"Yes, of course."*	· *"Compliment when I am amazed by their marketing campaign or some innovation in the product."* · *"Criticize when the product doesn't do what it claimed."* · *"Advise mostly when they ask for feedbacks through survey forms or when I am unhappy with their service."*	*"Sometimes I get a response while sometimes I don't. Often the same brand or company would respond in one case and would not respond in other."*
7.	*"Mostly No because I don't think it matters to a company."*	· *"Criticize when there is an illogical advertisement"*	*"Majorly No."*
8.	*"Yes, when they try to do something promising which even, I would like to see."*	· *"Compliment the firm when the innovation or idea s new and out of the box."* · *"Criticize when some product, brand or service have caused me a personal loss (time, money or any other such loss)."*	*"Mostly No, as I have never got a response on any tags or comments on social media."*
9.	*"Yes, when they inspire me."*	· *"Compliment when they come up with a brilliant idea to do something new or come out of a crisis."* · *"Criticize if the service is only concerned about profit generation and service level is really low."* · *"Advice only if asked in surveys or feedbacks."*	*"Yes, sometimes I get responses for criticism and also get reply of how they would want a chance to make things better this time."*
10.	*"Yes, when it matters to me."*	· *"Compliment when they come up with something disruptive in medical sciences which helps in saving more lives."* · *"Criticize for services especially in hospital chains and advice while giving the criticism."*	*"Yes, although they don't change the behavior often but I get responses which feels like being listened to but is not actually the case."*
11.	*"No, because I don't feel I am ever heard when I've tried in past."*	· *"Criticized because companies often don't listen to the customers post sale."*	*"No."*
12.	*"Yes, when something is relevant."*	· *"Compliment when I am really impressed by services (beauty chains, hotels, flights mainly)."* · *"Criticize when I feel like my complaints are not being heard."* · *"Advice in case there is a loophole in their service that they don't seem to notice (coupon code applications mainly)."*	*"Yes, often I've received mails and calls or comments on my tags stating how they are thankful or happy for the service they could provide."*
13.	*"Yes, when something is unique."*	· *"Compliment on a powerful advertisement."* · *"Criticize if company is indulged in unethical practices."* · *"Advice only in case I have good domain knowledge and I think my suggestion would be able to solve one of their problems."*	*"Sometimes, especially the local players have responded in a better way than multinational companies."*
14.	*"Yes, when it has clear visibility and impact on me."*	· *"Appreciate them usually if I like uniqueness of promotion campaign. Also, if they are expanding into new product segment which I am interested in."* · *"Criticize When I get to know about some unethical practices being followed in the firm through media."* · *"Advice sometimes regarding improvements in their product."*	*"Yes, mostly I get a reply within 24 hours of complaints or criticism especially."*
15.	*"Rarely since I don't think it matters to companies."*	· *"Being a strategy student, If I really like the strategy of the company.* *For ex. I really like the strategy of Jio coming into existence and disrupting the whole ecosystem."*	*"I don't think so as I've rarely criticized or advised but I haven't got any response for appreciation."*
16.	*"Not normally"*	· *"Appreciate When a firm delights its Customers."* · *"Criticize when they are not able to deliver their promises or failing to identify customer needs."* · *"Advice if asked in surveys"*	*"Not really as I never felt I got any substantial response after sending criticism or advice on social media."*
17.	*"No, since I don't think being a normal student or less volume customer, my point of view would matter to anyone."*	· *"Would have criticized only if I've been wronged otherwise not."*	*"Never."*

continued on following page

Table 4. Continued

Respondent	Question 1 Do you voice your concerns on social media?	Question 2 What was the type of conversation (criticism, appreciation, advice, feedback)?	Question 3 Do you think you're heard?
18.	*"Rarely."*	· *"Criticize When they don't take action against customer complaints. I took to Facebook and Twitter once, as a last resort to gain visibility against an airline which cancelled their flight at the very last moment."*	*"Yes, as these last resorts were often answered."*
19.	*"Yes, especially if its something of my interest."*	· *"Appreciate when a firm attracts new customers through its marketing campaign and create customer value through their product/ services offered. Cadbury-Age UK campaign."* · *"Criticize When firms don't respond positively to feedback from customers and go on doing things that they think would bring profit and not be beneficial to the customers. "*	*"Yes."*
20.	*"Yes"*	· *"Compliment when it has a clearly defined mission. Like Quora - to be a database of answers to all the questions possible."*	*"No, since I've never heard back from any company."*
21.	*"Yes, especially when I was having high expectations from the brand."*	· *"I only compliment as I don't think brands care for small comments. However, I always appreciate charitable cause done by brands."*	*"No."*
22.	*"Yes, if the creativity and simplicity with which the firm communicates its idea/strategy."*	· *"Appreciate When the firm is very much customer centric. Eg.: Amazon's delivery service. I had ordered a product at 7 pm and it was delivered on the very next day at 1 pm."* · *"Criticize When firms give very less importance to after sales service."*	*"Yes, as often ive got something or the other in comments or via email."*
23.	*"Yes."*	· *"Complement if something is a new perspective or philanthropic in nature. For ex. UNILEVER, For their ads which showcases natural resources crisis."* · *"Never criticized but advice for a friend's startup* *1) professional help in some of the areas for which I do have expertise.* *2) short sighted strategy.* *3) some marketing ideas as per my knowledge."*	*"Yes, face to face or on call is the most impactful; however, twitter is also reliable."*
24.	*"Yes, especially during mergers & Acquisitions as they interest me the most."*	· *"Criticize during forceful takeovers."*	*"No, since the decisions are already taken."*
25.	*"Yes, especially when I find something very unique about the strategy. I mostly comment to appreciate the strategic move of the management."*	· *"I appreciate a firm when it try to think outside the box and solve a problem for the people. Like I appreciated Yulu bikes for understanding the problem and conveniently bridging the gap between the metro stations and office premises for daily commuters."* · *"I criticize When they fail to look beyond their money making mindset and in the process harm innocent lives. Some pharmaceutical incidents."*	*"Rarely do I get any response"*
26.	*"Hardly once or twice."*	· *"Criticize when I don't like the product or service."*	*"No, never got any response thus stopped doing it."*
27.	*"Rarely."*	· *"Compliment when I am really impressed with their service."* · *"Criticize when I feel my complains are not being heard by the firm."*	*"Yes, sometimes."*
28.	*"Yes, due to uniqueness."*	· *"Compliment on a new strategy, and nice ad."* · *"Advice for takeovers."*	*"Yes, especially the small companies"*
29.	*"Yes."*	· *"Criticize and advice when there are certain visible loopholes or drawbacks."*	*"May be not as I rarely get any response."*
30.	*"Yes, on strategies."*	· *"Praise if I like the latest strategy."*	*"Sometimes (especially for lower end brands)."*
31.	*"No"*	· *"I have done it earlier both in the case of good service and bad service (especially for flights since I travel a lot) but the responses were abysmal, so I just figured out calling them is better than tagging them on social media."*	*"No."*
32.	*"Yes, especially during crisis."*	· *"Being a consultant, my travel needs are often without a notice. I am on Indigo's frequent fliers list and the tweet for my luggage missing was very well taken by them when the ground duty staff failed to help."*	*"Yes, I think public image and visibility to all makes it a more receptive method. Often the gap between ground duty staff and middle management is also narrowed with this approach."*

firms which had knowledge and understanding about its product, services, customers choice / needs, and expectations as also found by Zembik, (2014). Similarly, social media listening could be another tool in increasing the competitive advantage as any firm could proactively acquire useful information. The authors also discovered that social media was being used proactively by both the managers and customers in India as reported by the research of Bashir, Papamichail and Malik (2017). However, the hiatus would be varied from one firm to another firm. One must note that firms widely used social media as a part of post launch stages of new products as proved by the findings of Kenly and Poston, (2010). Similarly, in case of the social media-based sentiment analysis, sentiment towards a brand could suffer due to the exposure to a false claim spread through social media platforms as researched by Tuten and

Table 5. Response by Social Media Managers

Respondent	Question 1 Do you practice Social media listening?	Question 2 What were the cases in which you had engaged in social media listening but couldn't act? What were the underlying reasons behind this?	Question 3 How long does the decision-making process take, once you've identified something on social media? What was the process followed?
1.	*"Social media monitoring is a regular part of our work here. We monitor brand sentiment across globe. If we see anything troublesome, we inform business decision teams."*	*"Things like these keep happening every now and then, either due to our new offerings or due to competitors' offerings."*	*"The longest time is taken to confirm whether the risk is true or the just magnified version. Ideally if its critical immediate decisions are taken."*
2.	*"We are currently not involved in social media listening. However, our digital marketing team keep track of complaints and criticism if any under our brand name."*	*"Faulty products (which is a rare case) can sometimes be shared via twitter and we try to cater to all the comments."*	*"Since it is normally responding to complaints, we do the work within 3-4 business days."*
3.	*"Each brand monitoring heads in our company engages in social media listening. However, decision making involves the nod of whole department."*	*"Cannot be disclosed (mainly difficult to implement or profit prospectus is not so much)."*	*"Basis the wideness or no. of people talking about it, we have 3 decision making process each one has its own set of steps. It varies from 1 day to 9 working days for decision making."*
4.	*"I keep a track of public opinion. Our software here gives us a heads-up if something is not right. According to that we have a dedicated team to do and RCA but sometimes the underlying cause is not known which causes whole trouble."*	*"Inability to do Root-cause analysis (RCA)."*	*"The whole process of RCA and improving it can take anywhere from 1 day to 1 month. Depends on how fast we are able to get hang of the problem."*
5.	*"Did that during maggi crisis, even today there are a few negative sentiments owning to the problem that happened."*	*"We were not able to take any step because of involvement of different stakeholders including government. It has to be MD taking the decision since it was impacting an entire business unit."*	*"Depending on severity of situation and stakeholders can take as less than a few hours to a few weeks maybe."*
6.	*"My team is involved in social monitoring here. There are a few instances where we want to help a customer, but our business policy can sometimes stop us from doing so."*	*"In case of returns, even after its just 1 day post the timeline and there is no visible damage to offering."*	*"Decision making is often quick for us."*
7.	*"For us social media is basically responding to direct tags. Since it's a startup as we will increase in operation, we will look into dedicated tools for social listening."*	*"Haven't happen yet."*	*"The best thing about keeping track of tags is we can respond pretty quickly."*
8.	*"Being a service industry, we take social media very seriously. You will see a lot of tags on twitter pertaining to good or poor experiences by our fliers. We try to serve them ASAP."*	*"We are always able to take decisions. However, when immigration is involved things can get a bit slow."*	*"For us the time for response is normally less than an hour and our senior managers are also supportive as we are given the authority to take decisions without taking many people in the loop."*
9.	*"We have a dedicated software which gives us a real time data of what people are talking about with respect to our brands. Whenever we feel something needs an address, we micro analysis the situation to reach the root cause."*	*"There are a few cases of false alarm which makes things a bit difficult other than that we can take prompt action."*	*"Depending on the situation and severity the process can take from a few hours to a few weeks (unless a glitch or unseen circumstances happen)."*
10.	*"Ours is a relatively new brand for this company, therefore the social media team is on look out to see how customers are accepting it."*	*"Not till now."*	*"We take quick action zone wise if we find our brand lacking in a particular area (more ad time in our case)."*
11.	*"Our social media team have divided our market into 3 segments (hyper-users, normal users, occasional users), basis the zone our software collect data (frequency is high for low zone and low for high engagement zone)."*	*"Yes, when the cost of bringing the change is more than what we are currently getting."*	*"The action timeline varies from 3 business days to a quarter (in case of big commitments)."*

Perotti, (2017). However, the authors of this study also demonstrated that if firm managers were prompt enough to respond to the false claims, the damage could be undone. The implication of this research study was that the firm managers need not just only be vigilant about crisis management but should also strive to maintain a proactive responsive relation with external stakeholders (specially customers) based on severity of the situation.

Table 6. Thematic findings on social listening

Themes	Frequency	Extracted themes
Handling Crisis – Respondents impression of how the firm respond in case of a crisis.	12.5%	Successful crisis management lead to appreciation on social media.
Poor service – Customers impression of dissatisfactory services.	17.8%	Not being able to manage crisis efficiently, especially in-service sector (Delay in flights, missing luggage or delayed delivery) led to complaints.
Poor product – Respondents attitude when the product wasn't up to their expectations.	12.5%	Not being happy with the product or getting product different from the one posted online led to criticism which often went unanswered.
Good services – Customers attitude towards a brand if they were satisfied with the service provided to them.	12.5%	Good services (both pre and post-sale) led to praise on social media.
Good/extraordinary product – Respondents impression on getting a product that superseded their expectations.	8.9%	Value for money was often the most talked about trait by customers and getting a good product led to appreciation via social media platform.
Mergers and acquisitions – Customers interest in firm (negatives or positives) in cases of mergers and acquisitions.	33.9%	Customers interested in a particular company often tended to respond on M&A based on their knowledge.
Latest technology/Strategy – Respondents attitude towards a firm when they ushered a new technology or strategy in the market.	33.9%	An out of the box thinking and application of innovative thinking was most voiced information on social media.
CSR/Philanthropy – Customers evaluating companies on philanthropic dimension when they were interested in the CSR activities of firms.	14.2%	A good corporate social responsibility initiative led to appreciation on social media whereas the impression that the company wasn't giving back to the society led to criticism.

Figure 4. Difference in type of interaction (Offline vs Online)

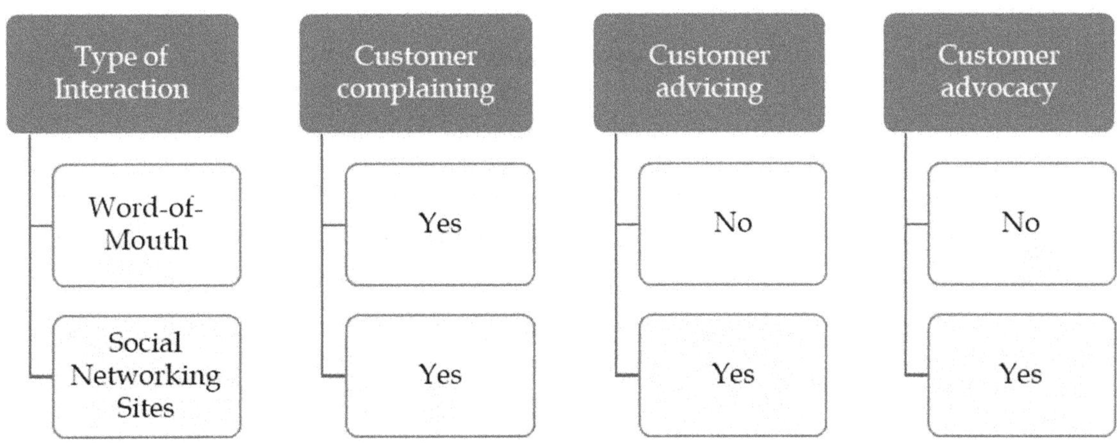

CONCLUSION

It would be important to comprehend that the Indian business landscape has been complex and competitive (Bhattacharyya, Rangarajan & Vyas, 2012). However, technology both in society as well as in organizations has made significant progress in this scenario (Verma & Bhattacharyya, 2016). There has been substantive cost as well as competitive pressures of doing business in India like many global markets, thus pricing of products and services has often been required to be competitive (Bhattacharyya & Deepak, 2012). Firm managers have to always undertake initiatives to be competitive in the marketplace specially like in the context of emerging markets like India (Bhattacharyya & Jha, 2014; Bhattacharyya, Jha & Fernandes, 2015). Inclusion of social listening would be a step in this direction. In this research, the scholars investigated the use of social listening and its impact on firm's strategy. Through the in-depth interviews conducted in context of goods and service sectors in Indian context, the research investigated the use of social listening in changing customer notions. With the help of customer interviews the authors argued that social listening had the potential to improve customer satisfaction and upend brand image. The analysis done by authors suggested that a formal use of social listening would help in developing new products, improving existing level of service, could also help companies in formulating better strategy. The authors argued that a proactive use of social media could not only reduce the risk of potential customer loss but could also increase the brand loyalty. Ultimately, while social media monitoring has been actively used in India, replacing it with social listening could help firm managers develop insights to provide strategic guidance to managers. Because of the growing investment in social media platforms by firms, this research had implications for managers of both goods and service sector. In the firm strategy context, wherein networking was vital to overcome communication barrier, this study demonstrated that social listening could represent an effective method for firms. This could be to access information, knowledge, data and managerial learning to facilitate strategy and innovation. However, firm managers should also be aware of ambiguity, wherein due to dynamic environment, not all the data that was generated could be trusted to give accurate representation of customer sentiments. By examining how and under what conditions social listening could influence strategy formation in firms, the authors have addressed its impact in firm's strategy making process. Since the likelihood of any information spreading over social media was more than by word of mouth (Tuten and Perotti, (2017), it was vital to monitor

Figure 5. Frequency vs Nature of conversation

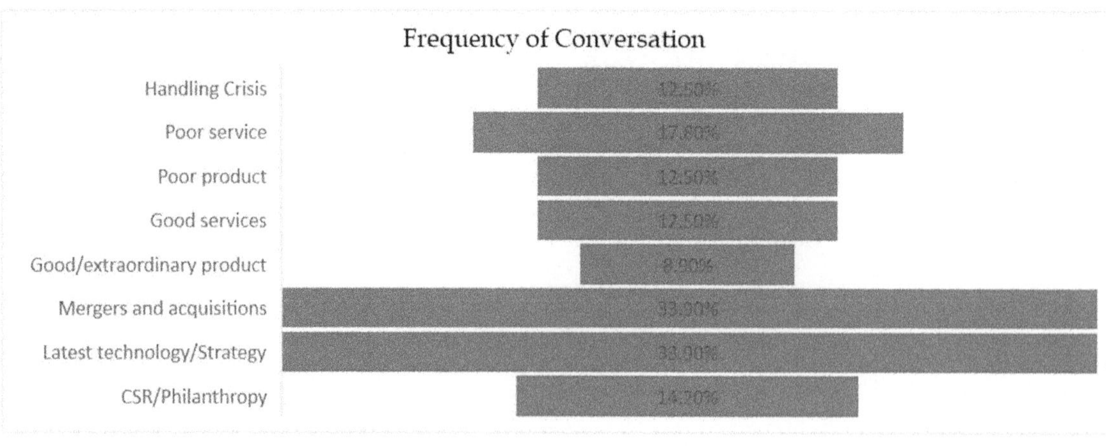

social media. Similarly, it would be better if firm managers engaged in precautionary measures to avoid the crisis altogether. It was also discovered that poor service and goods were one of the prime reasons why customers took to social media. Therefore, an understanding of why and how customers reacted on social media, could help firm managers in devising strategies to increase customer satisfaction. This was explained with the help of a set of frameworks presented in figures 4,5 and 6.

Whereas word of mouth was the primary carrier of information, it was rapidly being replaced by social networking sites (Curran, Treiber and Rossenblatt, 2018). Similar insights were gathered with the help of the questionnaire circulated to customers as represented in figure 5.

Social media users often voiced the concerns online due to several reasons, namely, towards securing response for crisis management, reflections regarding latest technology, satisfaction with the product

Figure 6. Customer satisfaction framework

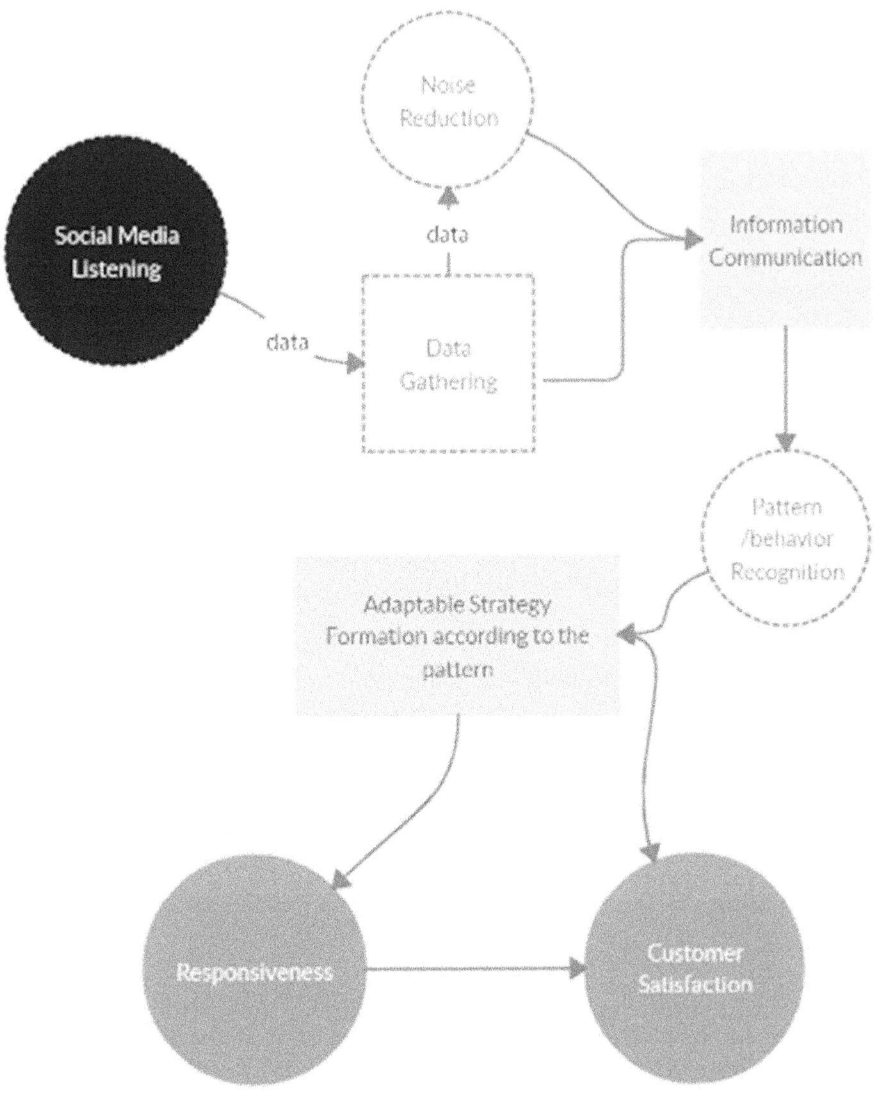

or service and such others. Based upon the study findings, one could argue that poor goods or services and marketing strategy led to maximum customer interactions online. A firm could benefit if it could be prompt enough to gather these insights and increase its responsiveness to customer's dissatisfaction or during crisis.

One must note that according to figure 6, for managers, once the data was collected from social media, in order to change it into information, redundant and non-useful data was required to be filtered out. After the process of data filtering, a behavioral pattern could be chalked out. This could be based upon the nature of customer digital footprint such as criticizing, advising, appreciating and informing. Based on these patterns, the type of strategy and timeline could be decided which would lead to increased responsiveness and efficiency. This would in turn lead to better customer satisfaction. Being a new area of research, the number of articles on social listening were relatively less. This also meant that the study conducted here could further be extended to more than just marketing or strategy and customer satisfaction. There was a clear increase in the number of research publications on related topics starting from the year 2014. Post 2014, a number of scholars had mentioned regarding the relevance and importance of social media monitoring. However, the ethical problem relating to individual data collection was also needed to be addressed. Future research might as well address social listening methods in more detail. In addition, research on return on investment component of social listening and noise reduction would be useful. Moreover, research on social media as a false information spreading channel could also be useful for companies as pointed out by Banerjee &Agarwal, (2012). Since social media has been user driven. Future research on identifying patterns and behaviors could also be an interesting topic of research. Competitor monitoring with the help of social listening could be a priority research agenda for managers to plan competitive strategies.

REFERENCES

Anderson, L. S., Bell, H. G., Gilbert, M., Davidson, J. E., Winter, C., Barratt, M. J., Win, B., Painter, J. L., Menone, C., Sayegh, J., & Dasgupta, N. (2017). Using Social Listening Data to Monitor Misuse and Nonmedical Use of Bupropion: A Content Analysis. *MIR Public Health and Surveillance*, *3*(1), 2369–2960. doi:10.2196/publichealth.6174 PMID:28148472

Banerjee, D. (2020). *Covid pandemic, social media and digital distancing*. Available at: https://www.newindianexpress.com/opinions/2020/may/06/covid-pandemicsocial-media-and-digital-distancing-2139724.html

Bashir, N., Papamichail, K. N., & Malik, K. (2017). Use of Social Media Applications for Supporting New Product Development Processes in Multinational Corporations. *Technological Forecasting & Social Change: An International Journal*, *120*(C), 176–183. doi:10.1016/j.techfore.2017.02.028

Bear, M. (2015). Survival of the fittest: Using social media to thrive in the 21st century. *Journal of Brand Strategy*, *4*(2), 106–113.

Berthon, P. R., Pitt, L. F., Plangger, K., & Shapiro, D. (2012). Marketing meets Web 2.0, social media, and creative consumers: Implications for international marketing strategy. *Business Horizons*, *55*(3), 261–271. doi:10.1016/j.bushor.2012.01.007

Bhattacharyya, S. S., & Deepak, P. K. (2012). Comprehending the changing global iron ore trade service system and the dynamics of pricing. *International Journal of Business and Globalisation*, *9*(1), 70–89. doi:10.1504/IJBG.2012.047523

Bhattacharyya, S. S., & Jha, S. (2014). Development of a model on profit orientation with organizational variables in the context of emerging economies. *Journal of Asia Business Studies*, *8*(3), 264–277. doi:10.1108/JABS-05-2013-0026

Bhattacharyya, S. S., Jha, S., & Fernandes, C. (2015). Determinants of speed to market in the context of the emerging Indian market. *Asia Pacific Journal of Marketing and Logistics*, *27*(5), 784–800. doi:10.1108/APJML-12-2014-0172

Bhattacharyya, S. S., Rangarajan, R., & Vyas, K. G. (2012). Reflections on mapping chaos in the business organisational landscape. *International Journal of Business Innovation and Research*, *6*(1), 76–116. doi:10.1504/IJBIR.2012.044258

Bhimani, H., Laure, A., & Barlatier, P. A. (2019). Social media and innovation: A systematic literature review and future research directions. *Technological Forecasting and Social Change: An International Journal*, *144*, 251–269. doi:10.1016/j.techfore.2018.10.007

Bolton, R., & Saxena-Iyer, S. (2009). Interactive services: A framework, synthesis and research directions. *Journal of Interactive Marketing*, *23*(1), 91–104. doi:10.1016/j.intmar.2008.11.002

Booth, N., & Matic, J. A. (2011). Mapping and leveraging influencers in social media to shape corporate brand perceptions. *Corporate Communications*, *16*(3), 184–191. doi:10.1108/13563281111156853

Chae, M., & Sheu, C. (2020). Exploring social media use in B2B supply chain operations. *Business Horizons*, *63*(2), 73-84.

Conn, G. (2020). *Managing Brand Communication During Covid-19*. Available at: https://blog.sprinklr.com/managing-brand-communication-covid-19/

Cui, R., Gallino, S., Moreno, A., & Zhang, D. J. (2018). The Operational Value of Social Media Information. *Production and Operations Management: An International Journal*, *27*(10), 1749–1769. doi:10.1111/poms.12707

Curran, T., Treiber, J., & Rosenblatt, M. (2018). Building Brands Through Social Listening. *Northeast Business & Economics Association*, *21*(1), 71–74.

Daniel, E. O. (2011). The Use of Social Media in the Supply Chain: Survey and extensions. *Intelligent Systems in Accounting, Finance and Management: An International Journal*, *18*(3), 121–144.

Denzin, N. K., & Lincoln, Y. S. (2008). Introduction: The discipline and practice of qualitative research. In N. K. Denzin & Y. S. Lincoln (Eds.), *Strategies of qualitative inquiry* (pp. 1–43). Sage Publications, Inc.

Dokyun, L., Kartik, H., & Harikesh, S. N. (2018). Advertising Content and Consumer Engagement on Social Media: Evidence from Facebook. *Journal of Management Science*, *64*(11), 4967–5460.

Elena, C. A. (2015). Social Media – a Strategy in Developing Customer Relationship Management. *Procedia Economics and Finance*, *39*, 785–790. doi:10.1016/S2212-5671(16)30266-0

Enginkaya, E., & Yilmaz, H. (2014). What Drives Consumers to Interact with Brands through Social Media? A Motivation Scale Development Study. *Procedia: Social and Behavioral Sciences, 148*, 219–226. doi:10.1016/j.sbspro.2014.07.037

Fuscaldo, D. (2019). *Facebook Now Has More Users in India Than in Any Other Country.* Available at: https://www.investopedia.com/news/facebook-now-has-more-users-india-any-other-country/

Graffigna, G., & Riva, G. (2015). Social media monitoring and understanding: An integrated mixed methods approach for the analysis of social media. *International Journal of Web Based Communities, 11*(1), 57–72. doi:10.1504/IJWBC.2015.067083

Habibi, H., Hamilton, C. A., Valos, M. J., & Callaghan, M. (2015). E-marketing orientation and social media implementation in B2B marketing. *European Business Review, 27*(6), 638–655. doi:10.1108/EBR-03-2015-0026

Hamel, G., & Prahalad, C. K. (1996). Competing in the New Economy: Managing out of Bounds. *Strategic Management Journal, 17*(3), 237–242. doi:10.1002/(SICI)1097-0266(199603)17:3<237::AID-SMJ829>3.0.CO;2-G

He, W., Zha, S., & Li, L. (2013). Social media competitive analysis and text mining: A case study in the pizza industry. *International Journal of Information Management, 33*(3), 464–472. doi:10.1016/j.ijinfomgt.2013.01.001

Johansson & Brynielsson. (2012). Estimating Citizen Alertness in Crises using SocialMedia Monitoring and Analysis. *EISIC '12: Proceedings of the 2012 European Intelligence and Security Informatics Conference*, 189–196.

Josephson, A., & Lambe, E. (2020). *Brand communications in time of crisis.* Available at: https://blog.twitter.com/en_us/topics/company/2020/Brand-communications-in-time-of-crisis.html

Juan, D. U., Feida, Z. H. U., & Ee Peng, L. I. M. (2012). Dynamic Label Propagation in Social Networks. *The 18th International Conference on Database Systems for Advanced Applications,* 194-209.

Kasper, H., Koleva, I., & Kett, H. (2012). Matching Corporate Goals with External Social Media Activities. In *The Semantic Web: ESWC 2012 Satellite Events in Heraklion, Greece, 2012* (pp. 233–244). Springer.

Kenly, A., & Poston, B. (2010). *Social Media and Product Innovation*. Available at: https://viewpoints.io/entry/social-media-and-product-innovation

Kohli, C., Suri, R., & Kapoor, A. (2015). Will social media kill branding? *Business Horizons, 58*(1), 35–44. doi:10.1016/j.bushor.2014.08.004

Lewis, C., Jillian, P., & Augustson, E. (2015). Social Listening: A Content Analysis of E-Cigarette Discussions on Twitter. *Journal of Medical Internet Research, 17*(10). PMID:26508089

Marshall, M. N. (1996). Sampling for qualitative research. *Family Practice, 13*(6), 522–526. doi:10.1093/fampra/13.6.522 PMID:9023528

Paniagua, J., & Sapena, J. (2014). Business performance and social media: Love or hate? *Business Horizons, 57*(6), 719–728. doi:10.1016/j.bushor.2014.07.005

Patroni, J., Briel, F. V., & Recker, J. (2020). Unpacking the social media–driven innovation capability: How consumer conversations turn into organizational innovations*", Information & management. The International Journal of Information Systems Applications*, 103267. doi:10.1016/j.im.2020.103267

Pham, P., & Gammoh, B. (2015). Characteristic of Social Media Marketing Strategy and Customer-Based Brand Equity Outcomes: A Conceptual Model. *International Journal of Internet Marketing and Advertising*, *9*(4), 321–337. doi:10.1504/IJIMA.2015.072885

Pragati. (2019). *Social media statistics in India.* Available at: https://www.talkwalker.com/blog/social-media-statistics-in-india

Reid, E., & Duffy, K. (2018). A netnographic sensibility: Developing the netnographic/social listening boundaries. *Journal of Marketing Management*, *34*(3-4), 263–286. doi:10.1080/0267257X.2018.1450282

Reiter, L., McHaney, R., & Connell, K. Y. H. (2017). Social media influence on purchase intentions: Instrument validation. *International Journal of Web Based Communities*, *13*(1), 54–72. doi:10.1504/IJWBC.2017.082719

Sangani, P. (2019). *Companies using tech to move Fast Moving Consumer Goods faster*. Available at: https://economictimes.indiatimes.com/industry/cons-products/fmcg/companies-using-tech-to-move-fast-moving-consumer-goods-faster/articleshow/72287883.cms?from=mdr

Scherl, L. M., & Smithson, M. (1987). A new dimension to content analysis: Exploring relationships among thematic categories. *Quality & Quantity*, *21*(2), 199–208. doi:10.1007/BF00167608

Schultz, A., & Parikh, J. (2020). *Keeping Our Services Stable and Reliable During the COVID-19 Outbreak.* Available at: https://about.fb.com/news/2020/03/keeping-our-apps-stable-during-covid-19/

Seale, C. (1999). Quality in qualitative research. *Qualitative Inquiry*, *5*(4), 465–478. doi:10.1177/107780049900500402

Shaikh, F. (2018). *Social Media Listening & Analytics - Market Overview (India)*. Available at: https://www.linkedin.com/pulse/social-media-listening-analytics-indian-market-overview-shaikh

Silverman, D. (2016). *Qualitative research.* Sage.

Singh, A., Shukla, N., & Mishra, N. (2017). Social media data analytics to improve supply chain management in food industries. *Transportation Research Part E, Logistics and Transportation Review*, *114*, 398–415. doi:10.1016/j.tre.2017.05.008

Steimer, S. (2017). *How to Reach a Broader Audience with Multicultural Social Listening*. Available at: https://www.ama.org/marketing-news/how-to-reach-a-broader-audience-with-multicultural-social-listening/

Tam, L., & Kim, J. N. (2019). Social media analytics: How they support company public relations. *The Journal of Business Strategy*, *40*(1), 28–34. doi:10.1108/JBS-06-2017-0078

Tuten, T., & Perotti, V. (2017). Lies, brands and social media. *Qualitative Market Research*, *22*(1), 5–13. doi:10.1108/QMR-02-2017-0063

Vaismoradi, M., Turunen, H., & Bondas, T. (2013). Content analysis and thematic analysis: Implications for conducting a qualitative descriptive study. *Nursing & Health Sciences*, *15*(3), 398–405. doi:10.1111/nhs.12048 PMID:23480423

Verma, S., & Bhattacharyya, S. S. (2016). Micro-foundation strategies of IOT, BDA, Cloud Computing. *Strategic Direction, VOL.*, *32*(8), 36–38. doi:10.1108/SD-06-2015-0093

Zembik, M. (2014). Social media as a source of knowledge for customers and enterprises. *Online Journal of Applied Knowledge Management*, *2*(2), 132–148.

Zhang, B., & Vos, M. (2014). Social media monitoring: Aims, methods, and challenges for international companies. *Corporate Communications*, *19*(4), 371–383. doi:10.1108/CCIJ-07-2013-0044

Zubielqui, G. C. D., & Jones, J. (2019). How and when social media affects innovation in start-ups. A moderated mediation model. *Industrial Marketing Management*, *85*, 209–220. doi:10.1016/j.indmarman.2019.11.006

Chapter 7
Demonetization and Movement Towards Digital Cashless Indian Economy:
Its Macroeconomic Effects

Rajib Bhattacharyya
Goenka College of Commerce and Business Administration, Kolkata, India

ABSTRACT

One of the greatest painful, un-stabilizing self-imposed macroeconomic blows on the Indian economy occurred in the absence of a short-term crisis when the government decided to announce a major change in the macroeconomic environment by demonetizing the high value currency notes – of Rs 500 and Rs 1000. These two denominations ceased to be legal tender from midnight of 8th of November 2016. The reasons offered for demonetization are two-fold: one, to control counterfeit notes that could be contributing to terrorism, in other words a national security concern; and second, to undermine or eliminate the "black economy." It has also been a step forward towards a digital cashless economy. In this study an attempt is being made to present a discussion on both the short- and long-run effects of demonetization. It attempts to throw light on the impact of some macroeconomic variables—GDP, sectoral composition, industrial production, inflation, employment—using secondary time-series analysis. The empirical analysis clearly reveals that contraction of currency in circulation was one of the most important factors responsible for decrease in GDP in India after the period of demonetization. Apart from the issue of transition, confronted by the banking system, the government initiative was needed to neutralize the short-term, medium-term, and long-term effects particularly on regularization of cash flows, withdrawals, income, employment, inflation, consumption, and production. Moreover, cyber and other digital security measures were also essential to curb any kinds of frauds and encourage people towards a more digital cashless economy.

DOI: 10.4018/978-1-7998-4787-8.ch007

INTRODUCTION

One of the greatest painful, un-stabilizing self-imposed macroeconomic blows on the Indian economy occurred in the absence of a short term crisis when the government decided to announce a major change in the macroeconomic environment by demonetizing the high value currency notes – of Rs 500 and Rs 1000. These notes ceased to be legal tender from the midnight of 8th of November 2016.Demonetization generally implies a systematic and independent process carried out to replace currencies generally of higher denominations with new currency units.Demonetization is one of the monetary measures adopted by a Government ideally to control demand pull inflationary pressures in the market. This is performed by imposing a restriction on currency notes to completely wipe them off the slate, thereby leading to lower circulation of cash in the economy.

The reasons offered for demonetization are two-fold: one, to control counterfeit notes that could be contributing to terrorism, in other words a national security concern and second, to undermine or eliminate the "black economy". It has also been a step forward towards a digital cashless economy. For proper implementation and conduct of policies in the public domain curbing black money is very essential as it has an adverse impact on both economic and social front.Technically speakingdemonetization is a liquidity shock; a sudden stop in terms of currency availability and so it created short term negative impact on the economy.Most middle and lower segments of the population who constitute the 'base of the pyramid' uses currency to meet their transactions. The daily wage earners, other labourers, small traders etc. who reside out of the formal economy lost income in the absence of liquid cash. Cash stringency compelled firms to reduce labour cost and thus reduces income to the poor working class. This, in turn, created a fall in the demand for mass consumption goods and the market suffered a short term recessionary situation.The information on demonetization was released suddenly and the worst affected was the common man. The social impact was also tremendous, particularly in case of serous patients undergoing emergency treatment or in case of some social gatherings or mishaps. Moreover, people who are not so much habituated in using digital platforms like old and retired people had to bear great hardships to maintain their regular expenditures.

Though the aim of the government was to unveil counterfeit currency from circulation, but surprisingly and contrary to the expectation almost 99 percent of demonetized currency notes were returned to the banking system. This was despite the fact that, in an effort to punish those with unaccounted cash, the Indian government introduced additional rules regarding the amount of discontinued currency that could be deposited into a bank account. But to get hold of the original amount, an accurate estimation was required of the amount of unaccounted cash in the country preceding demonetization.

Demonetization had immediate impact (short term) of wiping out of cash on both household and business transactions. In the medium term it has significant impact on the banking system and also a change mode of payment and tax system and in the long run it has its effect on some macroeconomic variables- GDP, sectoral composition, industrial production, inflation, employment.

LITERATURE SURVEY

Since the announcement of the demonetization in India, a huge body of literature has developed regarding its various aspects. Some of the important contributions in this field are discussed below. Agarwal et al (2018) conducted a comprehensive analysis of the impact of unexpected demonetization in India on payment digitization. They show that the drying-up of cash due to demonetization had led to a significant increase in the level of payment digitization and the rise applies to both traditional and non-traditional digital payment modes -- cards and e-wallets. However, the effects are stronger for regions that already had pre-existing digital infrastructure in place. Aggarwal and Narayan (2017), estimated the impact of India's demonetizationon domestic trade in agricultural commodities. They focused on short term effects up to 3 months after demonetizationfor 35 major agricultural commodities in 3000 regulated markets in India for the period 2011-2017. They found that the monetary contraction embodied in demonetization significantly impacted arrivals and prices, though the price impacts are perhaps more lasting. Ahluwalia (2016) tried to show that on rooting out black money from the system, there is a need to make distinction between black income and black wealth, as these are two different things.Bhavnani, and Copelovitch (2018) showed that the economic impact of demonetization was felt most acutely in relatively "unbanked" areas, where households and businesses lack access to the formal financial system and are most cash-dependent. Chanda (2016) tried to examine the immediate short run impact of the large and unexpected policy change on the informal sector. He also tried to point out the possible benefits of demonetization. Chanda and Cook (2019) examined the medium term effect of demonetization using both regional and household data. Using night-light data, they show that the economic activity was higher and socio-economic characteristics were lower in the district which had higher deposit growth during demonetization. Chadha and Sharma (2017), tried to examine the short-term and long-term economic impact of demonetization on various sectors of India, like agriculture, real estate, construction, manufacturing, financial, aviation, tourism and hospitality, telecom, healthcare and automobile. The worst affected sectors being financial and real estate, construction, tourism and hospitality. Chodorow-Reich et al (2018) developed a macro model to calibrate the aggregate effects. They too rely on district level estimates of night lights data and use elasticity. Dash (2017) tried to explore the socio economic effects of demonetization. Medina and Schneider (2018) obtained new results on the shadow economy for 158 countries all over the world are presented over 1991 to 2015. They estimated India's shadow economy to be on average almost 25 percent of GDP for the period 2004-2015.. Rasel, Hossian, Sultana, Kabir (2019) in their paper discuss the motives and after effects of demonetization decision taken by the Indian Government on November 10, 2016. In addition, it has tried to highlight the demonetization effects in some other countries. Rao and other (2016) tried to evaluate the short run and medium-term impacts that such a shock is expected to have on the economy. Further, the impact of such a move would vary depending on the extent to which the government decides to re-monetize. This paper elucidates the impact of such a move on the availability of credit, spending, and level of activity and government finances. RBI report (March, 2017) had provided an extensive preliminary assessment of various macroeconomic impacts of demonetization. The whole analysis is divided into five parts- growth and inflation, financial sector, financial markets, external sector and digital modes of payment. Shah (2017) seeks to study the impact of demonetization on common person, on agricultural sector and farmers of rural India. Shirley (2017) aims to examine the impact of demonetization on households, farming and fishing industry, jewelry and real estate and on IT sector. Singh (2017) tried to demonstrate the overall impact of demonetization on Indian economy. On the one hand he tried to show the short run loss in income and welfare loos of the deprived and daily wage earners. On the other, he points out the hidden benefits of demonetization. Vyas (2017) in his paper attempts to understand the impact of demonetization announced on November 8, 2016, if any, on employment by using the fast-frequency measures generated using Consumer Pyramids Household Survey (CPHS). He used data on two Waves preceding demonetization and two Waves after demonetization. He used data for seven quarters - 3 before and 4 after demonetization. He also used monthly and weekly data to understand the impact of demonetization.

OBJECTIVE OF THE STUDY AND METHODOLOGY

The present study attempts to examine both the short and long run effects of demonetization. It tries to analysis the immediate impact of wiping out of cash on both household and business transactions. The short-term effect on the economy would depend on the speed with which and the extent to which the cash is replaced by the authorities. In the medium term there would be certainly a significant impact on the banking system and also a change mode of payment and tax system. Lastly, it attempts to throw light on the impact of some macroeconomic variables- GDP, sectoral composition, inflation, employment, using secondary time-series data published by the Reserve Bank of India (RBI) and Centre for Monitoring Indian Economy (CMIE).

For the empirical analysis secondary quarterly time-series data from the official website of RBI is used regarding the two explanatory variables Currency in Circulation (CIC) and Credit-Deposit Ratio (CDR) and also for the dependent variable GDP at constant prices (at prices 2011-12) for the period March 2015 to December 2019. Multiple regression analysis is used to test the significance of the explanatory variables and Augmented Dickey Fuller (ADF) Test is used to check whether unit roots are stationary. Statistical package e-views have been used to test the result.

BRIEF HISTORY OF DEMONETIZATION IN INDIA

The Reserve Bank manages currency in India andderives its role in currency management on the basisof the Reserve Bank of India Act, 1934. Rs. 1000 and higher denomination notes were firstdemonetized in January 1946 and again in1978.The highest denomination note ever printedby the Reserve Bank of India was the Rs10,000 note in 1938 and again in 1954. Butthese notes were demonetized in January1946 and again in January 1978, according toRBI data.Rs 1,000 and Rs 10,000 bank notes were incirculation prior to January 1946. Higherdenomination banknotes of Rs 1,000, Rs 5,000 andRs 10,000 were reintroduced in 1954 and all of themwere demonetized in January 1978.

Facts and Figures of the Present Demonetization (8th November, 2016)

As per RBI Handbook on Statistics of Indian Economy 2015-16, a total of Rs.16.42 lakh crore (table-1) worth of currency was in circulation as at end-March 2016. Of this, Rs.14.18 lakh crore was in form of Rs.500 and Rs.1000 denomination notes, representing around 86 per cent (table-1) of the value of total currency and coins in circulation. In terms of number of notes in circulation, Rs.500 and Rs.1000 denomination notes represent about 2200 crore notes, which were about 26 per cent of total notes in circulation. During the year, 632,926 pieces of counterfeit notes were detected in the banking system, of which 95 per cent were detected by commercial banks. Denomination-wise, detection of counterfeit notes of Rs.100 and Rs.1000 increased in 2015-16 (Table-2).

SHORT RUN AND MEDIUM TERM ECONOMIC AND SOCIAL EFFECTS

Short run Effects

Table 1. Bank Notes in Circulation

Denomination	Volume (million pieces)			Value (Rs. Billion)		
	Mar '14	Mar '15	Mar '16	Mar '14	Mar '15	Mar '16
2 and 5	11698 (15.1)	11672 (13.9)	11626 (12.9)	46 (0.4)	46 (0.3)	45 (0.3)
10	26648 (34.5)	30304 (36.3)	32015 (35.5)	266 (2.1)	303 (2.1)	320 (1.9)
20	4285 (5.5)	4350 (5.2)	4924 (5.4)	86 (0.7)	87 (0.6)	98 (0.6)
50	3448 (4.5)	3487 (4.2)	3890 (4.3)	172 (1.3)	174 (1.2)	194 (1.2)
100	14765 (19.1)	15026 (18.0)	15778 (17.5)	1476 (11.5)	1503 (10.5)	1578 (9.6)
500	11405 (14.7)	13128 (15.7)	15707 (17.4)	5702 (44.4)	6564 (46.0)	7854 (47.8)
1000	5081 (6.6)	5612 (6.7)	6326 (7.0)	5081 (39.6)	5612 (39.3)	6326 (38.6)
Total	77330	83579	90266	12629	14289	16415

[Note: Figure in the parentheses represents the percentage share in the total]
[Source: Currency Management, RBI, Chapter-VII, pg. 89]

Table 2. Denomination-wise Counterfeit Notes Detected in the Banking System (April to March)

				2014-15		
2015-16	**Denomination**	**No. of Counterfeit Notes**	**Notes in Circulation**	**FICN as proportion of NIC**	**No. of Counterfeit Notes**	**Notes in Circulation**
FICN as proportion of NIC	**2 and 5**	0	11672000000	0	2	11626000000
0	**10**	268	30304000000	0.00000001	134	32015000000
0	**20**	106	4350000000	0.00000002	96	4924000000
0	**50**	7160	3487000000	0.00000206	6453	3890000000
0.0000017	**100**	181799	15026000000	0.0000121	221447	15778000000
0.0000141	**500**	273923	1328000000	0.00002087	261695	15707000000
0.0000167	**1000**	131190	5612000000	0.00002338	143099	6326000000
0.0000226	Total	694446	83579000000	0.00006791	632926	90266000000

[Notes:FICN = Fake Indian Currency Notes
NIC = Notes in Circulation
[Source: Currency Management, RBI, Chapter-VII, pg.92]

According to NITI Aayog, there are multiple benefits of demonetization. Firstly, it is supposed to wipe out most of the illegal cash accumulated over a number of years from the system. This will have a direct impact on inflation. Secondly, counterfeit currency circulating in the country has ceased to be of any value. Thirdly, it would curb the menace of corruption and terrorism as the existing black money will be of no use. Fourthly, it would bring back a lot of money outside the system back into the financial system which can be used by the banks for onward lending for commercial activities. This would not only improve the profitability of banks, but would also pave way for reduction of interest rates and partly address the problem of NPAs. Fifthly, it will help cleaning the process of election funding bringing more transparency and fairness in the manner of conduct of Elections. Sixthly, in due course of time, it would significantly help in improving tax collections as public would prefer to deal in white transactions by paying legitimate taxes. Seventhly, in respect of currency which is not deposited back in the banks a space would be created wherein outstanding liability of RBI can be extinguished paving way for additional resources for the Government for being used for public purpose in phases without impacting inflation. Eighthly, with clean-up of black money, asset prices especially real estate would further decline thus making housing more affordable for public at large. Ninthly, demonetization is viewed as a measure of sterilizing the money. RBI plays the pivotal role in this demonetization drive. Considering the banking sector, both public and private sector banks are facing the severe issue of Non-Performing Assets (NPA) or Bad loans. This demonetization measure will help banks to recover some bad loans and improve their financial position.Last, but not the least, it would significantly improve India's image in the global arena as the country which respects the rule of law and where businesses can flourish through legitimate means paving way for large scale investments both from within the country and abroad.

Demonetization technically is a liquidity shock; a sudden stop in terms of currency availability and so it created short term negative impact on the economy.Most middle and lower segments of the population who constitute the 'base of the pyramid' uses currency to meet their transactions. The daily wage earners, other labourers, small traders etc. who reside out of the formal economy lost income in the absence of liquid cash. Cash stringency compelled firms to reduce labour cost and thus reduces income to the poor working class. This, in turn, created a fall in the demand for mass consumption goods and the market suffered a short term recessionary situation.When liquidity shortage strikes, it is consumption that is going to be adversely affected first. This results in a fall in production, employment and tax revenue.The decision about ban on currency note has adversely affected the industrial sector. Trade across all facets of the economy was disrupted. Consumer goods sales are reported to have dropped by one-third. Farmers have difficulty buying seeds and fertilizer and selling crops and perishable products. The demonetization led to unavailability of cash to pay for food products. The reduction in demand that arose in turn led to a crash in the prices of crops. Farmers were unable to recover even the costs of transportation from their fields to the market from the low prices offered. This forced the farmers across the country to dump their products in desperation.

The information on demonetization was released suddenly and the worst affected was the common man. The social impact was drastic with marriages facing severe issues with cash transactions in marriages coming to a standstill. The impact on the health care sector was huge with most of the hospitals refused to accept the old currency. During the demonetization long queue of about 1 to 2 kilometer was seen in several parts. Despite of that it was not guarantee that the one will get money from the ATM or bank. Some people start moving to the bank from the last night. There was a severe shortage of cash. Some unscrupulous money traders tried to make profit hoarding money and lending at a high price.

Medium Term Effect

In the medium term, the effects would be related to the extent to which the currency is not replaced within the economy. If the entire currency is replaced, there would not be any major effects on the economy. However, it is to be expected that the entire currency would not be replaced – to the extent currency is extinguished and to the extent some of the currency remains as bank deposits, there would be some impact on the economy. The first effect would be a compression of the economy to the extent the extinguished currency was working as a medium of exchange. The currency that is placed in the banks but not withdrawn, it is argued, would generate an expansion in deposits in the economy. There are a number of transition issues that need to be managed for this transition to be effective: There is need for a significant upgrade of the banking infrastructure as well as in the telecom infrastructure that would provide the backbone for digital transactions. Apart from the technological issues, there is a behavioural change that is being expected in people from using cash as a medium of exchange to using other cash substitutes both for making payments and receiving payments. In the interim, until people adjust to the use of non-cash instruments, there would be an increased demand for the cash.

LONG RUN IMPACT OF DEMONETIZATION ON SOME MAJOR MACRO VARIABLES

GDP Growth

Quarterly Estimates of GDP at Constant Prices, 2011-12 series reveals in the third quarter (Q4) of financial year 2016-17, when the demonetization was implemented, the growth rate immediately started to dip down from 8.6 to 6.3 (Q4, 2016-17). Again it started to revive from Q2, 2017-18. But due to the world wide recessionary situation the growth rate again started to fall from the first quarter of 2018-19 and it continued the same trend thereafter.(table-3). So it seems clear that there has been a negative impact on the growth rate of GDP due to the demonetization..

Sectoral Composition

The growth in the 'agriculture, forestry and fishing', 'mining & quarrying', 'manufacturing', 'construction', and Electricity, gas, water supply & other utility services registered a steady decline after the implementation of the demonetization, whereas Trade, hotels, transport, communication and services related to broadcasting, 'financial, real estate and professional services' and Public Administration, defense and other services have registered a rise though suffering from an initial declining shock(table-4).

Index of Industrial Production (IIP)

The Quick Estimates of Index of Industrial Production (IIP) with base 2011-12 for the month of January 2020 stands at 137.1, which is about 2.0 percent higher as compared to the level in the month of January 2019. The Indices of Industrial Production for the Mining, Manufacturing and Electricity sectors for the month of January 2020 stand at 124.3, 137.6 and 155.6 respectively, with the corresponding growth rates of 4.4 percent, 1.5 percent and 3.1 percent as compared to January 2019. But the General Index

Table 3. Quarterly Estimates of GDP at Constant Prices, 2011-12 Series (Growth Rates of GDP before and after demonetization)

	Q1 (April – June)	Q2 (July – September)	Q3 (October – December)	Q4 (January – March)
2015-16	7.6	8.0	7.2	9.1
2016-17	8.7	9.7	8.6	6.3
2017-18	5.8	6.5	7.6	8.2
2018-19	7.1	6.2	5.6	5.7
2019-20	5.6	5.1	4.7	N.A.

[Source: Ministry of Statistics and Programme Implementation, Govt. of India (as on March 2020)]

Table 4. Annual Estimates of GDP (sector-wise) at Constant Prices, 2011-12 Series

	2015-16	2016-17	2017-18	2018-19	2019-20
1. Agriculture,forestry & fishing	0.6	6.8	5.9	2.4	3.7
2. Mining & quarrying	10.1	9.8	4.9	-5.8	2.8
3. Manufacturing	13.1	7.9	6.6	5.7	0.9
4. Electricity, gas, water supply & other utility services	4.7	10.0	11.2	8.2	4.6
5. Construction	3.6	5.9	5.0	6.1	3.0
6. Trade, hotels, transport, communication and services related to broadcasting	10.2	7.7	7.6	7.7	5.6
7. Financial, real estate & professional services	10.7	8.6	4.7	6.8	7.3
8. Public Administration, defense and other services	6.1	9.3	9.9	9.4	8.8
9. GVA at basic prices	8.0	8.0	6.6	6.0	4.9

[Source: Ministry of Statistics and Programme Implementation, Govt. of India (as on March 2020)]

for the month of January 2018 stands at 132.3, which is 7.5 percent higher as compared to the level in the month of January 2017. The Indices of Industrial Production for the Mining, Manufacturing and Electricity sectors for the month of January 2018 stand at 114.5, 133.8 and 149.5 respectively, with the corresponding growth rates of 0.1 percent, 8.7 percent and 7.6 percent as compared to January 2017. This clearly reveals the fact that the growth rate of overall industrial production as well as its various sectors have declined overtime due to the impact of demonetization.

Inflation

The impact of demonetization on inflation in the near-term stemmed mainly from moderation in food inflation, especially perishables, as inflation excluding food and fuel remained broadly unaffected.

Table 5. Index of Industrial Production (IIP)

		Index of Industrial Production (IIP)				
Industry Code	**Description**	Jan'16	Jan'17	Jan'18	Jan'19	Jan'20
5	**Mining**	105.3	114.4	114.5	119.1	124.3
10- 32	**Manufacturing**	120.8	123.1	133.8	135.5	137.6
35	**Electricity**	132.1	138.9	149.5	150.9	155.6
	General Index	119.5	123.1	132.3	134.4	137.1

[Source: Ministry of Statistics and Programme Implementation, Govt. of India,(Press Release- Jan2016- March2020]

Food Inflation

Food inflation declined from 3.7 per cent (year-on-year, y-o-y) in October 2016 to 2.6 per cent in November, to 2.0 per cent in December and further to 1.3 per cent in January 2017. This was mainly on account of vegetables and pulses. Vegetable prices declined by 6.2 per cent on a month-on-month (m-o-m) basis in November 2016 and further by 11.7 per cent in December 2016.

Inflation Excluding Food and Fuel

Even though discretionary consumer spending on items such as clothing and footwear, household goods and services, recreation and amusement, and personal care and effects (which constitute 16 per cent of the CPI basket) may have been impacted, the prices of these items weathered the transitory effects of the cash shortage as they are normally revised according to pre-set cycles and showed minimal changes post demonetization.

Table 5. **CPI Inflation in Select Groups** *(y-o-y in per cent)*

Category	Nov-15	Dec-15	Jan-16	Oct-16	Nov-16	Dec-16	Jan-17
Fuel & light	5.3	5.4	5.3	2.9	2.8	3.8	3.4
Clothing & footwear	5.8	5.7	5.7	5.2	5.0	5.0	4.7
Housing	5.0	5.1	5.2	5.1	5.0	5.0	5.0
Miscellaneous*	3.8	4.0	3.9	4.7	4.8	4.7	5.1
CPI-excluding Food-Fuel	4.7	4.9	4.7	4.9	4.9	4.9	5.1
* Includes household goods and services; health; transport and communication; recreation and amusement; education; and personal care and effects.							

[Source: RBI Report on Demonetization, March 10, 2017]

Figure 1 demonstrates the movements in CPI (y-o-y inflation) in pre and post demonetization period. It came down sharply during the first six months after demonetization following the RBI policy of Inflation targeting but thereafter it has shown upward trends except for a few months in 2018.

Figure 1. Movements in CPI (y-o-y inflation) in Pre and Post Demonetization period
[Source: RBI, Table No. 18; Consumer Price Index Base 2010 = 100]

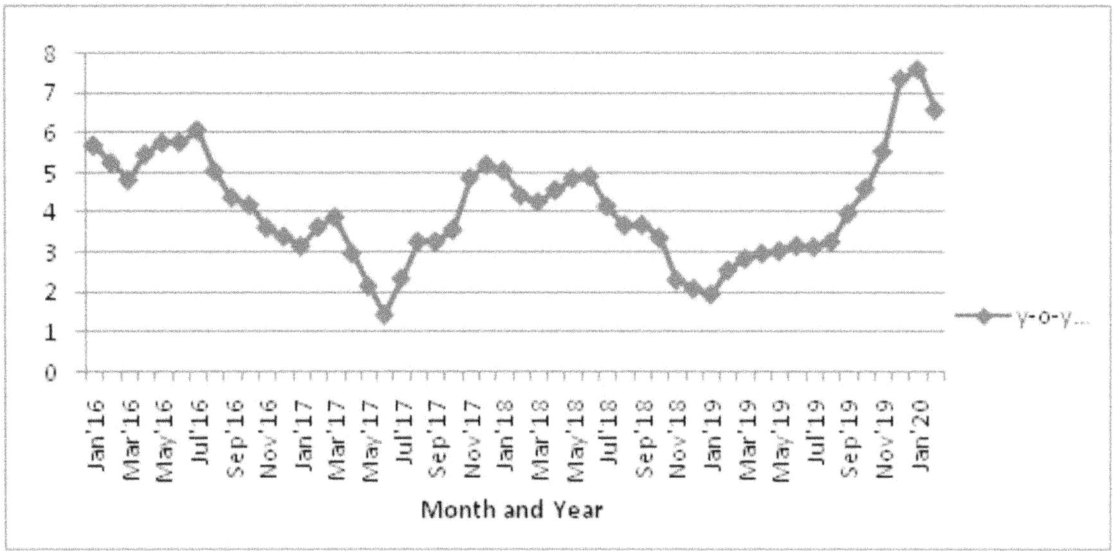

Employment Situation

Initially there was a fall in non-farm employment following demonetization, but after that it revived. Total nonfarm employment increased by 223,000 in May. Employment continued to trend up in retail trade, health care, and construction. The employment change for April revised down from 164,000 to 159,000, and the change for March revised up from 135,000 to 155,000. On net, employment over these months is 15,000 higher than previously reported (figure-2).

Figure 3 illustrates the changes in the unemployment rate in general and also separately for male and female during the pre and post demonetization period in India. Prior to demonetization the unemployment rate was as high as 24 percent. This sharply declined to about 9 percent during the first half of 2017, but thereafter there has been a steady upsurge in the unemployment rate. Moreover, throughout the entire period under consideration, the unemployment rate for male was higher than that of female.

EMPIRICAL ANALYSIS

Here our aim is to simply find out whether the two important monetary indicators viz. Currency in circulation (CIC) and Credit-Deposit ratio (CDR) are important determinants of the growth of GDP overtime. Secondary quarterly data from the official website of RBI is used regarding the two explanatory variables CIC and CDR and also for the dependent variable GDP at constant prices (at prices 2011-12) for the period March 2015 to December 2019. Because we all know there was a massive decrease in the Currency in circulation (CIC) and CDR during the time of change of legal tender under demonetization. Our regression equation is

Figure 2. Employment in total nonfarm (2015-2018)
[Source: Bureau of Labor Statistics, Current Employment Statistics, June 01, 2018]

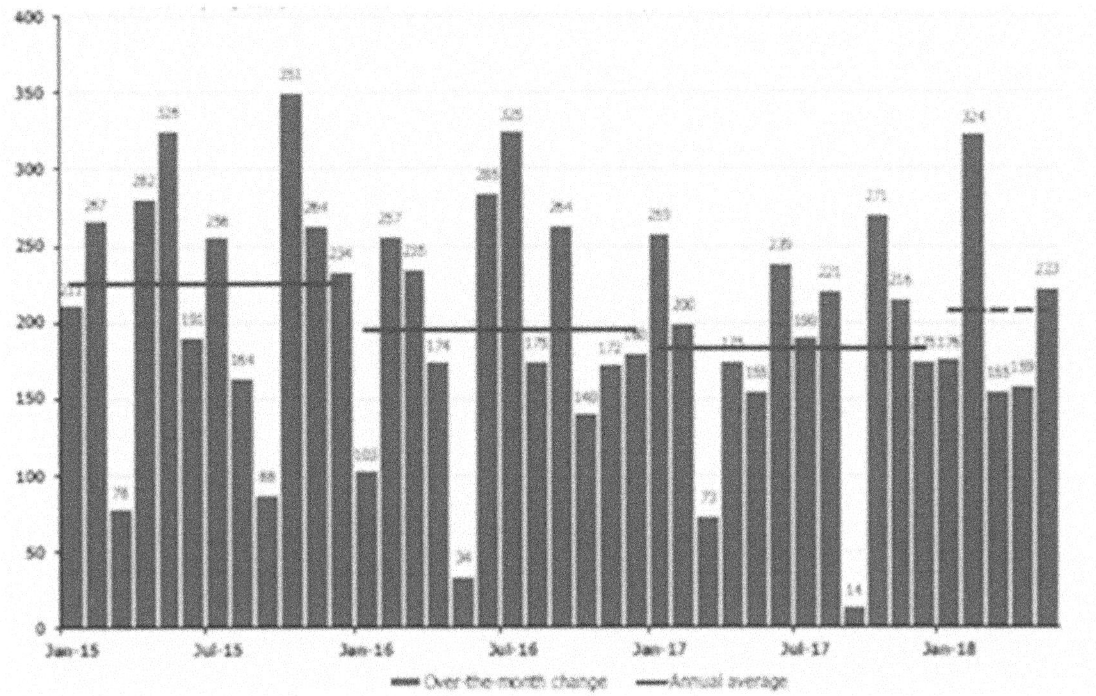

Figure 3. Changes in Unemployment Rate during Pre and Post Demonetization
[Source: Centre for Monitoring Indian Economy (CMIE), Jan2016- Dec-2019]

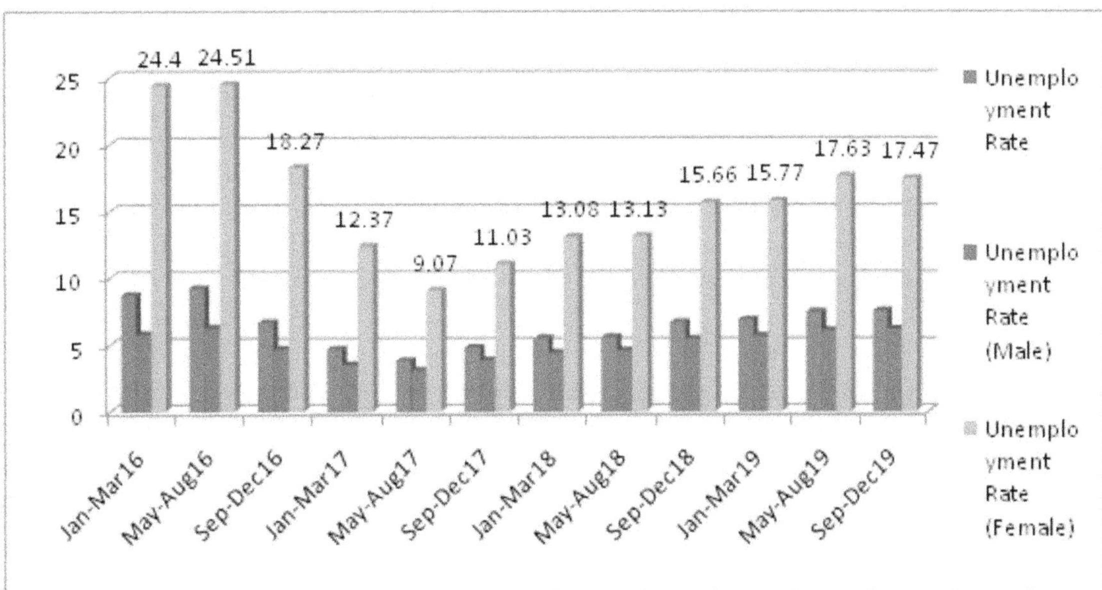

$$GDP = \propto_0 + \propto_1 CIC + \propto_2 d(CDR).$$

Before starting any time series analysis the ADF Unit root test is performed to check whether the series is stationary (detail is provided in the appendix Table 7). Both GDP and CIC are stationary at level whereas CDR is stationary at the first difference and hence our model specification is the one stated above.

Dependent Variable: GDP				
Method: Least Squares				
Variable	**Coefficient**	**Std. Error**	**t-Statistic**	**Prob.**
$\propto_0$	2100317.	273940.8	7.667048	0.0000
CIC	0.654845	0.153295	4.271792	0.0006
D(CDR)	21165.75	31435.09	0.673316	0.5104
R-squared	0.659582			
Durbin-Watson stat	0.798393			

The detail is provided in the appendix table 8. The above regression analysis shows that out of the two explanatory variables CIC is positive and significant whereas change in CDR also bears a positive sign but is insignificant.As demonetization created a huge spurt of bank deposits but created disincentives to credit expansion, so the impact of CDR on output was insignificant. So a fall in currency in circulation during demonetization had a negligible impact on GDP of India.

POLICY IMPLICATIONS

Initiative to Curtailing Black Money

Curtailment of black money has been one of the major thrust areas of the Government especially its recent initiative towards demonetization. In a common parlance, black money refers to the money which is generated through illegitimate means or by bypassing taxation system. Generation of black money in social, economic and political space has a debilitating effect on the conduct of public policy and the institutions of governance in the country. Black money together with counterfeit currency is also associated with crime and terrorism. While there is no official estimate of quantum of black money in India or abroad, a 2010 World Bank Report on shadow economies estimated it at 31 per cent of GDP of 162 countries in 2007 with India's estimate pegged at 20.7 per cent of GDP comparing favourably with the world average. There have been other estimates which have placed size of India's parallel economy at higher levels including a recent FICCI report which has estimated it to as high as 75 per cent of GDP.

There are many reasons for the creation of back money in India. Black money is increasing in India for the reasons of controls, permits, quotas and licenses. Higher rates of taxes has resulted a growing tendency of tax evasion among the tax payers. There is an upward tendency of supporting of political parties with the help of black money. Big trade houses are donating an enormous amount of black money to the political parties, especially the ruling party with the sole objective to tame the political leadership for deriving undue profit by manipulating policy decisions (Lekhi, 2003, 193). The reluctance to bring agricultural earnings in the realm of income tax has also contributed to creation of black money. Real estate transaction is a significant source of generating black money in India. Generation of black income in a country like India also results from other different activities like smuggling, property deals, bribery, kickbacks, commissions, concealment of income by professionals, artists etc.

Cashless Economy- A Move Towards Digitization

Themoveofdemonetizationshallusherinthenewera ofdigitaleconomyandelectronicpaymentsandreceipts. The change of currency notes and resultant cash crunch in the system has led to a new opportunity for the country i.e. to move towards a cashless or less cash society in the medium to long run. While India has come a long way from introduction of electronic funds transfer, the newer forms of payment have been developed in the recent years which hold significant potential to move towards a less cash economy. These include (i) Unified Payments Interface (UPI) which enables a person to transfer funds to any other person registered on UPI through mobile phone connected to internet; (ii) Digital wallets, such as SBI Buddy wherein money can be loaded to your mobile wallets (*e-batua*) and transferred to any other person using mobile numbers or bank details; (iii) Pre-paid, Debit or Credit Cards which can be used at ATMs, Point of Sales (PoS) Machines by swiping the cards; (iv) Aadhaar Enabled Payment Systems (AEPS) wherein funds can be transferred using Aadhaar numbers seeding with bank accounts; and (v) Unstructured Supplementary Service Data (USSD) wherein funds can be transferred from mobile phones without requiring access to internet connection. In the long run, this would provide a significant boost to the economy as more and more informal methods of business transactions migrate to the formal sector paving way for greater transparency, financial inclusion (both on deposits and credit side) and better tax compliance.

CONCLUDING REMARKS

The above analysis clearly shows that the phenomenon of demonetization is one of the largest self-inflicted macroeconomic shocks on the Indian economy in the absence of a short term crisis. Given the sheer size of the economy, the decision to withdraw 85 percent of the currency, all of a sudden, naturally has created short run disruption and disturbances. But in the medium and long run the repercussion effect is been reduced to a great extent. This is particularly true for India where a large section of the economyis comprised of the informal or unorganized sectorwhich functions on cash basis not illegal.GDP at 2011-12 prices in the fourth quarter (Q4) of financial year 2017-18 registered growth rate of 7.7 per cent as against 5.6 percent, 6.3 percent and 7.0 percent respectively, in the first three quarters, Q1, Q2 and Q3 of 2017-18. The growth rate started to drop after the first quarter of 2016-17. But after the demonetization in November 2016, the growth rate in the third quarter dropped to 6.8 and it fell further to 6.1 in Q4, 2016-17. Demonetization technically is a liquidity shock; a sudden stop in terms of currency availability. . Agriculture, forestry and fishing, mining & quarrying, manufacturing, and Electricity, gas, water supply & other utility services have fallen in their contribution as compared to the previous year. The impact of demonetization on inflation in the near-term stemmed mainly from moderation in food inflation, especially perishables, as inflation excluding food and fuel remained broadly unaffected. Initially there was a fall in non-farm employment following demonetization, but after that it revived. The reasons offered for demonetization are two-fold: one, to control counterfeit notes that could be contributing to terrorism, in other words a national security concern and second, to undermine or eliminate the "black economy". It has also been a step forward towards a cashless economy. But one must remember black money is not preserved only in the form of counterfeit notes, it also kept as investment real estate and gold. So, side by side these are also to be controlled by some means or other. Regarding movement towards digital cashless economy proper security measure needs to be taken for smooth online transaction and access to digital devices and operations must be available at low cost to common man. So we have to wait further to reap full benefits of demonetization utilizing adequate safeguards to digital transactions. The empirical analysis clearly reveals that contraction of currency in circulation was one of the most important factors responsible for decrease in GDP in India after the period of demonetization.

REFERENCES

Agarwal, S., Debarati, B., Pulak, G., Bhuvanesh, P. & Jian, Z. (2018). *Demonetization and Digitization.* Available at SSRN: https: //ssrn.com/abstract=3197990

Aggarwal, N., & Narayanan, S. (2017). *Impact of India's demonetization on domestic agricultural markets.* Indira Gandhi Institute of Development Research. Available at http://www.igidr.ac.in/pdf/publication/WP-2017-023.pdf

Bhavnani, R. R., & Copelovitch, M. (2018). *The Political Impact of Monetary Shocks: Evidence from India's 2016 Demonetization, January.* Available at SSRN: https://ssrn.com/abstract=3095228

Chadha, A., & Sharma, R. (2017). Demonetization: Economic impact on different sectors in India. International Journal of Latest Technology in Engineering. *Management and Applied Science*, *6*(6), 219–223.

Chanda, A. (2016). *Notes (and anecdotes) on Demonetization.* Accessed on 10th June, 2019, https://www.researchgate.net/publication/311908388_Notes_and_Anecdotes_on_Demonetization

Chanda, A., & Cook, C. J. (2019). *Who Gained from India's Demonetization? Insights from Satellites and Surveys.* Working Paper 2019-06, Department of Economics, Louisiana State University. Available at https://www.lsu.edu/business/economics/files/working papers/pap19_06.pdf

Chodorow, G. R., Gopinath, G., Mishra, M., & Naraynan, M. (2018). *Cash and the Economy: Evidence from India's Demonetization.* Working Paper, Harvard University. Available at https://scholar.harvard.edu/files/crgmn_ demonetization.pdf

Dash, A. (2017). A Study on Socio Economic Effect of Demonetization in India. *International Journal of Management and Applied Science, 3*(3).

Medina, L., & Schneider, F. (2018). *Shadow Economies Around the World: What Did We Learn Over the Last 20 Years?* IMF Working Paper WP/18/17.

PTI. (2016). Demonetisation to Pull Down GDP Growth: Montek Singh Ahluwalia. *Economic Times*. https://economictimes.indiatimes.com/news/economy/policy/demonetisation-to-pull-down-gdp-growth-montek-singh-ahluwalia/articleshow/55568179.cms

Rao, K., Mukherjee, S., Kumar, S., Sengupta, D. P., Tandon, S., & Nayudu, S. (2016). *Demonetization: Impact on the Economy*. National Institute of Public Finance and Policy New Delhi, Working Paper No. 182.

Rasel, M., Hossian, M.S., Sultana, A., & Kabir, M.H. (2019). Demonetization in India: An Evaluation. *Asian Journal of Economics, Business and Accounting, 12*(2), 1-12.

RBI. (2016a). *Annual Report, Table VIII 1 Banknotes in Circulation*. https://rbi.org.in/Scripts/BS_PressReleaseDisplay.aspx?prid=38520

RBI. (2016b). *Withdrawal of Legal Tender Status for Rs. 500 and Rs. 1000 Notes*. Reserve Bank of India(RBI) Notice. https://rbi.org.in/Scripts/BS_PressReleaseDisplay.aspx?prid=38520

RBI Report. (2017). *Macroeconomic Impact of Demonetization- A Preliminary Assessment*. Author.

Shah, A. Y. (2017). Impact of Demonetization on Rural India. *International Journal of Scientific and Research Publications, 7*(3).

Shirley, M. A. J. (2017). *Impact of Demonetization in India. International Journal of Trend in Research and Development*.

Singh, A. (2017). Impact of demonetization on Indian economy. *International Journal of Engineering and Management Research, 7*(3), 785–788.

Vyas, M. (2017). *Using Fast Frequency Household Survey Data to Estimate the Impact of Demonetization on Employment*. CMIE Working Paper.

APPENDIX

Table 7. Results of Unit Test (ADF)

Variable	t-Statistic	Probability	Critical value	Series Type
GDP	-26.73866	0.0001	-3.081002	S
CIC	-4.970983	0.0010	-3.040391	S
CDR	-2.148895	0.2295	-3.029970	NS
D(CDR)	-4.410416	0.0033	-3.040391	S

Table 8. Regression Results

Dependent Variable: GDP				
Method: Least Squares				
Date: 03/27/20 Time: 18:44				
Sample (adjusted): 6/01/2015 12/01/2019				
Included observations: 19 after adjustments				
Variable	Coefficient	Std. Error	t-Statistic	Prob.
C	2100317.	273940.8	7.667048	0.0000
CIC	0.654845	0.153295	4.271792	0.0006
D(CDR)	21165.75	31435.09	0.673316	0.5104
R-squared	0.659582	Mean dependent var		3247231.
Adjusted R-squared	0.604530	S.D. dependent var		306577.7
S.E. of regression	215798.9	Akaike info criterion		27.54602
Sum squared resid	7.45E+11	Schwarz criterion		27.69514
Log likelihood	-258.6872	Hannan-Quinn criter.		27.57126
F-statistic	10.16457	Durbin-Watson stat		0.798393
Prob(F-statistic)	0.001416			

Chapter 8
Augment Human Resource Proximity Plumbing Cybernation

Anant Deogaonkar
Shri Ramdeobaba College of Engineering and Management, India

Sampada Nanoty
M. S. University Vadodara, India

Archana Shrivastava
https://orcid.org/0000-0001-7955-3844
Jaypee Business School, Jaypee Institute of Information Technology, India

Geetika Jain
https://orcid.org/0000-0002-2733-3767
Amity University, Noida, India

ABSTRACT

The expeditious proliferation of artificial intelligence in the mainstream has rejigged the simplest processes of the various sectors in the most efficient way. With the advent of the era of cybernation, the work culture has been curbed with the timely developments and upgradation of the technology. Cybernation has propelled the growth of every respective sector of the vast corporate diaspora with time. The main aim of the cybernation being that of smoothening the complex, bulk tasks which exploit mass human energy, has seen much success in its purpose so far. But certain domains of the corporate diaspora still await the technological transformation of their respective processes. One such prominent domain and the real fuel of the corporate diaspora, the human resource has yet to expand its purview to imbibe and imbue cybernation in its certain processes. Human resource domain being the custodian of the corporate, wherein it is for the people and by the people though with the niche of Industry 4.0 beholds more space to expand the angle of understanding the term resource for the human, than human as an element

DOI: 10.4018/978-1-7998-4787-8.ch008

of resource in itself. Multifarious human resource processes can be enhanced further with apt utility of digitization in order to optimize the user interface and user experience, boosting the overall employee experience amidst the corporate. Several certain customary functions of the human resources entail the adaptation of automation in more nuanced way to evolve parallel with the digitalization. Moreover, the millennial era further looks up to a transformed human resource with higher echelons of functions to be performed, digitally evolved jobs, an automated work environment, work culture well acquainted with the artificial intelligence. The effect of cybernation on the business acumen of futuristic human resource leaders, working in the rapid concurrent era of disruptions, without losing the human touch, will carve the future human resource structure. Therefore, the intent of this chapter is to study the detailed implications of automation, digitalization, and cybernation in the domain of human resources and to study and examine the dynamically changing HR functions with technological interventions and disruptions by proposing a literature review.

OBJECTIVE

Through this chapter we propose to highlight the detailed implications of automation, digitalization and cybernation in the domain of Human Resource. We also examine the probable possibilities of impacts of dynamically changing HR functions with technological interventions and disruptions.

INTRODUCTION

Human resource management is an essential part of every company. Whether it's hiring new employees, training, or ensuring that local labor laws are complied with, HR processes are a vital part of every company.But HR has usually been thought of as a highly manual department process. They are used to rolling up their sleeves and getting the job done themselves. But all that's changing.Automation is invading the HR space, and very soon everything that can be automated, will be automated. Current HR staff need to adapt to the coming changes or get left behind in the dust.What does this mean for HR now and in the future? Are workers going to become obsolete? Are they going to find their job roles differ from what's typically expected of them? Let's take a closer look.HR automation is the process of enhancing the efficiency of the HR department by freeing employees from tedious manual tasks and allowing them to focus on complex tasks like decision making and strategizing. By automating standard and repetitive HR activities, organizations can reduce the cost and time they spend on manual HR planning and processing– Kissflow, (2018) HR Automation - The Future of Human Resource Process Management. https://kissflow.com/hr-process/

THE PRESENT STATUS OF HR

From the times of the conventional monotonous static tactics amidst the corporate, to this day's no break contemporary marathon era with unconventional processes easily automatic, the wheels of evolution and development have revolved at meteoric pace. The gradual involvement of technology over the years has seen itself as a part of even the most minimal tasks of our day to day lives. Even the functions and processes in the corporate world have been no exception to this. Cybernation has transmogrified every sphere of the corporate diaspora by aptly acquainting the respective areas with the artificial intelligence, digitalization and automation optimizing efficiency, accuracy and the precision in the varied functions performed. The domain of HR possessing vast purview of various functional people processes still leaves a room for automation of certain processes which yet exploits human as a resource. Humans are still themselves being the resources than being provided, resources and tools at their hands. Even today humans personally indulge in numerous mundane tasks which can be easily digitally substituted. Although with the introduction of industry 4.o several manual tasks have been mechanized smoothening the process, yet for certain HR functions there still prevails an element of doubt, questioning the involvement of technology and digitization pertaining to the fact that automatic functioning may turn out to be autocratic in the with time in the future and may lose the most important element of human touch in it. But due to this, many other mundane HR processes are refrained from automation, though it being the most efficient way of carrying out those processes. Also, for certain HR functions there still lingers dilemma about the adoption of cybernation in it questioning the existence of humanitarian part of work in it. Speaking of expanding the purview of Human Resources for plumbing cybernation in the Human Resource proximity at higher echelons, brings in several ethical dilemmas to be addressed. Each and every process amidst the Human Resources ought to be examined for proper amalgamation of the man and machine with respect to the particular function. Moreover, moving forward towards the direction of tech HR, the processes imperative to be automated and the processes demanding personal physical human involvement prominently ought to be sorted and bifurcated for the avoidance of the work disturbances due to the technological disruptions. The most common and largely thought of risk of adopting digital ways in Human Resource realm is that the expeditiously mushrooming machines and automation will risk the requirement of human existence in the organization and the work that is to be done by them. This can be tackled by proper assessment of the requirements and the nature of the varied Human Resource functions. The Artificial Intelligence itself being a by product of the human intelligence can't become a part of every humanitarian activity. Though it is for the advancement and the ease of the human tasks but only up to the extent of the simplification of the complex and tedious processes and not beyond the doubt of the need of human existence in the organization. Each workplace irrespective of the high level of cybernation and well equipped with the developing industrial standards such as 4.o, can't take over the humanist cognitive crucial involvement amidst the corporate environment. Therefore, further discussions in the chapter will pertain to signify the meaning of automation in the Human Resource realm. Moreover, further classification of the areas of HR, which are already automated, the functions that are yet to be adopted with digitalization, the areas of HR which behold the threat to humanist touch and the future scenario of the business acumen with the millennials curbing the HR architecture with the tech HR and the cybernation disruptions, shall be discussed via various themes in this chapter. To broadly examine and understand the optimal and efficiency increasing relationship between the man and the machine, to clarify both, the pros and cons of automation in the domain of the corporate fuel HR.

CYBERNATION AND HR

The realm of Human Resources has a wide plethora of functions directed towards the development and the modernization of the organization. Mainstream minimal HR tasks yet involving humans physically can easily be substituted by the digitalization and cybernation very efficiently. Beginning with a paperless work culture substituting it with digital forms to the data analytics software for systematic organization and management of the bulk and crucial data. In the human resources realm, "HR automation is the process of enhancing the efficiency of the HR department by freeing employees from tedious manual tasks and allowing them to focus on complex tasks like decision making and strategizing. By automating standard and repetitive HR activities, organizations can reduce the cost and time they spend on manual HR planning and processing"– Kissflow, (2018) HR Automation - The Future of Human Resource Process Management. https://kissflow.com/hr-process/ Without hampering the quality of the work, improving the work efficiency, with increased precision, easing the tasks and lessening the excess work burden of the humans, the cybernation in HR aptly plays its role towards the tech HR. Various cybernation interventions have reached and engaged in the respective HR areas by eliminating the need of humans to personally look after these minimalist and easily substitutable tasks. Handling many critical administrative tasks such as selecting profiles with certain skills, filing documents, feeding information, creating and sharing files, etc. These tasks may take hours if processed manually. - Abhishek Upadhyay (2019, July 26). What is HR Automation? - Techrseries (https://www.techrseries.com/primer/what-is-hr-automation/). The digital transformation officers, data scientists, data analysts, digital learning officers are some of the flourishing futuristic tech HR roles, the millennials will be prominently looking up to. Explicitly scrutinizing and reinterpreting the HR functions to integrate the organization's work culture with the pioneering business models will be the work of the millennial Human Resource leaders. By properly examining and understanding the various processes under the domain of Human Resources, the millennial Human Resource leaders accordingly will have to integrate the technology with the respective processes for the adoption of the dynamic business models. The workforce of the contemporary era ought to be tech savvy and upscale and acquaint itself with the digital methodologies to establish a synergy between the man and the machines, escalating the people experience in the organization. The Human Resource leaders of this era constantly need to abreast themselves parallel to the digital developments to stay relevant at the workplace. Cybernation provides greatly as a resource in itself to the Human Resources, diversifying the Human Resource realm. It provides an opportunity of smart work to the humans in the organization to skillfully take the advantage of the optimal utility of the artificial intelligence and the digital pathways to enhance the various work processes. The Human Resource leaders have to be supple to be able to make the best advantage of the technology and automation.

System Synchronizing (a Classic Example of Cybernation)

Laserfiche, comes up with an innovative and interesting concept of Enterprise Content Management (ECM). A streamline software which renders very efficiently within the economy of time. Organizations use this ECM for capturing, storing, securing and accessing information. Right from importing documents into a digital repository, whether they originate on paper or in a digital format to making information simpler to locate during an audit or records request – Laserfiche, (2019). What is Human Resources (HR) Automation https://www.laserfiche.com/ecmblog/what-is-hr-automation/#So cybernation, the digitalization, the artificial intelligence into action in the work environment, manage the vital administrative tasks, which though being of a critical nature are carried out with at most precision, which if manually done, consume a lot of time. The mundane tasks which are crucial to perform, mostly the on paper tasks, are easy to eliminate via the technological substitution. The intensive documentation, bulk data sharing, transferring of files, safe and systematic maintenance of records and many such allied tasks can be simplified by adoption of automation. Cybernation in the work culture reframes the workforce strategy widening the prospective of role of HR and increasing the expectations for the HR analytics. In fact, the comprehension and the ability of using the power of cybernation, proves to be the line separating those constantly updating their skills and being abreast with the dynamically evolving technological trends and those remaining marginalized. Employers had predicted earlier that around 17 percent of work will be automated by 2020, compared to about 5 percent in 2014, according to Willis Tower Watson, a global consulting company. – David Tobenkin (2019 February, 26) HR Needs to Stay Ahead of Automation - SHRM (https://www.shrm.org/hr-today/news/hr-magazine/spring2019/pages/hr-needs-to-stay-ahead-ofautomation.aspx). Also, Gartner in the past had predicted that by 2020 the Artificial Intelligence would have created more than jobs than it would be eliminating. It had envisaged a total of 2.3 million new jobs to have been created in lieu of 1.8 million jobs that would be redundant – Abhijit Rao (2020 March, 5) Tech Upskilling – The Why and How – Peoplematters (https://www.peoplematters.in/article/hr-technology/tech-upskilling-the-why-and-how24899). Therefore, adoption of automation proves to be a positive element fruitful in creating new and more creative jobs.

Uniformity in the Worldwide Cultures

The espousal of automation and digitalization increases the anticipation for uniformity and equanimity in the work culture ecosystem throughout the corporates in the world by paralleling the automation methods used for tasks and the involvement of artificial intelligence unlike the difference caused by when done physically by humans. This tech human integration would open the doors wide for the worldwide integration smoothening and easing the trade and business pathways across various nations. Moreover, it would also reduce the operational differences in the working styles and functions of the various organizations of the world. The best example of uniformity of operations is the industrial revolutions. Currently the corporates of the world have adopted the Industry 4.o. Curbing the current trends in automation and cyber-physical systems, Industry 4.o is the current market niche, driving the tech culture fueling the engines of the various corporate functions of the corporates across the globe. A majority of the leading organizations of the world have integrated their systems with the Industry 4.o therefore it's easy for one organization to establish a connection with the other organization due to the similar formats of their systems and processes. Easing the international integration will improve the economies of the International Human Resource. Aligning the various styles across various work cultures and the HR functions will escalate the echelons of the roles of the international Human Resource. It will provide more time and space for the higher level strategic discussions amidst the HR professionals from various countries promoting innovation and development of more prominent HR roles enriching the employees working experience.

CYBERNATION IMPERATIVE HUMAN RESOURCE AREAS

The realm of Human Resources has a profusion of varied processes. The compliance driven Human Resource processes are onerous and hulking. The tech HR tools grip the cybernation processes providing cost effective and time saving benefits easing the employee management. A majority of the core Human Resource processes possess a wide scope to be automated or to be digitalized, except for a few handful which require great level of personal human attention. Right from the basic process of recruitment and onboarding of the employees to the exit interviews all the processes are positively tech integrating. Either the entire process completely or if not wholly but at least a part of it holds a scope to be automated.

Recruitment and Onboarding

Processes such as recruitment and onboarding though mundane to the HR work culture are important and vital processes for an organization. Integrating these processes with the cybernation changes the panorama of the processes. Data analytics software and automation tools can function very fruitfully in the entire process. Right from the collection and systematic organization of data to the sending of bulk emails, sorting and forming respected required groups in accordance with the systematic arrangement and representation of data. Moreover, securely storing the information inputs made by the candidates. Right from the beginning each candidate profile is lucidly created and as the candidate goes through various processes the profile is auto updated with the respective progress. Further the record of the data is retained once the candidate is hired and becomes a part of the organization. Also, the organized and compiled data can be accessed and referred by the candidate timely, also automation makes the editing and additions an easy task to do. The major advantage of adopting automation in the recruitment and onboarding process is that the software required for this process is a very simple and streamlined software, easy to understand and use. The Human Resource employees with little technical knowledge can also create an automated workflow system using drag and drop interface or customize with a few readily available templates, no special IT experts or field specialists are required for this software development – Kissflow (2019 August, 27), Employee Onboarding, https://kissflow.com/hrprocess/employee-onboarding/

Timesheets and Leave Management

Further, the maintenance of the employee time sheets with automated calculations of the work hours, the leave approvals and the employee payroll. With due consideration about the hate towards the manually prepared timesheets which pose increased chances of neglect and other human errors, overall risking its reliability and being a reason of conflict amidst the organization, the automated time sheets are programmed to work with precision and accuracy. Moreover, the entire leave management becomes a lot easier with the automated software for the same. Both, the organization as well as the employees can track leave records of respective employees. With the software the information about the type of the leaves, the number of leaves taken, number of leaves still remaining, the leave policy everything is on the tips for the employee. So he or she can smoothly schedule meetings and also send timely email alerts for the ease of working, also helps a lot regulating the absenteeism. The preferred arrangement ought to be sufficiently vigorous to consistently deal with every one of the stages associated with leave the executives procedure: application, endorsement/dismissal, recording leaves, overseeing leave equalization, and examination. So the automated timesheets help increase the transparency amidst the employees in the organization. - Open HRMS, (2019 March, 18), Benefits of an automated leave management system https://www.openhrms.com/blog/benefits-of-automated-leave-management-system

Automating the Performance Management System

Integrating the Performance Management System with automation would have been a less acceptable idea initially but today most large organizations have already accepted and acquainted with this transition. Performance Management System being one of the core and most important Human Resource processes is no more an exception in the adoption of automation. Certain functions in the process of performance management system are indeed imperative to automation. Performance management system has been continuously evolving significantly throughout the last decade. Today's performance management system is a very dynamic process with continuous evaluation and measurement harnessing the development of the personnel and aligning it with the organization's mission. Rather than a mere annual event it has become a more interactive process. Therefore, the current ways of performance management work with a streamlined model, ready for customization and also user-friendly. Automating the performance management system is made easier with softwares such as Halogen, TalentSpace, Ceridian Dayforce and SAP Successfactors to name a few. All these softwares are well equipped with built-in functionalities which help in controlling and regulating the visibility, data updating with the user authorization specifics and the facilitation of data across other modules, like compensation planning. –Chiradeep BasuMallick (2018 July, 20) Automating Employee Performance Management -HR Technologist https://www.hrtechnologist.com/articles/performance-management-hcm/automating-employeeperformance-management/ Moreover, the Human Resource Information System (HRIS) is a great integrating agent when performance management is to be curated. According to a report by Deloitte, 76% of the organizations have reinvented their performance management process, making it continuous and 91% of these have better data for people decisions. Automation of the performance management system paralleling today's dynamic workplace, with talents and multitasking and the rapidly changing work roles, it's the holistic reviews that catapult the workplace. – Synergita (2019 July, 24), Performance Management Automation – The Future of Talent Management https://www.synergita.com/blog/performance-management-automation/

Exit Interviews and Off Boarding

With the changing perspectives of every process in the organization, the exit interviews and the off boarding process is also looked up to with an optimistic view rather than blatantly completing the formalities. The corporates these days look at the exit interviews and the off boarding process as an opportunity to understand and examine the reasons for the inflating attrition rates and to seek feedback from the leaving employees before they step out of the organization which may contribute to the growth and betterment of the organization. The overall process of offboarding can be made more systematic by integrating it with the automation. Automating the exit interviews and the overall offboarding process is especially very useful when the number of employees exiting are more in number. An automated system isn't burdened with the more number of employees, it can ensure systematic documentation imperative at the time of the resignation. It makes easy to preserve records for future audits. It makes the handling of checklists a very smooth and accurate task. Analytics create smart ways of bringing out employee responses more honestly and increases the participation in the exit interviews. Also, cybernation of the offboarding process and the exit interviews helps in hiring more wisely in the future by retaining the employee reviews and responses given at the time of the leaving. – Shivasankari Bhuvaneswaran, (2019 November, 12), Employee Offboarding – Kissflow https://kissflow.com/hr-process/employee-offboarding/exit-interviewprocess/ Above mentioned were some of the routine Human Resource processes which had certain areas having a scope for automation, in fact by integrating it with automation and analytics these processes relieved humans from cumbersome tasks which used to unnecessarily burden humans and also were prone to human errors. After overviewing the role of cybernation in the mundane Human Resource processes, it can be clearly observed that cybernation proves to be a resource to the humans in the organization, increasing the value of humans and curbing the perspective of HR professional, projecting them more as human assets rather than human resource. A recent KPMG report found that virtually all HR functions can be fully or partially automated. Of 21 responsibilities, KPMG found only five to be relatively less susceptible to automation: § People performance whole system architecture (building a high-performance work system). § HR and business strategy. § Organizational effectiveness. § Change management. § Employee relations. -David Tobenkin, (2019 February, 26), HR Needs to Stay Ahead of Automation – SHRM https://www.shrm.org/hr-today/news/hr-magazine/spring2019/pages/hr-needs-to-stay-aheadof-automation.aspx Despite of the advent of cybernation in the Human Resources domain and a majority of Human Resource functions integrating very well with automation, the futuristic relevance of the work of humans in the domain of HR seems to be at a risk. But clearly, cybernation cannot completely eliminate the need of humans in the workplace. The millennial Human Resource leaders are projected to be engaging themselves into more important and crucial tasks, the tasks of the processes involving human psyche. The processes that are more people oriented and can't be functional without the personal human touch in it. We are further going to discuss the futuristic relevance of the humans in the workplace, amidst the technological disruptions. How, even with the high level of cybernation the physical human presence in certain tasks is essential.

HUMAN RELEVANCE AMIDST THE CYBERNATION DISRUPTIONS

The all-pervasive cybernation amidst the corporate has impacted the work culture changing the implications of the style of jobs. With the integration of automation in each sphere of the Human Resource realm, the relevance of the humans in the work environment is a growing concern. The expeditious pace of development of the digitalization and the Artificial Intelligence interventions amidst the organization threatens the pace of the development of the employees synchronizing with it. While equipping our organizations with the digitally automated systems, it is very peremptory to ensure the optimal sustainability of the humans in the organizations. We have five generations in the workforce. Digitally native millennials and Gen Z are becoming a larger percent of the workforce. Each group has specific ways in which they like to consume information. Gen Y and Gen Z also expect on-demand access and support, much like we see in the consumer economy. It can clearly be observed that technology is ingraining deeper in the corporate functions and the Human Resources domain has no more remained an exception to this. We need to ensure that the technological intervention is much focused on the algorithms that are fair, interpretable, and based on valid data sets. The Artificial Intelligence must support our goal to create belonging in the workplace. – Jill Larsen, (2019 July, 30), Reskilling Human Resources for the Age of Automation – TLNT https://www.tlnt.com/reskilling-human-resources-for-the-age-of-automation/ Humans are the core of the organizations and moreover, the realm of Human Resources is the domain which is the people oriented domain of the corporate diaspora. Human Resources work for the people oriented functions, they work for the people and by the people. Therefore, it is vital to understand the fact that human requirement and involvement in the domain of the Human Resources is inevitable. In the concurrent era, it is important to upscale and upgrade skills rapidly. The millennial employees necessarily need to be more adaptive towards change and learn to be adjusting with the dynamic work environment, also they ought to increase their powers of grasping and assimilating quick. The key of staying relevant in the era of technological disruptions is creating an amazing talent brand and employee experience by provoking thought leadership and innovation. By taking the advantage of the fact that the monotonous tasks are taken care of by the technology, the HR personnel can engage more in the crucial and effective decision making processes. The Human Resource personnel can make the people experience in the organization more interactive and can make the workplace and the working style more comfortable for the employees of the organization. Also, they would be able to enhance the customer experience with the organization by personally being able to pay attention to the certain important issues which otherwise were hard to pay personal attention to. Right since the beginning man has been craving for appreciation. Appreciation is that satisfying need of the humans which is a great driver of motivation. Even the hierarchy of needs by Abraham Maslow marks the esteem needs and the self-actualization needs as the highest of all other basic needs. These needs directly trigger the human psyche. Praise and words of appreciation which fill the humans with the feelings of prestige and accomplishment. No programmed machine of artificial intelligence can have the degree of human emotions. A set of programmed expressions instilled in the Artificially Intelligent robots cannot be compared with the natural human emotions. The feeling of empathy can no way be explained and instilled in the machines. A human needs another human to share and care. The term millennial is paralleled by the term which has an increased focus and attention which is the mental health. With the rapidly increasing technological disruptions and dynamism in the work culture, it is indeed hard and stressful, staying abreast with the constant changes and upscaling regularly. Therefore, the futuristic Human Resources millennial leaders ought to imbibe the art of not just change management but also stress management. The best way of stress management comes out from the increased interpersonal human interaction. Hence, for making further developments and innovations humans need these person to person interactions which involve the human touch. Also, it is interesting to observe and understand a very important fact of the human psyche while speaking of the man v/s machine comparisons. Machines have been man's creation and man possesses high self-esteem, therefore man won't ever let the machines takeover his position.

CONCLUSION

Hence, it can be concluded from the above study that though the relevance of man with the increase of machines may be questioned but the real debate or comparison of man v/s machine turns out to be a futile one. The domain of Human Resources has always been the most people guarded corporate domain and though by automating the basic functions and processes, the futuristic relevance of humans is quite clearly secure. Man and Machines are ought to be working in synchronization. Corporates have been and are bound to develop with and by humans and the Human Resources guards the corporate periphery.

REFERENCES

Abhishek Upadhyay. (2019, July 26). *What is HR Automation? Techrseries*. Available at https://www.techrseries.com/primer/what-is-hr-automation/

BasuMallick. (2018, July 20). *Automating Employee Performance Management-HR Technologist*. Available at https://www.hrtechnologist.com/articles/performance-management-hcm/automating-employee-performance-management/

Bhuvaneswaran. (2019, November 12). *Employee Offboarding – Kissflow*. Available at https://kissflow.com/hr-process/employee-offboarding/exit-interview-process/

Kissflow. (2018). *HR Automation - The Future of Human Resource Process Management*. Available at https://kissflow.com/hr-process/

Kissflow. (2019, August 27). *Employee Onboarding*. Available at https://kissflow.com/hr-process/employee-onboarding/

Larsen. (2019, July 30). *Reskilling Human Resources for the Age of Automation – TLNT*. Available at https://www.tlnt.com/reskilling-human-resources-for-the-age-of-automation/

Laserfiche. (2019). *What is Human Resources (HR) Automation*. Available at https://www.laserfiche.com/ecmblog/what-is-hr-automation/

Open, H. R. M. S. (2019, March 18). *Benefits of an automated leave management system*. Available at https://www.openhrms.com/blog/benefits-of-automated-leave-management-system>

Rao. (2020, March 5). *Tech Upskilling – The Why and How – People matters*. Available at https://www.peoplematters.in/article/hr-technology/tech-upskilling-the-why-and-how-24899

Synergita. (2019, July 24). *Performance Management Automation – The Future of Talent Management*. Available at https://www.synergita.com/blog/performance-management-automation/

Tobenkin. (2019, February 26). *HR Needs to Stay Ahead of Automation – SHRM*. Available at https://www.shrm.org/hr-today/news/hr-magazine/spring2019/pages/hr-needs-to-stay-ahead-of-automation.aspx

Chapter 9
Huawei, China, and Ideological Tensions in the 5G Telecommunications Platforms

Bruno Mascitelli
Swinburne University of Technology, Australia

Mona Chung
North China University of Technology, China

ABSTRACT

While the COVID 19 pandemic has captured the attention of the geo-political agenda throughout 2020, pushing the Huawei controversy off the front pages of the news, the hysteria and suspicions around Huawei providing their lower cost telecommunications equipment to Western nations reached new crescendos in the move towards 5G communication platforms. The purpose of this chapter is to examine the recent series of escalating tensions between Huawei and Western nations. While there was a first run of tension with the 4G networks, it was to be repeated with the preparations for the 5G telecommunications platforms. Alongside this expansion was the parallel development of geo-political tensions between China and Western powers. This included ongoing tensions over the South China Sea, Taiwan's relationship with China, the Hong Kong issue, the trade war with the United States, and general diplomacy between China and the West. The chapter seeks to provide the likely result on how these tensions would be resolved.

INTRODUCTION

The purpose of this chapter is to explore and recount the ways which the hue and cry over Huawei and its competitive telecommunications equipment is dividing opinion and nations on its suitability for involvement in the telecommunications rollout. Moreover, this chapter seeks to examine the significance of this renewed Huawei exclusion from some western telecommunication projects and whether this is an ongoing cold war play out through the ongoing "strategic mistrust" between the two key sides or whether there is a genuine act of business fear of stronger competition. It should be said that some western na-

DOI: 10.4018/978-1-7998-4787-8.ch009

tions – not all are following the US lead and pursuing their own national interests and cheaper telecommunications platforms by using Huawei. At the same time the concerns about Huawei as a "security threat" may have some bearing on the decisions to impede its involvement in these 5G rollouts. Added to this is also the case of a not so discreet measure to hinder telecommunications competition in what is a ruthlessly competitive global industry, with strong US and global players. Whether it be due to Cold War legacies or business competition, these "commercial" exclusions do not sit well in this globalised economy. The concern by some western nations, and the pretence of a security threat felt by nations is largely due to the perceived "closeness" of Huawei to the Chinese State and leadership. Before addressing the recent tensions involving Huawei, it is worth drawing on some history and context to this standoff as a backdrop to this standoff.

The Origins of the Telecommunications Giant – Huawei

The origins of Huawei as a telecommunications giant and representative of China's growing international stature is instructive of both its growth as well as that of China. The telecommunications giant began as in 1987 by founder Ren Zhengfei in the industrial area of Shenzen, with only fourteen employees at the time. Much of the origins of Huawei is often focused around the early career of its founder. Ren worked in the civil engineering sector of the military reaching the rank of colonel where he also worked as Director of the Information Engineering Academy. For conscripts in the People's Liberation Army (PLA), this military experience was quite common in his generation and it is this association which has caught public attention from foreign observers and which is the purported evidence of the link between Huawei and the Chinese military. In the military Ren also worked on bridge building and civil construction, ironically almost not at all in the telecommunication field. After the disbandment of his PLA unit, Ren moved to the Shenzhen South Sea Oil Corporation (SSSOC), another state-owned enterprise (SOE) and in the late 1980s as the government began pushing telecommunications switch technology, he left SSSOC to start Huawei Technologies (Ahrens 2013). Ren was hugely influential in the company, although he only held only 1.3 per cent of the shares. The remaining shares are owned by all employees. Mindful of the perception and association with the PLA in his early days, he was then and more so now, unconcerned and dismissive of his early connection to the PLA.

As China began moving to a more market-oriented and open economy after the Deng's economic forms and open-door policy in 1979 (Chung 2010), that his strong interest in telecommunication activities eventually emerged (Lord 2012). In its start-up operations, Huawei engaged in reverse engineering in its early telecommunications business. It made no secret of copying Cisco, Fujitsu and others to the extent that it was also known as the "Cisco of China" (Buderi & Huang 2006: 206). These were important advances in its attempt to stand on its feet and thereby be able to engage in innovative telecommunications investing its profits into more research and development. Huawei made important advances from its early location in the Special Economic Zone of Shenzhen, one of China's initial experiments with the free market. Throughout the 1990s Huawei grew its commercial business across China and in 1992 the Chinese government urged China to become a leading player in global telecommunications. China was not content with being a customer of foreign technologies and information technology and saw telecommunications as being a truly innovative technology critical for nation building (Chung & Mascitelli 2014). At a certain point Huawei knew it needed to turn its attention also to the foreign market and for this purpose it was provided a US$10 billion line of credit by the China Development Bank and a $US600 million loan from China's Export-Import Bank (Wesley 2011:38). By 2005 Huawei's global sales had now outperformed its China sales making it one of the few telecommunication multinational firms in China. This strong international presence continued and by 2012 two-thirds of Huawei's business was located outside of China, making Huawei the world's largest telecoms vendor by revenue. In 2018 Huawei surpassed Sweden's Ericsson AB to become the world's largest telecom equipment supplier, despite moves by the U.S. and Australia to limit official use of products from the Chinese tech giant (Tan 2018).

A History of Allegations Against Huawei

The controversy around Huawei has a long history which according to one scholar goes back to 2001 when Indian security services accuse Huawei of aiding Taliban! Reports from India's intelligence agencies, led to the placing of Huawei's India operations on a watch list for "alleged business dealings with the Taliban, Pakistan and Iraq". At the time India's authorities were considering expelling 178 Chinese engineers working at the Bangalore R&D centre. The allegations were denied by Huawei as being "untrue" and the Company was "is in compliance with the United Nations' standards and regulations" (Magee 2019).

Not surprisingly the strongest objection to Huawei's operation came in 2003 from Cisco – now a strong US rival of Huawei. Cisco sued Huawei alleging that Huawei had "unlawfully copied intellectual property from the American networking infrastructure firm". The allegations related to Cisco's assertions that Huawei had copied Cisco IOS software, including source code, as well as documentation and other materials, plus infringements of Cisco patents. After years of legal exchanges Huawei and Cisco came to a settlement out of court in 2014, in exchange for a promise from Huawei to modify its product (Twain 2017).

In 2005 British Marconi came under fire for engaging in merger talks with Huawei and the other major Chinese telecommunications provider, ZTE. The negotiations for "potential business combinations" did not proceed very far before its collapse in 2006. Ultimately financial difficulties led to the collapse of Marconi in 2006, when much of the business was sold to the Swedish telco infrastructure company Ericsson (Associated Press 2005).

In 2007 the Bush administration was warned on a Huawei possible deal with 3Com. Following a joint venture between Cisco rival 3Com and Huawei in China called H3C Technology, Bain Capital agreed to buy 3Com in its entirety for more than $2 billion with minority equity financing from Huawei in 2007, translating to a 16.5 percent stake in the overall business. It was this that prompted elements within Congress to complain to Bush that the deal should not be approved by the Committee on Foreign Investment in the United States (Flynn & Bradsher, 2007). One Republican representative Ileana Ros-Lehtinen led the calls stating it would "be a grave error for US regulators to approve a deal that permits minority ownership in 3Com by one of the least transparent companies operating in China, a firm with shadowy ties to Chinese army and intelligence services." The deal failed, with Hewlett Packard ultimately picking up 3Com in late 2009 (Drawbaugh, 2007).

In March 2009 the UK government warned over BT 21CN network - Alex Allan, who was chairman of the Joint Intelligence Committee, told then-home secretary Jacqui Smith that the steps BT had taken to secure its network for the 21CN network transformation rollout in Britain might not have been adequate. Ministers heard that Britain hadn't paid "sufficient attention to the threat [from Huawei] in the past," according to one observer (Williams 2009) that GCHQ had also warned that the network would have been open for the targeting of attacks from China. Officials in Britain noted that the risk was low, but that the impact of such an attack would be high (Williams 2009).

In 2010 former GCHQ boss,Andrew Hopkins now an independent consultancy owner but previously a deputy director at GCHQ, joined Huawei and was based at the centre in Banbury. The Sunday Times noted that he was once head of engineering and procurement at GCHQ, having been around the intelligence world for 40 years. In the same year Huawei opened its Cyber Security Evaluation Centre (HCSEC) in Banbury, Oxfordshire. it was to be overseen by CESG, part of GCHQ, to test Huawei products and equipment for security holes (Kerbaj 2013). Huawei said at the time "The aim of this security centre is to address growing concerns from organisations, and from governments generally, about the safety of cyberspace and the need for built-in network protection to help society and businesses withstand malicious attacks from the outside" (Kerbaj 2013).

In 2011, John Suffolk, who had previously held a high-ranking position in the civil service as the government's CIO, joined Huawei from the role to head up the firm's global cybersecurity efforts. He had been CIO and senior information risk owner since 2006. He had to consult former British prime minister David Cameron for clearance to join Huawei, which was approved. As part of the agreement Suffolk would have to steer clear of direct work with government for two years - which included lobbying and government endorsements. Suffolk remains at Huawei (Hall 2011).

In 2012 matters escalated to new heights. Triggering the concern was 2012 Huawei being banned from Australia's National Broadband Network by the Australian government citing security concerns in March of that year (Ingraham 2012). This occurred even when Huawei had worked to create an oversight board to examine its equipment - with former foreign minister Alexander Downer leading the effort. At the time even Downer, certainly no friend of China, thought the "whole concept of Huawei being involved in cyber warfare is based on the company being Chinese" and that the scandal was "ridiculous" (ITNews 2012).

Some months later the US followed suite with the Australian Huawei verdict. In October a US House of Representatives Intelligence Committee report warned of the potential for state influence threats from both Huawei and ZTE. The report presented by the chairman of the committee, Mike Rogers, said that they had received allegations of strange behaviour from using equipment from Huawei and ZTE, including sending packets of data to China overnight. The report suggested to the Committee on Foreign Investment in the United States that contracts with Huawei or ZTE be blocked which is what happened.

Surprisingly in the same year British Prime Minister David Cameron met with Huawei founder Ren Zhengfei to confirm a £1.3 billion investment in Britain including research and development spend and its employee headcount. The meeting saw Huawei mark £650 million for operations work in the UK, and £650 million for procurement in the five years that would follow. Against the "Five Eyes" sentiment, Cameron noted that this Huawei investment "demonstrates once again that the UK is open for business" and that Britain valued the "important relationship with China" (Whittaker 2012). Ren Zhengfei responded accordingly "The UK is one of the most important European markets in which Huawei has invested. Over the past 11 years we have found its government to be transparent, efficient and practical. The UK is an open market, which welcomes overseas investment" (Whittaker 2012). While this was by no means Huawei's first major investment in the UK, it cemented future investment patterns before the more recent controversies erupted.

Soon after the block on Huawei in the US in 2012, American telecommunication carriers agree to block Huawei deals which began with Sprint Nextel which was acquired by Japanese conglomerate SoftBank, whereby the two entities agreed not to use technology from Huawei (Dyer & Kirchgaessner 2013). Huawei's response towards the US began to consolidate around an impossible situation whatever

Huawei did. In 2013 Eric Xu, who had become one of the three rotating Chairmen of the company made the statement that after these US pronouncements that Huawei is no longer interested in the US market.

On a visit to Australia in 2013 former CIA head Michael Hayden described Huawei as an "unambiguous national security threat to the US and Australia". In a statement to the Australian Financial Review he stated that "I reviewed Huawei's briefing paper…But God did not make enough slides on Huawei to convince me that having them involved in our critical communications infrastructure was going to be OK" (Smith & Joye 2014).

With Britain on the other hand, Cameron came under scrutiny and criticism for having engaged with Huawei. In late 2013 Cameron was forced to defend the use of Huawei investment following a visit of American senators insisting that Huawei equipment posed a security risk. Cameron responded by stating the UK-Huawei £1.3 billion deal whereby the UK had a "proper system in the UK for examining whether investments in the UK are pro-competitive and whether they're in the national interest". However, in a move behind the scenes Cameron ensured that further security checks took place at the Huawei security centre in Banbury. In 2014 numerous checks were made on the Huawei code and even after Huawei giving the entirety of its source code over to the info security experts at GCHQ but concluded that there was no evidence Huawei presented "any risk to the UK's national security," …"and no evidence of espionage" (Computer Weekly 2014).

In 2016 Huawei demonstrated its superiority over other vendors on security patching. Despite the long list of controversies and fears, Huawei performed remarkably well on security patching tests, when compared to other Android vendors such as Samsung and its other competitors (Magee 2019). Months later further allegations of industrial espionage emerged again in the US with the "'Tappy the Robot" controversy when it was alleged that Huawei had stolen IP from T-Mobile USA concerning a phone-testing robot used by American carrier Tappy. The Tappy controversy would return in January 2019 when the first assistant US attorney Annette Hayes described Huawei's actions as a "flagrant abuse of the law" (Eggerton 2019).

Matters escalated to fever pitch in the 2018 and 2019 period with greater pressure on decision making for 5G networks. Clearly the Huawei question would re-emerge and did so with a vengeance. Washington engaged in vigorous campaign with its allies to ban Huawei from its new 5G networks. US Officials briefed countries including Germany, Italy, and Japan, and the US was even considering increasing financial aid for countries that did not sign up to contracts with Chinese vendors. The Huawei response took little time to become public. They were "surprised by the behaviours of the US government" and that if a government's behaviour "extends beyond its jurisdiction, such activity should not be encouraged". In the UK, the US message was not being welcomed whole heatedly. Vodafone's incoming chief executive Nick Read backed Huawei - and described it as being "actively engaged" with British and European security agencies. "I think they're doing everything possible to ensure they remain a very serious and credible supplier" (Pham 2019). Another voice of support for Huawei came from Neil McRae, chief network architect for BT Group, described Huawei as the "only one true 5G supplier" at a Huawei event in London (Le Maistre 2019).

Meanwhile in 2016 the US had emerged with possible Iran sanction violations from Huawei. Prosecutors in New York had been investigating Huawei for the potential violation of US sanctions on Iran and concerned Huawei allegedly shipping products that originated in the USA to Iran, and therefore "a violation of US export and sanctions laws". Then in late 2018 came the extraordinary arrest in Canada of Huawei CFO Meng Wanzhou, Chief financial officer of Huawei and daughter of founder Ren Zhengfei where she was threatened with extradition to the USA - under the pretence of sanctions violations pertaining to

Iran. The accusations appear to relate to Meng serving on the board of a Hong Kong business Skycom which is alleged to have worked with Iran between 2009 and 2014. Huawei responded by stating that it "complies with all applicable laws and regulations where it operates, including applicable export control and sanction laws and regulations of the UN, US and EU" (Arthur 2018). This arrest was happening ironically at the same moment that President Xi and President Trump were attending the G20 meeting in Argentina where they were seeking a compromise on averting a US-China trade war as well as to de-escalate the growing tensions between these two countries. While the China-US trade tensions have remained, the fate of Meng Wanzhou and her extradition to the US is still being decided by the Canadian courts. The Huawei question has risen to become a global debate especially amongst advanced western nations in their endeavour to provide a policy towards the development of their 5G telecommunications platform. Most western nations involved, especially those involved in the "Five Eyes" group falling in line with excluding Huawei from their platforms while others have continued with their involvement with this Chinese company in their telecommunications rollout. In an interview with the BBC with Ren Zhengfei suggested that the arrest of his daughter was politically motivated and that there was "no way the US can crush us...Even if they persuade more countries not to use us temporarily, we can always scale things down a bit" (BBC 2019).

The Current State of Huawei Relations With Global Telecoms Providers

Fundamentally what is at issue was broader than an isolated arrest of a Huawei manager, as one observer aptly noted:

It is natural to assume that the detentions and restrictions on Huawei's use in core infrastructure are due to the rupture in US-China trade relations. However, these actions can best be understood through the prism of two clashing meta-trends: hi-tech's strategic importance across the realms of defence, commerce and social organisation under the leadership of the United States, and China's emergence as a rising military power under the auspices of the Communist Party (Friedlander 2018).

In early 2019 Huawei's founder,Ren Zhengfei in an interview in a round table to global media companies, the Financial Times, Wall Street Journal and Bloomberg denied that the Chinese government had asked for help to spy using the firm's technology. He went on to say "I love my country, I support the Communist Party...But I will not do anything to harm the world. I don't see a close connection between my personal political beliefs and the businesses of Huawei" (Magee 2019).

In February 2019 Trump announced that he would be discussing the possibility of dropping the charges against Huawei as part of the US-China trade deal under discussion. Huawei on the other hand remained defiant with its founder declaring that the US would not be able to crush Huawei. Throughout most of 2019, Trump threatened to legislate against any possible collusion of American companies with Huawei. This was followed by charges being prepared against the daughter of Huawei founder which included 23 charges including bank fraud, obstruction of justice and Intellectual theft. At the Davos World Economic Forum meeting in January 2019 a senior Huawei executive pressed by reporters to address restrictions against Huawei in various western countries, responded that Huawei could move its operations to nations where it was welcomed.

The Huawei concern took on importance as platforms were coming closer to the preparation of the 5G platforms. In the UK, throwing a spanner in the works, MI6 leader Alex Louder notes that blocking

Huawei from these telecommunications projects was not a good thing citing monopoly processes which would not be a good outcome. Suppliers should be accepted on the basis of their product and quality and "this has nothing to do with the country of origin…We should be insisting on the highest level of quality in any form of technology platform or service we choose to use and in particular security quality" (Magee 2019). The comments were equally endorsed by GCHQ director Robert Hannigan putting the "Five Eyes" united front against Huawei in difficulty.

The Role of the "5 Eyes" in the Huawei Campaign

The "Five Eyes" have been at the forefront of concern for Huawei. The Five Eyes alliance is an intelligence information sharing agreement between Canada, the United States, the United Kingdom, Australia and New Zealand. Its origins trace back to Anglo-American cooperation in World War II and with New Zealand joining in 1956. The challenge of what to do with Huawei has created fractures amongst this intelligence cooperation. With the United States, New Zealand and Australia already barring Huawei from their network, and the UK placing an extremely arduous configuration on the company's operations in the UK, Canada remains as the last fully undecided party.

In the case of Canada, the US Senate Intelligence committee warned Canada that its role in the intelligence alliance will be questioned should Canada decide to collaborate with Huawei. This is significant because it represents a possible turning point in the nuanced relationship, not only between members of the Five Eyes alliance, but between Canada and the United States. Canada is being strongly cautioned by the United States to choose "security over consumer convenience", who believe that Huawei is being controlled by the Chinese Communist Party. Despite Huawei's denial of involvement with the government, the fear regarding ties to the Chinese government resides in the Chinese law that mandates Chinese companies to cooperate with the government upon a request to do so.

The White House former security adviser in 2019 John Bolton, noted that Huawei was the tip of the iceberg in terms of Chinese penetration of western societies. He noted:

China's efforts to influence opinion in America via Confucius Centres and other ways trumped Russia's election hacking. …It is really far greater in magnitude than any other foreign effort we have seen in history to influence American opinion and it's not just confined to the United States…They are doing it in Australia and other countries – close friends of ours (Mitchell 2019).

Fractures within the "Five Eyes" have emerged over each nation's handling of Huawei involvement in their telecommunications operations for the 5G platform. In February 2019, pressure was brought to bear on the UK for failing to ban Huawei with the threat of being excluded from the Five Eyes organisation. The report stated:

Worries about security of UK networks following their exposure to Huawei may make the Five Eyes partners, and perhaps others such as France, Germany or Japan, less inclined to co-operate with the UK in the future (Bourke 2019).

Huawei has made many gestures to reassure its audience and client governments of its credentials and security record. Besides being prepared to "…offer complete and unrestricted access to our software source code and equipment" (Lord 2012), Huawei even appointed as its global cyber-security chief, former chief information officer of the British government, John Suffolk (Hall 2011). This approach by Huawei to find reliable representatives of the country who might be able quash any concern about security was adapted across a range of markets. In hindsight it is a strategy that did not have its desired effects (Chung & Mascitelli 2014). As one observer noted: "Even if the US and its allies in the Five Eyes intelligence network (the UK, Australia, Canada and New Zealand) completely opt out of dealing with Huawei, most countries in the world will adopt 5G networks based on Chinese technology" (Mahbubani 2019). What is fundamentally at issue for the "Five Eyes" is the dilemma and nexus between information sharing and security. However if Huawei, would provide its services at the lowest cost on the market, spearheads this movement, and could divide the Five Eyes alliance.

Moreover, the much-cited security concerns over these Chinese companies were to some observers, "exaggerated". As one scholar noted:

... the reaction to Huawei harks back to the fear in the 1980s of Japanese companies that were overtaking the U.S. auto industry and buying up iconic pieces of real estate, such as the Rockefeller building in New York... It was long thought that we were the number-one economy and China just supplied cheap labor... Now it is clear that China has a lot to offer in terms of innovation and industrial policy and state investment, and now people are scared (Guthrie cited in Kang 2013).

China and Huawei – Permanent US-China Distrust?

According to Shambaugh the rise of China has rendered it to be a major competitive player alongside traditional western powers:

It's mainly a competitive relationship in all areas, economic, strategic, political, ideological even cultural.... So this is a new characteristic of the relationship and we have to get used to the fact that we are going to get a tense relationship, we cannot continue to naively hope that the two sides will love each other and get along (Cited in Yingzi 2012).

This growing tension alluded to by Shambaugh has of course never really ceased especially since China entered the WTO in 2001. What has changed is China's ability to economically challenge and compete with developed nations and that includes the US. This standoff between growing Chinese economic penetration and irritation from the developed western economies about the encroaching economic nature of China has now touched new heights (Chung & Mascitelli 2014).

The exclusion of Huawei from the 5G telecommunications infrastructures in this case are even more pronounced with global campaigns to shut out Chinese firms and Chinese influence. An even more aggressive anti-China stance on trade promoted from the US White House and Donald Trump in a bi-partisan mode tells us that this will be a new norm. Complicating this new standoff is however a series of new factors which were not present a decade ago. First the Belt and Road initiative which is inducing numerous governments along the route and outside to subscribe to this infrastructure investment producing large projects and greater connectedness between Asia, Europe and Africa. Second is the fact that the US once the bastion of free trade is resorting to protectionism which is unsettling the global trade environment. A third factor is that China has emerged as a global power which a decade ago was not yet a fact and in another decade could see China being a bigger economy than the US. Finally, China is economically penetrating the globe and posing scenarios which are unsettling previous security arrangements and the global power environment.

The standoff on Huawei raises an ongoing state of affairs in relation to the US and China relations. While the Trump approach may have shaken US global order approach, especially in creating an uncertainty with US allies and rivals, the China issue is however bipartisan in approach. Trump has contributed little different to what Obama and previous democrats had declared over the years. The realisation that China was the enemy is a joint position agreed upon by both parties in the US system. The move of Trump to the White House in early 2017 produced some surprising foreign policy moves. The supportive view towards Brexit, the view of a German dominated European Union, the foreign affairs consequence of "making America great again" protectionist stance on American goods and services. Equally the shifting of the US Embassy from Tel Aviv to Jerusalem or even the implied softness towards Russia and its alleged interference in US elections. Trump national security advisor John Bolton, also national security advisor to George W Bush, in March 2019 issued further warnings on Huawei about "Manchurian" chips in Huawei technology which can be used for espionage (Mitchell 2019). However, what has not changed in the American rhetoric is its hostility and wariness towards China, a bipartisan approach shared with his predecessor in Barack Obama and firmly ingrained in US foreign policy. In early 2019 Democrat and Republican congressman introduced bills that would require the President to ban the export of US components to any Chinese telecommunications company that violates US sanctions or export control laws (The Age 2019, p. 19).

For US allies, the Trump factor has another dimension to it which the Democratic Party leadership and establishment is acutely aware of and which has been playing out since the arrival of Trump to the White House. While western security has been the mainstay of post war security, the slow decline of the US as a world power and the rise of China is placing many former US allies into dilemmas about future security and economic relations. The US decline which began long before the arrival of Trump and which has acquired greater awareness with US chastisement of NATO allies, Europe and the European Union with concern that "making America great again" where international institutions like the UN, the WTO had become too favourable of China and being

The fact that China continues to have a centrally planned economy where the State is the ultimate decider. While it has strands of a dual economy where State Owned Enterprises (SOEs) remain a key part of the economy and that it is still a centrally planned economy where capitalist enterprises do not run the economy or the country is the matter which confuses and upsets many western nations. Is this the extent of the threat?

CONCLUSION

Huawei is a giant Chinese telecommunications company which has become the focus of contract exclusion and finger pointing by certain western governments for allegedly being close to the Chinese government and spying on foreign nations. In its earlier days as a developing telecommunications provider, it also distributed Cisco products and eventually became a competitor to this American telecommunications powerhouse. Many of the allegations of impropriety from the US political establishment stemmed from Cisco allegations against Huawei. China's growth as a multinational has also coincided with the growth of China as a global economic and political power in the last two decades. For the purposes of 4G rollout, the US and Australia in 2012 the forefront initially excluded Huawei from their telecommunications infrastructure on the grounds of "national security". At the time the US stated that Huawei could not be free of influence from Beijing and could be used to undermine US and western security. Only months earlier a similar verdict was announced by the Australian (Labour) government in relation to bids for the National Broadband Network (NBN) from the Chinese Huawei. In both cases alleged closeness to the Chinese government and especially its intelligence arm was offered as the reason for barring Huawei from bidding. This Huawei has always denied.

With the upcoming 5g rollout the matter has resurfaced with predictable responses. The underlying characteristics keep evolving and China is becoming a bigger economic power and its multinationals are thriving alongside. It is unlikely that the standoff between the major western powers and Huawei will change anytime soon. No amount of denial from Huawei will change the distrust which has emerged especially from the US. The Chinese economy will continue to operate around its SOE's and the Chinese economy, as we saw with the Corona Virus response will have strong government input and regulation. At the same time the power of the US economy is in slow decline and the choices for other western powers will be to respond in what is in their own interest which might be no longer to follow the directives of the US. This is a line none of these nations wish to pursue but might pose themselves as a necessity which will traverse the geopolitical legacy of the past. Time will tell.

REFERENCES

Ahrens, N. (2013). *China's competitiveness: myth, reality and lessons for the United States and Japan: Case Study Huawei, February 2013.* Center for Strategic and International Studies.

Arthur, C. (2018). *Huawei, sanctions and software: everything you need to know.* The Guardian. https://www.theguardian.com/technology/2018/dec/08/huawei-sanctions-software-what-you-need-to-know

Associated Press. (2005). *China's Huawei pursues Britain's Marconi.* China Daily. https://www.chinadaily.com.cn/english/doc/2005-08/10/content_467796.htm

BBC. (2019). *The US cannot crush us, says Huawei founder, Interview with Huawei founder Ren Zhengfei.* BBC. https://www.bbc.com/news/business-47274679

Bourke, L. (2019). *Britain warned it must ban Huawei.* The Age.

Buderi, R., & Huang, G. (2006). *Guanxi: Microsoft, China and Bill Gates's plan to win the road ahead.* Random House.

Caldwell, C. (2012, Oct. 20). US consensus on free trade is breaking down. *Financial Times.*

Chung, M. (2010). *Doing business successfully in China.* Chandos Publishing.

Chung, M., & Mascitelli, B. (2014). *Huawei's Battle: Cold War or Commercial War? In Asian Business and Management Practices: Trends and Global Considerations.* IGI Publishing.

Drawbaugh, K. (2007). *Huawei-3Com deal threatens U.S. security: lawmakers.* Reuters Agency. https://www.reuters.com/article/us-3com-congress/huawei-3com-deal-threatens-u-s-security-lawmakers-idUSN1537679420071015

Dyer, G., & Kirchgaessner, S. (2013). *Sprint agrees to shun Huawei equipment*. Financial Times. https://www.ft.com/content/45e16976-97f0-11e2-97e0-00144feabdc0

Eggerton, J. (2019). *Huawei Indicted for Theft, Fraud and More: Justice points to effort to steal T-Mobile tech*. Broadcasting Cable.com. https://www.broadcastingcable.com/news/huawei-indicted-for-theft-fraud-and-more

Flynn, L., & Bradsher, K. (2007). *Bain and Chinese Company to Acquire 3Com*. New York Times. https://www.nytimes.com/2007/09/29/technology/29com.html

Friedlander, J. (2018). *How the arrest of Huawei's Meng Wanzhou may mark the start of the great China-US technology decoupling*. https://www.scmp.com/comment/insight-opinion/united-states/article/2179520/how-arrest-huaweis-meng-wanzhou-may-mark-start

Hall, K. (2011). *Former government CIO John Suffolk joins Huawei as head of cybersecurity*. Computer Weekly. https://www.computerweekly.com/news/2240105220/Former-government-CIO-John-Suffolk-joins-Huawei-as-head-of-cybersecurity

Ingraham, N. (2012). *Australia bans Huawei from bidding on broadband network buildout due to security concerns*. The Verge. https://www.theverge.com/2012/3/26/2903097/australia-ban-huawei-national-broadband-network-bid

ITNews. (2012). *Downer blasts Huawei links to cyber attacks: Former foreign minister blasts NBN ban*. https://www.itnews.com.au/news/downer-blasts-huawei-links-to-cyber-attacks-294934

Kerbaj, R. (2013). *Chinese firm Huawei hires former GCHQ chief*. The Sunday Times. https://www.thetimes.co.uk/article/chinese-firm-huawei-hires-former-gchq-chief-637q3f2583z

Le Maistre, R. (2018). *BT's McRae: Huawei Is 'the Only True 5G Supplier Right Now*. https://www.lightreading.com/mobile/5g/bts-mcrae-huawei-is-the-only-true-5g-supplier-right-now/d/d-id/747734

Lord, J. (2012). *National Press Club address*. Australian Financial Review. https://www.afr.com/rw/20092014/AFR/2012/10/24/-Photos-/030a5b50-1d7d-11e2-80929ae2fdd1541e_John%20Lord%20National-%20Press%20Club%20Address.pdf

Magee, T. (2019). *Huawei controversies timeline*. Computerworld UK. https://www.computerworld.com/article/3427998/huawei-controversies-timeline.html

Mahbubani, K. (2019). *The US strategy is not the best way to deal with Huawei*. Financial Times. https://www.ft.com/content/3d489be2-3e73-11e9-9499-290979c9807a

Mitchell, P. (2019, Mar. 12). Trump aide warns on Huawei. The Age.

Pham, M. (2019). *Vodafone chief slams Huawei exclusions*. Mobile World. https://www.mobileworldlive.com/featured-content/home-banner/vodafone-chief-slams-huawei-exclusions/

Smith, P., & Joye, C. (2014). *NSA spy praises Huawei ban*. Australian Financial Review. https://www.afr.com/policy/foreign-affairs/nsa-spy-praises-huawei-ban-20140508-itzhy

Tan, J. (2018). *Huawei Now World's Largest Telecom Equipment-Maker*. CX Daily Briefing. https://www.caixinglobal.com/2018-03-19/huawei-now-worlds-largest-telecom-equipment-maker-101223256.html

Twain, A. (2017). *Cisco Vs Huawei — Which One is the better Choice for Ethernet Switches?* Medium. https://medium.com/@lia640230/cisco-vs-huawei-which-one-is-the-better-choice-for-ethernet-switches-59ffd324117d

Wesley, M. (2011). *There goes the neighbourhood: Australia and the rise of Asia*. University of New South Wales Limited.

Whittaker, Z. (2012). *Huawei to invest $2B in U.K. amid ongoing 'spying' claims*. Cnet.com. https://www.cnet.com/news/huawei-to-invest-2b-in-u-k-amid-ongoing-spying-claims/

Williams, C. (2009). *BT network 'vulnerable to Chinese attack'*. The Register. https://www.theregister.co.uk/2009/03/30/huawei_threat/

Chapter 10
What Are the Leading Bank-Specific and Macroeconomic Factors Influencing Islamic Bank Performance?
New Evidence From MENA Countries

Mosharrof Hosen
https://orcid.org/0000-0002-9301-4318
Universiti Tunku Abdul Rahman, Kampar, Malaysia

ABSTRACT

Despite the proven sustainability and growth of Islamic banks during the financial crisis period, many scholars criticise the current performance of Islamic banks. Therefore, policymakers are continuously getting worried due to inconclusive finding of different research related to Islamic bank profitability. To shed the light of raising concern, this study investigates the issue from considering both macroeconomic and bank-specific factors. The annual cross-sectional data has been collected from 46 Islamic banks in 10 selected MENA countries over the period 2015-2019. The standardized pooled ordinary least square (OLS) approach's findings revealed that bank size, capital adequacy, GDP, and inflation have a significant positive impact on Islamic banks' return on asset, but asset quality has no significant effect on ROA. In contrast, most of the variables have an insignificant effect of ROE. Investors, financial analysts, and policymakers will get benefits from this study's results to secure their investment by successfully controlling the above-mentioned leading factors.

DOI: 10.4018/978-1-7998-4787-8.ch010

INTRODUCTION

In 2007-2008, during the global financial crisis, the financial world observed the limitation of conventional banking system where Islamic financial system showed its continuous sustainability and growth (Ftiti, Nafti, & Sreiri, 2013; Trad, Trabelsi, & Goux, 2017). Based on the statement published by Islamic Finance Development Report (IFDR) 2018[1], there are remarkably increased in Shariah-compliant assets which was $200 billion only during 2003 and raised to $2.44 trillion in 2017. Moreover, the Islamic financial system has been accepted by more than 80 countries and operating with around 1400 institutions, where the annual growth rate is 10 percent. However, Chowdhury, Haque, and Masih (2017) mentioned that Islamic banks' return on asset (ROA) and return on equity (ROE) have been decreasing continuously compared to prior of the global financial crisis. According to IFDR report 2018, Islamic financial institutions had experienced slow growth in 2018. Accordingly, having these conflicting statements motivate to revisit Islamic bank profitability in a relatively broader avenue through MENA countries.

Two maiden indicators could determine the profitability of any commercial bank such as return on asset and return on equity. Return on asset derived by net profit after tax is divided by total asset. ROA represents the organisational efficiency in order to manage their assets. On the other hand, ROE can be derived from the organisation's net profit after tax divided by equity capital. Investors can get profit from any investment from a bank based on the ROE. According to Ozili and Uadiale (2017), most of the banking regulatory bodies consider banks' profitability based on ROA and ROE.

In international settings, maximum number of financial institutions, generally banks, follow the traditional banking system as a benchmark of which the maiden intention is to maximise shareholders' profit regardless of borrowers' welfare. In contrary, the Islamic banking system, which is relatively new compared to conventional financing, is grabbing the researchers' attraction in many developed and developing countries because of its unique features. The Islamic banking system prohibits the interest-based transaction, which is the maiden element to increase profit of conventional banks. The Islamic bank follows the shariah rules by accepting profit and loss sharing principle between both parties. Investors in Islamic bank do not mention the profit rate while the banks receive money. So, it is evident that profit-loss sharing principle provides a better avenue for Islamic bank to sustain longer and healthy economic growth (Ibrahim et al., 2019; Mehta & Bhavani, 2017; Mokni & Rachdi, 2014).

Profit loss sharing and mark-up is commonly used as a shariah compliance principle to measure profitability in Islamic banks. As Islamic banking system completely follow the shariah principle, there should not be any transaction, money collection or payment, based on interest. In the context of profit lost sharing policy, the rate of return for any financial assets should not be pre-fixed. On the other hand, the rate of return of mark-up transaction, which is mainly used during the purchase-resale contract could be determined based on the benchmark. Therefore, the previous empirical study found that profit-loss sharing principle outperformed than mark-up principle, but most of the time Islamic bank used mark-up transaction for a short duration (Bidabad & Allahyarifard, 2019; Suzuki, Uddin, & Sigit, 2019). In the conventional banking system, the borrower is entirely responsible for any kind of risk, whereas the Islamic bank share risks with borrowers. Controlling risk is very much crucial for any bank because it directly impacts the profitability (Sobarsyah et al., 2020).

According to Akhtar, Akhter, and Shahbaz (2017), the Islamic bank's balance sheet considered depositors as shareholders of a bank, and there were no fixed liabilities existed. This feature helps Islamic bank to absorb any shock from the asset side, and it is automatically adjusted in the liability side as well. Moreover, the feature gives more uniqueness of Islamic banks to become more stable during the crisis period. On the other hand, during the financial crisis period, conventional banks cannot be stable because banks turn to liability management when any crisis arises in the asset side. Likewise, Islamic banks experience less bankruptcy compared to the conventional banks because all parties are considered as shareholders of a bank, and thus all transactions are executed based on trust.

Even though the profitability determinants of Islamic banks are a "vital phenomenon" to maintain sustainable economic growth, most of the previous study looked at this context into either Africa, Malaysia, or GCC countries. For example, the profitability of Islamic banks investigated by Chowdhury et al. (2017); Ftiti et al. (2013); Olson and Zoubi (2008) on GCC countries. Ibrahim et al. (2019); Mohamad et al. (2019); Rosly and Abu Bakar (2003) examined the issue from Malaysian banking sector perspective whereas Daoud and Kammoun, (2020); Akhtera, Majeedb, and Roubaudc (2019) looked into African countries. Likewise, most of the past studies studied determinants of Islamic bank profitability based on either internal or external factors. Moreover, a short period and small dataset were used in prior empirical studies. The previous studies evident that very less attention had been paid in the literature to investigate this issue from MENA countries. So, this study contributes to the body of knowledge by scrutinising Islamic bank profitability based on banks internal factors and macroeconomic factors with a larger dataset which is less common in literature.

In addition to the introductory section, the paper is organised as follows: Section 2 highlights the key challenges that are facing the Islamic bank, and following section outlines the most relevant empirical literature that underlined the research objectives. Research methodology, data, and variables are discussed in section 4. Section 5 presents the empirical results and a discussion based on economic intuition. The final section provides concluding remarks, limitations, future directions, and policy implications of the study.

KEY CHALLENGES OF ISLAMIC BANKS

As compared to conventional counterpart, Islamic banking system is relatively new, and it has significantly less research, especially for MENA countries. There are two maiden challenges faced by Islamic banks, such as *Shariah* compliance risk and credit risk. Islamic banks adhere to an ancient problem related to launching a new product. Still, every bank has their own *shariah* board which permits to launch a new product without ensuring international standard. So, the quality and features of the product could be different from other banks because shariah scholars follow a different school of thought. The previous empirical findings suggested that there should have a post-audit system and that the board committee must include scholars from different countries and of different school of thought (Iqbal, & Mirakhor, 1999; Narayan & Phan, 2019). Moreover, the Islamic banking system is also having challenges related to high government intervention, weak regulatory and advisory system, inefficient taxation system, lack of prudent legal and infrastructural framework.

In addition to legal and infrastructural challenges, Al-Wesabi (2020) posits that the performance of Islamic banks is also deteriorating due to the lack of knowledge of maintaining credit risk. The banks' utmost feature is collecting deposit from one party and loan it other party and efficiently performing these activities will generate profit (Broni et al., 2018). If a bank fails to select the right customers, then credit risk arises. The Islamic banks face credit risk problem concerning *mudarabah, mushrakah, istisnah*, and *salam* contracts. To minimize the risk pertaining to these contracts, most of the Islamic banks use a collateral system that permitted by Islamic shariah. The previous studies measured credit risk as a proxy of non-performing loan. If any client fails to return principal and/or interest in three consecutive months or ninety days, then it is considered as a non-performing loan (Hosen et al., 2020).

According to Lassoued (2018), three-quarters of Islamic banks' total risks are incurred through credit risk, and thus it is more liable for bank failure. Along with credit risk challenge, Islamic bank faces liquidity and market risk. Most of the Islamic bank's contracts follow profit-loss sharing (PLS) basis, but some contracts are also executed through non-PLS modes such as *ijarah* and *murabahah*. These contracts experience higher market risk compared to credit risk because of fixed return characteristics. The market share of *murabahah* contract is greater than total share of *mudarabah* and *musharakah*.

Aside from the credit risk, Bizri and Bizri (2017) pointed out that Islamic banks in MENA countries also faces some unique challenges that most of the time are ignored by researchers. The authors conducted an interview with customers and bank officials. In their analysis, they revealed that, Islamic banks face a challenge from industry, regulatory body, existing customers, product characteristics, social and economic development perception. However, in comparison with other financial industry, Islamic banking industry performance is outstanding. Other counterpart financial industries are continuously trying to attract more client from banks. As bank customers are becoming more aware of *shariah* rules and regulations nowadays, this has triggered bank officials to have sufficient knowledge about products and their shariah compliance status. The Islamic banks products must be acknowledged by *shariah* board. To launch any product, it needs thorough screening processes by *shariah* scholars. The scholars were also claiming that this process would increase the price of the product. Additionally, Islamic banks are continuously encountering social and economic uncertainties because when a bank enters any PLS contract with a client, the anticipation is that the economic growth will be increased, the unemployment rate will be decreased, and hence the standard of living will be improved.

THEORETICAL UNDERPINNING AND LITERATURE REVIEW

Theoretical Underpinning

There are two driven factors lead to determine the bank's profitability; internal and external. Internal factors are those which the banks usually can control by applying their sufficient management skills. On the other hand, external factors denote all outside influences which cannot be controlled directly, such as interest rate risk, inflation rate, GDP etc. The maiden intention of the banks is to maximise profits by efficiently managing their resources and skills. Below are some economic theories discussing how to increase profitability in any financial organisation.

Efficient structure theory

Efficient structure theory postulates that the profit of any financial institution will generate only if the company can successfully concentrate on the market structure as well as on employee's performance. When a bank becomes efficient through standard quality management, that will lead to less cost and hence will boost the profit. Efficient structure theory proposes two different hypotheses; Efficient structure X (ESX) and Efficient structure scale (ESS). Efficient structure X hypothesis proposes that, better management, sound technology, lower-cost strategy provide supreme efficiency of banks, and that will hit to bank's profits and market share. On the other hand, Efficient structure scale (ESS) hypothesis suggests that banks profit will be maximised if the massive scale of efficiency can be ensured in terms of operation.

Economies of scale theory

This theory explains that banks will get maximum profitability if they could manage efficient and large-scale service. Theoretically, a large bank can earn more profit compared to a smaller one because larger banks enjoy the cost advantage. Therefore, this study predicts that bank size might have a significant effect on banks' profitability. The previous researcher used these theories variables, including other macroeconomic factors, to investigate banks' profitability and performance. For example, Azad, Azmat, and Hayat (2019) examined Islamic and conventional banking performance in 20 countries over the year 2000 to 2015. The results discovered that bank size, along with other variables, has a significantly positive impact on bank performance.

Empirical Review

Currently, one of the most controversial and popular topics in the Islamic Finance arena is to check whether Islamic banks are just mimicking conventional banks or they really follow Islamic principle. There have been a lot of studies conducted to analyse the determinants of the Islamic and conventional banks' profitability and performance. Many of the studies tried to find the relation between different variables and the profitability of the banks and compare them with the Islamic and conventional systems. The variables varied from bank-specific factors, macroeconomic factors, industry factors, and other factors. To check the exact phenomenon, many studies were conducted in different countries and banks as well.

Mehta and Bhavani (2017) investigated 19 Islamic and non-Islamic commercial banks in the UAE analysing what were the leading factors affected performance and profitability. Annual bank data was collected from the period between 2006-2013. In this study, they found that cost efficiency, high capital adequacy ratio, and improvement of asset quality had a significant impact on profitability of the banks. The results further indicated that diversifying into non-traditional source revenue affected the profitability positively, however, it was negatively impacted in NIM.

Similarly, Mokni and Rachdi (2014) examined 15 conventional banks and 15 Islamic banks' profitability of MENA countries based on relatively advanced statistics GMM approach. The authors mentioned, based on a dynamic model specification, that the results had shown the significance of the determinants varied between Islamic and conventional banks. Some factors were found to affect traditional banks positively but affected Islamic banks negatively. For example, off-balance-sheet activities had a negative impact on Islamic banks, but positive impact on conventional banks. In addition, the authors also found that non-performing loans affected banks' profitability negatively due to the accumulation of unpaid loans that led to decreasing banks' returns. To sum up, their study suggested that Islamic and conventional banks' profitability reacted differently to several factors.

Eljelly (2013) tested the profitability of Sudanese banks by using the return on equity (ROE), return on assets (ROA), and net financing margin (MARG). Regarding ROA, he found that cost, liquidity, and size of the bank had significant positive impact. The previous factors were external, but regarding the internal factors, the author revealed that there had no impact on profitability. ROE and ROA were affected by the same set of internal variables. Regarding MARG, only two variables, cost and liquidity, were found significant.

Chowdhury, Haque, and Masih (2017) employed relatively advanced statistical methods such as Quantile regression, dynamic GMM, and Wavelet coherent approaches to analyse the internal and external performance determinants of GCC Islamic banks. Their findings showed that banks specific factors especially capital adequacy had significant influence on the performance of banks. The authors suggested that Islamic banks should increase equity financing rather than debt financing. They found that banks reacted more to banks specific factors rather than macroeconomic factors, which means that banks should have focused more on improving their internal operations, such as cost efficiency and capital adequacy.

In the same line, by employing panel regression model, Kalluru and Bhat (2008) discovered that Indian commercial banks' performance mostly depended on bank-specific variables such as capitalization, bank size and some other macroeconomic variables. Additionally, political parties' involvement and bank ownership had a significant positive impact on banks' profitability. Similarly, by employing a panel dataset from 1996–2005, Khediri and Khedhiri (2011) examined Tunisian deposit banks differentials in interest margins and profitability. The results revealed that better management quality was the key indicators of banks profitability. Therefore, the results also found a significant affiliation between greater bank size, higher capital ratio, and profitability.

Idris et al. (2011) revealed that Islamic banks in Malaysia reacted significantly to factors like bank size, asset quality, expenses management, and money supply. Bank size and money supply were positively related to the performance of banks, but asset quality and expenses management were negatively correlated. However, they found that factors capital ratio, liquidity, GDP, and inflation were significant determinants of Malaysian Islamic banks' profitability. Naseri, Bacha and Masih (2020) scrutinized banks' profitability and efficiency from 12 emerging countries by employing GMM approach which covered panel data from 2002 to 2013. To inspect this issue, the authors used both country-specific and bank-specific variables. The findings revealed that bank size had a significant impact on both bank efficiency and profitability for all countries. It was also observed that when bank size increased the efficiency and profitability consequently rose at a certain threshold level, the relationship became inverse after that threshold level. However, the findings found insignificant affiliation between the cost to asset ratio, cost to equity ratio, gross domestic product (GDP), inflation, efficiency and profitability.

In the same vein, Hosen, Broni and Uddin (2020) examined the bank-specific and macroeconomic determinants of non-performing loans which is considered one of the most important indicators of bank performance. A total of thirty banks, including both Islamic and conventional, were used by covering a set of panel data from 2014 to 2018. Pooled OLS estimation's results revealed that inefficiency had a significant effect on NPL in both conventional and Islamic banks in the context of Bangladesh. The result also mentioned negative rapport between NPL and loan to deposit ratio, which meant when LTD ratio rose the level of NPL decreased. More importantly, the findings revealed that Islamic bank capital structure was better than conventional banks. Unfortunately, the results failed to derive significant affiliation between diversification, bank size, credit growth, economic growth and NPLs.

From the above-discussed literature review, the author finds that the banking system by default is shaped in a framework where the objective is to increase the shareholder's wealth. Islamic banks should be the leading institutions to pave the way for a sustainable and more inclusive financial system. One of the most considerable risks to banks, both conventional and Islamic, is the failure to maintain sound asset quality. Lack of sound asset quality is the base upon which the Global Financial Crises in 2008, and all the previous financial crises took place. In this case, Islamic banks were relatively safe in comparison to the conventional ones. Accordingly, in this study, the author looks into the factors that could help Islamic banks sustain the crises. Economic crises are the reason why a country suffers. When these incidents take place, the public losses all their savings. In such situations, regulators need to emphasize on the importance of properly managing a variety of banking risks. Nevertheless, the requirements are tight as banks' asset proportion increases with the introduction of each Basel requirements. In lieu of these, the author investigated selected MENA countries Islamic banks performance from internal and external factors' perspective.

RESEARCH METHODOLOGY

Dependent Variables

Previous studies provided inconclusive results related to determining Islamic banks' profitability. Some studies explored profitability through ROA, and others used ROE. For example, Aziz (2017) mentioned that ROA could explain better profitability than ROE. On the other hand, Wasiuzzaman and Tarmizi (2010) employed both ROA and ROE to explore profitability. The authors reported that ROE could not determine bank leverage compared to ROA. Likewise, Anbar and Alper (2011) tested a research model by using both ROA and ROE. The authors advocated that both can explain the bank's profitability. So, to resolve all the problems raised, the current author inclined to use both ROA and ROE to determine profitability. ROA was measured through net profit divided by the company's total assets, and result showed as a percentage form; it supported how efficient are banks to maintain their assets. On the other hand, ROE was measured through net profit divided by shareholder's equity and result showed as a percentage form.

Independent Variables

This study used two types of independent variables, such as bank-specific and macroeconomic variables. Banks have ability to control their profitability by efficiently managing bank-specific factors but cannot control directly macroeconomic effects.

Bank specific independent variables

The bank can earn maximum profit by efficiently managing bank-specific factors. This study used three bank-specific variables that are as follows:

Bank size: Is characterized by the total assets of any bank. Most of the previous studies used the natural logarithm of total assets to measure the bank size. The current author predicts that bank size might have a significantly positive effect on bank profitability.

Asset quality: This is an essential phenomenon for any bank. It is also used to denote credit risk ratio. The bank ensures asset quality through loans divided by total assets. The previous study evident that it has a positive effect on profitability.

Capital adequacy: It could be measured through total equity divided by a total asset. The healthy percentage of the ratio indicates better capital adequacy. So, this study anticipates that capital adequacy might have positively related to profitability.

Macroeconomic independent variables

GDP growth: When gross domestic product growth turns to higher, people would have more money, and they will put that money into banks. So, the higher GDP ratio tends to impact on bank's profitability positively.

Inflation rate: denotes the increase or decrease consumers price index of all necessary goods and services. It affects the real value of cost and revenues. Inflation rate significantly effect the banking industries interest rate determination. This study anticipates the inflation rate would have a positive effect on bank's profitability.

Table 1. The particulars of variables

Classification of variables	Code	Name	Measurement	Source
Dependent variables	ROA	Return on asset	Net profit divided by total asset	Wasiuzzaman and Tarmizi (2010)
	ROE	Return on equity	Net profit divided by total equity	
Bank specific independent variables	LogA	Bank size	Natural logarithm of total assets	Aziz (2017)
	LAQ	Asset quality	Banks loans divided by total assets	Anbar and Alper (2011)
	CAQ	Capital adequacy	Total equity divided by total assets	
Macroeconomic variables	GDP	Gross domestic product	The annual GDP growth rate	Aziz (2017)
	INF	Inflation	The annual consumer price index	Anbar and Alper (2011)

Proposed Research Model

In order to scrutinise ten MENA countries, with a total of forty-six Islamic banks' profitability, the author proposed two different types of models.

Model (1):

$$ROA_i = \beta o + \beta_1 LogA_i + \beta_2 LAQ_i + \beta_3 CAQ_i + \beta_4 GDP_i + \beta_5 INF_i + \varepsilon_i \ldots\ldots\ldots\ldots\ldots\ldots \quad (1)$$

Model(2):

$$ROE_i = \beta o + \beta_1 LogA_i + \beta_2 LAQ_i + \beta_3 CAQ_i + \beta_4 GDP_i + \beta_5 INF_i + \varepsilon_i \ldots\ldots\ldots\ldots\ldots\ldots \quad (2)$$

where ROA, ROE, LogA, LAQ, CAQ, GDP, INF represents return on asset, return on equity, bank size, asset quality, capital adequacy, gross domestic product, and inflation respectively.

Data and Methodology

This study covers annual dataset over the period 2015-2019 of ten selected MENA listed countries (Bahrain, Egypt, Iran, Jordan, Kuwait, Qatar, Saudi Arabia, Tunisia, United Arab Emirates, and Yemen). The study collected forty-six Islamic banks cross-sectional data from the Bloomberg terminal and the international monetary fund (IMF) database. At first, the author intended to collect more data, but due to unavailability of data, especially newly established banks, the author was compelled to exclude some observations. To solve the research question, this study adopted regression equation, a number of standardized pooled ordinary least square (OLS), from Imran, Chowdhury and Hosen (2018). The OLS estimation mainly focused on Best Linear Unbiased Estimation (BLUE) (Broni et al., 2019). More importantly, this study ensured error term normality, absence of heteroskedasticity and outlier. When these assumptions hold, the estimation models can provide better significant results. Consequently, to ensure the robustness of models, different diagnostic tests were performed (see appendix A and B).

EMPIRICAL RESULT DISCUSSION

In order to solve the research question, three steps of statistical tests were applied with the help of Eviews and Stata software. At the first step, this study tested the nature of dataset by doing descriptive statistics and Pearson correlation test. Secondly, employed a number of standardized pooled ordinary least square (OLS) regression approach to test the proposed research model. Finally, the diagnostic test was done to ensure model authenticity.

Table 2 depicts the mean, standard deviation, minimum, maximum and total number of observations used in this study. The result shows, on average, during our estimated period, the mean value of ROA is 54.41% compared to 15.10% ROE where both profitability indicators minimum value is negative and maximum value is positive. Likewise, the mean value of bank size is 2.56, and the standard deviation is 59.98% which means all estimated banks have not equal asset level and both minimum and maximum value are positive. Therefore, asset quality also varied among different banks, but capital adequacy variable shows that almost all banks adequacy behaved similarly. In addition, the effect of GDP has changed among different bank because the standard deviation shows more than 50%. In the same vein, the mean value of inflation is 59.36%, and the standard deviation is 2.87% which means there is not much gap between different banks. The minimum and maximum value of inflation are -1.6015 and 5.3825, respectively.

Table 3 shows the correlation matrix among all the studied variables. The author advocated that most of past studies result deemed to be biased due to a high correlation between variables. The result reveals that most of the variables are significant at 1% and 5%. The highest correlation shows between inflation and GDP. The reason could be when GDP per capita is increased, people purchasing power is increased as well, and the economy has more money supply that leads to increase inflation level. The results also posit that bank size has a significantly positive relationship with ROA and ROE, which means that when bank size increase the level of return on asset and equity also rise. Likewise, asset quality has a positive rapport with ROA and ROE. When banks asset quality is better, the rate of return shows an upward trend. Similarly, capital adequacy tends to indicate positive affiliation with ROA and ROE. It

Table 2. Descriptive statistics

Variables	Mean	S.D.	Minimum	Maximum	Observation
ROA	0.5441	0.0494	-1.0561	4.2206	46
ROE	0.1510	0.0502	-1.6723	0.4845	46
LogA	2.5575	0.5998	0.3690	18.5302	46
LAQ	0.3821	0.3404	0.0327	0.5310	46
CAQ	0.0928	0.0169	-1.2510	3.5231	46
GDP	3.2314	0.5069	0.8319	15.2361	46
INF	0.5936	0.0287	-1.6015	5.3825	46

Note: ROA (return on asset), ROE (return on equity), LogA (bank size), LAQ (asset quality), CAQ (capital adequacy), GDP (gross domestic product), INF (inflation), S.D (standard deviation).

is clear that this study had no multicollinearity issue because the result shows a low (below 0.80) and a significant correlation between variables.

Table 3. Pearson correlation test result

Variables	ROA	ROE	LogA	LAQ	CAQ	GDP	INF
ROA	1						
ROE	.220**	1					
LogA	.031*	.089**	1				
LAQ	.050	.334**	.062**	1			
CAQ	.077**	.137**	.210**	.056	1		
GDP	.300**	.059	.245**	.087	.208**	1	
INF	.204**	.151**	.381**	.113*	.213**	.494**	1

**. Correlation is significant at the 0.01 level. *. Correlation is significant at the 0.05 level.

Note: ROA (return on assest), ROE (return on equity), LogA (bank size), LAQ (asset quality), CAQ (capital adequacy), GDP (gross domestic product), INF (inflation).

Table 4 illustrates the regression results for both models return on asset and return on equity. The table shows that the ROA model can explain more Islamic bank profitability than ROE model. This result includes a new insight to the body of knowledge because previous studies had confusion on which model should apply to determine Islamic bank profitability (Anbar & Alper, 2011).

ROA (return on assest), ROE (return on equity), LogA (bank size), LAQ (asset quality), CAQ (capital adequacy), GDP (gross domestic product), INF (inflation).

The above result indicates that R-Squared represents 51.61% variations in the ROA can be explained by the model, which includes the changes of all independent variables. Similarly, R- Squared shows 28.96% for ROE. The results indicate that ROA has more explanatory power than ROE. F statistic further shows that the variables are jointly significant in explaining the variations in the ROA.

The results indicate that bank size coefficient is 0.146837, which is statistically significant at $p<0.01$. If the bank wants to increase by 1% ROA, the bank size must need to increase by 14.68. On the other

Table 4. Regression result

Variables	Model(1) ROA	Model(2) ROE
Constant	23.7553** (0.0531)	12.9887** (0.0277)
LogA	0.146837*** (0.0000)	0.005758 (0.9388)
LAQ	0.0547 (0.1627)	0.23469 (0.2760)
CAQ	0.5118** (0.0538)	0.57635** (0.0280)
GDP	0.437048** (0.0118)	0.005367 (0.9779)
INF	0.012890* (0.0863)	0.086720** (0.0280)
R-Squared	0.516122	0.289635
Adjusted R-Squared	0.441679	0.180348
F-statistic	6.933144 (0.000046)	2.650223 (0.029743)
No of Observation	46	46

Note: Standard errors in parentheses. *** $p<0.01$, ** $p<0.05$, * $p<0.1$

hand, bank size has no significant effect on ROE model. The coefficient of asset quality is 0.0547, which indicates that if a bank wants to increase ROA by 1%, the level of asset quality should be increased by 5.47%, but unfortunately the model fails to provide significant evidence. In the context of 1% increase in ROE, the bank asset quality should be boosted up by 23.47%, which does not illustrate statistical significance. Another bank-specific variable, capital adequacy, shows statistical significance at 5%. If banks want to boost ROA by 1%, the capital adequacy should be increased by 51.18%, and that percentage is requiring even higher for ROE, which is 57.64%.

Moreover, macroeconomic variables such as GDP and inflation has a significant positive effect on return on asset. In contrary, only inflation has a significantly positive effect on return on equity. To ensure the estimated models' results are valid, this study further performed a different diagnostic test for both models (see appendix A and B). In order to ensure the models' robustness, regressions were run through Ramsey RESET Test, Breusch-Godfrey Serial Correlation LM test, Breusch-Pagan-Godfrey heteroskedasticity test, and Jargue Bera normality test. The results of the diagnostic test clearly indicated that both regressions findings were robust because autocorrelation, normality, heteroskedasticity, model misspecifications were no problem for this study.

CONCLUSIONS AND POLICY IMPLICATIONS

The preceding empirical analysis allowed to shed some light on the leading impacts of bank-specific and macroeconomic factors on Islamic banking performance. A set of cross-sectional data covered 2015-2019 were collected from ten selected MENA countries to address the research objective. More importantly, the study employed a number of standardized pooled OLS regression approach to purify the statistical results. The estimated model's findings indicated that Islamic banks' profitability measures responded positively to the increase in bank size, asset quality and capital adequacy. However, the evidence only illustrated significant affiliation with bank size and capital adequacy towards profitability, but insignificant relationship provided through asset quality. In addition, the results also indicated positive rapport with GPD and ROA. The finding revealed that when any country's economic condition is good, the stakeholders' intention to use banks increase. As a result, financial transactions would help banks to generate more profit. It was further pointed out that, only two variables, capital adequacy and inflation had significant impact on return on equity. The findings in this study were found to be intuitive and consistent with other previous studies.

Accordingly, policymakers need to consider these variables in order to increase banks' profitability. Since the ultimate objective of management is to maximize the value of the shareholders' equity, an optimal mix of returns and risk exposure should be pursued in order to increase the profitability of the bank. Hence, a comprehensive plan to identify objectives, goals, budgets, and strategies should be developed. The planning should encompass both internal and external performance dimensions. Since there is increasing innovation and deregulation in the financial service industry, internal and external competitiveness is becoming a critical factor in evaluating performance. This research is not out of limitation, even though the findings have a significant impact on banking industries performance determination. The current research was compelled to exclude some observations due to data unavailability. Future researcher could be extended by adding more bank-specific and macroeconomic variables and a longer period of data set. Likewise, future researchers may pay attention to compare the profitability between OIC and MENA countries Islamic banks.

ACKNOWLEDGMENT

This research received no specific grant from any funding agency in the public, commercial, or not-for-profit sectors.

REFERENCES

Akhtar, B., Akhter, W., & Shahbaz, M. (2017). Determinants of deposits in conventional and Islamic banking: A case of an emerging economy. *International Journal of Emerging Markets*, *12*(2), 296–309. doi:10.1108/IJoEM-04-2015-0059

Akhtera, W., Majeedb, M. U., & Roubaudc, D. (2019). Islamic Banking and Financial Inclusion: Evidence from Asian and African Markets. *Journal of Islamic Business and Management*, *9*(2), 341–354. doi:10.26501/jibm/2019.0902-007

Al-Wesabi, H. A. (2020). Credit risk of Islamic banks in GCC countries. *International. Journal of Banking & Finance*, *10*(2), 95–112. http://e-journal.uum.edu.my/index.php/ijbf/article/view/8476/1421

Anbar, A., & Alper, D. (2011). Bank specific and macroeconomic determinants of commercial bank profitability: Empirical evidence from Turkey. *Business and Economics Research Journal, 2*(2), 139-152. Retrieved from https://papers.ssrn.com/sol3/papers.cfm?abstract_id=1831345

Asma' Rashidah Idris, F. F. A., Asari, H., Taufik, N. A. A., Salim, N. J., Mustaffa, R., & Jusoff, K. (2011). Determinant of Islamic banking institutions' profitability in Malaysia. *World Appl. Sci. J, 12*, 1-7. Retrieved from http://citeseerx.ist.psu.edu/viewdoc/download?doi=10.1.1.390.3689&rep=rep1&type=pdf

Azad, A. S., Azmat, S., & Hayat, A. (2019). What determines the profitability of Islamic banks: Lending or fee? *International Review of Economics & Finance*, 1–15. doi:10.1016/j.iref.2019.05.015

Aziz, N. I. M. (2017). Islamic Banking Profitability: Roles played by Internal and External Banking Factors. *The Journal of Muamalat and Islamic Finance Research, 14*(1), 23–38. http://jmifr.usim.edu.my/index.php/jmifr/article/view/12

Ben Khediri, K., & Ben-Khedhiri, H. (2011). Determinants of bank net interest margin in Tunisia: A panel data model. *Applied Economics Letters, 18*(13), 1267–1271. doi:10.1080/13504851.2010.534052

Bidabad, B., & Allahyarifard, M. (2019). IT role in fulfillment of Profit & Loss Sharing (PLS) mechanism. *International Journal of Islamic Banking and Finance Research, 3*(2), 44–59. https://www.cribfb.com/journal/index.php/ijibfr/article/view/274. doi:10.46281/ijibfr.v3i2.274

Bizri, R., & Bizri, I. (2017). Challenges facing the Islamic Banking industry in the MENA region: A comparative study. *Proceeding Book of International Congress of Islamic Economy, Finance and Ethics.*

Broni, M. Y., Hosen, M., & Masih, M. (2019). Does a country's external debt level affect its Islamic banking sector development? Evidence from Malaysia based on Quantile regression and Markov regime-switching. *Quantitative Finance and Economics, 3*(2), 366–389. doi:10.3934/QFE.2019.2.366

Broni, M. Y., Hosen, M., & Saiti, B. (2018). The causality between stock market and banking sector: Evidence from dual banking system. *International Journal of Business and Society, 19*(3), 596–615. https://hdl.handle.net/20.500.12436/862

Chowdhury, M. A. F., Haque, M. M., & Masih, M. (2017). Re-examining the determinants of Islamic bank performance: New evidence from dynamic GMM, quantile regression, and wavelet coherence approaches. *Emerging Markets Finance & Trade, 53*(7), 1519–1534. doi:10.1080/1540496X.2016.1250076

Daoud, Y., & Kammoun, A. (2020). *Islamic Banking in North Africa: Emergence, Growth, and Prospects. In Growth and Emerging Prospects of International Islamic Banking*. IGI Global. doi:10.4018/978-1-7998-1611-9.ch005

Eljelly, A. M. (2013). Internal and external determinants of profitability of Islamic banks in Sudan: Evidence from panel data. *Afro-Asian Journal of Finance and Accounting, 3*(3), 222–240. doi:10.1504/AAJFA.2013.054424

Ftiti, Z., Nafti, O., & Sreiri, S. (2013). Efficiency of Islamic Banks During Subprime Crisis: Evidence of GCC Countries. *Journal of Applied Business Research, 29*(1), 285–304. doi:10.19030/jabr.v29i1.7615

Hosen, M., Broni, M. Y., & Uddin, M. N. (2020). What are the bank specific and macroeconomic elements influence non-performing loans in Bangladesh? Evidence from conventional and Islamic banks. *Green Finance*, *2*(2), 212–226. doi:10.3934/GF.2020012

Ibrahim, M. H., Salim, K., Abojeib, M., & Yeap, L. W. (2019). Structural changes, competition and bank stability in Malaysia's dual banking system. *Economic Systems*, *43*(1), 111–129. doi:10.1016/j.ecosys.2018.09.001

Imran, M., Chowdhury, M. A. F., & Hosen, M. (2018). Financial Development, Technological Development, and Poverty: A Cross-Sectional Study. In Management Strategies and Technology Fluidity in the Asian Business Sector (pp. 126-138). IGI Global. doi:10.4018/978-1-5225-4056-4.ch008

Iqbal, Z., & Mirakhor, A. (1999). Progress and challenges of Islamic banking. *Thunderbird International Business Review*, *41*(4-5), 381–405. doi:10.1002/tie.4270410406

Lassoued, M. (2018). Comparative study on credit risk in Islamic banking institutions: The case of Malaysia. *The Quarterly Review of Economics and Finance*, *70*, 267–278. doi:10.1016/j.qref.2018.05.009

Mehta, A., & Bhavani, G. (2017). What Determines Banks' Profitability? Evidence from Emerging Markets-the Case of the UAE Banking Sector. *Accounting and Finance Research*, *6*(1), 77–88. doi:10.5430/afr.v6n1p77

Mohamad, M. T., Sulaiman, A. A., Hamimah, K., & Muslim, N. (2019). The determinants of bank profitability: How Malaysian Islamic banks response to the financing risk. *Advances in Social Sciences Research Journal*, *6*(12), 1–15. doi:10.14738/assrj.612.7471

Mokni, R. B. S., & Rachdi, H. (2014). Assessing the bank profitability in the MENA region. *International Journal of Islamic and Middle Eastern Finance and Management*, *7*(3), 305–332. doi:10.1108/IMEFM-03-2013-0031

Narayan, P. K., & Phan, D. H. B. (2019). A survey of Islamic banking and finance literature: Issues, challenges and future directions. *Pacific-Basin Finance Journal*, *53*, 484–496. doi:10.1016/j.pacfin.2017.06.006

Naseri, M., Bacha, O. I., & Masih, M. (2020). Too small to succeed versus too big to fail: How much does size matter in banking? *Emerging Markets Finance & Trade*, *56*(1), 164–187. doi:10.1080/1540496X.2019.1612359

Olson, D., & Zoubi, T. A. (2008). Using accounting ratios to distinguish between Islamic and conventional banks in the GCC region. *The International Journal of Accounting*, *43*(1), 45–65. doi:10.1016/j.intacc.2008.01.003

Ozili, P. K., & Uadiale, O. (2017). Ownership concentration and bank profitability. *Future Business Journal*, *3*(2), 159–171. doi:10.1016/j.fbj.2017.07.001

Rosly, S. A., & Abu Bakar, M. A. (2003). Performance of Islamic and mainstream banks in Malaysia. *International Journal of Social Economics*, *30*(12), 1249–1265. doi:10.1108/03068290310500652

Sobarsyah, M., Soedarmono, W., Yudhi, W. S. A., Trinugroho, I., Warokka, A., & Pramono, S. E. (2020). Loan growth, capitalization, and credit risk in Islamic banking. *International Economics*, 1-18. doi:10.1016/j.inteco.2020.02.001

Suzuki, Y., Uddin, S., & Sigit, P. (2019). Do Islamic banks need to earn extra profits? A comparative analysis on banking sector rent in Bangladesh and Indonesia. *Journal of Islamic Accounting and Business Research, 10*(3), 369–381. doi:10.1108/JIABR-01-2017-0003

Trad, N., Trabelsi, M. A., & Goux, J. F. (2017). Risk and profitability of Islamic banks: A religious deception or an alternative solution? *European Research on Management and Business Economics, 23*(1), 40–45. doi:10.1016/j.iedeen.2016.09.001

Wasiuzzaman, S., & Tarmizi, H. A. B. A. (2010). Profitability of Islamic banks in Malaysia: an empirical analysis. *Journal of Islamic Economics, Banking and Finance, 6*(4), 53-68. Retrieved from https://www.researchgate.net/publication/236980854

ENDNOTE

1 Retrieved from https://www.worldfinance.com/awards/world-finance-islamic-finance-awards-2019

APPENDIX A: DIAGNOSTIC TEST FOR ROA

Table 5. Model Mis-specication

Ramsey RESET Test			
Equation: UNTITLED			
Specification: LROA C LLGL LPNIR LLRIL LILGL LILE LASSET			
Omitted Variables: Squares of fitted values			
	Value	df	Probability
t-statistic	0.460524	38	0.6478
F-statistic	0.212082	(1, 38)	0.6478
Likelihood ratio	0.256018	1	0.6129

Ho: There is no model mis-specification
Ha: There is model mis-specification

The above Ramsey Reset test that F-statistic value is 0.212082 and probability is 0.6474, which is indicating not to reject the null hypothesis. So, here is no model mis-specification.

Table 6. Autocorrelation

Breusch-Godfrey Serial Correlation LM Test:			
F-statistic	1.681532	Prob. F(2,37)	0.2000
Obs*R-squared	3.832735	Prob. Chi-Square(2)	0.1471

Ho: Error term is not autocorrelated
H1: Error term is autocorrelated

The table shows that F-statistic value is 1.681532, and p-value is 0.20000, i.e. means p-value is higher. This study fails to reject the null hypothesis. So, the error term is not autocorrelated.

Table 7. Heteroskedasticity

Heteroskedasticity Test: White			
F-statistic	1.948182	Prob. F(6,39)	0.0972
Obs*R-squared	10.60777	Prob. Chi-Square(6)	0.1013
Scaled explained SS	6.035259	Prob. Chi-Square(6)	0.4193

Ho: Variance is constant
H1: Variance is not constant

From the above statement's result show that Obs* R-squared value is 10.60777 and probability is 0.1013. So, the finding indicates to reject the null hypothesis.

Remedies of Heteroskedasticity Test

The above result depicts that, after correction of the heteroskedasticity problem, the standard error has been changed.

Table 8. White variance-covariance matrix

before correction			after correction		
Variable	Coefficient	Std. Error	Coefficient	Std. Error	t-Statistic
LPNIR	0.146837	0.07589	0.146837	0.071077	2.065889
LLRIL	117.0547	58.58201	117.0547	61.47202	1.904195
LLGL	-116.216	58.61966	-116.216	61.33564	-1.89476
LILGL	116.5118	58.59069	116.5118	61.34919	1.899158
LILE	-0.43705	0.165455	-0.43705	0.18187	-2.40307
LASSET	0.01289	0.074208	0.01289	0.084814	0.151984
C	-233.755	117.1813	-233.755	123.0215	-1.90012

From the above graph, it is clear that there has no structural break because all line is remaining within the range level.

Figure 1. Structural Stability
Ho: *No structural stability*
H1: **S***tructural stability*

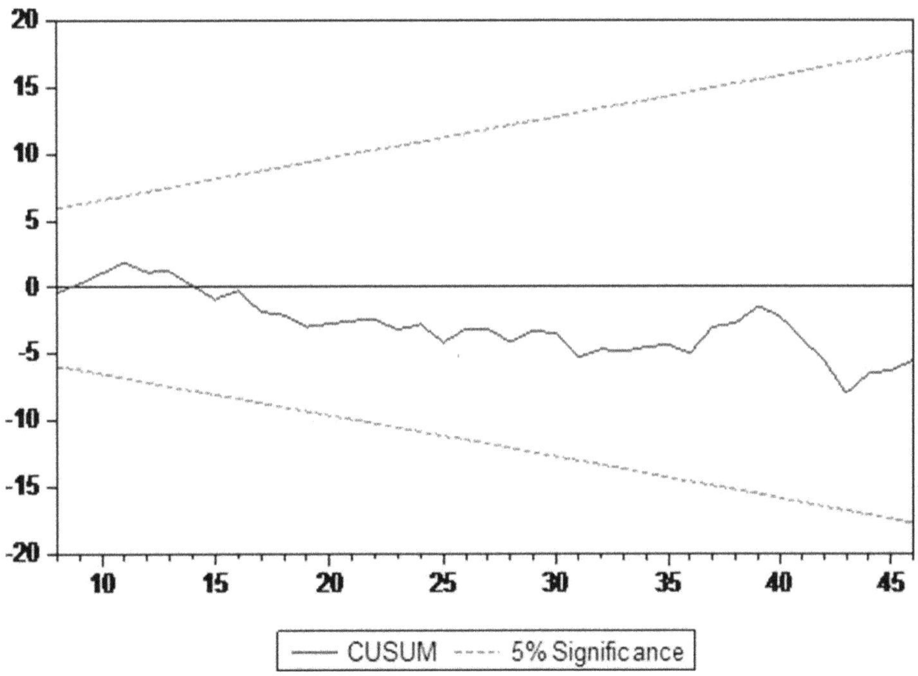

APPENDIX B: DIAGNOSTIC TEST FOR ROE

From the above result, F-statistic shows value 0.863403 and probability is 0.43. Here this study fails to reject the null hypothesis. So, the error is not autocorrelated.

Table 9. Auto-correlation Test

Breusch-Godfrey Serial Correlation LM Test:			
F-statistic	0.863403	Prob. F(2,37)	0.4300
Obs*R-squared	2.051113	Prob. Chi-Square(2)	0.3586

Ho: Error is not autocorrelated
H1: Error is autocorrelated

From the above result, F statistic value is 5.093307 and probability value is 0.0299, which requires to reject the null hypothesis. So, there is a model mis-specification.

Table 10. Model Mis-Specification

	Value	df	Probability
t-statistic	2.256836	38	0.0299
F-statistic	5.093307	(1, 38)	0.0299
Likelihood ratio	5.785951	1	0.0162

Ho: There is no model mis-specification
H1: There is model mis-specification

The above result indicates that Obs R-squared is 37.35601 and probability is 0.0534. So, the author should reject the null hypothesis.

Table 11. Heteroskedasticity Test

Heteroskedasticity Test: White			
F-statistic	3.457293	Prob. F(25,20)	0.0031
Obs*R-squared	37.35601	Prob. Chi-Square(25)	0.0534
Scaled explained SS	25.47356	Prob. Chi-Square(25)	0.4361

Ho: Variance is Constant
H1: Variance is not Constant

Remedies of Heteroskedasticity Problem

The above result illustrates that after correction of the heteroskedasticity problem, the standard error has been changed.

Table 12. White variance-covariance matrix

before correction			after correction		
Variable	**Coefficient**	**Std. Error**	**Coefficient**	**Std. Error**	**t-Statistic**
LPNIR	-0.00576	0.074378	-0.005758	0.081604	-0.070563
LLRIL	63.23469	57.41421	63.23469	63.60434	0.994188
LLGL	-62.5387	57.4511	-62.53874	63.46649	-0.985382
LILGL	62.57635	57.42272	62.57635	63.49032	0.985605
LILE	0.005367	0.162156	0.005367	0.158014	0.033965
LASSET	0.08672	0.072728	0.08672	0.078575	1.103657
C	-125.989	114.8453	-125.9887	127.3021	-0.989682

The above graph depicts that there have no structural breaks because the line remaining within the range.

Figure 2. Structural Stability Test
Ho: *No structural stability*
H1: *Structural stability*

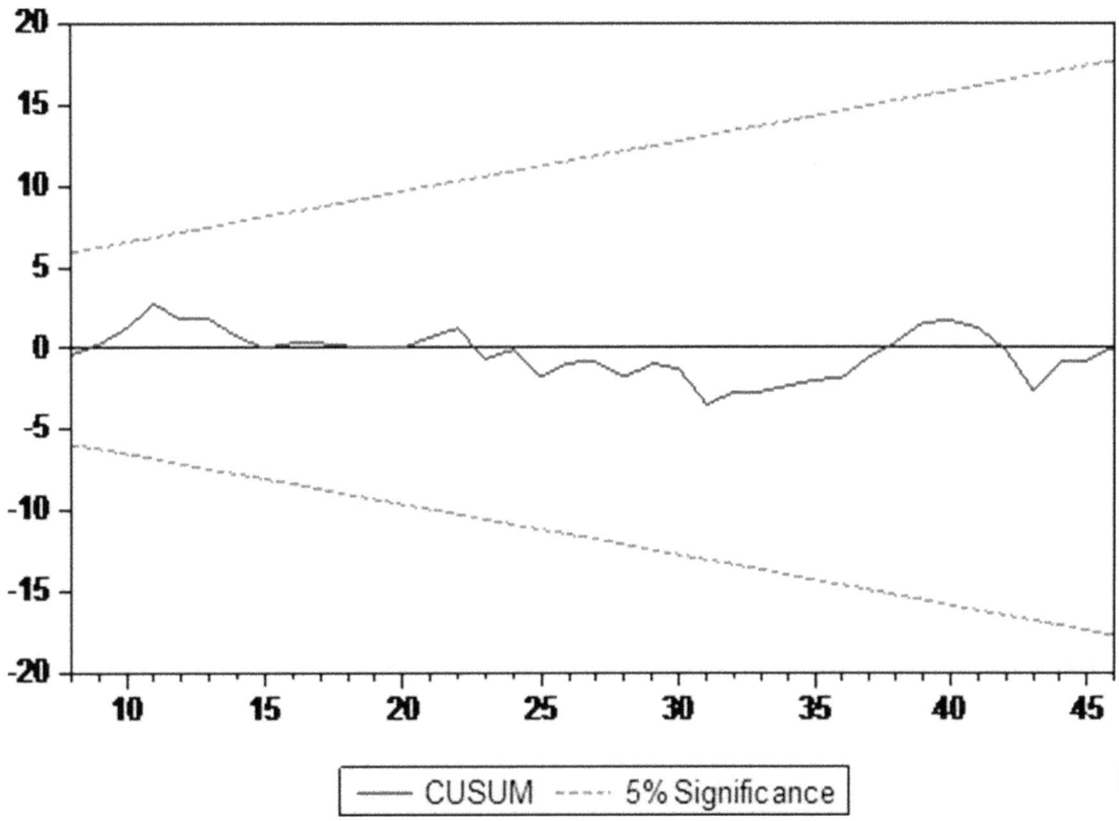

Chapter 11
Disruption and Innovation Trends in the QSR Industry:
Perspectives Drawn From India

Gaurav Nagpal
https://orcid.org/0000-0003-1957-7865
Birla Institute of Technology and Science, Pilani, India

Kanika Dawar
Birla Institute of Technology and Science, Pilani, India

Srutadipta Roy Choudhury
Birla Institute of Technology and Science, Pilani, India

Tanmay Singh
Birla Institute of Technology and Science, Pilani, India

ABSTRACT

The QSR (quick service restaurants) industry in the emerging economies such as India is undergoing a wave of disruption and re-engineering. Many global brands in QSR food servicing have resorted to technology and innovation in one or more aspects of their value chain in order to maintain leadership positions in a market that is facing some fast-growing competition from various channels, especially with the penetration that service aggregators like Zomato, Swiggy, and Uber Eats have managed to gain. This study aims to establish a general direction towards which the QSR industry is progressing in India by examining not only the current trends in India but also the trends that are prevalent worldwide and which have the potential of diffusion to emerging economies like India.

DOI: 10.4018/978-1-7998-4787-8.ch011

Figure 1. Disposable Income in India
Source: trandingeconomics.com

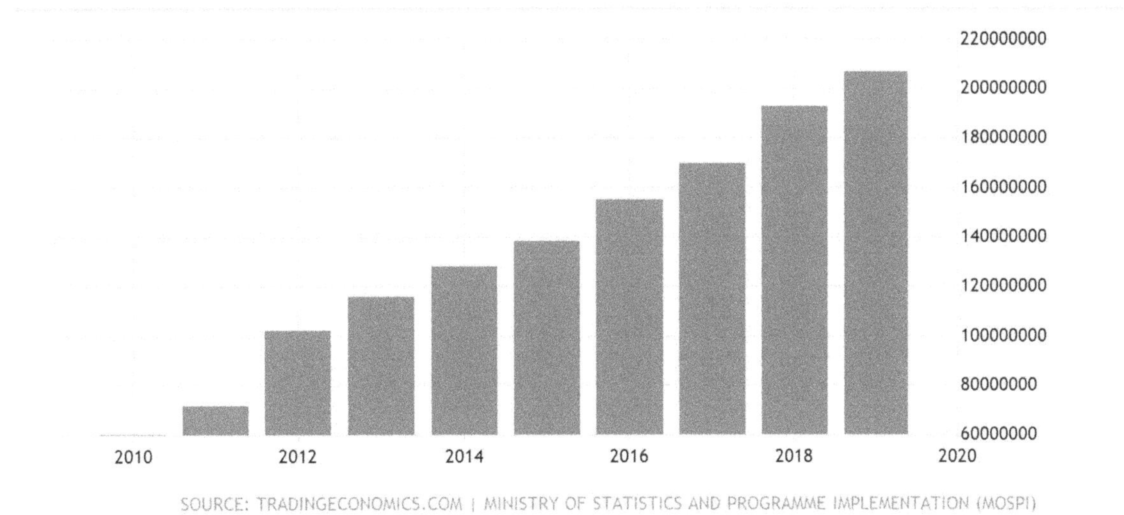

The Indian Food and Beverage industry is undergoing a wave of disruption and re-engineering driven by multiple factors, viz. the machine learning and artificial intelligence taking the front seat, the changing food habits of the consumer, the aggregation of demand and supply using technology, the tightening food safety norms, the increasing competitive intensity in the industry and the ever-innovating supply chains and processes.

Many global brands in food servicing and Quick Service restaurants (QSRs) like McDonald's, Domino's Pizza, KFC and Pizza Hut have resorted to technology and innovation in one or more aspects of their value chain in order to maintain leadership positions in a market that is facing some fast-growing competition from various channels, especially with the penetration that service aggregators like Zomato, Swiggy and Uber Eats have managed to gain. This study aims to establish a general direction towards which the QSR industry is progressing in India by examining the trends that are prevalent worldwide. The study also discusses in brief the implications of Covid-19 for this industry, and the lessons to learn from this crisis.

INTRODUCTION

India has been characterized as the fifth-largest country in the World in terms of nominal GDP and the third-largest in terms of purchasing power parity. Nearly 60% of India's GDP is driven by domestic private consumption and continues to remain the world's sixth-largest consumer market. According to 2017 PricewaterhouseCoopers (PwC) report, India's GDP at purchasing power parity could overtake that of the United States by 2050. India ranks second globally in food and agricultural production. As depicted in Figure 1, Disposable Personal Income in India increased to 206 INR Trillion in 2019 from 192 INR Trillion in 2018.

The key drivers of F&B industry in India are increasing consumer expectations on transparency, increase in consumer preference for plant based food, and increasing conscience towards health and wellness. These drivers combined with the potential of the Indian economy, gives the F&B industry enormous opportunities for growth and success.

Along with the economic patterns changing for the better, India is also adapting to the western tastes and cultures. India is now the world's 10th fastest growing market for specialist coffee and tea retail chains, valued at Rs. 2,570 crores in 2018, estimated to grow by 6.9% to Rs. 4,540 crores by 2023, as shown in Figure 2.

Figure 2. Market Size of coffee retail chain in India,2014-2025
Source: Grand View Research, Industry Analysis 2018

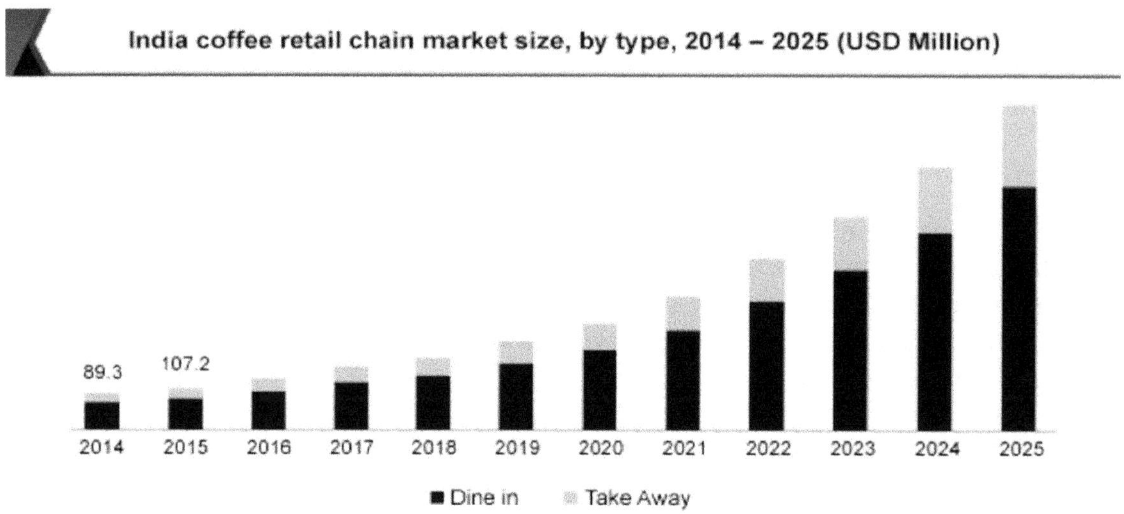

Figure 3. Projected share of organized and unorganized segment in the F&B market
Source: NRAI Food Services Report, 2019

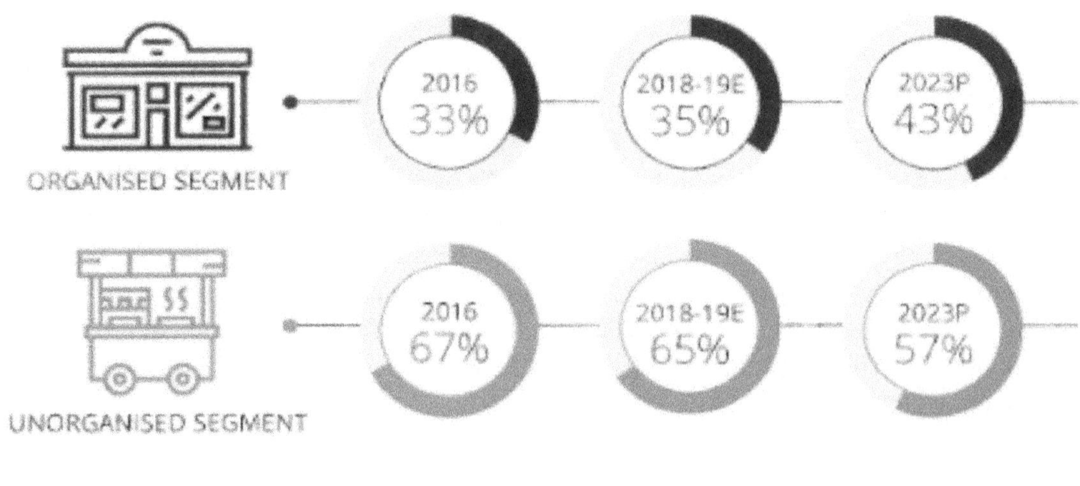

The Figure 3 illustrates that the share of the organized food and beverages market is poised to grow in the overall industry.

This is how this study has been structured. The Section 1 (the current section) lays down the introduction to the topic and the motivation behind this study. The Section 2 reviews the existing literature on service innovation. The Section 3 explains the research methodology. The Section 4 discusses the upcoming trends in the industry, and is the longest section of the paper. The effort has been made to touch upon every domain of QSR innovation in this section. The Section 5 discusses the lessons posed by the Covid-19 Crisis, and the Section 6 concludes the article.

LITERATURE REVIEW

The detailed study of the existing literature on the service innovation was reviewed and it was found that there is good amount of work done on this topic. In services industry, it is not as important to acquire customers as it is to have customers (Berry, 1980). Barras (1986) was among the early researchers who came up with the theory of service innovation. Managing the total experience of the customer right from prospecting till the product disposal and repeat purchasing assistance has become of paramount importance (Berry et al. 2002).

Innovation in the services industry acts as catalyst for the economic growth of services sector (Snyder et al. 2016). Quality of service delivery has a substantial influence on the customer satisfaction (Shostack, 1984 and Crosby et al. 1990) as well as on creation of new markets (Berry et al. 2006). The higher customer satisfaction can increase the customer loyalty (Cronin and Taylor, 1992). Bourke et al. (2020) showed that a structured approach to innovation benefits the professional services firms while explaining the same with an example of a legal services. Keaveney (1996) laid down the eight broad categories of reasons for customer switching in the service industries, all of which can be addressed by bringing innovation and use of technology or analytics.

Guile and Quin (1988) devoted a book to the technology-based innovation in the services industry. Increased digitalization has an influence on the business models of the firms by revolutionizing the product and service offerings (Rachinger et al. 2019). Soto-Acosta et al. (2018) suggested that the growth in information and communication technologies has expedited the innovation in the business models. With the advent of digitalization, there has been a transformation of services into "smart services" by building on the capabilities of smart products (Paukstadt et al. 2019).

Bitner (1992) proposed that the physical surroundings have an influence on the customers and employees in the services industry, and therefore, they need to be a part of the innovation ambit. Martin and Horne (1993) suggested that four factors determine the success of innovation- the work culture, the diversity of the R&D team, the experience with earlier innovations and the deployment of matrix organization. Uchupalanan (2000) examined the innovations in banking industry of Thailand, and proposed that the competitive strategy and IT enabled innovation are dynamically related to each other in financial services. Howells (2001) studied the innovation of services in OECD nations. Price promotions facilitate the retailers in driving the impulse buying (Hisseini et al. 2020). Cocreation of value is also gaining momentum in the services industry and helps meet the customer needs better (Ye & Kankanhalli, 2020).

Bitner (2008) advocated the use of service blueprinting as an effective tool for service innovation. Miles (2008) while examining the innovation pattern in services industry suggested that some service organizations behave very much like high technology manufacturing. He said that service innovation can be brought in via the routes of on-the-job creativity and project management. Gallouj and Djellal (2010) discussed social innovation and economics of innovation in the services industry. Marketing and management of services is significantly different from that of the physical goods (Lovelock & Wright, 2002). Karmarkar (2014) emphasized that the industrialization of services is a very complex topic by virtue of heterogeneity. Schachter (2018) said that the innovation can happen in the form of product, process, organization, marketing and technology.

The role of innovation in the management of services cannot be underplayed. Lack of innovations can cause the businesses to fail (Cole, 2019). While the firms need to innovate constantly, they also need to do so cautiously, as the mis-planned innovations can cause the decline of the firms (Christensen, 1997). The firms practicing service innovation need to be cautious of the fact innovation is not only concerned with building a research and development team, but also about the openness to new ideas, risks, change and failures (O'Reilly, 1997). The firms need to be adaptive enough to break, make and maintain the institutionalized rules of resource integration that is required for the service innovation as suggested by Huotari et al. (2016). Also, the service delivery executives need to be given full support and a conducive environment (Tajeddini et al. 2020). Innovation is not just a process but needs to be ingrained in the culture of the organization (Ghazzawi, 2009) and therefore, the innovation needs a lot of parenting (Ishlak, 2017).

Dasi et al (2017) studied the recent trends of digitalization in the telecom sector. Wang et al. (2019) studied how the innovation models have evolved in the automobile service industry over the period of time. Castro et al. (2020) studied the dynamics of service innovation on the evolution of fintech ecosystem. While there has been significant research on services innovation in general, and also some works on service innovation in BFSI and IT services, the work on the HoReCa (Hotels, Restaurants and Cafes) industry and QSR industry is missing. Therefore, this paper attempts to shed light on the innovations in the QSR industry from the perspectives of the emerging economy of India.

RESEARCH METHODOLOGY

This study is an exploratory research on the perspectives of the QSR industry. The insights presented in this paper have been collected on the basis of primary research as well as secondary research. The primary research has been done with the industry experts, the practitioners, the employees in the QSR industry, the customers and the suppliers to the industry through unstructured questionnaires that sought their comments on the latest and upcoming innovations. A wide variety of outlets represented by different QSR chains were visited in the metro towns of the country to seek the inputs of the respondents on the innovation trends. The sequence of questions asked to the respondents was self-evolving in nature on the basis of the answers provided by them. The secondary research data has been collected from the industry blogs, the industry magazines and the editorials available on the internet sources.

UPCOMING TRENDS

As the world progresses towards automation, AI/ML, Food and Beverage (F&B) industry is not far behind in finding use cases of technology into a business that has traditionally been conventional. Many brands, from food processing to food services have found and implemented solutions that take the industry a step ahead in the game. The upcoming sections will touch upon the entire value chain of a typical F&B organization, giving insights on the research and new developments being carried out in every aspect of the same. The entire value chain can be classified into seven broad components as shown in Figure 4. Let us have a look at the emerging trends in all these aspects.

Figure 4. Broad Components of a QSR value chain
Source: Self-Compilation by Authors

Procurement

The F&B players are tending towards a vertically integrated supply chain. As of now, the supply chain is operated in a manner where the activities are majorly outsourced to the third-party vendors but the control of the nodal firm remains on the entire supply chain.

Some of the major challenges of the procurement being faced by the industry are as follows:

- **Sourcing Locally:** Although the farm-to-fork concept is becoming increasingly popular, but, fresh local products are costlier and more difficult to source in adequate bulk quantities.
- **Supplier Management:** Food and beverage procurement generally involves a large number of suppliers - even for smaller businesses. A lot of work goes into building and maintaining a good working relationship with these suppliers. Once a supplier is chosen, businesses must monitor and manage their suppliers' service performance in terms of delivery, cost, quality, responsiveness, customer service and reliability. Furthermore, businesses must stay updated on changes in pricing, terms of trade, or product availability. Keeping track of all these processes and information is often tedious, meticulous, and prone to human errors.
- **Keeping up with Regulations:** As international brands penetrate into the Indian market, they ought to keep up with the changing regulations in the country. For the F&B operators with suppliers in multiple geographical locations, this challenge becomes multi-fold.

As more and more players enter the industry, the QSR industry is taking a chapter out of the FMCG book and tweaking its sourcing strategy in order to maintain competitive advantage and to stop the control from going into the suppliers' hand. One of the QSR giants, McDonalds has already moved to vertical integration in order to reduce costs and increase profits. They have contracted producers for growing own beef, meat processing, creating own spices, growing own potatoes and other vegetables and transporting their goods on their own. Even the land on which the restaurants are constructed, is sometimes owned by McDonalds.

Also, as the consumer becomes more cognizant of what to consume and what not to, the concept of "farm-to-fork" has become the USP of many food retailers and is expected to grow further into a strategy focus of many international brands in the near future. The main component of such strategies remains the quality check of ingredients procured from the farm. There are many startups, like ImpactVision and Scio, which have automated the quality check process using non-invasive computer vision technology which identifies the consistency and the quality of ingredients using AI/ML.

Product

Many international brands brought the international products to India and over a period of time, made these products the preference of Indians. Whether it was Dominos delivering Pizza in 30 minutes, or McDonalds providing burgers in a drive-through window, the product as well as the service of these brands became popular with the Indians in no time. According to a report by Nestle Professional, consumers need not travel to eat global food, because it is available locally; and only 20% of them get it through travel.

But with the changing trends of glocalization, the brands are incorporating the local preferences of the local consumer and personalize the product to local taste or flavor. Hence, the QSR brands are striving to achieve a balance between what they have to offer and what the customer wants. This balancing act is what made McDonald's offer a Mc Maharaja or a Mc Aloo Tikki to the Indian market or what made Haldiram's a household name.

Taking innovative products forward, many new concepts, like One Dish Wonders, a food chain that serves the food in only one dish, has positioned the concept as its specialty and core competence, and has starting gaining prevalence. Plant-based-food is also becoming popular with each passing day and the research is being conducted on generating plant-based meat and other plant-based products in order to cater to the needs of the health-conscious consumer.

Another area that is witnessing innovation in the industry is packaging. Packaging remains the first impression of the product offering of any organization. While it needs to be attractive on one hand, it also contributes immensely to the increasing plastic consumption in the society. Hence, the adaption of sustainable raw materials in packaging of the food products is a trend which should be here to say. In India, cardboard flask has created storm in tea sales. It keeps the tea warm and fresh for 90 minutes. Some of the major brands selling tea as their core product like ChaiPoint and Chaayos are using this and have shown 50% increase in delivery market. Zomato introduced tamper-proof packaging for food safety. 100% tamper-proof packaging is in an effort to add an extra layer of safety to food deliveries, present in small and large sizes for one to two food items and two to four food items, respectively. The package has been designed in such a way that after it is sealed by the restaurant, it can be broken only by cutting off the top-end strip. Zomato has already shipped more than three million tamper-proof packages to restaurants. Biaxially-oriented polypropylene (BOPP) and Cast Polypropylene (CP) are some other packaging materials that come from the same poly-olefin family of polymers and help in less consumption of plastics and overall lesser lamination cost. These materials are currently used by some packaged food brands like "Anshul" and "Funday". Some other examples of sustainable packaging include KFC Comestible Cup which is a double layer coating of white chocolate around biscuit wrapped in sugar paper is designed in the shape of a cup and can tolerate the heat of the espresso due to its texture and is edible. Carlsberg Green Fiber Bottle Packaging is made up of wood fiber in partnership with EcoXpac. Butter Better Environment-Friendly Breakfast consists of a great dose of butter covered with a biodegradable and recyclable wooden knife. New Fresh pack of Mars Drinks have eliminated the use of aluminum foil pack and reduced the carbon footprint by about 31%. Tim Hortons has introduced a new lid that is 100 per cent recyclable.

Operations

In this section, we shall discuss two important emerging trends- the use of blockchain, and the IOT based maintenance.

Blockchain for Supply Chain

An important revolution in the operations and supply chain activities of F&B firms is the adoption of the blockchain. The Blockchain refers to a digitalized, dispersed spreadsheet that records transactions and tracks assets in a business network. Since these assets are distributed by countless no. of computers in the business network worldwide, they cannot be controlled by a single person. Instead when a person uploads a transaction to the network, the systems run complex algorithms to check if the transaction is valid. If the transaction is binding, it is linked to the preceding transaction. This set of linked transactions is the blockchain.

The three properties of blockchain that have the capability to transform Supply Chain are:

- *Decentralization:* In a blockchain-based supply chain management, record keeping and provenance tracking become easy as the product information can be accessed through the help of embedded sensors and RFID tags.
- *Immutable*: The history of a product right from its origination to where it is in the present time can be traced through blockchain.
- *Transparency*: This type of accurate provenance tracking can be used to detect frauds in any part of the supply chain.

Figure 5 depicts how the blockchain technology is benefitting the operations in QSR industry. The entire supply chain can be made robust and secure by adopting the blockchain technology into its back-end operations.

IoT Based Predictive Maintenance

All Indian kitchens like KFC, Dominos, and Pizza Hut etc. have come up with unique ways of maintaining their restaurants over these years. There are numerous electrical and mechanical gadgets, ovens, sensors in a restaurant. The number of these equipment varies from a standalone restaurant to dine-out restaurants depending on the need. Over the years, every day these equipment are being checked for their functioning. As the technology advanced, big players in Indian QSR industry has adapted the change quite comprehensively.

Before 2010-11, Pizza Hut and Dominos could only manage their ovens by the temperature sensor attached to it. The Air Conditioners, chimneys were supposed to be in running condition always except in winters. The lighting in a restaurant was always illuminated in proper ways and sometimes irrespective of the lighting condition outside. These have been the case of most of the restaurants when they found the cost incurred for energy consumption, maintenance of all equipment and regular breakdown had a huge impact in their overall profit by the end of year. And this wasn't in control for most of the cases as equipment breakdown has led to a significant drop in sales in every part of the country.

Figure 5. Benefits of Blockchain for the F&B Industry
Source: Authors

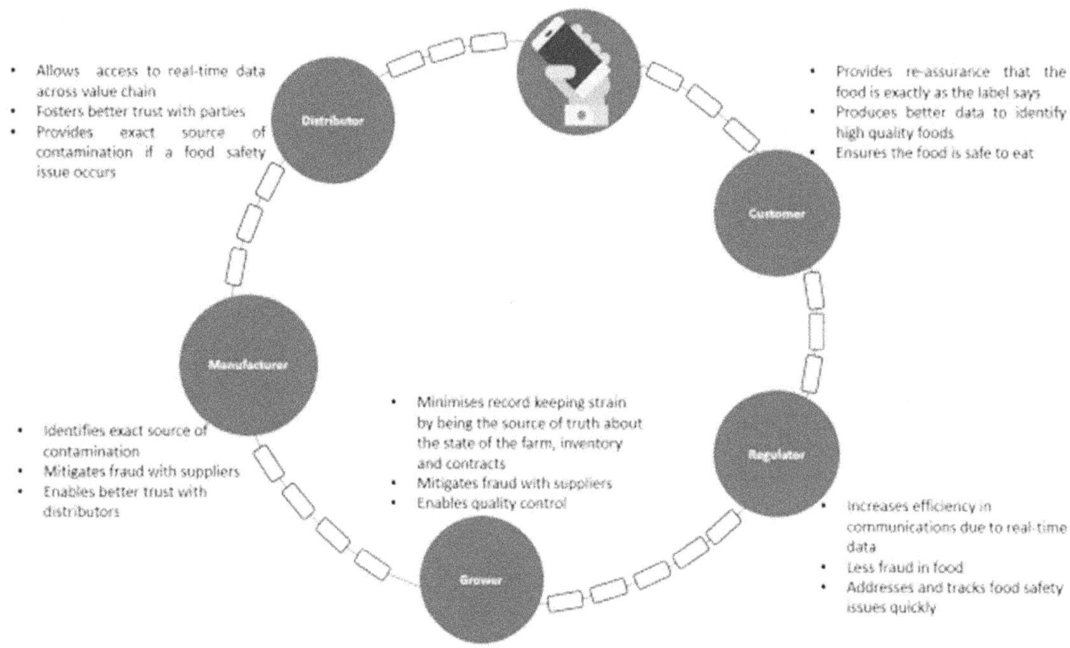

Loss in revenue will hardly be ever accepted by any board of directors and so disruptive innovations in this sector were being searched for immediately. IOT based sensors then came into picture. IOT-Internet of Things is a system of interrelated computing devices provided with UIDs (Unique Identifiers) that has the potential to capture data, feed into cloud system, send automatic alert and instruct to change/ adjust the devices/sensors according to the requirement. Today every restaurant has lots of such devices placed to perform very unique set of functions for e.g. Temperature sensors in oven- which detects any leak of extra heat, sensors which control the flow of gas in ovens, sensors in the make-line and customer area to assess the comfort of the employees and customers, door lock sensors in cold-rooms to reduce the time for door opening and closing, sensors in cold room issue warnings if the temperature falls below the desired value, pH sensors controlling the ACs according to the outside humidity, illumination sensors which instruct lights to turn off/dim/glow with the change in lighting outside the restaurant. These devices thus have taken complete control over the functioning of each equipment and send all the information regarding run time, energy consumption in cloud which can be accessed in web portals, can be seen, reviewed and decisions for future can be derived. One such decision is Predictive Maintenance.

All restaurants undergo preventive maintenance which includes periodic servicing and servicing based on complaints of equipment. Technicians are assigned based on the complaint and they repair the same. But these IOT over the years can collect data points where they can be analysed to know or predict when any device in restaurant is not performing to desired capacity over a period of time which ideally it should be and so in this way a prediction can be done on the health of the equipment which has the potential to breakdown in near future. This analysis will lead to a machine based decision making of corrective action where the equipment will be checked before its breakdown. This process is termed as 'Predictive Maintenance.'

Figure 6. Predictive Maintenance Architecture
Source: Industry 4.0 Predictive Maintenance, The Complete Guide, Seebo.com

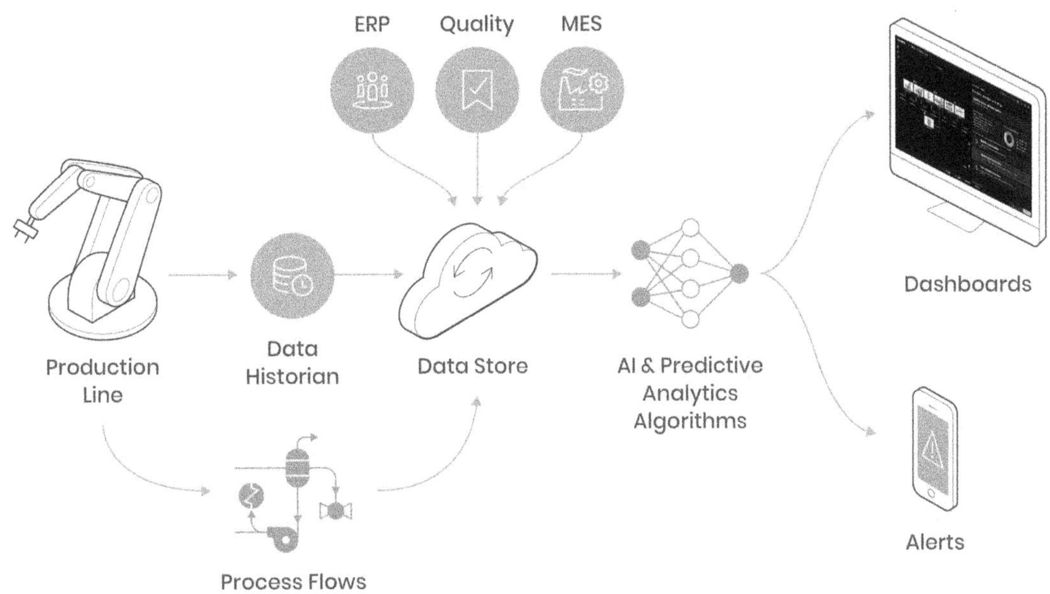

Figure 6 depicts how an IoT collects information and how this information is processed and alerts are rolled out after analysis.

The benefits of Predictive Maintenance include:

- **Reduce maintenance cost**: IOT based predictive maintenance utilizes historical data from multiple source including IOT devices and sensors to make accurate prediction about asset health, utilization and possibility of failure, enabling to take action based on this information. Thus avoidable costs can be reduced greatly and the reduction in the amount of time the machinery is down for maintenance
- **Increase Asset Utilization:** IoT based predictive maintenance enables more efficient use of assets by providing the ability to predict machine failure and reduce maintenance issues. It can help identify the causes of delays, whether internal/external and help set up processes to address the causes. The issues can also be detected even before it is operational and provide early warnings thus improving performance.
- **Extend Asset Life:** IoT based predictive maintenance enables one to monitor, maintain and optimize asset health for better availability, utilization and performance. Real time monitoring enables one to schedule maintenance, repairs and replacement of parts even before the event occurs thus extending the life of assets.
- **Improve Field crew efficiency:** Unplanned downtime or machine failure often requires reallocation of field service crews from other work locations to address the issue, or hiring of extra personnel or a complete rescheduling of other planned maintenance activities. This can be avoided

with IoT-based predictive maintenance, thus improving the utilization and response time of field service crew and reducing maintenance duration and asset downtime.

The opportunities that we have to improve businesses on this significant a scale are too valuable to leave unexplored. IoT data has left this opportunity wide open for QSR industry in our country working with machinery or anything that captures data. The enormously impactful case of predictive maintenance is just the beginning of the potential we'll see from the steady reduction in the cost of capturing data and calculating predictive outputs by AI or ML.

Product Pricing

The three key pricing innovations being adopted are charm pricing, price congruency and price discrimination. Let us discuss each of these one by one.

Charm pricing:

The players in the F&B industry are increasingly resorting to Charm pricing, also known as psychological pricing, for psychological influencing the customers who get swayed to buy the products or perceive the entire value proposition in a favorable way. Odd numbers are the foundation for charm pricing. The most common ending numbers are 9 and 5, which found that these cents endings accounted for 90% of the 840 prices being analyzed.

The driving forces of charm pricing are summarized below:

- *Specificity*: Charm pricing offers a level of explicitness, which mentally triggers a thought that the item is estimated at the best possible worth. This is particularly evident if the item is estimated partially, implying that the appeal cost shows up as penny esteem.
- *Perceived loss*: Consumers esteem an item dependent on misfortune instead of addition. Also, since most purchasers in the Western world read a cost from left to right, they are bound to lock onto the principal number they see as a grapple point. This implies Rs499 can feel like altogether under Rs500 from the initial introduction, despite the fact that there is only an Rs1 contrast.
- *Perceived gain*: something contrary to saw misfortune is likewise obvious, and buyers could utilize charm pricing as an approach to feel like they've set aside cash. The higher, adjusted value fills in as a stay point (Rs500), while the lower cost speaks to reserve funds (Rs499, which implies you spare Rs1. This follows a hypothesis that a .99 or .95 value finishing triggers a "deal" prompt in the shopper, who may accept the cost is limited.

Price Congruency:

We often observe that the firms use a smaller font with smaller price when reflecting a discount. Congruency of size and value will make the price drop seem larger. Although the bigger fonts might be more eye-catching, but keeping font size congruent to value emphasizes the price difference. Figure 7 depicts an example of how price congruency is used by organisations by covering $3/4^{th}$ area of packaging for a reduction in price from 12 to 10.

Figure 7. Example of Congruent Pricing

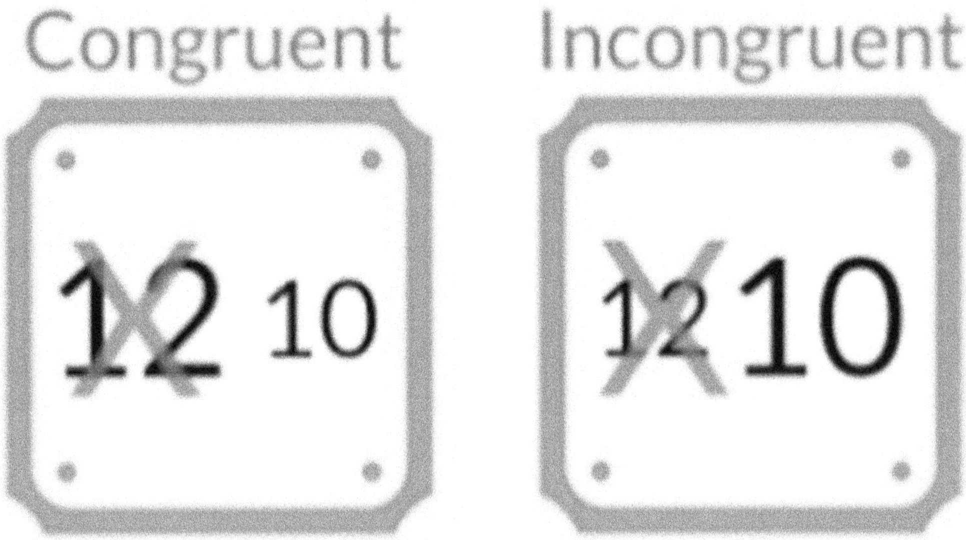

Implement slight Price Difference:

The players are seen to adjust their price to differ across the product line or to differ from a competitor's in order to increase the likelihood of making a sale. The marketers have discovered that identical prices for similar products make people over-analyse the product qualities, and that the different prices make the products seem more similar and are less likely to provoke "buyer's remorse".

Marketing

Marketing has always been a way of communication between the brand and the consumer. As the consumer becomes more susceptible to the marketing messages, the F&B industry is also inventing new means to pass the brand message onto the consumer. The industry is leveraging the marketing automation to reach the customer more effectively and efficiently, and to increase the breadth and depth of reach.

Taking leverage of the increased penetration of smartphones, the brands are able to communicate with the consumer at all times. The technology used to keep in touch with the customer either onsite or off the premises is known as "marketing automation" and is becoming a way forward for all the marketing activities carried out by brands. Marketing automation platforms can trigger direct correspondence that catches client eye while they're in the café, drives online networking collaboration, and promotes retention after they leave. Customer data, available readily with the brands, is used to measure customer sentiment in real time to project the lifetime value of a specific customer and to optimize and measure return visits.

There are multiple ways in which marketing automation benefits an organisation:

- *Rescuing Guests at Risk*: There's nothing more discouraging than not seeing a regular guest come back. To rescue those potentially lost guests, the players have incorporated a feature on their CRM platform that flags those people who have broken their regular visit pattern and sends an offer to encourage them to return.
- *Commemorating Milestones: The enablement of CRM has led the players to treat the customers in a more personalized manner. For example: the* guests who visit the restaurants more frequently are being offered a special treatment. The chains are sending an offer when customers reach pre-determined milestones such as their 10th, 25th, or 100th visit. Offers are also being generated annually, for example, on the anniversary of a customer's first visit to the restaurant.
- *Promoting Loyalty*: Many of the food chains are creating a virtual loyalty program that works like punch cards used in the good old "coffee club". Clients will get an offer each time they arrive at the quantity of visits indicated by the café.
- *Rolling Rewards*: Not each eatery foresees a similar degree of visitor recurrence. The players are tweaking rewards for recurrence and consistency dependent on a number of visits and timespan set by the individual café (for instance, 3 visits in 10 days); an offer is sent when clients meet these rules

There are multiple ways in which marketing automation is being adopted by different organisations in the form of Email marketing (using software like mail-chimp), customer Relationship Management (CRM) tools (like HubSpot and Microsoft dynamics), Graphic Designing tools (like Tableau) and even for proper marketing research analytics which play a great role in cost reduction.

Food Delivery

With the customer preferring to save the travel time and the traffic hassles, the food delivery seems to be a good option, more so for the chains that save on the overhead costs and are able to reach a wider market.

Online Food Delivery Market- India

We can also observe that the online food delivery is increasing at an exponential rate with the upcoming apps that aggregate the demand and the supply

The Figure 8 shows that online food delivery market in India is expected to boom to INR 614 Bn by 2023 with orders growing at 130% averaging around 370,000 orders per day.

There are various drivers of the growth in the online food delivery market. As can be derived from figure 9, the major drivers have been the increase of mobile phone users and the internet penetration which has exponentially increased in India over the span of last few years. It also depends on the discounts given by the aggregators to grab the attention of consumers more and to ease their lives.

As shown in the figure 10, India has shown an exponential increase in the market over last three years and has great potential in future too. Young professionals facing the shortage of time are the most valuable targets in this market and make about fifty percent of the pie. Also, females make the equal contribution and have been a major target segment due to their contribution in boosting the market. Income does not play a significant role as consumers earing middle and high income take about the same share of the pie.

The concept of cloud kitchens is becoming increasingly popular, especially among the food aggregators, in order to maximize the reach in food delivery. As shown in the figure 11, the rise of dark kitchens

Figure 8. Potential market of online food delivery from 2017-23
Source: Reference from Zomato Foodwork 2019

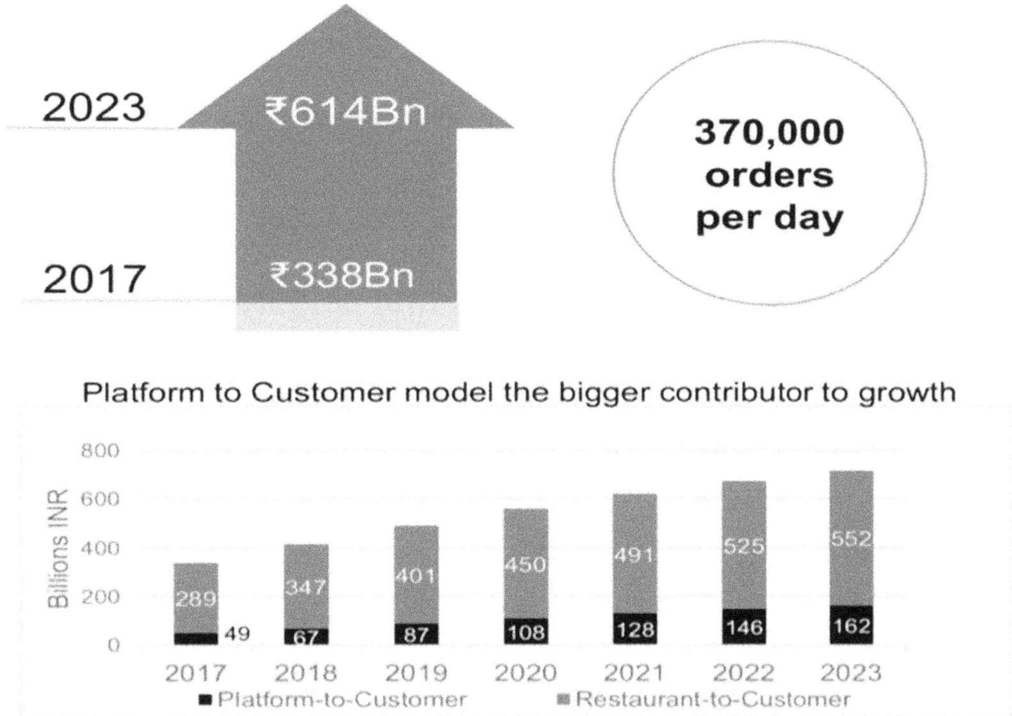

concept in India validates the potential of this industry in the future. Some startups like Fassos, Box8 and Freshmenu have been a great success working on this concept and have attracted great investment as well as customers. India

IoT based food delivery system

Advent of technology has drastically changed the way food delivery system works across the globe. Until 2010, it was mostly over call that an organization used to know the status of a delivery vehicle. Then came revolutionary devices and gadgets and that completely changed the way how operations are being handled today. One of such phenomenon is Internet of Things, in short **IoT**.

Influence of IoT on the food industry:

- **Improved Food Safety:** The paramount importance given by F&B industry is on food safety. Food and beverage companies adopted IoT to help in providing the best products & complying with FSMA regulations:
  Ö Temperature and humidity sensors: These sensors are used to monitor production state, shipping condition, temperature maintained in cold rooms so that the food products remain safe in a suitable environment.
  Ö The sensors also give data on violation of any the points and potential threat.

Figure 9. Growth Drivers of the Online food Delivery Market
Source: Self-compilation by Authors

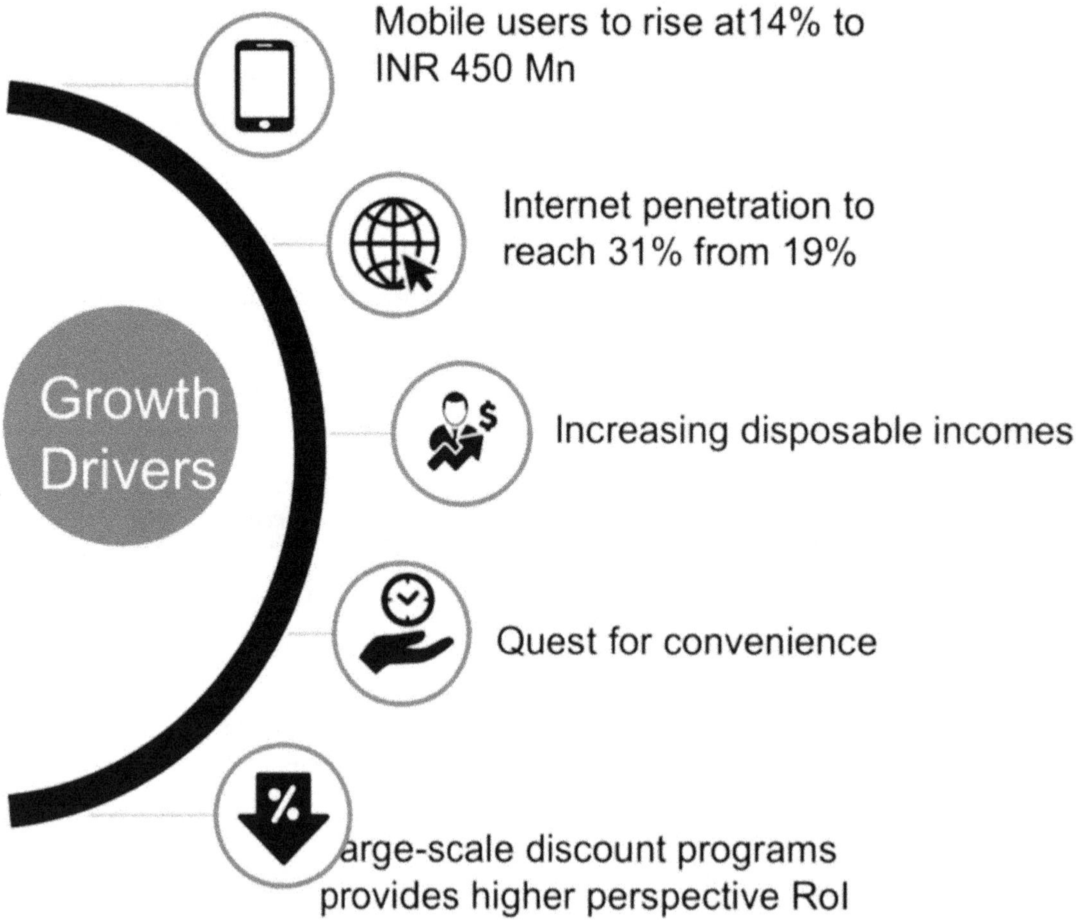

- Packaging industry is tagging any food package with sensors and these are fed into server of supply chain link. Any tempering with the sensors can easily be traced now and tracking process gets smoother.
- **Increases Operational Visibility:** In a business that is relied heavily on coordination, visibility of operations is crucial for effective and time bound actions. A well-defined IoT framework can act as the bridge between managers and detailed data giving a profound understanding of information such as real-time alerts, on-time conveyances, etc. This helps managers make informed decisions to avoid any unnecessary issues. IoT has proven its advantage in especialy warehouse operations with equipment like sensors and bar code readers, and has ultimately streamlined operations allowing for perceivability of stock and easy tracking of items.

Figure 10. Food delivery market trends in different geographies, gender and income range
Source: Compiled from various sources by authors

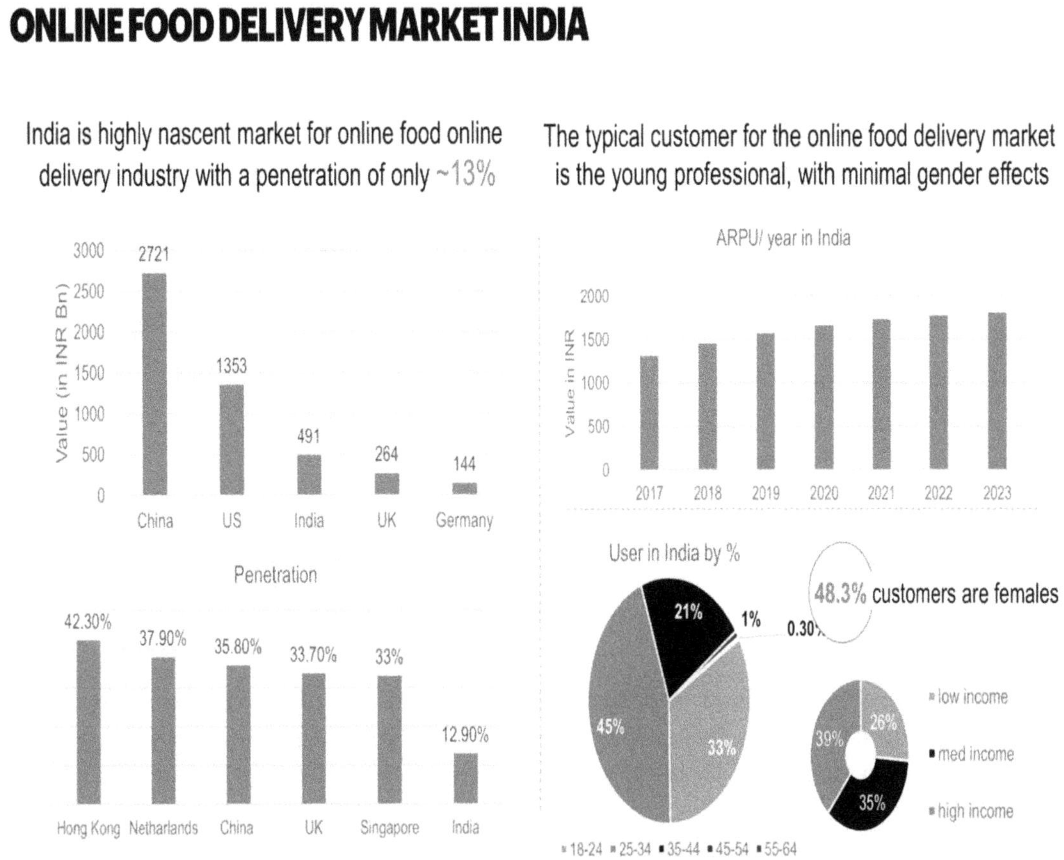

- **Route Optimisation:** Stock perceivability is crucial for any company to flourish, but it is not the only factor to be considered. Other factors like increased road time, fuel use, carbon imprints are also of major concern to any organisation. IoT innovation is helping in combating all this and more by allowing strategic use of company assets to reach planned destinations productively through open communication between drivers and armada managers. Along with improving real-time analytics, it also helps in achieving proficient arrangement of operations and increased client satisfaction.
- **Improvement of Real-time Tracking:** The fleet of cargos essentially the food items which are delivered in huge numbers are always a concern as there is an issue of rot. Through the real time tracking of the fleet managers can be aware of driver locations and any other issue the cargo is facing while on the road. IOTs nowadays can also aware managers about a heavy traffic. This helps them in better management of the fleet, smart driving options for the drivers and so on.
- **Productive Last-Mile Conveyance:** As of today companies like Rivigo are following a relay-driving technique where the fleet is carried to a certain place by a driver and from there another driver takes on for the later miles of the journey. On these stoppages, the company is indicated of

Figure 11. Market Reach due to the presence of Cloud Kitchens
Source: Compiled from various sources by authors

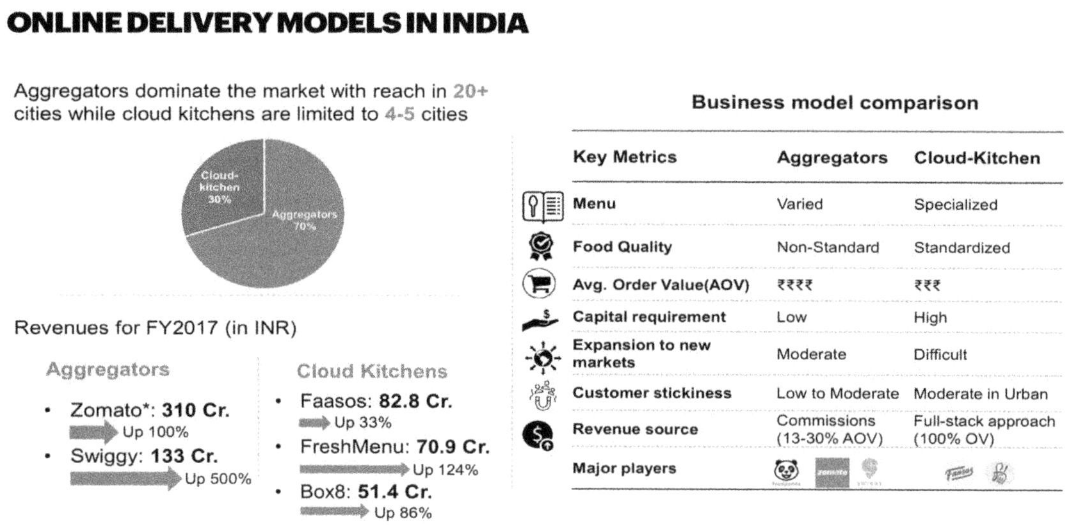

the fuel condition, weather forecast etc. These knowledge make the journey more seamless as well time saving on the last mile and the delivery is sure to achieve the target.

There is less doubt that IOT has impacted the total delivery part of supply chain, from improving visibility to real-time tracking, food safety and last-mile execution. Technology has always been a factor of constant change and so more no.of sophisticated devices are expected to arrive in time which will make analysis and decision making much smoother. As the ever expanding industry, the game will always be on being the best in the market and so such competitions will only open doors for further evolutions in supply chain.

Use of E-bikes for delivery in India

With a population of over 1.2 billion, India is besting the chart of the greatest client markets. India's 563 million youngsters making India gold dig for nourishment conveyance associations. According to a very reliable source, income in the Indian online nourishment conveyance section amounts to US$7,730M in 2019 which is required to cross US$12,536M by 2023, at the annual development rate of 12.8%. Two major players of Indian nourishment conveyance market are Zomato and Swiggy. Both unicorn status earned companies process more than 13 million requests in the month. In any case, because of low-margin business, poor gracefully demand ratio, over-reliance on gig laborers and cut-throat rivalry, the two of them are losing a heap of cash. In this way, they are attempting many ways to slice the operation cost and to have enough drivers to satisfy the demand. In 2019, Zomato tied up with many e-bicycle manufacturers of India to change over 40% of the armada to control assisted bicycles. At present, Zomato has a armada of more than 5000 e-bicycles and conveyance partners are conveying nourishment on e-bicycles in more than 12 urban communities of India. In his official statement, Zomato representative said that e-bicycles enable drivers to convey the nourishment on time and earn more.

Challenges on use of e-bicycles for conveyance in India

A portion of the issues looked in the Indian market by utilizing traditional conveyance strategies in India are:

- **Delivery drivers are earning less amid rising fuel cost**: However nourishment conveyance companies are offering generally excellent business chance to conveyance administrators, they are claiming that they cannot earn enough cash to endure easily. They have to spend a major percentage of their earning on the fuel and since they are free contractors, nourishment conveyance companies cannot pay them the fuel cost. This entire situation limits more conveyance administrators from joining the company which eventually decreases the request fill rate (percentage of requests satisfied) and so does the client satisfaction rate.
- **An wasteful driver tracking strategy**: As of now, a client can track the conveyance driver who is on his way to convey the nourishment, in the portable app. Be that as it may, many clients complain that they can't track conveyance drivers appropriately and it is valid. Conveyance drivers are tracked utilizing their telephone's location. In the event that they keep GPS on their telephones off, there is no other way to track them.
- **Congested urban areas causing a delay**: Indian urban communities are among the most blocked urban areas on the planet and to convey nourishment in such urban areas, conveyance drivers require 20-30% additional time. Because of this undesirable delay, clients get the nourishment late and conveyance drivers earn underneath average. In this way, both client satisfaction and driver satisfaction get affected, badly.

Increasing ecological issues: As the nourishment conveyance advertise in India grows, so does the quantity of bicycles on the streets, each emanating a critical carbon sum and at last adding to the unfavorable states of nature.

Advantages of E-bicycles:

With decreased resource cost, utilization of power which is a lot less expensive than fuel, and the diminished hustle of refuelling, in this way expanding the representative profitability; e-bicycles at last cut down the expenses brought about per conveyance, legitimately affecting the reality of the activities. The legislature of India is likewise concocting the spending intends to energize increasingly more E-vehicles and organizations and thus, Zomato, Swiggy, Domino's India have all begun and having trials with e-bicycles which will shape the following period of conveyance framework in India.

Customer Experience

Customer Experience enhancement remains at the crux of strategy of any QSR brand and there have been many trendy and technology-centric concepts that have come into play in the recent times. These concepts not only add as an effective attraction into the restaurant, but many of these tactics also play well into reducing costs by keeping operations cost at the minimum.

Technology has majorly affected the relationship between the restaurant and client by digitalizing the restaurant. From getting the customer to choose your offerings over the others, to enhancing his/her experience once the person is in the restaurant, digitalization has a role to play at every stage. The needs of the generation-z and millennial customer are especially centred around a digitalized restaurant even if it is as basic as dining in a Wi-Fi enabled restaurant.

The consumption patterns of the customers are often dependent on the stage of need felt by the customer is in. Figure 12 shows how Maslow's need hierarchy can be used to determine the consumption needs of the customer by basing them on the stage of need according to one's age and experience. This is further be utilized by organizations to determine their value propositions and messaging to different customer groups and segments.

Figure 12. Consumer's Hierarchy of needs
Source: Authors

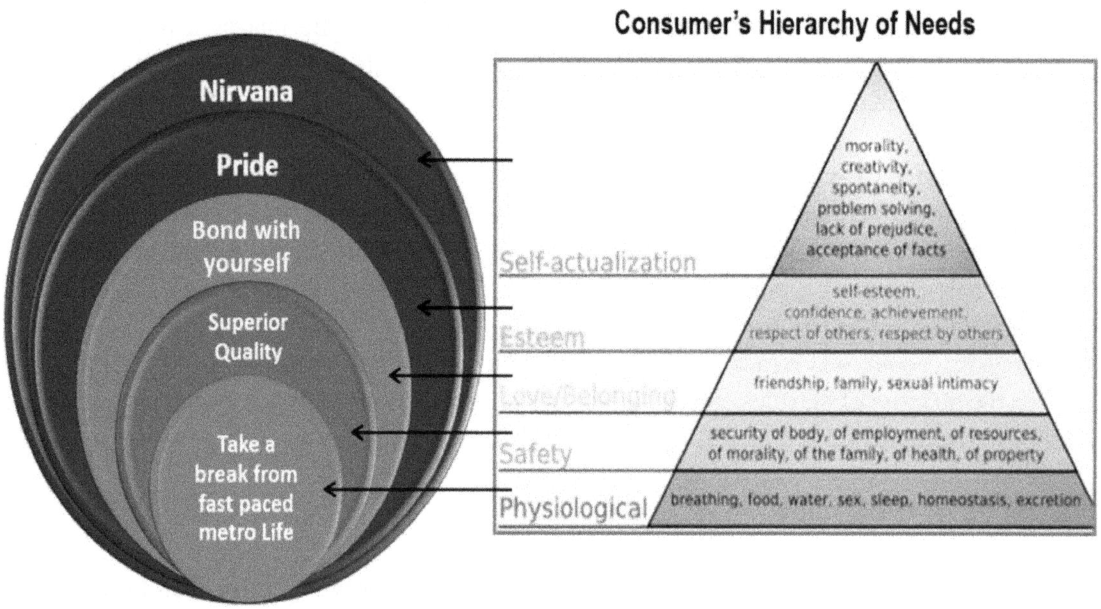

Live Kitchens

One of the many trends that have caught up with Indian kitchens over the years is live cooking. Live cooking is a culinary art form which involves the chef, who prepares the dish in the open and serves it at the table. Several cuisines are now prepared live in many restaurants in India.

Live kitchen concept for QSRs allows the customers to see how clean the kitchen is, admire the expertise of the chef, and review how well their meals are being prepared. These types of the kitchens also allow the clients to see the quality of ingredients and the culinary used. The biggest advantage of a live kitchen is the engagement between the chefs and the guests.

Live cooking makes the whole dining experience more interactive and lively. It helps the guests in customising their favourite dishes from the existing menu. Dishes such as Kothu Parothas, Pastas, Noodles,

Chinese Fried Rice are big hits at our establishment and it is quite interesting for the guests to add sauces, vegetables and watch the chef whip up a special meal before their eyes, said Chef Kailash Gundupalli, Executive Chef, ibis & Novotel Bengaluru Techpark

A Russian pizza chain called Dodo's Pizza took the concept of live kitchens to customers' homes by installing web cams in the restaurant kitchens which can be streamed on the customer app against an order placed with the restaurant.

Display-in-store

When you walk into a retail store or supermarket, you'll notice some shelves are more decorated to grab attention. Or there may be a few standees with specific products displayed. All these are examples of in-store displays, which are critical to the marketing strategies of stores and brands. In-store displays can be broadly categorized into three types: Window display, to attract attention and draw customer into a store; Point-of-purchase display, to encourage customers to make a last-minute buying decision and Standees, to make the customer aware of the offerings of the restaurant. This could be details of an ongoing offer or product related information (benefits and/or how to use the product).

In-store displays are an effective way of upselling, cross-selling and increasing the overall basket value of a customer. While in-store displays are focused on boosting sales, they can also be a highly effective branding tool. So, there are two essential things to consider when designing an in-store display most important being information. A customer should be given enough information to make a purchase decision. At the same time, the text needs to be big and crisp, to attract customers from a distance. Second is the design which needs to be attractive and impactful, while adhering to the brand guidelines of the organization.

Taking these conventional ways forwards and accommodating the technology in order to enhance the customer experience, many brands have started using screens greeting the customers by their names and displaying personalized offers for each customer using technologies like computer vision. This enhances the return rate of the customer as the customer feels more value and connected to the brand. Also, integrating these systems with the Point-of-sale systems deployed, gives the consumer insights to the company which can be analyzed objectively and quantitatively when in search of scope of improvements.

Service Robots

Robotics is another aspect in the era of automation which is the eventual future of the QSR industry. According to a study, 47% of the QSR diners prefer a self-ordering kiosk to customize their orders. These statistics combined with the internet and technology penetration in India, lead to a very high potential success for service robots in India.

The number of robots in the global food industry is well over 30,000, while the number of robots per 10,000 employees rose from 62 in 2013 to 84 in 2018.

Though the use of technology increases consistency and has a high potential of reducing costs, the feasibility of each tech application should be measured by keeping various aspects in mind, customer engagement level being just one of the aspects. For example, a restaurant might consider deploying robots in activities like butchery where chances of injury are high, but not so in dine-in services, where people might prefer the human touch.

Figure 13. Comparatives of various advancements by different food chains
Source: Authors

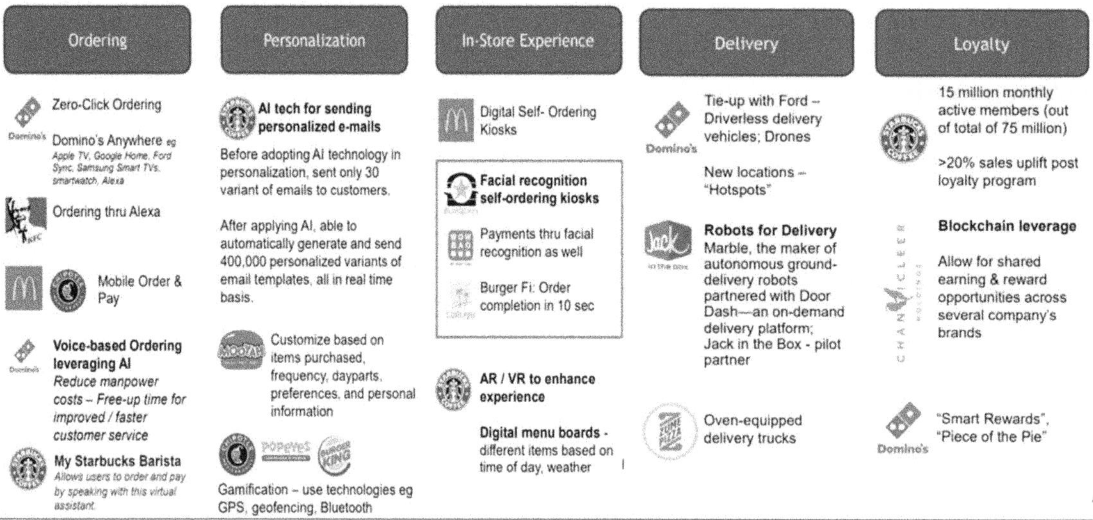

Figure 13 depicts the adaptation of the latest technological advances by different food chains around the globe. These activities have helped the companies to increase their brand awareness as well as customer engagement and also to map their brand image, of being the first one to start a new moment using mobile applications and websites.

CRISIS MANAGEMENT LESSONS FROM COVID-19

One thing that the recent COVID-19 pandemic has shown the organizations across industries is the need for an effective and robust crisis management system. The QSR sector was one of the worst impacted sectors due to the novel coronavirus pandemic across globe. Along with the strategies to evolve and make the business future-proof, there are certain practices that will be considered by all organizations in the near future.

Global supply chains: The reliability on supply chains panning across countries has been the major cause of the scale of impact QSR industry had to face. The organizations will thus be reconsidering reliance and dependency on a single supplier rather than a network of suppliers. The firms will be looking forward to build a partner ecosystem to mitigate any future risks. The consumer will also be questioning the sourcing of ingredients from certain specific areas which were the most affected by the disease and will thus be inclining towards products which are locally sourced.

Hygiene and safety protocols: The newly implemented "Zero Contact Delivery" by many QSR brands proved to be a vital step in assuring the customers that the product they are receiving is being delivered safely. These protocols will be staying back even after the pandemic situation is dealt with due the post-pandemic paranoia of the customers. Hence, the organizations need to make their cash-less delivery optimized and ready for upscale. The social distancing and "no touch" serving will also be prevalent once the lockdown restrictions are lifted and the restaurants are open for dine-in services.

Online Sale Boost: The pandemic has taught the customers how safe and convenient is online ordering. The seniors have also caught up to speed with online ordering and thus there might be a reduction in dine-in and increase in online delivery post-pandemic.

Adaption of technology: The only way to reduce human touch on the food served to customer, and hence ensure its safety is by adopting technology and automation into the business processes.

CONCLUSION

The above discussion makes it very evident that F&B industry is on the verge of major disruptions carried out through technology and process improvements. We have seen, how technology has taken over the entire value chain of a restaurant. The time isn't far away, where companies can think about operating a man-less store. Self-ordering kiosks taking the orders, a robo-chef preparing the dishes and a service robot serving those dishes to the customer. Technology is paving its way into styling the F&B industry into a Food Technology industry serving India tech-enabled food. The applications of technology are not just superficial but have actual business use cases that are focused on reducing costs and increasing the profits by taking informed data-driven decisions to improve the working of an organization in this industry overall. Apart from this, we see the industry moving towards more sustainable practices, covering the aspects of financial sustainability (lean restaurants, smart pricing, cost-effective procurement and delivery, sourcing risk mitigation), social sustainability (high levels of sensitivity to the consumer liking and disliking, customer responsiveness, personalization features in CRM, enhanced customer experience and in-spirit adherence food safety norms) and environmental sustainability (green packaging, plant based meet, e-bikes for delivery).

REFERENCES

Barras, R. (1986). Towards a theory of innovation in services. *Research Policy*, *15*(4), 161–173. doi:10.1016/0048-7333(86)90012-0

Berry, L., Carbone, L., & Haeckel, S. (2002). Managing the Total Customer Experience. *MIT Sloan Management Review*, 43.

Berry, L., Shankar, V., Parish, J., Cadwallader, S., & Dotzel, T. (2006). Creating New Markets Through Service. *MIT Sloan Management Review*, 47.

Berry, L. L. (1980). Services Marketing Is Different. *Business (Atlanta, Ga.)*, *30*(May), 24–29.

Bitner, M. J. (1992). Servicescapes: The impact of physical surroundings on customers and employees. *Journal of Marketing*, *56*(1), 57–71. doi:10.1177/002224299205600205

Bourke, J., Roper, S., & Love, J. H. (2020). Innovation in legal services: The practices that influence ideation and codification activities. *Journal of Business Research, 109*, 132–147. doi:10.1016/j.jbusres.2019.11.057

Castro, P., Rodrigues, J. P., & Teixeira, J. G. (2020). Understanding FinTech Ecosystem Evolution Through Service Innovation and Socio-technical System Perspective. In H. Nóvoa, M. Drăgoicea, & N. Kühl (Eds.), *Exploring Service Science. IESS 2020. Lecture Notes in Business Information Processing* (Vol. 377). Springer. doi:10.1007/978-3-030-38724-2_14

Christensen, C. W. (1997). *The innovator's dilemma: When new technologies cause great firms to fail.* Harvard University Press.

Cole, B. M. (2019). *Innovate or Die: How a lack of innovation can cause business failure.* www.forbes.com

Cronin, J. J. Jr, & Taylor, S. A. (1992). Measuring Service Quality: A Reexamination and Extension. *Journal of Marketing, 56*(July), 55–68. doi:10.1177/002224299205600304

Crosby, L. A., Evans, K. A., & Cowles, D. (1990). Relationship Quality in Services Selling: An Interpersonal Influence Perspective. *Journal of Marketing, 54*(July), 68–81. doi:10.1177/002224299005400306

Dasí, À., Elter, F., Gooderham, P.N., & Pedersen, T. (2017). New Business Models In-The-Making in Extant MNCs: Digital Transformation in a Telco. In *Breaking up the Global Value Chain* (Advances in International Management, Vol. 30). Emerald Publishing Limited. doi:10.1108/S1571-502720170000030001

Gallouj, F., & Djellal, F. (Eds.). (2010). *The handbook of innovation and services.* Edward Elgar. doi:10.4337/9781849803304

Ghazzawi, I. (2019). Cirque Du Soleil: Innovation is more culture than just a process. *Journal of Case Research and Inquiry, 5*, 201–236.

Guile, B. R., & Quin, J. B. (1988). *Managing Innovation: Cases from the Services Industries.* National Academy Press.

Hosseini, S., Haghverdi, F., Mohammad, S. M., & Hajipour, E. (2020). The effect of price promotions on impulse buying: The mediating role of service innovation in fast moving consumer goods. *International Journal of Business Information Systems, 33*(3), 320. doi:10.1504/IJBIS.2020.105828

Howells, J. (2001). The nature of innovation in services. In *OECD, innovation and productivity in services, OECD proceedings industry, services and trade.* Paris: Organization for Economic Cooperation and Development (OECD).

Huotari, K. K., Edvardsson, B., Jonas, J. M., Sorhammar, D., & Witell, L. (2016).. . *Journal of Business Research, 69*(8), 2964–2971. doi:10.1016/j.jbusres.2016.02.029

Ishlak, W. (2017). Creating an innovation culture. *McKinsey Quarterly.* https://www.mckinsey.com/business-functions/strategy-and-corporate-finance/our-insights/creating-an-innovation-culture

Karmarkar, U. (2014). The industrialization of services. In E. Baglieri & U. Karmarkar (Eds.), *Managing Consumer Services.* Springer. doi:10.1007/978-3-319-04289-3_2

Keaveney, S. M. (1995). Customer Switching Behavior in Service Industries: An Exploratory Study. *Journal of Marketing*, *59*(2), 71–82. doi:10.1177/002224299505900206

Lovelock, C., & Wright, L. (2002). *Principles of service marketing and management* (2nd ed.). Prentice Hall.

Martin, C. R., & Horne, D. A. (1993). Services innovation: Successful versus unsuccessful firms. *International Journal of Service Industry Management*, *4*(1), 49–65. doi:10.1108/09564239310024985

Miles. (2008). Patterns of innovation in service industries. *IBM Systems Journal*, *47*(1), 115-128. doi: . doi:10.1147j.471.0115

Ø

O'Reilly, B. (1997). The secrets of America's most admired corporations: New ideas, new products. *Fortune*, *135*, 60–64.

Paukstadt, U., Strobel, G. & Eicker, S. (2019). *Understanding services in the era of the internet of things: a smart service taxonomy*. Academic Press.

Rachinger, M., Rauter, R., Müller, C., Vorraber, W., & Schirgi, E. (2019). Digitalization and its influence on business model innovation. *Journal of Manufacturing Technology Management*, *30*(8), 1143–1160. doi:10.1108/JMTM-01-2018-0020

Schachter, M. (2018). The nature and variety of innovation. *International Journal of Innovation Studies*, *2*(2), 65–79. doi:10.1016/j.ijis.2018.08.004

Shostack, L. (1984). Designing Services that Deliver. *Harvard Business Review*, *62*, 133–139.

Snyder, H., Witell, L., Gustafsson, A., Fombelle, P., & Kristensson, P. (2016). Identifying categories of service innovation: A review and synthesis of the literature. *Journal of Business Research*, *69*(7), 2401–2408. doi:10.1016/j.jbusres.2016.01.009

Soto-Acosta, P., Del Giudice, M., & Scuotto, V. (2018). Emerging issues on business innovation ecosystems: The role of information and communication technologies (ICTs) for knowledge management (KM) and innovation within and among enterprises. *Baltic Journal of Management*, *13*(3), 298–302. doi:10.1108/BJM-07-2018-398

Tajeddini, K., Martin, E., & Altinay, L. (2020). The importance of human-related factors on service innovation and performance. *International Journal of Hospitality Management*, *85*(102431), 102431. doi:10.1016/j.ijhm.2019.102431

Uchupalanan, K. (2000). Competition and IT-based innovation in banking services. *International Journal of Innovation Management*, *4*(4), 455–490. doi:10.1142/S1363919600000238

Wang, C. N., Day, J. D., & Farid, M. (2019). Service Innovation Model of the Automobile Service Industry. *Applied Sciences (Basel, Switzerland)*, *9*(12), 2403. doi:10.3390/app9122403

Ye, H., & Kankanhalli, A. (2020). Value Cocreation for Service Innovation: Examining the Relationships between Service Innovativeness, Customer Participation, and Mobile App Performance. *Journal of the Association for Information Systems*, 294–312. doi:10.17705/1jais.00602

Chapter 12
The CSR Performance and Earning Management Practice on the Market Value of Conventional Banks in Indonesia

Saarce Elsye Hatane
https://orcid.org/0000-0002-3797-1623
Petra Christian University, Indonesia

Amadea Nathania Pranoto
Petra Christian University, Indonesia

Josua Tarigan
Petra Christian University, Indonesia

Josephine Alexandra Susilo
Petra Christian University, Indonesia

Ang Jonathan Christianto
Petra Christian University, Indonesia

ABSTRACT

This study examined the effect of the components of corporate social responsibility (CSR) and earnings management on market value, measured using Tobin's Q. CSR is measured by using KLD Index, while earnings management used discretionary loan loss provision. The GMM-SYS (generalized method of moment system) dynamic panel data method is employed to examine the research framework on conventional banks listed in Indonesia Stock Exchange. Among six components in CSR disclosures, only corporate governance, environmental and product disclosures are favorable for bank's market value.

DOI: 10.4018/978-1-7998-4787-8.ch012

Furthermore, earnings management had a positive impact on market value. Empirical result indicated that CSR functions as a part of bank strategic moves in order to survive the highly dynamical business environment. Since CSR inflicts additional costs for the company, they must perform CSR efficiently while maintaining a strong relationship with shareholders. This study contributes to CSR and financial management literature by finding the nature of CSR effects as future strategic investment.

INTRODUCTION

The banking sector in Indonesia (Hatane et al., 2019) is experiencing a slowdown from decreasing credit quality within the last five years. In 2016, President Joko Widodo also enacted a regulation for banks to reduce their loan rates (Nugroho, 2016). While the government tried to lower the interest rate, banks were facing a series of bad credits. The rise of non-performing loans caused by bad credits has presented a challenge for banks in restoring public trust and building clear, transparent business numbers. On the other hand, banks must also comply with the regulation and reduce lending rates. As a result, banks are indirectly required to implement social, ethical, and responsible approach in their business environment to regain public trust. Corporate social responsibility (CSR) has become a global trend for companies in gaining public trust as well as achieving sustainability. Companies seek to show their concern for the community while promoting organizational participation and position in the market. By applying CSR, firms can benefit from better positioning, even if this necessitates them in spending extra costs. However, having a good image and good firm quality on the market can encourage employees to work productively and achieve higher financial performance (Devie et al. 2018).

CSR in banking is related to its environment, community, and products (Aracil, 2019). The main product of a bank is any facility or service related to cash management, therefore, the important elements for the welfare of banks are finance, customers, and society. A socially responsible bank is accountable to take on responsibility for the impact of its activities on society. Concern for environmental sustainability by banks gave rise to the concept of green banking. The need to adopt green banking practices is considered very important because of its environmental, corporate, and social benefits for the economy (Ibe-Enwo et al. 2019). Secondly, to gain customer and society trust, banks need integrity and transparency to operate (Banking for society, n.d.). Banks are means used by the public to invest their funds. Therefore, banks are very important to have a high level of transparency.

When a company is being transparent by divulging what struggles are being faced, it is doing voluntary disclosure. Yim et al. (2019) contended that by voluntarily disclosing information, the company doing CSR is signaling the public on its quality. To increase customer confidence, companies must reduce information asymmetry. Earnings management is often related to information asymmetry because the concept of earnings management is to manipulate earnings. In the process, profit manipulation can be done to make the company look profitable in that period. However, a socially-responsible corporate has a low incentive to manage earnings (Hong & Andersen, 2011); in other words, a company with poor CSR activities has a higher rate of earnings management. It is hoped that by running CSR well enough, while also having a low level of earnings management, banks have a better reputation and firm market value will increase.

Based on previous studies, it is generally agreed that CSR activities increase market value (Aras et al., 2018; Cho et al., 2019). Feng et al. (2017) said that different type of CSR has a different effect on the market value. However, on the contrary, Omar & Zallom (2016) found that some CSR components can lower market value. Moreover, Chtourou & Triki (2017) argued instead that as long as it does not harm the company, CSR can be implemented for long-term business sustainability purposes. Therefore, studies on the impact of CSR and financial performance have yielded inconclusive results. Additionally, many prior studies discuss the impact of CSR on financial performance on non-financial companies (Oh and Park, 2015; Sial et al. 2018; Gangi et al, 2018; Ho et al. 2019). There are limited studies found on the impact of CSR and earnings management on the market value of the banking sector. Whereas, the banking sector plays an important role in maintaining a country's economic stability and wealth (Hatane et al. 2019). Moreover, most studies focus on the CSR of Islamic banks, however not on conventional banks. To fill in the literature gap, this research provides valuable insight into CSR and its relation with the market value of banks listed in the Indonesia Stock Exchange (*Bursa Efek Indonesia*, BEI). This research tries to give insights into how CSR can be a strategic approach to achieve sustainability. Its influence on the environment, society, and communities has to, therefore, be measured with different perspectives. In order to achieve the objective, this study uses the KLD Index as a multidimensional approach in measuring CSR performances. Therefore, making the objective of this study is to test the impact of CSR and earnings management on the market value of conventional banks in Indonesia. Section 2 states the background theory of CSR and earnings management, followed by prior researches on CSR and financial performance relationships. Then, in Section 3, the research methodology is explained. Finally, Section 4 discusses the results and solutions; Section 5 provides conclusions and limitations.

BACKGROUND

Corporate social responsibility is associated with voluntary acts by a company in social or environmental forms to propose society's welfare (Omar & Zallom, 2016). Various practices are taken by a company ranging from donating money, to concern for the environment, and to promote the firm's transparency. Preserving the environment, the concept of green banking comes into action. Green banking promotes environmentally friendly practices and reduces the carbon footprint of banking activities. It aims to improve operations and technology together by making environmentally friendly client habits in banking activities, thus benefiting the community as well. CSR practices aren't limited to donations and environmentally recycle, but also on the willingness to reveal factual issues that happen to the company. On top of that, the responsibility practices done by a company can become their strategy to enhance the corporate's reputation (Devie et al. 2018). Moreover, on gaining public trust, banks shall promote transparency by signaling the public. In the long term, CSR is a strategic approach in navigating dynamic business activities and reaching a sustainable environment (Carini et al., 2017).

Companies adopting social responsibility practices reduce information asymmetry (Su et al., 2014) and prevent adverse selection (Yu et al., 2017). This is often linked with signaling theory. Signaling theory explains firms' efforts to signal the public regarding their motivation and goodwill (Yu et al., 2017). Information asymmetry arises from inside information that is not being published by one party. It occurs when a party (in a situation) has more information than the other party, or in other words, one of the parties benefits from the information in its possession. Signaling theory discusses information asymmetry between two parties where the source of asymmetric information is mainly related to information about quality or intention (Su et al., 2014). Quality concerns about how one party reacts by showing its true attitudes toward receiving premium benefits from the other party. The intention relates to how to diminish the possibility of a moral hazard resulting from the behavior of the parties exchanging information.

Yim et al., (2019) argues that companies engaged in CSR provide a signal to society about their high quality. It is most likely that the company doing CSR performances are perceived to be more honorable by showing altruistic values toward society. In that case, they are less likely to possess a moral hazard. Yu et al., (2017) states that based on signaling theory, companies can provide intangible information through voluntary disclosure to strengthen their competitive advantage and capability in the market. As a company discloses its CSR performances voluntarily, a company not only shows that it is complying with the laws and regulations but also to declare its legitimacy. Deegan (2002) mentioned legitimacy theory is developing voluntary, social, and environmental disclosures to fulfill their social contract that enables the recognition of the organization's objectives. It is a system that backs up the business organization during turbulence. Adhering to the legal obligation is a prerequisite to meet the responsibility (Mullerat & Brennan, 2005). When the social expectation rises and the organization's activities do not meet moral values, an entity should defend itself through legitimate economic and social actions. Companies that are practicing CSR are considered to be more respectable since they demonstrate altruistic values in addition to their legitimate obligations (Gras-Gil et al., 2016). Through the integration of CSR performance, banks indirectly have an impact on society that is being sustainable. Encouraging social and environmental responsibility toward sustainability can increase firm market value (Aras et al., 2018; Cho et al., 2019). By implementing CSR, firms can benefit from better market positioning. Thus the research hypothesis for this paper is formed:

Hypothesis One: Corporate social responsibility positively affects market value.

Based on agency theory, conflict of interest may push managers to manage earnings. In the banking industry, the manager's motivation to manage profits is to minimize profit volatility from time to time (Othman & Mersni, 2014). Loan Loss Provision (LLP) is used by banks as a proxy to manage earnings. The purpose of this is to set aside a certain amount to be used as a bad debt reserve. Manipulation is a part of information asymmetry. Normally, socially responsible firms have low incentives to manage earnings. In other words, firms with poor CSR activities have a higher activity level of earnings management (Gras-Gil et al. 2016). A high activity level of earnings management can mislead financial statement users. The low quality of information generated from the adverse selection can affect a company's market value investor (Ujah et al., 2017). A company with a high level of integrity and credibility will acquire the public's trust (Mukherjee & Nuñez, 2019), and so raises its market value. Market value embodies investors' opinions on a company, which is reflected in the equity market value. Market value can also depict future profits through investors' evaluation. Banks with integrity and high credibility can increase public trust (Mukherjee and Nuñez, 2019). Thus, the second hypothesis is formed:

Hypothesis Two: Earnings management negatively affects market value.

To capture the multi-dimension of CSR, this paper uses an extensively used approach, the KLD Index formulated by Kinder, Lydenberg, and Domini to measure CSR (Devie et al., 2018; Ho et al., 2019;

Chantziaras et al., 2020). The index is divided into two categories: strengths and concerns. Strengths refer to the additional ability of a firm; concerns are matters concerning the inability to achieve the goal of strengths. While under the two categories, seven components comprise of *Community, Corporate governance, Diversity, Employee relations, Environment, Human rights*, and *Products* (Sun & Rakhman, 2013).

RESEARCH METHODOLOGY

Sampling and Data Collection

The study used secondary data taken from annual reports, financial reports, Bloomberg databases, and other trustworthy sources. The population in this study is 42 conventional banks listed in Indonesia Stock Exchange (BEI). The banks must have continuously published annual reports in 2012-2018. They must also have the necessary information as needed for variable measurement. The sample is thus 31 companies in the banking sector, with a seven-year observation period from 2012-2018.

The purpose of the research is to investigate whether CSR and earnings management affects market value in a positive, negative, or neutral way. To resolve the endogeneity problem, this study uses the GMM-SYS (generalized method of moment system) dynamic panel data method (Lin *et al.*, 2018) since GMM has the largest correction effect on coefficients. The problem of endogeneity stems from the fact that causality can run in both the direction of independent to dependent variables and vice versa. A reciprocal relationship can happen between both variables. The GMM-SYS method was developed to overcome the correlation problem between the dependent variable and any existing error in the GMM estimator (Oh & Park, 2015).

Dynamic panel data has three steps in testing the validity and reliability of a model:

1. Arellano-Bond test

The Arellano-Bond test is done to diagnose any serial correlation. The null hypothesis of the test is that there exists autocorrelation on *error*. The null hypothesis of the Arellano-Bond test for serial correlation is:

- **H0:** there is no autocorrelation
- H0 is rejected if p-value < 1%, 5%, 10%

Arellano-Bond test has two orders, AR 1 and AR 2 as seen in Table 1. The test is consistent if H0 is rejected (on three significant levels of 1, 5, and 10%) on AR 1, but is not rejected on AR 2 (Lin *et al.*, 2018). As seen in Table 1, H0 is rejected as the p-value is 0.0581 which is significant on a 10% level. For AR2, it is supposed to be above a significant level, and the value agrees with the theory, 0.3691.

2. Sargan test

On the GMM model, it is important to know the validity of the instrumental variable which amount exceeds the estimated parameter (over-identification). The Sargan test tries for the validity of over-identification restrictions, on where p-values are reported. The null hypothesis of the Sargan test is:

- **H0:** the limit of over-identification is valid
- H0 is rejected if p-value < 1%, 5%, 10%

For this test, it is expected for the p-value to be above the significant levels of 1, 5, and 10%; in other words, the null hypothesis is not rejected. The Sargan test on over-identifying restrictions presents a higher p-value, implying that there is no over-identification problem, and so it can be said that the model is valid. As shown in Table 1, the Sargan test resulted in 0.2596 which aligned with the theory implying there is no problem exists concerning over-identification.

3. Wald test

This test is used in simultaneously testing the significance of parameters that are used for the model between dependent and independent variables, distributed in asymptotic Chi-square, with null hypothesis stating that there is no relationship in the estimated model, and H0 is rejected if the p-value is < α. The Wald test is used to determine if the variables employed in the tested model are simultaneously significant. Therefore, the null hypothesis of the Wald test is:

- **H0:** there are no relations between variables in the model.
- H0 is rejected if p-value < 1%, 5%, 10%

The Wald test is expected to reject the null hypothesis, with rejection occurring if p-value < 1%, 5%, 10%, and so the rejection of the null hypothesis in the Wald test becomes the objective of the estimator (Habimana, 2016). As seen in Table 1, the result of the Wald test is 0.0000, which rejected the null hypothesis with a p-value of < 1%.

Table 1. Validity and reliability test

Test for AR(1) errors	z = -1.89504	[0.0581]
Test for AR(2) errors	z = -0.898199	[0.3691]
Sargan over-identification test	Chi-square(19) = 22.5101	[0.2596]
Wald (joint) test	Chi-square(12) = 22196.8	[0.0000]
Sum squared residual	2.592302	
S.E. of regression	0.122411	

Table 1 shows that the model is valid and reliable as it has fulfilled the three requirements of validity and reliability test.

Measurements

Measurement of Corporate Social Responsibility

Following previous studies (Matuszak *et al.*, 2019; Chantziaras *et al.*, 2020), the measurement used for CSR is KLD Index. KLD Index was developed to support social studies and comprehensively measure a company's social activities. KLD Index was chosen to measure CSR since this index is multidimensional, thus capable of picturing the company from a variety of dimensions. The KLD Index has been used as a CSR measurement tool in various studies. There are seven empirical indicators: *community*, *corporate governance*, *diversity*, *employee relations*, *environment*, *human rights*, and *product*. These components are further separated into two categories, which are *strength* (the company's strength or advantages) and *concern* (any problem inside or related to the company that needs special attention). Every bank that has fulfilled the *strength* or *concern* are numbered 1, and 0 when it doesn't. To make the data more reliable, each data are calculated as a ratio (value divided by the average). The KLD Index used in this study is a holistic approach from both the good and the bad sides of the company to measure social performance. The following is a brief explanation of the CSR components:

1. Community

Discusses the treatment of a company on its surrounding community. Community activities can be through donations, financial aid, or social support towards the community in the vicinity of or outside the company's environment.

2. Corporate governance

This refers to a set of policies or regulations that affect the process of management and control in a company or corporation.

3. Diversity

Relates to the diversity of board members and employees. A company is said to have more diversity when it has a Chief Executive Officer that is a woman or a member of a minority group; when it has made important progress in promoting women and/or minority groups; when it has a diverse board of directors; when it provides benefit, care, and job for disabled people; and other forms of diversity.

4. Employee relations

Refers to the relations among the company employees.

5. Environment

This refers to how the company acts regarding its surrounding environment.

6. Human rights

Relates to the rights and obligations of the company's consumers and employees, as dictated by the law.

7. Product

The most important category; this part explores the quality and detail of a product that is developed by a company. In this study, a bank's financial service is the product.

Measurement of Earnings Management

Earnings management in the banking sector is achieved through the reduction of discretionary accruals from the total accrual. For this sector, earnings management is often reflected by Loan Loss Provision (LLP) (Othman & Mersni, 2014; Ujah *et al.*, 2017). Banks use LLP to manage their earnings. The total accrual is represented by LLP. Table 2 displays the operational definition to measures the bank's earnings management. The empirical indicator is LLP obtained from:

$$LLP = \text{Non-discretionary LLP (NDLLP)} + \text{Discretionary LLP (DLLP)} \quad (1)$$

Thus, DLLP is obtained by subtracting NDLLP from LLP. Based on previous research (Othman & Mersni, 2014), the estimation method utilized to find DLLP is:

$$DLLPit = LLPit - [\beta 0 + \beta 1\ NPLit - 1 + \beta 2\ \Delta\ NPLit + \beta 3\ \Delta\ TLit]. \quad (2)$$

Where:

Table 2. The operational definition of earnings management

Component of Earnings Management	Definition
Loan loss provision (LLP*it*)	The total of loan loss provision on bank *i* in year *t*, divided by an initial credit balance
Non-performing loans (NPL*it* – 1)	The opening balance of non-performing loans on bank *i* in year *t*, divided by an initial credit balance
ΔPL*it*	The difference of non-performing loans on bank *i* in year *t*, divided by an initial credit balance
ΔL	The difference of total credit on bank *i* in year *t*, divided by an initial credit balance

Measurement of Market Value

The empirical indicator employed to measure market value is Tobin's Q. Tobin's Q does not only provide a snapshot of a company's value but also investors' view on the company which is reflected from the equity value. Tobin's Q is calculated from the *market value of equity* (market capitalization) plus *total liabilities* and divided by *total assets* (Nawaz, 2017). Table 3 presents the operational definition of each variable that is examined in the research model.

To test the hypotheses and see the effect of the CSR components and earnings management have on the market value of conventional banks in Indonesia, the following regression model is employed:

$$TOBQit = \beta 0 + \beta 1COMit + \beta 2CGit + \beta 3DIVit + \beta 4EMPit$$
$$+ \beta 5ENVit + \beta 6HRit + \beta 7PRODit + \beta 8DLLPit + \beta 9SIZEit + \beta 10CARit + \beta 11LDit + \varepsilon$$

Measurement of Control Variables

1. Firm Size (SIZE)

Based on market capitalization, the size of the company can be reflected from the total assets owned by the company. Measurement of company size is done to distinguish quantitatively between large companies and small companies. The natural logarithm of total assets is known as the proxy for firm size. Thus, it is evident that firm size reflects the financial performance of a company (Nawaz, 2017).

2. Capital adequacy ratio (CAR)

Capital Adequacy Ratio (CAR) is the ratio of a capital structure owned by the company. CAR is obtained from the average total equity divided by the average total assets. In developing countries, a stable capital structure is very important especially for financial institutions because it can help in dealing with a crisis (Menicucci and Paolucci 2016). Thus, CAR can reflect how sturdy the company's capital structure is. The higher the value of CAR, the better the capital structure of the company.

3. Loan to deposit (LD)

Loan to deposit is used to represent external financing (Othman and Mersni, 2014). To be able to obtain external financing, banks report low LLP to reduce perceived risk and to increase reported income, so that it provides appealing numbers to the eyes of investors. A high LD ratio shows that total loans are greater than deposits. Therefore, banks need to withdraw more deposits from customers to increase liquidity. For that matter, bank managers have an incentive to report low LLP. Thus, the level of earnings management through DLLP is negatively related to the demand for external financing. The variables and their definitions are as follows.

RESEARCH RESULTS AND ANALYSIS

The analysis of the descriptive statistics of each variable is explained in this part. Table 4 briefly illustrates the data used in this study, by using several parameters such as mean, median, standard deviation (S.D.), minimum, and maximum values.

As shown in Table 4, each CSR component in the data has a uniformly distributed value as seen from the standard deviation (S.D.), which is close to 0 (unbiased), except for CAR and LD. This is shown in the standard deviation (S.D.) column that seven components have a value of less than 1 (*the community*

Table 3. Variables definition

Variable	Definition
CSR components	COM = Community CG = Corporate governance DIV = Diversity EMP = Employee relations ENV = Environment HR = Human rights PROD = Product For each component, the difference from the total score of *strength* and the total score of *concern* is divided by the number of categories. The components and categories of details are included in the Appendix.
Tobin's Q (TOBQ)	Market capitalization plus total liabilities divided by total assets
Discretionary loan loss provision (DLLP)	The measurement of earnings management (total accruals minus non-discretionary accruals)
Firm Size (SIZE)	Natural logarithm of total assets
Capital adequacy ratio (CAR)	The average of total equity divided by the average of total assets
Loan-to-deposit ratio (LD)	Total loan divided by total deposit

has a value of 0.176, *corporate governance* 0.173, and so on). However, based on the *mean* values shown, all banks on average have a high CAR value of 13.929. As regulated by the Financial Services Authority Regulations (*Otoritas Jasa Keuangan*, OJK) Number 03/2016, the capital structure standard for the banking sector ranges from 8% to 14%, and this percentage varies depending on the bank's ranking. The higher the ranking, the higher is the capital structure, which is demanded by Financial Services Authority Regulations, to secure company assets. The *mean* of CAR is 13.929, thus on average, all banks in the sample have a good quality of CAR without considering the ranking. Thus, high data distribution (S.D.) on CAR which is 5.041 has no significant effect.

Table 4. Descriptive statistics analysis

Variable	Mean	Median	S.D.	Minimum	Maximum
Community (COM)	0.753	0.714	0.176	0.000	1.000
Corporate Governance (CG)	0.872	1.000	0.173	0.000	1.000
Diversity (DIV)	0.290	0.375	0.181	-0.125	0.500
Employee (EMP)	0.610	0.571	0.224	0.000	1.000
Environment (ENV)	0.681	0.833	0.308	0.000	1.000
Human Rights (HR)	0.521	0.500	0.214	0.000	1.000
Product (PROD)	0.733	0.750	0.190	0.000	1.000
DLLP	-0.001	-0.002	0.013	-0.030	0.077
Firm Size	30.975	30.786	1.938	26.961	34.799
CAR	13.929	13.279	5.041	0.137	35.514
LD	86.688	87.255	14.821	43.460	146.376
Tobin's Q	1.072	1.025	0.152	0.529	1.593

In contrast, LD exhibits a very large deviation, meaning the LD from the Indonesian conventional banks' sample is highly variable as we can see from the S.D. which is 14.821. LD illustrates external funding (Othman & Mersni, 2014), considering each bank has a different funding structure depending on its size. This result can be explained as a consequence of rising bad credit up through 2016. There exists a highly difficult condition for banks, causing widespread data distribution (Sari, 2016). An explanation is then derived that banks that suffer from unstable capital structure need additional capital. They must use external funding in order to maintain their liquidity. *Diversity* has a minus minimum score of -0.125. This means that the *concern* issues exceed the *strengths*. High *concern* for *diversity* arises because of the *non-representation* issue, that is, the lack of women on the board of directors when the research is conducted.

Table 5. Hypotheses testing (CSR components)

Variable	Conventional Banks (DP)		Significance Results
	Coefficient	P-value	
Tobin's Q (t-1)	0.893408	<0.0001***	
Const	−0.155595	0.0157**	
Community	−0.0384439	0.0663*	Sig -
Corporate Governance	0.0915947	<0.0001***	Sig +
Diversity	−0.0375903	0.0105**	Sig -
Employee relations	−0.0234789	0.0069***	Sig -
Environment	0.0208300	0.0443**	Sig +
Human rights	0.0120698	0.4266	In Sig
Product	0.0486374	<0.0001***	Sig +
DLLP	1.28258	<0.0001***	Sig +
Size	0.00224933	0.1599	In Sig
CAR	0.00220793	0.0004***	Sig +
LD	0.00101749	<0.0001***	Sig +

Notes: * p<0.10 (weakly significant); **p<0.05 (significant); ***p<0.01 (highly significant).

Table 5 exhibits the test result on the impact of each CSR and earnings management, along with the control variables (Size, CAR, LD), on market value.

The research agrees with Feng *et al.* (2017) that every component has a different effect on market value. As seen in Table 5 of the significant results column, four out of seven CSR components positively affect market value, three of them affect significantly, and one is insignificant, which is *human rights*. The three components which affect negatively are *community*, *diversity*, and *employee relations*. This is shown by the minus coefficients of −0.0384439, −0.0375903, and −0.0234789 consecutively. Results are contrary to previous studies which found that all CSR activity has a positive significant relationship with market value (Aras *et al.*, 2018; Cho *et al.*, 2019). Conforming to Omar & Zallom (2016), *the community* negatively impacts market value.

Tobin's Q contains the equity market value components which involve investors' reasoning in determining firm value. Yet, DLLP which indicates the existence of earnings management instead raises market value. This is consistent with the output of the negative significant impact some CSR components have on Tobin's Q. During the administration of President Joko Widodo, the government imposed a reduction in loan interest rates (Nugroho, 2016). Bad credit became the main problem of Indonesian banks, which could logically explain this situation. *The community* has a negative value (coefficient of –0.0384439) since there are more *concerns* than *strengths* due to negative economic impact (an aspect of *Community*), namely bad credit, during the observation period. The *diversity* value is also negative because of the lack of women on the board of directors' composition, causing higher *concern* value compared to *strength*. Banks can improve their *diversity* as it is an internal factor. Tang (2019) wrote that from 2016 through 2018, bank employees suffered from lay-offs due to digitalization and automation processes, these results in negative impact by *employee relations*. What happened to these banks is an unavoidable outside factor. Banks are pressured to reduce lending rates, but at the same time, they are facing bad credits. As a result, banks are not liquid and face a crisis in obtaining working capital. Working capital is used to fund the banks' daily operational activities and is obtained from current assets minus current liabilities. According to Megeid (2017), if a bank faces a liquidity crisis, it is necessary to borrow additional funds in order to fulfill liquidity requirements and raise loan loss provision. This is supported by the data in Table 5, which shows that Loan-to-Deposit (LD) correlates positively with Tobin's Q (a positive coefficient of 0.00101749), meaning market value (Tobin's Q) grows when Loan-to-Deposit increases. To resolve the lack of working capital, banks chose to apply for long-term external funding to fund the organization, instead of short-term funding. This leads to an increase in total loans. Supposed that in the observation period the economic condition is normal, both *community* and *employee relations* might generate positive results, and therefore six CSR components (*community, corporate governance, diversity, employee relations, environment,* and *products)* would positively impact market value.

Corporate governance, environment, and *product* have a significant positive impact on market value as seen by the positive coefficients of 0.0915947, 0.0208300, and 0.0486374 consecutively. *The human rights* component has a positive impact on market value but not significantly. Therefore, management must pay attention to developing CSR activities related to corporate governance, environment, and products.

Looking at a different perspective, these banks displayed transparency by doing voluntary disclosure on factual ongoing information, in this case, bad credit. Banks demonstrated high integrity by being transparent (Mukherjee & Nuñez, 2019) since they chose to do voluntary disclosure. This act reduces information asymmetry and thus acknowledges the signaling theory. By this theory, a company gives out a positive signal to the public that there are no hidden motives to harm customers, by this means society; instead, they were facing a financial crisis. The result shown in Table 5 may be caused by the possibility that investors choose to see the result of the company's financial performance. Investors value financial statements more compared to the CSR section (ACCA, 2008). They contend that being transparent and accountable towards the society and environment does not benefit company profitability, so they choose to see only the final result of financial performance. Therefore, this affects the equity market value, which resulted in a significant negative impact of CSR on Tobin's Q.

In this study, it is hypothesized that earnings management negatively affects market value because of the adverse selection of information by management. However, in this result, the second hypothesis is rejected since earnings management affects market value positively (as seen in the coefficient of DLLP is 1.28258 with positive significance result). This result isn't consistent with the previous study that said loan loss provisions are negatively related to banking performance (Wu et al., 2016). It is found that by reserving provisions, banks have a better result. During the observation period, banks are facing a financial crisis, which was bad credit. Due to the economic impact, banks need liquid assets. To cope with the situation, they set aside LLP to be used as a bad debt reserve. This can logically explains the situation why earnings management resulted in a positive impact on banking performance, which is market value in this study.

Control Variable Analysis

The research model also considers three control variables: Firm Size (SIZE), Capital Adequacy Ratio (CAR), and Loan-to-Deposit (LD). The finding of the control variables analysis is summarized in Table 5. Only CAR and LD are consistent in playing their roles as control variables, shown by significant results of 0.0004*** and <0.0001*** consecutively with a p-value of less than 1% (highly significant). Contrary to previous studies, SIZE does not significantly influence financial performance (Nawaz, 2017). A large bank does not necessarily have a better performance than a smaller bank. Therefore, firm size is not a significant factor. On the other hand, CAR and LD both significantly affect market value. CAR captures a market-based approach and consists of total assets and total equity. A strong and significant link is found between CAR and Tobin's Q. Tobin's Q includes equity market value, which explains why CAR is significant to Tobin's Q. A significant positive relationship is also found on LD to Tobin's Q. In other words, external funding as reflected by LD enhances market value. As the bank increases external funding (total loans), its equity level also rises, and so does its loan-to-deposit rate.

SOLUTIONS AND RECOMMENDATIONS

Managers of conventional banks should make a budget plan in advance before doing CSR, to make sure that the benefits from CSR outweigh its costs. For the bad credit, banks must prepare a portfolio on liquidity risk. In case it occurs in the future, banks are ready to face without practicing excess earnings management by reserving a high value of DLLP. Banks should also increase the diversity in the board of directors, for example by giving the female employee a chance for duty, enforcing equal rights. Since *corporate governance, environment,* and *product* are positively impacting market value, managers are recommended to develop CSR activities relating to them. The environment is one of the most prominent CSR components in this study. This component assesses how banks contribute positively or at least not to pollute the environment. Banks do not directly damage the environment. The concept of green banking is developing along with the attention of the banking industry in protecting the environment. Green banking is translated as an effort by banks to prioritize the fulfillment of sustainability in lending or operational activities. The use of energy, water, and other natural resources in banking activities is not as severe as the use by other sectors, such as mining and processing industries. To enhance developing CSR activities related to *environment* and *product*, banks can adopt the concept of green banking. Green banking practices can be in the form of paperless banking, internet banking, paperless automated teller machines (ATMs), renewable energy and energy efficiency can be implemented by adopting energy-saving technologies, installing solar panels to create alternative energy, recycling and recyclable products (Kumar & Prakash, 2018). However, banking cannot necessarily be released from the problem of increasing environmental degradation. By providing loans or financing to its customers, banks can be a trigger for activities that have an impact on the environment.

Regulators are expected to make appropriate considerations related to the interests of stakeholders. In this study, it is found that banks tend to focus on environmental greening activities and donations to the surrounding community. They overlook the innovation of *product* components, specifically not emphasizing disclosure related to green banking. Thus, it is recommended for banks to focus on disclosure of product innovation with the concept of green banking. Since business moves dynamically, any CSR measurement used must be adapted for its era. It is recommended that future studies pay attention to the existing popular movements, as there is a chance for CSR measurement methods to evolve in the future. Hence, future research should use a measurement that has been adjusted with the existing period.

CONCLUSION

The purpose of this study is to recognize the impact of CSR and earnings management on the market value of conventional banks. The study uses data taken from annual reports and Bloomberg database between 2012 and 2018. The first hypothesis examines the relationship between CSR, as an independent variable, and market value. CSR consists of seven components which comprise of *community*, *corporate governance*, *diversity*, *employee relations*, *environment*, *human rights*, and *product*. The result shows that each CSR component has a differing influence on market value. The second hypothesis tests the effect of earnings management on market value. The second hypothesis is not accepted as there is a significant positive effect of DLLP on market value. When a bank experiences bad credits, it needs working capital, so it sets to borrow from external parties increasing loan loss provision. This explains why earnings management positively impacts market value. However, if the excess practice of earnings management is done, it results in information asymmetry and could harm the company's reputation.

CSR should have been able to help banks increase market value. However, during the observation period, a series of bad credits and mass lay-offs caused by digitalization and automation happened, therefore resulted in differing influences on market value. Nevertheless, there are logical causes that explain why *community*, *diversity*, and *employee relations* have a negative effect. As long as it does not harm the organization, CSR is a good approach for the company in achieving business sustainability (Devie *et al.* 2018). Suppose the economic condition is fairly normal during the period, it leads to a better result. Investors can support CSR activities carried out by banks to achieve business sustainability goals that can also minimize business risks in the future.

LIMITATIONS

The research has several limitations; one being the number of the bank sample size used is very limited, considering not all conventional banks in Indonesia made their data available. Future studies should research all conventional banks in Indonesia. Additionally, this study only investigated market value, and only used a single measurement for market value using Tobin's Q. Measurement of a company's financial performance can be done from more than one side, which is not only market value, it can also be viewed from the profitability or return on investment. Therefore, the next studies should also employ more thorough data with a better approach and holistic measurement.

REFERENCES

ACCA. (n.d.). *Social and environmental narrative reporting: analysts' perceptions*. https://www.acca-global.com/gb/en/technical-activities/technical-resources-search/2008/november/perceptions-narrative-reporting.html

Aracil, E. (2019). Corporate social responsibility of Islamic and conventional banks. *International Journal of Emerging Markets*, *14*(4), 582–600. doi:10.1108/IJOEM-12-2017-0533

Aras, G., Tezcan, N., & Furtuna, O. K. (2018). The value relevance of the banking sector multidimensional corporate sustainability performance. *Corporate Social Responsibility and Environmental Management*, *25*(6), 1062–1073. doi:10.1002/csr.1520

Banking for Society. (n.d.). What do we mean by corporate social responsibility and socially responsible banking? Author.

Carini, C., Comincioli, N., Poddi, L., & Vergalli, S. (2017). Measure the performance with the market value added: Evidence from CSR companies. *Sustainability*, *9*(12), 2171.

Chantziaras, A., Dedoulis, E., Grougiou, V., & Leventis, S. (2020). The impact of religiosity and corruption on CSR reporting: The case of U.S. banks. *Journal of Business Research*, *109*, 362–374. doi:10.1016/j.jbusres.2019.12.025

Cho, S., Chung, C., & Young, J. (2019). Study on the relationship between CSR and financial performance. *Sustainability*, *11*(2), 343. doi:10.3390u11020343

Chtourou, H., & Triki, M. (2017). Commitment in corporate social responsibility and financial performance: A study in the Tunisian context. *Social Responsibility Journal*, *13*(2), 370–389. doi:10.1108/SRJ-05-2016-0079

Deegan, C. (2002). Introduction: The legitimising effect of social and environmental disclosures – a theoretical foundation. *Accounting, Auditing & Accountability Journal*, *15*(3), 282–311. doi:10.1108/09513570210435852

Devie, D., Liman, L. P., Tarigan, J., & Jie, F. (2018). Corporate social responsibility, financial performance and risk in Indonesian natural resources industry. *Social Responsibility Journal*, *16*(1), 73–90. doi:10.1108/SRJ-06-2018-0155

Feng, M., Wang, X., & Kreuze, J. G. (2017). Corporate social responsibility and firm financial performance. *American Journal of Business*, *32*(3/4), 106–133. doi:10.1108/AJB-05-2016-0015

Gangi, F., Mustilli, M., & Varrone, N. (2019). The impact of corporate social responsibility (CSR) knowledge on corporate financial performance: Evidence from the European banking industry. *Journal of Knowledge Management*, *23*(1), 110–134. doi:10.1108/JKM-04-2018-0267

Gras-Gil, E., Manzano, M. P., & Fernández, J. H. (2016). Investigating the relationship between corporate social responsibility and earnings management: Evidence from Spain. *BRQ Business Research Quarterly*, *19*(4), 289–299. doi:10.1016/j.brq.2016.02.002

Habimana, O. (2016). Do flexible exchange rates facilitate external adjustment? A dynamic approach with time-varying and asymmetric volatility. *International Economics and Economic Policy*, *14*(4), 625–642. doi:10.100710368-016-0341-7

Hatane, S. E., Octavia, F., & Florentina, J. (2019). The comparison of earnings management practices in Indonesia's Islamic banks and conventional banks. *Advances in Economics. Business and Management Research*, *69*, 127–131.

Ho, A. Y.-F., Liang, H.-Y., & Tumurbaatar, T. (2019). The impact of corporate social responsibility on financial performance: Evidence from commercial banks in Mongolia. *Advances in Pacific Basin Business, Economics and Finance*, 109–153.

Hong, Y., & Andersen, M. L. (2011). The relationship between corporate social responsibility and earnings management: An exploratory study. *Journal of Business Ethics*, *104*(4), 461–471. doi:10.100710551-011-0921-y

Ibe-Enwo, G., Igbudu, N., Garanti, Z., & Popoola, T. (2019). Assessing the relevance of green banking practice on bank loyalty: The mediating effect of green image and bank trust. *Sustainability*, *11*(17), 4651. doi:10.3390u11174651

Kumar, K., & Prakash, A. (2018). Developing a framework for assessing sustainable banking performance of the Indian banking sector. *Social Responsibility Journal*, *15*(5), 689–709. doi:10.1108/SRJ-07-2018-0162

Lin, W., Ho, J., & Sambasivan, M. (2018). Impact of corporate political activity on the relationship between corporate social responsibility and financial performance: A dynamic panel data approach. *Sustainability*, *11*(1), 60. doi:10.3390u11010060

Matuszak, Ł., Różańska, E., & Macuda, M. (2019). The impact of corporate governance characteristics on banks' corporate social responsibility disclosure. *Journal of Accounting in Emerging Economies*, *9*(1), 75–102. doi:10.1108/JAEE-04-2017-0040

Megeid, N. S. A. (2017). Liquidity risk management: Conventional versus Islamic banking system in Egypt. *Journal of Islamic Accounting and Business Research*, *8*(1), 100–128. doi:10.1108/JIABR-05-2014-0018

Menicucci, E., & Paolucci, G. (2016). The determinants of bank profitability: Empirical evidence from European banking sector. *Journal of Financial Reporting and Accounting*, *14*(1), 86–115. doi:10.1108/JFRA-05-2015-0060

Mukherjee, A., & Nuñez, R. (2019). Doing well by doing good: Can voluntary CSR reporting enhance financial performance? *Journal of Indian Business Research*, *11*(2), 100–119. doi:10.1108/JIBR-07-2018-0199

Mullerat, R., & Brennan, D. (2005). Corporate social responsibility: The corporate governance of the 21st century. International Bar Association.

Nawaz, T. (2017). Momentum investment strategies, corporate governance and firm performance: An analysis of Islamic banks. *Corporate Governance: The International Journal of Business in Society*, *17*(2), 192–211. doi:10.1108/CG-03-2016-0052

Nugroho, B. P. (2016). *Jokowi: I will find a way to reduce loan interest rate*. https://finance.detik.com/moneter/d-3119293/jokowi-saya-akan-cari-jalan-agar-bunga-kredit-turun

Oh, W., & Park, S. (2015). The relationship between corporate social responsibility and corporate financial performance in Korea. *Emerging Markets Finance & Trade*, *51*(3), 85–94. doi:10.1080/1540496X.2015.1039903

Omar, B. F., & Zallom, N. O. (2016). Corporate social responsibility and market value: Evidence from Jordan. *Journal of Financial Reporting and Accounting*, *14*(1), 2–29. doi:10.1108/JFRA-11-2014-0084

Othman, H. B., & Mersni, H. (2014). The use of discretionary loan loss provisions by Islamic banks and conventional banks in the Middle East region. *Studies in Economics and Finance*, *31*(1), 106–128. doi:10.1108/SEF-02-2013-0017

Sari, E. V. (2016). *September 2016 non-performing loans is higher than last year*. https://www.cnnindonesia.com/ekonomi/20161107114502-78-170819/kredit-macet-september-2016-lebih-tinggi-dibanding-tahun-lalu

Sial, M., Zheng, C., Khuong, N., Khan, T., & Usman, M. (2018). Does firm performance influence corporate social responsibility reporting of Chinese listed companies? *Sustainability*, *10*(7), 2217. doi:10.3390u10072217

Su, W., Peng, M. W., Tan, W., & Cheung, Y.-L. (2014). The signaling effect of corporate social responsibility in emerging economies. *Journal of Business Ethics*, *134*(3), 479–491. doi:10.100710551-014-2404-4

Sun, L., & Rakhman, F. (2013). CFO financial expertise and corporate social responsibility. *International Journal of Law and Management*, *55*(3), 161–172. doi:10.1108/17542431311327619

Tang, W. (2019). *Banks lay off employees due to automation, digitalization*. https://www.thejakartapost.com/news/2019/03/31/banks-lay-off-employees-due-to-automation-digitalization.html

Ujah, N. U., Brusa, J., & Okafor, C. E. (2017). The influence of earnings management and bank structure on bank performance. *Managerial Finance*, *43*(7), 761–773. doi:10.1108/MF-12-2015-0329

Wu, Y. C., Wei Kiong Ting, I., Lu, W. M., Nourani, M., & Kweh, Q. L. (2016). The impact of earnings management on the performance of ASEAN banks. *Economic Modelling*, *53*, 156–165. doi:10.1016/j.econmod.2015.11.023

Yim, S., Bae, Y. H., Lim, H., & Kwon, J. (2019). The role of marketing capability in linking CSR to corporate financial performance. *European Journal of Marketing*, *53*(7), 1333–1354. doi:10.1108/EJM-08-2017-0526

Yu, H.-C., Kuo, L., & Kao, M.-F. (2017). The relationship between CSR disclosure and competitive advantage. *Sustainability Accounting. Management and Policy Journal*, *8*(5), 547–570.

APPENDIX

Table 6.

Categories	Strengths	Concerns
Community	Generous giving	Investment controversies
	Innovative giving	Negative economic impact
	Housing support	Indigenous people relations
	Education support	Tax disputes
	Peoples relations	Other Concerns
	Non-US giving	
	Voluntary programs	
	Other strength	
Corporate governance	Limited compensation	High Compensation
	Ownership strength	Ownership concern
	Transparency strength	Transparency concern
	Accountability strength	Accountability concern
	Public policy strength	Public policy concern
	Other strength	Other concerns
Diversity	CEO	Controversies
	Promotion	Non-representation
	Board of directors	Other concerns
	Work-life benefits	
	Women and minority	
	Employment of the disabled	
	Gay and lesbian policies	
	Other strength	
Employee relations	Union relations	Union relations
	No-layoff policy	Health and safety concern
	Cash profit sharing	Workforce reductions
	Employee involvement	Retirement benefits concern
	Retirement benefits	Other concern
	Health and safety	
	Other strengths	
Environment	Beneficial products	Hazardous waste
	Pollution prevention	Regulatory problems
	Recycling	Ozone depleting chemicals
	Clean energy	Subtantial emissions
	PPE	Agriculture chemicals
	Other strengths	Climate change
		Other concern
Human rights	Positive record in Indonesia	Labor right concern
	Indigenous people relations	Indigenous people relations concern
	Labor rights strength	Other concerns
	Other strengths	
Products	Quality	Product safety concern
	R&D, innovation	Marketing contracting concern
	Benefits to economically disadvantage	Antitrust
	Other strength	Other concern

Chapter 13
Retailing in Indonesia:
A Deeper Look Into the World's Growing Market

Adilla Anggraeni
Binus Business School, Bina Nusantara University, Indonesia

Ayuphita Tiara Silalahi
https://orcid.org/0000-0002-0984-5558
Binus Business School, Bina Nusantara University, Indonesia

ABSTRACT

The chapter discusses Indonesia's retailing landscape. The retail sector itself can be considered to be one of the most promising in Asia due to the high populations, growing middle class, higher purchasing power, and shifting spending habits. The discussion revolves along the state of online and offline retailing in Indonesia, including the current trends and discussion of luxury retailing. The technological advancement was proven to have shifted how people do retailing activities. The chapter discusses the trends in luxury retail as well as the challenges facing luxury retailers doing business in Indonesia, which may include counterfeiting. Counterfeiting is one of the prevailing issues in Indonesian retailing behaviours, targeting consumers who are aware that they have indeed purchased counterfeited items.

INTRODUCTION

Retailing in Indonesia has been a subject of many studies, as the retail sector itself is projected to have a compound annual growth rate (CAGR) of 13.8% by 2024. In terms of segmentation, Indonesian's retail market can be segmented by product category, distribution channel, and market dynamics.

The retail sector itself can be considered to be one of the most promising in Asia due to the high number of populations, growing middle class, higher purchasing power and shifting spending habits.

In 2017, Asia's private consumption was affected by higher prices for food, electricity, and fees for vehicle registration. In 2018, the condition was better as the private consumption was fueled by lower credit cost, increasing employment, and an expansion of social welfare.

DOI: 10.4018/978-1-7998-4787-8.ch013

However, it should be noted that household consumption in Indonesia has slowed down in recent years, which is regrettable since this sector has been one of the main driving factors for the economy, and is considered to be more important than investment, exports, and government spending. Indonesia's food and beverage market plays a crucial role.However, its position in the global F&B market is uncertain, as Indonesia relies on imported products for its F&B retail market such as wheat, dairy, or processed food products (mordorintelligence.com, 2019).

Retailing trends vary over the years. Some may be impacted by the advancement of technology, some are influenced by the shifting of consumer behaviours, as well as the economic conditions of the country. Despite the changes and the relatively turbulent environment, retailers have thrived by adapting their strategies and making some changes to fit the environment.

This chapter will discuss the retailing landscape in Indonesia, covering topics such as offline retailing, online retailing and luxury retailing.

Offline Retailing

This section will discuss about the trends of retailing in Indonesia, including faith-based retailing which is one of many manifestations of social changes driven by the growing position of Islam in society.

In addition to that, this section will also discuss types of offline retailers in Indonesia and the trends that may have shaped the offline retailers in the recent years.

There are different types of traditional retailers in Indonesia, a relatively small retail establishment which usually operate their own stores and operate their business by themselves with 2-5 employees and usually involve their family members. However, there is one type of traditional retailer who sells merchandise openly in the pedestrian area namely street hawker. There are some types of traditional retailers known in this country: 1). traditional (wet) market, 2). small kiosk, called warung, 3). mom and pop store, and 4). street hawker. (Sunanto, 2012)

The convenient retailers market is dominated by two big players; Indomaret and Alfamart. Faith-based retailers, such as Shodaqo (literal meaning: charity) have also seen some growth. This type of retailer was seen as a partner that can strengthen the traditional small kiosks due to its economic sharing principles (kontan.co.id). The convenience retailers are popular due to its convenience location, relatively large assortment of merchandise and its operational hours.

In 2017, Indonesia's retail giant Mitra Adi Perkasa (MAP) closed two of its major department stores; Lotus and Debenham (jakartapost.com, 2017). This move was made pretty closely after MAP, who is behind some lifestyle brands such as Starbucks, Nike, Adidas, Lacoste and many more announced its foray into the e-commerce market. The move was seen as a way to salvage the offline retailers market which have seen better days.

Jakartaglobe.id reported that Aprido (Indonesian Retailer Association) has estimated that retail sales have shrunk by 8 percent to Rp 30 trillion ($2.25 billion) in the first quarter of 2017, compared with the same period in 2016. This may be due to the new government's plan to access bank clients' credit card data which was off limits under Indonesia's bank secrecy rule for tax purposes may have caused people to hold back their shopping activities.

The consultancy firm PwC Indonesia, said that internet access growth has enabled the consumers to have access to a vast selection of products globally at more affordable prices. The power has shifted from the producers to consumers and this has been enabled by fast growth in internet access, allowing consumers to have access to vast a selection of goods from the global market at relatively low prices. This situation has also put pressures on retailers to offer better value and more convenience to consumers.

Convenience retailers still dominate the Indonesian market. In 2018, Indomaret and Indomaret Point (owned by retail group Indomarco Prismatama), as its line extension were the top selling retailers, earning a combined US$4.89 billion in sales. The convenience store chains beat its closest competitor Alfamart, owned by Sumber Alfaria Trijaya, which booked US$3.97 billion in sales.

In recent years it is evident, offline retailers in Indonesia have been facing fierce competitors from their online counterparts. As a result, they called for 'equal treatment' from the government. It was acknowledged that aggressive competition between online and offline retailers has caused retail giants to suffer huge losses. For example, a publicly listed grocery store, Hero Supermarket closed 26 of its stores and laid off 532 employees as part of its efficiency measures in 2019 (jakartapost.com, 2019).

The advancement of technology on the other hand, has enabled both offline and online retailers to co-exist as a part of omnichannel retailing. In fact, some retailers have resorted to online stores as a way to survive. Besides providing their services at the brick and mortar stores, some mom-and-pop stores have utilized the country's growing electronic marketplace to sell their products (dailysocial.id). An example of this is GrabKios that is empowered by Grab Indonesia. This new type of retailer equips the small shop owners (called 'warung' in Indonesian) with the necessary technology to manage transactions. This program also offers the agents additional business promises, such as provision of mobile credit top ups, bill payments, purchase of travel tickets and fund transfer service. (snapcart.global, 2017).

Offline retailers may also be subject to the practice of showrooming. This indicates a practice where the information search or research takes place in a brick and mortar setting; however the purchases take place in the online setting; something that Indonesian consumers evidently do (Astari, Huliselan, & Jong, 2017). A previous study for example, indicates that webroomers may perceive greater time and and effort savings as well as may perceive themselves to be making the right purchases more compared to showroomers (Flavian, Guarrea and Orus, 2020).

Showrooming behaviour may mean that even though the consumers may visit the stores, they do not necessarily make any purchase. This can pose a challenge to the offline retailers, as the number visitors does not necessarily correspond with the sales figure.

Online Retailing

Over the last few years, a large number of brick and mortar retail landscape has been closing down on a catastrophic level, that it was labelled 'retail apocalypse' (Helm, Kim, & Van Riper, 2020) indicating a permanent restructuring of physical retailing with the steady increase of electronic retailing. Though this trend toward fewer physical stores is not uniquely occurring in the United States, however it is the most visible market with more than 7000 stores closing in 2016 (Isidore, 2017). The retail landscape in Indonesia is also facing a major shift toward the electronic retailing fueled by the changing behavior of its consumers that strives for convenience as its foremost reason. More than 95% of Indonesian retailers have expanded to online stores, through having its own website, social media account, or joining e-commerce marketplaces to fulfil consumer demand and an increased competition. This transition of the retail landscape has increased not only competition but also power structure between consumers and retailers; and it's definitely tilting in favor towards the consumers (Rezabakhsh, Bornemann, Hansen, & Schrader, 2006).

The online retailing sector in Indonesia is particularly promising due to the high number of social media users. Data gathered by We Are Social and Hootsuite indicated Indonesia's 150 million internet users spend an average of 8 hours and 36 minutes connecting, discovering, and shopping every single day (The Jakarta Post, 2020) more than any other country in the world. Moreover, Indonesia is considered as the highest country who adopts e-commerce acumen, thanks to its 67.6% demographic bonus of 15 to 64 years old and tech-savvy, resulting in more than 90 percent of conducting business online (CNN Indonesia, 2020). With accelerated growth of Indonesian telecommunications infrastructure and internet connectivity becoming more affordable, especially in mobile phones, Indonesia's e-commerce market sits at $12.2 billion in 2018 and a forecast of $53 billion in 2025 according to tech giant Google and Singapore's Temasek (Bisara, 2019) and with that comes the prospect of creating more than 26 million jobs both directly and indirectly (Silaen, 2019).

As Southeast Asia's biggest emerging market, Indonesia is home to various unicorn startups. Startup refers to new businesses accelerated by the existence of the digital platform with unicorn defined as startups that have values of more than 1 billion dollars. With more than 225 unicorns across the globe, four are Indonesian made startups: Go-Jek, Traveloka, Tokopedia, and Bukalapak with a total estimated valuation of more than Rp108,3trillion or equivalent of US $7581billion (Cinthyana, 2018).

Online retail business in Indonesia is huge and growing. Underpinning this growth are the micro, small and medium enterprises (MSMEs) and these establishments are also going online (businesswire, 2019). The MSMEs are crucial to the economy as they have helped improve the socio-economic outcomes and created new emerging markets both domestic and abroad (jakartapost.com, 2020). Various types of e-commerce are available in Indonesia ranging from beauty, FMCG, banking, transportation, travel to fashion and food and beverage with various price segments from low to luxury goods. Combined with accelerated stability of internet infrastructure, low data costs, a growing number of youthful, middle class population with bank accounts, a more secure payment aggregator, and ease of use of online application - serve as crucial enablers for continuing e-commerce growth. The exponential growth also propelled by intense use of smartphones as a lifestyle where it increasingly becomes more convenient to conduct online shopping. With 195 million smartphone users in Indonesia and only 30 million who have conducted online shopping, the growth of potential online shoppers is huge (Bisara, 2019).

E-commerce in a nutshell is a process of selling and buying goods, services and information or the transmitting of funds over electronic means primarily via the Internet networks. It refers to any online retail, online shopping and online transaction conducted via the Internet either as Business-to-Business (B2B), Business-to-Consumer (B2C), Consumer-to-Consumer (C2C), and Consumer-to-Business (C2B).

Unlike other countries, Indonesians prefer to conduct online trading using informal channels of social media platforms such as Facebook, Twitter, Line, WhatsApp and Instagram to avoid paying commission or taxes (Tan, 2019). Although as recently as April 2019, the Indonesian government in an effort to protect the local manufacturers as well as to levy taxation on imported goods in the electronic marketplace issued a Government Regulation No. 80/2019 (GR80) on Trade via Electronic Systems which imposed a 10% tax on transaction on online platforms (Reuters, 2019). In 2016, these social e-commerce made up 36% of online retail in Indonesia, however the number fell to 19% in 2018 due to various reasons of counterfeit or poor quality goods, poor customer experience and unreliable sellers.

Concurrently, these issues triggered a turn of formal channel of electronic-retailing (e-tailing) and propelled the market to grow to 81% in 2018 (Tan, 2019). 80% of Indonesia's e-commerce market is dominated by C2C players demonstrated by the four biggest players: Shopee, Bukalapak, Tokopedia, and Lazada. However, due to the change in the business model, the B2C market, with the four biggest players in Indonesia - BukaMall, Official Store Tokopedia, LazMall, and Shopee Mall – all are extending to have their own B2C arm, is expected to grow by 35% in 2023 (RedSeer, 2019; Tan, 2019).

E-commerce changed the course of consumer purchase with its convenience of 24/7 transaction availability and globally accessibility where it has evolved to encompass a wide variety of goods and services (Bakos, 2001). As a result, this growing trend has allowed local businesses to increase and blossom in the online market. Changes in social lifestyles also drives many businesses to digitize their physical store to encourage sales as well as to meet the needs of the changing behavior of their customers. Reports on e-commerce concurrently define the top drivers of shifting consumers motivation to shop online due to practicality, price, product range and fast delivery (Deloitte, 2017; RedSeer, 2019; Tan, 2019).

Practicality or Convenience: The number one reason for consumer motivation to shop online is the practicality factor. Buying goods in a brick and mortar store is constrained by time and distance. With online shopping, transactions could be done anytime and, in any location, as long as internet connection is on.

Price Comparisons: The fascination of hunt bargains among many Indonesian consumers causes them to take lower-price deals that many online retailers offer. The reports stated that the 26% online platform allows its users to conduct price comparison between different stores prior to purchase. This benefit encourages buyers, especially those who are price sensitive, to assess all price options and provide freedom to choose a store that gives the best price for the goods they are searching.

Product range: The third driver of consumer motivation to shop online is the availability of product choices (17%). It allows e-commerce buyers to have the option of obtaining the best goods available, both local or international sellers, which at times becomes unavailable in a physical store or within the area closest to the buyer.

Fast delivery: Speed of delivery is also a contributing factor to the consumer's motivation to migrate from being offline shoppers to make purchases online – more so than having offline touchpoints and fast internet connectivity.

Though Indonesian's e-commerce is still in its nascent stage compared to China and the United States respectively, its growth projection is promising. To capture this value, Indonesian MSMEs need clear rules from the government that should be applied consistently and at the same time not create additional burdens that could restrict the ability for MSMEs to scale operations and trade. Thus, the GR80 initiatives should encompass national digital policies that are practical, provide more choice and control to the consumers, and align with international best practices and standards (jakartapost.com, 2020).

Luxury Retailing

Indonesia's appetite in terms of luxury retails is considered to be the highest in Asia. In 2016, sales of luxury goods in Indonesia grew by 84% from 2015, recording the largest online luxury sales growth in Asia (accommerce.asia, 2017). Since 2013, Indonesia and other Southeast Asian nations, including Malaysia, Vietnam and Thailand, are the new engines of luxury growth within the Asia region. Southeast Asia had 11 percent growth in the personal luxury goods market in the 2012-2013 period, compared with 6 percent globally, the study said. The growth proliferates due to social media and digital marketing with renowned young influencers

The luxury retailing in Indonesia is supported by different factors, such as the increasing number of high net worth individuals as well as the ongoing growth in the country's tourism industry. (medium.com). In general, the ones within the age group of 35-39 years old are the majority highest earners, followed by those within the age range of 30-34 years old. The typical profile of individuals in these age groups are young, highly educated professionals who have managed to climb the career ladder in various companies. These individuals usually have young families, and are often in the market for various products and services, such as consumer electronics, cars, luxury goods and memorable experiences (luxurysociety.com).

There are many different luxury brands operating in Indonesia, including Louis Vuitton, Gucci, Prada, Balenciaga as well as Bottega Venetta. These luxury brands exist in the form of online retailers. Some of the retailers, such as Masari, have a physical store as well. Brands such as Louis Vuitton, Gucci, Christian Dior, Burberry and Hugo Boss contribute to the luxury fashion sectors as the five largest luxury brands in Indonesia.

There are however, some challenges for luxury retailers in Indonesia, including counterfeiting. Many Indonesians purchase counterfeited handbags and accessories knowingly, despite understanding that purchasing those goods leads to negative consequences. There is little that authorities can do if the brands whose products have been counterfeited do not file any complaints (insideindonesia.org).

Retailing and Consumer Behaviours

It has been acknowledged that the existence of technology may have shifted the customer journey in retailing. For example, the customer journey may not be as linear as moving from pre-purchase to purchase and post purchase; but the process itself may be iterative with looping aspects (Grewal and Roggeveen, 2020). For example, the consumer may utilize technology such as artificial intelligence (AI) and IoT to determine when the inventory level is low so that they can make replenishment purchases. In this case, the consumer may jump from the pre-purchase to post-purchase stage with technology handling the purchase stage more effectively. This suggests how the retailers can actually benefit immensely from the utilization of big data (Dekimpe, 2019).

Consumption trends in Indonesia were also characterized by cultures. Korean cosmetics and beauty products are some of the items that have started to gain popularity among Indonesian consumers in recent years. The growth of market trends in these products seems quite significant, and most likely have been triggered by the growing interests especially among young people, in Korean pop music (K-pop) and Korean drama (K-drama). Competition in cosmetics products between South Korean and Japanese manufacturers in Indonesia has been fiercer in recent years, and Korean cosmetics brands have experienced significant market growth over time (Delloitte, 2019).

Some examples of Korean brands that have gained popularity include Innisfree and The Faceshop, which are the skincare and cosmetic brands currently sold in their own outlets across different shopping malls in Indonesia. It has been noted as well how the Indonesian millennials spend 50% of their disposable incomes to purchase products/services in 4S categories: skin, sugar, sun and screen (Wibowo, 2020), highlighting the importance that they place in taking care of their skin.

Across most product categories, Indonesians are not only faithful to brands, but also show a strong preference for local brands. Seventy five percent of the respondents surveyed by McKinsey in 2014, on average, have stated that they already have a preferred brand in mind when they go into stores to buy home and personal care products; and more than two-thirds said the same for food and beverage items. (McKinsey, 2014). This brings forward both challenges and opportunities to retailers operating in Indonesia.

The existence of new payment systems with attractive promotions such as cashback, free delivery and installment, have increased the consumption. Food retailers in particular, have benefited from the existence of the promotional activities. Variety of promotions have been noted to increase impulse spending for food retailers. The promotions are usually given on a daily basis; with more promotions given to commemorate special events such as Independence Day.

CONCLUSION

The discussion on Indonesian retailing landscape is by no means exhaustive. There are other aspects that could be discussed in the future, for example how retailers can survive with the changes in economic situations that may have led people to tighten their belts and reduce consumption. In addition to that, discussion on retails would not be completed without consideration on how technologies may further shape the retailing landscape. Combining accelerated growth in e-commerce, technology acumen and demographic bonus, Indonesian retailing landscape can be seen as the promised land. Further discussion on self-service technology, omnichannel effectiveness, and retailing logistics can further sharpen the insights on Indonesian retailing landscape.

REFERENCES

Akhaya, P. (2020, January 30). *Indonesian e-commerce site Blibli embraces New Retail with BlibliMart launch*. Academic Press.

Amirio, D. (2016). Mitra Adiperkasa announces own marketplace. *The Jakarta Post.* Retrieved from: https://www.thejakartapost.com/news/2016/02/19/mitra-adiperkasa-announces-own-marketplace.html

Arismunandar, A. (2018, August 20). *Indonesian Retailers Need Better Digital Integration*. Jakarta Globe. Retrieved from: https://jakartaglobe.id/business/indonesian-retailers-need-better-digital-integration/

Astari, I. S., Huliselan, J. J., & Jong, M. T. T. (2017). Customer showrooming behaviour and the effect on salesperson performance. *DeReMa Jurnal Manajemen*, *12*(2), 187–213. doi:10.19166/derema.v12i2.525

Bakos, Y. (2001). The emerging landscape for retail E-commerce. *The Journal of Economic Perspectives*, *15*(1), 69–80. Advance online publication. doi:10.1257/jep.15.1.69

Bisara, D. (2019). *Indonesia's E-commerce Market Larger Than Estimated; Consumer Habits Changing: Study*. Retrieved from https://jakartaglobe.id/business/indonesias-ecommerce-market-larger-than-estimated-consumer-habits-changing-study/

Businesswire. (2019, April 11). *Retail Market in Indonesia 2019-2023 | Growth in E-Commerce to Boost Growth | Technavio*. Retrieved from https://www.businesswire.com/news/home/20191004005209/en/Retail-Market-Indonesia-2019-2023-Growth-E-Commerce-BoostLB-C64i

Cinthyana, L. (2018). *A Brief Look At 4 Unicorn Startups in Indonesia*. Retrieved from https://indonesiatatler.com/arts-culture/business/gen-t-a-brief-look-at-4-unicorns-in-indonesia

Cochrane, J. (2013, November 20). Luxury Brands Find A Home in Indonesia. *The New York Times.* Retrieved from: https://www.nytimes.com/2013/11/21/fashion/Luxury-Finds-a-Home-in-Indonesia.html

Dekimpe, M. (2019). Retailing and retailing research in the age of big data analytics. *International Journal of Research in Marketing*. Advance online publication. doi:10.1016/j.ijresmar.2019.09.001

Deloitte. (2017). *Deloitte Consumer Insights*. Retrieved from https://www2.deloitte.com/id/en/pages/consumer-industrial-products/articles/consumer-insights-id-2017.html

Dwijayanto, A. (2018, March 19). *Tahun ini, Hydro Perdana targetkan punya 500 gerai Sodaqo Mart dan 212 Mart, Kontan*. Retrieved from: https://industri.kontan.co.id/news/tahun-ini-hydro-perdana-targetkan-punya-500-gerai-sodaqo-mart-dan-212-mart

Fitriani, E. (2017, April 6). *More Retailers to Expand Into e-Commerce to Survive*. Retrieved from: https://jakartaglobe.id/news/more-retailers-to-expand-into-e-commerce-to-survive

Flavian, C., Gurrea, R., & Orus, C. (2020). Combining channels to make smart purchases: The role of webrooming and showrooming. *Journal of Retailing and Consumer Services*, *52*, 101923. doi:10.1016/j.jretconser.2019.101923

Fomicheva, E. (2018, January 20). *The Retail Sector: The Market of Fashion, Luxury and Premium-Class Goods: Indonesia*. Retrieved from: https://medium.com/@ekaterina.fomicheva25/the-retail-sector-the-market-of-fashion-luxury-and-premium-class-goods-indonesia-929a920e409d

Helm, S., Kim, S. H., & Van Riper, S. (2020). Navigating the 'retail apocalypse': A framework of consumer evaluations of the new retail landscape. *Journal of Retailing and Consumer Services*, *54*. Advance online publication. doi:10.1016/j.jretconser.2018.09.015

Indonesia, C. N. N. (2020, April 11). *Tren dan Peluang Industri E-Commerce di Indonesia 2020*. Retrieved from https://www.cnnindonesia.com/teknologi/20200205204206-206-472064/tren-dan-peluang-industri-e-commerce-di-indonesia-2020

Indonesia-investments.com. (2016, September 12). *E-commerce market Indonesia: Online Retail Growing Strongly*. Retrieved from: https://www.indonesia-investments.com/news/todays-headlines/e-commerce-market-indonesia-online-retail-growing-strongly/item7179

Indonesia-investments.com. (2017, December 13). *E-Commerce in Indonesia: Many Consumers Look Offline, Buy Online*. Retrieved from: https://www.indonesia-investments.com/news/todays-headlines/e-commerce-in-indonesia-many-consumers-look-offline-buy-online/item8410

Isidore, C. (2017, December). *Retail's toughest year: A record for store closings*. Retrieved from https://money.cnn.com/2017/12/26/news/companies/retail-toughest-year-store-closings/index.html

Kaushik, P. (2019, October 29). The Indonesian retail market is tipped for astronomical growth, but cashless payments will be key to realising its potential. *Asean Today*. Retrieved from: https://www.aseantoday.com/2019/10/the-indonesian-retail-market-is-tipped-for-astronomical-growth-but-cashless-payments-will-be-key-to-realising-its-potential/

KrAsia. (2019, November 20). *Offline Programs are Getting Tech Players More Customers in Indonesia*. Retrieved from: https://dailysocial.id/post/offline-programs-are-getting-tech-players-more-customers-in-indonesia

Mufti, R. R. (2018, September 26). Indomaret tops retailer list with US$4.89b in sales. *The Jakarta Post*. Retrieved from: https://www.thejakartapost.com/news/2018/09/25/indomaret-tops-retailer-list-with-us4-89b-in-sales.html

Mybusiness.Singtel.com. (n.d.). *Online retailing in Indonesia: What SMEs should know*. Retrieved from: https://mybusiness.singtel.com/techblog/online-retailing-indonesia-what-smes-should-know

Putri, A. S. (2020, January 29). *Inovasi Toko Offline Tanpa Kasir Pertama Hadir di Indonesia*. Retrieved from: https://www.fimela.com/lifestyle-relationship/read/4166318/inovasi-toko-offline-tanpa-kasir-pertama-hadir-di-indonesia

Razdan, R., Das, M., & Sohoni, A. (2014, January 1). *The evolving Indonesian Consumer*. McKinsey Report. Retrieved from: https://www.mckinsey.com/business-functions/marketing-and-sales/our-insights/the-evolving-indonesian-consumer

RedSeer. (2019). *Indo E-Tailing: Poised To Grow More Than 4x Over 2018-2023*. Retrieved from https://redseer.com/newsletters/indo-e-tailing-poised-to-grow-more-than-4x-over-2018-2023/

Reuters. (2019). *Indonesia to lower threshold for import taxes on e-commerce goods*. Retrieved from https://www.thejakartapost.com/news/2019/12/24/government-to-lower-threshold-for-import-taxes-on-e-commerce-goods.html

Rezabakhsh, B., Bornemann, D., Hansen, U., & Schrader, U. (2006). Consumer power: A comparison of the old economy and the internet economy. *Journal of Consumer Policy*, *29*(1), 3–36. Advance online publication. doi:10.100710603-005-3307-7

Shihab, S. (2019, October 2). *Post fast fashion: The future of fashion and the rise of resale*. The Jakarta Post. Retrieved from: https://www.thejakartapost.com/life/2019/10/02/post-fast-fashion-the-future-of-fashion-and-the-rise-of-resale.html

Silaen, L. (2019, April 11). *95% Indonesian Retailers Expands to Online Stores amid the Digital Era - The Insiders Stories*. Retrieved from https://theinsiderstories.com/95-indonesian-retailers-expands-to-online-stores-amid-the-digital-era/

Singh, P. (2019, April 6). *What Makes Indonesia the Fastest Rising E-commerce Country*. Retrieved from: https://www.entrepreneur.com/article/331838

Snapcart. (2017, March 9). *The coexistence of offline and online grocery shopping*. Retrieved from: https://snapcart.global/the-coexistence-of-offline-and-online-grocery-shopping

Tan, Z. (2019). *Three trends in Indonesia's e-commerce sector, as told by RedSeer*. Retrieved from https://kr-asia.com/three-trends-in-indonesias-e-commerce-sector-as-told-by-redseer

Tang, W. (2019, February 1). Offline retailers call for equal treatment. *The Jakarta Post*. Retrieved from:https://www.thejakartapost.com/news/2019/02/01/offline-retailers-call-for-equal-treatment.html

Techwire Asia. 2019, October 29). *Why offline retailers in Indonesia should bank on e-payment solutions*. Retrieved from: https://techwireasia.com/2019/10/why-offline-retailers-in-indonesia-should-bank-on-e-payment-solutions/

The Jakarta Post. (2017, October 26). *Lotus, Debenhams in Indonesia to close down by year's end.* The Jakarta Post. Retrieved from: https://www.thejakartapost.com/life/2017/10/26/lotus-debenhams-in-indonesia-to-close-down-by-years-end.html

The Jakarta Post. (2018, March 20). After Sodaqo Mart, 212 Mart, Hydro to introduce Rinjani Mart. *The Jakarta Post.* Retrieved from: https://www.thejakartapost.com/news/2018/03/20/after-sodaqo-mart-212-mart-hydro-to-introduce-rinjani-mart.html

The Jakarta Post. (2020, April 21). In challenging times, digital economy and e-commerce can chart a path toward recovery. *The Jakarta Post.* Retrieved from: https://www.thejakartapost.com/academia/2020/04/21/in-challenging-times-digital-economy-and-e-commerce-can-chart-a-path-toward-recovery.html

The Jakarta Post. (2020, April 11). *How Indonesians embrace the digital world.* Retrieved from https://www.thejakartapost.com/academia/2019/03/18/how-indonesians-embrace-the-digital-world.html

Wibowo, A. (2020, January 10). *Paying for the glow: Indonesian skincare e-commerce market trends.* Janio Asia. retrieved from: https://janio.asia/sea/indonesia/indonesia-skincare-ecommerce-trends/

Wira, N. N. (2020, January 28). Indonesian beauty trends to look out for in 2020. *The Jakarta Post.* Retrieved from: https://www.thejakartapost.com/life/2020/01/28/indonesian-beauty-trends-to-look-out-for-in-2020.html

Wong, E. (2019, March 18). How Indonesians embrace the digital world. *The Jakarta Post.* Retrieved from https://www.thejakartapost.com/academia/2019/03/18/how-indonesians-embrace-the-digital-world.html

Chapter 14
Automation of VAT System:
A Pathway of Domestic Resource Mobilization

Biplob Kumar Nandi
East West University, Bangladesh

Md. Humayun Kabir
https://orcid.org/0000-0002-5648-197X
East West University, Bangladesh

Nandini Roy
University of Dhaka, Bangladesh

ABSTRACT

The automated tax system has been taken as an effective tool for modernizing the tax system. The automated tax system can easily store all types of reported income, and it makes the tax submission procedure easy and convenient, resulting in reducing the compliance cost. The main objective of this chapter is to explain the necessity of an automated value added tax (VAT) system for raising domestic resource mobilization and how automation can be a better alternative to finance sustainable development goals projects. The secondary data was collected from the National Board of Revenue, Bangladesh. This study explains that the entire VAT system's automation can reduce the taxpayers' incentive to evade tax by reducing the tax compliance and taking bribes of tax officials. In sum, automation of the tax system would ultimately be pragmatic tax reform for the financing in the SDG projects.

INTRODUCTION

Tax evasion has been a universal and persistent problem, mostly in developing economies, with a severe economic consequence of having a shortage of resources to finance public projects (Galtung, 1995; Fjeldstad, 1996). Tax evasion and fraud in the tax administration have been taken place a complex phenomenon in public finance, which has several detrimental effects on the economy. The persistent

DOI: 10.4018/978-1-7998-4787-8.ch014

tax evasion in an economy hampers the tax efforts, and the loss of revenue can suggest a reduction in public services, including the resource allocation in the human capital and welfare programs. Besides, the higher level of tax evasion can seriously hinder the equity of taxation and economic growth (Shleifer & Vishny, 1993; Galtung, 1995; Hendriks et al., 1999; Cheng & Zeng, 2015).

Bangladesh, a rising economy with a persistent high average per capita growth, is one of the lowest tax revenue performers compared to the other developing economies[1]. Although Bangladesh has taken various reforms for the modernization of the tax system, the overall tax effort reflects below the potential. In addition, the higher level of tax evasion erodes the scope of tax revenue generation and escalates the informal economy's size. The broader informal economy, ultimately, creates the vicious cycle of domestic resource mobilization (Bird, 1992; Tanzi & Shome, 1993). Tax evasion is a behavioral, cultural, and political phenomenon. The tax evasion would be worsened when the taxpayers under-report their income bribing tax officials (Slemrod & Yitzhaki, 2000; Cerqueti & Coppier, 2009).

The automated tax system has been taken a useful tool for modernizing the tax system. The automated tax system can easily store all types of reported income, and it makes the tax submission procedure easy, resulting in reducing the compliance cost. Moreover, the chance of contact between taxpayers and tax officials will probably be zero in the automated tax system, which implies that collusion between taxpayers and tax officials for providing and taking bribes would be impossible. Even if there has been existed collusion, the cost of evasion will be significantly high because the probability of getting caught will increase. Thus, automation in any tax system has compliance costs with almost nothing; lowering the cost of tax compliance encourages taxpayers to pay the actual tax liabilities.

Over the last decade, Bangladesh has experienced sustained growth, ranging between 6 and 8 percent, while tax to GDP ratio has remained stagnant, hovering around 9 percent, on average. Bangladesh requires enormous resources, amounting to 928.5 billion USD by 2031, achieving the first phase of Sustainable Development Goals (SDGs)[2]. Ministry of Planning, Bangladesh has also set the target of financing in numerous SDG projects; almost 80 percent will be collected from the domestic resource. Furthermore, Bangladesh is on the track of LDC graduation period, the opportunity of low-cost financing, soft loans from multi-national agencies and donor countries, would be narrower after 2026. Thus, the demand for increasing tax revenue has been rocketed, financing numerous public projects.

National Board of Revenue (NBR), Bangladesh, the absolute authority of tax collection, has reported the tax evasion from the VAT of 892 billion of Taka during the fiscal year, 2017-18. This tax authority has affirmed that the lack of adequately reported income and the absence of an automated system have created the opportunities for taxpayers to evade tax. VAT system in Bangladesh has two types of the tax payment system, including the online and offline VAT returns[3]. As there is no bound obligation for taxpayers submitting their tax returns online, a tiny portion of the VAT payers uses the online tax submission procedure. That is why this offline tax submission has been opening up the way to evade tax as well as providing bribes to the tax officials, implying the persistent increases in the VAT evasion. For the fulfillment of domestic resource demand, there is no option for Bangladesh without taking further tax reforms, including domestic-based VAT. Without massive reforms, implementing only the full automation in the VAT system, Bangladesh can raise the tax revenue significantly.

This chapter's main objective is to explain the necessity of an automated VAT system for raising domestic resource mobilization and how automation can be a better alternative to financing SDG projects. The rest of the paper is composed of five more sections. Literature review and overview of the Bangladesh VAT system have been presented in sections two and three, respectively. Section four provides the theory and the conceptual framework of tax evasion, and data and methodology are discussed in section five.

Section six presents revenue gains and the possibility of financing options in numerous SDGs projects, and challenges and policy recommendations are presented in the final section.

BACKGROUND

Tax evasion has been taken place a prominent interest in doing research. Empirical studies about VAT evasion are still scanty. However, all of the empirical findings suggest that the entire tax system's automation has kept tax compliance and corruption at a minimum. A country's central and local budget is based on the country's tax revenue collection, but the tax collection procedure became more and more complicated over the years. The increasing level of technological advances can solve the problem related to tax systems (Campbell & Hanschitz, 2018). Besides, automation boosts up the tax efficiency. Isaac and Lilian (2010) investigated the automation of custom tax administration in Uganda and found a positive correlation among automation, tax revenue collection effectiveness, and cost of tax administration. On the other hand, the researcher also found a negative connection between automation and tax clearance time. Automation in the tax administration helps increase the tax revenue because of the tax authority's greater effectiveness in revenue collection. The revenue collection would be significant if the whole administration procedure between taxpayers and tax collectors are digitalized. Gitaru (2017) concluded that automation in tax administration had increased the revenue collection at an increasing rate.

Digitalization in the tax administration process enables the automated tax revenue collection and helps tax authorities detect tax compliance. The adaptation of information technology in tax administration is costly, but it can be categorized as a business's strategic decision. Tax authority needs to adopt and disseminate tax laws on a uniform basis, providing quality services to the taxpayers, and improving tax compliance besides collecting tax revenue in due time from right taxpayers. The authors also defined that the e-tax system is a system that offers electronic registration, filing, and payment of tax as well as education and information to taxpayers. The authors concluded that information technology (IT) could help a country's tax administration achieve long-term goals – collecting tax revenue from the right taxpayer in due time and applying uniform laws and regulations (Jimenez, Mac an tSionnaigh, & Kamenov 2013).

Furthermore, Pitić, Radosavljević, Babin, and Erić (2019) explained that the digitalization process of tax administration through digital technologies like data analytics, big data, and Blockchain. Digital technologies accelerate the efficiency of tax revenue collection. The researchers concluded that the automation process is improving traditional tax services and helping the tax administration to offer new services for the taxpayers. Jimenez et al. (2013) stated that the changing nature of business due to technological innovation, the tax administrators are using modern information technology to collect tax from taxpayers. On the other hand, Clavey, Pemberton, Loeprick, and Verhoeven (2019) pointed out, "tax administrations in developing economies can benefit from rules that are relatively simple and certain in the application. In particular, this is because such rules can be administered by smaller tax administrations, with limited resources and staff with less experience and expertise." Furthermore, Campbell and Hanschitz (2018) clarified that the unreported income by an individual taxpayer or by a corporate taxpayer could eliminate by the adoption of online tax accounts. The authors also suggested an epistemic tax policy that will help tax authorities to monitor the expected and actual tax collection results.

Nam, Parsche, and Schaden (2001) analyzed the quantification of value added tax (VAT) evasion and fraud in European Union (EU) countries and computed the hypothetical tax revenues and find the time-lag problem in VAT collection. The researchers also found a direct connection between the level of tax rates of a country and the degree of tax evasion. Moreover, Bellon, Chang, Dabla-Norris, Khalid, Lima, Rojas, and Villena (2019) examined the impact of electronic invoicing (e-invoicing) of firms' tax compliance in Peru and found that e-invoicing has increased a firm's sales by five percentage points in the first year of reformation from traditional to the automated system. The researchers also found that electronic invoicing can lower the tax compliance costs of different firms and ultimately improve tax compliance. In Peru, the value added tax collection significantly increase because the tax administration concentrated more on smaller firms.

Moreover, tax can be deducted automatically and instantly from business or a corporation through the online platform of a tax authority; when a company is making transactions, the tax authority is receiving notification of the transaction and deducting the value added tax amount for that particular transaction (Campbell & Hanschitz, 2018). This strategy mentioned above can enhance transparency and the optimal effectiveness of tax administration. However, Schwebkea, Brinkb, Hansenc, and Kellihera (2019) analyzed the role of trustworthiness in tax filing and tax compliance and found that if taxpayers use tax agency reconciliation system (TAR), then the complexity of tax filing process, errors in the filing process and administrative costs reduce for both the revenue authority and the taxpayers. Besides, Sawyer and James (2018) pointed out that digitalization is increasingly becoming a tool to detect and reduce tax evasion and avoidance. Digitalization or automation in the tax system can reduce the tax administration's operating costs in the long term compared with traditional or partially analogs tax systems even though the initial cost of setting up digital technology is substantial. Kitsios, Jalles, and Verdier (2019) stated that "digitalization can improve tax compliance by enhancing operational efficiency and the quality of the information in trade transactions."

On the other hand, De Mello (2009) examined the connection between revenue authority and taxpayers using differential games instead of a principal-agent relationship framework. The author found that VAT efficiency (i.e., the ratio of collections as a share of consumption to the statutory tax rate) is negatively correlated with the statutory rate and cost of tax administrations. Additionally, the study concluded that value added tax efficiency would be higher in countries where stricter laws and regulations are followed. On the other hand, Terada-Hagiwara, Gonzales, and Wang (2019) presented that digitalization raises issues of VAT collection, particularly in business-to-consumer (B2C) and consumer-to-consumer (C2C) transactions. First, the cost of collecting VAT on low-value transactions of goods may be higher than the tax revenue collected. Second, the complexity of VAT collection on service and intangible transactions makes taxation of cross-border, online transactions difficult.'

Chege, Kiragu, Lagat, and Muthoni (2015) investigated the effects of electronic fiscal devices (EFDs) on value added tax collection in Tanzania by using regression analysis and found a significant relationship between VAT collection and roll-out. On the other hand, the study showed an insignificant relationship between VAT collection and enforcement of EFDs and compliance checks. They also concluded that the use of fiscal electronic devices and their efficiency depends heavily on the roll-out, and compliance and enforcement also play a role. Gordon and Nielsen (1997) estimated that tax evasion costs could be reduced by raising the value-added tax (VAT) rate relative to the income tax rate. Moreover, Mohammed and Gel (2014) proved that due to the introduction of electronic tax register machines (ETRS) by the Ethiopia Revenue and Customs Authority, the amount of direct tax revenue (i.e., corporate income tax), indirect tax revenue and the accumulated tax revenue has increased in Ethiopia.

While reviewing those studies, it was found that significant studies have proved that automation and the digitalization of the entire tax system have kept the tax compliance and corruption at a minimum.

However, no study was conducted for the necessity of an automated VAT system for raising domestic resource mobilization and how automation can be a better alternative to financing SDG projects.

MAIN FOCUS OF THE CHAPTER

Overview of VAT System in Bangladesh

The tax structure is fundamental for an ideal tax system. The ideal tax system must ensure the equity and efficiency of taxation. For the equity of taxation, the share of direct tax should be higher than that of the indirect tax. On the other hand, the tax efficiency depends on the tax performance of an economy, which implies that when tax revenue starts to increase, the efficiency of tax gradually rises. In general, tax collection in developing countries is highly dominated by indirect tax. The primary source of indirect tax has been observed the Value Added Tax (VAT), and the performance of VAT efforts, ultimately, determines the overall tax performance.

Figure 1. Tax performance of Bangladesh and its comparators
Source: World Development Indicators, World Bank, and Authors' Estimates

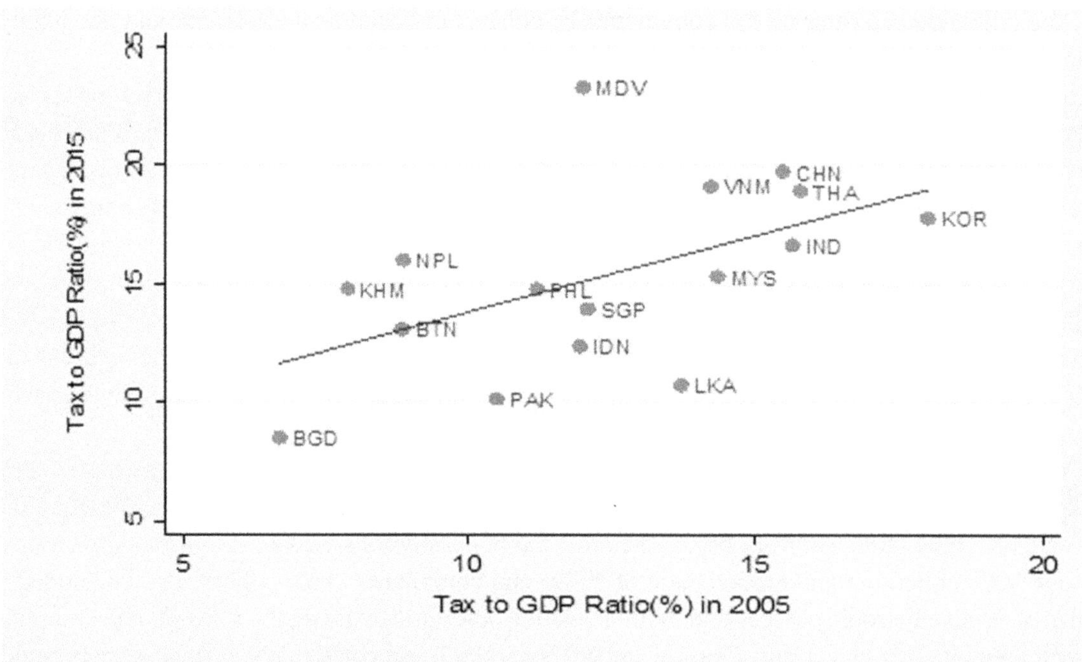

The scatter plot depicts in the figure-1 represents the convergence of tax among the selected developing and developed countries of South and East Asian region. This diagram explains how the tax performance improves with the initial condition over the current decade; the initial tax to GDP ratio was placed in 2005. We have seen that the position of Bangladesh is in the south-west corner compared with

Figure 2. Tax performance: Correlation between Tax-to-GDP and VAT-to-GDP in 2015
Source: World Development Indicators, World Bank, and Authors' Estimates

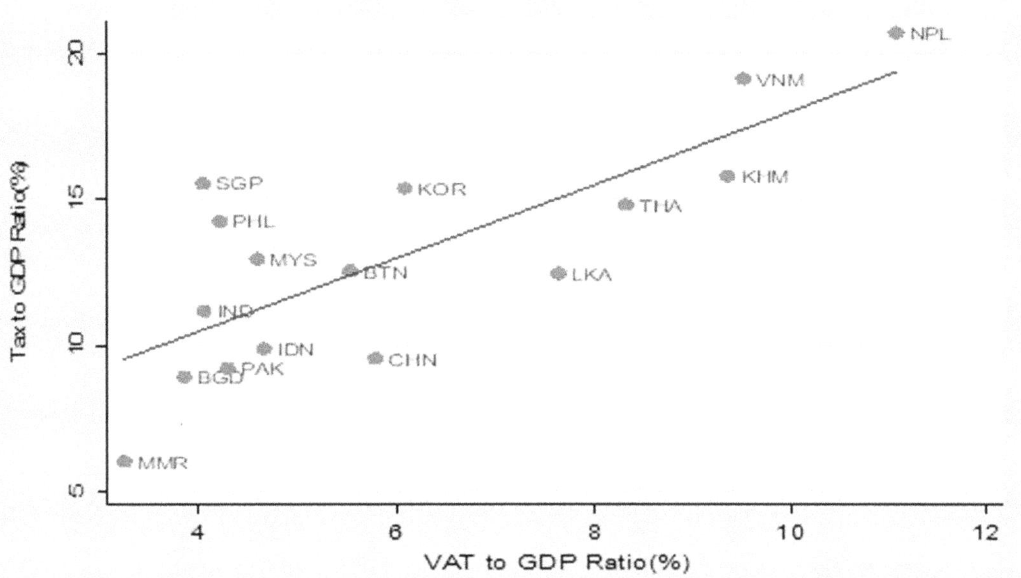

other comparators, such as Cambodia, Indonesia, India, and Vietnam. During the year 2005, the tax to GDP ratio was around 7.2 percent; surprisingly, this ratio is hovering around at 9.1 percent in 2015. In terms of gaining tax efficiency, Bangladesh is far lagging than other comparators. The scatter plot in the figure-2 shows the strong association between Value Added Tax (VAT) and the overall tax performance. This indicates that VAT revenue has the significantly largest shares among sample countries, and the overall revenue collection is highly dominated by VAT. Thus, VAT productivity should be higher for more revenue collection from VAT. Figure-3 represents VAT productivity among the comparators of Bangladesh[4]. The higher value of VAT productivity implies that higher tax has been collected from the existing base, with the given level of effective VAT rate. From the figure-3, it is observed that the VAT productivity of Bangladesh is significantly below than comparator countries, indicating that Bangladesh has enormous potential in VAT if further reforms would be possible to implement.

During the first two decades of Bangladesh, trade-based taxes dominated the tax structure, customs duties alone, accounting for about a third of tax revenue. This scenario, however, started to change after the introduction of VAT from the beginning of 1991. Since the beginning of VAT implementation, Bangladesh had taken numerous prudent tax reforms to abolish the cascading problem of the sales tax system. When VAT was introduced, the share of VAT revenue increased; it recorded from 24.6 percent during the period 1990-2000 to 36.8 percent in 2011-19. A more dramatic change is depicted for custom duties, with its share declining to 12.6 percent of the total tax revenue over the period between 2011 and 2019. The reduced share of customs revenue also reflects a better integration of Bangladesh with the global economy by removing tariff rates. Since the early 1990s, the reduction of average tariff rates was significantly higher, resulting in revenue loss from custom duty and supplementary import. This

Figure 3. Value added tax productivity among selected countries in 2015
Source: World Development Indicators, World Bank, and Authors' Estimates

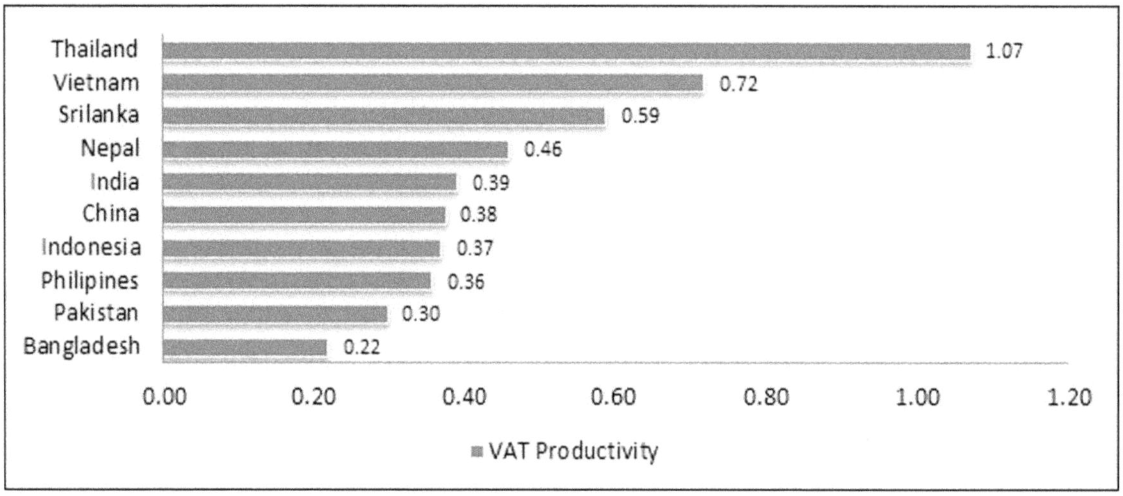

loss from the trade-based taxes has mainly been compensated through the expansion of VAT coverage to many services, wholesale, and retail, as well as the continued increased share from direct tax.

Figure 4. Tax structure during pre and post vat regime in Bangladesh
Source: National Board of Revenue, Bangladesh

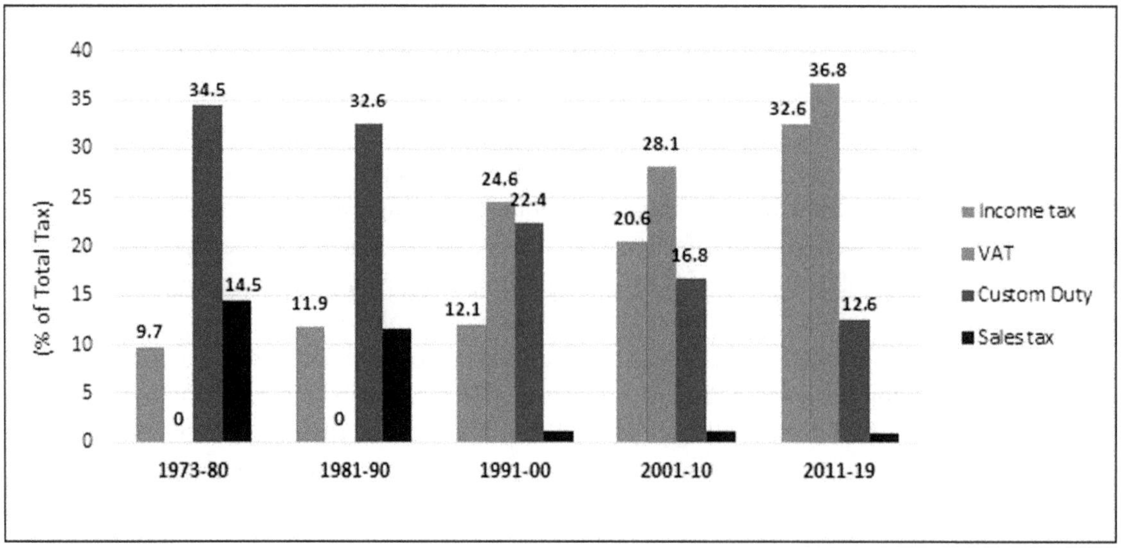

From the figure-4, the impact of the implementation of VAT on tax structure, suggesting VAT is more effective than sales tax. There is no doubt that the progress of VAT has contributed significantly to increasing the overall tax revenue. However, the VAT base still suffers due to the existing tariff value system[5], long listed exemptions, prevailing reduced rates, and some implemented unequal treatments. The key feature of the VAT system in Bangladesh is highlighted in the Box-I below.

Box 1. Summary of Bangladesh VAT System

Characteristics of VAT System	Exemptions and Deductions	Current tax status with rates
❑ Invoice method VAT applied to manufactures ❑ VAT is applicable to imports and selected services and goods at the domestic wholesales and retails	❑ Firms with turnover less than Tk. 8 million per annum. ❑ 3.0 percent turnover tax is applicable to small retailer and no rebate is allowed on inputs ❑ Education, public administration, housing and charitable health services, cold storage, travel agency, indenting firm, construction faces a reduced tax without credit from invoiced tax	❑ 15 percent at standard rate ❑ Fixed VAT amounting Tk. 14,000 for small retailers of Dhaka City Corporation ❑ Fixed VAT amounting TK. 10,000 for small retailers of Chittagong City Corporation ❑ Fixed VAT amounting TK. 7,200 for small retailers of other city corporations ❑ Fixed VAT amounting TK. 3,600 for small retailers of all districts ❑ Truncated rates of 1.5%, 2.5%, 4.5%, 5% and 5.5% in cases where invoice method is difficult to apply. 3% for land development firm ❑ IT enabled service provider's fixation of VAT deductible at source at the rate of 4.5%. It varies in others types-services provided by commercial importers and businesses (3%), construction firms (7.5%), furniture manufacturers (6%), furniture sellers (4%) and procurement providers (4%).
❑ Exports are exempted from VAT	**Goods Exempted:**	
❑ VAT is levied on the base inclusive of Customs duties and supplementary duties ❑ Distortion–chain base system-i.e. tariffs values and truncated base ❑ Wholesalers and retailers may register for VAT (those who want to engage in standard VAT system)	❑ Animals, meat, eggs, hides, fish, vegetables, fruit, grain, flour, cattle and poultry feed, primary milk products, insecticides, jute cuttings, oilseeds, ❑ A few chemicals and drugs, fertilizers, domestic textiles. Cottage industries (defined as a unit with an annual turnover of less than taka 6 million and a capital; investment in machinery of less than taka 4 million). Some plastics, metal products, electricity used in the agricultural sector and a wide range of machinery and scientific apparatus.	

Source: National Board of Revenue, Bangladesh

The current tariff values hinder the full utilization VAT base because tariff values allow the truncated tax base. Apart from the truncated VAT base, the higher level of VAT evasion has been contributed to lowering the VAT revenue. The amount of evasion follows the increasing trend, and this trend seems to be robust due to the absence of a fully automated tax system. In the lack of automation, many taxpayers can submit their return through offline, which is an antiquated payment system. Ultimately, taxpayers can easily hide their sales information because it is challenging to uncover unreported documents about sales revenue by tax officials. Moreover, taxpayers can quickly contact tax officials directly. Consequently, they have a higher chance of offering bribes to tax officials and escaping the bulk tax.

Theoretical Aspect and Conceptual Framework

Theory of Tax Evasion

The economic models of tax evasion (Becker, 1968; Becker & Stigler, 1974; Cerquti & Coppier, 2009) suggests that tax evasion is inversely related to tax compliance. This implies that the tax system's complexity, unscrupulous acts of tax officials, and higher expenditure in preparing tax returns increase the compliance cost. The tax evasion theory asserts that the optimum level of evasion is determined when the Marginal Benefit (MB) equals the Marginal Cost (MC) per dollar non-reported income or sales revenue. According to the theory, the marginal benefit is simply the tax rate when a taxpayer is capable of evading. On the other hand, the marginal cost of tax evasion depends on the penalty and the probability of getting caught, if a taxpayer is caught. Thus, a rational taxpayer is engaged in tax evasion until the benefits of committing the crime are larger than the risk of getting caught and the costs of punishment.

Conceptual Framework: Automation and Tax Evasion

The conceptual framework in association with tax evasion and automation is formulated under the assumption that the VAT system's automation will reduce the compliance cost and tax officials' opportunity to take bribes. This framework of a fully automated tax system also assumes that all account information of registered taxpayers will be appropriately stored, and tax liability will be calculated automatically, resulting in a hassle-free and straightforward tax system. Moreover, taxpayers do not need to contact tax officials when they want to submit their tax returns, implying that tax officials' opportunities for taking bribes and unnecessary delaying tendency by officials to approve the legal tax return will decrease. Under the tax system without automation, the complexity of tax calculation, unscrupulous acts (taking bribes) of tax officials, and the cost of preparing tax returns (bookkeeping) are high, the compliance cost of tax return, thus, increases; and taxpayers have become to be demotivated, resulting in that the level of tax evasion would increase. Besides, if taxpayers want to hide their actual sales turnover, they can easily do it, and tax officials can make it challenging to uncover unreported information. This situation would be more shocking if the taxpayers are dishonest; they demand bribes and allow taxpayers to evade. Therefore, tax returns in the system without automation would create a greater risk of higher evasion.

The VAT system of Bangladesh has two types of the payment system- offline and online. Since the VAT system is not fully automated, taxpayers can submit their returns either by using old-fashioned submission through offline or online payment, which is not obligatory for all taxpayers. Hoping to increase more compliance and lowering the level of evasion, the Bangladesh government has taken initiatives for VAT automation through VAT Online Project (VOP)[6]. Under this project, the government wants to include all of the firms who are active taxpayers; but they do not submit their online returns. The government of Bangladesh believes that the compliance and bribes cost would be almost zero under the full automated tax system. If the tax system is fully automated, the probability of getting caught increases, and eventually, the incentive for tax evasion decreases. Under the full automation, taxpayers are bound to submit their returns online, they do not need to contact officials, and ultimately, bribe cost per taxpayer should be almost nothing. This conceptual framework of the automated VAT system supports the relationship between automation and tax compliance, which is directly inverse, indicating that taxpayers' incentive to evade tax would be high because they have to pay actual tax, penalty, and money they spend for bribes if they are caught.

Methodology

Consider there is n number of active firms, and of them, only q firms submit their return trough online; thus, (n-q) firms are the outside of online tax submission. As the online VAT return is not mandatory, it is assumed that (n-q) firms who are avoiding online tax returns, they used to evade some proportion of actual tax liability. This is a natural phenomenon because taxpayers contact dis-honest officials and offer bribes to avoid tax liability. Underlying all of these assumptions, the maximum gain from tax evasion is simply the gap between the optimal evasion (maximum benefit from evasion) and the cost of evasion. Therefore, we assume that active VAT payers who return their tax through offline also pay some proportion of tax, so their willingness to pay for actual tax liability is less than or equal to the total evasion cost. Under this consideration, we can express the equation below:

$$\left(t_p - t_a\right) \geq E_{cb} + E_{com} \tag{1}$$

In equation (1), t_p represents the optimal level of tax evasion per taxpayer, and t_a denotes to the actual tax liability per taxpayer who submit tax through offline. E_{cb} indicates the cost of providing bribes to the tax officials by per taxpayer, E_{com} is the compliance cost of the manipulation actual revenue report. The total cost of evasion is the sum of money taxpayers have to pay as a bribe to the dishonest officials and extra money they have to pay for audit for the manipulation of bookkeeping records. In general, manipulation costs would be high in the offline tax payment because it takes more time to prepare a fake report to escape the actual tax liability. A non-active taxpayer in online submission always wants to increase the gap between the optimum level of tax evasion (benefits from tax evasion) and the cost of evasion with the given tax rate. For the calculation of additional revenue gain from automation, it is required to estimate the optimum level of evasion, t_p, actual tax liability from the existing tax system, t_a, the total cost of tax evasion, $\left(E_{cb} + E_{com}\right)$.

Optimal Tax Evasion

According to the theory of tax evasion (Becker, 1974), the optimum level of tax is determined when marginal benefit (MB) equals marginal cost (MC) per dollar of non-reported income. Because of the lack of data on non-reported income, we have the data of VAT gap as a proxy for non-reported income. VAT gap is the difference between potential and actual tax. If this gap has positive value, it implies the tax evasion in the tax system. In this study, marginal benefit per dollar non-reported income is simply the VAT rate, t, and it is assumed to be fixed. Therefore, the amount of benefit is the amount tax evasion. In contrast, marginal cost depends on the probability of getting caught and penalty. It is considered that marginal cost function will be an upward sloping curve, meaning that marginal cost per dollar of VAT evasion will increase. This study has assumed the marginal cost function in the equation below:

$$MC(x) = P + \beta x \tag{2}$$

Here, p stands for the probability of getting caught, and x represents the amount of VAT evasion. The value of β takes value ranging between 0 and 1. When β increases to 1, taxpayer's tendency to evade more, and the amount of evasion will be high. Similarly, the marginal benefit of per dollar tax evasion will follow the function below:

$$MB(x) = t \tag{3}$$

For simplicity, we use the t for the effective VAT rate, which is simply the VAT revenue divided by the VAT base[7]. Equating the equation-2 and 3, the solution of the value of x will provide the optimum level of tax evasion (t_p). In Bangladesh, the penalty for tax evasion is significantly minimal. Therefore, we can represent the equation-1, such as the following:

$$t_a + \left(E_{Cb} + E_{com}\right) \leq t_p \tag{4}$$

Here, t_p stands for the benefit from tax evasion, t_a is the actual tax liability, and $\left(E_{Cb} + E_{com}\right)$ is the cost of evasion that includes the bribes and the cost of compliance for the preparation of fake reports. We predict that a rational taxpayers always be careful about the total cost (expenditure) and total benefit during the illegal activities. Equation-4 shows that a rational taxpayer wants to evade tax until total costs of evasion will be less than or equal to the total benefits.

Estimation of Revenue Gains

The underlying assumption of the estimation of revenue gains is that VAT payers in the offline are also active, but, they usually evade some portion of their actual payment through the manipulation or hiding their actual information in the absence of full automated system. For the calculation simplicity, we have represented the equation-4 as an equality constraint, such as:

$$t_a + \left(E_{Cb} + E_{com}\right) = t_p \tag{5}$$

Under the full automated VAT system, (n-q) firms are bound to submit their returns through the online. As a result, the total cost of evasion generating from bribes to tax officials and compliance costs would be zero. Thus, $t_a = t_p$ in the long-run, but it would be $t_a < t_p$ in the short-run. Because taxpayers have initial fixed cost (installation cost of automation procedure, for example, software, equipment purchasing for automated system, fees to tax authority), government should design an incentive mechanism that attracts to the taxpayers. With taking this issue, our short-run assumption is that government will allow some incentives (tax rebate) for taxpayers, which will follow $t_a < t_p$. In the long-run, $\left(E_{Cb} + E_{com}\right)$ will be zero, $\left(E_{Cb} + E_{com}\right)$ is bored by taxpayers to escape actual tax. Since the total cost of evasion must be lower or equal to the total tax evasion (benefit), taxpayers will comply the full amount of tax that they usually want to evade in the offline payment system. Using the average VAT tax liabilities per taxpayer, we have estimated the additional revenue gain in the long-run by using the equation below:

$$Additional\ Revenue\ gain\left(V_g\right) = \left(t_P - t_a\right) \times \left(n - q\right) \tag{6}$$

The revenue gain will be determined in the equation-6, which is simply the multiplication of $\left(t_P - t_a\right)$, the amount of tax evasion (benefit gained without automation) by (n-q) is the total number of non-active online taxpayers. Alternatively, this equation shows that the maximum revenue gain from full automation; taxpayers are willing to pay this amount when the compliance cost and bribes are zero.

Empirical Analysis

The estimation of additional revenue from the fully automated VAT system has been followed- (i) data collection and basic variables setting, (ii) calculation of average actual VAT liability, (iii) the optimum level of tax evasion, and finally, (iv) total revenue gain.

Data Collection and Variable Construction

Data used in this estimation is secondary data collected from the Annual Report, the fiscal year 2017-18 published by the National Board of Revenue (NBR), Bangladesh. All data are annual data. As NBR has published the tax evasion related data only for the fiscal year of 2017-18, we have less scope to elaborate this estimation from year to year. We have calculated the total number of non-active firms in the online payment system by the subtraction between total registered firms, including active and non-active taxpayers, and the number of firms submitting tax through online actively. The average VAT liability is calculated by taking the ratio of VAT revenue collected by the government to the total number of active VAT payers, including online and offline. The probability of getting caught is estimated by using the assumption of how many cases are hanging in the judiciary system that is related to tax evasion. With the given number of taxpayers, if the number of cases of tax defaulter increases, we have assumed that the probability of getting caught increases. Each of defaulter has a non-reported income; they have a probability distribution function that represents the probability of getting caught if they evade corresponding with the level of non-reported income across the group.

Empirical Findings

The method of estimation is discussed in detail in section-5. Based on this discussed methodology, the additional revenue gain has been estimated. Variables, which are used for estimation, are reported in the table-1. First of all, we have shown the baseline scenario, and this scenario is treated by taking into consideration of full automation. The baseline scenario is designed by the assumption that all of the non-active taxpayers in the offline system are included.

Baseline Scenario

To estimate the optimum level of evasion, the effective VAT rate is the marginal benefit of per unit non-reported sales revenue. Because there are multiple VAT rates in Bangladesh, the effective VAT rate has been used. The value of the effective VAT rate is 0.038 or 3.8 percent, while the standard VAT rate is 15 percent. Marginal benefit (MB) function for the theory of optimal evasion has been taken a form, such as:

$$\mathrm{MB} = 0.038 \tag{7}$$

The marginal cost of tax evasion has been estimated by using the equation below:

$$MC = 0.014 + 0.46x \tag{8}$$

Table 1. Estimation of optimal evasion and revenue gain under full automation

Components	FY18
Part-A: Estimation of Optimal VAT Evasion	
Total VAT evasion, In billion BDT	129.24
Probability of getting caught, if a firm evades(P)	0.014
Effective VAT rate (%) (t)	0.038
Coefficient of VAT Gap (Potential – actual VAT) (β)	0.46
Optimum VAT evasion per firm, In billion BDT(t_p)	0.053
Part-B: Estimation of VAT Gains due to Automation	
Actual VAT tax liability per firm, In billion BDT(t_a)	0.012
Revenue gain due to automation, In billion BDT***	892.98
Revenue gain due to automation as % GDP	3.97
Memorandum Items	
No of active VAT payers (online and offline) (n)	57022
No of active VAT payers (online) (q)	35000
No of firms evading tax	778
No of Registered Firms (Cumulative)	825052
VAT revenue, In billion BDT	682.2
GDP, In billion BDT	**22505**

Source: Authors' Estimates

*** indicates the formula of $(t_P - t_a)\times(n-q)$

The equation-8 shows that marginal cost follows an increasing function of the VAT gap, implying that the tax gap is 46%, on an average, with the given level of potential tax. The value of 0.014 is the probability of getting caught It is estimated to take the ratio of cases in the court related to tax evasion to the number of non-active VAT payers online. When the number of fraudulent cases increases, given the non-active online VAT payers' chance of getting caught increases. The variable, x, stands for the VAT gap, indicating that the magnitude of the VAT gap determines the marginal cost of evasion.

With the lack of data on non-reported income across taxpayers, the average rate of the VAT gap has been used to formulate the marginal cost function. VAT gap indicates the average rate of evasion with the existing base and administrative efficiency. The average value of the estimated VAT gap, which is projected by Mansur, Yunus, and Nandi (2011) and Langford and Ohlenburg (2015)[8]. Moreover, our assumptions have been justified with this value because several estimates of the VAT gap for developing economies takes value between 0.40 and 0.7 (Clotfelter, 1983; Blumenthal, Christian, Slemrod, & Smith, 2001; Bania, Gray, & Stone, 2007). In general, the VAT gap coefficient lies between 0 and 1, when the VAT gap reaches closer to1, the amount of evasion will be smaller.

According the theory of optimum evasion, equilibrium occurs when marginal benefit (MB) and marginal cost (MC) are the same. Substituting the MB and MC function in the equilibrium condition, we can get:

$$MB = MC \tag{9}$$

$$0.038 = 0.014 + 0.46x \tag{10}$$

Solving the equation-10, we have estimated the value of optimal tax evasion, t_p, per firm, which is the amount of BDT 0.053 billion in the fiscal year of 2017-18. Under the existing VAT system, the maximum amount of tax that a firm can evade, is simply BDT 0.053 billion. This also implies the maximum gain or benefit, the offline taxpayers might receive if they can evade tax.

In the existing VAT system, there are 57022 active firms; however, NBR has reported only 35000 firms to submit their tax return through online. Since we assume that all the active firms submit their return through online under the full automation, the remaining of 22022 firms will be included in the online payment system. In case of full automation, all of the non-active firms in the online are bound to submit their returns through online. As a result, the total cost of evasion generating from bribes to tax officials and compliance costs would be zero. With the absence of automation, the cost of bribes and compliance from tax complexity are the expenditure that taxpayers have to pay for the evasion. Since in the earlier we assume offline taxpayers will evade some proportion of actual tax, this amount of evasion must be greater than or equal to the total cost of evasion. From the equation-5, we can rewrite in the long-run under full automation as: $(t_p - t_a) = (E_{Cb} + E_{com})$. Thus, the taxpayers want to comply the full amount of tax, which is the gap between optimum level evasion and the portion of actual tax they have already paid. The argument behind this gap is that the amount of $(E_{Cb} + E_{com})$ is saving in the full automation, and if the tax payer is not willing to pay the amount of $(t_p - t_a)$, they must be caught. Moreover, they have to pay this amount plus penalty cost of evasion. Applying the equation-6, we have estimated the revenue gain of BDT 893 billion, which is equivalent to 3.97 percent of GDP.

Sensitivity Analysis

The baseline scenario is the optimistic scenario. If this optimistic scenario is possible to achieve, Bangladesh should require to improve administrative efficiency, reduce corruption, and to ensure law and order. The tariff value system, moreover, should be eliminated for broadening the VAT base. We assume that it takes time, and the tax authority should offer some incentives in the short-run. For establishing the fully automated VAT system by non-active firms in the online, they would require setting costs. Underlying these factors, we have formulated the four different scenarios taking with the issue of full and partial automation. In the full automation, we have considered that 22022 firms would be included, while a fraction of firms is in the partial automation. Assumptions of four scenarios under full and partial automation are depicted in the table-2.

In the sensitivity analysis, we have assumed that the government requires tax rebates in the initial period of automation so that non-active offline firms may be encouraged to enter in the online payment

Table 2. Description of four scenarios under full and partial automation

Scenario	Partial Automation	Full Automation
Scenario-1	Willingness to Pay: 40% of tax evasion Additional offline Firms: 25% of total	Willingness to Pay: 40% of tax evasion Additional offline Firms: 100% included
Scenario-2	Willingness to Pay: 60% of tax evasion Additional offline Firms: 50% of total	Willingness to Pay: 60% of tax evasion Additional offline Firms: 100% included
Scenario-3	Willingness to Pay: 80% of tax evasion Additional offline Firms: 75% of total	Willingness to Pay: 80% of tax evasion Additional offline Firms: 100% included
Scenario-4	Willingness to Pay: 100% of tax evasion Additional offline Firms: 80% of total	Willingness to Pay: 80% of tax evasion Additional offline Firms: 100% included

Source: Authors' Estimates

system. Initially, the non-active offline firms have to incur automation fees and the installation cost of equipment for the full automation process. Partial automation in figure-5 has shown that non-active offline firms are willing to comply with 40 percent of the amount of the gap between optimum evasion and actual tax, and 25 percent of firms will enter into the online payment. On the other hand, scenario-4, for example, represents 100 percent willingness to comply and 80 percent of the new firm inclusion. The additional revenue gain from scenario-1 has estimated to 0.40 percent of GDP, while it is estimated to 3.17 percent of GDP from the scenario-4. In the case of the full automation system, the additional revenue gain has been registered to range between 1.59 percent and 3.97 percent of GDP.

Scope of Financing SDG Projects

Achieving the Lower Middle-Income Country (LMIC) in 2016, Bangladesh has kept an ambitious target of reaching the Higher Middle-Income Country (HMIC) by 2031. Although Bangladesh has experienced higher economic growth over the last decade, labor productivity growth does not increase in line with growth momentum. The growth theory suggests that labor productivity, employees' skills, and innovation are fundamental to maintaining sustained economic growth in the long run. Bangladesh has also experienced structural transformation; however, the expansion of the industry has been taken place almost stagnant. The lack of export diversification is a potential hindrance; the lack of infrastructure for industrial expansion has further intensified the challenges of increasing labor productivity and innovation. It is evident that Bangladesh has a vast advantage in population dividends; it is possible to capitalize on this advantage when additional employment is created along with industrial expansion. For the utilization of population dividend advantage, industrial expansion, and increasing labor productivity are considered as a necessary condition; however, Bangladesh faces huge resource constraint. The government can catalyze the mitigation of resource constraints to allocate more resources in numerous infrastructure, welfare, and human capital projects. Thus, the adequacy of the domestic resource is vital to mitigate the rocketed demand of resources for infrastructure and human development.

Seventeen goals in the SDGs are inclusive for sustainable development. Bangladesh has already taken several initiatives to meet the SDG target by 2031. If Bangladesh can achieve the SDG targets, Bangladesh can quickly reach a higher middle-income status. Most of the infrastructure projects are financed from the external sources; the opportunities for soft loans from the donor and multi-national agencies have also been contracted. Furthermore, the stagnant of tax revenue collection is intensifying

Figure 5. Sensitivity analysis of VAT revenue gain during automation (as % of GDP)
Source: Authors' Estimates

Components	FY18
Part-A: Estimation of Optimal VAT Evasion	
Total VAT evasion, In billion BDT	129.24
Probability of getting caught, if a firm evades(??)	0.014
Effective VAT rate (%) (t)	0.038
Coefficient of VAT Gap (Potential – actual VAT) (??)	0.46
Optimum VAT evasion per firm, In billion BDT($??_{??}$)	0.053
Part-B: Estimation of VAT Gains due to Automation	
Actual VAT tax liability per firm, In billion BDT($??_{??}$)	0.012
Revenue gain due to automation, In billion BDT***	892.98
Revenue gain due to automation as % GDP	3.97
Memorandum Items	
No of active VAT payers (online and offline) (n)	57022
No of active VAT payers (online) (q)	35000
No of firms evading tax	778
No of Registered Firms (Cumulative)	825052
VAT revenue, In billion BDT	682.2
GDP, In billion BDT	**22505**

the challenges of financing in the SDG projects. Figure-6 represents the estimated resources, which are required to reach the SDGs targets. Based on the report of the Ministry of Planning, Bangladesh, 66.3 billion USD per year will be required to achieve the investment target of 982.48 billion USD throughout of 2017 and 2031.

Figure-7 and table-3 depict the required resources for achieving the specific SDG goals and the source of targeted financing that is estimated by the Ministry of Planning, Bangladesh. The quality of education and good health have been prioritized significantly represented in SDG3 and SDG4. The higher priorities in these two sectors support the idea of improving human capital leading to labor productivity. The highest priority is assigned to the goal of SDG-13, which is related to climate change, implying

Figure 6. Year-wise additional cost for achieving SDG targets
Source: GED, Ministry of Planning, Bangladesh

Scenario	Partial Automation	Full Automation
Scenario-1	Willingness to Pay: 40 % of tax evasion Additional offline Firms: 25% of total	Willingness to Pay: 40 % of tax evasion Additional offline Firms: 100% included
Scenario-2	Willingness to Pay: 60 % of tax evasion Additional offline Firms: 50% of total	Willingness to Pay: 60 % of tax evasion Additional offline Firms: 100% included
Scenario-3	Willingness to Pay: 80 % of tax evasion Additional offline Firms: 75% of total	Willingness to Pay: 80 % of tax evasion Additional offline Firms: 100% included
Scenario-4	Willingness to Pay: 100 % of tax evasion Additional offline Firms: 80% of total	Willingness to Pay: 80 % of tax evasion Additional offline Firms: 100% included

that Bangladesh wants to contribute to green growth to ensure environmental sustainability. The goal of SDG7, SDG-8, and SDG-9 have an allocation of USD 536 billion, which includes clean energy, decent work, and industrial innovation, and infrastructure development.

Figure 7. Goal-wise additional cost in billion USD during fy2017 to fy30
Source: GED, Ministry of Planning, Bangladesh

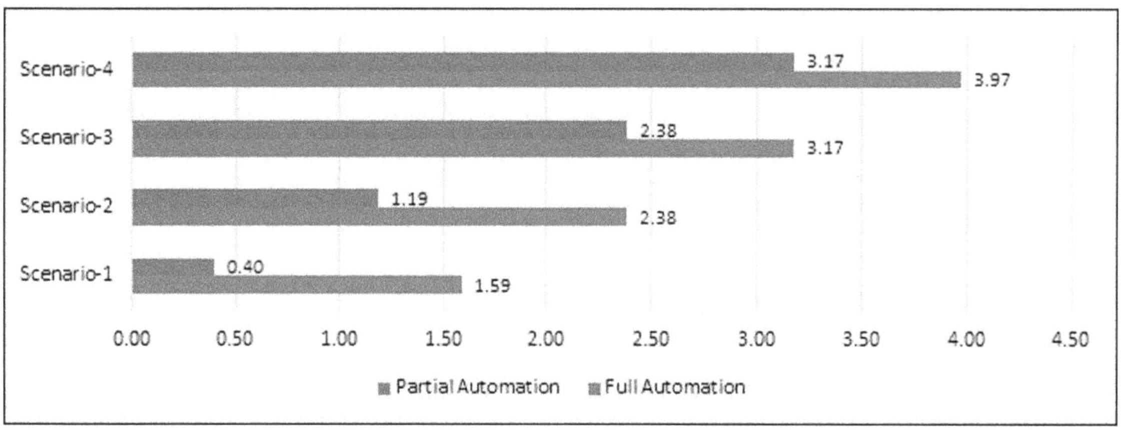

From the topmost priorities, it has been observed that Bangladesh focuses on rapid industrialization through increasing labor productivity and new job creation. To achieve all of these targets, higher allocation in human capital, infrastructure, innovation, and skills-enhancing training is well justified. In the context of reality, Bangladesh has a huge investment gap in infrastructure and human capital projects. Based on the World Bank report, Bangladesh requires to invest as much as BDT 471 billion per year to mitigate the investment target BDT 4,081 billion in the lower bound case and BDT 5,539 billion in the upper bound case for transports, electricity, and WSS by 2020[9]. If we look at the financing strategies, shown in table-3, it has been observed that 85.11 percent fund of SDG projects would be collected from domestic resources. Therefore, Bangladesh should take prudent tax reform policies for the modernization of the tax system, which can contribute to the scarcity of the domestic resource.

Table 3. Financing strategy for implementation of SDGs (USD in billion)

Components of Financing	FY17-20	FY21-25	FY26-30	FY17-30
Total additional amount from domestic sources (85.11% of total)	107.72	257.49	430.87	796.09
Total additional amount from external sources (14.89% of total)	22.07	43.15	67.17	132.39
Total additional amount from both external and domestic sources (100%)	129.79	300.64	498.04	928.48
Annual average additional amount from domestic sources	26.93	51.5	86.17	56.86
Annual average additional amount from external sources	5.52	8.63	13.43	9.46
of Which:				
Foreign Direct Investment (FDI)	2.73	6.45	10.7	6.91
Grants and aid	2.79	2.17	2.74	2.55

Source: GED, Ministry of Planning, Bangladesh

VAT is the primary source of domestic resource mobilization, and this system has a huge tax gap. This is the high time for Bangladesh to reform the VAT system through the implanting of full automation. Automated VAT system will reduce the tax gap and improve tax efficiency with tax evasion minimization. This study has estimated the additional revenue gain due to the full automation, which is robust. This study also suggests that the additional revenue gain would account for ranging between 1.59 and 3.97 percent of GDP if the VAT system would be fully automated, with the same base. According to the estimation reported in table-3, Bangladesh requires investment from domestic resources for the financing of SDGs, which is the amount of 26 billion USD, on an average per year, and 10.05 percent of GDP. Only automation from the VAT system can fulfill almost half of SDG financing from the domestic resource. Therefore, the digitalization of the overall tax system can foster domestic resource mobilization and contribute to employment generation and sustained economic development.

FUTURE RESEARCH DIRECTIONS

In this study, the necessity of an automated VAT system for raising domestic resource mobilization and how automation can be a better alternative to finance SDG projects are evaluated for Bangladesh. Corruption has been taken place the central issue of tax evasion; however, the behavioral issues of tax evasion would be a more dynamic research topic in the future. The research about the issue of behavioral aspects of tax officials and taxpayers would be more appealing because the various incentive mechanisms would be an ideal fiscal policy instrument for the solution of tax evasion. In addition to this aspect, there remains potential scope to explore how the inclusion of the informal economy affects the optimum level of evasion, with the given level of corruption and administrative efficiency.

CONCLUSION

The persistent tax evasion can create the sluggishness of domestic resource mobilization in Bangladesh. As Bangladesh currently faces the external financing constraints, there is no better alternative without boosting up the domestic resource mobilization. Moreover, the persistent level of tax evasion can have detrimental effects on the redistribution, which violates the tax equity, and this trend, ultimately, would hinder the pace of economic growth through thwarting the continued public capital accumulation. This scenario would worsen when the significant resource gap is widened for financing in the development of human capital. Undoubtedly, Bangladesh badly needs to raise domestic-based tax efforts. That is the reason, and VAT is the ideal option for Bangladesh; there exists a lot of VAT potential. It is very shocking that the VAT system currently suffers from the existing truncated base, long listed exemptions, and multiple rates.

Along with drawbacks, if the tax evasion in the VAT system has been taken place a permanent issue, the persistent higher tax evasion will be intensified the VAT gap. Theory and empirical studies suggest that tax evasion is a behavioral and cultural problem. It is the complex outcome of administrative inefficiencies, bribes taken by dishonest tax officials, and the inability of uncovered non-reported income with the absence of full.

REFERENCES

NBR Annual Report, 2017-18, *National Board of Revenue, Bangladesh.*

Bania, N., Gray, J. A., & Stone, J. A. (2007). Growth, taxes, and government expenditures: Growth hills for US states. *National Tax Journal, 60*(2), 193–204. doi:10.17310/ntj.2007.2.02

Becker, G. S. (1968). Crime and punishment: An economic approach. In *The economic dimensions of crime* (pp. 13–68). Palgrave Macmillan. doi:10.1007/978-1-349-62853-7_2

Becker, G. S., & Stigler, G. J. (1974). Law enforcement, malfeasance, and compensation of enforcers. *The Journal of Legal Studies, 3*(1), 1–18. doi:10.1086/467507

Bellon, M. M., Chang, J., Dabla-Norris, M. E., Khalid, S., Lima, F., Rojas, E., & Villena, P. (2019). *Digitalization to Improve Tax Compliance: Evidence from VAT e-Invoicing in Peru.* International Monetary Fund. doi:10.5089/9781513513713.001

Bird, R. M. (1992). *Tax policy and economic development.* Johns Hopkins Univ Pr.

Blumenthal, M., Christian, C., Slemrod, J., & Smith, M. G. (2001). Do normative appeals affect tax compliance? Evidence from a controlled experiment in Minnesota. *National Tax Journal, 54*(1), 125–138. doi:10.17310/ntj.2001.1.06

Campbell, D. F., & Hanschitz, G. (2018). *Digitalization of Tax: Epistemic Tax Policy.* Academic Press.

Cerqueti, R., & Coppier, R. (2009). Tax revenues, fiscal corruption and "shame" costs. *Economic Modelling, 26*(6), 1239–1244. doi:10.1016/j.econmod.2009.06.005

Chege, A., Kiragu, N., Lagat, C., & Muthoni, G. (2015). Effect of electronic fiscal devices on VAT collection in Tanzania: A case of Tanzania revenue authority. *European Journal of Business and Management, 7*(33), 125–133.

Clavey, C., Pemberton, J. L., Loeprick, J., & Verhoeven, M. (2019). *International Tax Reform.* Digitalization, and Developing Economies.

Clotfelter, C. T. (1983). Tax evasion and tax rates: An analysis of individual returns. *The Review of Economics and Statistics*, *65*(3), 363–373. doi:10.2307/1924181

De Mello, L. (2009). Avoiding the value added tax: Theory and cross-country evidence. *Public Finance Review*, *37*(1), 27–46. doi:10.1177/1091142108316588

Fjeldstad, O. H. (1996). *Tax evasion and corruption in local governments in Tanzania: Alternative economic approaches*. Academic Press.

Galtung, F. (1995). Current strategies for combating corruption: A study of corruption in the tax administration. *Berlin: Transparency International Occasional Working Paper*, (8).

Gitaru, K. (2017). *The Impact Of System Automation On Revenue Collection in Kenya Revenue Authority: A Case Study of SIMBA*. Academic Press.

Gordon, R. H., & Nielsen, S. B. (1997). Tax evasion in an open economy: Value-added vs. income taxation. *Journal of Public Economics*, *66*(2), 173–197. doi:10.1016/S0047-2727(97)00044-3

Hindriks, J., Keen, M., & Muthoo, A. (1999). Corruption, extortion and evasion. *Journal of Public Economics*, *74*(3), 395–430. doi:10.1016/S0047-2727(99)00030-4

Isaac, N. N., & Lilian, L. (2010). Automation and customs tax administration: Empirical evidence from Uganda. *African Journal of Business Management*, *4*(11), 2241.

Jimenez, G., Mac an tSionnaigh, N., & Kamenov, A. (2013). Information Technology for Tax Administrations. *USAID Bureau for Economic Growth, Education and Environment, Office of Economic Policy.* http://pdf. usaid. gov/pdf_docs/PNAEA485. pdf

Kitsios, E., Jalles, J., & Verdier, G. (2019). *Reducing Tax Evasion from Cross-Border Fraud: The role of Digitalization*. Academic Press.

Langford, B., & Ohlenburg, T. (2015). *Tax revenue potential and effort*. International Growth Centre Working Paper. Available at: https://www. theigc. org/wp-content/uploads/2016/01/Langford-Ohlenburg-2016-Working-paper. pdf

Macroeconomic Outlooks for the Perspective Plan. (2014). Ministry of Planning, Bangladesh.

Mansur, A. H., Yunus, M., & Nandi, B. K. (2011). An evaluation of the tax system in Bangladesh. In *Conference on Linking Research to Policy: Growth and Development Issues in Bangladesh, Dhaka, December* (*Vol. 20*). Academic Press.

Mohammed, H. K., & Gela, Z. D. (2014). Challenges of electronics tax register machine (ETRS) to businesses and its impact in improving tax revenue. *International Journal (Toronto, Ont.)*, *5*(3), 2305–1493.

Nam, C. W., Parsche, R., & Schaden, B. (2001). *Measurement of value added tax evasion in selected EU countries on the basis of national accounts data*. Academic Press.

Pitić, G., Radosavljević, G., Babin, M., & Erić, M. (2019). Digitalization of the tax administration in Serbia. *Ekonomika preduzeća*, *67*(1-2), 131-145.

Sawyer, A. J., & James, S. (2018). *Digitalization of Tax: Comparing New Zealand and United Kingdom Approaches*. Academic Press.

Schwebkea, J., Brinkb, W., Hansenc, V., & Kellihera, C. (2019). *Analyzing the role of trustworthiness in tax filing and tax compliance behavior through an automated return*. Academic Press.

Slemrod, J., & Yitzhaki, S. (2002). Tax avoidance, evasion, and administration. In *Handbook of public economics* (Vol. 3, pp. 1423–1470). Elsevier.

Tanzi, V., & Shome, P. (1993). A primer on tax evasion. *Staff Papers*, *40*(4), 807–828. doi:10.2307/3867611

Terada-Hagiwara, A., Gonzales, K., & Wang, J. (2019). *Taxation Challenges in a Digital Economy—The Case of the People's Republic of China*. Academic Press.

ADDITIONAL READING

Cerqueti, R., & Coppier, R. (2009). Tax revenues, fiscal corruption and "shame" costs. *Economic Modelling*, *26*(6), 1239–1244. doi:10.1016/j.econmod.2009.06.005

De Mello, L. (2009). Avoiding the value added tax: Theory and cross-country evidence. *Public Finance Review*, *37*(1), 27–46. doi:10.1177/1091142108316588

Galtung, F. (1995). Current strategies for combating corruption: A study of corruption in the tax administration. *Berlin: Transparency International Occasional Working Paper*, (8).

Hindriks, J., Keen, M., & Muthoo, A. (1999). Corruption, extortion and evasion. *Journal of Public Economics*, *74*(3), 395–430. doi:10.1016/S0047-2727(99)00030-4

Mansur, A. H., Yunus, M., & Nandi, B. K. (2011). An evaluation of the tax system in Bangladesh. In *Conference on Linking Research to Policy: Growth and Development Issues in Bangladesh, Dhaka, December* (Vol. 20).

Nam, C. W., Parsche, R., & Schaden, B. (2001). Measurement of value added tax evasion in selected EU countries on the basis of national accounts data.

Sawyer, A. J., & James, S. (2018). Digitalization of Tax: Comparing New Zealand and United Kingdom Approaches.

Slemrod, J., & Yitzhaki, S. (2002). Tax avoidance, evasion, and administration. In *Handbook of public economics* (Vol. 3, pp. 1423–1470). Elsevier.

KEY TERMS AND DEFINITIONS

Automated Tax System: A tax system integrated with advanced technology to collect taxes from taxpayers.

Economic Growth: The increasing level of the production of economic goods and services in a period compared with the previous period.

Indirect Tax: Indirect tax charged on goods and services (e.g., value added tax).

National Board of Revenue: The revenue authority of Bangladesh.

Public Finance: Public finance is a branch of economics which concerned with government revenue and expenditure.

Sustainable Development Goals: Some distinct goals with an objective to end poverty.

Tax Evasion: It is an illegal activity for avoiding tax by the taxpayers.

VAT Efficiency: The ratio of collections as a share of consumption to the statutory tax rate.

ENDNOTES

1 Bangladesh has a tax to GDP ratio of 7.8 percent, on an average throughout 2011-17, while South Asian countries have an average of 12.97 percent. For emerging economies, the tax to GDP ratio has reached to 23.25 percent, on an average, during 2011-2017. Bangladesh has a lower tax to GDP ratio due to the complexity of tax submission, lack of automation, and inefficiency in the tax administration.

2 This estimated value is taken from the report of GED, Ministry of Planning, Bangladesh.

3 In Bangladesh, the number of active VAT payers (online and offline) is 57022; out of the total VAT payers, the number of active VAT payers is 35000. In the fiscal year 2017-18, a total of 778 firms evaded value added tax.

4 VAT productivity is the ratio of VAT as % of GDP to the Standard VAT rate. Higher productivity suggests that revenue grows faster relative to the VAT base with the given level of standard VAT rate.

5 VAT is imposed on the market value addition. However, the VAT system's tariff value is an administrative market value addition that is fixed by tax officials. Tariff value reduces the VAT base because the market value addition in the tariff value system is lower than the actual value addition, which is determined from sale price minuses purchase price.

6 VAT Online Program Project will introduce automation, including on-line VAT taxpayer services, and improve transparency in the VAT administration system. The project will support the government to implement the new VAT law, which comes into effect in 2015, aims to reduce administrative costs, and seek to increase the number of active registered taxpayers from 35,00 to 85,000 in 2019-2020.

7 In Bangladesh, VAT is allowed value addition of manufacturing and service sectors, and there are also multiple rates. As consequence, agricultural value addition is excluded when the effective VAT rate is calculated. We have also deducted some portion of the service sector because all services are not allowed for VAT coverage.

8 VAT gap is calculated by taking the difference between tax potential and actual tax. The tax frontier model has been used by the author to calculate VAT potential. Tax potential is measured by using

the tax effort index, taking the ratio of actual VAT to GDP ratio to the predicted value of VAT to GDP. The tax effort index ranges between 0 and 1. We have assumed the average VAT effort index value is to 0.54, suggesting that 46 percent of VAT base has not fully utilized to collect revenue due to lack of automation, corruption, and inefficiency of tax administration.

9 See Andres et al. (2013) for the description of the methodology for computing these estimates. World Bank estimates the investment requirement of $59 billion in lower bound and $79.5 billion of investment requirement in upper bound for electricity, transports, and WSS to mitigate investment gaps in these sectors.

Chapter 15
An Overview of Emerging Technologies in the Indian Retail Industry

Nilesh Kumar
Amity University, Jharkhand, India

ABSTRACT

With the arrival of several new players, Indian retail has become one of the most dynamic and fast industries. With the advancement in technology, internet, engineering, many retailers are adopting and using the internet of things, big data technology, RFID, and other technical software and programs to enhance customer experience, customer engagement through which retailers are improving efficiency. In particular, many customer-oriented internet of things technologies, such as augmented reality, smart shopping carts, smart displays, and RFID tags, are expected to change the way customers experience retail shopping. For this study, the secondary data has been explored and studied. The purpose of this chapter is to study how emerging technologies like big data and IoT implementation are transforming organizational practices and thereby generating potential benefits in the retail industry.

INTRODUCTION

Indian retail is experiencing tremendous growth with the changing demographics and one improving the quality of life of city people. Retail Sector is the most thriving sector in the Indian economy. With a growing economy, improved income dynamics, increasing awareness and a heavy customer base, India is fast becoming one of the most potential markets for domestic and global retailers. The main purpose of this document is to be strategic analyze the Indian retail trade. Retail is one of the largest industries in India and one of the largest sources of employment in the country. According to India Brand Equity Foundation report the Indian retail market has approximately 14 million outlets and is the largest retail destination in the world.

Retailing in India is one of the pillars of its economy, accounting for 14 to 15 percent of GDP. The Indian retail market is estimated at US $ 450 billion and is one of the top five retail markets in the world

DOI: 10.4018/978-1-7998-4787-8.ch015

in terms of economic value. India is one of the fastest growing retail markets in the world with 1.2 billion people (Foreign direct investment (FDI) in the multi-brand retail sector in India - A boon or bane - IEEE Conference Publication, 2020). Most Indian stores take place in open markets or in millions of small, independent supermarkets and shops. Shoppers are usually outside the store, ask what they want and cannot take a product off the shelf or investigate it. Retailing in India is essentially manned small shops. In 2010, about 4 percent of the industry accounted for larger-sized convenience stores and supermarkets, and these were only present in large urban centers. About 40 million Indians (3.3% of the Indian population) work in retail and logistics in India (Elahi et al, 2013).

The retail market in India is estimated to reach $ 1.1-1.3 trillion in 2025, down from $ 0.7 trillion in 2019, and is growing at a compound annual growth rate (CAGR) of 9-11%, driven by socio-demographic and economic factors such as urbanization, income growth and emergence in nuclear families (Jha, 2020, para.1).

India is the fifth largest retail destination worldwide. The country is among the highest in the world in per capita availability. Retail sales in India are experiencing exponential growths, with retail development not only taking place in the major cities and metros, but also in the cities of Tier-II and Tier-III. Healthy economic growth, changing demographic profile, rising disposable incomes, urbanization, changing tastes and consumer preferences are the other factors driving growth in the organized retail market in India. The Indian population participates in online retailing on a large scale ("Indian Retail Industry Analysis," 2018, para.2).

The online retail market is expected to grow from $ 6 billion to $ 70 billion in FY15-FY20. The increasing participation of foreign and private players has boosted Indian retail. India's price competitiveness is attracting large retailers to use it as a sourcing base. Global retailers such as Walmart, GAP, Tesco and JC Penney are increasing their purchasing from India and moving from third party purchasing offices to setting up their own fully managed purchasing and purchasing offices. The government of India has implemented reforms to attract FDI in retail. The government of India has approved 51 percent FDI in multi-brand retail and increased the FDI limit to 100 percent from 51 percent in single-brand retail, and plans to allow 100 percent FDI in e-commerce, under the agreement that the products sold must be manufactured in India to take advantage of the liberalized regime (IBEF,n.d).

The retail ecosystem in India is at the forefront of change and has evolved. 2019 was an interesting year for Indian retail - it is undergoing a sea of transformation, experiencing exponential growth and expanding not only in the country's major cities and metros, but also in the cities and towns of Tier II and III. Retailers learn how to balance strategies between online and physical sales. There are many factors driving this growth in the organized retail market in India. The most important of these are healthy economic growth, changing demographic profile, increasing disposable incomes, urbanization, changing tastes and consumer preferences. Retail is going to undergo a seismic shift to become much more diverse and vibrant, something that will only continue as consumers evolve and expect experience offerings and multi-channel connection.

BACKGROUND

The retail industry in India is witnessing a massive overhaul, as traditional retailers are making way for new sizes. These modern retail formulas offer a wide variety of customers and provide an ideal shopping experience with a fusion of product, entertainment and service, all less than one roof. Now the consumer has multiple options to choose from, from the retailer to the most sophisticated supermarkets, department stores, squares and malls that supply the latest quality products. The food and groceries; health and beauty; clothing; jewelry; and consumer durables are the fastest growing categories of organized retail. Hypermarkets, shopping centers, supermarkets are consumers' favorite shops. In addition, there are different consumer product preferences shop formulas are as follows: food and grocery, health and beauty service market; clothing and clothing, catering services and an entertainment center; books, music and gifts - convenience store and shopping centers; watches, mobile, accessories and pharmaceutical hypermarket; footwear department store. International fame and product availability and brand communication are the characteristics that drive organized retail in India and organized retail is preferred for its convenience and variety (Ravi Kiran & Deepika Jhamb, 2011).

India is home to more than 1.2 billion inhabitants and the second largest retail market in the world. Retail in India continues to maintain momentum, driven by economic and social developments and population growth. Key factors in retail growth are robust economic growth, growing tourism, growing population, growing youth segment, changing consumer trends, increasing purchasing power and penetration of international players. Retail sales in the India region will grow with a CAGR of 16.3% over 2013-18 ("Indian Retail Industry - Major trends, Growth and Opportunities 2020 – 2025", para.1).

India's position over the period in Asia is most optimistic, with an expected CAGR of over 16.3%, followed by Indonesia with a CAGR of 14%. The total size of Indian retail in 2013 is $ 534 USD (IBEF, n.d).

India's retail trade is driven by rising disposable income, consumer confidence and increasing wealthy individuals. The Indian retail market has become more robust after the arrival of international retail chains. The retail market is severely affected by low GDP per capita and high youth unemployment.

Liberal retail policies and the removal of trade barriers and restrictions on foreign investment and links with the World Trade Organization (WTO) are helping to boost retail growth in India. India has recently made its policy liberal, which will contribute to more growth and facilitate business.

Information technology advances are rapidly changing the retail industry. In particular, the emergence of the Internet of Things (IoT) offers retailers strategic opportunities to engage customers and transform their shopping experience. IoT is a new technology where retail services are delivered to users through smart or intelligent objects or devices. IoT is considered a clear step in the evolution of retail as it combines the physical and virtual dimensions of the retail environment to create a seamless and personalized shopping experience tailored to the needs of the customer. It is claimed that the implementation of IoT in retail is expected to bring a significant increase in efficiency to retailers and customers in terms of cost savings, time savings and improved accessibility. In addition, IoT increases value through interconnectedness and networks, improved intelligence and improved behavior (Balaji et al., 2018)

According to Gartner (2015), IoT is identified as one of the major strategic technology trends expected to reform retail opportunities until 2020. Some of the notable applications of IoT in retail are products with radio frequency identification (RFID), smart shopping carts, near field communication systems, smart shopping carts and virtual mirrors etc. Given the rapid growth of IoT in retail, it is critical for academics and retailers to understand the adoption process.

According to Gartner (2020) forecasts that global IT retail spending will drop by 13.3% in 2020 to $ 196.8 billion in constant US dollars, from $ 227.1 billion in 2019. Expenditure is expected to recover to average growth rates five-year 10.6% to reach an estimated $ 270.5 billion by 2024.

Despite the growing interest in the adoption of digital technologies and big data analysis, a clear picture of the dynamics of application and the benefits of implementing big data in literature is lacking, especially in specific industries such as retail, one dimension of the service world. Especially empirical

Table 1. IoT Endpoint Market by Segment, 2018-2020, Worldwide (Installed Base, Billions of Units)

Segment	2018	2019	2020
Utilities	0.98	1.17	1.37
Government	0.40	0.53	0.70
Building Automation	0.23	0.31	0.44
Physical Security	0.83	0.95	1.09
Manufacturing & Natural Resources	0.33	0.40	0.49
Automotive	0.27	0.36	0.47
Healthcare Providers	0.21	0.28	0.36
Retail & Wholesale Trade	0.29	0.36	0.44
Information	0.37	0.37	0.37
Transportation	0.06	0.07	0.08
Total	**3.96**	**4.81**	**5.81**

Source: Gartner (August 2019)

studies on this subject are lacking. Studies in this field usually consist of recently published conceptual research Most of the empirical research focuses on the health industry, and some also in the food industry. (Santoro et al., 2018)

According to Barney (1986) without the implementation of big data, retail companies cannot support business strategies for cost leadership or differentiation. Big data management helps companies to achieve and exploit their business strategy. Another theoretical implication concerns the relationship between the implementation of big data, the competences required to use data analysis and the sharing of data.

METHODOLOGY

For this article we have collected the secondary data through journals, articles, research papers, review papers, government reports available on websites. The article which we have considered for the study was homogenous to the topic. In this research paper we have reviewed few relevant articles. It was then observed and explained for this article to get the outcome.

MAIN FOCUS OF THE CHAPTER

Information technology is the application of computers to store, retrieve, send, and manipulating data often in the context of a company or another company. Information technology as defined by the Information Technology Association of America (ITAA), the research, design, development, implementation, support or management of computerized information systems, especially software applications and computer hardware. Includes the computer and information system industries, information technology is the ability to import, process, store, export electronically, send and receive data and information, including text, images, sound, and video, as well as the ability to operate all types of machines electronically.

The emerging technology changes many aspects of retail - from customer experience to supply chain management and in many other ways. In the ultra-competitive retail sector, traditional sources of decision making - such as sales history, experience and executive intuition - are now insufficient. Today's successful retail leaders rely on up-to-date data, statistics and solid facts to support their business decisions, including:

Customer Experience Decisions: To make effective, customer-focused decisions, retailers and brands use retail analytics to anticipate customer needs and provide a seamless customer experience. Retail customer analytics can also help you improve the customer experience and loyalty by knowing exactly which buyers buys which products - and personalizes your marketing based on customer data. According to Accenture, delivering a good shopping experience improves customer satisfaction, repeat purchases, customer loyalty, customer referrals, revenue, and customer engagement.

Strategic Decisions: Retail companies' functions often operate in silos - meaning their data insights are fragmented and stored across the organization. To get a comprehensive overview of business results, including consumer trends and growth strategies, your company needs to unify and integrate all its data. Consolidating your data can help you make better business decisions faster by using one reliable source of information about your products and customers. In addition, using a retail dashboard gives you a high-level overview of your key performance metrics, including pricing, promotion, and catalog movements.

Operational Decisions: To improve operational performance across all channels, data analysis from retailers can help retailers and suppliers track store-level demand in real time to ensure best-selling items stay in stock. By understanding promotional performance, you can customize your marketing, forecasting, and replenishment tactics and identify seasonal trends, popular items, and cross-selling opportunities to maximize revenue. These transformations bring new challenges. The increased deployment of new technologies such as smart mobile devices and social networks and the increasing importance of in-store technology solutions are creating new opportunities and challenges for retailers. As the boundaries between online and physical channels blur, a new approach to channel integration is emerging: the Omni channel, which aims to provide a seamless customer experience regardless of the channel. This introduction presents the results of focus group discussions on the role of information technology in retail, new business models and the future role of traditional stores as e-commerce progresses. Key issues that emerged from the discussion included the need for channel integration, the impact of mobile technologies, the growing role of social media, the changing role of physical stores, the need to respond to diverse customer requirements, the balance between personalization and privacy, and finally the re-design of the supply chain (Piotrowicz et al., 2014)

Internet of Things (IoT) is, in its most basic way, a network of devices connected to sensors. It allows these devices to communicate, analyze, and share data about the physical world through cloud-based software platforms and other networks.

The industry has undergone a complete makeover in the past decade, powered by technologies such as machine learning, artificial intelligence and IoT. The latter is already used by more than 50% of the major retailers worldwide. It continues an upward trend. Retail IoT applications are located in many areas of the industry, including industrial sensors for production, in-store analyzers, connectivity systems that aggregate forms of customer engagement both online and offline. Sparklabs predicted "exponential growth in the IoT space - from 2.5 billion devices in 2017 to 5.4 billion in 2020." Whatever the outcome, IoT will make retail forever different (Evdokimov et.al, 2011).

In the other hand Big data describes a large amount of data that is used to reveal patterns, trends and associations, especially related to human behavior and interactions. Historically, it has been defined by three key factors: volume, speed and variety. For retail, big data means a better understanding of consumer shopping behavior and attracting new customers. Retail big data analytics enable companies to make customer recommendations based on their purchase history, resulting in personalized shopping experiences. These super large datasets also help predict trends and make strategic decisions based on market analysis.

Smart business decision making requires you to know your facts and figures in terms of business. To quickly understand how your business is performing, a retail dashboard helps with strategic oversight and decisions. Data analysis can help you optimize your prices by following competitive price and discount strategies. To ensure you have the right product mix, use data analysis to check the courage and depth of competitors' catalogs and identify their newly launched products. Which products are hot in your rivals' range? Track fast-selling products from competing brands to optimize the positioning of your product site. What distinguishes your brand? Compare items you have in common with your competitors and the unique products you offer.

As a leader among retail analysis companies, Intelligence Node is a user-friendly software platform for retail analysis. Stay ahead of your rivals by closely following your competition and market trends with our proprietary retail analysis software. Get quick and timely insight into the pricing, promotion, and catalog movements of your leagues to plan ahead with precision and confidence.

There are following ways that how these technologies are used in Retail Industry-

Predict Expenditure

One of the most common ways in which big data is collected in retail is through loyalty programs. Today, it is also collected through credit card transactions, IP addresses, user logins and more. As more information is gathered, retailers can historically analyze the ebb and flow of shopping and spending by consumers to predict future spending and make personalized recommendations. Amazon uses big data to recommend items to you based on your previous searches and purchases.

Personalize Customer Experience

Big data can create opportunities for retailers to deliver better customer experiences. Costco uses their data collection to keep customers healthy.

Demand Forecast in Retail

In addition to big data, some algorithms analyze social media trends and web browsing to predict the next big thing in retail. Perhaps one of the most interesting data points for predicting demand is the weather.

Customer Journey Analytics

The customer journey is not a straight line. It is a zig-zag about channels from research to purchase. The only way to get a grip on the customer journey and create better experiences is to use big data. Big data can help retailers answer questions such as: Where are customers actually looking for product information? Where do we lose them? What are the most effective ways to reach them and force them to purchase?

Improved Supply Chain Management

IoT solutions such as RFID tags and GPS sensors can be used by retailers to get a comprehensive view of the movement of goods from manufacturing to in-store placement until a customer buys them. The information collected, such as the time spent on transportation or the temperature at which the product was stored, etc., can be analyzed in real time. This data proves to be useful, especially during the transportation of perishable products, where storage temperature is crucial. According to some experts, about three-quarters of retailers plan to modernize their supply chain management with IoT solutions

Better Customer Service

IoT also helps physical retailers by generating insights into customer data while creating opportunities to leverage that data. For example, retail IoT applications can synthesize data from video surveillance cameras, mobile devices, and social media websites, helping sellers better predict customer behavior.

Smarter Inventory Management

Inventory management can be a headache. A lack of accurate inventory tracking can lead to stockouts and overstock, costing retailers worldwide billions. IoT can address these issues by automating inventory visibility. Using smart inventory management solutions based on in-store sensors, RFID tags, beacons, video surveillance and digital price tags, retailers can improve their purchasing planning. When product inventory is low, the system offers to reorder the correct amount based on the analyzes obtained from IoT data.

Automated Handling

Check-out is an operation that is the most labor-intensive and often disapproving process for customers. When the cash lines are too long, many people leave without buying anything, resulting in lost profit. To prevent customers from leaving without purchases, retailers can use IoT solutions to automate point-of-sale (PoS) systems. Automated PoS can read tags on any product when the customer leaves the store and automatically reloads via a mobile payment app.

Important Organizational Elements Necessary for IoT Success

Culture

- A clear understanding of the business strategy to confirm that IoT compatible solutions are consistent with business strategy
- An approach that prioritizes impact and potential benefits of IoT investments around customer needs
- Coordination between IT and operations, marketing, supply chain and other business stakeholders confirm that IoT compatible solutions are designed and implemented for business needs
- A willingness to test - and fail - quickly to do that find the right mix of solutions

- Reduce silos between business-related and IT initiatives on IoT by building cross-functional project teams consisting of IT, Marketing, Operations and Supply Chain
- Reduce internal competition for resources and experience
- Prioritize turnover increase versus cost reduction opportunities for IoT (for example, use cost-saving benefits to fund revenue improvement initiatives)
- Use agile development techniques to improve implementation times for new IoT-related functionality
- Create a new privacy policy that carefully considers the new relationships businesses will have with consumers and their data and how they will interact in the real world

Basic Technology Capabilities Required for IoT Success

Big data / analysis

- Compatibility and use of existing data warehouses and database solutions for IoT applications for the benefits
- Local and own data management vs. cloud solutions to support IoT analytics
- Middleware solutions and data exchange that optimize search speed for real-time analysis
- In-memory computing Infrastructure
- Bluetooth LE Beacons that identify and send messages to registered consumers and unregistered devices who respond when the customer enters a store
- RFID for inventory management
- Network security policies and services to insure the customer data is safe throughout the supply chain applications
- Web services / APIs that control how devices send receive and process information
- API management strategy to provide the business with API monitoring and visibility to get the best results
- App factories
- Development and debug tools
- Embedded operating systems

The study explains India's situation and predicts retail growth. Reporting on growth, market trends, progress, challenges, opportunities, and technologies used growth forecasts, large companies, emerging companies and projects etc. in retail in India. In addition, the report also discusses the economic conditions and future projections of the current economic scenario and the impact of current policy changes in the economy, the reasons and implications for the growth of this sector.

CONCLUSION

Implementing these technologies like IoT, Big Data solutions can provide valuable insights for retailers. Such solutions can facilitate streamlined innovation in retailing and thus it will be helpful for customer experiences to increase profits for the marketers. With typical technological solutions, retailers are digitizing physical stores, retailers able to study the demand prior to the requirements, predictions of the expenditures of consumers and other valuable insights which can have a huge return on investment through improved supply chain efficiency, increased marketing conversions and more. It is therefore clear that technologies like IoT and Big Data have the power to improve the customer experience and increase brand loyalty which will increase the profit and will help to boom the industry. Overall, it is interesting to highlight that retail firms deeply and steadily use IoT and big data analytics to improve processes. Over the years, consumer demand has increased and the retailers were ready to meet this increase, technology evolved rapidly to support this growth. It is technology that helps retailers to score intense competition. Consumers expect more value and higher service levels. As a result, the technology continues to grow and retailers are looking for ways to measure technical business value and the effective use of technical resources. Retailers want to get more value from technologies and make them spend their limited resources on ways that improve their total offer to the customer. With change customer demands and expectations are increasing rapidly, organizations must be able to respond quickly in sequence to take advantage of revenue opportunities.

REFERENCES

Aruna, V., & Abdul Gafoor, A. (2012). Foreign direct investment (FDI) in the muli-brand retail sector in India - A boon or bane. *IEEE-International Conference On Advances In Engineering, Science And Management (ICAESM -2012)*, 32-35.

Balaji, M. S., Roy, S. K., Sengupta, A., & Chong, A. (2018). User acceptance of IoT applications in retail industry. In Technology Adoption and Social Issues: Concepts, Methodologies, Tools, and Applications (pp. 1331-1352). IGI Global. doi:10.4018/978-1-5225-5201-7.ch061

Caro, F., & Sadr, R. (2019). The Internet of Things (IoT) in retail: Bridging supply and demand. *Business Horizons*, *62*(1), 47–54. doi:10.1016/j.bushor.2018.08.002

EGHAM. (2019,August 29). Retrieved from https://www.gartner.com/en/newsroom/press-releases/2019-08-29-gartner-says-5-8-billion-enterprise-and-automotive-io

Elahi, D., Rehman, A., & Misra, A. (2013). An Empirical Study of the Businessmen Perception of Various Issues and Challenges Associated with FDI in Indian Retail Sector. *GBAMS: VIDUSHI*, *5*(2).

Evdokimov, S., Fabian, B., & Gunther, O. (2011). *RFID and the internet of things: Technology, applications, and security challenges*. Now Publishers Inc.

Gawankar, S. A., Gunasekaran, A., & Kamble, S. (2020). A study on investments in the big data-driven supply chain, performance measures and organisational performance in Indian retail 4.0 context. *International Journal of Production Research*, *58*(5), 1574–1593. doi:10.1080/00207543.2019.1668070

Ghazal, A., Rabl, T., Hu, M., Raab, F., Poess, M., Crolotte, A., & Jacobsen, H. A. (2013, June). BigBench: towards an industry standard benchmark for big data analytics. In *Proceedings of the 2013 ACM SIGMOD international conference on Management of data* (pp. 1197-1208). 10.1145/2463676.2463712

Gong, W., & Tian, G. (2012). Dynamic Evolution of IOT Application's Business Mode in Retail. In *ICLEM 2012* (pp. 1165–1172). Logistics for Sustained Economic Development—Technology and Management for Efficiency. doi:10.1061/9780784412602.0179

Gregory, J. (2015). *The Internet of Things: revolutionizing the retail industry.* Accenture Strategy.

Indian retail industry analysis. (2018, July7). Retrieved from https://www.indiaretailing.com/2018/07/07/research/indian-retail-industry-analysis/

Indian Retail Industry - Major trends, Growth and Opportunities (2020 - 2025). (n.d.). Retrieved from https://www.mordorintelligence.com/industry-reports/indian-retail-industry

Jha, L. (2020, February 26). India's retail market to touch $1.1-1.3 trillion by 2025: BCG. *LIVE Mint.* Retrieved from https://www.livemint.com/industry/retail/india-s-retail-market-to-touch-1-1-1-3-trillion-by-2025-bcg-11582714221778.html

Kiran, R., & Jhamb, D. (2011). A strategic framework for consumer preferences towards emerging retail formats. *Journal of Emerging Knowledge on Emerging Markets, 3*(1), 25.

Piotrowicz, W., & Cuthbertson, R. (2014). Introduction to the special issue information technology in retail: Toward omnichannel retailing. *International Journal of Electronic Commerce, 18*(4), 5–16. doi:10.2753/JEC1086-4415180400

Santoro, G., Fiano, F., Bertoldi, B., & Ciampi, F. (2018). Big data for business management in the retail industry. *Management Decision.*

Shankara, P., Mahanta, P., Arora, E., & Srinivasamurthy, G. (2015, October). Impact of internet of things in the retail industry. In *OTM Confederated International Conferences" On the Move to Meaningful Internet Systems"* (pp. 61-65). Springer. 10.1007/978-3-319-26138-6_9

Chapter 16
Innovative Technology and Human Resource Management

Sachin Soonthodu
https://orcid.org/0000-0003-1899-7008
Garden City University, India

Susheela Shetty
Brindavan College, Bangalore, India

ABSTRACT

Technology plays a crucial role in inclusive growth of modern human management systems. Recruitment, hiring, training, retaining, workplace administration, and optimizing workforce environment are the major functions of human resources management. Adopting innovative technology within the organisation enables the managers to accumulate and deliver the information as well as communicate with employees more effectively. India, as one of the developed countries, is successfully integrating technology in human resource management systems to ensure market-driven product and service development. Technology makes jobs easy; at the same time, it threatens the job market by reducing the human resource requirement to perform particular tasks. An effective human resource management should have the ability to integrate technology and the human resource for the better development of an organisation. This theoretical study focuses on various technologies adopted by the human resource management to make the workplace effective and highly productive.

INTRODUCTION

Managing people is the basic objective human resource management department of every organisation. In this context recruiting and retaining of talented human resource is top priority of an organisation. Organisations constantly strive to make sure that the employees are happy and don't feel to quit at any situations. Modern competitors are interested in reaching out the top talents of rivals by offering good packages and other benefits, so that the employee would feel to leave the company. Modern organisations understand that it is not only the salary influences employees but also the other factors that makes them

DOI: 10.4018/978-1-7998-4787-8.ch016

to be motivated to work for an organisation. Surrounding environment, supervisor-subordinate relationship, non monitory benefits, organisational support, reward and recognition, participatory management and organisations adaptability are the other factors motivate employees towards their job. On the other hand, organisations need to adopt innovative skills and technology to keep the employees updated to the competitive market. To achieve this, companies update themselves to innovative technology.

Technological approach to human resource management aims at building an employee's team, committed to make the organisation highly competitive. The digital revolution made the human resource managers to adopt innovative technology in-order to make their work easier and to take better decisions. From recruitment to retirement/change of company, an employee has to go through various phases of involvement and activities, which must be tracked by the human resource department. Networking, Job training, and attendance management etc seek technological support. Today many companies offer cloud based solutions to manage the technical and software related issues of human resource management. Thus technology has become the integrated part of human resource management. This theoretical chapter focuses on various issues of technology and human resource management, advices the pros and cons of technology implication in human resource management. The study may guide the governmental and non-governmental organisations to adopt and implement various innovative techniques that make the employees motivated, so that the work productivity increases.

Review of Literature

Human resource management is the process of recruiting people, training and compensating them and developing the policies and strategies to retain them for a longer duration of time (OUH). Storey (1995) defines Human Resource Management as 'a distinctive employee management approach which has primary objective of achieving competitive advantage through deploying highly capable and committed workforce by integrating cultural, structural and personal techniques'. Human Resource Management acts as a key role in the production process, and through that the entire business organisation reaches out the business goals and objectives. According to Guest (1987), a) commitment, b) flexibility, c) quality, and integration are the key elements of human resource management. Mathis and Johnson (2004) identify 7 major activities if human resource department, i.e., social, cultural, legal, economic political, technological, environmental, and global, which serve the competitive advantages of the business organisation.

Technology is defined as the science or knowledge put into practical to fins solution to problems or invents useful tools. Volti (2009) defines technology as 'a system created by humans that uses knowledge and organisation to produce objects and techniques for the attainment of specific goals. Technology has significant influence on the human resource management. Carroll (2017) identifies technology as something created through ordering, exhibiting organisation whose aspects function with a purpose that can provide some benefits'. The major objective of technology impletion in human resource management is to benefit both employees and the organisation to function in a better way. In other words, technology makes human resources more efficient and maximises output and minimises the possible problems.

Today organisations adopt innovative technology to keep a track on the production, services, customer service, and employee involvement. Selvam (2015) while studying the role of technology in human resource management identifies various areas which include recruiting, training, data storage and retrieval, performance management, communication and motivating knowledge workers. The study concludes that technology has positive impact on the internal operations of organisations.

There is interlinking between Business organisation, human resource performance and the innovative technology. Paul and Jeffrey (1998) believe that the employee performance decides the growth of an Organisation. Employee performance is the direct outcome of employee satisfaction. An integrated developmental practice adopted by human resource department of an organisation has greater impact on employee satisfaction and thereby induces employee performance (Huselid, 1995). Therefore, human resource department has to adopt innovative technologies that influence the inclusive growth of an organisation.

Global Human Resource Management has adopted innovative technology for quality enhancement of products and the services. India is the second largest country in Asia with a population of 137 billion, has highest degree of professionalism. Human resource is major contributor to the economic development of a country. By understanding the importance of human resource in the growth and development of a country, personnel management in India had emerged in the early 1920's and the concept is highly influenced by national culture, national institutions, unions, society and the government and non-governmental organisations. (Saini and Budhwar, 2004). India, being one of the most populated countries, has immense supply of quality human resource in all the sectors. Human resource plays vital role in achieving sustainable goals and Millennium Development Goals by expanding equal opportunity to all sections of the society (Chetia, 2014). Over the past two decades, HDI score of India has been improved drastically. Production and service sector in India are more emphasizing on adopting automated technology. Studies found that nearly 70 percent of firms in India have automated more than half of their human resource function, which includes their day-to-day operations (Tanwar, 2019). This includes various management functions such as recruitment, job processing, training and development, performance management and communication etc. Highest level of employee engagement, maximum return for investment and creating future ready workplace are the major reasons for adopting innovative technology in human resource management. Direct relationship between innovative technology and human resource development has positive impact on economic development. Improvements in human resource practices play crucial role in the constant rise of India's technological sector (Khare, 2018). As technological development speeded up across the world, it is the human resource departments must focus on making the work environment future friendly.

Today India has emerged as the start up capital of the world, pushing thousands of young entrepreneurs to take up challenging role. Having world's largest young population, highly educated and energetic men and women, the country has wide opportunity to implement highly innovative practices in human resource management (Josh, 2017)

Technology and Human Resource Management

Identifying and hiring the talented workforce is a continuous and the toughest job for human resource managers. Human resource manager has to identify the available jobs, publicize the requirements, recruit and select the right candidates. Once the selection process is completed, employees must be inducted, followed by training and development. Further, the HR has the responsibility of deciding salary and benefits, carry out all day-to-day tasks of employee management. This process should continue till the employee continues to serve for the organisation. Managing these tasks in medium and large scale organisations is the biggest challenge for the Human resource team. This is because the employees keep on joining and quit the organisation, thus the role of HR team becomes highly challenging. Innovative technology plays key role in employee recruitment, daily activities, salary and wage administration and exit process of the organisation.

As an emerging economic giant, 23 percent of Tech-start-ups in India are concerned with HR technology. Over 85 percent of business organisations opt for technology enabled HR processes. (People works, 2013)

Innovative Technologies in Human Resource Management:

In the modern world it is highly difficult to recruit and retain talented human resource, which is one of the most strategic HR decisions. In order to reach the highest return on the human capital investment organisations replace the traditional system with cloud based and software based innovative technology, which also leads to high productivity of employees. Organisations look into organisational viability, cost effectiveness and employee adoptability while implementing human resource technology. Today, human resource development organisations are integrating with software developers to develop software's for effective solution for prevailing issues.

Analytics

Human resource analytics is tool used by the professionals to evaluate the employees and applying analytical processes on the human resource within the organisation. The main purpose of analytics is to gather data of employees, and analyse it to make better decisions to improve the quality of human resources. The main objectives of HR analytics are to examine the employee turnover rate and the effects of employee turnover organisational financial performance and predict the employees who would quit the organisation. Human resource analysis has 5 broad areas including a) Employee churn analytics b) Organisational culture analytics b) Capacity analytics d) Capability analytics and e) Leadership analytics, which are based on the objectives and the purpose that needs to be served. Thus HR analytics, through hypothetical predictions supports the managers to take a fair decision on their employees.

Artificial Intelligence

HR managers adopt Artificial Intelligence (AI) in recruitment process to make the hiring easy and efficient. Artificial Intelligence matches the job profile and candidates skills required for a job to make smart recruitment processes. Artificial intelligence scrutinizes a number of applications among the pool of applicants to make the smart decision to hire the talented candidates. It provides personalised HR support to employees, removes bias in evaluation process and supports greater speed and convenience. Based on the suggestions of Artificial Intelligence HR managers make final decisions on candidates to appear for face to face interview. Thus AI removes the human biases and benefits the human resource team to handle the common questions and requests.

Artificial intelligence has greater role in employee retention. The software analyses an employee's computer activity, browsing, emails etc and stores the data. Based on these data, AI detects the changes, predicts the possibility of employees thinking of quitting the job and reports it to the management.

Chatbots

Chatbot is a software programme designed for internet conversation via auditory or textual methods. This is designed to understand how a person would behave as a conversation partner, which generally adopted by the customer service organisations to analyse customer behaviour and information acquisition. Peoplesoft, Workday and Kronos are some popular HR Chatbots. Over 2% of business organisations across the world use chatbot to boost their business activities and customer communication. HR team invests much time on managing day-to-day activities that could be handled by the chatbots by amplifying their capabilities. This software serves in answering FAQ's aggregates employee participation in training and development programmes and helps in annual self assessment. Chatbox automates end-to-end recruitment process such as screening candidates, scheduling interview and finalizing candidates etc. Many business organisations adopt Chatbot to for goal tracking, employee survey, performance review and also to track paid leave related issues.

Virtual and Augmented Reality (VR and AR)

Today, business organisations move forward in adopting Virtual reality and augmented reality to understand the employees at various levels such as recruitment, training and development, and day-to-day activities. In the recruitment process virtual Reality is used in creating a stimulated work environment to make better hiring decisions. Business organisations effectively utilize AR and AV technology in tackling training programmes, to create work simulation and to hold meetings with the employees without making them physically present in the board room. VR and AI technology helps the HR team to analyse employee's ability to think critical while decision making, create artificial work environment, which could save cost and time. Training and development programme becomes more effective with the inclusion of video and audio presentation which can be easily performed by Virtual Reality and Augmented Reality. This technology also helps the HR recruiters to select right resumes and to communicate with candidates during the selection process.

Blockchain

Blockchain is digital information technology platform used to store in a public database. Blockchain stores the information of participating transactions and distinguishes from other blocks. This database consists of several blocks and each block could store thousands of transactions. Blockchain helps the HR team to get information about the candidate applied for a particular job and acts as a quick guide in verifying candidature, work experience, employment record and salary and other information through real time information. Blockchain supports smart contract between the employee and employer, retains the employee records until he works for the organisation. This technology also helps the human resource department to maintain the confidentiality pertaining to employee's personal information, work history and other related information. Blockchain also helps the organisation to store the biometric data, to maintain a centralised system for employee auditing in a business organisation. Block chain facilitates real-time payments to contingent workers also helps in SWOT analysis of the business firm.

Internet of Things

Internet of things is a web enabled smart device and sensors connected through the internet and connecting people, their devices with the objective of performing multiple tasks at a time. Human resource management uses internet of things to augment better engagement of employees in order to develop a qualified work environment. Smart devices such as mobiles and tablets connect the employees within organisation to make better communication though messaging apps and networking sites. HR also uses internet of things to enable better recruitment process, to measure employee behaviour within the organisation. Large organisations with huge number of employees can easily track the employees and their activities, without signing in into the organisation. Business analysts predict that future human industry will be replaced with speech, voice and signals to make the business entity more effective. Internet of things enables continuous performance management by providing flexible workplace and healthy working environment. In other words internet of things focuses on fitness and productivity of employees and improves the work environment. Business organisations also install devices such as cameras and sensors to determine the periodical requirements such as maintenance, repair etc based on internet of things. Internet of things also focuses on peoples analytics such as, personal behaviour, employee stress, health and hygiene requirement, toxic behaviour, task engagement and quality time spent etc. Human resource manager can easily supervise the employees sitting at a remote place. This helps the human resource management to judge the overall performance of an individual.

Cognitive Technology

Cognitive technology is a computer application that imitates functions of human brains through various methods such as natural language processing, data mining and pattern recognition. Cognitive technology is an artificial intelligence technology interacting human brain with technology which will play vital role in the areas of automation and machine learning. It helps the HR managers in decision making process and assists them in enhancing end-to-end employee experiences. In the recruitment process, the HR managers judge the ability of the candidate by various contextual elements such as meaning, time, location, video and audio texts etc to identify the emotions of the candidate. This helps the HR managers to evaluate the capability of the candidate to adjust to the working environment. Cognitive analytics gets into various sources of data of a candidate such as professional experience, performance standards etc and also allows the employees to interact with the machines in a natural language within a natural environment. This makes employees to be comfortable in their work environment. Further, cognitive technology like a human being understands analyses and solves the problems by thinking remembering and reasoning. This technology is highly useful in complex judgement and high interactions with huge data. HR managers in large scale organisations can make quick decisions with the implication of cognitive technology.

Social Media

Social Medias are the simple, easy, quick and popular mode of communication. Various social network sites such as Facebook, Whatsapp, LinkedIn and Twitter not only connect the people but in the modern world acts as a major contributor to analyse the ability and personality of a person. Hence modern business organisations study the social network profile of a person who has applied for a particular job.

Many business organisations advertise the job openings and invite applications through social networks. Further, social network profiles help the HR team to trace the skills and experiences and also the areas of interest of a job applicant. Identifying potential candidates and screening is easy and cost saving through social networking. Social networks such as LinkedIn encourage the candidates to apply for a designated job. Today social networks function as the ambassadors of a company's corporate culture and play a vital role in managing the reputation of the company.

Employee Self-service Software

Employee self-service software is designed to assist and guide the employees to take care of various job related and human resource related tasks, which is otherwise conducted by the human resource department. Through ESS software employees are authorised to access various HR related issues such as payroll, perks and incentives, personal details, etc which reduces the burden of HR department. The HR has the responsibility of approving the details and the information which is updated by the employees. The information may include the personal details such as updating name, contact details, address, and work experience etc. Some ESS systems allows the employees to update the bank details, payroll information and also applying for leave and vacation etc. ESS system allows the employees to exercise control over their own information, at the same time and labour cost of HR department. Employees can access to the information anywhere and anytime, making the employees feeling empowered, which results in increased productivity.

Performance Solutions

Performance solution or performance management system is the software that helps the human resource managers to keep a track on its employees, analyse and evaluate their performance. Performance management system gathers data on the employees overall productivity and reports it to the management in the form of regular feedback. The software helps in better transparency in evaluating the performance of an employee. This includes employee appraisal, 360 degree feedback system and compensation management system. The performance solutions analyses the data of every employee, evaluates the performance and reports it to the management. This process saves the time and reduces the temper of managers. CakeHR, ELMO, GroSum and SAP SuccessFactors are some of the performance management system software's used by the different business organisations.

Benefit Management Platform

Benefit management platform includes different types of software's having the primary objective of automating the employee benefits on fingertips. Employees can access to various benefits, perks and the privileges at anytime through mobile phones and tablets. The employees are also permitted to edit and save their personal information though the Benefit Management Platform. This software offers access to 360 degree appraisal, feedback report, and organisational chart, so those employees need not to physically present at the HR office for any sort of information. This automated software has greater advantage of saving time and operational cost of the human resource department. Paycor is one such software which is used worldwide.

Cloud Technology and SaaS

Cloud based technology is an internet enabled technology or service from a remote location which allows a user to access the information anywhere in the world. Software as a Service (SaaS) is one of the three categories of cloud computing in which third party is authorised to purchase and use the software for their customers. Major advantage of SaaS is that the business organisations need not to install the software in their office systems or computers. SaaS supports HR team in tracking job applications, communicating the candidates, conducting online interview etc. An employee has direct access to attendance, performance appraisal and feedback, leave management, vacation and holiday supports, payroll and other self services. The SaaS enhances the productivity of employees and at the same time authorises the human resource team to have real time access to the employee information. Salesforce, SAP, Oracle and Microsoft are the leading SaaS software providers.

Bring Your Own Technology (BYOT)

Bring Your Own Technology (BYOT) also referred as Bring Your Own Device (BYOD) is a popular work environment in which an organisation insists its employees to bring their own computerised devices such as mobile phones and tablets, which are compact in nature. This is a popular technique adopted by many business organisations who supply minimum electronic devices and internet facilities. This kind of technology is very famous in large scale organisation, institutions etc, where supplying devices and big data is a difficult task. In this situation, management directs the employees to install the software or applications in the device that they bring in. The HR team can directly access the employees and their personal information through the installed applications. The employees can access to emails, leave application, attendance, performance appraisal and feedback and pop-ups etc through their own device. People often have much acquaintance to their own devices, which is comfort and handy, saves the time and operational cost of the organisation. Many organisations provide local networked internet/Wi-Fi to their employees to browse the applications. Some organisations disable the external networks so that, an employee can access only the internal internet facility through their device.

Mobile Workforce Management

Mobile Workforce Management (MVM) includes various categories of software and devices used to manage the employees or the people work outside the organisation. This generally includes field workers and the remote staff who manage their work through installed applications and software. MVM's are scheduled to connect, track, communicate and analyse the employees outside the organisation. This technology focuses on customer services and client communication in medium and large scale organisations. MVM's are helps the employees who prefer work from home and remote locations. The technology has real-time access to employee-customer meetings, quick feedback on the products and services etc. The management has direct access over the activities and the performance of employee who operates through MVM's.

Employee Scheduling Software

Employee Scheduling Software automates the creation, maintenance and update of employee schedule. This technology includes software and mobile applications that tracks employee log in and log out time, over time performance, leave and vacation and the tasks to be performed at a particular point of time. This software has unique features such as creating work chart, swap shifts, workplace analysis, removing unnecessary staff, interfacing to payroll and analysing employee engagement in a particular task. The main objective of employee scheduling software is to make sure that the employees concentrate on the job in an organised manner for the timely completion of priority tasks. Employee schedule software often checks to-do-list, work progress and reminds upcoming deadlines. Based on the software's report, the management can take a firm decision on performance of employee and employee retention. When I Work, Ximble, HotSchedules and Deputy are a few best employee schedule software and applications.

Performance Management Software

Performance Management Software is a technology or application that helps the management team to assess the performance and productivity of an employee. This technology reduces the paperwork burden of the human resource team by implementing online monitoring system. PMS allows the management team to track, monitor and report the performance of employee so that compensation management becomes easy. PMS can easily differentiate high performing employees from others by answering simple questions and analysing the back-end data. Modern PMS's are updated with latest feedback system, automated reminders on work scheduled, work in progress and the task completed. The Manager and HR team can easily monitor the work in progress, task completed, and contribution to company's growth to evaluate the performance of employees. BambooHR, Namely, CleaCompany and IBM Talent management are a few popular performance management software technologies.

Benefits of Innovative Technology

Technology advancement in human resource management brought considerable change in the structural and functional dimensions of the organisation. Technology has reduced administrative and financial burden of business organisations. This lead to revolutionary change as the overall process became faster, accurate and compact in nature. Software and technology applications have reduced the burden of paperwork. Meanwhile, recruitment and hiring process is expensive and time consuming without modern technology. The prevailing technology and applications are the alternative choice to reduce this burden as they are user friendly and economical in nature. Thus, technology has reduced the operational cost of the human resource department.

Modern human resource technology is developed to explicit accurate output on recruitment, hiring, training and development, payroll, compensation management, and performance appraisal etc. Effective implementation of these automated processes enhances the efficiency of both employees and the organisation. Identifying, selecting and managing the talented and skilled human resource are difficult task to a human resource manager. Today's organisations understood that the employees leave organisation due poor facilities, lack of attention from the employer and poor appraisal system. Technology enables the management to take fair decision on the factors of motivation for employees. Modern technology enhances scope for talent improvisation of the skilled human resource within the organisation.

Both employees and employers can instantly access the information which is readily available. Instant accessibility to information and real time data empowers the team leaders and the managers to easily manage the workflow. Scientifically developed software applications reduce the possible errors so that the management will have room for easy implementation of policies. Employees enjoy the ownership of applications, authorised to edit and modify personal information, involve in the constructive feedback and appraisal system brings transparency overall administrative system boosts them to feel empower empowered. This results in employee job satisfaction. There is higher scope for merit so that the rate of return is very high. Innovative technology minimises cross cultural barriers.

Innovative technology enables the HR managers to prepare the organisation to be the future ready workplace. HR managers have larger scope to assess the employees and develop plans to address organisational issues. Reaching out general public through Social Medias is a new trend to construct goodwill about the organisation. Social networks such as LinkedIn are the popular source of job search for job seekers wherein business organisations have considered these sites as the pool of talent acquisition.

Innovative technology pulled off the conventional organisational environment into a convenient operational system. Employees can initiate, operate and complete the assigned task simply log-in to applications and portals, sitting at a home. A field representative need not to report in the office every morning and evening, perhaps he will be tracked at any point of time. Communication between the subordinates and the supervisors has become handy. Interviews with the right candidates may happen thousands of kilometres away from the corporate office. Through virtual tours, augmented reality training and development becomes easy task, time saving and cost effective.

Role of Innovative Technology in Human Resource Management in India

Today technology has reached every sphere of human life making human lives better and easier. In the countries like India Innovative technology in Human Resource management is used for two major purposes. It is used to attract, hire, retain and maintain the talented workforce in the administration for the optimum utilization of these human talents. On the other hand Innovative technology is used to make the duties and responsibilities of the Human Resource Department easy. This can be done through adopting various applications and the softwares in the work environment. HR technology is used by all the span of management such as the employees, supervisors, managers and the HR department to make the work faster and efficient. This reduces the amount of administrative works of the business organization. The Managers can also take effective business decisions through the innovative HR technology.

- Strategic Alignment
- Business Intelligence
- Effectiveness and Efficiency.

Mrs. B Vijayalakshmi Murthy (2015) finds following reasons for implementing Innovative Technology in Human Resource Management in India.

- External Environmental forces
- Organisational Structural Characteristics
- Culture of the Organization
- Success rate of past Human Resource Innovations

- Consultants and their influence
- Insistence of Top Management
- Competitive strategy
- Competitiveness of the industry
- Cost reduction
- To increase the services of Human Resource Management Department
- To provide more satisfying work experience to the employees.
- Effective management of resources.

Maruti, one of the leading automobile giants of India was struggling in retain the human resources in their company. The MNC's and the international brands were the tough competitors to Maruti and they had a successful poaching of employees. Eternally Maruti realized that, lack of technological advancement is the major reason for employee turnover in the company and later started implementing innovative programs and employee benefit schemes. Today Maruti has satisfied work force who contribute for the best performance of the company.

Technology giants such as Infosys and Wipro are highly concerned about the welfare of employees. They adopt innovative training and development programmes, international exchange activities and technology based management system that makes employees highly satisfied with the company. Companies such as Ranbaxy, BioCon and ITES etc have adopted massive technology implication programme on Human Resource to ensure quality output and better performance with high degree of employee satisfaction.

Innovative technology is the priority of every business organization in India. Nearly 70 percent of companies have automated their Human Resource Functions for day to day operations. Analytics, Artificial Intelligence, Chatbots and the Cognitive Technology are the top innovative technologies adopted by Indian business organizations. In India, Innovative technology is the top priority in the areas such as HR operations, Performance Management, Recruitment and Learning and Development.

Cost saving is the other priority to involve Innovative Technology in Human Resource Management in India. Companies look for big save in HR operations, managing workforce and employee engagement through innovative technology. Integrating various functions in the human resource system and monitoring the employees are the other reasons for innovative technology in Human Resource Management.

Today Indian business organizations adopt innovative technology for talent acquisition, on-boarding of employees and performance management. Smart recruitment, better employee communication and strategic management of business firm are the other advantages of innovative technology in Human Resource Management. Indian business organizations also eye at social media hiring and behavioral analysis of potential employees through Innovative technology. Many business organizations are using application programmes for recruitment, browse the information of potential employees through social networks and offer online on-boarding process in India. Indian companies also adopted innovative technology in reporting, performance management, talent engagement, learning and development and talent pipeline of the employees. Indian corporate companies are entering into new breed of corporate learning tools and intelligent self service tools. Business organizations also entering into cloud based platforms.

Challenges in Adopting Innovative Technology

Human resource departments in business organisations adopt innovative technology to meet the competition successfully. Large scale organisations are highly flexible in nature hence they adopt innovative practices to survive in the market. However small and medium scale organisations face budgetary constraints as evolving into innovative technology is expensive. Once the technology is adopted, organisations need to timely update of these software and applications. This may incur high expenditure. Lack of knowledge and skills on the modern technology is the other constraint to adopt the innovative technology. Employees require timely training and skill building programmes to understand the technology. Resistance to change is common in the work environment. Managing change from employees' side requires strong HR policies. Over emphasis on technology may kill the personal and interpersonal skill and techniques of employees. Human capital cannot be treated as machines. Modern world has the fear that, high dependency on technology and computers cut-down employment, which further leads to economic and social crisis. Data security, manipulation of data becomes major to the business organisations. When the technology is handled by hundreds of people within the organisation, data theft and hacking might be the common issue.

Innovative technology widens opportunity, so that the employee turnover rate may increase. Business organisations often diversify the technology to keep the employees motivated. Depending on an outdated version of software or application de-motivates the work force. It is equally important that the organisations must supply ancillary services along with the innovative technology. For example, Wi-Fi or mobile data along with the mobile phone or tablets, internet connect to desktops and projectors. Besides these organisations must recruit technical expertise that can quickly handle the operational issues. Organisational culture greatly affects adaptation of innovative technology hence the organisation should be flexible enough to adopt swift changes.

CONCLUSION

Change is a common attribute of every business organisation. Any organisation that resists the change lasts in a short period of time. In the modern business entity, human resource department plays a vital role. Managing people is a difficult task. Integrating technology and human resource opened a new horizon in the fields of human resource management. Decades ago, people mastered machines but today technology controls people. Today's world expects smart work than hard work. Indian corporate companies and the business organisations are focusing on to innovative technology in the process of recruitment, training and development and the employee management process of the organization. As a result Indian companies witness shift paradigm in the entire process of the business organizations. Innovative technology in human resource management widens the opportunity to both employees and employers to perform the task on a mutual benefit. Both employees and the management should be open to accept and adopt changes in and around the business organisation. Technology should develop think tanks and enhance skills and create more opportunities. From this perspective, modern human resource departments should focus on the technology that integrate people, motivate them to work in a better work environment for quality output.

REFERENCES

Bersin, J. (2017). *HR and HR Technology in India: Growth, Purpose and Value*. SHRM.

Chetia, J. (2014, April). Human Resource Development and the Context of India. *International Journal of Humanities and Social Science*, *2*(4).

Guest. (1987). Human Resource Management and Industrial Relations. *Journal of Management Studies, 24*, 203-521. doi:10.1111/j.1467-6486.1987.tb00460.x

Human Resource Management, the Open University of Hongkong (OUH). (n.d.). Retrieved on 24th December 2019, http://www.opentextbooks.org.hk/system/files/export/32/32088/pdf/Human Resource Management_32088.pdf

Huselid, M. (1995). The impact of human resource management on turnover, productivity, and corporate performance. Academy of Management Journal, 38, 635-672.

Khare, P. (2018). *The role of HR and the rice of India's Tech Industry*. BIEF Blog.

La Shun, L. (2017). A comprehensive definition of technology from an Ethological Perspective. *Journal of Social Sciences*, *6*(4), 126. doi:10.3390ocsci6040126

Lawrence, P., & Pfeffer, J. (1998). The human equation: Building Profits by Putting People First. *Administrative Science Quarterly*, *43*(4), 956. doi:10.2307/2393627

Mathis, R. L., & John, J. (2004). *Human Resource Management.* South-Western Publisher.

People Works. (2013). *The future of HR technology in India*. Author.

Saini, D. (2004). *Budhwar, Pawan*. Human Resource Management in India. doi:10.4324/9780203157053

Selvam. (2015). Study on role of technology in Human Resources Management. *International Journal of Applied Research*, *1*(7), 472-475.

Storey, J. (1995). *Human Resource Management: A critical Text*. Routledge Publication.

Tanwar, S. (2019). *Indian companies are investing in human resource technologies to cut costs.* scroll.in.

Vijayalakshmi Murthy, B. (2015). *Innovative HR practices in IT industry of India – an Empirical Study*. http://www.vesasc.org/InnovativeHR_Practices_Mrs_Murthy_Nov_2015.pdf

Volt, R. (2009). Society and Technological Change (7th ed.). Worth Publications.

Chapter 17
Consumer Perception and Purchase Intention Towards Refurbished Smart Phones:
A Circular Consumption Perspective

Nishant Kumar
Amity University, Noida, India

Divya Mohan
Delhi Institute of Advanced Studies, India

ABSTRACT

Circular economy is a global economic model that focuses to transform linear consumption in a circular system by minimizing waste and preserving the cost of materials. Refurbishment can be useful to recover value from old products and to minimize waste. Based on the insights from literature, a deductive research approach has been used to examine consumer understanding about refurbished smart phone and their purchase intention. A survey based on barriers, perceived risk, and benefits associated with refurbished phones was conducted. Multiple analyses of variance were employed to identify the effect of demographic parameters on refurbishing dimensions. Multiple regression was used to identify prominent predictors in determining purchase intention towards refurbished products. The study demonstrates a fine level of awareness among people about refurbished phone, and they link it to environmental benefits. A major concern among consumers was performance issue and financial risk involved in purchasing refurbished smart phones. Financial benefits are key aspects behind promoting refurbished.

DOI: 10.4018/978-1-7998-4787-8.ch017

INTRODUCTION

The economy at present intends a circular system in which the materials and resources are sustained till the end. The circular economy aims at ways to minimize cot by implementing resource planning strategies (D'Amato et al., 2018, and Ghisellini et al. 2016). The increased circularity encourages production of goods in additional cycles. The production of second hand goods at lower prices helps customers' to save money and simultaneously also avoids wastage of materials. The circular economy seeks to transform linear consumption in a circular system by minimizing waste and preserving the cost of materials which leads to well-being of society (Kalioujny et al., 2016).

Refurbishment in smart phone market has seen an increase of 9% in the Indian Market in year 2019. The transition of the restructuring segment from the unorganized sector to the organized in countries such as India is also underway, which is opening up opportunities for refurbished products (*livemint.com*, 2020).). According to an industry-leading e-tailer, the renewed sector multiplies on an annual basis. The demand for refurbished products generally comes from level II and III cities in India. The young population or middle class largely look for good quality electronics and that too reasonably priced (Chanda, 2019). Industry observers say that the trend of refurbishment is driven by the declining product life cycles of smartphones as it has reduced from four years to a year now and consequently a greater number of phones entering the refurbishment cycle. Due to their high prices, cars are currently estimated to hold a 60% share in the organized part of this market, while electronics, including smartphones, have 25% and other products generally of household category claim 15% (Devika, 2020).

In recent trends, most big companies are planning to move from linear business production to circular business model. This shifting phase is not easy as it requires circumstantial changes like changes in legislation, new financing techniques and changes in behaviour of the consumers in accumulation to the changes inside the companies. It is anticipated that refurbished product market will reach $12-15 in the year 2020. Refurbishment is a process which is concerned with undoing a product, reinstating and testing the small parts including the entire product to its originality. After refurbishing a product it is expected to perform same as it was in original performance (Parker, Riley, Robinson, Symington, 2015). Unlike disposal, repairs do not require complete dismantling of goods. In the process of remanufacturing, a used product is turned into a fresh product. It is the process of bring back value to the used product and giving it the same shape as it was first in its new condition with original specifications. It leads to reduction in energy, cost of material and production (Gray&Charter, 2008). Slowly and steadily, organized retailers are taking place in market instead of unorganized local vendors. This is because of the prior's ability to completely transform the product and give it a "new look" and feel. Most of the firms have their firm fingers on the organized sector and also their concentration on standardizing and expanding the pre-owned electronic device market. Many organized players like GreenDust, Reboot, Overcart, Togofogo (individual entrants) and Ebay, Mazon (E Commerce Portals) are trying to grab this opportunity. The aim of these market players is to create an active marketplace which gives consumers choice to choose products with warranty and services attached. In India, there is a healthy competition experienced by all big market players and the existing companies have succeeded to develop interest amongst the buyers to invest into refurbished products as these products are equally comparable to the new products (Soumitra Gupta, CEO, Togofogo). Also at the same time there are market players creating a marketplace for merchants to sell branded refurbished product in addition to overstock aging inventory. Approximately 10% to 50% of the mobile phones sold in country are to be of surplus value and only 4-5% out of it are refurbished (Saurabh Rai, CEO, Surpluss.in).

This study contributes by investigating the likelihood of various encouragements to improve the purchase intent of refurbished smartphones. Second, previous research has clearly depicted that people differ in their awareness of restored smartphones. Still, there is a lack of full understanding of the specific customer groups suitable for selling refurbished smartphones. Explicitly, in this study the research has been conducted to investigate consumer responses towards refurbished smartphones and prominent factors contributing toward their purchase intention.

BACKGROUND

The products engineered in a state closer to the original product are considered to be circular products (Bocken et al., 2016). Circular products eradicates environmental costs while performing intrusions to the products' commercial state (den Hollander et al., 2017; Lieder and Rashid, 2016). "Circular consumption" refers to consumer decision making processes in relation to restored products. Therefore, understanding consumer decision making process is significant to analyses the purchase intention of consumers for restored smartphones.

There is lack of knowledge and consideration for refurbished products in customers' mind. Environmental concerns and mindfulness towards refurbishment reinforces customers' intention to purchase refurbished smartphones (Shu San Gan, 2019). It is clear, that to sell refurbished mobile phones it is necessary to attract customers' towards it (Atasu et al., 2010; Guide & Li, 2010; Jiménez-Parra et al., 2014). The study that examines the response of customers' towards refurbished products mainly emphasis on customers' wish to pay for refurbished mobile phones (Hamzaoui Essoussi and Linton, 2010; Harms and Linton, 2015; Hazen et al., 2012; Michaud and Llerena. 2011), which demarcates the amount which customers' are ready to spend for a given product. The studies depicts that as compared to new products customers' are ready to pay less for refurbished products. In addition, existing researches has studies prevailing models for acceptance of products to elucidate the aspects that impacts the purchase for refurbished products (Jiménez-Parra et al., 2014; Khor & Hazen, 2016; Wang & Hazen, 2015; Wang et al., 201). The issues discovered included the outlook of consumers towards a subjective factor which is refurbishment, (Khor and Hazen, 2016), consumer thoughtfulness about the quality of the restored products. It also includes the cost of restored products and its impact on environment (Wang and Hazen, 2015; Wang et al., 2013), as well as personal inspirations and marketing mix influence on consumers (Jiménez-Parra et al., 2014). Although these studies gives an intense information on customers' response for refurbished products, but is just an overview of the factors influencing customers' perception for refurbishment. While deciding upon the implementation of restoration process the organizations requires detailed information to analyze the incentives which will enhance the purchasing intent of customers' for the restored smartphones. It also analyzes the consequences of these incentives on different customers' group (Bocken, Schuit, 2018).

It has been studied that giving products again a new life through refurbishment is worthwhile for companies (Atasu et al., 2008; Linton, 2008). Precisely, previous research has surveyed functional problems of restoration (Jiménez-Parra, Rubio, and Vicente-Molina 2014), management aspects, such as pricing (Subramanian & Subramanyam, 2012) and sales cannibalization (Atasu et al., 2010). For successfully implementing refurbishment, researchers have defined phases of product design to make restoration at ease (Nilsson et al., 2016), by reduction of total number of components (Ijomah et al., 2007).

CONCEPTUAL CHANGE: THE EKB MODEL

The EKB model (Engel et al. 1968) is the base for this theoretical framework. EKB model is a consumer decision making model which is widely accepted. This model symbolizes the consumer decision-making process as a step by step process that occurs in a number of phases, which are a pre-purchase phase, an orientation phase, an evaluation phase and a post-purchase phase. The cognitive decision-making process is demonstrative of functional products, of high participation. Therefore, the EKB model has been studies to comprehend the acceptance of customers' for refurbished smartphones (Van Weelden et al., 2016).

Figure 1.
Source: Consumer decision-making-process for factors effecting acceptance of refurbished mobile phones (Van Weelden et al., 2016)

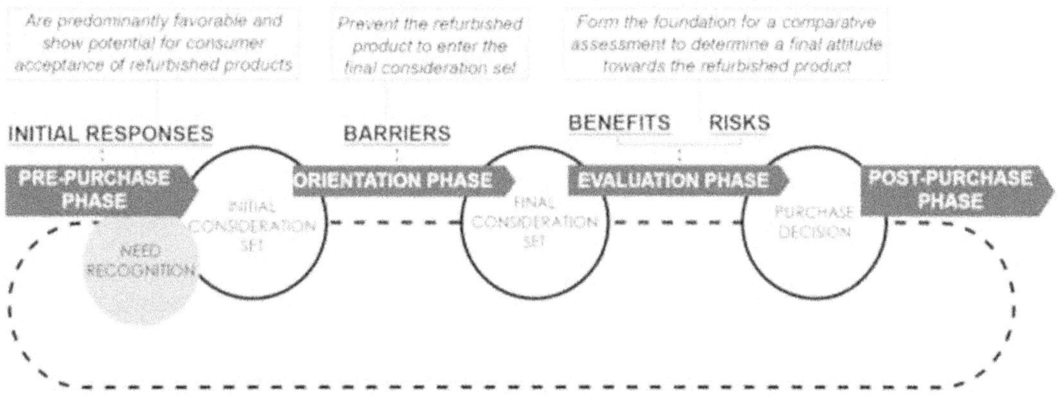

Orientation Phase: Barriers

One of the biggest drawbacks is that refurbished smartphones are not available in all markets. Although if refurbished mobile phones are available, there are two barriers that is Lack of Awareness and mis-understanding about refurbished mobile phones which deters them to be a part of alternatives while consumers' take decisions of purchasing a final product after evaluating alternatives, (Van Weelden et al., 2016). Many of the customers remain unaware of refurbished smartphones available and they miss the chance of including it in their alternatives (Wang, Y., & Hazen, B. T. 2016). The visual appearance of remanufactured mobile phones is also a hindrance for acceptance because customer's feel it to be less beautiful as compared to new mobile phones. Moreover, they presume it be less desirable and have a connotation that it may not function as the original one (Mugge, Jockin, and Bocken 2017).

Evaluation Phase: Benefits & Risk

In this phase it has been studied that different target groups have different perception towards refurbished products. Although Consumers' are prepared to buy refurbished products at a low price as they find it as a cheaper alternative to satisfy their need (Mugge, Jockin, and Bocken 2017). These financial benefits motivates customers' to purchase refurbished smartphones (Jiménez-Parra et al., 2014; Wang & Hazen; 2015; Young et al., 2010). It has also been found that environmental benefits are an incentive for customers' to buy refurbished smartphones. Generally the customers' are ready to pay for refurbished phones with eco certification (Harms and Linton, 2016; Mugge et al., 2017). Inspite of all the environmental benefits, it is not possible to modify the perception of customers' for refurbished smartphones (Harms & Linton, 2015; Van Weelden et al., 2016; Young et al., 2010).

Apparently, in this phase the risk linked with refurbished smartphones are also observed. The perceived risk (performance, financial, time and obsolescence) have an adverse effect on customers' acceptance for refurbished phones (Van Weelden et al. 2016). The wearing away of the smartphones makes it less wanted because it remind consumers' of its previous use and develops negative impact in their mind that it may not function perfectly as compared to a new one (Van Weelden et al., 2016; Wang & Hazen; 2015; Wang et al., 2013), (Herjanto et al. 2016), (Hazen et al., 2017;Wang and Kuah, 2018); Also if the prices of refurbished smartphones are high then it is not considered by customers' in their decision making process because there are causes that affect the accomplishment of remanufacturing engagement like its feasibility and remaufacturability (Kirchherr, J.; Reike, D.; Hekkert, M., 2017), (Rizos, V.; Tuokko, K.; Behrens, A., 2017).

CHAPTER FOCUS AND MEASURES

A survey was conducted to measure Indian consumer Perception and Purchase Intention towards Refurbished Smart Phones. Questionnaire was designed with a brief introduction to refurbishing in order to make respondents familiar with research context. Questions were based on the orientation (Barriers) and evaluation phase (Risk and Benefits) of Consumer decision-making-process for factors effecting acceptance of refurbished mobile phones (Van Weelden et al., 2016). Respondents were asked to rate their purchase intention, perceived benefit and perceived risk for refurbished smart phones. Scales were adopted from the literature (Table 1) and measured on five point Likert scale ranging from 1(Strongly Disagree) to 5 (Strongly Agree).

Respondents were targeted through online survey form. Link of the same was mailed and also circulated through email and social media groups. Target population of the study includes diverse demographic of respondents from Delhi/ NCR region (India). A total of 650 questionnaires were distributed and only 247 questionnaires complete in all aspects were considered for the study, yielding a response rate of 38%. Demographic profile of respondents included in study is represented in Table 2.

Out of total 247 respondents 61.53% were male and rest females. Majority of the respondents fall in the age group of 18-30 years followed with other groups. There is a percentage wise difference of around 6% among student and service personals followed with other professionals. 38.86% of the respondents were graduate followed with 34.41% Post graduate and rest others. Most of the customers look for aspirational brands as compared to others while going for refurbished smart phone purchase.

Reliability coefficient was computed and reliability measure for all the seven constructs ranges in between .719 to .805, well above the defined threshold of .70 (Nunnally and Bernstein 1994, DeVellis 2003).

The result of Kaiser-Meyer-Olkin Measure of Sampling Adequacy (KMO) .843, indicates the presence of sufficient inter- correlations in the data set and appropriateness of factor analysis. Significant test statistics result for Bartlett's test of Sphericity represents that correlation matrix is not an identity

Table 1. Construct Definition

Construct	Code	Statement	Source
Purchase Intention	PI1	Intend to invest in refurbished smart phones.	Chen and Barns (2007) Truong (2003) Suh and Han (2003)
	PI2	Willing to purchase refurbished smart phones.	
	PI3	Recommendation to others.	
Awareness	AR1	Familiarity with refurbished smart phones	Wang et al., (2013)
	AR2	Familiarity with quality of refurbished smart phones	
	AR3	Familiarity with performance of refurbished smart phones	
Financial risk	FR1	Substantial risk with expenditure in refurbished smart phone.	DelVecchio & Smith, (2005)
	FR2	Loss of money if refurbished phone does not work	
	FR3	Regret with purchase of refurbished phone	
	FR4	Concern with the cost of refurbished phone.	
Lack of thrill and newness	TN1	Lack of enjoyment refurbished phone.	Van Weelden et al., (2016)
	TN2	Lack of freshness with refurbished phone.	
	TN3	Perceived as inferior in quality	
Environmental benefits	EB1	Refurbished phones are environment friendly	Van Weelden et al., (2016) Mugge et al., (2017)
	EB2	Refurbished phones can help in developing sustainable future	
	EB3	Refurbished phones has environmental benefits	
Financial benefits	FB1	A refurbished phone has more financial benefits as compared to new phone.	Van Weelden et al., (2016) Mugge et al., (2017)
	FB2	Better brand preference at Low Price for refurbished phones as compared to new phones.	
	FB3	Promotional offers are more interesting on refurbished phones as compared to new phone.	
	FB4	More features at fewer prices in refurbished phones.	
Performance risk	PR1	Performance of refurbished phone a matter of concern	Stone& Grønhaug, (1993)
	PR2	Concern with the reliability of refurbished phone	
	PR3	Concerned with the level of benefit that is expected from refurbished phones.	

Table 2. Demographic Profile

Variables	Frequency	Percentage (%)
Gender		
Male	152	61.53
Female	95	38.46
Age group		
18-30	116	46.96
31-45	70	28.34
46-60	39	15.78
60+	23	9.31
Occupation		
Services	94	38.05
Business	44	17.81
Student	77	31.17
Other	32	12.95
Education Qualification		
Graduate	96	38.86
Post Graduate	85	34.41
Professional Courses	66	26.72
Refurbished Brand Preference		
Aspirational Brands (Apple, Samsung, Nokia, Motorola)	137	55.46
Others	110	44.53

matrix. The result from reliability statistics and measure of sampling adequacy rivals the appropriateness of scales used and data gathered for this study.

Factor analysis was performed to validate the constructs and only factors with an Eigen value of 1.0 with factor loading above 0.5 were retained for further investigation. Model explains a total variance of 68.16% and represents clear distinction in consumers' mind about refurbished smart phones.

RESPONSE TOWARDS REFURBISHED SMART PHONE

Multivariate Analysis of Variance (MANOVA) is used for measuring the effect of demographic parameters on barriers and evaluation of refurbished smart phones. As per the results in Table 3, Model I represents statistically significant difference across different occupational groups regarding refurbishing dimensions, Wilks' $\lambda = .864$, $F = 4.523$, $p <. 001$. The significant F indicates that there exists a difference among different occupation categories regarding the understanding of Awareness, Financial Risk, Lack of thrill and newness, Environmental benefits, Financial benefits and Performance risk for refurbished smart phones. Based on mean scores it is observed that business personal perceive that there is lack of thrill and newness in refurbished phones where as students associate performance risk with refurbished

Table 3. Result Reliability and Factor Analysis

Factors	Items	Factor Loading	% Variance	Cronbach Alpha
Purchase Intention	PI1	.765	8.16	.732
	PI2	.811		
	PI3	.615		
Awareness	AR1	.756	7.92	.759
	AR2	.522		
	AR3	.714		
Financial risk	FR1	.895	15.92	.719
	FR2	.827		
	FR3	.820		
	FR4	.715		
Lack of thrill and newness	TN1	.578	6.28	.776
	TN2	.633		
	TN3	.809		
Environmental benefits	EB1	.577	9.56	.805
	EB2	.785		
	EB3	.889		
Financial benefits	FB1	.758	10.40	.780
	FB2	.729		
	FB3	.802		
	FB4	.770		
Performance risk	PR1	.697	9.92	.754
	PR2	.684		
	PR3	.806		

Note: Factor Analysis- Extraction Method: Principal Component Analysis, Rotation Method: Varimax with Kaiser Normalization.

phones. Interesting aspect is service personals associate financial risk but they recognize environmental benefits with such products too.

Model II shows a significant effect of age group on refurbishing dimensions, (Wilks' $\lambda = .793$, $F = 5.035$, $p <. 001$). Financial risk and financial benefits were not as important as other dimension hence found as insignificant. Individuals with the age group of 15-30 years identify it as environment friendly but associate financial risk with these products also. Respondents with the age group 31-45 years feel refurbished as inferior as compared to new smart phones. Model III exhibits significant effect of education qualification on refurbishing dimensions (Wilks' $\lambda = .692$, $F = 4.523$, $p <. 001$). Mean score represents those respondents with graduation as background feels refurbished phones are financially beneficial but shows concern with performance of such phones. Other category respondents mean score shows higher in Awareness, Financial Risk, Lack of thrill and newness and Environmental benefits. Customer brand choice with refurbished smart phone shows significant effect on refurbishing dimensions (Wilks' $\lambda = .575$, $F = 8.217$, $p <. 001$). Consumer choice with aspirational brand shows high mean score for

Table 4. MANOVA Results

MODEL I Dependent Variable	Source (Occupation)				F	Significance level
	Business	**Service**	**Student**	**Others**		
Awareness	3.075	2.999	3.226	4.641	2.260	.020
Financial risk	4.185	4.646	3.298	4.301	3.818	.010
Lack of thrill and newness	3.484	3.29	3.59	3.182	2.906	.034
Environmental benefits	4.661	4.794	4.185	4.169	4.638	.003
Financial benefits	*3.045*	*3.085*	*3.029*	*2.849*	*.740*	*.529*
Performance risk	3.035	3.235	4.806	2.695	4.331	.005
MODEL II Dependent Variable	**Source (Age Group)**				**F**	**Significance level**
	18-30	31-45	46-60	60+		
Awareness	3.200	3.158	3.552	3.125	6.595	.000
Financial risk	*4.435*	*4.399*	*4.369*	*4.763*	*2.146*	*.074*
Lack of thrill and newness	3.200	3.573	3.297	3.420	3.578	.007
Environmental benefits	5.833	4.625	5.404	4.944	5.002	.001
Financial benefits	*2.665*	*2.994*	*3.110*	*2.671*	*.843*	*.498*
Performance risk	3.444	2.866	2.760	2.701	10.930	.000
MODEL III Dependent Variable	**Source (Education Qualification)**				**F**	**Significance level**
	Graduate	Post Graduate	Professional Courses			
Awareness	2.494	3.083	3.534		8.978	.000
Financial risk	2.447	2.835	3.447		7.357	.000
Lack of thrill and newness	4.598	4.632	3.848		11.27	.000
Environmental benefits	2.767	4.585	3.534		19.09	.020
Financial benefits	5.484	5.208	3.589		21.11	.000
Performance risk	3.396	2.398	2.674		1.773	.032
MODEL IV Dependent Variable	**Source (Brand Preference)**				**F**	**Significance level**
	Aspirational Brands (Apple, Samsung, Nokia, Motorola)		Other Brands			
Awareness	3.475		3.610		3.765	.005
Financial risk	3.253		3.523		6.595	.000
Lack of thrill and newness	*4.396*		*4.726*		*2.146*	*.074*
Environmental benefits	3.597		2.972		3.578	.007
Financial benefits	5.404		4.894		5.002	.001
Performance risk	*3.117*		*2.967*		*.843*	*.498*

environmental and financial benefits for refurbished phones. For other brands customer posses sufficient knowledge about refurbishing but associate financial risk with the refurbished product.

FACTORS INFLUENCING PURCHASE INTENTION

A multiple regression was conducted to evaluate the impact of barriers and risk & benefits associated with refurbished smart phone on consumer purchase intention. Purchase intention was taken as dependent variable and Awareness, Financial Risk, Lack of thrill and newness, Environmental benefits, Financial benefits and Performance risk was considered as independent variables.

Table 5. Result Multiple Regression

	Dependent Variable (Purchase Intention)			
Independent Variable	*B*	*SE B*	*B*	*Significance level*
Awareness	.182	.065	.186	.005
Financial risk	-.380	.052	-.423	.000
Lack of thrill and newness	-.166	.050	-.175	.001
Environmental benefits	.176	.048	.204	.000
Financial benefits	*.097*	*.065*	*.094*	*.139*
Performance risk	-.484	.055	-.622	.000

Tests for multicollinearity indicate very low value of VIF & Tolerance for Model hence no multicollinearity has been assumed among the independent variables. The test of independence is satisfied as the value of Durbin-Watson was found to be equal to 1.56, which is well below the defined threshold limit. The regression model was significant ($F(6,243) = 33.49$, $p < .001$), and predictors explained 33.49% variance in the outcome variable consumer purchase intention. A significant positive effect was found for Awareness ($\beta = .186, p < .05$) and Environmental benefits ($\beta = .204, p < .05$), suggesting that people with better knowledge about refurbished smart phone and its environmental benefits are more inclined toward purchasing refurbished smart phones. Significant negative effect were found for Financial risk ($\beta = -.423$, $p < .05$), Lack of thrill and newness ($\beta = -.175$, $p < .05$) and Performance risk ($\beta = -.622$, $p < .05$). The strength of association with purchase intension is stronger in case of risk as compared to benefits for refurbished smart phones. Performance of refurbished product is a major concern among consumers. Refurbished smart phones are not perceived as new, reliable and profitable by consumers. Refurbished smart phones are promoted as financially beneficial ($\beta = .094, p = .139$) product but interestingly it has found to be insignificant from consumer perspective. Based on findings of study purchase intention purchase intention is a linear combination of Awareness, Environmental benefits, Financial risk, Lack of thrill and newness and Performance risk.

Purchase Intention = 1.27 + .182 Awareness + .176 Environmental benefits + (-.380) Financial risk + (- .166) Lack of thrill and newness + (-.484) Performance risk + ε

IMPLICATION AND GLOBAL SCENARIO

Circular economy a regenerative system recently stimulated refurbishing in order to minimize waste through sustainable consumption. The growing use of electronic products and rapidly evolving technologies leads to volumes of electronic waste in both regions, developed and developing. In the recent past, it has been witnessed that people replace electronic products such as smart phones and other electronic devices if it slows down in its performance or breaks due to mishandling else also if a new model is offered on the market. These factors are enormously increasing e-waste worldwide. The need to reduce e-waste is expected to positively affect the growth of the global market for refurbished and used cell phones during the predicted period (Global Market Study on Refurbished and Used Mobile Phones: Increasing Initiatives to Reduce e-Waste Driving Market Growth, 2020). Though years back refurbishment was not given importance but now it can be clearly observed that it is full of opportunities and is given priority by manufacturers and retailers. Refurbished products are easily accepted as a preference for electronic items. Subsequently, manufacturers and retailers can gain high from refurbishment so are being much thoughtful towards refurbished products and towards consumers who are interested in these products. They will definitely loose the incentive of huge amount of customers if they do not focus on refurbished market (Rallo, 2018). In developed countries such as the United Kingdom, Italy, Germany, France and the United States, most users of the loyal consumer base are tech savvy. They generally look for replacing their old mobile phones with latest available in the market. Nonetheless, they search for new technology at affordable price. This is the major objective that users in developed nations wish to purchase refurbished products with newer features but priced less (Global Used and Refurbished Phones Market Study - NSYS GROUP, 2020). Many organizations are now progressing towards refurbished market and it is advisable to go ahead as it will increase the customer base by aligning best strategies for growing market.

Growing commercial and environmental interest in refurbishing, this study explains consumer acceptance toward refurbished product. This work contributes to the literature of refurbishing and boosts different strategies in circular economy. Using EKB model (Engel et al., 1968) barriers, perceived risk and benefits were used to understand consumer perspective toward refurbished product and their influence on purchase intention. Factor analysis was used to validate the constructs extracted from literature in current research context. Result from factor analysis reflects consumers clear understanding related with Awareness, Financial Risk, Lack of thrill and newness, Environmental benefits, Financial benefits, Performance risk and purchase intention. Multiple Analyses of Variance was used to check the effect of respondents demographic parameters (Occupation, gender, education qualification and brand preference) on factors associated with barriers, perceived risk and benefits of refurbished smart phone. Results clearly depict that customers are having fine level of awareness about refurbished smart phones but major concern is the performance. Customers feel that the refurbished phones are not new and a sense of inferiority as compared to new phones. Financial and environmental benefit with aspirational brands are the drivers for customer's inclination toward refurbished smart phone and literature suggest that refurbished phones sold with strong brand image helps in building purchase intention (Hamzaoui Essoussi & Linton, 2014). Multiple regression was conducted to evaluate the impact of barriers, risk & benefits of refurbishing on consumer purchase intention. Among the five significant predictors to purchase intension, performance risk was having strongest association with the outcome variable followed with financial risk. Customers still associate reliability issue, investment concern and expected benefit from refurbished phones as their top priority. Financial benefit associated with refurbished smartphone was found to be insignificant in majority of the cases. Most of the firms use financial benefit as a handy tool for marketing refurbished products but customers are not giving due importance to it and the findings are in accordance with Mugge et. al (2017). As per the findings of research customer associate risk and barriers more with refurbished phones as compared to benefits. Customers still associate reliability issue, investment concern and expected benefit from refurbished phones as their top priority. and ensure customers that nowhere these products are inferior as compared to new phones. Companies need to position refurbished product as a suitable alternative to new product by adding some unique values to it. The increase in use of data has compelled consumers to look for refurbished smart phones. Due to heavy demand most of the aspirational brands are coming with heavy discount. Top electronic distributers has already started to operate in this segment in order to cater consumer needs, But lack of communication from marketers in terms benefits and its distinctiveness of refurbished products has positioned consumers in a confused state. Industry could use the insights of this research in order to develop market strategy which can provide environmental benefits as well as commercial benefits.

REFERENCES

Atasu, A., Guide, V. D. R. Jr, & Van Wassenhove, L. N. (2010). So what if remanufacturing cannibalizes my new product sales. *California Management Review*, *52*(2), 56–76. doi:10.1525/cmr.2010.52.2.56

Atasu, A., Sarvary, M., & Van Wassenhove, L. N. (2008). Remanufacturing as a marketing strategy. *Management Science*, *54*(10), 1731–1746. doi:10.1287/mnsc.1080.0893

Bocken, N. M. P., de Pauw, I., van der Grinten, B., & Bakker, C. (2016). Product design and business model strategies for a circular economy. *Journal of Industrial and Production Engineering*, *32*(1), 67–81. doi:10.1080/21681015.2014.1000399

Bocken, S., Schuit, C. S. C., & Kraaijenhagen, C. (2018). Experimenting with a circular business model: Lesson from eight cases. *Environmental Innovation and Societal Transitions*, *28*, 79–95. Advance online publication. doi:10.1016/j.eist.2018.02.001

Chanda, N. S. (2019, May 13). *Refurbished goods industry in India: Is Flipkart's promise really worth it?* IMS Proschool Offers Courses in Data Science, Digital Marketing, IFRS, ACCA, CFA, Business Analytics, Financial Modeling, CIMA, CFP Courses. https://www.proschoolonline.com/blog/refurbished-goods-industry

Chen, Y. H., & Barns, S. (2007). Initial trust and online behaviour. *Industrial Management & Data Systems*, *107*(1), 21–36. doi:10.1108/02635570710719034

D'Amato, D., Droste, N., Allen, B., Kettunen, M., Lähtinen, K., Korhonen, J., Leskinen, P., Matthies, B. D., & Toppinen, A. (2017). A. Toppinen Green, Circular, Bio economy, A Comparative Analysis of Three Sustainability Avenues. *Journal of Cleaner Production*, *168*, 716–734. doi:10.1016/j.jclepro.2017.09.053

den Hollander, M. C., Bakker, C. A., & Hultink, E. J. (2017). Product Design in a Circular Economy: Development of a Typology of Key Concepts and Terms. *Journal of Industrial Ecology*, *21*(3), 517–525. doi:10.1111/jiec.12610

DeVellis, R. F. (2003). *Scale development: Theory and applications*. Sage Publications.

Engel, J. F., Kollat, D. T., & Blackwell, R. D. (1968). *Consumer behavior*. Holt, Rinhart & Winston.

Ghisellini, P., Cialani, C., & Ulgiati, S. (2016). A review on Circular Economy: The Expected Transition to a Balanced Interplay of Environmental and Economic Systems. *Journal of Cleaner Production, 114*, 11–32. doi:10.1016/j.jclepro.2015.09.007

Global Market Study on Refurbished and Used Mobile Phones. Increasing Initiatives to reduce e-Waste Driving Market Growth. (2020, January). https://www.persistencemarketresearch.com/market-research/refurbished-and-used-mobile-phones-market.asp

Global Used and Refurbished Phones Market Study - NSYS GROUP. (2020). https://nsysgroup.com/en/media/articles/globalused-and-refurbished-phones-market-study

Gray, C., & Charter, M. (2008). Remanufacturing and Product Design. *International Journal of Product Development, 6*(34).

Guide, V. D. R. Jr, & Li, J. (2010). The potential for cannibalization of new products sales by remanufactured products. *Decision Sciences, 41*(3), 547–572. doi:10.1111/j.1540-5915.2010.00280.x

Hamzaoui Essoussi, L., & Linton, J. D. (2010). New or recycled products: How much are consumers willing to pay? *Journal of Consumer Marketing, 27*(5), 458–468. doi:10.1108/07363761011063358

Harms, R., & Linton, J. D. (2016). Willingness to pay for eco-certified refurbished products: The effects of environmental attitudes and knowledge. *Journal of Industrial Ecology, 20*(4), 893–904. doi:10.1111/jiec.12301

Hazen, Overstreet, R. E., Jones-Farmer, L. A., & Field, H. S. (2012). The role of ambiguity tolerance in consumer perception of remanufactured products. *International Journal of Production Economics, 135*(2), 781–790. doi:10.1016/j.ijpe.2011.10.011

Ijomah, W. L., McMahon, C. A., Hammond, G. P., & Newman, S. T. (2007). Development of design for remanufacturing guidelines to support sustainable manufacturing. *Robotics and Computer-integrated Manufacturing, 23*(6), 712–719. doi:10.1016/j.rcim.2007.02.017

Jiménez-Parra, B., Rubio, S., & Vicente-Molina, M.-A. (2014). Key drivers in the behavior of potential consumers of remanufactured products: A study on laptops in Spain. *Journal of Cleaner Production, 85*, 488–496. doi:10.1016/j.jclepro.2014.05.047

Kalioujny, B., Ermushko, J., & Zhavoronok, A.V. (2016). *Establishment of a strategy of circular economy increasing the well-being of society: comparison of two national policies*. Academic Press.

Khor, K. S., & Hazen, B. T. (2017). Remanufactured products purchase intention and behaviour: Evidence from Malaysia. *International Journal of Production Research, 55*(8), 2149–2162. doi:10.1080/00207543.2016.1194534

Kirchherr, J., Reike, D., & Hekkert, M. (2017). Conceptualizing the circular economy: An analysis of 114 definitions. *Resources, Conservation and Recycling, 127*, 221–232.

Lieder, M., & Rashid, A. (2016). Towards circular economy implementation: A comprehensive review in context of manufacturing industry. *Journal of Cleaner Production, 115*, 36–51.

Linton, J. D. (2008). Assessing the economic rationality of remanufacturing products. *Journal of Product Innovation Management, 25*(3), 287–302. doi:10.1111/j.1540-5885.2008.00301.x

Michaud, C., & Llerena, D. (2011). Green consumer behaviour: An experimental analysis of willingness to pay for remanufactured products. *Business Strategy and the Environment, 20*(6), 408420.

Mugge, R., Jockin, B., & Bocken, N. (2017). How to sell refurbished smartphones? An investigation of different customer groups and appropriate incentives. *Journal of Cleaner Production, 147*, 284–296. doi:10.1016/j.jclepro.2017.01.111

Nunnally, J. C., & Bernstein, I. H. (1994). *Psychometric Theory* (3rd ed.). McGraw-Hill.

Parker, Riley, & Robinson. (2015). Remanufacturing Market study. *Horizon 2020*, Grant Agreement No. 645984, A report by ERN.

Rallo. (2018). The Rise of Refurbished Products. *Liquidity Services – A Better Future for Surplus,* 3-10

Rizos, V., Tuokko, K., & Behrens, A. (2017). *The Circular Economy: A Review of Definitions, Processes and Impacts*. Centre for European Policy Studies.

Shu, S. G. (2019). Analyzing Remanufacturability of Mobile Phones using DEMATEL Approach. *Jurnal Teknik Industri, 21*(1), 33–42. doi:10.9744/jti.21.1.33-42

Singh, D. (2020). *Amazon, Flipkart eyeing refurbished goods market in India: Will the bet pay off?* Financial Express.

Subramanian, R., & Subramanyam, R. (2012). Key Factors in the Market for Remanufactured Products. *Manufacturing & Service Operations Management, 14*(2), 315–326. doi:10.1287/msom.1110.0368

Suh, B., & Han, I. (2003). The impact of customer trust and perception of security control on acceptance of electronic commerce. *International Journal of Electronic Commerce, 7*(3), 135–164. doi:10.1080/10864415.2003.11044270

Van Weelden, E., Mugge, R., & Bakker, C. (2016). Paving the way towards Circular Consumption: Exploring Consumer Acceptance of Refurbished Mobile Phones in the Dutch Market. *Journal of Cleaner Production, 113*, 743-754.

Wang, Wiegerinck, V., Krikke, H., & Zhang, H. (2013). Understanding the purchase intention towards remanufactured product in closed-loop supply chains: An empirical study in China. *International Journal of Physical Distribution & Logistics Management, 43*(10), 866–888. doi:10.1108/IJPDLM-01-2013-0011

Wang, P., & Kuah, A. T. H. (2017). Green marketing cradle-to-cradle: Remanufactured products in Asian markets. *Thunderbird International Business Review, 60*(5), 783–795. doi:10.1002/tie.21925

Wang, Y., & Hazen, B. T. (2015). (in press). Consumer product knowledge and intention to purchase remanufactured products. *International Journal of Production Economics*. Advance online publication. doi:10.1016/j.ijpe.2015.08.031

Wang, Y., & Hazen, B. T. (2015). Consumer product knowledge and intention to purchase remanufactured products. *International Journal of Production Economics*. Advance online publication. doi:10.1016/j.ijpe.2015.08.031

Wang, Y., & Hazen, B. T. (2016). Consumer product knowledge and intention to purchase remanufactured products. *International Journal of Production Economics, 181*(B), 460-469. doi:10.1016/j.ijpe.2015.08.031

Young. (2010). Sustainable consumption: Green Consumer Behaviour When Purchasing Products. *Sustainable Development*, *18*(1), 20–31.

Chapter 18
Women Managers and Generations:
A Study of Obstacles

Kanchan Chandar Tolani
Shri Ramdeobaba College of Engineering and Management, Nagpur, India

Pritam Bhadade
Shri Ramdeobaba College of Engineering and Management, Nagpur, India

Kavita Patil
Dhanwate National College, Nagpur, India

Archana Shrivastava
Jaypee Business School, Jaypee Institute of Information Technology, India

ABSTRACT

The number of women in organizations is increasing in most countries, but the representation of women in managerial positions is still disproportional. The percentage of women in leadership positions globally is only 29%. Grant Thornton annual survey 2019 reveals that India still ranks the fifth lowest in having women in managerial roles. Thus, though diversity at work is increasing, there are still fewer women in the boardroom. The main reason for this is the hurdles and obstacles that women managers face. The chapter studies the various obstacles faced by women managers. Also, it takes into account the role of generation and aims at comparing the hurdles faced by women managers belonging to Generations X and Y. The study is undertaken with special reference to the banking sector. Major findings reveal that there is a difference in obstacles faced by women managers belonging to Generations X and Y.

DOI: 10.4018/978-1-7998-4787-8.ch018

INTRODUCTION

The number of women in organizations is increasing in most countries. Women are also entering into those sectors which were traditionally dominated by men. The rate at which women are becoming entrepreneurs is nearly twice that of men (Zellner, 1994). Even the percentage of women in managerial roles has increased across the globe in recent years (Powell and Graves, 2003). But despite all this, the representation of women in managerial positions is still disproportional (Linehan, 2008). The percentage of women in leadership positions globally records to only 29%. Grant Thornton annual survey 2019 reveals that India still ranks the fifth lowest in having women in managerial roles. Thus, though diversity at work is increasing, the number of women in the boardroom level is still less (Hillman, Shropshire, and Cannella, 2007).

Women today are no more willing to be a peripheral part of the workforce. They wish to take up senior positions and are willing to earn a good amount of money. But many researchers found that even if women have a high level of qualifications and the desire to achieve something professionally, not many get to fulfill it. As there are still many barriers that stop women from being successful (Chenevert and Tremblay, 2002). Women mangers tend to encourage employee development and are better than male managers when it comes to team building at work (Chenevert and Tremblay, 2002). Women are believed to improve the company's overall performance when occupying managerial roles. They are considered better managers than their male counterparts (Cristian Dezs and David Gaddis Ross, 2012). As women managers play a crucial role in the development of the organization, companies must find a way to retain these talented and high potential managers. And one way they can do this is by creating a favorable organization culture (Cooper, 2001). As many studies suggest that women consider unfavorable organizational culture and norms as a bigger obstacle than societal and family issues (Lyness and Thompson). Many women managers leave managerial roles because of a lack of support from subordinates and seniors and bad work culture (AgnieszkaLipińska-Grobelny, 2010).

As per (Tolani, Bhadade & Sao, 2018), the issues and challenges faced by women belong to different generations are not the same. The expectations of women brought up in the dissimilar historical background and economic conditions will not be the same. The majority of women manager currently at work belongs to Generation X and Generation Y. Generation X is more adaptive and ready to learn new things. They like to have work-life balance, job stability and prefer to give importance to personal life (Janet Bickel, 2005, FGI, 2004, Santos & Cox, 2000). On the other hand, Generation Y, have very high expectations. They are smart, good at the use of technology, frequently upgrade skills and like to hop job for better opportunities (Kim, 2008, Eddy S.W. Ng, 2010, Sara De Hauw et al, 2010, Ng et al, 2010).

Thus organizations should focus on modifying their policies and practices and aim at creating a culture that is conducive for the advancement and retention of women employees. Companies should make constant efforts to increase diversity across the organization (Cooper, 2001).

The current paper aims at understanding the various obstacles faced by women occupying leadership roles. It also aims at finding the strategies that the companies can adopt to eliminate these obstacles. Several studies in the past have focused on understanding the issues of women managers but there is a very little study conducted considering the role of Age and Generation. A study conducted by Jyrkinen, M, &McKie L, 2012 supports the argument that women belonging to different age groups experience different challenges and their way of responding to these challenges is also different. In this study, we have attempted to compare the obstacles faced by Generation X and Generation Y women managers.

LITERATURE REVIEW

Obstacles Faced by Women Managers

Various studies on women managers reveal that there are various obstacles that women experience at the individual, organizational, and societal level (Karam & Afioni, 2013).

One of the major obstacles faced by women at the workplace which prevents their advancement to the top position is the **"glass ceiling"**. This phenomenon is prevalent in various organizations (Simpson and Altman, 2000). Though many women are acquiring managerial positions today, the glass ceiling still exists (Meyerson and Fletcher, 2000). According to Stroh, Langlands, & Simpson, (2004), Glass ceiling is nothing but a set of barriers at the workplace which are stopping the women employees from setting their foot in the upper management. And even if they get into a top position they find it hard to survive there. Glass ceiling also hinders the career development of women employees. In most organizations, it is the lack of organizational support, mentoring, and networking (Vlado Dimovski, 2010). Glass ceiling as a barrier largely influences the career of women (David, 2001; Mavin, 2000).

Another challenge that women at managerial roles need to deal with is the **''queen bee syndrome''** (Keeton, 1996). It is a condition where women who have reached the upper management are not willing to extend any support or help to the women aspiring to reach the top (Ng & Chiu, 2001). These are those women who are not ready to break the cycle, as they had struggled hard to reach to the top, they want other women to also go through that same set of issues. These women have taken efforts to create their space in the male-dominated culture. Thus they do not let other women enter easily (Staines, Tavris, & Jayaratne, 1974). A study conducted by Belle Derks (2015) suggests that women exhibiting "queen bee syndrome" do three things: 1) Avoiding social contact with other women. 2) Endorsing the current gender hierarchy. 3) Presenting themselves like men. Queen bee syndrome leads to a lack of support for women and creates unavailability of women mentors for aspiring women juniors. (Fox, 2005)...

Among the various obstacles faced by women managers, one most prevalent obstacle is the **gender stereotype** (Karam & Afioni, 2013). This obstacle is considered as most disruptive for women managers. (Claudia Peus, 2015). Women experience a lack of cross-gender support, difficulty in accessing the social network, isolation, clubbism (Kauser &Tlaiss, 2011) and all of these affect adversely women manager's morale and performance (Ikhlas A. Abdalla1, 2015). Gender stereotypes, bad attitudes towards women, and cultural biases are hindering the performance of women managers across all the settings (Vlado Dimovski, 2010). Leadership roles have always been associated with male gender and this trend continues to persist in various places even today (Eagly, 2007; Heilman, 2001; Powell, Butterfield, & Parent, 2002). Women are always considered suitable for a supportive role and are never considered for central activities (Dasgupta & Asgari, 2004).

Work-family conflict is also a major issue that affects women managers (Heilman & Okimoto, 2008). Many women managers are unable to focus on their work effectively as they do not receive support from their family members. A researcher states that family support plays a crucial role in the advancement of women (Karam & Afioni, 2013). Many women managers say that is very hard to balance both work and family especially when you are handling crucial responsibilities at work and there is a lack of organizational and family support (Guendouzi, 2006). They are always trying to figure out whether to put family first or work. This dilemma is created mostly because of the lack of women- friendly organizational policies and lack of support from the family members (Maume, 2006). The Organization must strive to make policies to ensure that women find it easy to carry out all the roles such as women, a mother, a wife, and a manager effectively. (José M. Coronel, 2010).

Few researchers suggest that some barriers to women managers are also **individual-centered**, such as personality traits, attitude, confidence, and risk-taking capacity, etc. (Powell, 2000). Inner drive and self-efficacy play an important role for a women manager to succeed in their career. Women's lack of self-interest, self-confidence, and inclination are considered as major blocks to the career advancement of women employees (Peus & Traut-Mattausch, 2007).

Gen X & Gen Y

People belonging to Generation X and Generation Y have different historical backgrounds, thus the characteristics and attitudes of these two generations are very dissimilar (Reisenwitz & Iyer, 2009). Thus they exhibit different behaviors and expectations at work (Tolani, Bhadade & Sao, 2018).

Generation X born from 1961 to1979 (Gurau, 2012), are also called Baby Busters. It is a diligent and reliable generation (Gursoy, Maier & Chi, 2008). Generation X individuals are also called as Latchkeys generation as it was the first generation, whose parents were working and many of these people had witnessed parental divorce. Because of these life experiences, this generation puts family first and likes to have work-life balance (Janet Bickel, 2005). They give their family and personal life more priority and are not willing to sacrifice it for work (Cole et.al, 2002). This generation is more adaptive to changes and is willing to learn new ways of doing things (FGI, 2004). Though generation X was the first generation to use technological devices such as computers, laptop on a day to day basis, with rapid technological advancement, this generation is not as technologically urbane as the new generations. But as this generation is a highly adaptable, they constantly try to learn the new technology. When it comes to career and job, this generation constantly makes efforts to develop skills and qualifications which can aid in their career development (Santos & Cox, 2000). Thus this generation is result-oriented and highly focused (Tolani, Bhadade & Sao, 2018). Generation X individuals as compared to the new generation individuals prefer job stability, they consider job decision as an important decision and they prefer hopping jobs only if they get better salaries and growth prospects (Tulgan, 2000). This generation has witnessed a major recession and financial crises of the 1980s and 1990s (Galambos, 2014). Thus when making an investment or financial decision, this generation gets very cautious. (Crumpacker & Crumpacker, 2007).

Generation Y born from 1978 to 1994 (Sheahan, P, 2005), are also called Millennials and Eco boomers (Howe and Strauss, 2003). Millennials are poised, smart, and enthusiastic and curious individuals (Kim, 2008). This generation continually upgrades their skills and likes to be successful (Eddy S.W. Ng, 2010). But when it comes to their career, they frequently hop jobs and are always looking for better opportunities. This generation has very high standards and expectations when it comes to the workplace, and job (Sara De Hauw et al, 2010). This generation believes that a good workplace is one where the employees are treated well, and the health and wellbeing of the employee is important (Andrea Hershatter, 2010). According to Millennials, a conducive work environment is one where employees are treated as assets and they should be valued (Diane Randall Andrews, 2013). As this generation is born and brought up in the age of social media, they have high social needs, they like to maintain good interpersonal relationships at work (Ng et al, 2010). This generation of employees prefers working in teams. They are excellent collaborators (Dougan et al., 2008). They like to set team goals and believe in exhibiting team spirit (Gursoy et al., 2008).This generation as compared to the previous generations is more technologically, as they have been using various technological devices right from childhood.

Thus this generation expects technological sophistication at their workplaces. Generation Y individuals put a lot of emphasis on flexibility at work (Iyet & Reisenwitz, 2009). As compared to Generation X, they prefer work-life integration over work life balance. As they are technologically urbane, they believe we can complete our work from anywhere, anytime without compromising on life. As this generation employees are unique and must be dealt with differently than the previous generations.

RESEARCH METHODOLOGY

Objectives of the Study:

Based on identified research gaps from the review of the literature, the following broad objective was constructed.

- To determine various obstacles faced by women managers.

The following hypotheses were formulated and this empirical study tests those hypotheses.

The Null Hypothesis

- There is no significant difference between obstacles faced by women managers at the workplace among the different age groups.
- There is no significant difference between obstacles faced by women managers at the workplace among different marital statuses.
- There is no significant difference between obstacles faced by women managers at the workplace among different years of experience.

Data Collection Method:

This study has adopted an online mode for data collection. The primary data has been collected by using a structured questionnaire for the study. As the study focuses on understanding the various obstacles faced by women managers at the workplace hence the questionnaire for the study is designed on the following parameters.

1. Workplace Ecosystem
    a. Work life balance
    b. Occupational Health
    c. Work values
2. Gender Discrimination
    a. Pay & Promotion
    b. Gender Stereotypes
3. Home & Work Conflict
    a. Children
    b. Family (In-laws)

   c. Husband
4. Cultural Factors
   a. Societal Norms
   b. Perception
5. Individual Self

Sample Size:

The data for the study has been collected using a structured questionnaire. For the collection of data, a total of 120 women managers working in the banking industry have been reached. Out of 120, 99 respondents have filled the questionnaire and 3 responses were rejected due to incomplete information. Hence 96 valid responses were considered for the study. The random sampling technique is used to sample from the population. The sample comprised of 45.8% i.e. 44 respondents from age group of 30-40, 37.5% i.e.36 respondents from 40-50 and 16.67% i.e.16 respondents from 50-60.

MANOVA analysis is carried out to identify to the impact of various dependent variables on fixed factors i.e. age, marital status, experience vs obstacles.

DATA ANALYSIS AND FINDINGS

To determine the various obstacles faced by the women managers, MANOVA analysis was carried out by taking age, marital status, and work experience as fixed factors. The findings of the analysis have been put in the given below table.

Comparison of Responses Among age Groups

As anticipated and demonstrated in Table 1, the age has a significant impact on all the dependent variables (age vs obstacles; Wilks' Lambda = 0.00, $p < 0.05$).

Table 1. Age Vs. Obstacles

Multivariate Tests[a]									
Effect		Value	F	Hypothesis df	Error df	Sig.	Partial Eta Squared	Noncent. Parameter	Observed Power[d]
Age	Pillai's Trace	1.907	72.355	42.000	148.000	.000	.954	3038.924	1.000
	Wilks' Lambda	.000	439.359[b]	42.000	146.000	.000	.992	18453.066	1.000

There is a statistical significant difference between responses among age groups i.e. 30-40, 40-50, and 50-60. They are significantly different on work-life balance, occupational health, work values, job aspects, pay & promotion, family and societal norms.

Comparison of Responses Among Different Marital Status Groups

As anticipated and demonstrated in Table 2, the marital status has a significant impact on all the dependent variables (marital status vs obstacles; Wilks' Lambda = 0.01, $p < 0.05$)

Table 2. Marital status Vs. Obstacles

Multivariate Tests[a]										
Effect		**Value**	**F**	**Hypothesis df**	**Error df**	**Sig.**	**Partial Eta Squared**	**Noncent. Parameter**	**Observed Power[d]**
Marital_Status	Pillai's Trace	1.833	38.705	42.000	148.000	.000	.917	1625.617	1.000
	Wilks' Lambda	.001	120.662[b]	42.000	146.000	.000	.972	5067.800	1.000

They are significantly different on all parameters. As their marital status is changing they are different on the workplace ecosystem, gender discrimination, home & work conflict, cultural factors, and self as obstacles

Comparison of Responses Among Different Experience Groups

As anticipated and demonstrated in Table 3, the experience at the current position has significant impact on all the dependent variables (experience vs obstacles; Wilks' Lambda = 0.01, $p < 0.05$)

Table 3. Experience Vs. Obstacles

Multivariate Tests[a]									
Effect		**Value**	**F**	**Hypothesis df**	**Error df**	**Sig.**	**Partial Eta Squared**	**Noncent. Parameter**	**Observed Power[d]**
Experience	Pillai's Trace	2.577	22.822	60.000	225.000	.000	.859	1369.316	1.000
	Wilks' Lambda	.001	34.474	60.000	218.627	.000	.903	2038.992	1.000

There is a statistical significant difference between responses of groups having different years of experience i.e. less than a year, 1-5 years, 6-10 years, 11-15 years.

RESEARCH IMPLICATIONS

Women managers today are an important part of organizations, the policymakers thus should try and understand their problems and attempts must be made to resolve them. This study will help the policymakers to understand the obstacles faced by women managers and will suggest to them the ways by which they can help women managers to overcome these obstacles.

FINDINGS AND CONCLUSION

It has been found in the study that the major obstacles faced by women managers which hinders their growth include lack of work-life balance, majority of women managers feel that they don't get enough time to fulfill their family responsibilities or to pursue their hobbies. Women managers often need to sacrifice on their social life, family time, or "me time" to be productive or creative at work. As women managers don't get enough time to focus on their health, many women occupying managerial roles suffer from various health issues such as obesity, hair fall, anemia, anxiety, depression, and stress.

Another obstacle faced by women managers is home and work conflict. The majority of women managers suggest that one reason they can't grow in their career is the lack of family support. Some women managers who are married with children feel very guilty that they are unable to give enough time to their children.

One of the obstacles in the various cultural barriers that women managers face. People at work make perceptions about their character, competence, and reputation the way they like. Also, the lack of enough female managers as role models at the workplace creates issues for women managers.

The Study also reveals that there is a significant difference in the obstacles faced by women managers belonging to Generation X and Y. Obstacles faced by women managers are different for women who are single, who are married, and for those who are married with children. The number of years of experience of the women managers has an impact on the obstacles faced by her.

The Study suggests that some ways by which companies can help women managers to overcome these obstacles are by providing a fair and transparent workplace which is gender-neutral. Providing flexibility to women managers at work such as flexible working hours, work from home facility, crèche facility in the company can help women managers to achieve work-life balance. Some women also feel that mentoring facility and wellness programs for women can also help them in overcoming their obstacles.

LIMITATIONS AND FUTURE RESEARCH DIRECTION

The study is restricted to women managers belonging to the banking sector. Thus further studies can be done to understand the obstacles faced by women managers working in other sectors. The results of the research cannot be generalized as it is limited to women managers of India. Thus research can be carried out on women managers of other countries and a cross country analysis can also be done.

ANNEXURE

Table 4. Questionnaire

You get enough_time_to_fulfill_your_family_responsibilities
You get time_to_pursue_your_hobbies
You can smoothly_balance_your_work_and_life
organization_pay_adequate_attention_towards_women_employees_and_their_problems
Your organization_has_a_facility_of_work_from_home
organization_has_a_day_care_centre_facility_for_children
Your organization_has_flexible_work_timings
I_often_have_to_sacrifice_my_social_life,_family_time,_or_me_time_to_be_able_to_get_creative_and_productive_with_my_career
Mentoring_program_for_women_at_work_can_help_in_resolving_a_lot_of_problems_that_women_managers_face
Are_you_suffering_from_health_issues_like_obesity,_hair_fall,_and_anemia_due_to_work_pressure?
You_suffer_from_work_stress_due_to_excessive_work_pressure
Do_you_suffer_from_any_health_complications_like_High_Blood_pressure,_Diabetes_or_any_other_disease_due_to_work_pressure?
Do_you_experience_issues_like_anxiety,_depression,_sadness_or_any_other_psychological_stress_due_to_work_pressure?
Promotion_in_company_is_done_on_the_basis_of_merit
Your_company_policies_are_fair_and_transparent
Superiors_give_due_value_to_suggestions_put_by_women_employees
You_get_proper_cooperation_from_the_people_working_with_you
You_have_a_proper_grievance_redressal_system_for_employees_in_your_company?
Your_job_contribute_towards_your_personal_growth_and_development
Your_job_provide_you_with_an_opportunity_to_bring_out_your_best_potential_for_the_organization
Do_you_get_regular_feedback_on_your_work_performance_in_order_to_improve
Your_excellence_in_performance_is_rewarded_in_your_job
There_are_no_pay_disparity_based_on_gender
While_promoting_an_employee,_gender_of_the_employee_is_not_a_deciding_factor
You_are_required/expected_to_work_more_than_other_male_managers
There_are_not_enough_female_managers_as_role_models_in_your_workplace
Different_treatments_at_work_to_male_and_female_employees_occupying_the_similar_position
Subordinates_(people_working_under_you)_do_not_take_your_commands_seriously_as_you_are_a_female_manager
Subordinates_give_same_amount_of_respect_to_both_male_and_female_managers
Men_consider_women_as_women_and_not_professional_colleagues
Your_child_help_you_in_your_work_at_home
You_are_able_to_attend_all_the_school_meetings/commitments_of_your_child
You_donâ€™t_give_enough_time_to_your_children_because_of_your_job
You_feel_guilty_that_your_child_spends_most_of_the_time_in_day_care/or_with_a_helper_at_home
If_given_a_choice,_you_would_leave_the_job_and_prefer_to_stay_with_children_at_home
You_are_satisfied_with_your_child_care_or_other_caregiver_arrangement
You_feel_your_children_experience_loneliness_as_you_are_working
``
Your_work_often_gets_disrupted_by_family_commitments_and_responsibilities
You_face_several_difficulties_at_home_for_working
Your_family_forces_you_to_quit_your_job_and_asks_you_to_pay_attention_to_home_responsibilities
Your_spouse_share_the_parenting,_childcare_work
Your_spouse_helps_you_sufficiently_in_housekeeping_tasks
Your_spouse_feels_inferior_as_you_are_in_a_managerial_post
Your_spouse_feels_is_jealous_of_you_as_you_earn_more_than_him
You_make_valuable_contribution_to_your_family_finances
Your_spouse_value_your_contribution_to_family_finances
Work_Environment_is_equally_conducive_for_both_working_women_and_working_men
Your_colleagues_and_subordinates_are_supportive_and_caring
Your_male_subordinates_make_you_feel_uncomfortable
Experienced_instances_of_sexual_harassment_at_your_workplace
Getting_support_from_other_women_is_a_challenge
People_at_work_make_perceptions_about_your_(women_managers')_character,_the_way_they_like
People_at_work_make_perceptions_about_your_(women_managersâ€™)_competence,_the_way_they_like
People_at_work_make_perceptions_about_your_(women_managersâ€™)_reputation,_the_way_they_like
You_donâ€™t_get_enough_â€œme_timeâ€
You_feel_you_donâ€™t_get_quality_time_with_your_partner
You_donâ€™t_get_time_to_spend_with_your_family_and_friends
You_are_unable_to_focus_on_your_health
Your_job_gives_you_a_sense_of_confidence
You_often_feel_that_you_are_tired_and_you_need_some_time_off
I_often_have_to_sacrifice_on_my_social_life_to_be_able_to_get_creative_and_productive_with_my_career
I_often_have_to_sacrifice_on_my_"me_time"_to_be_able_to_get_creative_and_productive_with_my_career.
You_are_able_to_overcome_challenges_faced_by_you_to_a_large_extent

REFERENCES

Abdalla, I. A. (2015). Being and Becoming a Leader: Arabian Gulf Women Managers' Perspectives. *International Journal of Business and Management*, *10*(1), 25.

Afiouni, F., Karam, C. M., & El-Hajj, H. (2013). The HR value proposition model in the Arab Middle East: Identifying the contours of an Arab Middle Eastern HR model. *International Journal of Human Resource Management*, *24*(10), 1895–1932. doi:10.1080/09585192.2012.722559

Agars, M. D. (2004). Reconsidering the impact of gender stereotypes on the advancement of women in organizations. *Psychology of Women Quarterly*, *28*(2), 103–111. doi:10.1111/j.1471-6402.2004.00127.x

Alimo-Metcalfe, B. (2010). An investigation of female and male constructs of leadership and empowerment. *Gender in Management*, *25*(8), 640–648. doi:10.1108/17542411011092309

Bickel, J., & Brown, A. J. (2005). Generation X: Implications for faculty recruitment and development in academic health centers. *Academic Medicine*, *80*(3), 205–210. doi:10.1097/00001888-200503000-00003 PMID:15734801

Chênevert, D., & Tremblay, M. (2002). Managerial career success in Canadian organizations: Is gender a determinant? *International Journal of Human Resource Management*, *13*(6), 920–941. doi:10.1080/09585190210134282

Cooper Jackson, J. (2001). Women middle managers' perception of the glass ceiling. *Women in Management Review*, *16*(1), 30–41. doi:10.1108/09649420110380265

Coronel, J. M., Moreno, E., & Carrasco, M. J. (2010). Work–family conflicts and the organizational work culture as barriers to women educational managers. *Gender, Work and Organization*, *17*(2), 219–239. doi:10.1111/j.1468-0432.2009.00463.x

Cotter, D. A., Hermsen, J. M., Ovadia, S., & Vanneman, R. (2001). The glass ceiling effect. *Social Forces*, *80*(2), 655–681. doi:10.1353of.2001.0091

Crumpacker, M., & Crumpacker, J. M. (2007). Succession planning and generational stereotypes: Should HR consider age-based values and attitudes a relevant factor or a passing fad? *Public Personnel Management*, *36*(4), 349–369. doi:10.1177/009102600703600405

Dasgupta, N., & Asgari, S. (2004). Seeing is believing: Exposure to counterstereotypic women leaders and its effect on the malleability of automatic gender stereotyping. *Journal of Experimental Social Psychology*, *40*(5), 642–658. doi:10.1016/j.jesp.2004.02.003

Dasgupta, N., & Asgari, S. (2004). Seeing is believing: Exposure to counterstereotypic women leaders and its effect on the malleability of automatic gender stereotyping. *Journal of Experimental Social Psychology*, *40*(5), 642–658. doi:10.1016/j.jesp.2004.02.003

De Hauw, S., & De Vos, A. (2010). Millennials' career perspective and psychological contract expectations: Does the recession lead to lowered expectations? *Journal of Business and Psychology*, *25*(2), 293–302. doi:10.100710869-010-9162-9

Derks, B., Van Laar, C., & Ellemers, N. (2016). The queen bee phenomenon: Why women leaders distance themselves from junior women. *The Leadership Quarterly*, *27*(3), 456–469. doi:10.1016/j.leaqua.2015.12.007

Derks, B., van Laar, C., Ellemers, N., & Raghoe, G. (2015). Extending the queen bee effect: How Hindustani workers cope with disadvantage by distancing the self from the group. *The Journal of Social Issues*, *71*(3), 476–496. doi:10.1111/josi.12124

Dezsö, C. L., & Ross, D. G. (2012). Does female representation in top management improve firm performance? A panel data investigation. *Strategic Management Journal*, *33*(9), 1072–1089. doi:10.1002mj.1955

Dimovski, V., Skerlavaj, M., & Man, M. M. K. (2010). Comparative analysis of mid-level women managers' perception of the existence of glass ceiling in Singaporean and Malaysian organizations. *International Business & Economics Research Journal, 9*(8).

Dimovski, V., Skerlavaj, M., & Man, M. M. K. (2010). Comparative analysis of mid-level women managers' perception of the existence of glass ceiling in Singaporean and Malaysian organizations. *International Business & Economics Research Journal, 9*(8).

Eagly, A. H. (2007). Female leadership advantage and disadvantage: Resolving the contradictions. *Psychology of Women Quarterly*, *31*(1), 1–12. doi:10.1111/j.1471-6402.2007.00326.x

Guendouzi, J. (2006). "The guilt thing": Balancing domestic and professional roles. *Journal of Marriage and the Family*, *68*(4), 901–909. doi:10.1111/j.1741-3737.2006.00303.x

Gursoy, D., Maier, T. A., & Chi, C. G. (2008). Generational differences: An examination of work values and generational gaps in the hospitality workforce. *International Journal of Hospitality Management*, *27*(3), 448–458. doi:10.1016/j.ijhm.2007.11.002

Heilman, M. E. (2001). Description and prescription: How gender stereotypes prevent women's ascent up the organizational ladder. *The Journal of Social Issues*, *57*(4), 657–674. doi:10.1111/0022-4537.00234

Heilman, M. E. (2012). Gender stereotypes and workplace bias. *Research in Organizational Behavior*, *32*, 113–135. doi:10.1016/j.riob.2012.11.003

Heilman, M. E., & Okimoto, T. G. (2008). Motherhood: A potential source of bias in employment decisions. *The Journal of Applied Psychology*, *93*(1), 189–198. doi:10.1037/0021-9010.93.1.189 PMID:18211144

Hershatter, A., & Epstein, M. (2010). Millennials and the world of work: An organization and management perspective. *Journal of Business and Psychology*, *25*(2), 211–223. doi:10.100710869-010-9160-y

Hillman, A. J., Shropshire, C., & Cannella, A. A. Jr. (2007). Organizational predictors of women on corporate boards. *Academy of Management Journal*, *50*(4), 941–952. doi:10.5465/amj.2007.26279222

Howe, N., & Strauss, W. (2003). *Millennials go to college: Strategies for a new generation on campus: Recruiting and admissions, campus life, and the classroom*. American Association of Collegiate Registrars and Admissions Officers.

Jyrkinen, M., & McKie, L. (2012). Gender, age and ageism: Experiences of women managers in Finland and Scotland. *Work, Employment and Society*, *26*(1), 61–77. doi:10.1177/0950017011426313

Kanter, R. M. (1977). *Men and women of the corporation*. Basic Books.

Keeton, K. B. (1996). Characteristics of successful women managers and professionals in local government: A national survey. *Women in Management Review, 11*(3), 27–34. doi:10.1108/09649429610117434

King, E. D. (2006). Report from SIOP: Current industrial/organizational psychology perspectives of women in organizations. *Equal Opportunities International, 25*(3), 215–218. doi:10.1108/02610150610687854

Krahn, H., & Galambos, N. (2014). Work values and beliefs of ' Generation X' and 'Generation Y'. *Journal of Youth Studies, 17*(1), 92–112. doi:10.1080/13676261.2013.815701

Lawless, J. L., & Fox, R. L. (2005). *It takes a candidate: Why women don't run for office*. Cambridge University Press.

Levy, M., & Powell, P. (2000). Information systems strategy for small and medium sized enterprises: An organisational perspective. *The Journal of Strategic Information Systems, 9*(1), 63–84. doi:10.1016/S0963-8687(00)00028-7

Linehan, M., & Scullion, H. (2008). The development of female global managers: The role of mentoring and networking. *Journal of Business Ethics, 83*(1), 29–40. doi:10.100710551-007-9657-0

Lipińska-Grobelny, A., & Wasiak, K. (2010). Job satisfaction and gender identity of women managers and non-managers. *International Journal of Occupational Medicine and Environmental Health, 23*(2), 161–166. doi:10.2478/v10001-010-0015-6 PMID:20630833

Livingstone, D. W., Pollock, K., & Raykov, M. (2016). Family binds and glass ceilings: Women managers' promotion limits in a 'knowledge economy'. *Critical Sociology, 42*(1), 145–166. doi:10.1177/0896920514532663

Lyness, K. S., & Thompson, D. E. (1997). Above the glass ceiling? A comparison of matched samples of female and male executives. *The Journal of Applied Psychology, 82*(3), 359–375. doi:10.1037/0021-9010.82.3.359 PMID:9190144

Maume, D. J. (2006). Gender differences in restricting work efforts because of family responsibilities. *Journal of Marriage and the Family, 68*(4), 859–869. doi:10.1111/j.1741-3737.2006.00300.x

Mavin, S. (2000). Approaches to careers in management: Why UK organisations should consider gender. *Career Development International, 5*(1), 13–20. doi:10.1108/13620430010309323

Meyerson, D., & Fletcher, J. (2000). A modest manifesto for shattering the glass ceiling. *Harvard Business Review, 78*(1), 127–140.

Ng, C. W., & Chiu, W. C. (2001). Managing equal opportunities for women: Sorting the friends from the foes. *Human Resource Management Journal, 11*(1), 75–88. doi:10.1111/j.1748-8583.2001.tb00033.x

Ng, E. S., Schweitzer, L., & Lyons, S. T. (2010). New generation, great expectations: A field study of the millennial generation. *Journal of Business and Psychology, 25*(2), 281–292. doi:10.100710869-010-9159-4

Peus, C., Braun, S., & Knipfer, K. (2015). On becoming a leader in Asia and America: Empirical evidence from women managers. *The Leadership Quarterly, 26*(1), 55–67. doi:10.1016/j.leaqua.2014.08.004

Peus, C., & Traut-Mattausch, E. (2007). *Factors influencing women managers' success*. Academic Press.

Peus, C., & Traut-Mattausch, E. (2008). Manager and mommy? A cross-cultural comparison. *Journal of Managerial Psychology*, *23*(5), 558–575. doi:10.1108/02683940810884531

Pitta, D., & Gurău, C. (2012). A life-stage analysis of consumer loyalty profile: Comparing Generation X and Millennial consumers. *Journal of Consumer Marketing*.

Powell, G. N., Butterfield, D. A., & Parent, J. D. (2002). Gender and managerial stereotypes: Have times changed? *Journal of Management*, *28*(2), 177–193. doi:10.1177/014920630202800203

Powell, G. N., & Graves, L. M. (2003). *Women and Men in Management* (3rd ed.). Sage Publications.

Reisenwitz, T. H., &Iyer, R. (2009). Differences in Generation X and Generation Y: Implications For The Organization And Marketers. *Marketing Management Journal, 19*(2).

Santos, S. R., & Cox, K. (2000). Workplace adjustment and intergenerational differences between matures, boomers, and Xers. *Nursing Economics*, *18*(1), 7. PMID:11029913

Schmitt, M. T., Ellemers, N., & Branscombe, N. R. (2003). Perceiving and responding to gende discrimination in organizations. In S. A. Haslam, D. Van Knippenberg, M. J. Platow, & N. Ellemers (Eds.), *Social identity at work: Developing theory for organizational practice* (pp. 277–292). Psychology Press.

Sheahan, P., & Sheahan, P. (2005). Generation Y: Thriving and surviving with generation Y at work. Prahran: Hardie Grant Books.

Son, J., & Kim, S. S. (2008). Internet users' information privacy-protective responses: A taxonomy and a nomological model. *Management Information Systems Quarterly*, *32*(3), 503–529. doi:10.2307/25148854

Staines, G., Tavris, C., & Jayaratne, T. E. (1974). *The queen bee syndrome*. Academic Press.

Stroh, L. K., Langlands, C. L., & Simpson, P. A. (2004). Shattering the glass ceiling in the new millenium. In M. S. Stockdale & F. J. Crosby (Eds.), *The psychology and management of workplace diversity* (pp. 147–167). Blackwell.

Stroh, L. K., Langlands, C. L., Simpson, P. A., Stockdale, M. S., & Crosby, F. J. (2004). Shattering the glass ceiling in the new millennium. *The psychology and management of workplace diversity*, 147-167.

Tlaiss, H., & Kauser, S. (2011). The impact of gender, family, and work on the career advancement of Lebanese women managers. *Gender in Management*, *26*(1), 8–36. doi:10.1108/17542411111109291

Tolani, K., Bhadade, P., & Sao, R. (2018). Gen X and Gen Y Women Managers: Challenges and Issues. Helix: The scientific. *Explorer*, *6*, 5.

Tulgan, B. (2000). *Managing Generation X: How to bring out the best in young talent*. WW Norton & Company.

Appendix 1

Table 5 Profile of Respondents

Respondent Characteristics	Study N = 96
Gender Male Female	0 (0%) 96 (100%)
Age 30–40 years 40–50 years 50–60 years	44 (45.83) 36 (37.5) 16 (16.6)
Marital status Single Married Married with children	36 (37.5) 28 (29.16) 32 (33.33)
Education level Undergraduate Postgraduate	40 (41.66%) 56 (58.33%)
Education Stream Engineering Commerce/Business Science Arts	20 (20.83%) 48 (50%) 20 (20.83%) 8 (8.33%)
Work Experience Less than a year 1-5 years 6-10 years 11-15 years	4 (4.12%) 52 (54.16%) 28 (29.16%) 12 (12.5%)

Chapter 19
Perceived Tourist Harassment in Tourist Destinations:
A Study of Southern Coastal Belt of Sri Lanka

Shamila Rasanjani Wijesundara
Uva Wellassa University, Sri Lanka

Athula Gnanapala
Sabaragamuwa University of Sri Lanka, Sri Lanka

ABSTRACT

Tourism is a fast-growing industry in the world. Many developing countries have recognized the economic contribution of the tourism industry towards to country; therefore, it has been included as an integral part of their development strategies. Sri Lanka continues to use tourism as one of the incomes earning strategy of its nation. At present, a huge tourism development is continued while accepting severe issues occurs itself like tourist harassment. The nature of the harassment is different from destination to destination, and this study mainly aims to identify the harassment in Sri Lanka. The study carried out in Southern Coastal Belt, considering foreign tourists as the sample to the study. A pretested questionnaire was distributed among 600 foreigners to collect primary data for the study, and 530 questionnaires were valid for the analysis. The collected data was analyzed through exploratory factor analysis, which revealed six major types of harassment in Sri Lanka as a result of tourist consumption process throughout the vacation.

DOI: 10.4018/978-1-7998-4787-8.ch019

INTRODUCTION

Tourism was an activity in which relatively few participated regularly, and was primarily confined to Europe, North America and a small number of locations in other parts of the world. Because, travel was difficult, uncomfortable, expensive and frequently dangerous (Stephan, 1998) as perceived by the travelers. With the time passes, people used to travel despite of perceived complications as diversified motives appeared in the travel destinations. These motives are varied in world-wide travel destinations according to the potential resources they have to attract travelers. Availability of resources for tourism in a destination may decides the capacity of its economy to generate income via tourism. Sri Lanka is one of the best destination to travel in the world because of its unique collection of features like, landscape, misty hills, rare and unique wild life, rich culture and tradition, tropical weather, sandy beaches, manmade attractions, warm hospitality and friendly people etc. Hence, Sri Lanka Tourism has been playing an important role in its economy being remained as the third foreign exchange earner in 2017. However, tourism is not a source to generate only the benefits to any economy. Jayawardena (2013) explained six key challenges faced by Sri Lanka tourism; infrastructure development, attracting investors, finding adequate numbers of trained staff, conservation of fauna and flora, clear destination positioning and harassment of tourists. Among them, the present study focuses to identify the types of tourist harassment occurring in tourist destination in Sri Lanka while finding major reasons to overcome the tourist harassment.

THEORETICAL BACKGROUND

Harassment is a legal term and has different meanings in different jurisdictions (Otoo at el., 2019). As they explained in same study, tourist harassment is pervasive and may occur at any time or place within the tourism experience. Paying of deep attention will be needed on tourism experience gained by the tourists, because, as Kozak (2007) discussed "hospitality" and harassment" are words identifying two different aspects of a national culture and of a tourist's experience. Purely, negative tourist experience. Meanwhile, positive experience make the tourists satisfied. Now, it is clear that one of the negative consequences arising from tourist-host interactions is the conflict of tourist harassments (Chepkwony & Kangogo, 2013). Meanwhile, Chepkwony and Kangogo (2013) and Barnett (2001) considered that tourists expect to be accorded with warm welcome any time they interact with the host community in the course of their holiday. These expectations of tourists and the warm welcome in terms of food, a place to rest and nice conversation by the host community should be interacted together to keep a well balance between two parties in order to achieve tourism development in the destination. However, the increase of tourist harassment than the feeling of hospitality will cause to leak of economic benefits from destinations. On oppose, it adds more costs to the tourism industry in an economy to implement a proper mechanism in order to overcome the harassment issues. Further, the situation will cause to downfall of global tourism.

According to Sri Lanka Tourist Police, 48 cases in 2010, 82 cases in 2011 and 90 cases in 2012 were recorded as tourism related crimes which included sexual harassment, harassment, frauds, selling illegal gems, charging extra money, not confirming the service before the arrival, providing bad service, robbery, breaking trust, stealing money and property etc., in island wide. Even though, the cases have been divided in to two broader groups like, Case Against Tourist (CAT) and Cases From Tourists (CFT) in order to handle them effectively, the number of cases happened in each year have been increased.

However, as stated by McElory et al. (2007), although terrorism and crime are more serious tourism threats, harassment is one of the most pervasive and least studied problems affecting destinations across the globe. Further, they mentioned tourist harassment as a neglected area of study, and perhaps the least well understood.

TOURISM INDUSTRY IN SRI LANKA

Tourism industry in Sri Lanka has a long historical journey being one of the oldest industries in Sri Lanka. SLTDA (2016) shows the historical evidences for the existence of travel in Ceylon even before the advent of Buddhism; with the travel by Thappassu and Bhalluka, two brothers engaged in trading, continued trade relations with Rome, Greece and East Asian countries like China, and attracting over 5000 Buddhist monks from foreign lands for education purposes. As it mentioned, it was not until the 18th century that travel and tourism was considered an exploitable and commercial exercise. The Government Tourist Bureau (GTB), prior to year 1966 was entrusted with the task of developing and promoting tourism (SLTDA, 2016). As reported in SLTDA (2016), GTB could not effectively undertake any development activity of tourist facilities, services and marketing due to constraints such as limited budgets and poor institutional capacity. However, according to Ceylon Tourist Board (as cited by Buultgens et al., 2016), the potential of tourism to contribute to the country's economic development was initially articulated in 1960s with the release of the first Tourism Management Plan in 1967. With these facts, it is evident that tourism industry is one of Sri Lanka's oldest industries. SLTDA (2018) reported that Sri Lanka has always been an ideal destination to transit and visit since the Silk Route merchants travelled to the East. Further, it discussed the similarity of tea industry and tourism industry. Anyhow, Lokuhetti et al., (2013) mentioned that Sri Lanka commenced organized tourism in 1966 and recorded its highest arrivals record in the pre conflict era, in 1982. After 1983, Sri Lanka faced enumerable challenges due to war and the war ended in 2009. The end of the 26 year war has created an opportunity for Sri Lanka to become a peaceful and one of the fastest growing tourism destinations in the world. Although Sri Lanka has a long history as a tourist destination, there have been ups and downs in the tourism industry in Sri Lanka in recent decades, particularly between 2003 and 2009 due to political violence and the separatist war interspersed with a number of peace episodes (Fernando et al, 2015). After the civil war, tourist arrivals to Sri Lanka have been increased dramatically. The Government identified tourism as a fast emerging potential growth sector in the economy in terms of foreign exchange earnings, employment creation, infrastructure development and regional development (Mathivathany & Sasitharan, n.d.). As they further, explain the up liftmen of the tourism not only benefits for the industry itself but, also supports many other sectors such as agriculture, fisheries, construction, and many more as a multi earning industry. As a result of that many self-employments had been developed while opening up the industries even for the small and medium sector. In line with that, essential needs like telecommunication, infrastructure, hotels, drinking water, sanitary facilities and electricity has been developed by the involvement of public and private sector. So that, for the first time in the history, tourist arrivals reached to new milestone of 2,333,796 (2 million) arrivals in 2018 registering 10.3 percent increase compared to 2017 (SLTDA, 2018). In the same year, as tourism played an important role in the Sri Lankan economy being the third foreign exchange earner after the workers' remittances and textile & garments. After the war, Sri Lanka demonstrated remarkable recovery being one of the booming and dynamic industries in the economy. So that, Ministry of Economic Development launched a Tourism Development Strategy for a five year from

2011 to 2016 with a massive marketing campaign under the slogan of " Sri Lanka- Wonder of Asia". Due to the varied of strategies implemented, now, tourism has become the main driver of economy. Tourism commonly contributes for increasing the income, changing of lifestyles, generating direct and indirect employment, increasing investment opportunities etc. as the economic benefits. According to Welgamage (2014), set of activities related to tourism includes transportation, communication, hotel and food, shopping and entertainment and tourism can generate jobs directly through hotels, restaurants, nightclubs, taxis, and souvenir sales, and indirectly through the supply of goods and services needed by tourism related businesses. In terms of employment, the total number in employment, both direct and indirect, in the tourism sector in 2017 can be estimated as 359,215 (SLTDA, 2017). According to Ranasinghe (2011) many countries give a significant importance for the tourism sector since it is able to generate more foreign earnings towards country and the government of Sri Lanka gives a significant priority to this sector and large number of investors are entering into the sector both large and small scale.

Tourist Attractions in Sri Lanka

Sri Lanka has been filled with natural attractions and man-made attractions where welcome foreigners from every corner of the world. Gnanapala and Sandaruwani (2016) mentioned that Sri Lanka has a massive potential to offer value-added products that could meet the expectations of high-end tourist markets with the rich natural reserves and abundant cultural heritages. As a result of the mixture of golden beaches, rich cultural heritage, diverse landscapes, and a significant number of wildlife, Sri Lanka is classified as one of the most popular tourist destinations in the region (Lai, 2002). Moreover, he further mentioned that Sri Lanka offers a plethora of options for tourists among them beach destinations, favorable climate, rich cultural heritage, national parks and wildlife. Sri Lanka is a glorious paradise in the world and it has been popular because of its geographical location (Mathivathany & Sasitharan, n.d.) As Peebles (2006) explained Sri Lanka has a tropical climate, warm and moist around all the year since it is just situated north of the equator. In addition to that, Sri Lanka is one of the countries where people could experience different nature of climate within two to three hour drive. For an instance, travelers those pass Banadarawela, Ella, Wellawaya and end in Kathatagama, could be able to experience cool climate and as well as hot climate during their journey. According to SLTDA (2018) the culture of Sri Lanka was made up by various influential factors such as, different religious, colonialization by the Dutch, the Portuguese and the British and close connections with India as a neighboring country etc. Additionally, during the last century, Sri Lanka has changed remarkably with global developments, economic growth and intense competition in developed countries. And also, Sri Lankans have ventured overseas and received global exposure on the activities involved. Consequently, this resulted in the integration of the western culture into the Sri Lankan community. Hence, Sri Lanka has diversified culture spread all over the country which is loved by foreigners. Today, cultural tourism has been become more important and popular among the travelers who need to fulfill their cultural needs. For an example, Polonnaruwa, Anuradhapura and Kandy which is known as cultural triangle, Sigiriya rock, Dambulla Cave Temple, Adams' Peak are few attractions visited under cultural tourism. Further, food culture is somewhat different from other Asian countries due to usage of spices, cooking methods, food habits, food belief etc. However, it has enormous amount of culture and heritage-based resources (de Silva, 2000). With regard to the national parks and wildlife reserves, the country has abundant bird life with 251 species resident and no less than 21 indigenous to the island (Mathews, 2000). Based on the national parks and wildlife reserves, different concepts of tourism like, adventure tourism, sustainable tourism, eco-tourism etc. have been marketed by the service providers. According to Fernando et al, (2015), Sri Lanka has 1,585 km of coastline, with Hikkaduwa and Unawatuna as well-known for excellent scuba diving, Mirissa where famous for viewing of whales and dolphins, Tangalle which is promoted as a diving destination and Trincomalee known for its natural harbor with two relatively unexplored beaches. Addition to that, Lai (2002, p 210) states "The southwestern coast is best from November to April and the east coast is best from April to September. Some popular beach spots on the southwestern coast include: Ambalangoda, home of devil-dancing and mask-making; Hikkaduwa, a popular underwater sports site with coral gardens". Therefore, considering that, the country has been marketing for sun, sea and sand.

Market Profile of Sri Lanka Tourism

Tourism demand and supply of Sri Lanka tourism has been mainly focused under the market profile. Tourist arrival is one of the indicators to measure the tourism demand in a country. Tourist arrivals to Sri Lanka during the year 2017 amounted to 2,116,407, registering a 3.2 percent increase since 2016 (SLTDA, 2017). SLTDA analyze the tourist arrivals according to the regional markets. The identified regional markets are America - North, Asia - North East, Asia - South East, Asia - South, Australasia, Europe -West, Europe – East, Middle East and other. Among them, Europe-West was the largest regional market from 2014 to 2017 continuously. The second largest was Asia- South and Middle East shows a drop of tourist arrivals to Sri Lanka from 2015.

According to SLTDA (2017) there are major top ten markets where India being the leading tourism producer to the country. China was the second largest tourism producer and UK was the third. Rest of the listed top ten countries were Germany, France, Maldives, Australia, Russia, USA and Japan. As argued by Fernando et al., (2016), It demonstrates that Sri Lanka's heavily dependence on traditional western tourist markets has declined. On the other hand, emerging Asian economies such as India and China are becoming important tourist markets for Sri Lanka. The tourists receiving from all around the world are classified in to different categories by Sri Lanka tourism based on their purpose of visit to the country in order to measure their motives to visit the country and on the other hand to keep them as data base which is needed for the service supply. SLTDA (2016) records that the majority of the tourist had visited for the purpose of pleasure/holiday (83.4 percent), followed by visiting friends and relatives (11.5 percent). Rest of the share was distributed among the purposes such as business (1.8 percent), convention & meetings (0.8 percent), health (0.6 percent), sports (0.4 percent), official (0.3 percent) and other purposes (1.2 percent). So that, service providers can use these information for plan their business focusing the highlights of the purposes of visiting the country. The average duration of stay of tourists in Sri Lanka during the year 2016 increased to 10.2 nights from 10.1 nights which was recorded in the year of 2015. Further, from the total tourists travelled to Sri Lanka in 2016, 54.7 per cent were female while the rest of the 45.3 per cent were male. There was no significant difference of the proportion in terms of gender. As revealed by the SLTDA (2017), majority of the tourists (42.5 percent) were in between 20 to 39 years of age which is usually called as "young ages". However, another important fact is that Sri Lanka tourism receives majority of tourists fallen under professional category with the percentage of 33 followed by the categories of businessman and educationalist with 19 percent for each. Accessibility to a destination and availability of carriers are another significant criterias for travel decisions. Top three airlines carrying 1.1 million tourists to Sri Lanka were Sri Lankan Airlines, Emirates and Qatar Airlines (SLTDA, 2017).

When turning in to supply side of the tourism in Sri Lanka, it requires to address the needs and wants of diverse of travelers visiting Sri Lanka. SLTDA (2016) mentioned that the total room capacity of the country has in classified, unclassified, boutique hotels and supplementary accommodation units for facilitating the tourists has increased in the same year. It was an increase of 382 units with 22,336 rooms from 354 units with 19,376 rooms in the previous year in tourist hotels and 1,558 units in 2016 from 1,409 units in 2015 in supplementary accommodation establishments. Anyhow, Ministry of Economic Development (2011) targeted and identified the increasing room capacity from 22000 to 45000 in hotels and the informal accommodation sector (guest houses, rest houses, holiday bungalows, home stays and youth hostels) in order to cater the expected number of tourists which was 2.5 million by the year of 2016. But, at the end of the year 2017, the total number of establishments in the registered list of accommodation at SLTDA amounted to 2,094 with 35,986 rooms. The total capacity consisted of 401 tourist hotels and 1,693 supplementary establishments. With the fulfillment of accommodation, employees are needed to cater for the travelers. The Labour Demand Survey by the Department of Census & Statistics (as cited in SLTDA, 2017) analysed the demand for labour within tourism as a subsector, covering the service industry for accommodation and food, as well as transportation providers.

Issues and Challenges Faced by Sri Lanka Tourism

Even though, Sri Lanka is filled with a pool of tourist attractions to attract tourists and gain large number of benefits, it faces many issues due to the increase of number of arrivals. According to SLTDA (2013), tourists who departed from the country had given several suggestions such as the need of better roads, better transport service for them, minimizing environmental pollution etc. while making the negative comments on variation of food available and the standard of the hotels. Lokuhetty (2013) discussed the main challenges which would Sri Lanka face in reaching its optimistic tourism targets under six broad categories incorporate with the six strategies identified. The challenges were infrastructure development, attracting investors, finding adequate numbers of trained staff, conservation of fauna and flora, clear destination positioning and harassment of tourists. Reconstruction work, conservation, rebuilding communities, rebuilding tourism brand, expanding tourism research and restructuring tourism bureaucracies were the strategies presented in line with the challenges. As an addition, Fernando et al, (2016) proved that the industry is facing a shortage of trained workers because of decades of neglect in training tourism workforce due to civil disturbances. Further, they highlighted that even though, government and private sector involve with training staff for tourism industry, still it suffers with severe shortage of employees in the hotel sector. However, the authorities who conduct the training programs to fill the existing human resource gap in the industry should not only target to train them in terms of skills, but, also from attitudes as well to deliver a quality service. Further, as mentioned by Ministry of Economic Development (2011), Sri Lanka Tourism targets the high end tourism moving away from low cost tourism. But, attracting quality tourists has been a major challenge given the state of existing tourism related infrastructure and support (Fernando at el. 2015) as well as the ensuring safety of tourists. Lai (2002), discussed some challenges faced by Sri Lanka Tourism and suggested to improve the existing transportation system for dispersing tourism activities to a greater geographical region and to improve the existing level of accommodation, health and safety network, and on-site facilities. Further, Li, Y.and Wen J. (2015) explained that there are two factors affecting travel decisions on destinations. As they stated, one is about tourists, like the leisure time, disposable money and so on; the other is about the destinations, such as the tourism resource, accessibility and safety. However, it is evident that academic scholars have concentrated on safety and security of the tourists in their studies. More recently, attention has turned to exploring the social impacts of tourism and important research is emerging in this area (Chandralal, 2010) since tourist harassment or visitor harassment have been increased in many destinations like Sri Lanka. As a global phenomenon, tourist harassment is rife in the west and other non-African destinations (Otoo at el. 2019). Tourist harassment being unpleasant behaviors towards to tourist, they closely tied to the existing social structures and can be occurred in different forms in different occasions. For an instance, Ranasinghe (2010) emphasized to take necessary actions by the government to improve the infrastructure facilities while giving a significant attention for road development in order to reduce the traffic jams. Oppose to and with regard to that, availability of poor transport facilities, waiting long time in the traffic, spending long hours on travelling, playing loud music within transport facility, disturbances from vendors and beggars etc. could be the harassment associated with infrastructure facilities subsequently the incidents make traveler unhappy oy annoyed. The hassle free visit around should be facilitated and appropriate legal regulations are recommended to create a conductive environment for tourists (Ranasinghe, 2010). For an instance, the current legislation restricting the issue of liquor licenses to establishments within 500 meters of schools and places of worship (Business Times, 2010). But, it is wise worthy to inform tourists before visiting those establishments, because of their expectations to fulfill the food and beverage requirements together. On the other hand, there are some tourism related businesses which are not registered under Sri Lanka Tourist Board (SLTB) and reported some harassment with in the business premises. For an instance, the surf bar and restaurant in Mirissa, where eight Dutch tourists assaulted over the weekend, was not registered with the SLTB, as stipulated by the Tourism Act No.38 of 2005 (Sunday Observer, 2018/04/15). However, it has been revealed that the establishment had obtained the liquor license despite being an unregistered tourist establishment. Now, it is proved that the genuine need of proper and active legal system to the industry. Furthermore, Lai (200) suggested to formulate comprehensive policies and criteria for tourism development in and adjacent to coastal areas, heritage sites, ecologically sensitive areas, and National Parks. The culture and history are considered as one of the major travel motives of the tourists visit Sri Lanka (Pathirana and Gnanapala, 2015) and the tourists would like to accompany with the tour guides to make the journey more quality, safe, memorable and effective. Specially, in Sigiriya area, they highlighted the issues related to the tourism industry such as, selling goods forcefully, availability of poor sanitary facilities, inconvenience situation from animals like street dogs and also the harassment from the site guides/helpers at site, vendors etc. Rathnayake and Wijesundara (2015) mentioned that the cases of tourists being robbed, murdered or sexually harassed are reported often in several destinations in Sri Lanka. The way of reporting was most probably through newspaper articles and media. However, recently, a 38 years old Czech tourist who was holidaying with his girlfriend was being robbed by a group of three men in a van and the tourist lost 500 Euros, credit cards, driving license, and insurance documents. Further, the theft of cash, cameras, ipads, laptops, communication equipment and also loss of travel documents were recorded from the same area. In conclusion to that, carrying or keeping worth equipment and utensils is in a danger. Moreover, not only the outside of the hotels, but also inside of the hotel premises, some harassment done by hotel staff were recorded. For an instance, in a more serious vein, a hotel employee attempted to rape a 35 year old female tourist while she was asleep in her room (Sri Lanka Brief, 2013/04). Anyhow, this situation should not be continued as it badly affect to the entire tourism industry. On the other hand, Lai (2002) suggested to educate foreign tourists to be sensitive and respect local customs; and encourage community involvement in planning and managing tourism development. In Sri Lanka context, some of the local communities hesitate to accept and engage in tourism industry due to the associated risks in terms of socio-cultural. This situation can be a base for tourist harassments from the host community. However, it is clear that many of the issues and challenges arose from the host community due to their perception on tourism industry.

OBJECTIVES OF THE PRESENT STUDY

Amidst to the present situation, three main objectives were set out for the study. The objective were to identify the types of tourist harassment in tourist destination in Southern Coastal Belt of Sri Lanka, to observe the reasons for taking place of tourist harassment in the tourist destinations and finally to identify the solutions for overcoming tourist harassment in Southern Coastel Belt of Sri Lanka.

Methodology and Result Discussion

The research site of the study was limited to the coastal belt of Southern Province which consists of three (03) districts namely Galle, Matara and Hambanthota and nearly fifteen (15) popular beach tourism destinations are situated such as Benthota, Balapitiya, Ambalangoda, Hikkaduwa, Galle, Unawatuna, Koggala, Weligama, Matara, Mirissa, Polhena, Dondra, Dickwella, Tangalle and Hambanthota. All of the foreign tourists select southern coastal belt as one of the main tourist destinations while visiting in Sri Lanka. According to the SLTDA (as cited in Samarathunga, 2018) illustrated that the majority of the tourists visiting the country are either starts or ends their journey from a beach destination. There were two reasons to select Southern coastal belt; visiting the area by many of the tourists being first reason, the second was records of the increased number of tourist harassment continuously through media and tourist police from the area.

The respondent for the study were foreign tourists who visited Southern Coastal belt of Sri Lanka. Comprising self-reported indicators on variables, a pre tested questionnaire with open-ended and closed-ended questions was developed as survey instrument for collecting primary data from the sample. The questionnaire consisted with three parts; Part 'A' for collecting demographic data of the sample with categorical data, Part 'B' for identifying types of tourist harassment with scale data and Part 'C' for observing reasons for tourist harassment and identifying strategies to overcome tourist harassment in Southern coastal belt of Sri Lanka with open ended questions.

Among 600 questionnaire, 530 were useful and they were entered to Statistical Package for the Social Sciences (SPSS) 21 version while employing Exploratory Factor Analysis (EFA) to identify the most important indicators in the questionnaire. Because, Hair et al. (2006) suggested that EFA can be applied for reduction of data through identification of representative variables from a larger set of variables for further application of multivariate analysis. Principal Component Analysis was employed for exploratory factor analysis with KMO & Bartlett's Test of Sphericity in order to ensure that the data matrix has sufficient correlations to justify the application of factor analysis. KMO & Bartlett's Test of Sphericity is a measure of sampling adequacy that is recommended to check the case to variable ratio for the analysis being conducted (Sriram, 2012). In statistics, while the KMO ranges from 0 to 1, the world-over accepted index is over 0.6. Also, the Bartlett's Test of Sphericity relates to the significance of the study and thereby shows the validity and suitability of the responses collected to the problem being addressed through the study. For the factor analysis to be recommended suitable, the Bartlett's Test of Sphericity must be less than 0.05. Considering that, the same test was applied for the 36 items under Tourist Harassment. According to the SPSS output of tourist harassment, KMO value of 0.610 is in accepted level and the Bartlett's Test of Sphericity recorded a value of 0.000 which is less than 0.05. Therefore, it was concluded that satisfactory factor analysis can be employed with the available data set.

According to the EFA output, six (6) factors were extracted as dimensions/types of tourist harassment based on factor loadings (as shown in the Table 1) and they were named accordingly as the Consumption Based Harassment (7 items), Expression Based Harassment (5 items), Community Based Harassment (5 items), Vocal Based Harassment (3 items), Sexuality Based Harassment (2 items) and Drugs Based Harassment (2 items).

Types of Tourist Harassment in Coastal Tourist Destinations

According to the EFA output shown in the table 01, mainly six (06) types of harassment were identified which are occurred in the tourist destination Southern Coastal Belt of Sri Lanka.

1. Consumption Based Harassment (ConBH)

There were 7 indicators lorded together as per the factor loadings. The indicators illustrate the nature of harassment happened to tourist when consumption attempts are made during their vacation in destinations in Southern Coastal Belt. Particularly, the consumption attempts of the tourists were related to their financial needs, the service needs and shopping needs.

2. Expression Based Harassment (ExpBH)

In here, mainly 5 indicators implicate to identify the Expression Based Harassment in the tourist destination. They are predominantly in the form of either verbal or physical, but as a result of the communication process in between tourists and harassers.

3. Community Based Harassment (ComBH)

As same as ExpBH, Community Based Harassment are shown by 5 indicators with the factor loading. ComBH are mainly associated with the behaviours of community people lived in the tourist destinations.

4. Vocal Based Harassment (VocBH)

There were 3 indicators found to express the nature of Vocal Based Harassment which were directly occurred verbally. But, they have occurred as face to face harassment or distance harassment.

5. Sexuality Based Harassment (SexBH)

Under Sexuality Based Harassment, 2 indicators were found to express the nature of SexBH. In here, particularly they happened as a result of involvement with tourism service providers.

6. Drugs Based Harassment (DruBH)

Table 1. Factors Extracted from EFA for Tourist Harassment

Rotated Component Matrix[a]						
	Component					
	1	2	3	4	5	6
I was overcharged for my consumption during my travel	.745					
I was provided incorrect financial information on requested service	.721					
Vendors forced me to enter their shops when I do window shopping	.720					
I was forced to purchase by local vendors when I engaged with tourism activities such as sun bathing, sightseeing, excursions, travelling etc.	.719					
Vendors used non-physical acts such as cat talks, leers to encouraging purchase	.657					
I experienced financial frauds when I exchange foreign currencies and use my debit/credit cards for payment	.656					
Vendors charged for unused services and adding on extra charges	.525					
The reasons for beating were misunderstanding, miscommunication, language barriers, cultural issues etc.		.889				
I experienced beating while engaging with tourism activities		.865				
I started beating first and then I was beaten		.854				
I understood that beating is an initiative of interacting with tourists		.848				
Vendors did not allow me to buy what I really needed		.561				
They followed me until I offer something for them			.872			
I was approached by different types of beggars such as adults, children, disabled, performance, story tellers, passive, buskers, forcing-service etc. at many destinations in Sri Lanka			.786			
When I offered something for one person, more beggars gathered around me			.635			
Vendors used abusive and intimidating language when purchase was refused			.574			
I did not receive promised service which I paid for			.513			
I experienced cat calls during my stay in Sri Lanka				.872		
I faced verbal harassment such as cat talks, leers, blaming etc. in the destination				.794		
I felt that verbal harassment is used to encourage purchase, look at local people etc.				.784		
When I ignored their behavior, they harassed me in other forms of harassment such as verbal, pestering, beating etc.					.866	
As I felt, sexual harassment is a way of encouraging towards to their business ex: beach boys, tour guides, hotel staff					.836	
I understood that people around me during my travel helped for drug peddling						.881
I was forced to buy/use drugs during my travel						.837
Extraction Method: Principal Component Analysis. Rotation Method: Varimax with Kaiser Normalization.						
a. Rotation converged in 7 iterations.						

Source: Survey Data, 2018

Like SexBH, only 2 factors were loaded to understand the nature of Drugs Based Harassment which are directly linked with drug usage, drug purchasing and forcing for drugs etc.

The Reasons for Taking Place of Tourist Harassment in the Tourist Destinations

The second objective of the study was to observe the reasons happened to tourist harassment in the destination. To achieve that, an open ended question was asked in the pre-tested questionnaire. The question was "What would be the reasons for happening tourist harassment in the tourist destinations in Southern Coastal Belt of Sri Lanka?" With the comprehensive analysis, the following can be presented as major reasons to occur tourist harassment in the destinations.

1. Level of care made by tourist on consumption needs/activities

Here, it can be guessed that the harassers or perpetrators may have considered whether the tourists directly care or indirectly care on consumption activities. Because, the harassment where tourists mostly agreed depend on the level of care or aware made by the tourists. For an example, perpetrators can overcharge on consumption if he or she feels that the tourists are not much caring the activity. Simply, it is called "ignorance".

2. Demography of the tourists

Majority of the tourist respondents were in young ages being first time visitors to Sri Lanka with the purpose of leisure. Hence, they have been spent money more on their consumption activities and since they are first time visitors to Sri Lanka, may have face higher rate of harassment (Chepkwony, 2013; de Albuquerque & McElory, 2001) on their consumption activities. On oppose, since the majority from Europe countries, perpetrators have been focused the type of tourists to interact (SLCSR, 2015; Ajagunna, 2006). Therefore, demographic of the tourists may possibly influence on perpetrators to do harassment based on consumption.

3. Misapprehension of information/behaviour

When the tourism happened in a destination it usually deals with different cultures; norms, believes, behaviours, expressions, languages etc. But, suggestive selling, product or service promotion, selling available goods/service with the vendors, vendor competition, expectation of high earn and making interest of local products are happened in order to provide necessary products and services for the tourists. With these activities misapprehension can be happened and it will be depend on the level of perception or understanding of host culture.

4. Nature of the place for tourism activities

It was observed that beaches and streets are the hotspots for happening harassment (Chepkwony & Kangogo, 2013; McElory et al, 2007; Rathnayake &Wijesundara, 2015). In the streets, even though there is a possibility to ignore the harassment, there is no ignorance on the beach. Because, majority of the foreigners expect to spend whole day in the beach. On the other hand, retaining foreigners in the beach or destination is important for other group of community people those who provide the goods and services for the guests. In conclusion, it is a matter of host community people creating two groups with different characteristics and directly influence on tourist behaviour and their activities.

5. Huge competition among service providers

There are plenty of service providers around the Southern Castel belt. But, the similarity of them is making efforts to sell a same featured product/service for the tourists while giving a competition for the competitors in the destination. And also, they are purely depended on tourism industry facing economical fluctuations due to seasonal businesses. Hence, everybody gives a huge competition beating to their own people in order to catch tourists for their business. Finally, it comes to tourist as a matter of harassment not as a way of fulfilment of their travel needs.

The Solutions for Overcoming Tourist Harassment in Southern Coastal Belt of Sri Lanka

The third objective of the present study was to find out the solutions for overcoming the tourist harassment in Southern Coastal of Sri Lanka. An open-ended question as "What do you suggest to overcome the harassment happened in Southern Coastal Belt of Sri Lanka?" was inserted to the questionnaire to know the tourists suggestions in details. However, they have given valuable opinions from their perspective. The given suggestions were summarized as follows.

1. Organizing language courses not only for direct interactive people but also for government officers since they are dealing with tourists at government establishments without having language proficiency like, German, French, Russian
2. Formalizing the language learning of beach boys by providing a certificate or letter etc. to make better relationship with government and also to deal with tourists in a professional manner
3. Building a "Performers zone" for vendors and beggars as they are entertained by the tourists since it displays the local culture
4. Prohibiting begging activities at the beach by beggars, male or female with kids
5. Establishing police patrols at the beach for ensuring safety and security of the people and properties
6. Issuing precautions on possible accidents, risks, risky people, environment changes etc.
7. Be aware on access of outside service providers with or without licenses
8. Frequently check-up on licenses or permission, temporary arranged illegal but, usual vendor huts and people who different in nature
9. Giving permission and schedule to conduct entertainment shows by beach restaurants at the beach.
10. Stopping communication of worst information via media and word of mouth.
11. Maintaining and taking actions to black list the harassers and not allowing them to go for other jobs
12. Introducing new three-wheelers for tourists in different places for ensuring safety and security on travel
13. Introducing shop list for shopping avoiding unusual overcharging, providing poor quality goods, etc.

14. Educating parents on impacts of children involvement in tourism industry without schooling
15. Conducting health clinics at the beaches for people like beach boys, vendors, beggars to mainly avoid spread of diseases
16. Providing trailer bikes for police officers in order to access speedy to the locations

According to the findings of the present study, it is true that tourist to Southern Coastal Belt face different harassment during their vacation. The study presents the nature of the harassment that they face, the reasons to occur the harassment and the solutions for overcoming the harassment from their perspective. From that, it is easy to identify the expectations of travellers from the host destination and it would be a better opportunity for the host community to understand about their customers. Through that, major problems which will be bases for harassment can be avoided. However, when making attempts to minimize tourist harassment, equal concern should be given to tourists and host community as they are bound to the chain of tourism. Moreover, the proposed solutions can be applied in global context to overcome the business failures occurred due to tourist harassment.

CONCLUSION

At present, Sri Lanka Tourism has been given a major attention on tourist harassment and ensuring safety and security of the tourists who travelled to Sri Lanka. And also, varied harassment happened to tourists were published through the media. Considering the potential influence of tourist harassment on tourist arrivals to the country, this study mainly focused to find out the types of tourist harassment, the reasons to happened them and solutions to overcome the harassment. As the results revealed, six main tourist harassment were identified namely Consumption Based Harassment, Expression Based Harassment, Community Based Harassment and Vocal Based Harassment, Sexuality Based Harassment and Drug Based Harassment. However, the proposed solutions to overcome tourist harassment will be mainly based on the host community and the facilities available within the destinations for tourist consumption process. Simply, it means there are more to satisfy the travelers visiting Southern Coastal Belt of Sri Lanka. Hence, this study shows the nature of harassment and it will be a significant base for tourism planners in the country to build Sri Lanka as a harassment free destination.

FUTURE RESEARCH

The present study deals with perspective of tourists only. But, it is necessary to know the perspective of harassers who are labelled by the community; vendors, beggars, children, beach boys etc. Because, potential harassers or the labelled people may see the incidents in a different aspect with their societal and educational backgrounds. Knowing the tourists' perspective and harassers' perspective, then the gap between hospitality and tourist harassment can be identified.

REFERENCES

Ajagunna, I. (2006). Crime and harassment in Jamaica: Consequences for sustainability of the tourism industry. *International Journal of Contemporary Hospitality Management, 18*(3), 253–259. doi:10.1108/09596110610658652

Cohen, R. (1984). The Sociology of tourism: Approaches, issues and findings. *Annual Review of Sociology, 10*(1), 373–392. doi:10.1146/annurev.so.10.080184.002105

Cortina, J. (2002). Big things have small beginnings: An assortment of "minor" methodological misunderstandings. *Journal of Management, 28*(3), 339–362. doi:10.1177/014920630202800305

De Albuquerque, K., & McElroy, J. L. (2001). Tourist harassment: Barbados survey results. *Annals of Tourism Research, 28*(2), 477–492. doi:10.1016/S0160-7383(00)00057-8

Gnanapala, W. K. A., & Sandaruwani, J. A. R. C. (2016). Impacts of Tourism Development in Cultural and Heritage Sites: An Empirical Investigation. *International Journal of Economics and Business Administration, 6*(2), 68–78.

Jayawardena, C. (2013). Innovative solutions for future tourism development in Sri Lanka (2013-2026). *Worldwide Hospitality and Tourism Themes, 5*(5), 512–531. doi:10.1108/WHATT-05-2013-0033

Jenkins, J. (1991). Tourism Development Strategies. In *Developing Tourism Destinations, 61-77, Harow*. Longman.

Kotler, P., Keller, K. L., Khoshi, A., & Jha, M. (2012). *Marketing Management: A South Asian perspective* (13th ed.). Pearson Education-India.

Kozak, M. (2007). Tourist harassment: A marketing perspective. *Annals of Tourism Research, 34*(2), 384–399. doi:10.1016/j.annals.2006.10.003

Lokuhetty, A., Jayawardhana, C., & Mudadeniya, D. (2013). Developing a shared vision for tourism in post-war Sri Lanka. *Worldwide Hospitality and Tourism Themes, 5*(5), 486–494. doi:10.1108/WHATT-05-2013-0030

Lopes, S. D. F. (2011). Destination image: Origins, developments and implications. PASOS. *Revista de Turismo y Patrimonio Cultural, 9*(2), 305–315. doi:10.25145/j.pasos.2011.09.027

Mason, P. (2008). *Tourism Impacts, Planning and Management*. Routledge.

McElroy, J. L., Tarlow, P., & Carlisle, K. (2007). 5 Tourist Harassment and Responses. *Analysis, Behaviour and Strategy, 94*.

Pathirana, D., & Gnanapala, W. A. (2015). Tourists' Harassment at Cultural Sites in Sri Lanka. Tourism. *Leisure and Global Change, 2*(1), 42–56.

Pearce, P., (1982). Perceived Changes in Holiday Destinations. *Annals of Tourism Research, 9*, 145-164.

Peter, M. (2008). *Tourism impacts, planning and management*. Butterworth-Heinemann.

Ranasinghe, J. (2012). Tourists' Satisfaction and Behavioral Intentions: An Empirical Evidence from Tourism Industry in Sri Lanka. *Proceedings of International Conference on Business Management.*

Ranasinghe, R., & Deyshappriya, R. (2012). *Analyzing the significance of tourism on Sri Lankan economy.* Retrieved from https://www.kln.ac.lk/fcms/ICBI2012/images/ICBM/dccs/TRM001.pdf

Rathnayake, R. D., & Wijesundara, W. G. (2015). *Tourist perception on harassments in Sri Lanka (with special reference to Mount Lavinia).* Academic Press.

Sharpley, R. (2002). Rural tourism and the challenge of tourism diversification: The case of Cyprus. *Tourism Management, 23*(3), 233–244.

Sieber, S. D. (1973). The integration of fieldwork and survey methods. *American Journal of Sociology, 78*(6), 1335–1359. doi:10.1086/225467

Sri Lanka Tourism Development Authority. (2016). *Annual Statistical Report 2015.* Sri Lanka Tourism Development Authority.

Sri Lanka Tourist Police. (2012). *Statistical Records.* Sri Lanka Tourist Police.

Compilation of References

Abdalla, I. A. (2015). Being and Becoming a Leader: Arabian Gulf Women Managers' Perspectives. *International Journal of Business and Management, 10*(1), 25.

Abhishek Upadhyay. (2019, July 26). *What is HR Automation? Techrseries.* Available at https://www.techrseries.com/primer/what-is-hr-automation/

Abukari, A. J., & Abdul-Hamid, I. K. (2018). Corporate social responsibility reporting in the telecommunications sector in Ghana. *International Journal of Corporate Social Responsibility, 3*(1), 2. doi:10.118640991-017-0025-9

ACCA. (n.d.). *Social and environmental narrative reporting: analysts' perceptions.* https://www.accaglobal.com/gb/en/technical-activities/technical-resources-search/2008/november/perceptions-narrative-reporting.html

Adams, C. A. (2002). Internal organisational factors influencing corporate social and ethical reporting. *Accounting, Auditing & Accountability Journal, 15*(2), 223–250. doi:10.1108/09513570210418905

Aerts, W., & Cormier, D. (2009). Media legitimacy and corporate environmental communication. *Accounting, Organizations and Society, 34*(1), 1–27. doi:10.1016/j.aos.2008.02.005

Afiouni, F., Karam, C. M., & El-Hajj, H. (2013). The HR value proposition model in the Arab Middle East: Identifying the contours of an Arab Middle Eastern HR model. *International Journal of Human Resource Management, 24*(10), 1895–1932. doi:10.1080/09585192.2012.722559

Agars, M. D. (2004). Reconsidering the impact of gender stereotypes on the advancement of women in organizations. *Psychology of Women Quarterly, 28*(2), 103–111. doi:10.1111/j.1471-6402.2004.00127.x

Agarwal, S., Debarati, B., Pulak, G., Bhuvanesh, P. & Jian, Z. (2018). *Demonetization and Digitization.* Available at SSRN: https: //ssrn.com/abstract=3197990

Agentestudio.com. (2019). *User-Centered Design: Principles, Processes and Examples | AGENTE.* Available at: https://agentestudio.com/blog/user-centered-design-examples

Aggarwal, N., & Narayanan, S. (2017). *Impact of India's demonetization on domestic agricultural markets.* Indira Gandhi Institute of Development Research. Available at http://www.igidr.ac.in/pdf/publication/WP-2017-023.pdf

Ahrens, N. (2013). *China's competitiveness: myth, reality and lessons for the United States and Japan: Case Study Huawei, February 2013.* Center for Strategic and International Studies.

Ajagunna, I. (2006). Crime and harassment in Jamaica: Consequences for sustainability of the tourism industry. *International Journal of Contemporary Hospitality Management, 18*(3), 253–259. doi:10.1108/09596110610658652

Akhaya, P. (2020, January 30). *Indonesian e-commerce site Blibli embraces New Retail with BlibliMart launch.* Academic Press.

Akhtar, B., Akhter, W., & Shahbaz, M. (2017). Determinants of deposits in conventional and Islamic banking: A case of an emerging economy. *International Journal of Emerging Markets*, *12*(2), 296–309. doi:10.1108/IJoEM-04-2015-0059

Akhtera, W., Majeedb, M. U., & Roubaudc, D. (2019). Islamic Banking and Financial Inclusion: Evidence from Asian and African Markets. *Journal of Islamic Business and Management*, *9*(2), 341–354. doi:10.26501/jibm/2019.0902-007

Alazzani, A., & Wan-Hussin, W. N. (2013). Global Reporting Initiative's environmental reporting: A study of oil and gas companies. *Ecological Indicators*, *32*, 19–24. doi:10.1016/j.ecolind.2013.02.019

Ali, N. (2015). *The Role of Cement Industry in the Economic Development of Pakistan*. EduPedia Publications (P) Ltd.

Alimo-Metcalfe, B. (2010). An investigation of female and male constructs of leadership and empowerment. *Gender in Management*, *25*(8), 640–648. doi:10.1108/17542411011092309

Al-Tuwaijri, S. A., Christensen, T. E., & Hughes, K. (2004). The relations among environmental disclosure, environmental performance, and economic performance: A simultaneous equations approach. *Accounting, Organizations and Society*, *29*(5–6), 447–471. doi:10.1016/S0361-3682(03)00032-1

Al-Wesabi, H. A. (2020). Credit risk of Islamic banks in GCC countries. *International. Journal of Banking & Finance*, *10*(2), 95–112. http://e-journal.uum.edu.my/index.php/ijbf/article/view/8476/1421

Amirio, D. (2016). Mitra Adiperkasa announces own marketplace. *The Jakarta Post.* Retrieved from: https://www.thejakartapost.com/news/2016/02/19/mitra-adiperkasa-announces-own-marketplace.html

Anbar, A., & Alper, D. (2011). Bank specific and macroeconomic determinants of commercial bank profitability: Empirical evidence from Turkey. *Business and Economics Research Journal, 2*(2), 139-152. Retrieved from https://papers.ssrn.com/sol3/papers.cfm?abstract_id=1831345

Anderson, L. S., Bell, H. G., Gilbert, M., Davidson, J. E., Winter, C., Barratt, M. J., Win, B., Painter, J. L., Menone, C., Sayegh, J., & Dasgupta, N. (2017). Using Social Listening Data to Monitor Misuse and Nonmedical Use of Bupropion: A Content Analysis. *MIR Public Health and Surveillance*, *3*(1), 2369–2960. doi:10.2196/publichealth.6174 PMID:28148472

Andrikopoulos, A., Samitas, A., & Bekiaris, M. (2014). Corporate social responsibility reporting in financial institutions: Evidence from Euronext. *Research in International Business and Finance*, *32*, 27–35. doi:10.1016/j.ribaf.2014.02.001

Aracil, E. (2019). Corporate social responsibility of Islamic and conventional banks. *International Journal of Emerging Markets*, *14*(4), 582–600. doi:10.1108/IJOEM-12-2017-0533

Aras, G., Tezcan, N., & Furtuna, O. K. (2018). The value relevance of the banking sector multidimensional corporate sustainability performance. *Corporate Social Responsibility and Environmental Management*, *25*(6), 1062–1073. doi:10.1002/csr.1520

Archel, P., Husillos, J., Larrinaga, C., & Spence, C. (2009). Social disclosure, legitimacy theory and the role of the state. *Accounting, Auditing & Accountability Journal*, *22*(8), 1284–1307. doi:10.1108/09513570910999319

Aribi, Z. A., & Gao, S. S. (2012). Narrative disclosure of corporate social responsibility in Islamic financial institutions. *Managerial Auditing Journal*, *27*(2), 199–222.

Arismunandar, A. (2018, August 20). *Indonesian Retailers Need Better Digital Integration.* Jakarta Globe. Retrieved from: https://jakartaglobe.id/business/indonesian-retailers-need-better-digital-integration/

Arthur, C. (2018). *Huawei, sanctions and software: everything you need to know.* The Guardian. https://www.theguardian.com/technology/2018/dec/08/huawei-sanctions-software-what-you-need-to-know

Aruna, V., & Abdul Gafoor, A. (2012). Foreign direct investment (FDI) in the muli-brand retail sector in India - A boon or bane. *IEEE-International Conference On Advances In Engineering, Science And Management (ICAESM -2012)*, 32-35.

Aruwa, S., & Hemen, A. (2011). Corporate social responsibility and organizational performance in Nigeria: A survey of the cement industry. *Journal of Entrepreneurship Research*, *1*(1), 57–74. doi:10.1093/icesjms/16.3.384

Askari Bank. (2013). *Annual Report of Askari Bank Limited for 2013*. http://akbl.com.pk/wp-content/uploads/2014/12/Askari-AR-2013.pdf

Asma' Rashidah Idris, F. F. A., Asari, H., Taufik, N. A. A., Salim, N. J., Mustaffa, R., & Jusoff, K. (2011). Determinant of Islamic banking institutions' profitability in Malaysia. *World Appl. Sci. J*, *12*, 1-7. Retrieved from http://citeseerx.ist.psu.edu/viewdoc/download?doi=10.1.1.390.3689&rep=rep1&type=pdf

Associated Press. (2005). *China's Huawei pursues Britain's Marconi*. China Daily. https://www.chinadaily.com.cn/english/doc/2005-08/10/content_467796.htm

Astari, I. S., Huliselan, J. J., & Jong, M. T. T. (2017). Customer showrooming behaviour and the effect on salesperson performance. *DeReMa Jurnal Manajemen*, *12*(2), 187–213. doi:10.19166/derema.v12i2.525

Atasu, A., Guide, V. D. R. Jr, & Van Wassenhove, L. N. (2010). So what if remanufacturing cannibalizes my new product sales. *California Management Review*, *52*(2), 56–76. doi:10.1525/cmr.2010.52.2.56

Atasu, A., Sarvary, M., & Van Wassenhove, L. N. (2008). Remanufacturing as a marketing strategy. *Management Science*, *54*(10), 1731–1746. doi:10.1287/mnsc.1080.0893

Awan, A. G., & Akhtar, N. (2014). The impact of Corporate Social Responsibility (CSR) on profitability of firms: A case study of fertilizer and cement industry in Southern Punjab, Pakistan. *International Journal of Development and Economic Sustainability*, *2*(4), 1682–1690.

Azad, A. S., Azmat, S., & Hayat, A. (2019). What determines the profitability of Islamic banks: Lending or fee? *International Review of Economics & Finance*, 1–15. doi:10.1016/j.iref.2019.05.015

Aziz, N. I. M. (2017). Islamic Banking Profitability: Roles played by Internal and External Banking Factors. *The Journal of Muamalat and Islamic Finance Research*, *14*(1), 23–38. http://jmifr.usim.edu.my/index.php/jmifr/article/view/12

Azizul Islam, M. (2017). CSR Reporting and Legitimacy Theory: Some Thoughts on Future Research Agenda. In M. Aluchna & S. Idowu (Eds.), *The Dynamics of Corporate Social Responsibility* (pp. 323–339). doi:10.1007/978-3-319-39089-5_17

Babich, N. (2019). *Principles of Human-Centered Design*. Available at: http://babich.biz/principles-of-human-centered-design/

Badke-Schaub, P., & And Frankenberger, E. (1999). Analysis of design projects. *Design Studies*, *20*(5), 465–480. doi:10.1016/S0142-694X(99)00017-4

Bakhtina, K., & Goudriaan, J. W. (2011). CSR reporting in multinational energy companies. *Transfer: European Review of Labour and Research*, *17*(1), 95–99. doi:10.1177/1024258910396308

Bakos, Y. (2001). The emerging landscape for retail E-commerce. *The Journal of Economic Perspectives*, *15*(1), 69–80. Advance online publication. doi:10.1257/jep.15.1.69

Balaji, M. S., Roy, S. K., Sengupta, A., & Chong, A. (2018). User acceptance of IoT applications in retail industry. In Technology Adoption and Social Issues: Concepts, Methodologies, Tools, and Applications (pp. 1331-1352). IGI Global. doi:10.4018/978-1-5225-5201-7.ch061

Banerjee, D. (2020). *Covid pandemic,social media and digital distancing.* Available at: https://www.newindianexpress.com/opinions/2020/may/06/covid-pandemicsocial-media-and-digital-distancing-2139724.html

Banerjee, S. (2020). Institutionalization of Corporate Social Responsibility (CSR) in India and Its Effects on CSR Reporting: A Case Study of the Petroleum and Gas Industry. In N. Mitra & R. Schmidpeter (Eds.), *Mandated Corporate Social Responsibility* (pp. 141–157). CSR, Sustainability, Ethics & Governance. doi:10.1007/978-3-030-24444-6_8

Bania, N., Gray, J. A., & Stone, J. A. (2007). Growth, taxes, and government expenditures: Growth hills for US states. *National Tax Journal, 60*(2), 193–204. doi:10.17310/ntj.2007.2.02

Banking for Society. (n.d.). What do we mean by corporate social responsibility and socially responsible banking? Author.

Barras, R. (1986). Towards a theory of innovation in services. *Research Policy, 15*(4), 161–173. doi:10.1016/0048-7333(86)90012-0

Bashir, N., Papamichail, K. N., & Malik, K. (2017). Use of Social Media Applications for Supporting New Product Development Processes in Multinational Corporations. *Technological Forecasting & Social Change: An International Journal, 120*(C), 176–183. doi:10.1016/j.techfore.2017.02.028

BasuMallick. (2018, July 20). *Automating Employee Performance Management-HR Technologist.* Available at https://www.hrtechnologist.com/articles/performance-management-hcm/automating-employee-performance-management/

BBC. (2019). *The US cannot crush us, says Huawei founder, Interview with Huawei founder Ren Zhengfei.* BBC. https://www.bbc.com/news/business-47274679

Bear, M. (2015). Survival of the fittest: Using social media to thrive in the 21st century. *Journal of Brand Strategy, 4*(2), 106–113.

Beattie, V. (2014). Accounting narratives and the narrative turn in accounting research: Issues, theory, methodology, methods and a research framework. *The British Accounting Review, 46*(2), 111–134. doi:10.1016/j.bar.2014.05.001

Bebbington, J., Unerman, J., & O'Dwyer, B. (2014). *Sustainability accounting and accountability* (2nd ed.). Routledge.

Beck, A. C., Campbell, D., & Shrives, P. J. (2010). Content analysis in environmental reporting research: Enrichment and rehearsal of the method in a British–German context. *The British Accounting Review, 42*(3), 207–222.

Becker, G. S. (1968). Crime and punishment: An economic approach. In *The economic dimensions of crime* (pp. 13–68). Palgrave Macmillan. doi:10.1007/978-1-349-62853-7_2

Becker, G. S., & Stigler, G. J. (1974). Law enforcement, malfeasance, and compensation of enforcers. *The Journal of Legal Studies, 3*(1), 1–18. doi:10.1086/467507

Belal, A. R., & Cooper, S. (2011). The absence of corporate social responsibility reporting in Bangladesh. *Critical Perspectives on Accounting, 22*(7), 654–667.

Bellon, M. M., Chang, J., Dabla-Norris, M. E., Khalid, S., Lima, F., Rojas, E., & Villena, P. (2019). *Digitalization to Improve Tax Compliance: Evidence from VAT e-Invoicing in Peru.* International Monetary Fund. doi:10.5089/9781513513713.001

Ben Khediri, K., & Ben-Khedhiri, H. (2011). Determinants of bank net interest margin in Tunisia: A panel data model. *Applied Economics Letters, 18*(13), 1267–1271. doi:10.1080/13504851.2010.534052

Berry, L. L. (1980). Services Marketing Is Different. *Business (Atlanta, Ga.), 30*(May), 24–29.

Berry, L., Carbone, L., & Haeckel, S. (2002). Managing the Total Customer Experience. *MIT Sloan Management Review*, 43.

Berry, L., Shankar, V., Parish, J., Cadwallader, S., & Dotzel, T. (2006). Creating New Markets Through Service. *MIT Sloan Management Review*, 47.

Bersin, J. (2017). *HR and HR Technology in India: Growth, Purpose and Value*. SHRM.

Berthelot, S., Coulmont, M., & Thibault, K. (2013). Sustainability Content on Oil and Gas Company Websites. *Business and Management Research*, *2*(1), 94–103. doi:10.5430/bmr.v2n1p94

Berthon, P. R., Pitt, L. F., Plangger, K., & Shapiro, D. (2012). Marketing meets Web 2.0, social media, and creative consumers: Implications for international marketing strategy. *Business Horizons*, *55*(3), 261–271. doi:10.1016/j.bushor.2012.01.007

Bhattacharyya, S. S., & Deepak, P. K. (2012). Comprehending the changing global iron ore trade service system and the dynamics of pricing. *International Journal of Business and Globalisation*, *9*(1), 70–89. doi:10.1504/IJBG.2012.047523

Bhattacharyya, S. S., & Jha, S. (2014). Development of a model on profit orientation with organizational variables in the context of emerging economies. *Journal of Asia Business Studies*, *8*(3), 264–277. doi:10.1108/JABS-05-2013-0026

Bhattacharyya, S. S., Jha, S., & Fernandes, C. (2015). Determinants of speed to market in the context of the emerging Indian market. *Asia Pacific Journal of Marketing and Logistics*, *27*(5), 784–800. doi:10.1108/APJML-12-2014-0172

Bhattacharyya, S. S., Rangarajan, R., & Vyas, K. G. (2012). Reflections on mapping chaos in the business organisational landscape. *International Journal of Business Innovation and Research*, *6*(1), 76–116. doi:10.1504/IJBIR.2012.044258

Bhavnani, R. R., & Copelovitch, M. (2018). *The Political Impact of Monetary Shocks: Evidence from India's 2016 Demonetization, January*. Available at SSRN: https://ssrn.com/abstract=3095228

Bhimani, H., Laure, A., & Barlatier, P. A. (2019). Social media and innovation: A systematic literature review and future research directions. *Technological Forecasting and Social Change: An International Journal*, *144*, 251–269. doi:10.1016/j.techfore.2018.10.007

Bhuvaneswaran. (2019, November 12). *Employee Offboarding – Kissflow*. Available at https://kissflow.com/hr-process/employee-offboarding/exit-interview-process/

Bickel, J., & Brown, A. J. (2005). Generation X: Implications for faculty recruitment and development in academic health centers. *Academic Medicine*, *80*(3), 205–210. doi:10.1097/00001888-200503000-00003 PMID:15734801

Bidabad, B., & Allahyarifard, M. (2019). IT role in fulfillment of Profit & Loss Sharing (PLS) mechanism. *International Journal of Islamic Banking and Finance Research*, *3*(2), 44–59. https://www.cribfb.com/journal/index.php/ijibfr/article/view/274. doi:10.46281/ijibfr.v3i2.274

Bird, R. M. (1992). *Tax policy and economic development*. Johns Hopkins Univ Pr.

Bisara, D. (2019). *Indonesia's E-commerce Market Larger Than Estimated; Consumer Habits Changing: Study*. Retrieved from https://jakartaglobe.id/business/indonesias-ecommerce-market-larger-than-estimated-consumer-habits-changing-study/

Bitner, M. J. (1992). Servicescapes: The impact of physical surroundings on customers and employees. *Journal of Marketing*, *56*(1), 57–71. doi:10.1177/002224299205600205

Bizri, R., & Bizri, I. (2017). Challenges facing the Islamic Banking industry in the MENA region: A comparative study. *Proceeding Book of International Congress of Islamic Economy, Finance and Ethics*.

Bloxham, E. (2011). Corporate governance and sustainability: New and old models of thinking. *Journal of Sustainable Finance and Investment*, *1*(1), 77–80. doi:10.3763/jsfi.2010.0003

Blumenthal, M., Christian, C., Slemrod, J., & Smith, M. G. (2001). Do normative appeals affect tax compliance? Evidence from a controlled experiment in Minnesota. *National Tax Journal*, *54*(1), 125–138. doi:10.17310/ntj.2001.1.06

Bocken, N. M. P., de Pauw, I., van der Grinten, B., & Bakker, C. (2016). Product design and business model strategies for a circular economy. *Journal of Industrial and Production Engineering*, *32*(1), 67–81. doi:10.1080/21681015.2014.1000399

Bocken, S., Schuit, C. S. C., & Kraaijenhagen, C. (2018). Experimenting with a circular business model: Lesson from eight cases. *Environmental Innovation and Societal Transitions*, *28*, 79–95. Advance online publication. doi:10.1016/j.eist.2018.02.001

Bolton, R., & Saxena-Iyer, S. (2009). Interactive services: A framework, synthesis and research directions. *Journal of Interactive Marketing*, *23*(1), 91–104. doi:10.1016/j.intmar.2008.11.002

Bonsón, E., & Bednárová, M. (2015). CSR reporting practices of Eurozone companies Prácticas en la presentación de informes sobre RSC de las empresas de la Eurozona. *Cómo Citar Este Artículo*, *18*(2), 182–193. doi:10.1016/j.rcsar.2014.06.002

Booth, N., & Matic, J. A. (2011). Mapping and leveraging influencers in social media to shape corporate brand perceptions. *Corporate Communications*, *16*(3), 184–191. doi:10.1108/13563281111156853

Boratynska & Huseynov. (2017). An innovative approach to food security policy in developing countries. *Journal of Innovation & Knowledge*, *2*, 39–44. www.elsevier.es/jik

Boratynska, K., & Huseynov, R. T. (2017). An innovative approach to food security policy in developing countries. *Journal of Innovation & Knowledge*, *2*(1), 39–44. www.elsevier.es/jik. doi:10.1016/j.jik.2016.01.007

Bourke, J., Roper, S., & Love, J. H. (2020). Innovation in legal services: The practices that influence ideation and codification activities. *Journal of Business Research*, *109*, 132–147. doi:10.1016/j.jbusres.2019.11.057

Bourke, L. (2019). *Britain warned it must ban Huawei*. The Age.

Bowering, G., Crone, P. P., & Kadi, W. (2012). *The Princeton Encyclopedia of Islamic Political Thought*. Princeton University Press., doi:10.2307/j.ctt1r2g6m

Branco, M. C., & Rodrigues, L. L. (2007). Issues in corporate social and environmental reporting research : An overview. *Issues in Social and Environmental Accounting*, *1*(1), 72–90.

Branco, M. C., & Rodrigues, L. L. (2008). Social responsibility disclosure: A study of proxies for the public visibility of Portuguese banks. *The British Accounting Review*, *40*(2), 161–181.

Broni, M. Y., Hosen, M., & Masih, M. (2019). Does a country's external debt level affect its Islamic banking sector development? Evidence from Malaysia based on Quantile regression and Markov regime-switching. *Quantitative Finance and Economics*, *3*(2), 366–389. doi:10.3934/QFE.2019.2.366

Broni, M. Y., Hosen, M., & Saiti, B. (2018). The causality between stock market and banking sector: Evidence from dual banking system. *International Journal of Business and Society*, *19*(3), 596–615. https://hdl.handle.net/20.500.12436/862

Buderi, R., & Huang, G. (2006). *Guanxi: Microsoft, China and Bill Gates's plan to win the road ahead*. Random House.

Businesswire. (2019, April 11). *Retail Market in Indonesia 2019-2023 | Growth in E-Commerce to Boost Growth | Technavio*. Retrieved from https://www.businesswire.com/news/home/20191004005209/en/Retail-Market-Indonesia-2019-2023-Growth-E-Commerce-BoostLB-C64i

Caldwell, C. (2012, Oct. 20). US consensus on free trade is breaking down. *Financial Times*.

Campbell, D. F., & Hanschitz, G. (2018). *Digitalization of Tax: Epistemic Tax Policy*. Academic Press.

Carini, C., Comincioli, N., Poddi, L., & Vergalli, S. (2017). Measure the performance with the market value added: Evidence from CSR companies. *Sustainability*, *9*(12), 2171.

Caro, F., & Sadr, R. (2019). The Internet of Things (IoT) in retail: Bridging supply and demand. *Business Horizons*, *62*(1), 47–54. doi:10.1016/j.bushor.2018.08.002

Casadei, A., & Amadei, F. (2010). The competitive influence of corporate social responsibility and corporate social disclosure in Italian small and medium sized companies: Focus on disclosure and competitive drivers 1. *Social and Environmental Accountability Journal*, *30*(1), 13–25.

Castro, P., Rodrigues, J. P., & Teixeira, J. G. (2020). Understanding FinTech Ecosystem Evolution Through Service Innovation and Socio-technical System Perspective. In H. Nóvoa, M. Drăgoicea, & N. Kühl (Eds.), *Exploring Service Science. IESS 2020. Lecture Notes in Business Information Processing* (Vol. 377). Springer. doi:10.1007/978-3-030-38724-2_14

Central Bureau of Statistics (CBS). (2010). Indonesia in Number Book. In Statistical Yearbook of Indonesia 2010. Badan Pusat Statistik, BPS.

Central Bureau of Statistics (CBS). (2011). Indonesia in Number Book. In Statistical Yearbook of Indonesia 2011. Badan Pusat Statistik, BPS.

Central Bureau of Statistics (CBS). (2011). Indonesia in Number Book. Statistical Yearbook of Indonesia 2011. Badan Pusat Statistik, BPS. ISSN/ISBN: ISSN/ISBN: 0126-2912

Central Bureau of Statistics (CBS). (2013). *CBS Strategies Data*, CV. Nasional Indah. ISSN: 2087-2011

Central Bureau of Statistics (CBS). (Badan Pusat Statistik, BPS) (2010). Indonesia in Number Book. Statistical Yearbook of Indonesia 2010. Badan Pusat Statistik, BPS. ISSN/ISBN: 0126-2912

Cerqueti, R., & Coppier, R. (2009). Tax revenues, fiscal corruption and "shame" costs. *Economic Modelling*, *26*(6), 1239–1244. doi:10.1016/j.econmod.2009.06.005

Chadha, A., & Sharma, R. (2017). Demonetization: Economic impact on different sectors in India. International Journal of Latest Technology in Engineering. *Management and Applied Science*, *6*(6), 219–223.

Chae, M., & Sheu, C. (2020). Exploring social media use in B2B supply chain operations. *Business Horizons*, *63*(2), 73-84.

Chanda, A. (2016). *Notes (and anecdotes) on Demonetization.* Accessed on 10th June, 2019, https://www.researchgate.net/publication/311908388_Notes_and_Anecdotes_on_Demonetization

Chanda, A., & Cook, C. J. (2019). *Who Gained from India's Demonetization? Insights from Satellites and Surveys*. Working Paper 2019-06, Department of Economics, Louisiana State University. Available at https://www.lsu.edu/business/economics/files/working papers/pap19_06.pdf

Chanda, N. S. (2019, May 13). *Refurbished goods industry in India: Is Flipkart's promise really worth it?* IMS Proschool Offers Courses in Data Science, Digital Marketing, IFRS, ACCA, CFA, Business Analytics, Financial Modeling, CIMA, CFP Courses. https://www.proschoolonline.com/blog/refurbished-goods-industry

Chantziaras, A., Dedoulis, E., Grougiou, V., & Leventis, S. (2020). The impact of religiosity and corruption on CSR reporting: The case of U.S. banks. *Journal of Business Research*, *109*, 362–374. doi:10.1016/j.jbusres.2019.12.025

Chaudhry, M., Mughal, S. L., & Zafar, F. (2014). Corporate Social Disclosure : A Case Study On Petroleum Industry Of Pakistan. *International Journal of Business and Marketing*, *2*(1), 1–18.

Chege, A., Kiragu, N., Lagat, C., & Muthoni, G. (2015). Effect of electronic fiscal devices on VAT collection in Tanzania: A case of Tanzania revenue authority. *European Journal of Business and Management*, *7*(33), 125–133.

Chênevert, D., & Tremblay, M. (2002). Managerial career success in Canadian organizations: Is gender a determinant? *International Journal of Human Resource Management*, *13*(6), 920–941. doi:10.1080/09585190210134282

Chen, Y. H., & Barns, S. (2007). Initial trust and online behaviour. *Industrial Management & Data Systems*, *107*(1), 21–36. doi:10.1108/02635570710719034

Chetia, J. (2014, April). Human Resource Development and the Context of India. *International Journal of Humanities and Social Science*, *2*(4).

Ching, H. Y., & Gerab, F. (2017). Sustainability reports in Brazil through the lens of signaling, legitimacy and stakeholder theories. *Social Responsibility Journal*, *13*(1), 95–110. doi:10.1108/SRJ-10-2015-0147

Cho, C. H., Choi, J.-S., Kwak, Y.-M., & Patten, D. M. (2013). An Empirical Investigation of the Extensiveness of Stand-Alone Environmental Reporting in South Korea. *Social and Environmental Accountability Journal*, *33*(2), 91–103.

Cho, C. H., Michelon, G., Patten, D. M., & Roberts, R. W. (2015). CSR disclosure: The more things change…? *Accounting, Auditing & Accountability Journal*, *28*(1), 14–35. doi:10.1108/AAAJ-12-2013-1549

Cho, C. H., & Roberts, R. W. (2010). Environmental reporting on the internet by America's Toxic 100: Legitimacy and self-presentation. *International Journal of Accounting Information Systems*, *11*(1), 1–16. doi:10.1016/j.accinf.2009.12.003

Chodorow, G. R., Gopinath, G., Mishra, M., & Naraynan, M. (2018). *Cash and the Economy: Evidence from India's Demonetization*. Working Paper, Harvard University. Available at https://scholar.harvard.edu/files/crgmn_demonetization.pdf

Choi, B. B., Lee, D., & Psaros, J. (2013). An analysis of Australian company carbon emission disclosures. *Pacific Accounting Review*, *25*(1), 58–79.

Cho, S., Chung, C., & Young, J. (2019). Study on the relationship between CSR and financial performance. *Sustainability*, *11*(2), 343. doi:10.3390u11020343

Chowdhury, M. A. F., Haque, M. M., & Masih, M. (2017). Re-examining the determinants of Islamic bank performance: New evidence from dynamic GMM, quantile regression, and wavelet coherence approaches. *Emerging Markets Finance & Trade*, *53*(7), 1519–1534. doi:10.1080/1540496X.2016.1250076

Christensen, C. W. (1997). *The innovator's dilemma: When new technologies cause great firms to fail*. Harvard University Press.

Chtourou, H., & Triki, M. (2017). Commitment in corporate social responsibility and financial performance: A study in the Tunisian context. *Social Responsibility Journal*, *13*(2), 370–389. doi:10.1108/SRJ-05-2016-0079

Chung, M. (2010). *Doing business successfully in China*. Chandos Publishing.

Chung, M., & Mascitelli, B. (2014). *Huawei's Battle: Cold War or Commercial War? In Asian Business and Management Practices: Trends and Global Considerations*. IGI Publishing.

Cinthyana, L. (2018). *A Brief Look At 4 Unicorn Startups in Indonesia*. Retrieved from https://indonesiatatler.com/arts-culture/business/gen-t-a-brief-look-at-4-unicorns-in-indonesia

Clavey, C., Pemberton, J. L., Loeprick, J., & Verhoeven, M. (2019). *International Tax Reform*. Digitalization, and Developing Economies.

Clotfelter, C. T. (1983). Tax evasion and tax rates: An analysis of individual returns. *The Review of Economics and Statistics*, *65*(3), 363–373. doi:10.2307/1924181

Cochrane, J. (2013, November 20). Luxury Brands Find A Home in Indonesia. *The New York Times*. Retrieved from: https://www.nytimes.com/2013/11/21/fashion/Luxury-Finds-a-Home-in-Indonesia.html

Cohen, R. (1984). The Sociology of tourism: Approaches, issues and findings. *Annual Review of Sociology*, *10*(1), 373–392. doi:10.1146/annurev.so.10.080184.002105

Cole, B. M. (2019*). Innovate or Die: How a lack of innovation can cause business failure.* www.forbes.com

Conn, G. (2020). *Managing Brand Communication During Covid-19*. Available at: https://blog.sprinklr.com/managing-brand-communication-covid-19/

Cooper Jackson, J. (2001). Women middle managers' perception of the glass ceiling. *Women in Management Review*, *16*(1), 30–41. doi:10.1108/09649420110380265

Coronel, J. M., Moreno, E., & Carrasco, M. J. (2010). Work–family conflicts and the organizational work culture as barriers to women educational managers. *Gender, Work and Organization*, *17*(2), 219–239. doi:10.1111/j.1468-0432.2009.00463.x

Cortina, J. (2002). Big things have small beginnings: An assortment of "minor" methodological misunderstandings. *Journal of Management*, *28*(3), 339–362. doi:10.1177/014920630202800305

Cotter, D. A., Hermsen, J. M., Ovadia, S., & Vanneman, R. (2001). The glass ceiling effect. *Social Forces*, *80*(2), 655–681. doi:10.1353of.2001.0091

Court, A. W., Culley, S. J., & And Mcmahon, C. A. (1996). Information access diagrams: A technique for analysing the usage of design information. *Journal of Engineering Design*, *7*(1), 55–75. doi:10.1080/09544829608907927

Cronin, J. J. Jr, & Taylor, S. A. (1992). Measuring Service Quality: A Reexamination and Extension. *Journal of Marketing*, *56*(July), 55–68. doi:10.1177/002224299205600304

Crosby, L. A., Evans, K. A., & Cowles, D. (1990). Relationship Quality in Services Selling: An Interpersonal Influence Perspective. *Journal of Marketing*, *54*(July), 68–81. doi:10.1177/002224299005400306

Crumpacker, M., & Crumpacker, J. M. (2007). Succession planning and generational stereotypes: Should HR consider age-based values and attitudes a relevant factor or a passing fad? *Public Personnel Management*, *36*(4), 349–369. doi:10.1177/009102600703600405

Cui, R., Gallino, S., Moreno, A., & Zhang, D. J. (2018). The Operational Value of Social Media Information. *Production and Operations Management: An International Journal*, *27*(10), 1749–1769. doi:10.1111/poms.12707

Curran, T., Treiber, J., & Rosenblatt, M. (2018). Building Brands Through Social Listening. *Northeast Business & Economics Association*, *21*(1), 71–74.

D'Amato, D., Droste, N., Allen, B., Kettunen, M., Lähtinen, K., Korhonen, J., Leskinen, P., Matthies, B. D., & Toppinen, A. (2017). A. Toppinen Green, Circular, Bio economy, A Comparative Analysis of Three Sustainability Avenues. *Journal of Cleaner Production*, *168*, 716–734. doi:10.1016/j.jclepro.2017.09.053

Daniel, E. O. (2011). The Use of Social Media in the Supply Chain: Survey and extensions. *Intelligent Systems in Accounting, Finance and Management: An International Journal*, *18*(3), 121–144.

Daoud, Y., & Kammoun, A. (2020). *Islamic Banking in North Africa: Emergence, Growth, and Prospects. In Growth and Emerging Prospects of International Islamic Banking*. IGI Global. doi:10.4018/978-1-7998-1611-9.ch005

Darwis, V. (2012). Food Self-Reliance Movement through the Village Food Resilience Program: Analyses and Constraints. *Agricultural Policy Analysis Journal, 10*(2), 159–179.

Darwis, V., & Rusastra, I. W. (2011, June). Optimizing Rural Community Empowerment through Integrating PUAP and Desa Mandiri Pangan Programs. *Agricultural Policy Analysis Journal., 9*(2), 125–142.

Dasgupta, N., & Asgari, S. (2004). Seeing is believing: Exposure to counterstereotypic women leaders and its effect on the malleability of automatic gender stereotyping. *Journal of Experimental Social Psychology, 40*(5), 642–658. doi:10.1016/j.jesp.2004.02.003

Dash, A. (2017). A Study on Socio Economic Effect of Demonetization in India. *International Journal of Management and Applied Science, 3*(3).

Dasí, À., Elter, F., Gooderham, P.N., & Pedersen, T. (2017). New Business Models In-The-Making in Extant MNCs: Digital Transformation in a Telco. In *Breaking up the Global Value Chain* (Advances in International Management, Vol. 30). Emerald Publishing Limited. doi:10.1108/S1571-502720170000030001

de Aguiar, T. R. S., & Fearfull, A. (2010). Global climate change and corporate disclosure: Pedagogical tools for critical accounting? *Social and Environmental Accountability Journal, 30*(2), 64–79. doi:10.1080/0969160X.2010.9651824

De Albuquerque, K., & McElroy, J. L. (2001). Tourist harassment: Barbados survey results. *Annals of Tourism Research, 28*(2), 477–492. doi:10.1016/S0160-7383(00)00057-8

De Hauw, S., & De Vos, A. (2010). Millennials' career perspective and psychological contract expectations: Does the recession lead to lowered expectations? *Journal of Business and Psychology, 25*(2), 293–302. doi:10.100710869-010-9162-9

De Mello, L. (2009). Avoiding the value added tax: Theory and cross-country evidence. *Public Finance Review, 37*(1), 27–46. doi:10.1177/1091142108316588

de Villiers, C., Low, M., & Samkin, G. (2014). The institutionalisation of mining company sustainability disclosures. *Journal of Cleaner Production, 84*(1), 51–58. doi:10.1016/j.jclepro.2014.01.089

de Villiers, C., & van Staden, C. J. (2006). Can less environmental disclosure have a legitimising effect? Evidence from Africa. *Accounting, Organizations and Society, 31*(8), 763–781. doi:10.1016/j.aos.2006.03.001

de Villiers, C., & van Staden, C. J. (2012). New Zealand shareholder attitudes towards corporate environmental disclosure. *Pacific Accounting Review, 24*(2), 186–210. doi:10.1108/01140581211258470

Deegan, C. (2002). Introduction: The legitimising effect of social and environmental disclosures - a theoretical foundation. Accounting. *Auditing and Accountability, 15*(3), 282–311. doi:10.1108/09513570210435852

Deegan, C., Rankin, M., & Voght, P. (2000). Firms' Disclosure Reactions to Major Social Incidents: Australian Evidence. *Accounting Forum, 24*(1), 101–130. doi:10.1111/1467-6303.00031

Dekimpe, M. (2019). Retailing and retailing research in the age of big data analytics. *International Journal of Research in Marketing*. Advance online publication. doi:10.1016/j.ijresmar.2019.09.001

Deloitte. (2017). *Deloitte Consumer Insights*. Retrieved from https://www2.deloitte.com/id/en/pages/consumer-industrial-products/articles/consumer-insights-id-2017.html

den Hollander, M. C., Bakker, C. A., & Hultink, E. J. (2017). Product Design in a Circular Economy: Development of a Typology of Key Concepts and Terms. *Journal of Industrial Ecology, 21*(3), 517–525. doi:10.1111/jiec.12610

Denzin, N. K., & Lincoln, Y. S. (2008). Introduction: The discipline and practice of qualitative research. In N. K. Denzin & Y. S. Lincoln (Eds.), *Strategies of qualitative inquiry* (pp. 1–43). Sage Publications, Inc.

Derks, B., Van Laar, C., & Ellemers, N. (2016). The queen bee phenomenon: Why women leaders distance themselves from junior women. *The Leadership Quarterly*, *27*(3), 456–469. doi:10.1016/j.leaqua.2015.12.007

Derks, B., van Laar, C., Ellemers, N., & Raghoe, G. (2015). Extending the queen bee effect: How Hindustani workers cope with disadvantage by distancing the self from the group. *The Journal of Social Issues*, *71*(3), 476–496. doi:10.1111/josi.12124

Designorate. (2019). *Characteristics of Human-Centered Design*. Available at: https://www.designorate.com/characteristics-of-human-centered-design/

DeVellis, R. F. (2003). *Scale development: Theory and applications*. Sage Publications.

Devie, D., Liman, L. P., Tarigan, J., & Jie, F. (2018). Corporate social responsibility, financial performance and risk in Indonesian natural resources industry. *Social Responsibility Journal*, *16*(1), 73–90. doi:10.1108/SRJ-06-2018-0155

Dezsö, C. L., & Ross, D. G. (2012). Does female representation in top management improve firm performance? A panel data investigation. *Strategic Management Journal*, *33*(9), 1072–1089. doi:10.1002mj.1955

Dimovski, V., Skerlavaj, M., & Man, M. M. K. (2010). Comparative analysis of mid-level women managers' perception of the existence of glass ceiling in Singaporean and Malaysian organizations. *International Business & Economics Research Journal, 9*(8).

Ding, D. K., Ferreira, C., & Wongchoti, U. (2016). *Does it pay to be different? Relative CSR and its impact on firm value*. doi:10.1016/j.irfa.2016.06.013

DKP. (2005). A food insecurity atlas of Indonesia, 2005. Dewan Ketahanan Pangan.

DKP. (2009). Panduan Penyusunan Peta Ketahanan dan Kerentanan Pangan di Indonesia: A Food Security and Vulnerability Atlas of Indonesia (FSVA). Jakarta: Dewan Ketahanan Pangan dan World Food Programme.

Dokyun, L., Kartik, H., & Harikesh, S. N. (2018). Advertising Content and Consumer Engagement on Social Media: Evidence from Facebook. *Journal of Management Science*, *64*(11), 4967–5460.

Dong, S., & Burritt, R. (2010). Cross-sectional benchmarking of social and environmental reporting practice in the Australian oil and gas industry. *Sustainable Development*, *18*(2), 108–118.

Dragomir, V. D. (2010). Environmentally sensitive disclosures and financial performance in a European setting. *Journal of Accounting & Organizational Change*, *6*(3), 359–388.

Drawbaugh, K. (2007). *Huawei-3Com deal threatens U.S. security: lawmakers*. Reuters Agency. https://www.reuters.com/article/us-3com-congress/huawei-3com-deal-threatens-u-s-security-lawmakers-idUSN1537679420071015

Duff, A. (2014). Corporate social responsibility reporting in professional accounting firm. *The British Accounting Review*, *48*, 74–86. doi:10.1177/0021943608317111

Dumay, J., & Cai, L. (2014). A review and critique of content analysis as a methodology for inquiring into IC disclosure. Journal of Intellectual Capital, 15(2), 264–290. doi:10.1108/JIC-01-2014-0010

Dumay, J., & Cai, L. (2015). Using content analysis as a research methodology for investigating intellectual capital disclosure: A critique. *Journal of Intellectual Capital*, *16*(1), 121–155. doi:10.1108/JIC-04-2014-0043

Dumay, J., Guthrie, J., & Farneti, F. (2010). Gri Sustainability Reporting Guidelines For Public And Third Sector Organizations. *Public Management Review*, *12*(4), 531–548. doi:10.1080/14719037.2010.496266

Du, S., & Vieira, E. T. (2012). Striving for Legitimacy Through Corporate Social Responsibility: Insights from Oil Companies. *Journal of Business Ethics, 110*(4), 413–427. doi:10.100710551-012-1490-4

Dwijayanto, A. (2018, March 19). *Tahun ini, Hydro Perdana targetkan punya 500 gerai Sodaqo Mart dan 212 Mart, Kontan.* Retrieved from: https://industri.kontan.co.id/news/tahun-ini-hydro-perdana-targetkan-punya-500-gerai-sodaqo-mart-dan-212-mart

Dyer, G., & Kirchgaessner, S. (2013). *Sprint agrees to shun Huawei equipment.* Financial Times. https://www.ft.com/content/45e16976-97f0-11e2-97e0-00144feabdc0

Eagly, A. H. (2007). Female leadership advantage and disadvantage: Resolving the contradictions. *Psychology of Women Quarterly, 31*(1), 1–12. doi:10.1111/j.1471-6402.2007.00326.x

Eggerton, J. (2019). *Huawei Indicted for Theft, Fraud and More: Justice points to effort to steal T-Mobile tech.* Broadcasting Cable.com. https://www.broadcastingcable.com/news/huawei-indicted-for-theft-fraud-and-more

EGHAM. (2019,August 29). Retrieved from https://www.gartner.com/en/newsroom/press-releases/2019-08-29-gartner-says-5-8-billion-enterprise-and-automotive-io

Elahi, D., Rehman, A., & Misra, A. (2013). An Empirical Study of the Businessmen Perception of Various Issues and Challenges Associated with FDI in Indian Retail Sector. *GBAMS: VIDUSHI, 5*(2).

Elena, C. A. (2015). Social Media – a Strategy in Developing Customer Relationship Management. *Procedia Economics and Finance, 39*, 785–790. doi:10.1016/S2212-5671(16)30266-0

Elijido-Ten, E. (2011). Media coverage and voluntary environmental disclosures: A developing country exploratory experiment. *Accounting Forum, 35*(3), 139–157.

Eljayash, K. M., James, K., & Kong, E. (2012). The Quantity and Quality of Environmental Disclosure in Annual Report of National Oil and Gas Companies in Middle East and North Africa. *International Journal of Economics and Finance, 4*(10), 201–217. doi:10.5539/ijef.v4n10p201

Eljelly, A. M. (2013). Internal and external determinants of profitability of Islamic banks in Sudan: Evidence from panel data. *Afro-Asian Journal of Finance and Accounting, 3*(3), 222–240. doi:10.1504/AAJFA.2013.054424

Engel, J. F., Kollat, D. T., & Blackwell, R. D. (1968). *Consumer behavior.* Holt, Rinhart & Winston.

Enginkaya, E., & Yilmaz, H. (2014). What Drives Consumers to Interact with Brands through Social Media? A Motivation Scale Development Study. *Procedia: Social and Behavioral Sciences, 148*, 219–226. doi:10.1016/j.sbspro.2014.07.037

Evdokimov, S., Fabian, B., & Gunther, O. (2011). *RFID and the internet of things: Technology, applications, and security challenges.* Now Publishers Inc.

Faisal, F., Tower, G., & Rusmin, R. (2012). Legitimising Corporate Sustainability Reporting Throughout the World. *Australasian Accounting Business & Finance Journal, 6*(2), 19–34. https://ro.uow.edu.au/aabfj/vol6/iss2/3/?utm_source=ro.uow.edu.au%2Faabfj%2Fvol6%2Fiss2%2F3&utm_medium=PDF&utm_campaign=PDFCoverPages

Falcon, W. P., & Naylor, R. L. (2005). Rethinking food security for the twenty-first century. *American Journal of Agricultural Economics, 85*(5), 1113–1127. doi:10.1111/j.1467-8276.2005.00797.x

FAO. (1996). Rome Declaration on World Food Security and World Food Summit Plan of Action. World Food Summit, Rome, Italy.

FAO. (2006). The State of Food Insecurity in the World 2006. Food and Agriculture Organization of the United Nations.

Feng, M., Wang, X., & Kreuze, J. G. (2017). Corporate social responsibility and firm financial performance. *American Journal of Business*, *32*(3/4), 106–133. doi:10.1108/AJB-05-2016-0015

Fitriani, E. (2017, April 6). *More Retailers to Expand Into e-Commerce to Survive*. Retrieved from: https://jakartaglobe.id/news/more-retailers-to-expand-into-e-commerce-to-survive

Fjeldstad, O. H. (1996). *Tax evasion and corruption in local governments in Tanzania: Alternative economic approaches*. Academic Press.

Flavian, C., Gurrea, R., & Orus, C. (2020). Combining channels to make smart purchases: The role of webrooming and showrooming. *Journal of Retailing and Consumer Services*, *52*, 101923. doi:10.1016/j.jretconser.2019.101923

Flynn, L., & Bradsher, K. (2007). *Bain and Chinese Company to Acquire 3Com*. New York Times. https://www.nytimes.com/2007/09/29/technology/29com.html

Fomicheva, E. (2018, January 20). *The Retail Sector: The Market of Fashion, Luxury and Premium-Class Goods: Indonesia*. Retrieved from: https://medium.com/@ekaterina.fomicheva25/the-retail-sector-the-market-of-fashion-luxury-and-premium-class-goods-indonesia-929a920e409d

Friedlander, J. (2018). *How the arrest of Huawei's Meng Wanzhou may mark the start of the great China-US technology decoupling*. https://www.scmp.com/comment/insight-opinion/united-states/article/2179520/how-arrest-huaweis-meng-wanzhou-may-mark-start

Friedman, A. L., & Miles, S. (2001). Socially Responsible Investment and Corporate Social and Environmental Reporting in the UK: An Exploratory Study. *The British Accounting Review*, *33*(4), 523–548. doi:10.1006/bare.2001.0172

Ftiti, Z., Nafti, O., & Sreiri, S. (2013). Efficiency of Islamic Banks During Subprime Crisis: Evidence of GCC Countries. *Journal of Applied Business Research*, *29*(1), 285–304. doi:10.19030/jabr.v29i1.7615

Fuscaldo, D. (2019). *Facebook Now Has More Users in India Than in Any Other Country.* Available at: https://www.investopedia.com/news/facebook-now-has-more-users-india-any-other-country/

Gallouj, F., & Djellal, F. (Eds.). (2010). *The handbook of innovation and services*. Edward Elgar. doi:10.4337/9781849803304

Galtung, F. (1995). Current strategies for combating corruption: A study of corruption in the tax administration. *Berlin: Transparency International Occasional Working Paper*, (8).

Gandhi, V. P., & Marsh, R. (2003). *Development and Poverty Reduction: Do Institutions Matter? A Study on the Impact of Local Institutions in Rural India*. Contributed Paper, The 25th International Conference of Agricultural Economists, Durban, South Africa.

Gangi, F., Mustilli, M., & Varrone, N. (2019). The impact of corporate social responsibility (CSR) knowledge on corporate financial performance: Evidence from the European banking industry. *Journal of Knowledge Management*, *23*(1), 110–134. doi:10.1108/JKM-04-2018-0267

Gao, S., Heravi, S., & Xiao, J. Z. (2005). Determinants of corporate social and environmental reporting in Hong Kong: A research note. *Accounting Forum*, *29*(2), 233–242.

Gao, Y. (2011). CSR in an emerging country: A content analysis of CSR reports of listed companies. *Baltic Journal of Management*, *6*(2), 263–291.

Gawankar, S. A., Gunasekaran, A., & Kamble, S. (2020). A study on investments in the big data-driven supply chain, performance measures and organisational performance in Indian retail 4.0 context. *International Journal of Production Research*, *58*(5), 1574–1593. doi:10.1080/00207543.2019.1668070

Ghazal, A., Rabl, T., Hu, M., Raab, F., Poess, M., Crolotte, A., & Jacobsen, H. A. (2013, June). BigBench: towards an industry standard benchmark for big data analytics. In *Proceedings of the 2013 ACM SIGMOD international conference on Management of data* (pp. 1197-1208). 10.1145/2463676.2463712

Ghazzawi, I. (2019). Cirque Du Soleil: Innovation is more culture than just a process. *Journal of Case Research and Inquiry*, *5*, 201–236.

Ghisellini, P., Cialani, C., & Ulgiati, S. (2016). A review on Circular Economy: The Expected Transition to a Balanced Interplay of Environmental and Economic Systems. *Journal of Cleaner Production*, *114*, 11–32. doi:10.1016/j.jclepro.2015.09.007

Giannarakis, G. (2014). The determinants influencing the extent of CSR disclosure. *International Journal of Law and Management*, *56*(5), 393–416. doi:10.1108/IJLMA-05-2013-0021

Gitaru, K. (2017). *The Impact Of System Automation On Revenue Collection in Kenya Revenue Authority: A Case Study of SIMBA*. Academic Press.

Global Market Study on Refurbished and Used Mobile Phones. Increasing Initiatives to reduce e-Waste Driving Market Growth. (2020, January). https://www.persistencemarketresearch.com/market-research/refurbished-and-used-mobile-phones-market.asp

Global Used and Refurbished Phones Market Study - NSYS GROUP. (2020). https://nsysgroup.com/en/media/articles/globalused-and-refurbished-phones-market-study

Gnanapala, W. K. A., & Sandaruwani, J. A. R. C. (2016). Impacts of Tourism Development in Cultural and Heritage Sites: An Empirical Investigation. *International Journal of Economics and Business Administration*, *6*(2), 68–78.

Gong, W., & Tian, G. (2012). Dynamic Evolution of IOT Application's Business Mode in Retail. In *ICLEM 2012* (pp. 1165–1172). Logistics for Sustained Economic Development—Technology and Management for Efficiency. doi:10.1061/9780784412602.0179

Gordon, R. H., & Nielsen, S. B. (1997). Tax evasion in an open economy: Value-added vs. income taxation. *Journal of Public Economics*, *66*(2), 173–197. doi:10.1016/S0047-2727(97)00044-3

Graffigna, G., & Riva, G. (2015). Social media monitoring and understanding: An integrated mixed methods approach for the analysis of social media. *International Journal of Web Based Communities*, *11*(1), 57–72. doi:10.1504/IJWBC.2015.067083

Gras-Gil, E., Manzano, M. P., & Fernández, J. H. (2016). Investigating the relationship between corporate social responsibility and earnings management: Evidence from Spain. *BRQ Business Research Quarterly*, *19*(4), 289–299. doi:10.1016/j.brq.2016.02.002

Gray, C., & Charter, M. (2008). Remanufacturing and Product Design. *International Journal of Product Development*, *6*(34).

Gray, R. (2006). Social, environmental and sustainability reporting and organisational value creation?: Whose value? Whose creation? *Accounting, Auditing & Accountability Journal*, *19*(6), 793–819. doi:10.1108/09513570610709872

Gregory, J. (2015). *The Internet of Things: revolutionizing the retail industry*. Accenture Strategy.

Grewal, B., Grunfeld, H., & Sheehan, P. (2012). *The contribution of agricultural growth to poverty reduction*. ACIAR Impact Assessment Series Report No. 76. Australian Centre for International Agricultural Research.

Guendouzi, J. (2006). "The guilt thing": Balancing domestic and professional roles. *Journal of Marriage and the Family, 68*(4), 901–909. doi:10.1111/j.1741-3737.2006.00303.x

Guest. (1987). Human Resource Management and Industrial Relations. *Journal of Management Studies, 24*, 203-521. doi:10.1111/j.1467-6486.1987.tb00460.x

Guide, V. D. R. Jr, & Li, J. (2010). The potential for cannibalization of new products sales by remanufactured products. *Decision Sciences, 41*(3), 547–572. doi:10.1111/j.1540-5915.2010.00280.x

Guile, B. R., & Quin, J. B. (1988). *Managing Innovation: Cases from the Services Industries*. National Academy Press.

Gursoy, D., Maier, T. A., & Chi, C. G. (2008). Generational differences: An examination of work values and generational gaps in the hospitality workforce. *International Journal of Hospitality Management, 27*(3), 448–458. doi:10.1016/j.ijhm.2007.11.002

Guthrie, J., Cuganesan, S., & Ward, L. (2008). Industry specific social and environmental reporting: The Australian Food and Beverage Industry. *Accounting Forum, 32*(1), 1–15. doi:10.1016/j.accfor.2007.10.001

Guthrie, J., Petty, R., Yongvanich, K., & Ricceri, F. (2004). Using content analysis as a research method to inquire into intellectual capital reporting. *Journal of Intellectual Capital, 5*(2), 282–293. http://www.emeraldinsight.com/doi/abs/10.1108/14691930410533704

Habibi, H., Hamilton, C. A., Valos, M. J., & Callaghan, M. (2015). E-marketing orientation and social media implementation in B2B marketing. *European Business Review, 27*(6), 638–655. doi:10.1108/EBR-03-2015-0026

Habimana, O. (2016). Do flexible exchange rates facilitate external adjustment? A dynamic approach with time-varying and asymmetric volatility. *International Economics and Economic Policy, 14*(4), 625–642. doi:10.100710368-016-0341-7

Hahn, R., & Kühnen, M. (2013). Determinants of sustainability reporting: A review of results, trends, theory, and opportunities in an expanding field of research. *Journal of Cleaner Production, 59*, 5–21. doi:10.1016/j.jclepro.2013.07.005

Hall, K. (2011). *Former government CIO John Suffolk joins Huawei as head of cybersecurity*. Computer Weekly. https://www.computerweekly.com/news/2240105220/Former-government-CIO-John-Suffolk-joins-Huawei-as-head-of-cyber-security

Hamel, G., & Prahalad, C. K. (1996). Competing in the New Economy: Managing out of Bounds. *Strategic Management Journal, 17*(3), 237–242. doi:10.1002/(SICI)1097-0266(199603)17:3<237::AID-SMJ829>3.0.CO;2-G

Hamzaoui Essoussi, L., & Linton, J. D. (2010). New or recycled products: How much are consumers willing to pay? *Journal of Consumer Marketing, 27*(5), 458–468. doi:10.1108/07363761011063358

Harms, R., & Linton, J. D. (2016). Willingness to pay for eco-certified refurbished products: The effects of environmental attitudes and knowledge. *Journal of Industrial Ecology, 20*(4), 893–904. doi:10.1111/jiec.12301

Hatane, S. E., Octavia, F., & Florentina, J. (2019). The comparison of earnings management practices in Indonesia's Islamic banks and conventional banks. *Advances in Economics. Business and Management Research, 69*, 127–131.

Hazen, Overstreet, R. E., Jones-Farmer, L. A., & Field, H. S. (2012). The role of ambiguity tolerance in consumer perception of remanufactured products. *International Journal of Production Economics, 135*(2), 781–790. doi:10.1016/j.ijpe.2011.10.011

Heilman, M. E. (2001). Description and prescription: How gender stereotypes prevent women's ascent up the organizational ladder. *The Journal of Social Issues, 57*(4), 657–674. doi:10.1111/0022-4537.00234

Heilman, M. E. (2012). Gender stereotypes and workplace bias. *Research in Organizational Behavior*, *32*, 113–135. doi:10.1016/j.riob.2012.11.003

Heilman, M. E., & Okimoto, T. G. (2008). Motherhood: A potential source of bias in employment decisions. *The Journal of Applied Psychology*, *93*(1), 189–198. doi:10.1037/0021-9010.93.1.189 PMID:18211144

Helm, S., Kim, S. H., & Van Riper, S. (2020). Navigating the 'retail apocalypse': A framework of consumer evaluations of the new retail landscape. *Journal of Retailing and Consumer Services*, *54*. Advance online publication. doi:10.1016/j.jretconser.2018.09.015

Hershatter, A., & Epstein, M. (2010). Millennials and the world of work: An organization and management perspective. *Journal of Business and Psychology*, *25*(2), 211–223. doi:10.100710869-010-9160-y

He, W., Zha, S., & Li, L. (2013). Social media competitive analysis and text mining: A case study in the pizza industry. *International Journal of Information Management*, *33*(3), 464–472. doi:10.1016/j.ijinfomgt.2013.01.001

Hillman, A. J., Shropshire, C., & Cannella, A. A. Jr. (2007). Organizational predictors of women on corporate boards. *Academy of Management Journal*, *50*(4), 941–952. doi:10.5465/amj.2007.26279222

Hindriks, J., Keen, M., & Muthoo, A. (1999). Corruption, extortion and evasion. *Journal of Public Economics*, *74*(3), 395–430. doi:10.1016/S0047-2727(99)00030-4

Ho, A. Y.-F., Liang, H.-Y., & Tumurbaatar, T. (2019). The impact of corporate social responsibility on financial performance: Evidence from commercial banks in Mongolia. *Advances in Pacific Basin Business, Economics and Finance*, 109–153.

Hong, Y. C., & Choi, I. (2011). Three dimensions of reflective thinking in solving design problems: A conceptual model. *Educational Technology Research and Development*, *59*(5), 687–710. doi:10.100711423-011-9202-9

Hong, Y., & Andersen, M. L. (2011). The relationship between corporate social responsibility and earnings management: An exploratory study. *Journal of Business Ethics*, *104*(4), 461–471. doi:10.100710551-011-0921-y

Hoover, C. (2019). Human-Centered Design vs. Design-Thinking: How They're Different.... *MovingWorlds Blog*. Available at: https://blog.movingworlds.org/human-centered-design-vs-design-thinking-how-theyre-different-and-how-to-use-them-together-to-create-lasting-change/

Hosen, M., Broni, M. Y., & Uddin, M. N. (2020). What are the bank specific and macroeconomic elements influence non-performing loans in Bangladesh? Evidence from conventional and Islamic banks. *Green Finance*, *2*(2), 212–226. doi:10.3934/GF.2020012

Hossain, M., & Andrew, J. (2006). *Corporate Social and Environmental Disclosure in Developing Countries : Evidence from Bangladesh*. Asia Pacific Conference on International Accounting Issues. https://ro.uow.edu.au/commpapers/179/

Hosseini, S., Haghverdi, F., Mohammad, S. M., & Hajipour, E. (2020). The effect of price promotions on impulse buying: The mediating role of service innovation in fast moving consumer goods. *International Journal of Business Information Systems*, *33*(3), 320. doi:10.1504/IJBIS.2020.105828

Howells, J. (2001). The nature of innovation in services. In *OECD, innovation and productivity in services, OECD proceedings industry, services and trade*. Paris: Organization for Economic Cooperation and Development (OECD).

Howe, N., & Strauss, W. (2003). *Millennials go to college: Strategies for a new generation on campus: Recruiting and admissions, campus life, and the classroom*. American Association of Collegiate Registrars and Admissions Officers.

Hsieh, Y.-C. (2012). Hotel companies' environmental policies and practices: A content analysis of their web pages. *International Journal of Contemporary Hospitality Management*, *24*(1), 97–121.

Human Resource Management, the Open University of Hongkong (OUH). (n.d.). Retrieved on 24th December 2019, http://www.opentextbooks.org.hk/system/files/export/32/32088/pdf/Human Resource Management_32088.pdf

Huotari, K. K., Edvardsson, B., Jonas, J. M., Sorhammar, D., & Witell, L. (2016)... *Journal of Business Research*, *69*(8), 2964–2971. doi:10.1016/j.jbusres.2016.02.029

Huselid, M. (1995). The impact of human resource management on turnover, productivity, and corporate performance. Academy of Management Journal, 38, 635-672.

Ibe-Enwo, G., Igbudu, N., Garanti, Z., & Popoola, T. (2019). Assessing the relevance of green banking practice on bank loyalty: The mediating effect of green image and bank trust. *Sustainability*, *11*(17), 4651. doi:10.3390u11174651

Ibrahim, F., & Barr, S. (2010). Reconfiguring IT and the Cultural Dimension in Knowledge Management Practices, International Journal of Knowledge. *Culture and Change Management*, *9*(11), 27–43.

Ibrahim, F., Edgar, D., & Reid, V. (2009). Assessing The Role Of Knowledge Management In Adding Value: Moving Towards A Comprehensive Framework. *Journal of Information & Knowledge Management*, *8*(4), 1–12. doi:10.1142/S0219649209002397

Ibrahim, M. H., Salim, K., Abojeib, M., & Yeap, L. W. (2019). Structural changes, competition and bank stability in Malaysia's dual banking system. *Economic Systems*, *43*(1), 111–129. doi:10.1016/j.ecosys.2018.09.001

Idemudia, U. (2011). Corporate social responsibility and developing countries: Moving the critical CSR research agenda in Africa forward. *Progress in Development Studies*, *11*(1), 1–18. doi:10.1177/146499341001100101

Ijomah, W. L., McMahon, C. A., Hammond, G. P., & Newman, S. T. (2007). Development of design for remanufacturing guidelines to support sustainable manufacturing. *Robotics and Computer-integrated Manufacturing*, *23*(6), 712–719. doi:10.1016/j.rcim.2007.02.017

Imran, M., Chowdhury, M. A. F., & Hosen, M. (2018). Financial Development, Technological Development, and Poverty: A Cross-Sectional Study. In Management Strategies and Technology Fluidity in the Asian Business Sector (pp. 126-138). IGI Global. doi:10.4018/978-1-5225-4056-4.ch008

Indian Retail Industry - Major trends, Growth and Opportunities (2020 - 2025). (n.d.). Retrieved from https://www.mordorintelligence.com/industry-reports/indian-retail-industry

Indian retail industry analysis. (2018, July7). Retrieved from https://www.indiaretailing.com/2018/07/07/research/indian-retail-industry-analysis/

Indonesia, C. N. N. (2020, April 11). *Tren dan Peluang Industri E-Commerce di Indonesia 2020*. Retrieved from https://www.cnnindonesia.com/teknologi/20200205204206-206-472064/tren-dan-peluang-industri-e-commerce-di-indonesia-2020

Indonesia-investments.com. (2016, September 12). *E-commerce market Indonesia: Online Retail Growing Strongly*. Retrieved from: https://www.indonesia-investments.com/news/todays-headlines/e-commerce-market-indonesia-online-retail-growing-strongly/item7179

Indonesia-investments.com. (2017, December 13). *E-Commerce in Indonesia: Many Consumers Look Offline, Buy Online*. Retrieved from: https://www.indonesia-investments.com/news/todays-headlines/e-commerce-in-indonesia-many-consumers-look-offline-buy-online/item8410

Ingraham, N. (2012). *Australia bans Huawei from bidding on broadband network buildout due to security concerns*. The Verge. https://www.theverge.com/2012/3/26/2903097/australia-ban-huawei-national-broadband-network-bid

Invisionapp.com. (2019). *User-centered design: Definition, examples, and tips | Inside Design Blog*. Available at: https://www.invisionapp.com/inside-design/user-centered-design-definition-examples-and-tips/

Iqbal, Z., & Mirakhor, A. (1999). Progress and challenges of Islamic banking. *Thunderbird International Business Review, 41*(4-5), 381–405. doi:10.1002/tie.4270410406

Isaac, N. N., & Lilian, L. (2010). Automation and customs tax administration: Empirical evidence from Uganda. *African Journal of Business Management, 4*(11), 2241.

Ishlak, W. (2017). Creating an innovation culture. *McKinsey Quarterly*. https://www.mckinsey.com/business-functions/strategy-and-corporate-finance/our-insights/creating-an-innovation-culture

Isidore, C. (2017, December). *Retail's toughest year: A record for store closings*. Retrieved from https://money.cnn.com/2017/12/26/news/companies/retail-toughest-year-store-closings/index.html

Islam, M. A. (2010). Social and Environmental Accounting Research: Major Contributions and Future Directions for Developing Countries. *Social and Environmental Accounting Research: Major Contributions and Future Directions for Developing Countries, 16*(2), 27–43.

Islam, M. Azizul, & Deegan, C. (2008). Motivations for an organisation within a developing country to report social responsibility information: Evidence from Bangladesh. *Accounting, Auditing & Accountability Journal, 21*(6), 850–874.

ITNews. (2012). *Downer blasts Huawei links to cyber attacks: Former foreign minister blasts NBN ban*. https://www.itnews.com.au/news/downer-blasts-huawei-links-to-cyber-attacks-294934

Jahdi, K. S., & Acikdilli, G. (2009). Marketing Communications and Corporate Social Responsibility (CSR): Marriage of Convenience or Shotgun Wedding? *Journal of Business Ethics, 88*(1), 103–113. doi:10.100710551-009-0113-1

Javaid Lone, E., Ali, A., & Khan, I. (2016). Corporate governance and corporate social responsibility disclosure: Evidence from Pakistan. Corporate Governance. *The International Journal of Business in Society, 16*(5), 785–797.

Jayanti, R. K., & Rajeev Gowda, M. V. (2014). Sustainability dilemmas in emerging economies. *IIMB Management Review, 26*(2), 130–142. doi:10.1016/j.iimb.2014.03.004

Jayawardena, C. (2013). Innovative solutions for future tourism development in Sri Lanka (2013-2026). *Worldwide Hospitality and Tourism Themes, 5*(5), 512–531. doi:10.1108/WHATT-05-2013-0033

Jenkins, J. (1991). Tourism Development Strategies. In *Developing Tourism Destinations, 61-77, Harow*. Longman.

Jha, L. (2020, February 26). India's retail market to touch $1.1-1.3 trillion by 2025: BCG. *LIVEMint*. Retrieved from https://www.livemint.com/industry/retail/india-s-retail-market-to-touch-1-1-1-3-trillion-by-2025-bcg-11582714221778.html

Jimenez, G., Mac an tSionnaigh, N., & Kamenov, A. (2013). Information Technology for Tax Administrations. *USAID Bureau for Economic Growth, Education and Environment, Office of Economic Policy*. http://pdf. usaid. gov/pdf_docs/PNAEA485. pdf

Jiménez-Parra, B., Rubio, S., & Vicente-Molina, M.-A. (2014). Key drivers in the behavior of potential consumers of remanufactured products: A study on laptops in Spain. *Journal of Cleaner Production, 85*, 488–496. doi:10.1016/j.jclepro.2014.05.047

Jiufang, T., Xiaohua, L., & Jiuhong, T. (2009). Environmental Disclosure of Chemical Industry: Evidence from Chinese A-Share Market. *Zhongguo Renkou Ziyuan Yu Huanjing, 7*(1), 23–29. doi:10.1080/10042857.2009.10684906

Jo, H., & Na, H. (2012). Does CSR Reduce Firm Risk? Evidence from Controversial Industry Sectors. *Journal of Business Ethics, 110*(4), 441–456. doi:10.100710551-012-1492-2

Johansson & Brynielsson. (2012). Estimating Citizen Alertness in Crises using SocialMedia Monitoring and Analysis. *EISIC '12: Proceedings of the 2012 European Intelligence and Security Informatics Conference*, 189–196.

Josephson, A., & Lambe, E. (2020). *Brand communications in time of crisis*. Available at: https://blog.twitter.com/en_us/topics/company/2020/Brand-communications-in-time-of-crisis.html

Juan, D. U., Feida, Z. H. U., & Ee Peng, L. I. M. (2012). Dynamic Label Propagation in Social Networks. *The 18th International Conference on Database Systems for Advanced Applications,* 194-209.

Jyrkinen, M., & McKie, L. (2012). Gender, age and ageism: Experiences of women managers in Finland and Scotland. *Work, Employment and Society*, *26*(1), 61–77. doi:10.1177/0950017011426313

Kalioujny, B., Ermushko, J., & Zhavoronok, A.V. (2016). *Establishment of a strategy of circular economy increasing the well-being of society: comparison of two national policies*. Academic Press.

Kamal, A., Yingjie, M., & Ali, A. (2019). Significance of Billion Tree Tsunami Afforestation Project and Legal Developments in Forest Sector of Pakistan. *International Journal of Law and Society*, *1*, 157.

Kamla, R., & Rammal, H. G. (2013). Social reporting by Islamic banks: Does social justice matter? *Accounting, Auditing & Accountability Journal*, *26*(6), 911–945. doi:10.1108/AAAJ-03-2013-1268

Kansal, M., Joshi, M., Babu, S., & Sharma, S. (2016). Reporting of Corporate Social Responsibility in Central Public Sector Enterprises: A Study of Post Mandatory Regime in India. *Journal of Business Ethics*, 1–19.

Kanter, R. M. (1977). *Men and women of the corporation*. Basic Books.

Karmarkar, U. (2014). The industrialization of services. In E. Baglieri & U. Karmarkar (Eds.), *Managing Consumer Services*. Springer. doi:10.1007/978-3-319-04289-3_2

Kasper, H., Koleva, I., & Kett, H. (2012). Matching Corporate Goals with External Social Media Activities. In *The Semantic Web: ESWC 2012 Satellite Events in Heraklion, Greece, 2012* (pp. 233–244). Springer.

Kaushik, P. (2019, October 29). The Indonesian retail market is tipped for astronomical growth, but cashless payments will be key to realising its potential. *Asean Today*. Retrieved from: https://www.aseantoday.com/2019/10/the-indonesian-retail-market-is-tipped-for-astronomical-growth-but-cashless-payments-will-be-key-to-realising-its-potential/

Keaveney, S. M. (1995). Customer Switching Behavior in Service Industries: An Exploratory Study. *Journal of Marketing*, *59*(2), 71–82. doi:10.1177/002224299505900206

Keen To Design. (2019). *Human Centred Design and it's Process - Keen to Design*. Available at: https://www.keentodesign.com.au/human-centred-design/

Keeton, K. B. (1996). Characteristics of successful women managers and professionals in local government: A national survey. *Women in Management Review*, *11*(3), 27–34. doi:10.1108/09649429610117434

Kemp, L. J., & Vinke, J. (2012). CSR reporting: A review of the Pakistani aviation industry. *South Asian Journal of Global Business Research*, *1*(2), 276–292.

Kenly, A., & Poston, B. (2010). *Social Media and Product Innovation*. Available at: https://viewpoints.io/entry/social-media-and-product-innovation

Kent, P., & Zunker, T. (2013). Attaining legitimacy by employee information in annual reports. *Accounting, Auditing & Accountability Journal*, *26*(7), 1072–1106. doi:10.1108/AAAJ-03-2013-1261

Kerbaj, R. (2013). *Chinese firm Huawei hires former GCHQ chief.* The Sunday Times. https://www.thetimes.co.uk/article/chinese-firm-huawei-hires-former-gchq-chief-637q3f2583z

Khan, L. J. C., & Bathurst, R. J. (2018). Institutional impacts on corporate social responsibility: A comparative analysis of New Zealand and Pakistan. *International Journal of Corporate Social Responsibility, 3*(1). Advance online publication. doi:10.118640991-018-0026-3

Khan, M. H.-U.-Z., Halabi, A. K., & Samy, M. (2011). Corporate social responsibility (CSR) reporting: A study of selected banking companies in Bangladesh. *Journal of Business and Management, 6*(2), 42–47. doi:10.1108/17471110910977276

Khan, M., & Hassan, A. (2019). Environmental Reporting in Pakistan's Oil and Gas Industry. *International Research Journal of Business Studies, 12*(1), 15–29. doi:10.21632/irjbs.12.1.15-29

Khan, M., Hassan, A., Tarbert, H., & Harrison, C. (2020). CSR reporting: A review of research and agenda for future research. *Management Research Review.*

Khare, P. (2018). *The role of HR and the rice of India's Tech Industry.* BIEF Blog.

Khor, K. S., & Hazen, B. T. (2017). Remanufactured products purchase intention and behaviour: Evidence from Malaysia. *International Journal of Production Research, 55*(8), 2149–2162. doi:10.1080/00207543.2016.1194534

Kilian, T., & Hennigs, N. (2013). Corporate social responsibility and environmental reporting in controversial industries. *European Business Review, 26*(1), 79–101. doi:10.1108/EBR-04-2013-0080

Kiliç, M., Kuzey, C., & Uyar, A. (2015). The impact of ownership and board structure on Corporate Social Responsibility (CSR) reporting in the Turkish banking industry. Corporate Governance. *The International Journal of Business in Society, 15*(3), 357–374. doi:10.1108/CG-02-2014-0022

Killian, S., & O'Regan, P. (2016). Social accounting and the co-creation of corporate legitimacy. *Accounting, Organizations and Society, 50*, 1–12. doi:10.1016/j.aos.2016.02.004

King, E. D. (2006). Report from SIOP: Current industrial/organizational psychology perspectivesof women in organizations. *Equal Opportunities International, 25*(3), 215–218. doi:10.1108/02610150610687854

Kiran, R., & Jhamb, D. (2011). A strategic framework for consumer preferences towards emerging retail formats. *Journal of Emerging Knowledge on Emerging Markets, 3*(1), 25.

Kirat, M. (2015). Corporate social responsibility in the oil and gas industry in Qatar perceptions and practices. *Public Relations Review, 41*(4), 438–446. doi:10.1016/j.pubrev.2015.07.001

Kirchherr, J., Reike, D., & Hekkert, M. (2017). Conceptualizing the circular economy: An analysis of 114 definitions. *Resources, Conservation and Recycling, 127*, 221–232.

Kissflow. (2018). *HR Automation - The Future of Human Resource Process Management.* Available at https://kissflow.com/hr-process/

Kissflow. (2019, August 27). *Employee Onboarding.* Available at https://kissflow.com/hr-process/employee-onboarding/

Kitsios, E., Jalles, J., & Verdier, G. (2019). *Reducing Tax Evasion from Cross-Border Fraud: The role of Digitalization.* Academic Press.

Kohli, C., Suri, R., & Kapoor, A. (2015). Will social media kill branding? *Business Horizons, 58*(1), 35–44. doi:10.1016/j.bushor.2014.08.004

Kolk, A., Hong, P., & van Dolen, W. (2010). Corporate social responsibility in China: An analysis of domestic and foreign retailers' sustainability dimensions. *Business Strategy and the Environment*, *19*(5), 289–303. doi:10.1002/bse.630

Kotler, P., Keller, K. L., Khoshi, A., & Jha, M. (2012). *Marketing Management: A South Asian perspective* (13th ed.). Pearson Education-India.

Kozak, M. (2007). Tourist harassment: A marketing perspective. *Annals of Tourism Research*, *34*(2), 384–399. doi:10.1016/j.annals.2006.10.003

Krahn, H., & Galambos, N. (2014). Work values and beliefs of ' Generation X′ and 'Generation Y'. *Journal of Youth Studies*, *17*(1), 92–112. doi:10.1080/13676261.2013.815701

KrAsia. (2019, November 20). *Offline Programs are Getting Tech Players More Customers in Indonesia*. Retrieved from: https://dailysocial.id/post/offline-programs-are-getting-tech-players-more-customers-in-indonesia

Krasodomska, J. (2015). CSR disclosures in the banking industry. Empirical evidence from Poland. *Social Responsibility Journal*, *11*(3), 406–423. doi:10.1108/SRJ-02-2013-0019

Krippendorff, K. (2004). Intrinsic Motivation and Human-Centered Design. *Theoretical Issues in Ergonomics Science*, *5*(1), 43–72. doi:10.1080/1463922031000086717

Krippendorf, K. (1980). *Content analysis: An introduction to its methodology*. Sage Publications.

Kumar, K., & Prakash, A. (2018). Developing a framework for assessing sustainable banking performance of the Indian banking sector. *Social Responsibility Journal*, *15*(5), 689–709. doi:10.1108/SRJ-07-2018-0162

Kuruppu, S., & Milne, M. J. (2010). Dolphin deaths, organizational legitimacy and potential employees' reactions to assured environmental disclosures. *Accounting Forum*, *34*(1), 1–19. doi:10.1016/j.accfor.2009.12.001

La Shun, L. (2017). A comprehensive definition of technology from an Ethological Perspective. *Journal of Social Sciences*, *6*(4), 126. doi:10.3390ocsci6040126

Laine, M. (2009). Ensuring legitimacy through rhetorical changes?: A longitudinal interpretation of the environmental disclosures of a leading Finnish chemical company. *Accounting, Auditing & Accountability Journal*, *22*(7), 1029–1054.

Langford, B., & Ohlenburg, T. (2015). *Tax revenue potential and effort*. International Growth Centre Working Paper. Available at: https://www. theigc. org/wp-content/uploads/2016/01/Langford-Ohlenburg-2016-Working-paper. pdf

Larsen. (2019, July 30). *Reskilling Human Resources for the Age of Automation – TLNT*. Available at https://www.tlnt.com/reskilling-human-resources-for-the-age-of-automation/

Laserfiche. (2019). *What is Human Resources (HR) Automation*. Available at https://www.laserfiche.com/ecmblog/what-is-hr-automation/

Lassoued, M. (2018). Comparative study on credit risk in Islamic banking institutions: The case of Malaysia. *The Quarterly Review of Economics and Finance*, *70*, 267–278. doi:10.1016/j.qref.2018.05.009

Lawless, J. L., & Fox, R. L. (2005). *It takes a candidate: Why women don't run for office*. Cambridge University Press.

Lawrence, P., & Pfeffer, J. (1998). The human equation: Building Profits by Putting People First. *Administrative Science Quarterly*, *43*(4), 956. doi:10.2307/2393627

Le Maistre, R. (2018). *BT's McRae: Huawei Is 'the Only True 5G Supplier Right Now*. https://www.lightreading.com/mobile/5g/bts-mcrae-huawei-is-the-only-true-5g-supplier-right-now/d/d-id/747734

Levy, M., & Powell, P. (2000). Information systems strategy for small and medium sized enterprises: An organisational perspective. *The Journal of Strategic Information Systems, 9*(1), 63–84. doi:10.1016/S0963-8687(00)00028-7

Lewis, C., Jillian, P., & Augustson, E. (2015). Social Listening: A Content Analysis of E-Cigarette Discussions on Twitter. *Journal of Medical Internet Research, 17*(10). PMID:26508089

Lieder, M., & Rashid, A. (2016). Towards circular economy implementation: A comprehensive review in context of manufacturing industry. *Journal of Cleaner Production, 115*, 36–51.

Lindstrom, M. (2008). *Buyology: How Everything we believe about, why we buy is wrong*. Random House Business.

Linehan, M., & Scullion, H. (2008). The development of female global managers: The role of mentoring and networking. *Journal of Business Ethics, 83*(1), 29–40. doi:10.100710551-007-9657-0

Linstrom, M. (2005). *Brand Sense: How to Build Powerful Brands through Touch, Taste, Smell, Sight and Sound.* Kogan Page Publishers.

Linton, J. D. (2008). Assessing the economic rationality of remanufacturing products. *Journal of Product Innovation Management, 25*(3), 287–302. doi:10.1111/j.1540-5885.2008.00301.x

Lin, W., Ho, J., & Sambasivan, M. (2018). Impact of corporate political activity on the relationship between corporate social responsibility and financial performance: A dynamic panel data approach. *Sustainability, 11*(1), 60. doi:10.3390u11010060

Lipińska-Grobelny, A., & Wasiak, K. (2010). Job satisfaction and gender identity of women managers and non-managers. *International Journal of Occupational Medicine and Environmental Health, 23*(2), 161–166. doi:10.2478/v10001-010-0015-6 PMID:20630833

Livingstone, D. W., Pollock, K., & Raykov, M. (2016). Family binds and glass ceilings: Women managers' promotion limits in a 'knowledge economy'. *Critical Sociology, 42*(1), 145–166. doi:10.1177/0896920514532663

Lock, I., & Seele, P. (2016). *The credibility of CSR (corporate social responsibility) reports in Europe. Evidence from a quantitative content analysis in 11 countries*. doi:10.1016/j.jclepro.2016.02.060

Lock, I., & Seele, P. (2015). Analyzing sector-specific CSR reporting: Social and environmental disclosure to investors in the chemicals and banking and insurance industry. *Corporate Social Responsibility and Environmental Management, 22*(2), 113–128. doi:10.1002/csr.1338

Lokuhetty, A., Jayawardhana, C., & Mudadeniya, D. (2013). Developing a shared vision for tourism in post-war Sri Lanka. *Worldwide Hospitality and Tourism Themes, 5*(5), 486–494. doi:10.1108/WHATT-05-2013-0030

Lopes, S. D. F. (2011). Destination image: Origins, developments and implications. PASOS. *Revista de Turismo y Patrimonio Cultural, 9*(2), 305–315. doi:10.25145/j.pasos.2011.09.027

Lord, J. (2012). *National Press Club address*. Australian Financial Review. https://www.afr.com/rw/20092014/AFR/2012/10/24/-Photos-/030a5b50-1d7d-11e2-80929ae2fdd1541e_John%20Lord%20National-%20Press%20Club%20Address.pdf

Lovelock, C., & Wright, L. (2002). *Principles of service marketing and management* (2nd ed.). Prentice Hall.

Lu, Y., & Abeysekera, I. (2015). What Do Stakeholders Care About? Investigating Corporate Social and Environmental Disclosure in China. *Journal of Business Ethics*. https://link.springer.com/content/pdf/10.1007%2Fs10551-015-2844-5.pdf

Lund-Thomsen, P., Lindgreen, A., & Vanhamme, J. (2016). Industrial Clusters and Corporate Social Responsibility in Developing Countries: What We Know, What We do not Know, and What We Need to Know. *Journal of Business Ethics, 133*(1), 9–24. doi:10.100710551-014-2372-8

Lyness, K. S., & Thompson, D. E. (1997). Above the glass ceiling? A comparison of matched samples of female and male executives. *The Journal of Applied Psychology*, *82*(3), 359–375. doi:10.1037/0021-9010.82.3.359 PMID:9190144

Macroeconomic Outlooks for the Perspective Plan. (2014). Ministry of Planning, Bangladesh.

Magee, T. (2019). *Huawei controversies timeline*. Computerworld UK. https://www.computerworld.com/article/3427998/huawei-controversies-timeline.html

Mahadeo, J. D., Oogarah-Hanuman, V., & Soobaroyen, T. (2011). Changes in social and environmental reporting practices in an emerging economy (2004–2007): Exploring the relevance of stakeholder and legitimacy theories. *Accounting Forum*, *35*(3), 158–175.

Mahbubani, K. (2019). *The US strategy is not the best way to deal with Huawei.* Financial Times. https://www.ft.com/content/3d489be2-3e73-11e9-9499-290979c9807a

Majeed, S., Aziz, T., & Saleem, S. (2015). The Effect of Corporate Governance Elements on Corporate Social Responsibility (CSR) Disclosure: An Empirical Evidence from Listed Companies at KSE Pakistan. *International Journal of Financial Studies*, *3*(4), 530–556.

Malik, M. S., & Kanwal, L. (2016). Impact of Corporate Social Responsibility Disclosure on Financial Performance: Case Study of Listed Pharmaceutical Firms of Pakistan. *Journal of Business Ethics*, ●●●, 1–10.

Mansur, A. H., Yunus, M., & Nandi, B. K. (2011). An evaluation of the tax system in Bangladesh. In *Conference on Linking Research to Policy: Growth and Development Issues in Bangladesh, Dhaka, December* (*Vol. 20*). Academic Press.

Marshall, M. N. (1996). Sampling for qualitative research. *Family Practice*, *13*(6), 522–526. doi:10.1093/fampra/13.6.522 PMID:9023528

Marsh, J. R. (1997). *The capture and utilization of experience in engineering design.* Cambridge University.

Martin, C. R., & Horne, D. A. (1993). Services innovation: Successful versus unsuccessful firms. *International Journal of Service Industry Management*, *4*(1), 49–65. doi:10.1108/09564239310024985

Marzouk, M., Linsley, P., & Verma, S. (2017). Risk reporting. *The Routledge Companion to Accounting and Risk*, *24*(1), 64–81. doi:10.4324/9781315716756

Mason, P. (2008). *Tourism Impacts, Planning and Management.* Routledge.

Mathis, R. L., & John, J. (2004). *Human Resource Management.* South-Western Publisher.

Matuszak, Ł., Różańska, E., & Macuda, M. (2019). The impact of corporate governance characteristics on banks' corporate social responsibility disclosure. *Journal of Accounting in Emerging Economies*, *9*(1), 75–102. doi:10.1108/JAEE-04-2017-0040

Maume, D. J. (2006). Gender differences in restricting work efforts because of family responsibilities. *Journal of Marriage and the Family*, *68*(4), 859–869. doi:10.1111/j.1741-3737.2006.00300.x

Mavin, S. (2000). Approaches to careers in management: Why UK organisations should consider gender. *Career Development International*, *5*(1), 13–20. doi:10.1108/13620430010309323

McElroy, J. L., Tarlow, P., & Carlisle, K. (2007). 5 Tourist Harassment and Responses. *Analysis, Behaviour and Strategy, 94.*

Medina, L., & Schneider, F. (2018). *Shadow Economies Around the World: What Did We Learn Over the Last 20 Years?* IMF Working Paper WP/18/17.

Medium. (2019). *Top 4 Principles of Human-Centered Design*. Available at: https://uxplanet.org/top-4-principles-of-human-centered-design-5e02751e65b1

Megeid, N. S. A. (2017). Liquidity risk management: Conventional versus Islamic banking system in Egypt. *Journal of Islamic Accounting and Business Research*, *8*(1), 100–128. doi:10.1108/JIABR-05-2014-0018

Mehta, A., & Bhavani, G. (2017). What Determines Banks' Profitability? Evidence from Emerging Markets-the Case of the UAE Banking Sector. *Accounting and Finance Research*, *6*(1), 77–88. doi:10.5430/afr.v6n1p77

Menicucci, E., & Paolucci, G. (2016). The determinants of bank profitability: Empirical evidence from European banking sector. *Journal of Financial Reporting and Accounting*, *14*(1), 86–115. doi:10.1108/JFRA-05-2015-0060

Merkelsen, H. (2011). Institutionalized Ignorance as a Precondition for Rational Risk Expertise. *Risk Analysis*, *31*(7), 1083–1094. doi:10.1111/j.1539-6924.2010.01576.x PMID:21284683

Meyerson, D., & Fletcher, J. (2000). A modest manifesto for shattering the glass ceiling. *Harvard Business Review*, *78*(1), 127–140.

Michaud, C., & Llerena, D. (2011). Green consumer behaviour: An experimental analysis of willingness to pay for remanufactured products. *Business Strategy and the Environment*, *20*(6), 408420.

Michelon, G., Pilonato, S., & Ricceri, F. (2015). CSR reporting practices and the quality of disclosure: An empirical analysis. *Critical Perspectives on Accounting*, *33*, 59–78. doi:10.1016/j.cpa.2014.10.003

Miles. (2008). Patterns of innovation in service industries. *IBM Systems Journal*, *47*(1), 115-128. doi: . doi:10.1147j.471.0115

Mitchell, P. (2019, Mar. 12). Trump aide warns on Huawei. The Age.

Mohamad, M. T., Sulaiman, A. A., Hamimah, K., & Muslim, N. (2019). The determinants of bank profitability: How Malaysian Islamic banks response to the financing risk. *Advances in Social Sciences Research Journal*, *6*(12), 1–15. doi:10.14738/assrj.612.7471

Mohammed, H. K., & Gela, Z. D. (2014). Challenges of electronics tax register machine (ETRS) to businesses and its impact in improving tax revenue. *International Journal (Toronto, Ont.)*, *5*(3), 2305–1493.

Mokni, R. B. S., & Rachdi, H. (2014). Assessing the bank profitability in the MENA region. *International Journal of Islamic and Middle Eastern Finance and Management*, *7*(3), 305–332. doi:10.1108/IMEFM-03-2013-0031

Momin, M. A., & Parker, L. D. (2013). Motivations for corporate social responsibility reporting by MNC subsidiaries in an emerging country: The case of Bangladesh. *The British Accounting Review*, *45*(3), 215–228. doi:10.1016/j.bar.2013.06.007

Mufti, R. R. (2018, September 26). Indomaret tops retailer list with US$4.89b in sales. *The Jakarta Post*. Retrieved from: https://www.thejakartapost.com/news/2018/09/25/indomaret-tops-retailer-list-with-us4-89b-in-sales.html

Mugge, R., Jockin, B., & Bocken, N. (2017). How to sell refurbished smartphones? An investigation of different customer groups and appropriate incentives. *Journal of Cleaner Production*, *147*, 284–296. doi:10.1016/j.jclepro.2017.01.111

Mukherjee, A., & Nuñez, R. (2019). Doing well by doing good: Can voluntary CSR reporting enhance financial performance? *Journal of Indian Business Research*, *11*(2), 100–119. doi:10.1108/JIBR-07-2018-0199

Mullerat, R., & Brennan, D. (2005). Corporate social responsibility: The corporate governance of the 21st century. International Bar Association.

Muttakin, M. B., & Khan, A. (2014). Determinants of corporate social disclosure: Empirical evidence from Bangladesh. *Advances in Accounting*, *30*(1), 168–175.

Mybusiness.Singtel.com. (n.d.). *Online retailing in Indonesia: What SMEs should know*. Retrieved from: https://mybusiness.singtel.com/techblog/online-retailing-indonesia-what-smes-should-know

Nam, C. W., Parsche, R., & Schaden, B. (2001). *Measurement of value added tax evasion in selected EU countries on the basis of national accounts data*. Academic Press.

Narayan, P. K., & Phan, D. H. B. (2019). A survey of Islamic banking and finance literature: Issues, challenges and future directions. *Pacific-Basin Finance Journal, 53*, 484–496. doi:10.1016/j.pacfin.2017.06.006

Naseri, M., Bacha, O. I., & Masih, M. (2020). Too small to succeed versus too big to fail: How much does size matter in banking? *Emerging Markets Finance & Trade, 56*(1), 164–187. doi:10.1080/1540496X.2019.1612359

Naser, K., Al-Hussaini, A., Al-Kwari, D., & Nuseibeh, R. (2006). Determinants of Corporate Social Disclosure in Developing Countries: The Case of Qatar. *Advances in International Accounting, 19*, 1–23.

Nawaz, T. (2017). Momentum investment strategies, corporate governance and firm performance: An analysis of Islamic banks. *Corporate Governance: The International Journal of Business in Society, 17*(2), 192–211. doi:10.1108/CG-03-2016-0052

Nazir, M. (2010). Corporate Social Disclosure in Pakistan: A Case Study of Fertilizers Industry. *Journal of Commerce, 2*(1), 1–11. http://www.ciitlahore.edu.pk/Papers/Abstracts/146-8588969319825962058.pdf

NBR Annual Report, 2017-18, *National Board of Revenue, Bangladesh.*

Ng, C. W., & Chiu, W. C. (2001). Managing equal opportunities for women: Sorting the friends from the foes. *Human Resource Management Journal, 11*(1), 75–88. doi:10.1111/j.1748-8583.2001.tb00033.x

Ng, E. S., Schweitzer, L., & Lyons, S. T. (2010). New generation, great expectations: A field study of the millennial generation. *Journal of Business and Psychology, 25*(2), 281–292. doi:10.100710869-010-9159-4

Nobanee, H., & Ellili, N. (2015). Corporate sustainability disclosure in annual reports: Evidence from UAE banks: Islamic versus conventional. *Renewable & Sustainable Energy Reviews, 55*, 1336–1341.

Nonaka, I. (1991, Nov.). The Knowledge Creating Company. *Harvard Business Review*, 96–104.

Norman, D. A., & Verganti, R. (2011). *Incremental and Radical Innovation: design research versus technology and meaning change*. 5th Conference on Designing Pleasurable Products and Interfaces, Politecnico di Milano, Milano, Italy.

NovoEd. (2019). Available at: https://plusacumen.novoed.com/#!/courses/design-kit-2019-3/flyer

Nugroho, B. P. (2016). *Jokowi: I will find a way to reduce loan interest rate*. https://finance.detik.com/moneter/d-3119293/jokowi-saya-akan-cari-jalan-agar-bunga-kredit-turun

Nunnally, J. C., & Bernstein, I. H. (1994). *Psychometric Theory* (3rd ed.). McGraw-Hill.

Nyahunzvi, D. K. (2013). CSR reporting among Zimbabwe's hotel groups: A content analysis. *International Journal of Contemporary Hospitality Management, 25*(4), 595–613.

Ø

O'Reilly, B. (1997). The secrets of America's most admired corporations: New ideas, new products. *Fortune, 135*, 60–64.

Odera, O., Scott, A., & Gow, J. (2016). An Examination of the Quality of Social and Environmental Disclosures by Nigerian Oil Companies. Corporate Governance. *The International Journal of Business in Society, 16*(2), 400–419.

Oh, W., & Park, S. (2015). The relationship between corporate social responsibility and corporate financial performance in Korea. *Emerging Markets Finance & Trade*, *51*(3), 85–94. doi:10.1080/1540496X.2015.1039903

Olson, D., & Zoubi, T. A. (2008). Using accounting ratios to distinguish between Islamic and conventional banks in the GCC region. *The International Journal of Accounting*, *43*(1), 45–65. doi:10.1016/j.intacc.2008.01.003

Omar, B. F., & Zallom, N. O. (2016). Corporate social responsibility and market value: Evidence from Jordan. *Journal of Financial Reporting and Accounting*, *14*(1), 2–29. doi:10.1108/JFRA-11-2014-0084

Open, H. R. M. S. (2019, March 18). *Benefits of an automated leave management system.* Available at https://www.openhrms.com/blog/benefits-of-automated-leave-management-system>

Othman, H. B., & Mersni, H. (2014). The use of discretionary loan loss provisions by Islamic banks and conventional banks in the Middle East region. *Studies in Economics and Finance*, *31*(1), 106–128. doi:10.1108/SEF-02-2013-0017

Ozili, P. K., & Uadiale, O. (2017). Ownership concentration and bank profitability. *Future Business Journal*, *3*(2), 159–171. doi:10.1016/j.fbj.2017.07.001

Paasch, A., Garbers, F., & Hirsch, T. (2010). Agricultural Trade and the Human Right to Food: The Case of Small Rice Producers in Ghana, Honduras, and Indonesia. In Food Ethics. DOI doi:10.1007/978-1-4419-5765-8_8

Pahuja, S. (2009). Relationship between environmental disclosures and corporate characteristics: A study of large manufacturing companies in India. *Social Responsibility Journal*, *5*(2), 227–244.

Paniagua, J., & Sapena, J. (2014). Business performance and social media: Love or hate? *Business Horizons*, *57*(6), 719–728. doi:10.1016/j.bushor.2014.07.005

Parker, Riley, & Robinson. (2015). Remanufacturing Market study. *Horizon 2020*, Grant Agreement No. 645984, A report by ERN.

Pathirana, D., & Gnanapala, W. A. (2015). Tourists' Harassment at Cultural Sites in Sri Lanka. Tourism. *Leisure and Global Change*, *2*(1), 42–56.

Patroni, J., Briel, F. V., & Recker, J. (2020). Unpacking the social media–driven innovation capability: How consumer conversations turn into organizational innovations*", Information & management. The International Journal of Information Systems Applications*, 103267. doi:10.1016/j.im.2020.103267

Patten, D. M. (1992). Intra-industry environmental disclosures in response to the Alaskan oil spill: A note on legitimacy theory. *Accounting, Organizations and Society*, *17*(5), 471–475. doi:10.1016/0361-3682(92)90042-Q

Patten, D. M., & Zhao, N. (2014). Standalone CSR reporting by U.S. retail companies. *Accounting Forum*, *38*(2), 132–144. doi:10.1016/j.accfor.2014.01.002

Paukstadt, U., Strobel, G. & Eicker, S. (2019). *Understanding services in the era of the internet of things: a smart service taxonomy.* Academic Press.

Pearce, P., (1982). Perceived Changes in Holiday Destinations. *Annals of Tourism Research, 9*, 145-164.

People Works. (2013). *The future of HR technology in India.* Author.

Peter, M. (2008). *Tourism impacts, planning and management.* Butterworth-Heinemann.

Peus, C., & Traut-Mattausch, E. (2007). *Factors influencing women managers' success.* Academic Press.

Peus, C., Braun, S., & Knipfer, K. (2015). On becoming a leader in Asia and America: Empirical evidence from women managers. *The Leadership Quarterly*, *26*(1), 55–67. doi:10.1016/j.leaqua.2014.08.004

Peus, C., & Traut-Mattausch, E. (2008). Manager and mommy? A cross-cultural comparison. *Journal of Managerial Psychology*, *23*(5), 558–575. doi:10.1108/02683940810884531

Pham, M. (2019). *Vodafone chief slams Huawei exclusions*. Mobile World. https://www.mobileworldlive.com/featured-content/home-banner/vodafone-chief-slams-huawei-exclusions/

Pham, P., & Gammoh, B. (2015). Characteristic of Social Media Marketing Strategy and Customer-Based Brand Equity Outcomes: A Conceptual Model. *International Journal of Internet Marketing and Advertising*, *9*(4), 321–337. doi:10.1504/IJIMA.2015.072885

Piotrowicz, W., & Cuthbertson, R. (2014). Introduction to the special issue information technology in retail: Toward omnichannel retailing. *International Journal of Electronic Commerce*, *18*(4), 5–16. doi:10.2753/JEC1086-4415180400

Pitić, G., Radosavljević, G., Babin, M., & Erić, M. (2019). Digitalization of the tax administration in Serbia. *Ekonomika preduzeća, 67*(1-2), 131-145.

Pitta, D., & Gurău, C. (2012). A life-stage analysis of consumer loyalty profile: Comparing Generation X and Millennial consumers. *Journal of Consumer Marketing*.

Powell, G. N., Butterfield, D. A., & Parent, J. D. (2002). Gender and managerial stereotypes: Have times changed? *Journal of Management*, *28*(2), 177–193. doi:10.1177/014920630202800203

Powell, G. N., & Graves, L. M. (2003). *Women and Men in Management* (3rd ed.). Sage Publications.

Pragati. (2019). *Social media statistics in India.* Available at: https://www.talkwalker.com/blog/social-media-statistics-in-india

PTI. (2016). Demonetisation to Pull Down GDP Growth: Montek Singh Ahluwalia. *Economic Times*. https://economictimes.indiatimes.com/news/economy/policy/demonetisation-to-pull-down-gdp-growthmontek-singh-ahluwalia/articleshow/55568179.cms

Putri, A. S. (2020, January 29). *Inovasi Toko Offline Tanpa Kasir Pertama Hadir di Indonesia.* Retrieved from: https://www.fimela.com/lifestyle-relationship/read/4166318/inovasi-toko-offline-tanpa-kasir-pertama-hadir-di-indonesia

Quisumbing, A. R. (2003). Household Decisions, Gender, and Development A Synthesis of Recent Research. An earlier. Food Policy, 20, 407–423.

Rachinger, M., Rauter, R., Müller, C., Vorraber, W., & Schirgi, E. (2019). Digitalization and its influence on business model innovation. *Journal of Manufacturing Technology Management*, *30*(8), 1143–1160. doi:10.1108/JMTM-01-2018-0020

Rahaman, A. S., Lawrence, S., & Roper, J. (2004). Social and environmental reporting at the VRA: Institutionalised legitimacy or legitimation crisis? *Critical Perspectives on Accounting*, *15*(1), 35–56. doi:10.1016/S1045-2354(03)00005-4

Rallo. (2018). The Rise of Refurbished Products. *Liquidity Services – A Better Future for Surplus,* 3-10

Ranasinghe, R., & Deyshappriya, R. (2012). *Analyzing the significance of tourism on Sri Lankan economy.* Retrieved from https://www.kln.ac.lk/fcms/ICBI2012/images/ICBM/dccs/TRM001.pdf

Ranasinghe, J. (2012). Tourists' Satisfaction and Behavioral Intentions: An Empirical Evidence from Tourism Industry in Sri Lanka. *Proceedings of International Conference on Business Management*.

Rao, K., Mukherjee, S., Kumar, S., Sengupta, D. P., Tandon, S., & Nayudu, S. (2016). *Demonetization: Impact on the Economy*. National Institute of Public Finance and Policy New Delhi, Working Paper No. 182.

Rao. (2020, March 5). *Tech Upskilling – The Why and How – People matters.* Available at https://www.peoplematters.in/article/hr-technology/tech-upskilling-the-why-and-how-24899

Rasel, M., Hossian, M.S., Sultana, A., & Kabir, M.H. (2019). Demonetization in India: An Evaluation. *Asian Journal of Economics, Business and Accounting, 12*(2), 1-12.

Rathnayake, R. D., & Wijesundara, W. G. (2015). *Tourist perception on harassments in Sri Lanka (with special reference to Mount Lavinia).* Academic Press.

Razdan, R., Das, M., & Sohoni, A. (2014, January 1). *The evolving Indonesian Consumer.* McKinsey Report. Retrieved from: https://www.mckinsey.com/business-functions/marketing-and-sales/our-insights/the-evolving-indonesian-consumer

RBI Report. (2017). *Macroeconomic Impact of Demonetization- A Preliminary Assessment.* Author.

RBI. (2016a). *Annual Report, Table VIII 1 Banknotes in Circulation.* https://rbi.org.in/Scripts/BS_PressReleaseDisplay.aspx?prid=38520

RBI. (2016b). *Withdrawal of Legal Tender Status for Rs. 500 and Rs. 1000 Notes.* Reserve Bank of India(RBI) Notice. https://rbi.org.in/Scripts/BS_PressReleaseDisplay.aspx?prid=38520

RedSeer. (2019). *Indo E-Tailing: Poised To Grow More Than 4x Over 2018-2023.* Retrieved from https://redseer.com/newsletters/indo-e-tailing-poised-to-grow-more-than-4x-over-2018-2023/

Reid, E., & Duffy, K. (2018). A netnographic sensibility: Developing the netnographic/social listening boundaries. *Journal of Marketing Management, 34*(3-4), 263–286. doi:10.1080/0267257X.2018.1450282

Reisenwitz, T. H., &Iyer, R. (2009). Differences in Generation X and Generation Y: Implications For The Organization And Marketers. *Marketing Management Journal, 19*(2).

Reiter, L., McHaney, R., & Connell, K. Y. H. (2017). Social media influence on purchase intentions: Instrument validation. *International Journal of Web Based Communities, 13*(1), 54–72. doi:10.1504/IJWBC.2017.082719

Relano, F., & Paulet, E. (2012). Corporate responsibility in the banking sector: A proposed typology for the German case. *International Journal of Law and Management, 54*(5), 379–393. doi:10.1108/17542431211264269

Reuters. (2019). *Indonesia to lower threshold for import taxes on e-commerce goods.* Retrieved from https://www.thejakartapost.com/news/2019/12/24/government-to-lower-threshold-for-import-taxes-on-e-commerce-goods.html

Rezabakhsh, B., Bornemann, D., Hansen, U., & Schrader, U. (2006). Consumer power: A comparison of the old economy and the internet economy. *Journal of Consumer Policy, 29*(1), 3–36. Advance online publication. doi:10.100710603-005-3307-7

Rizos, V., Tuokko, K., & Behrens, A. (2017). *The Circular Economy: A Review of Definitions, Processes and Impacts.* Centre for European Policy Studies.

Rosly, S. A., & Abu Bakar, M. A. (2003). Performance of Islamic and mainstream banks in Malaysia. *International Journal of Social Economics, 30*(12), 1249–1265. doi:10.1108/03068290310500652

Rusliyadi, M., Mohd, H., Jamil, A., & Anshari, M. (2020). Analysis of Food Security Policy by Participatory Poverty Assessment (PPA) Effort: Case in Indonesia. In P. Ordoñez de Pablos, M. Almunawar, & M. Abduh (Eds.), Economics, Business, and Islamic Finance in ASEAN Economics Community (pp. 105-127). Hershey, PA: IGI Global. doi:10.4018/978-1-7998-2257-8.ch006

Rusliyadi, M., Bin Hj. Mohd. Jamil, A., Maseleno, A., Tri Kumalasari, R., & Othman, M. (2019). Agricultural extension policy, agricultural growth and poverty reduction in Indonesia. *IACSIT International Journal of Engineering and Technology*, *7*(4), 5539–5550. doi:10.14419/ijet.v7i4.13337

Rusliyadi, M., & Jamil, A. B. (2020). Participatory Poverty Assessment Effort in Food Security and Extension Policy: Evidence From Indonesia. In V. Erokhin & T. Gao (Eds.), *Handbook of Research on Globalized Agricultural Trade and New Challenges for Food Security* (pp. 481–499). IGI Global. doi:10.4018/978-1-7998-1042-1.ch024

Rusliyadi, M., Jamil, A., Mohd, B., & Kumalasari, R. T. (2019). Analysis of household food security policy: Case of food security village programme, Indonesia. *Asian Journal of Agriculture and Rural Development*, *9*(1), 19–32.

Rusliyadi, M., & Libin, W. (2018). Agriculture development programs for poverty reduction evidences from Indonesia and china - comparative study case. *Asian Journal of Agriculture and Rural Development*, *8*(2), 104–118.

Saini, D. (2004). *Budhwar, Pawan*. Human Resource Management in India. doi:10.4324/9780203157053

Salomone, R., & Galluccio, G. (2001). Environmental Issues and Financial Reporting Trends: A Survey in the Chemical and Oil & Gas Industries. *SSRN Electronic Journal* (FEEM Working Paper No. 32.2001). doi:10.2139srn.278240

Sangani, P. (2019). *Companies using tech to move Fast Moving Consumer Goods faster*. Available at: https://economictimes.indiatimes.com/industry/cons-products/fmcg/companies-using-tech-to-move-fast-moving-consumer-goods-faster/articleshow/72287883.cms?from=mdr

Santoro, G., Fiano, F., Bertoldi, B., & Ciampi, F. (2018). Big data for business management in the retail industry. *Management Decision.*

Santos, S. R., & Cox, K. (2000). Workplace adjustment and intergenerational differences between matures, boomers, and Xers. *Nursing Economics*, *18*(1), 7. PMID:11029913

Sari, E. V. (2016). *September 2016 non-performing loans is higher than last year*. https://www.cnnindonesia.com/ekonomi/20161107114502-78-170819/kredit-macet-september-2016-lebih-tinggi-dibanding-tahun-lalu

Satriawan, Oktavianti. (2012). Upaya Pengentasan Kemiskinan Pada Petani Menggunakan Model Tindakan Kolektif Kelembagaan Pertanian. *Jurnal Ekonomi Pembangunan*, *13*(1), 96–112.

Sawyer, A. J., & James, S. (2018). *Digitalization of Tax: Comparing New Zealand and United Kingdom Approaches*. Academic Press.

Schachter, M. (2018). The nature and variety of innovation. *International Journal of Innovation Studies*, *2*(2), 65–79. doi:10.1016/j.ijis.2018.08.004

Scherl, L. M., & Smithson, M. (1987). A new dimension to content analysis: Exploring relationships among thematic categories. *Quality & Quantity*, *21*(2), 199–208. doi:10.1007/BF00167608

Schmitt, M. T., Ellemers, N., & Branscombe, N. R. (2003). Perceiving and responding to gende discrimination in organizations. In S. A. Haslam, D. Van Knippenberg, M. J. Platow, & N. Ellemers (Eds.), *Social identity at work: Developing theory for organizational practice* (pp. 277–292). Psychology Press.

Schultz, A., & Parikh, J. (2020). *Keeping Our Services Stable and Reliable During the COVID-19 Outbreak*. Available at: https://about.fb.com/news/2020/03/keeping-our-apps-stable-during-covid-19/

Schwebkea, J., Brinkb, W., Hansenc, V., & Kellihera, C. (2019). *Analyzing the role of trustworthiness in tax filing and tax compliance behavior through an automated return*. Academic Press.

Seale, C. (1999). Quality in qualitative research. *Qualitative Inquiry*, *5*(4), 465–478. doi:10.1177/107780049900500402

Securities and Exchange Commission of Pakistan. (2013). *CSR Guidelines*. https://www.sustainablebankingnetwork.org/upload/file/2019/0819/1566184721324559.pdf

Selvam. (2015). Study on role of technology in Human Resources Management. *International Journal of Applied Research, 1*(7), 472-475.

Shah, A. Y. (2017). Impact of Demonetization on Rural India. *International Journal of Scientific and Research Publications, 7*(3).

Shaikh, F. (2018). *Social Media Listening & Analytics - Market Overview (India)*. Available at: https://www.linkedin.com/pulse/social-media-listening-analytics-indian-market-overview-shaikh

Shankara, P., Mahanta, P., Arora, E., & Srinivasamurthy, G. (2015, October). Impact of internet of things in the retail industry. In *OTM Confederated International Conferences" On the Move to Meaningful Internet Systems"* (pp. 61-65). Springer. 10.1007/978-3-319-26138-6_9

Sharif, M., & Rashid, K. (2014). Corporate governance and corporate social responsibility (CSR) reporting: An empirical evidence from commercial banks (CB) of Pakistan. *Quality & Quantity, 48*(5), 2501–2521. doi:10.100711135-013-9903-8

Sharpley, R. (2002). Rural tourism and the challenge of tourism diversification: The case of Cyprus. *Tourism Management, 23*(3), 233–244.

Sheahan, P., & Sheahan, P. (2005). Generation Y: Thriving and surviving with generation Y at work. Prahran: Hardie Grant Books.

Sheil, D., & Liswanti, N. (2006). Scoring the importance of tropical forest landscapes with local people: Patterns and insights. *Environmental Management, 38*(1), 126–136. doi:10.100700267-005-0092-7 PMID:16508796

Shihab, S. (2019, October 2). *Post fast fashion: The future of fashion and the rise of resale*. The Jakarta Post. Retrieved from: https://www.thejakartapost.com/life/2019/10/02/post-fast-fashion-the-future-of-fashion-and-the-rise-of-resale.html

Shirley, M. A. J. (2017). *Impact of Demonetization in India. International Journal of Trend in Research and Development.*

Shostack, L. (1984). Designing Services that Deliver. *Harvard Business Review, 62*, 133–139.

Shu, S. G. (2019). Analyzing Remanufacturability of Mobile Phones using DEMATEL Approach. *Jurnal Teknik Industri, 21*(1), 33–42. doi:10.9744/jti.21.1.33-42

Sial, M., Zheng, C., Khuong, N., Khan, T., & Usman, M. (2018). Does firm performance influence corporate social responsibility reporting of Chinese listed companies? *Sustainability, 10*(7), 2217. doi:10.3390u10072217

Sieber, S. D. (1973). The integration of fieldwork and survey methods. *American Journal of Sociology, 78*(6), 1335–1359. doi:10.1086/225467

Silaen, L. (2019, April 11). *95% Indonesian Retailers Expands to Online Stores amid the Digital Era - The Insiders Stories*. Retrieved from https://theinsiderstories.com/95-indonesian-retailers-expands-to-online-stores-amid-the-digital-era/

Silverman, D. (2016). *Qualitative research*. Sage.

Singh, P. (2019, April 6). *What Makes Indonesia the Fastest Rising E-commerce Country*. Retrieved from: https://www.entrepreneur.com/article/331838

Singh, A. (2017). Impact of demonetization on Indian economy. *International Journal of Engineering and Management Research, 7*(3), 785–788.

Singh, A., Shukla, N., & Mishra, N. (2017). Social media data analytics to improve supply chain management in food industries. *Transportation Research Part E, Logistics and Transportation Review*, *114*, 398–415. doi:10.1016/j.tre.2017.05.008

Singh, D. (2020). *Amazon, Flipkart eyeing refurbished goods market in India: Will the bet pay off?* Financial Express.

Slemrod, J., & Yitzhaki, S. (2002). Tax avoidance, evasion, and administration. In *Handbook of public economics* (Vol. 3, pp. 1423–1470). Elsevier.

Smith, P., & Joye, C. (2014). *NSA spy praises Huawei ban*. Australian Financial Review. https://www.afr.com/policy/foreign-affairs/nsa-spy-praises-huawei-ban-20140508-itzhy

Snapcart. (2017, March 9). *The coexistence of offline and online grocery shopping*. Retrieved from: https://snapcart.global/the-coexistence-of-offline-and-online-grocery-shopping

Snyder, H., Witell, L., Gustafsson, A., Fombelle, P., & Kristensson, P. (2016). Identifying categories of service innovation: A review and synthesis of the literature. *Journal of Business Research*, *69*(7), 2401–2408. doi:10.1016/j.jbusres.2016.01.009

Sobarsyah, M., Soedarmono, W., Yudhi, W. S. A., Trinugroho, I., Warokka, A., & Pramono, S. E. (2020). Loan growth, capitalization, and credit risk in Islamic banking. *International Economics*, 1-18. doi:10.1016/j.inteco.2020.02.001

Son, J., & Kim, S. S. (2008). Internet users' information privacy-protective responses: A taxonomy and a nomological model. *Management Information Systems Quarterly*, *32*(3), 503–529. doi:10.2307/25148854

Soto-Acosta, P., Del Giudice, M., & Scuotto, V. (2018). Emerging issues on business innovation ecosystems: The role of information and communication technologies (ICTs) for knowledge management (KM) and innovation within and among enterprises. *Baltic Journal of Management*, *13*(3), 298–302. doi:10.1108/BJM-07-2018-398

Sri Lanka Tourism Development Authority. (2016). *Annual Statistical Report 2015*. Sri Lanka Tourism Development Authority.

Sri Lanka Tourist Police. (2012). *Statistical Records*. Sri Lanka Tourist Police.

Staines, G., Tavris, C., & Jayaratne, T. E. (1974). *The queen bee syndrome*. Academic Press.

Stanny, E. (2013). Voluntary Disclosures of Emissions by US Firms. *Business Strategy and the Environment*, *22*(3), 145–158.

Static1.squarespace.com. (2019). Available at: https://static1.squarespace.com/static/55ca3eafe4b05bb65abd54ff/t/574737f89f7266ddad87a3cf/1464285179544/294+van+der+Bijl-Brouwer.pdf

Steimer, S. (2017). *How to Reach a Broader Audience with Multicultural Social Listening*. Available at: https://www.ama.org/marketing-news/how-to-reach-a-broader-audience-with-multicultural-social-listening/

Storey, J. (1995). *Human Resource Management: A critical Text*. Routledge Publication.

Stroh, L. K., Langlands, C. L., Simpson, P. A., Stockdale, M. S., & Crosby, F. J. (2004). Shattering the glass ceiling in the new millennium. *The psychology and management of workplace diversity*, 147-167.

Stroh, L. K., Langlands, C. L., & Simpson, P. A. (2004). Shattering the glass ceiling in the new millenium. In M. S. Stockdale & F. J. Crosby (Eds.), *The psychology and management of workplace diversity* (pp. 147–167). Blackwell.

Studio Frankly. (2019). *Desirable, Feasible and Viable: three important lenses - Studio frankly*. Available at: https://frankly.studio/desirable-feasible-and-viable-three-important-lenses/

Subramanian, R., & Subramanyam, R. (2012). Key Factors in the Market for Remanufactured Products. *Manufacturing & Service Operations Management*, *14*(2), 315–326. doi:10.1287/msom.1110.0368

Suh, B., & Han, I. (2003). The impact of customer trust and perception of security control on acceptance of electronic commerce. *International Journal of Electronic Commerce*, *7*(3), 135–164. doi:10.1080/10864415.2003.11044270

Sumiani, Y., Haslinda, Y., & Lehman, G. (2007). Environmental reporting in a developing country: A case study on status and implementation in Malaysia. *Journal of Cleaner Production*, *15*(10), 895–901. doi:10.1016/j.jclepro.2006.01.012

Sun, L., & Rakhman, F. (2013). CFO financial expertise and corporate social responsibility. *International Journal of Law and Management*, *55*(3), 161–172. doi:10.1108/17542431311327619

Susanto, H., Chen, C. K., & Almunawar, M. N. (2018). Revealing Big Data Emerging Technology as Enabler of LMS Technologies Transferability. In *Internet of Things and Big Data Analytics Toward Next-Generation Intelligence* (pp. 123–145). Springer. doi:10.1007/978-3-319-60435-0_5

Su, W., Peng, M. W., Tan, W., & Cheung, Y.-L. (2014). The signaling effect of corporate social responsibility in emerging economies. *Journal of Business Ethics*, *134*(3), 479–491. doi:10.100710551-014-2404-4

Suzuki, Y., Uddin, S., & Sigit, P. (2019). Do Islamic banks need to earn extra profits? A comparative analysis on banking sector rent in Bangladesh and Indonesia. *Journal of Islamic Accounting and Business Research*, *10*(3), 369–381. doi:10.1108/JIABR-01-2017-0003

Sweeney, L., & Coughlan, J. (2008). Do different industries report Corporate Social Responsibility differently? An investigation through the lens of stakeholder theory. *Journal of Marketing Communications*, *14*(2), 113–124. doi:10.1080/13527260701856657

Syed, M. A., & Butt, S. A. (2017). Financial and non-financial determinants of corporate social responsibility: Empirical evidence from Pakistan. *Social Responsibility Journal*, *13*(4), 780–797. doi:10.1108/SRJ-08-2016-0146

Synergita. (2019, July 24). *Performance Management Automation – The Future of Talent Management.* Available at https://www.synergita.com/blog/performance-management-automation/

Tajeddini, K., Martin, E., & Altinay, L. (2020). The importance of human-related factors on service innovation and performance. *International Journal of Hospitality Management*, *85*(102431), 102431. doi:10.1016/j.ijhm.2019.102431

Tam, L., & Kim, J. N. (2019). Social media analytics: How they support company public relations. *The Journal of Business Strategy*, *40*(1), 28–34. doi:10.1108/JBS-06-2017-0078

Tamvada, M. (2020). Corporate social responsibility and accountability: A new theoretical foundation for regulating CSR. *International Journal of Corporate Social Responsibility*, *5*(1). Advance online publication. doi:10.118640991-019-0045-8

Tan, J. (2018). *Huawei Now World's Largest Telecom Equipment-Maker.* CX Daily Briefing. https://www.caixinglobal.com/2018-03-19/huawei-now-worlds-largest-telecom-equipment-maker-101223256.html

Tan, Z. (2019). *Three trends in Indonesia's e-commerce sector, as told by RedSeer.* Retrieved from https://kr-asia.com/three-trends-in-indonesias-e-commerce-sector-as-told-by-redseer

Tang, W. (2019). *Banks lay off employees due to automation, digitalization.* https://www.thejakartapost.com/news/2019/03/31/banks-lay-off-employees-due-to-automation-digitalization.html

Tang, W. (2019, February 1). Offline retailers call for equal treatment. *The Jakarta Post.* Retrieved from:https://www.thejakartapost.com/news/2019/02/01/offline-retailers-call-for-equal-treatment.html

Tanwar, S. (2019). *Indian companies are investing in human resource technologies to cut costs.* scroll.in.

Tanzi, V., & Shome, P. (1993). A primer on tax evasion. *Staff Papers*, *40*(4), 807–828. doi:10.2307/3867611

Techwire Asia. 2019, October 29). *Why offline retailers in Indonesia should bank on e-payment solutions.* Retrieved from: https://techwireasia.com/2019/10/why-offline-retailers-in-indonesia-should-bank-on-e-payment-solutions/

Terada-Hagiwara, A., Gonzales, K., & Wang, J. (2019). *Taxation Challenges in a Digital Economy—The Case of the People's Republic of China.* Academic Press.

The Interaction Design Foundation. (2019). F*rom Prototype to Product: Ensuring Your Solution is Feasible and Viable.* Available at: https://www.interaction-design.org/literature/article/from-prototype-to-product-ensuring-your-solution-is-feasible-and-viable

The Jakarta Post. (2017, October 26). *Lotus, Debenhams in Indonesia to close down by year's end.* The Jakarta Post. Retrieved from: https://www.thejakartapost.com/life/2017/10/26/lotus-debenhams-in-indonesia-to-close-down-by-years-end.html

The Jakarta Post. (2018, March 20). After Sodaqo Mart, 212 Mart, Hydro to introduce Rinjani Mart. *The Jakarta Post.* Retrieved from: https://www.thejakartapost.com/news/2018/03/20/after-sodaqo-mart-212-mart-hydro-to-introduce-rinjani-mart.html

The Jakarta Post. (2020, April 11). *How Indonesians embrace the digital world.* Retrieved from https://www.thejakartapost.com/academia/2019/03/18/how-indonesians-embrace-the-digital-world.html

The Jakarta Post. (2020, April 21). In challenging times, digital economy and e-commerce can chart a path toward recovery. *The Jakarta Post.* Retrieved from: https://www.thejakartapost.com/academia/2020/04/21/in-challenging-times-digital-economy-and-e-commerce-can-chart-a-path-toward-recovery.html

Tilling, M. V., & Tilt, C. a. (2010). The edge of legitimacy: Voluntary social and environmental reporting in Rothmans' 1956-1999 annual reports. *Accounting, Auditing & Accountability Journal, 23*(1), 55–81.

Tilt, C. A. (2016). Corporate social responsibility research: The importance of context. *International Journal of Corporate Social Responsibility, 1*(1), 1–9. doi:10.118640991-016-0003-7

Tlaiss, H., & Kauser, S. (2011). The impact of gender, family, and work on the career advancement of Lebanese women managers. *Gender in Management, 26*(1), 8–36. doi:10.1108/17542411111109291

Tobenkin. (2019, February 26). *HR Needs to Stay Ahead of Automation – SHRM.* Available at https://www.shrm.org/hr-today/news/hr-magazine/spring2019/pages/hr-needs-to-stay-ahead-of-automation.aspx

Tolani, K., Bhadade, P., & Sao, R. (2018). Gen X and Gen Y Women Managers: Challenges and Issues. Helix: The scientific. *Explorer, 6*, 5.

Trad, N., Trabelsi, M. A., & Goux, J. F. (2017). Risk and profitability of Islamic banks: A religious deception or an alternative solution? *European Research on Management and Business Economics, 23*(1), 40–45. doi:10.1016/j.iedeen.2016.09.001

Tran, T. T. M., Aluko, O., & Beddewela, E. (2016). The Impact of Institutional Environment on Corporate Social Responsibility Disclosure. *Academy of Management Proceedings, 2016*(1), 17827. doi:10.5465/ambpp.2016.17827

Tulgan, B. (2000). *Managing Generation X: How to bring out the best in young talent.* WW Norton & Company.

Tuten, T., & Perotti, V. (2017). Lies, brands and social media. *Qualitative Market Research, 22*(1), 5–13. doi:10.1108/QMR-02-2017-0063

Twain, A. (2017). *Cisco Vs Huawei — Which One is the better Choice for Ethernet Switches?* Medium. https://medium.com/@lia640230/cisco-vs-huawei-which-one-is-the-better-choice-for-ethernet-switches-59ffd324117d

Uchupalanan, K. (2000). Competition and IT-based innovation in banking services. *International Journal of Innovation Management*, *4*(4), 455–490. doi:10.1142/S1363919600000238

Ujah, N. U., Brusa, J., & Okafor, C. E. (2017). The influence of earnings management and bank structure on bank performance. *Managerial Finance*, *43*(7), 761–773. doi:10.1108/MF-12-2015-0329

Ullah, H., & Afjalur, M. (2015). Corporate social responsibility reporting practices in banking companies in Bangladesh. *Journal of Financial Reporting and Accounting*, *13*(2), 200–225.

Vaismoradi, M., Turunen, H., & Bondas, T. (2013). Content analysis and thematic analysis: Implications for conducting a qualitative descriptive study. *Nursing & Health Sciences*, *15*(3), 398–405. doi:10.1111/nhs.12048 PMID:23480423

Van Weelden, E., Mugge, R., & Bakker, C. (2016). Paving the way towards Circular Consumption: Exploring Consumer Acceptance of Refurbished Mobile Phones in the Dutch Market. *Journal of Cleaner Production, 113*, 743-754.

Vani, M., & Murali, K. P. (2015). Corporate Social Responsibility: A Glance At the Practices of Cement Industry. *International Journal Of Marketing*, *4*(8), 79–100.

Verma, S., & Bhattacharyya, S. S. (2016). Micro-foundation strategies of IOT, BDA, Cloud Computing. *Strategic Direction, VOL.*, *32*(8), 36–38. doi:10.1108/SD-06-2015-0093

Vijayalakshmi Murthy, B. (2015). *Innovative HR practices in IT industry of India – an Empirical Study*. http://www.vesasc.org/InnovativeHR_Practices_Mrs_Murthy_Nov_2015.pdf

Volt, R. (2009). Society and Technological Change (7th ed.). Worth Publications.

Von Hippel, E. (2005). *Democratizing Innovation*. MIT Press. doi:10.7551/mitpress/2333.001.0001

Vurro, C., & Perrini, F. (2011). Making the most of corporate social responsibility reporting: Disclosure structure and its impact on performance. *Corporate Governance*, *11*(4), 459–474. doi:10.1108/14720701111159280

Vyas, M. (2017). *Using Fast Frequency Household Survey Data to Estimate the Impact of Demonetization on Employment*. CMIE Working Paper.

Waheed, M. A. A. (2014). Approach to fire-related disaster management in high density urban-area. *Procedia Engineering*, *77*, 61–69. doi:10.1016/j.proeng.2014.07.007

Wang, C. N., Day, J. D., & Farid, M. (2019). Service Innovation Model of the Automobile Service Industry. *Applied Sciences (Basel, Switzerland)*, *9*(12), 2403. doi:10.3390/app9122403

Wang, P., & Kuah, A. T. H. (2017). Green marketing cradle-to-cradle: Remanufactured products in Asian markets. *Thunderbird International Business Review*, *60*(5), 783–795. doi:10.1002/tie.21925

Wang, Wiegerinck, V., Krikke, H., & Zhang, H. (2013). Understanding the purchase intention towards remanufactured product in closed-loop supply chains: An empirical study in China. *International Journal of Physical Distribution & Logistics Management*, *43*(10), 866–888. doi:10.1108/IJPDLM-01-2013-0011

Wang, Y., & Hazen, B. T. (2015). (in press). Consumer product knowledge and intention to purchase remanufactured products. *International Journal of Production Economics*. Advance online publication. doi:10.1016/j.ijpe.2015.08.031

Wasiuzzaman, S., & Tarmizi, H. A. B. A. (2010). Profitability of Islamic banks in Malaysia: an empirical analysis. *Journal of Islamic Economics, Banking and Finance, 6*(4), 53-68. Retrieved from https://www.researchgate.net/publication/236980854

Weiler, A. M., Hergesheimer, C., Brisbois, B., Wittman, H., Yassi, A., & Spiegel, J. M. (2014). Food sovereignty, food security and health equity: A meta-narrative mapping exercise. *Health Policy and Planning*, *30*(8), 1078–1092. doi:10.1093/heapol/czu109 PMID:25288515

Wesley, M. (2011). *There goes the neighbourhood: Australia and the rise of Asia*. University of New South Wales Limited.

Whittaker, Z. (2012). *Huawei to invest $2B in U.K. amid ongoing 'spying' claims*. Cnet.com. https://www.cnet.com/news/huawei-to-invest-2b-in-u-k-amid-ongoing-spying-claims/

Wibowo, A. (2020, January 10). *Paying for the glow: Indonesian skincare e-commerce market trends*. Janio Asia. retrieved from: https://janio.asia/sea/indonesia/indonesia-skincare-ecommerce-trends/

Williams, C. (2009). *BT network 'vulnerable to Chinese attack'*. The Register. https://www.theregister.co.uk/2009/03/30/huawei_threat/

Wira, N. N. (2020, January 28). Indonesian beauty trends to look out for in 2020. *The Jakarta Post*. Retrieved from: https://www.thejakartapost.com/life/2020/01/28/indonesian-beauty-trends-to-look-out-for-in-2020.html

Wired. (2019). *Why Human-Centered Design Matters*. Available at: https://www.wired.com/insights/2013/12/human-centered-design-matters/

WiseStep. (2019). *How to Solve Unemployment in a Country: Best Tips - WiseStep*. Available at: https://content.wisestep.com/solve-unemployment-country-best-tips/

Wong, E. (2019, March 18). How Indonesians embrace the digital world. *The Jakarta Post*. Retrieved from https://www.thejakartapost.com/academia/2019/03/18/how-indonesians-embrace-the-digital-world.html

Wu, Y. C., Wei Kiong Ting, I., Lu, W. M., Nourani, M., & Kweh, Q. L. (2016). The impact of earnings management on the performance of ASEAN banks. *Economic Modelling*, *53*, 156–165. doi:10.1016/j.econmod.2015.11.023

Yapa, P. W. S., Harvey, D., & Ellis, G. (2005). Disclosure of Corporate Environmental Policies in Annual Reports: Further Evidence Incorporating a National Ideology–An Australian Study. *Journal of Asia-Pacific Business*, *6*(1), 75–90.

Ye, H., & Kankanhalli, A. (2020). Value Cocreation for Service Innovation: Examining the Relationships between Service Innovativeness, Customer Participation, and Mobile App Performance. *Journal of the Association for Information Systems*, 294–312. doi:10.17705/1jais.00602

Yim, S., Bae, Y. H., Lim, H., & Kwon, J. (2019). The role of marketing capability in linking CSR to corporate financial performance. *European Journal of Marketing*, *53*(7), 1333–1354. doi:10.1108/EJM-08-2017-0526

Young. (2010). Sustainable consumption: Green Consumer Behaviour When Purchasing Products. *Sustainable Development*, *18*(1), 20–31.

Yu, H.-C., Kuo, L., & Kao, M.-F. (2017). The relationship between CSR disclosure and competitive advantage. *Sustainability Accounting. Management and Policy Journal*, *8*(5), 547–570.

Zembik, M. (2014). Social media as a source of knowledge for customers and enterprises. *Online Journal of Applied Knowledge Management*, *2*(2), 132–148.

Zhang, B., & Vos, M. (2014). Social media monitoring: Aims, methods, and challenges for international companies. *Corporate Communications*, *19*(4), 371–383. doi:10.1108/CCIJ-07-2013-0044

Zhang, J., Guo, H. T., Li, B., & Wang, W. (2008). *The Influence of Financial Factors on Environmental Information Disclosure in China Chemical Industry*. doi:10.2139srn.1305005

Zubielqui, G. C. D., & Jones, J. (2019). How and when social media affects innovation in start-ups. A moderated mediation model. *Industrial Marketing Management*, *85*, 209–220. doi:10.1016/j.indmarman.2019.11.006

About the Contributors

Patricia Ordóñez de Pablos is a professor in the Department of Business Administration in the Faculty of Business and Economics at The University of Oviedo (Spain). She completed her education in The London School of Economics (UK). Her teaching and research interests focus on the areas of strategic management, knowledge management, organizational learning, human resource management, intellectual capital, information technologies, with special interest in Asia (Bhutan, China, Laos, Myanmar). She is Editor-in-Chief of the International Journal of Learning and Intellectual Capital (IJLIC) and International Journal of Asian Business and Information Management (IJABIM), respectively. She has edited books for IGI-Global, Routledge and Springer.

Miltiadis D. Lytras is Associate Professor at Deree- ACG with a research focus on semantic web, knowledge management and e-learning, with more than 100 publications. He has co-edited more than 45 special issues in International Journals (IEEE Transaction on Knowledge and Data Engineering, IEEE Internet Computing, IEEE Transactions on Education, Computers in Human Behaviour, Interactive Learning Environments, Journal of Knowledge Management, Journal of Computer Assisted Learning) and has authored/(co-)edited 42 books (e.g. Open Source for Knowledge and Learning Management, Ubiquitous and Pervasive Knowledge Management, Intelligent Learning Infrastructures for Knowledge Intensive Organizations, Semantic Web Based Information Systems, China Information Technology Handbook, Real World Applications of Semantic Web and Ontologies, Web 2.0: The Business Model, etc.). He (has) serves(ed) as the (Co) Editor in Chief of 8 international journals (e.g., International Journal on Semantic Web and Information Systems, International Journal of Knowledge Society Research, International Journal of Knowledge and Learning, International Journal of Technology Enhanced Learning).

* * *

Adilla Anggraeni is a faculty member of Binus Business School International Undergraduate Program. Her research interests include Consumer Behaviour, Retail Management, and Luxury Branding.

Rajib Bhattacharyya is an Associate Professor in Economics, Goenka College of Commerce and Business Administration, Kolkata, India. He obtained his bachelor degree in Economics from St Xavier's College, Kolkata and his Master degree in Economics, from University of Calcutta. He did his M.Phil and Ph.D in Economics, both from the University of Calcutta. He has 19 years of teaching experience at the UG and PG levels. His fields of interests are International Trade, Finance, Development Economics, and Women & Development. He has contributed a good number of articles in reputed national and international journals/ books viz. IGI Global (USA), Emerald (U.K.) and Springer.

Ang Jonathan Christianto is completing a bachelor's degree in Business Accounting from Petra Christian University. While completing his title, he took the CMA certification class held by the university. He also completed an internship program at PT. Sumber Cipta Multiniaga for two months in the finance department. This company is a branch of PT. Djarum, the fourth largest cigarette company in Indonesia. His job during his internship was to help process financial data and the final balance of each branch account in eastern Indonesia which was used to prepare weekly and monthly financial statements which would then be sent to the head office.

Mona Chung received her doctorate from Monash University in Melbourne. Dr Chung is a bi-cultural business expert in doing business with China in particular negotiations. She addresses the major issue - overcoming the cultural gap between Westerners and Chinese in commerce and education. Dr Chung specialises in strategic planning, management and marketing practice for international organisations with the understanding of the culture of Chinese market first. Her major contribution from her PhD to knowledge is the Chung Model which has been tested, applied and approved in practice to improve the outcome of businesses. As a bi-cultural consultant she short-circuits processes and produce results that increase efficiency by between 70% and 50%. Dr Chung is in a unique position not only she has the theoretical tools but also the practical experiences. She has published 6 books and over 90 publications. She is an expert in cross-cultural communication.

Athula Gnanapala is a Senior Lecturer attached to the Dept. of Tourism Management, Faculty of Management Studies, Sabaragamuwa University of Sri Lanka. Presently, he also serves as the Head of the department Programme Coordinator of the M.Sc. in Ayurvedic Hospital Management Programme. Dr. Gnanapala obtained his first degree, B.Sc. in Tourism Management from the Sabaragamuwa University of Sri Lanka in 1997, after that he followed the M.Sc. in Management degree at the University of Sri Jayewardenapura. He has obtained his Doctoral degree in Tourism Management from the Xiamen University, P.R. China. His research interests include consumer behavior in tourism including motivation, perception & satisfaction, sustainable tourism planning & development, tourism and green marketing etc. He has published his research findings in both national and international reputed journals and other publications. He disseminates his expertise as a reviewer of nationally and internally recognized journals, tourism consultant, editorial member, scientific committee member for international symposiums, etc.

Saarce Elsye Hatane is a lecturer in the Accounting Department of Universitas Kristen Petra, Indonesia. She is majoring in Management Accounting and holding Certified Management Accountant from International Certified Management Accountant, Australia. She also has a Chartered Accountant designation from Indonesia Accountant Body. She is a trainer for Certified Management Accountant course in East Java, Indonesia. Besides, she also gives training in finance and cost accounting for the small enterprises in Surabaya, Indonesia. She has experiences in publishing research articles in some reputable journals which are indexed by Scopus. Her research areas are corporate governance, intellectual capital, social responsibility, and knowledge management. Besides, Ms Saarce also a reviewer in some reputable international journals indexed by Scopus. She became the head of Business Accounting

Program in Universitas Kristen Petra since 2013 until now, 2020. She also gives business consultation for some small and medium enterprises in Indonesia.

Mosharrof Hosen is currently a Doctor of Philosophy (PhD) candidate of the Faculty of Business and Finance, Universiti Tunku Abdul Rahman (UTAR), Malaysia. He obtained his Master of Science in Islamic Finance in 2017, from INCEIF (AACSB-Accredited), Malaysia. Prior that, he finished Bachelor of Business Administration (Major in Banking and Finance) from IIUC in 2015. He is working as a research assistant under the faculty of Business and Finance, UTAR. His research interest includes financial econometrics, economics, organizational behaviour, knowledge management, Islamic finance and accounting, educational system. He is an executive editor at International Research Journal of Education and Leadership Management (IRJELM). He has published several international refereed journals including Journal of Economics, Finance and Administrative Science (JEFAS), International Journal of Social Economics (IJSE), Quantitative Finance and Economics (QFE), International Journal of Business and Society (IJBS), International Journal of Financial Studies (IJFS), International Journal of Asian Business and Information Management (IJABIM), Asia-Pacific Social Science Review (APSSR). He has reviewed research articles from international journals such as International Journal of Emerging Market (IJEM), Journal of Financial Economic Policy (JFEP), Journal of Islamic Accounting and Business Research (JIABR), Journal of Economics, Management and Trade (JEMT), Asian Journal of Research in Computer Science (AJRCS), Asian Journal of Economics, Business and Accounting (AJEBA), Asian Journal of Advanced Research and Reports (AJARR).

Fahmi Ibrahim is Assistant Professor of School of Business, Universiti Teknologi Brunei (UTB), Brunei Darussalam. He gained his PhD from Glasgow Caledonian University, Glasgow, UK and MSc in Business Information Technology Systems (BITS) from University of Strathclyde, Glasgow, UK. He has a wide range of academic experience, gained in further and higher education establishments in the Brunei Darussalam and UK. This experience includes module and programme development, programme leadership, and international collaboration. Her current teaching and research areas are in the field of Strategic Management, Knowledge Management, and Intellectual Capital Management, Management Information Systems (MIS), Operations Management within public, private and SMEs organisations. His consultancy experience is in the area of Business Transformation particularly in SMEs. The consultancy expertise is supported by and complemented by his research interests. His research output includes book chapters, journal articles and conference papers. In recent years his research interest has evolved to be contextualised around the strategic development of organisations in complex and transitional environments.

Md. Humayun Kabir is a Lecturer at the Department of Business Administration, East West University, Dhaka, Bangladesh. His research interest includes dividend policy, financial inclusion, financial markets, and so forth.

Muzammal Khan is a lecturer in the School of Business and Creative Industries at the University of the West of Scotland situated in beautiful Scotland, UK. He is graduated with a PhD from the university in which he is currently working. He is an author of several publications and a researcher in the field of business ethics and entrepreneurship research. Currently, he is supervising a PhD project that investigates the impact of culture on women entrepreneurship in a developing country. He is keen to conduct further research on interdisciplinary topics.

Nilesh Kumar possesses experience of two years in corporate and more than five years in academic institutions as an academician and non-academic profile as well. He has done his Masters in marketing management and Post-graduation in international business. He is also pursuing his Ph.D. from Ranchi University in marketing. He has served in various colleges of Ranchi. He has published a few quality research papers and book chapters in journals & conferences. He is an exceptional speaker and an expert in giving training in soft skills.

Nishant Kumar is currently working in Amity School of Business, Amity University Noida. He has more than 9 years of experience including Academics Corporate and worked on various National & International Research Projects. He has published research papers in Journals of repute. He has presented papers at various National & International conferences in the prestigious institutes like IIM Bangalore, IIM Indore and University of Mumbai.

Bruno Mascitelli moved to academia in 2000 after spending two decades working for the Australian government in the trade and investment promotion. He then joined the US Consulate in Melbourne where he spent a further two years promoting US companies in the Australian market. In 2000 he joined academia and undertook a PhD in the area of European politics. Bruno's research areas of interest include migration, international business, political economy. He has published 22 books and over 60 journal articles.

Divya Mohan is working as faculty Delhi Institute of Advanced Studies, India. Her Research interest mainly includes Recycling, Refurnishing and Circular Economy. She presented her research in national and International level followed with its publication.

Fadzliwati Mohiddin is a Deputy Dean, School of Business, Brunei University of Technology, Brunei Darrusalam.

Gaurav Nagpal is an Assistant Professor in Management Department of Birla Institute of Technology and Science Pilani. His area of expertise is Operations and Supply Chain Management, Operations Research, Industrial Engineering, Business Statistics and Data Analytics. He received his Bachelor's degree in Mechanical Engineering from YMCA Institute of Engineering in 2005. Post that, he completed his MBA from Indian Institute of Foreign Trade, New Delhi. He has been a GATE topper with 99.83 percentile (AIR-41) in mechanical engineering. He has also done EPMBD from IIM Calcutta, and is CSCP qualified from APICS. He is currently pursuing his PhD from BITS Pilani in the area of inventory management. He has twelve years of industry experience, of which the former seven years were into Operations and supply chain profiles with NTPC, Daimler India Commercial Vehicles and with Escorts Agri-machinery Group. After that he worked for five years in business strategy, planning and analysis profiles. Before joining BITS as Assistant Professor in 2018, he was working with the leading grocery e-Commerce firm "Grofers" as Associate Director- Business Planning and Analysis.

Biplob Nandi is a Senior Lecturer at the Department of Economics, East West University, Dhaka, Bangladesh. His research interest includes macroeconomic modeling, fiscal and debt behavior in developing countries, analysis of firm and industry behavior, and so forth.

Sampada Nanoty is a Graduate Scholar, Maharaja Sayajirao Gaikwad University, Vadodara, Gujarat, India.

Amadea Nathania Pranoto is completing her bachelor's degree in Business Accounting from Petra Christian University. She is on the last semester of studying and currently working on finishing her thesis about Corporate Social Responsibility. While also completing her degree, she attends the Certified Management Accountant course held by the university. Currently, she takes a part in managing the small family business of butchery. In the business, she is now in charge of the financial recording and development of the business. Her occupations include the bookkeeping, preparing financial reports, and providing strategic insights to advance the business in the long run.

Nandini Roy has completed Master of Business Administration from the University of Dhaka, Bangladesh.

Mohamed Saleem is a Dean School of Business, Brunei University of Technology.

Desi Setiana received a BSc and MSc in Psychology Behavior of Information Technology, respectively from University of Indonesia and University of Brunei. She is researcher at the Ministry of Law and Human Right, Republic of Indonesia. Her research interests are in the areas of Psychology of Information Security, User Behaviour toward Cyberbullying, IT Emerging Technology for Psychology Education. She is now in-pipeline to pursuing Ph.D in IT Psychology for Cyberbullying and Security Protection for Prisoners.

Susheela Shetty is an assistant Professor in the Department of Business Administration, Brindavan College, Bangalore has more than 5 years of Experience in teaching at both graduate and post graduate level. She has completed her Masters of Business Administration at Mangalore University and Master of Journalism and Mass Communication at University of Mysore. Her areas of interest includes Business Administration, Human Resource Management and Innovative Technology in Human Resource Management.

Archana Shrivastava is working as professor at Jaypee School of Business, JIIT University, Noida.

Ayuphita Silalahi is the deputy head of program of International Business program in Binus Business School. Bina Nusantara University. Her research interests include marketing communication and social media marketing. She has been teaching since 2011 and teaches various classes such as marketing communication, interpersonal communication, public speaking, and other classes of similar topics.

Sachin Soonthodu is an Assistant Professor in the Department of Tourism, Garden City University has more than 10 years of experience in teaching both at graduate and postgraduate level. He has pursued Masters of Business Administration (Tourism) from Mangalore University and PGDCA from MAHE. He has qualified UGC- NET in 2009 and K-SET in 2015 and at present engaged in doctoral research at Karnataka Folklore University, Haveri. He is the principal investigator for the Minor Research Project funded by UGC. He also served as the visiting faculty for IATA study centers in Bangalore. Currently he is also associated with research on temples of Kodagu district of Karnataka. His key skills include

Travel and Tourism Management, Tourism Geography, Indian Architecture, Airline and Cargo Management, Marketing Management and Business Administration. His passion includes research, Hindu Architecture, Travel, Photography and Blogging.

Heru Susanto is a researcher at Research Center for Informatics, the Indonesian Institute of Sciences; and an Honorary Professor in the department of Information Management at College of Management, Tunghai University, Taichung, Taiwan. He is also a Visiting Professor at School of Business, University Technology of Brunei. Dr. Susanto has worked as an IT professional in several roles, including Web Division Head of IT Strategic, and Prince Muqrin Chair for Information Security Technologies. His research interests are in Information Security, 5G Technologies, Grid Application, Big Data, Business Process Re-engineering, and e-Marketing. Dr. Susanto received a BSc in Computer Science; an MBA in Marketing Management; an MSc in Information Systems; and a PhD in Information Security from Tunghai University and University of Brunei. Dr. Heru has successfully authoring 8 books entitled: Information Security Management Systems, Business Process Reengineering an ICT Approach, The Emerging Technology of Big Data, Human Capital through ICT, Chemical Technology and Informatics in Chemistry with Applications. He also has more than 90 publication in journals, and book chapters.

Josephine Alexandra Susilo was completing her bachelor's degree in Business Accountancy from Petra Christian University. She was applied course in Management Accounting, certified by International Certified Management Accounting, Australia. Currently, she was took part in managing her small family business of jewelry. Yet, also running of her small beverage business. In her small beverage business, she becomes the administrator, the barista and the financial recording too. Her occupations in her small beverage business is brewing the coffee, maintaining the quality taste, promoting on social media, spreading through personal messages, and conceiving the new ideas for her menu. Her obligations is pressing the capital to get a high profits.

Josua Tarigan has an experience in Accounting Education for more than fifteen years. Besides that almost two years experience in ERP related (Siemens Company) and also several years in freelance consulting. Have been interacting directly with several companies in Indonesia, Singapore, Malaysia, Bangkok, Vietnam, Myanmar, Korea, Japan, Hongkong, Macau, Shenzen, Dubai, Europe (Germany, Chezh, Austria, Spain, Netherland, Belgium, France & Switzerland) and United States of America (USA). Have strong knowledge and skill in the area of Strategic Management Accounting, Finance & Auditing Information System. Serve also as a visiting lecturer in Germany (Berlin & Munich) for Financial Management course and a reviewer for Journal of Asia Business Studies (Q1-Emerald); International Journal of Emerging Markets (Q2-Emerald) & Nankai Business Review International (Q3-Emerald). He also become Editorial Board for ASEAN Journal of Management & Innovation (AJMI) and Jurnal Akuntansi Keuangan (JAK). He has been recently invited as keynote speakers at Rangsit University (Thailand) international conference. Additionally, proficient in both written and spoken english, computer literate with excellent interpersonal, communication and intercultural skills.

Shamila Wijesundara, since joining the Uva Wellassa University, has been involved with teaching related to Tourism and Hospitality Management. Her research interest includes human resource management in tourism, food and beverage, host-guest relation, etc.

Index

A

Accountability 4, 7, 19-25, 27, 211
Artificial Intelligence 93, 131-135, 138-139, 174, 220, 252, 261, 263, 268
Assistance Role 43
Automated Tax System 225-226, 232-233, 246
Automation 93, 131-138, 140, 177, 184-185, 192, 194, 208, 210, 213, 225-229, 232-240, 242, 244, 246-247, 263

B

Banking Sector 11, 17, 26, 120, 155, 165-167, 198-199, 201, 204, 206, 211-212, 286, 293
Barriers 250, 267, 271, 274-275, 277, 280-282, 287-289, 293, 295
Before and After analysis 60
Big Data 93, 220, 222, 227, 248, 250-253, 255-257, 265
Black Money 115-117, 120, 126-128

C

Cashless Economy 115-116, 128
China 25, 28, 42, 58, 72, 141-144, 146-150, 219, 245, 284, 302, 304
Circular economy 271-272, 281-284
Community Perception 29, 32
Content Analysis 1, 4-7, 19-20, 22-23, 25-26, 28, 95, 99, 110, 112-114
Corporate Social Responsibility 1-2, 19-28, 197-200, 203, 211-213
Corporate Social Responsibility Reporting 1, 19-20, 22, 26-27, 213
Credit-Deposit ratio 118, 124
Currency in Circulation 115, 118, 124, 126, 128
Customer voice 95
Cybernation 131-138

D

Data Breach Prevention 76
Demonetization 115-116, 118, 120-129
Developing Country 1, 4, 22-23, 27-28, 30, 44
digital disruption 173
Digital Ecosystem 77, 79, 93
Digitization 115, 117, 127-128, 131-133
DSS (Decision Support System) 94

E

Earnings management 197-201, 204-205, 207-213
Economic Growth 30, 44, 154-156, 158, 176, 226, 239, 243-244, 246, 249-250, 303
Employee experience 131-132, 139
enhanced customer experience 173, 194
Environmental 1-2, 4-5, 7-28, 42, 59, 65, 194, 197-200, 209, 211, 241, 259, 267, 271, 273, 275, 277, 280-283, 297, 305

F

Food Security 29-32, 42-47, 58-65, 71-73
Food Security Analysis at household level 60, 71
Food Security and Extension Policy 42-43, 58, 72
Food Self Sufficiency Village Programme Indonesia 29

G

Generalized Method of Moment System 197, 201
Gross Domestic Product 158, 160-162

H

Huawei 141-143, 145, 147-152
Human Factors 76-77
Human Resource 131-140, 258-270, 295, 297, 305
Human-Centered Design 76-85, 91-93

I

Impacts 2, 6, 15, 17, 24, 32, 35, 40, 60, 70-71, 82, 117, 132, 154, 163, 207, 210, 273, 284, 306, 312-313
India 13-14, 20, 24, 26, 28, 42, 58, 95-97, 105, 108, 112-113, 115-118, 120, 122-124, 126-129, 131, 143, 173-175, 177, 179, 186, 190-192, 194, 230, 248-250, 255-258, 260-261, 267-268, 270-272, 275, 282, 284, 286-287, 293, 303-304
Indirect Tax 228-229, 246
Indonesia 30-31, 41-42, 44-45, 58-62, 67, 71-72, 76, 167, 197-199, 201, 205, 210, 212, 215-224, 230, 250
Indonesia's conventional banks 197
innovation 56, 71, 77-78, 82, 85, 92-94, 98, 108, 111-114, 135, 139, 148, 164, 173-174, 176-177, 179, 188, 194-196, 210, 227, 239, 241, 248, 255, 258, 282, 284
Innovation Management 94, 196, 284
Innovation Management Capabilities 94
Innovation Management Culture 94
Innovation Management Strategy 94
Innovation Management Structure 94
Institutional Role 43
IoT 114, 180-183, 186-189, 220, 248, 250-252, 254-257
Islamic banks profitability 153

K

KLD Index 197, 199-200, 203

L

Leaders 35, 46-47, 49, 70, 132, 134, 138-139, 252, 267, 286, 295-296
Legitimacy Theory 3, 5, 20, 26, 28, 200
luxury retailing 215-216, 219

M

Managers 85, 94-100, 103, 105-106, 108-110, 187-188, 200, 205, 209, 258-261, 263-264, 267, 286-291, 293, 295-298
Market Value 198-201, 204-205, 207-211, 213, 246
MENA countries 153-157, 159-160, 163-164

N

National Board of Revenue 225-226, 231-232, 236, 243, 246

O

Obstacles 286-288, 290-293
offline 97, 107, 215-217, 219, 222-223, 226, 232-236, 238-239, 246, 252
online 24, 27, 95, 107, 109-110, 114, 128, 184-187, 189, 194, 215-223, 226-228, 233-239, 246, 249, 252, 265-266, 268, 275, 282, 284, 290
ordinary least square (OLS) 153, 161

P

Perceived Risk and Benefits 271, 281
Polluting Sectors 2-3, 9, 28
product design 82, 173, 273, 282-283
Public Finance 129, 225, 244-246

Q

QSR Industry 173-174, 177-178, 180, 183, 192-193

R

Refurbished phone 271
retail 2, 26, 96, 124, 175, 192, 215-218, 221-222, 231, 248-257
Retail Technology 248
return on asset (ROA) 153-154
return on equity (ROE) 153-154, 157

S

Secondary time-series analysis 115
SECP 2-4, 7, 9, 17-18, 28
Sectors 1-3, 5-11, 16-19, 24, 28, 43, 56, 58, 61, 63, 98-99, 108, 117, 121-122, 128, 131, 164, 193, 209, 220, 240, 246-247, 260, 287, 293, 302
Securities Exchange Commission of Pakistan 28
Short and Long run Impact 115
smart pricing 173, 194
Social 2, 4-5, 7-9, 11-28, 31, 34, 37-39, 45, 52, 61, 64, 66-70, 79, 95-101, 103-107, 109-114, 116, 119-120, 126, 146, 156, 166, 177, 194, 197-200, 203, 211-213, 215-219, 250, 252-254, 256, 259, 263-264, 267-270, 275, 288-289, 293, 295-296, 298, 306-307
Social media listening 95-100, 105, 113
Social media marketing 95, 113
Social media marketing strategy 95, 113
Source Information Role 43
Strategic Investment 198

strategic mistrust, 141
sustainability 4, 20-26, 29-30, 39, 44, 57, 62, 64, 67, 82, 93, 138, 153-154, 173, 194, 198-200, 209-213, 241, 282, 313
Sustainable Development Goals 225-226, 246

T

Tax Administration 225, 227-228, 244-247
Tax Compliance 127, 225-228, 232-233, 243, 245
Tax Evasion 126, 226-228, 232-238, 242-246
Tax Revenue 120, 225-231, 239, 244
Technology 29, 33, 42-43, 56, 58, 67, 72, 76-77, 80, 82, 85, 92-93, 99, 108-109, 128, 131, 133-134, 138-139, 141-144, 146-151, 156, 166, 173-174, 176-177, 179-180, 184, 186, 189-190, 192, 194, 196, 199, 216-217, 220-221, 227-228, 244, 246, 248, 250-252, 255-259, 261-263, 265-270, 281, 286-287, 289
The Institutional Impact 29
Tobin's Q 197, 204, 207-210
Tourist Destination 300-302, 307-308
Tourist Harassment 300-302, 306-313
Tourists Satisfaction 300

U

UEBA (User and Entity Behaviour Analytics) 94
Usability Enhancement 76
US-China 141, 146, 148
User Experience 76-77, 80, 132

V

VAT Efficiency 228, 246
VAT Evasion 226-227, 232, 234
VAT productivity 230, 246
Volume of Reporting 6, 17
Voluntary Guidelines 1-2, 4-5, 7, 9-10, 16-17, 19, 28

W

Women 31, 35-40, 45, 62, 66, 73, 203, 207-208, 260, 286-291, 293, 295-298

Lightning Source UK Ltd.
Milton Keynes UK
UKHW032018280920
370690UK00003B/50